Anti-Money Laundering and the Law

This book provides a distinctive and critical analysis of the anti-money laundering (AML) measures that have been put in place in Türkiye and the United Kingdom.

The work presents a comparative analysis of if, and to what extent, the AML regimes in these jurisdictions are fit for purpose in countering some of the most pressing predicate crimes. It investigates the AML regimes relating to tackling the riskiest/ most prevalent predicate crimes, that is, drug trafficking and tax crimes, thereby filling a significant gap within the current literature. The study provides insights into the effectiveness and efficiency of national AML frameworks adopted by Türkiye and the UK in addressing distinct crimes, thereby identifying essential features of an optimum AML ecosystem that could effectively address predicate crimes regardless of their nature. This novel approach offers a detailed analysis of the law in books and law in practice elements of the AML regimes in Türkiye and the United Kingdom which will set the tone for conducting similar studies in other jurisdictions.

The book will be of interest to academics, researchers and policy-makers working in the areas of Financial Crime, Law Enforcement and Comparative Law.

Engin Erken is a major in the General Command of Gendarmerie (Türkiye). Engin completed his PhD at the Research Centre for Financial and Corporate Integrity at Coventry University. During his PhD studies, Engin participated as a research assistant in three EU-funded projects, namely VIRTEU (https://www.corporatecrime.co.uk/virteu), PROTAX (https://protax-project.eu), and TRACE (https://trace-illicit-money-flows.eu). Engin is currently a lecturer in crime prevention strategies at Gendarmerie and Coast Guard Academy (Türkiye). His research focuses on law enforcement practices in countering financial crimes with a specific interest in preventing money laundering and its underlying predicate offences.

Umut Turksen is Professor in Law at the Centre Financial and Corporate Integrity of Coventry University. Umut is a business-facing legal academic, and he is interested in the practical application of the law in innovation, societal security, and development. He has provided consultancy and training to prestigious international businesses and government projects. He led the EU funded project 'PROTAX', which focused on countering tax crimes in Europe, and he is currently coordinating another EU funded project, TRACE, (https://trace-illicit-money-flows.eu) which aims to create technology-based solutions (including AI) for tracking illicit money and virtual asset flows. In addition to his expertise in financial crime, societal security, risk and compliance, Umut has published extensively on energy law and security, international trade law and development, and arbitration. See, https://pureportal.coventry.ac.uk/en/persons/umut-turksen for further details.

The Law of Financial Crime

Series Editors

Nicholas Ryder Professor of Law

Cardiff University, School of Law and Politics, UK.

Dr. Lachmi Singh Associate Lecturer

Bristol Law School, University of the West of England, UK.

Sam Bourton Lecturer in Law

the University of the West of England, UK.

While a growing number of high-profile financial crime cases have hit the headlines recently the topic of financial crime is also generating much attention amongst academics and practitioners. This series will be the first to be dedicated to the law of financial, or economic, crime and offers a platform for important and original research in this area.

Books in the series will cover traditional subjects of financial crime including money laundering, terrorist financing, fraud, market abuse, insider dealing, market manipulation, tax evasion, bribery and corruption. But broader legal and regulatory issues will also be covered as well as emerging areas of concern such as the risks to stability of the financial system posed by financial crime. Emphasis will be placed on comparative approaches to the subject considering legislation across a number of jurisdictions as well as international regulations where appropriate, giving the series a truly global outlook.

The titles in the series are primarily aimed at an audience of researchers, scholars and practitioners in the area but should also be of interest to policy makers, law enforcement agencies, financial regulatory agencies, as well as people employed within the financial services sector.

Available titles in this series include:

Beneficial Ownership and Legal Responsibility
Concealment, Avoidance and Impunity
Paul Beckett

Tax Evasion and the Law
A Comparative Analysis of the UK and USA
Sam Bourton

Anti-Money Laundering and the Law
Comparative Approaches to Countering Predicate Crimes
Engin Erken and Umut Turksen

For more information about this series, please visit: www.routledge.com/The-Law-of-Financial-Crime/book-series/FINCRIME

Anti-Money Laundering and the Law

Comparative Approaches to Countering Predicate Crimes

Engin Erken and Umut Turksen

Routledge
Taylor & Francis Group
LONDON AND NEW YORK

First published 2025
by Routledge
4 Park Square, Milton Park, Abingdon, Oxon OX14 4RN

and by Routledge
605 Third Avenue, New York, NY 10158

Routledge is an imprint of the Taylor & Francis Group, an informa business

British Library Cataloguing-in-Publication Data
A catalogue record for this book is available from the British Library

ISBN: 978-1-032-72658-8 (hbk)
ISBN: 978-1-032-73925-0 (pbk)
ISBN: 978-1-003-46668-0 (ebk)

DOI: 10.4324/9781003466680

Typeset in Galliard
by Apex CoVantage, LLC

Contents

Tables

Acronyms

AFN	Account Forfeiture Notice
AFO	Account Freezing Order
AML	Anti-Money Laundering
AMLD	Anti-Money Laundering Directive
ARA	Assets Recovery Agency
ARIS	Asset Recovery Incentivisation Scheme
CBCFC	Coordination Board for Combatting Financial Crimes
CDD	Customer Due Diligence
CDF	Contractual Disclosure Facility
CE	Customs Enforcement
CGC	Coast Guard Command
CPS	Crown Prosecution Service
CTF	Counter-Terrorist Financing
DAML	Defence Against Money Laundering
DATF	Defence Against Terrorism Financing
DNFBPs	Designated Non-Financial Businesses and Professions
DPA	Deferred Prosecution Agreement
EC	European Commission
EFECC	European Financial and Economic Crime Centre
EMIS	Entegre Mali İstihbarat Sistemi
ESW	Egmont Secure Web
EU	European Union
EUROPOL	European Union Agency for Law Enforcement Cooperation
FATF	Financial Action Task Force
FCA	Financial Conduct Authority
FIs	Financial Institutions
FIU	Financial Intelligence Unit
FO	Forfeiture Order
FSRBs	FATF-Style Regional Bodies
GCG	General Command of Gendarmerie
GDP	Gross Domestic Product
GDS	General Directorate of Security

GNAT	Grand National Assembly of Türkiye
HMRC	Her Majesty's Revenue and Customs
HMT	HM Treasury
IMF	International Monetary Fund
INTERPOL	International Criminal Police Organisation
JFAC	Joint Financial Analysis Centre
JIT	Joint Investigation Team
JMLIT	Joint Money Laundering Intelligence Task Force
KOM	Kaçakçılık ve Organize Suçlarla Mücadele
KPI	Key Performance Indicator
KYC	Know Your Customer
LEAs	Law Enforcement Agencies
MASAK	Mali Suçları Araştırma Kurulu
MER	Mutual Evaluation Report
ML	Money Laundering
MLA	Mutual Legal Assistance
MoI	Ministry of Interior
MoJ	Ministry of Justice
MoT	Ministry of Trade
MoTF	Ministry of Treasury and Finance
MoU	Memoranda of Understanding
MS	Member States
NA	Not Available
NATO	North Atlantic Treaty Organization
NCA	National Crime Agency
NECC	National Economic Crime Centre
NRA	National Risk Assessment
OECD	Organisation for Economic Cooperation and Development
OFAC	Office of Foreign Assets Control
OPBAS	Office for Professional Body Anti-Money Laundering Supervision
PEPs	Politically Exposed Persons
POCA	Proceeds of Crime Act
PPP	Public-Private Partnership
RBA	Risk-Based Approach
RO	Restraint Order
ROCUs	Regional Organised Crime Units
SARs	Suspicious Activity Reports
SFO	Serious Fraud Office
SNRA	Supranational Risk Assessment
SOCA	Serious Organised Crime Agency
STRs	Suspicious Transaction Reports
TADOC	Turkish International Academy against Drugs and Organized Crime
TF	Terrorist Financing

TUBIM	Turkish Monitoring Centre for Drugs and Drug Addiction
UK	United Kingdom
UKFIU	United Kingdom Financial Intelligence Unit
UN	United Nations
UNODC	United Nations Office on Drugs and Crime
UNSCRs	United Nations Security Council Resolutions
USA	United States of America
UWOs	Unexplained Wealth Orders
WB	World Bank

Acknowledgements

Dr. Engin Erken

I dedicate this book to my awesome parents, Münevver Erken and Emin Erken, who have always been there and supported me no matter what the circumstances are. Rest in peace, Dad! This book would not have been possible without the support and encouragement of several exceptional people. I would like to take this opportunity to show my gratitude to those who have continuously assisted me along this rough journey. I would like to thank my co-author, Prof. Umut Turksen, for his invaluable insight that has reinforced the rigour of the book. I would also like to thank the Turkish General Command of Gendarmerie, and the Gendarmerie and Coast Guard Academy for their continuous support that enabled the publication of this book. In particular, I want to thank my wife, Duygu Erken, and my son, Emirhan John Erken, for their unwavering love, and unconditional moral and emotional support, and for tolerating my disappearances due to long working hours.

Prof. Umut Turksen

It is not often that we in the academia get a chance to work with law enforcement personnel to write a book. This is one of those rare instances which has been a great pleasure and an important learning experience for me. So, I thank my co-author, Engin, for his diligent, insightful, and critical approach to research and the topics that we examine in this book. I would also like to thank Prof. Nigel Berkeley, Prof. Panos Andrikopoulos, Dr. Adam Abukari and all the staff at the Research Centre for Financial and Corporate Integrity, Coventry University and the Turkish Gendarmerie and Cost Guard Academy for their support and generosity over the years without which this research or the book would not have been possible.

Acknowledgments

1 Introduction

1.1 The Context and the Contribution of the Study

The term money laundering (ML) was mentioned for the first time in modern literature during the prominent Watergate Scandal in 1973.[1] The expression originates in the disguising practices utilised by the infamous Al Capone, as he used (in the literal sense of the word) launderettes to establish a cash-intensive business network, thereby camouflaging his illegal sources of income to render them ostensibly legitimate.[2] In fact, given that ML refers to disguising the illicit origins of proceeds of crime, its existence dates back to early times, suggesting that it is as old as the ancient crimes of primitive history. However, the elevated levels of the international illicit drug trade and associated growing concerns in the 1980s have motivated governments to consider ML as a problem that should be addressed collaboratively.[3] The United States of America (USA) is the first jurisdiction that criminalised ML in 1986, and over 170 countries, including Türkiye and the UK, have outlawed it since then.[4] In other words, as Rossel and others aptly posit, the prevalence of the legal instruments prescribing the ML sphere has increased on par with the recognition of the offence itself.[5]

1 Friedrich Schneider and Ursula Windischbauer, 'Money Laundering: Some Facts' (2008) 26(3) European Journal of Law and Economics 387.
2 Brigitte Unger, 'Can Money Laundering Decrease?' (2013) 41(5) Public Finance Review 658.
3 Norman Mugarura, 'The Institutional Framework Against Money Laundering and Its Underlying Predicate Crimes' (2011) 19(2) Journal of Financial Regulation and Compliance 174; Jason Campbell Sharman, 'Power and Discourse in Policy Diffusion: Anti-Money Laundering in Developing States' (2008) 52(3) International Studies Quarterly 635.
4 Sharman (n 3).
5 Lucia Rossel and others, 'The Implications of Making Tax Crimes a Predicate Crime for Money Laundering in the EU: Building a Legal Dataset of Tax Crimes and Money Laundering in the European Union' in Brigitte Unger, Lucia Rossel and Joras Ferwerda (eds), *Combatting Fiscal Fraud and Empowering Regulators: Bringing Tax Money Back into the COFFERS* (OUP 2021).

DOI: 10.4324/9781003466680-1

The financial world considers ML as the series of actions by which offenders strive to hide the origin and ownership of the proceeds of their illicit activities.[6] The concealment techniques utilised by offenders have no limits and range from using mobile devices,[7] cash couriers or money mules[8] to financial institutions (FIs)[9] and even legal practitioners, such as lawyers or professional enablers in a general sense,[10] depending on the creativity of the intellectual capabilities of the perpetrators. ML is often considered a three-stage process, commencing with the placement phase, followed by the layering step, and concluding with the integration stage.[11] The placement phase is where criminal proceeds are introduced and placed in the legitimate economy or platforms (e.g., purchasing antiques and real estate). The layering represents the step where offenders aim to obscure and hide the proceeds of crime by relocating the funds (e.g., a series of transactions between numerous accounts and jurisdictions). The integration refers to the stage where money launderers reintegrate their illicit proceeds/assets into the legitimate financial system (e.g., cancelling an insurance policy after paying the premium).[12] As the close reading of the aforementioned definition connotes, the ML offence is predicated upon an underlying crime (i.e., predicate crime), perpetration of which generates illegitimate revenues, constituting the crux of the phenomenon. That is to say, eliminating or at least minimising the prevalence of ML offences depends on impeding associated predicate crimes, which has been one of the incentives behind determining the scope of this book.

ML has been a significant national and international concern because of its adverse effects on (the integrity of) the global economy.[13] According to a study conducted by International Monetary Fund (IMF) in 1996, the amount of money that is laundered was around 2 to 5% of the global gross domestic

6 Mark Pieth and Gemma Aiolfi, *A Comparative Guide to Anti-Money Laundering: A Critical Analysis of Systems in Singapore, Switzerland, the UK and the USA* (Edward Elgar Publishing 2004).

7 James Whisker and Mark Eshwar Lokanan, 'Anti-Money Laundering and Counter-Terrorist Financing Threats Posed by Mobile Money' (2019) 22(1) Journal of Money Laundering Control 158.

8 Muhammad Subtain Raza, Qi Zhan and Sana Rubab, 'Role of Money Mules in Money Laundering and Financial Crimes: A Discussion Through Case Studies' (2020) 27(3) Journal of Financial Crime 911.

9 Stefan D Cassella, 'Illicit Finance and Money Laundering Trends in Eurasia' (2019) 22(2) Journal of Money Laundering Control 388.

10 Michael Levi, 'Making Sense of Professional Enablers' Involvement in Laundering Organized Crime Proceeds and of Their Regulation' (2020) 24(1) Trends in Organized Crime 96; Katie Benson, *Lawyers and the Proceeds of Crime: The Facilitation of Money Laundering and Its Control* (Routledge 2020).

11 Mark Button, Branislav Hock and David Shepherd, *Economic Crime: From Conception to Response* (Routledge 2022); Nicholas Ryder, 'The Financial Services Authority and Money Laundering: A Game of Cat and Mouse' (2008) 67(3) Cambridge Law Journal 635.

12 ibid.

13 Schneider and Windischbauer (n 1).

product (GDP),[14] which then amounted to between USD 590bn and USD 1.5tn, where the former figure was approximately equivalent to the value of Spain's economic output.[15] United Nations Office on Drugs and Crime (UNODC) posits that the estimated amount of money laundered around the world annually is currently between USD 800bn and USD 2tn.[16] A more recent jurisdiction-specific estimation by the National Crime Agency (NCA) indicates that offenders reportedly launder GBP 90bn in the UK per annum.[17] Likewise, the think tank Global Financial Integrity estimates that Türkiye lost USD 8.4bn through illicit financial flows between 2006 and 2015,[18] which may shed light on the total amount of money laundered in the country annually. More specifically, whilst the amount of illicit money that flowed out of Türkiye was USD 8.4bn, the fraudulent invoicing resulted in the inflow amount of USD 16.9bn in the previously mentioned period.[19] These estimations on the scale of the phenomenon indicate that also the calculation of its extent is challenging because there is no visible data on the amount of money laundered (i.e., shadow economy), which is evident in the enormous marginal difference in the prediction interval. However, given the estimated magnitude of the problem globally and nationally concerning Türkiye and the UK, investigating the role of AML structures in addressing the predicament, thereby identifying characteristics of an optimum AML framework, deserves close examination.

In an economic environment where ML activities are in operation, foreign investors can be discouraged, and global capital flows can be falsified.[20] Furthermore, they may hinder the efficient use of resources, thereby causing welfare losses.[21] In addition to their economic impact, these illegal activities also deteriorate the integrity of the criminal justice system and diminish public confidence in the state and the financial sector, thereby enhancing the prevalence

14 Peter J Quirk, 'Macroeconomic Implications of Money Laundering' (1996) International Monetary Fund Working Paper WP/96/66 <www.elibrary.imf.org/doc/IMF001/04385-9781451962123/04385-9781451962123/Other_formats/Source_PDF/04385-9781455295791.pdf> accessed 21 May 2020.

15 FATF, 'How Much Money Is Laundered Per Year?' <www.fatf-gafi.org/faq/moneylaundering/> accessed 21 May 2020. See also Dennis Cox, *An Introduction to Money Laundering Deterrence* (John Wiley & Sons 2015).

16 UNODC, 'Money Laundering' <www.unodc.org/unodc/en/money-laundering/overview.html> accessed 26 June 2022.

17 HL Deb 1 May 2018, vol 640, col 192.

18 Global Financial Integrity, 'Illicit Financial Flows to and from 148 Developing Countries: 2006–2015' (January 2019) <https://gfintegrity.org/report/2019-iff-update/> accessed 21 May 2020.

19 ibid.

20 IMF, 'Factsheet: IMF and the Fight Against Money Laundering and the Financing of Terrorism' <www.imf.org/en/About/Factsheets/Sheets/2016/08/01/16/31/Fight-Against-Money-Laundering-the-Financing-of-Terrorism> accessed 13 July 2022.

21 ibid.

of criminal activities and terrorism.[22] Moreover, the recent developments in technology, communication, and transportation domains have made it easier for criminals to launder money as the world is more interconnected, allowing them to move and/or relocate their illicit proceeds smoothly (e.g., the use of cryptocurrencies and non-fungible tokens).[23] Consequently, the harm caused by these activities is not limited to a single jurisdiction where they have been conducted because of the destabilising consequences on other economies. As 'the globalisation of crimes requires globalised solutions',[24] enhancing national and international security and prosperity, protecting institutions and legitimate businesses, and maintaining the political stability of governments require AML authorities and the private sector to address the problem in solidarity nationally and internationally. That is to say, given that a chain is no stronger than its weakest link, enhancing the overall competency of the global financial ecosystem requires improving and ensuring the adequacy and effectiveness of each component actor's national AML efforts. Therefore, identifying characteristics of an optimum AML structure that could effectively counter all predicate crimes regardless of their nature would benefit the global AML regime, including its national constituents, such as Türkiye and the UK.

The global reach of the acknowledgment of these adverse impacts posed by the phenomenon has engendered global responses. The initiatives at the United Nations (UN) level, starting with the 1988 UN Vienna Convention, led, amongst others (see Chapter 2), to the establishment of the Financial Action Task Force (FATF) and the creation of FATF Recommendations.[25] FATF Recommendations, which guide national governments in structuring effective AML measures and demonstrate fundamental requirements for relevant stakeholders, such as obliged entities, have been recognised as essential minimum international standards for combating ML and financing of terrorism.[26] The principal aim of AML standards has been to starve criminals of their illegal assets by enabling recovery of these assets, thereby eradicating predicate crimes. Furthermore, these standards have been created to ensure that '[f]inancial systems and the broader economy are protected from the threats of money laundering and the financing of terrorism and proliferation,

22 Peter Alldridge, 'Money Laundering and Globalization' (2008) 35(4) Journal of Law and Society 437; Unger (n 2).

23 Robert Stokes, 'Virtual Money Laundering: The Case of Bitcoin and the Linden Dollar' (2012) 21(3) Information & Communications Technology Law 221.

24 Rossel and others (n 5) 239.

25 The political consensus on the gravity of the illicit drug trade predicament was ensured at the 1988 UN Vienna Convention; and the Financial Action Task Force (FATF) was created by the Paris Summit Meeting of the G-7 to implement efficient procedures against ML activities in 1989. See Michael Levi and William Gilmore, 'Terrorist Finance, Money Laundering and the Rise and Rise of Mutual Evaluation: A New Paradigm for Crime Control?' in Mark Pieth (ed), *Financing Terrorism* (Springer 2002).

26 Michael Levi and Peter Reuter, 'Money Laundering' (2006) 34(1) Crime and Justice 289.

thereby strengthening financial sector integrity and contributing to safety and security'.[27] From a predicate crimes perspective, whilst the initial AML policies (e.g., the 1990 Recommendations) exclusively focused on addressing drug-related financial offences, the scope of the devoted efforts gradually expanded (i.e., in 1996, 2003, and 2012) to a broader framework concentrating on all crimes, including terrorism, generating ill-obtained gains.[28] However, it remains questionable whether national AML structures established to address ML deriving from drug trafficking are effective in tackling other predicate crimes with unique characteristics. This inquiry has been another consideration for determining the scope of this study.

FATF Recommendations are soft laws that do not have the same binding power as harnessed by conventional legal instruments.[29] Accordingly, jurisdictions do not always transpose such soft law provisions into national legislation uniformly, as evident, for instance, in Türkiye and the UK's national AML compositions. Furthermore, this diversification is more apparent between the discrete law disciplines, such as common law and civil law, as the UK and Türkiye adopt, respectively. For example, Rossel and others observe that whilst common law jurisdictions (e.g., Ireland and the UK) prescribe harsher punishments for ML than tax crimes, civil law jurisdictions (e.g., Germany and Hungary) impose more severe penalties for tax crimes.[30] However, interestingly, Türkiye, as a civil law country, stipulates harsher punishments for ML than tax crimes.[31] Similar to the differences in determining predicate crimes and sanctions imposed on them, the types and compositions of state authorities responsible for AML are varied. For example, the financial intelligence unit (FIU) in Türkiye embraces an administrative model of FIU as many other civil law jurisdictions, such as France[32] and Belgium.[33] The UK, on the other hand, adopts a law enforcement type of FIU. However, it is necessary to state

27 FATF, 'An Effective System to Combat Money Laundering and Terrorist Financing' <www.fatf-gafi.org/publications/mutualevaluations/documents/effectiveness.html> accessed 22 August 2022.
28 Levi and Gilmore (n 25).
29 Georgios Pavlidis, 'Financial Action Task Force and the Fight Against Money Laundering and the Financing of Terrorism: Qua Vadimus?' (2020) 28(3) Journal of Financial Crime 765.
30 Rossel and others (n 5).
31 Whilst Article 359 of Law No 213 (Tax Procedure Law) 1961, depending on the gravity of the crime, stipulates three separate imprisonment terms consisting of 18 months–3 years, 3–5 years, and 2–5 years, Article 282 of TCC 2004 prescribes 3–7 years imprisonment for money launderers, as discussed in Chapter 3 in detail.
32 Ministère de l'Économie, des Finances et de la Relance, 'TRACFIN' <www.economie.gouv.fr/tracfin> accessed 22 May 2020. See also Genevieve Bardin, 'Compliance and Anti-Money Laundering Regulation in France' (2002) 10(2) Journal of Financial Crime 135.
33 CTIF-FCI, 'Anti-Money Laundering and Countering the Financing of Terrorism System' <www.ctif-cfi.be/website/index.php?lang=en> accessed 22 May 2020. See also John G Goldsworth, Wouter H Muller and Christian H Kälin, 'Belgium' in John G Goldsworth, Wouter H Muller and Christian H Kälin (eds), *Anti-Money Laundering: International Law and Practice* (John Wiley & Sons 2012).

that many other common law jurisdictions, such as the USA,[34] Australia,[35] and Canada,[36] adopt an administrative type of FIU in contrast with the UK. Although embracing a particular type of FIU has certain advantages and disadvantages, as discussed in Chapter 2, it is more important to consider how effectively the FIU is utilised in countering ML rather than the type of FIU adopted. Therefore, it is crucial to investigate the differences created by these approaches and scrutinise the underlying reasons that generate strengths and deficiencies relating to impeding ML and its underlying predicates across distinct law disciplines, another inspiration behind settling on the focal point of this study.

As the FATF Recommendations indicate, any success in countering ML offences depends on countering also the predicate crimes. In other words, if the global economic *fora* desire to overcome ML, the swamp of predicate crimes, the root of the problem, should be addressed. This can be achieved by eliminating deficiencies that increase the occurrence of predicate crimes and that simplify the laundering of the proceeds derived from such (predicate) offences. That is to say, given that offenders decide to commit particular offences after evaluating the potential costs and benefits of involving those crime opportunities (i.e., the rational choice perspective),[37] the differences in the AML frameworks affect each jurisdiction's efficacy as the perpetrators exploit the weaknesses accordingly. For example, it would be reasonable to expect a criminal to disguise the proceeds of their crime in a jurisdiction where the underlying offence is not a predicate crime as it technically eliminates the risk of committing ML given its definition. Therefore, it is paramount to investigate the effectiveness of the current AML structures of Türkiye and the UK in tackling predicate crimes to comprehend their respective competencies, thereby identifying any hurdles standing in the way of their AML effectiveness and adopting an optimum AML regime.

The notion of predicate offences is defined as 'the underlying criminal offence that gave rise to the criminal proceeds which are the subject of a money laundering charge'.[38] However, its definition and categories vary from

34 Financial Crimes Enforcement Network, 'FinCEN' <www.fincen.gov> accessed 13 July 2022.

35 Australian Government, 'Australian Transaction Reports and Analysis Centre (AUSTRAC)' <www.austrac.gov.au/about-us/austrac-overview> accessed 13 July 2022. See also Neil Jensen, 'Creating an Environment in Australia Hostile to Money Laundering and Terrorism Financing: A Changing Role for AUSTRAC' (2008) 5(5) Macquarie Journal of Business Law 93.

36 Government of Canada, 'Financial Transactions and Reports Analysis Centre (FINTRAC)' <www.fintrac-canafe.gc.ca/fintrac-canafe/1-eng> accessed 22 May 2020. See also Jeffrey R Simser, 'Canada's Financial Intelligence Unit: FINTRAC' (2020) 23(2) Journal of Money Laundering Control 297.

37 Derek B Cornish and Ronald V Clarke, 'Understanding Crime Displacement: An Application of Rational Choice Theory' (1987) 25(4) Criminology 933.

38 R Bell, 'Abolishing the Concept of "Predicate Offence"' (2003) 6(2) Journal of Money Laundering Control 137.

one jurisdiction to another, as is the case for Türkiye and the UK. Following Recommendation 3 of the FATF,[39] jurisdictions flexibly adopt the relevant definition as per their jurisdiction-specific priorities and characteristics. More specifically, the FATF Recommendations allow jurisdictions to embrace an all-crimes, a threshold, a list-based approach, or a combination of such procedures in determining the extent of predicate crimes.[40] For instance, whilst Türkiye describes predicate offences by reference to a minimum imprisonment threshold of six months, the UK, on the other hand, defines them by reference to all crimes, as discussed in Chapters 3 and 4, respectively. In other words, there is no global uniformity even around the definitional stance of the concept amongst the authorities, which would doubtlessly affect the efficacy of each jurisdiction in handling the phenomenon, another reference point to be considered within this book.

As discussed in the following chapters (i.e., Chapters 3 to 6), on par with the international developments relating to AML practices in the global sphere, Türkiye and the UK have taken significant steps to ensure their structural congruency and integrity with the international financial world. In order to create a safe and secure environment for their citizens, Türkiye and the UK have long been dealing with various organised crime syndicates and associated ML activities. The geographical location of Türkiye, which plays a bridging role by linking Asia, Europe, Africa, and the Middle East, facilitates the illicit trafficking of humans and illegal goods and attracts transnational organised crime groups.[41] Türkiye's geographical position, the destabilised war-torn neighbours, such as Iraq and Syria, rugged and porous borders, and economic and political struggles create an environment where ML activities could take place relatively smoothly. For instance, the Corruption Perception Index 2021 ranks Türkiye as 96/180 whilst scoring 38/100,[42] where a higher score indicates a healthier economic environment. The Financial Secrecy Index 2022 ranks the country as 59/141, suggesting the amount of illicit financial flows is rather high.[43] The Rule of Law Index 2021 ranks Türkiye as 117/139,[44] which may give insight into the relatively weak adherence to the rule of law and the associated

39 FATF, 'International Standards on Combatting Money Laundering and the Financing of Terrorism & Proliferation: The FATF Recommendations' (Updated March 2022) <www.fatf-gafi.org/media/fatf/documents/recommendations/pdfs/FATF%20Recommendations%202012.pdf> accessed 26 June 2023.

40 ibid. See Interpretive Note to Recommendation 3.

41 Sule Toktas and Hande Selimoglu, 'Smuggling and Trafficking in Turkey: An Analysis of EU-Turkey Cooperation in Combating Transnational Organized Crime' (2012) 14(1) Journal of Balkan and Near Eastern Studies 135.

42 Transparency International, 'Corruption Perception Index – Countries: Turkey' <www.transparency.org/en/cpi/2021/index/tur> accessed 11 July 2023.

43 Tax Justice Network, 'Financial Secrecy Index 2022: Turkey' <https://fsi.taxjustice.net> accessed 11 July 2023.

44 World Justice Project, 'WJP Rule of Law Index 2021: Turkey' <https://worldjusticeproject.org/rule-of-law-index/country/Turkey> accessed 17 August 2023.

challenges of law enforcement and AML in Türkiye. Therefore, given that ML is an integral element of transnational organised crime,[45] the exploitable geostrategic position of the country makes Türkiye more vulnerable to being exposed to relevant predicate offences, thus making it an ideal jurisdiction to be included in the study.

On the other hand, as one of the pivotal financial centres in the world, the UK is continuously being targeted by a significant amount of ML attempts and activities.[46] Even though the existing AML legislation and enforcement mechanisms are seemingly well developed in the UK (see Chapters 4 and 6), it is still regarded as a jurisdiction where ML activities take place in significant numbers. For example, as estimated by Ferwerda and others, 40% of all ML in the 36 OECD countries[47] occur only in two jurisdictions, namely the USA and the UK.[48] As an indicator of the jurisdiction's current economic climate, the Corruption Perception Index 2021 ranks the UK as 11/180 whilst scoring 78/100,[49] and the Financial Secrecy Index 2022 estimates it as 13/141.[50] The Rule of Law Index 2021 ranks the UK as 16/139.[51] Although these rankings suggest that the UK is in a better position than Türkiye in preventing ML and associated predicate crimes,[52] revealing underlying reasons that still generate unsatisfactory outcomes for the jurisdiction entails scrutinising the legal and institutional AML composition adopted by the UK. Therefore, in order to identify how such structural AML differences impact the prevalence of and the effectiveness in tackling predicate crimes, the UK is included in this comparative study.

Despite all their efforts (e.g., undertaking NRAs and identifying ML risks accordingly), the criticisms regarding both jurisdictions' effectiveness in their

45 Mugarura (n 3); Sharman (n 3).

46 For example, ML is estimated to cost every household in the UK GBP 255 annually. See Law Commission, 'Money Laundering: Summary' (June 2019) 2 <https://s3-eu-west-2.amazonaws.com/lawcom-prod-storage-11jsxou24uy7q/uploads/2019/06/6.5612_LC_Anti-money-laundering-summary_v6.pdf> accessed 17 August 2023.

47 It is necessary to note that there are 38 OECD member jurisdictions. The study undertaken by Ferwerda and others does not include Colombia (2020) and Costa Rica (2021), which recently became OECD members. See OECD, 'Our Global Reach: Member Countries' <www.oecd.org/about/members-and-partners/> accessed 11 July 2023.

48 Joras Ferwerda and others, 'Estimating Money Laundering Flows with a Gravity Model-Based Simulation' (2020) 10(1) Scientific Reports <https://doi.org/10.1038/s41598-020-75653-x> accessed 11 July 2023.

49 Transparency International, 'Corruption Perception Index – Countries: United Kingdom' <www.transparency.org/en/cpi/2021/index/gbr> accessed 11 July 2023.

50 Tax Justice Network, 'Financial Secrecy Index 2022: United Kingdom' <https://fsi.taxjustice.net> accessed 11 July 2023.

51 World Justice Project, 'WJP Rule of Law Index 2021: United Kingdom' <https://worldjusticeproject.org/rule-of-law-index/country/2021/United%20Kingdom/> accessed 17 August 2023.

52 For example, for a discussion on how corruption and ML are intertwined, see Raffaella Barone, Donato Masciandaro and Friedrich Schneider, 'Corruption and Money Laundering: You Scratch My Back, I'll Scratch Yours' (2022) 73(1) Metroeconomica 318.

AML ecosystem have not ended. For instance, in 2010, Türkiye was identified as a country with critical AML insufficiencies by the FATF International Co-operation Review Group, whereby the FATF commenced a monitoring process on Türkiye.[53] However, Türkiye had not been subject to this process since 2014, when the FATF recognised Türkiye's success in addressing the previously identified deficiencies,[54] until its recent inclusion in the jurisdictions under increased monitoring.[55] In other words, Türkiye's extensive efforts in tackling ML seem to fail to address the phenomenon effectively. Although the UK's recent AML efforts are notable, they have not fully dealt with the problem of being an ML haven. For instance, Keatinge argues that the current AML arrangements in the UK are ineffective in identifying ML activities and that most of the data within SARs is worthless.[56] According to Lindenberg, the UK enables criminals to launder their illicit gains as it is relatively easy to form a company in its offshore territories. Similarly, Sikka opines that it is effortless to set up a business in the UK as the control process does not check the accuracy of the information provided (e.g., name and address) by entrepreneurs and that the deficiencies associated with the UK's AML system stem from the improper institutional arrangements.[57] These facts clearly illustrate that AML frameworks adopted by Türkiye and the UK comprise some deficiencies, suggesting that adjusting the focal point of related efforts to concentrate on predicate crimes may curtail the phenomenon, another inductive force behind this study.

The eagerness to eliminate the serious consequences of ML activities has inspired many scholars to investigate the current AML structures to critique whether they are effective in preventing ML offences. However, whilst numerous studies examine and compare the effectiveness of AML compositions in impeding ML offences across the existing literature,[58] their respective outcomes in reducing predicate crimes remain underexplored. Furthermore, comparative

53 FATF, 'Improving Global AML/CFT Compliance: Update On-Going Process' (February 2010) <www.fatf-gafi.org/countries/d-i/greece/documents/improvingglobalamlcftcomplianceupdateon-goingprocess-february2010.html> accessed 22 May 2023.

54 FATF, 'Outcomes of the Plenary Meeting of the FATF, Paris' (22–24 October 2014) <www.fatf-gafi.org/documents/news/plenary-outcomes-october-2014.html> accessed 22 May 2023.

55 FATF, 'Jurisdictions Under Increased Monitoring' (March 2022) <www.fatf-gafi.org/publications/high-risk-and-other-monitored-jurisdictions/documents/increased-monitoring-march-2022.html#turkey> accessed 10 June 2022.

56 Chris Stokel-Walker, 'Why the UK Is Losing Its Costly Battle against Money Laundering' *Wired* (10 December 2018) <www.wired.co.uk/article/money-laundering-in-the-uk-russian-banks> accessed 22 May 2023.

57 ibid.

58 Nicholas Ryder, *Money Laundering – An Endless Cycle? A Comparative Analysis of the Anti-Money Laundering Policies in the United States of America, the United Kingdom, Australia and Canada* (1st edn, Routledge 2012); Christoph Wronka, 'Anti-Money Laundering Regimes: A Comparison Between Germany, Switzerland and the UK with a Focus on the Crypto Business' (2022) 25(3) Journal of Money Laundering Control 656.

studies devoted to comparing common law and civil law jurisdictions are limited, and no academic work particularly juxtaposes Türkiye and the UK in this context. In this framework, it is important to critically examine the current AML legal and operational structures of Türkiye and the UK and identify their strengths and weaknesses in countering prominent predicate crimes, thereby identifying also the unique characteristics of an optimum AML composition. This monograph fills this gap in the extant literature as it analyses AML structures adopted by Türkiye and the UK and their effectiveness in impeding predicate crimes from a comparative perspective. More importantly, it is deduced that this study could be the first of its kind, implementing a comprehensive approach, particularly in relation to the role of AML structures (adopted by Türkiye and the UK) in impeding predicate crimes.

Consequently, the authors investigate and compare the current legal and institutional AML structures embraced by Türkiye and the UK. In doing so, they aim at revealing the underlying reasons that generate differences in the prevalence of and the effectiveness in impeding underlying predicate crimes for ML in these jurisdictions, thereby identifying specific characteristics of an optimum AML structure. Given that it would be impossible to scrutinise such effects on all predicate crimes in the confines of this book, the study examines only two predicate crimes, namely illicit drug trafficking and tax offences, that constitute some of the highest risks for Türkiye and the UK. Additionally, given that the nation-specific characteristics associated, amongst others, with historical, geographical, cultural, socio-legal, and political backgrounds play a crucial role in establishing AML regimes, the study seeks to reveal such factors that create different AML approaches and effectiveness.

Comparing the organisational AML structures of the two jurisdictions has at least a threefold relevance. Firstly, as two non-member European States of the European Union (EU),[59] Türkiye and the UK share commonalities as the two representatives of international *fora* as they are both members of various global organisations, such as the Group of Twenty (G20),[60] the FATF,[61] the Egmont Group,[62] Council of Europe,[63] and the North Atlantic Treaty Organization (NATO),[64] indicating their common strategic vision in their approach to international matters, including AML. Secondly, as they belong to two distinct law disciplines, namely common law and civil law, it is believed that this

59 European Union, 'Country Profiles' <https://europa.eu/european-union/about-eu/countries_en> accessed 5 May 2023.

60 G20, 'Participants' <https://g20.org/en/about/Pages/Participants.aspx> accessed 5 May 2023.

61 FATF, 'FATF Members and Observers' <www.fatf-gafi.org/about/membersandobservers/> accessed 13 July 2023.

62 Egmont Group, 'Members by Region' <https://egmontgroup.org> accessed 13 July 2023.

63 Council of Europe, '46 Member States' <www.coe.int/en/web/portal/46-members-states> accessed 2 July 2023.

64 NATO, 'NATO Member Countries' <www.nato.int/cps/en/natohq/nato_countries.htm> accessed 5 May 2023.

divergence point may contribute to acknowledging the underlying reasons generating diverse outcomes in impeding predicate crimes across such disciplines. Finally, the relative scarcity of studies comparing jurisdictions relating to their potency in hindering predicate offences rather than in AML practices, and the absence of research comparing particularly Türkiye and the UK in this end (as the literature review has revealed), underpin the need for this book. It is believed that comparison of Türkiye with one of the biggest financial centres in the world provides an excellent opportunity to contribute with an extensive study that might inspire and pave the way for developing a more effective AML composition. It is also hoped that further comparative studies would be conducted to determine if and to what extent various AML regimes result in reducing predicate crimes.

1.2 Aims and Objectives of This Book

Our study has identified (see Chapter 8) that whilst an AML regime may be effective in tackling particular crimes (e.g., *conventional* offences), it may show deficiencies in countering others with more sophisticated elements (e.g., tax crimes). Therefore, the ultimate purpose of this book is to identify key characteristics of an optimum AML structure that could effectively address predicate crimes regardless of their nature. Accordingly, the main research aim has been to demonstrate whether and how differences between the legal and institutional AML structures may impact the effectiveness in tackling and the prevalence of predicate crimes, thereby underlining the unique features of an optimum AML regime capable of addressing all predicate offences. In other words, this study has aimed (i) to reveal the underlying reasons associated with the relevant AML legal frameworks accounting for the prevalence of different types of predicate crimes in Türkiye and the UK; (ii) to unveil the essential divergence points between the two institutional AML structures and their impact on the varying predicate crime prevalence in these jurisdictions; and (iii) to shed light on the areas in need of reform, thereby enhancing the effectiveness in the fight against ML and its underlying predicates. With these aims in mind, the study has addressed three main questions: (i) whether the differences between the AML legal frameworks adopted by Türkiye and the UK impact the prevalence of predicate crimes (if so, how?); (ii) whether the unique characteristics of the two institutional AML structures result in dissimilar predicate crime prevalence; and (iii) what would be the necessary steps to be taken to ensure the optimum AML composition, thereby reducing predicate crimes and increasing the recovery of criminal assets through a fit-for-purpose AML mechanism?

1.3 Scope and Limitations of This Book

Although Türkiye and the UK share commonalities in their approach to international matters, including AML, they are representatives of two distinct *strata* relating to their level of development as the former is a developing country, whereas the latter is recognised as a developed jurisdiction.[65] The literature review has revealed that there is no study examining the impact of AML regimes in impeding predicate crimes (i.e., drug trafficking and tax crimes). Accordingly, this study has utilised literature written on AML and predicate crimes as distinct areas of inquiry. Accordingly, this book is the first of its kind and makes an original contribution to literature with its comparative analysis of two AML regimes and their impact on predicate crimes.

The sources of data utilised in the book consist of legal instruments (i.e., case law and statutes), publicly available reports of relevant competent authorities (e.g., annual reports of the UKFIU and MASAK), and other pertinent secondary sources, such as mutual evaluation reports (MERs) by the FATF. Considering the room for bias in self-reporting, the validity of the research findings depends on the trueness of the annual reports investigated.

In the confines of this book, the comparative analysis is limited to Türkiye and the UK. However, notwithstanding its geographical extent, it is believed that the research approach and outcomes may be applicable for jurisdictions of similar characteristics and backgrounds, as the research focus reframes the AML domain by taking a different approach. In addition to its geographical coverage, the temporal framework encompasses the last 40 years relating to AML efforts by Türkiye and the UK, as the international recognition of ML dates back to the 1980s.[66]

Lastly, although AML and CTF concepts are intertwined and go hand in hand, CTF efforts and, therefore, the associated predicate crimes of terrorism origins are excluded from the scope of the study, as CTF has recently been studied in detail by academia (see, for instance, Basaranel and Turksen).[67] Additionally, it is important to note the difference between ML and reverse ML: Whilst ML refers to disguising practices of illegal proceeds derived from an underlying crime, the notion of reverse ML, on the other hand, stands for the concealing of the source of legitimate money, which is to be used to finance future criminal activities (e.g., financing of terrorism).[68] In other words, whilst AML efforts concern the origins of criminal proceedings, CTF efforts focus on the expenditure of such funds.[69] Therefore, as the study inves-

65 United Nations, *World Economic Situation and Prospects 2022* (United Nations Publication 2022) 153–54 <https://desapublications.un.org/file/728/download?_ga=2.182751270.1838915455.1661156885-1130433834.1661156885> accessed 17 August 2023.

66 United Nations Convention Against Illicit Traffic in Narcotic Drugs and Psychotropic Substances 1988.

67 Burke U Basaranel and Umut Turksen, *Counter-Terrorist Financing Law and Policy: An Analysis of Turkey* (Routledge 2019).

68 Stefan D Cassella, 'Reverse Money Laundering' (2003) 7(1) Journal of Money Laundering Control 92.

69 OECD, *Money Laundering and Terrorist Financing Awareness Handbook for Tax Examiners and Tax Auditors* (OECD Publishing 2019) 25 <www.oecd.org/tax/crime/money-laundering-and-terrorist-financing-awareness-handbook-for-tax-examiners-and-tax-auditors.pdf> accessed 1 February 2023.

tigates predicate offences rather than the unlawful use of legitimate property, the concept of reverse ML is not scrutinised in this book.

1.4 Structure and Methodologies Employed in the Book

The book has been divided into nine chapters consisting of one introduction chapter; one chapter investigating international AML efforts; two chapters examining AML legal frameworks adopted by Türkiye and the UK; two chapters scrutinising institutional AML structures embraced by Türkiye and the UK; one thematic comparison chapter analysing convergence and divergence points of the two AML regimes and evaluating the overall AML effectiveness of the two jurisdictions; one chapter exploring the impacts of differences in the AML compositions on the prevalence of and the effectiveness in tackling predicate crimes; and one conclusion chapter.

The first chapter comprises five sections. It introduces the context and contribution of the study, thereby explaining research interests and pointing out the gaps within the literature. After setting out aims and objectives of the book, it outlines the key areas of inquiry and the questions this study endeavours to answer. The third section outlines the scope and limitations of the study, whereby it postulates whether research findings apply to other jurisdictions constituting the global economic system. The following section describes the research design and methodology embraced to address the research aims and objectives. The final chapter outlines the structure of the book by summarising each chapter.

Chapter 2 inquires into the international AML regime, thereby delineating competent authorities of the global financial world and investigating the role of each component in ensuring a more hostile environment for the nefarious ML activities and their underlying predicates. More specifically, it delves into the function of the UN, FATF, Egmont Group of Financial Intelligence Units, International Monetary Fund (IMF), World Bank (WB), and the EU in directing and coordinating the global AML efforts. In doing so, it examines the evolution of the global AML ecosystem, thereby exploring the development of the scope of predicate crimes at the international level.

Chapters 3 (Türkiye) and 4 (the UK) (i) examine the evolution of national AML legal frameworks established by the two jurisdictions; (ii) scrutinise principal AML legal instruments therein, thereby explaining how they may empower or incapacitate AML efforts; and (iii) shed light on areas that would benefit from reform, thereby eliminating the obstacles hampering AML efforts. Chapters 5 (Türkiye) and 6 (the UK) (i) analyse institutional AML structures adopted by the two jurisdictions; (ii) investigate judicial systems, legal sources, and the hierarchy between them; and (iii) inquire into competent AML authorities therein, thereby outlining their powers, duties, and organisational structures. By doing so, they point out the current competency and potential drawbacks of AML stakeholders in Türkiye and the UK, including the judiciary, prosecutors, LEAs, and FIUs. In other words, these four chapters aim to demonstrate the essential divergence points between the two legal and institutional AML frameworks, thereby preparing a basis for investigating the impacts of such structural differences on the prevalence of and the effectiveness in tackling predicate crimes.

Chapter 7 is devoted to a thematic comparison (e.g., obliged entities and obligations) of the AML compositions of Türkiye and the UK. In light of legal and institutional AML differences identified in the previous chapters and based on empirical evidence from Türkiye and the UK (e.g., the number of STRs/SARs, prosecutions/convictions secured, and the asset recovery figures), Chapter 7 compares and explores the overall AML effectiveness of the two jurisdictions. Although the core focus of the book has been to identify the impacts of AML heterogeneities on the prevalence of and the effectiveness in tackling predicate crimes, Chapter 7, from a broader AML perspective, aspires to provide a solid basis for a predicate-crime-specific investigation as undertaken in Chapter 8.

The penultimate chapter focuses on two of the most prevalent/highest risk predicate crimes, namely illicit drug trafficking and tax offences, for the two jurisdictions as case studies. It starts with explaining the underlying reasons for their selection as case studies. Then, it examines how the differences between legal and institutional AML regimes adopted by Türkiye and the UK (may) impact the prevalence of/the effectiveness in tackling these particular and complex predicate crimes. By doing so, it underlines the unique characteristics of an optimum AML structure that would address all predicate crimes regardless of their nature, be it conventional (e.g., illicit drug trafficking) or with more sophisticated elements (e.g., tax crimes).

The final chapter, Chapter 9, discusses and synthesises research findings against the provided background throughout the study, thereby pointing out justifications for the two administrations' divergent experiences within the AML realm. In doing so, it addresses the first two research questions. It concludes by putting forward suggestions for competent authorities, relevant stakeholders, and practitioners, thereby addressing the last research question. Lastly, it proffers potential research areas for future researchers that would further enrich the literature.

Before moving further, it is crucial to clearly define the terms of effectiveness and efficiency, which have been used frequently throughout the book. The most recent FATF Methodology utilised for assessing jurisdictions regarding their technical compliance with the FATF Recommendations and the effectiveness of their AML/CTF systems defines the term effectiveness as 'the extent to which the defined outcomes are achieved'.[70] Concerning the defined outcomes in this context, the FATF determines 11 immediate

70 FATF, 'Methodology for Assessing Technical Compliance with the FATF Recommendations and the Effectiveness of AML/CTF Systems' (updated October 2021) 15 <www.fatf-gafi.org/media/fatf/documents/methodology/FATF%20Methodology%2022%20Feb%202013.pdf> accessed 31 December 2023.

outcomes (e.g., confiscation), which feed into three intermediate outcomes and lead to the high-level objective of an 'effective' AML/CTF framework.[71] In other words, the FATF assesses the AML effectiveness of jurisdictions against these benchmarks. However, a close examination of these criteria (see footnote 71) indicates that they are not crystal clear due to the subjective nature of the phenomenon and the vagueness of the defined outcomes. For example, Immediate Outcome 6 reads as '[f]inancial intelligence and all other relevant information are appropriately used by competent authorities for money laundering and terrorist financing investigations',[72] where the meaning of 'appropriately' can be interpreted in varied ways across jurisdictions. For example, there are significant differences between Türkiye and the UK regarding sharing financial intelligence between competent AML authorities due to the differing discretion rights in this context (see Chapter 8). In other words, as argued by Pol, the defined outcomes stipulated by the FATF are 'often ambiguous, unrealisable or lacking measurability'.[73] Furthermore, each assessor may evaluate the AML effectiveness of a country diversely. As a corroborative statement, the FATF Methodology states that '[t]he assessment process is reliant on the judgement of assessors',[74] suggesting that different assessors may conclude differently regarding the effectiveness of an AML regime. Similarly, the Wolfsberg Group, in their Statement on Effectiveness concerning FIs, determines three main components of an effective AML/CTF regime, which comprise (i) complying with the AML/CTF legal framework; (ii) providing 'highly useful information' to competent AML authorities; as well as (iii) establishing a 'reasonable' and risk-based control mechanism to mitigate ML/TF risks.[75] As evident in this statement, effectiveness indicators adopted by the Wolfsberg Group also contain vague expressions (e.g., highly useful and reasonable). In other words, as Goldby aptly posits, 'there is no consensus

71 Intermediate Outcomes refer to (i) mitigating ML/TF risks through policy, coordination, and cooperation; (ii) preventing proceeds of crime (and funds concerning TF) from entering the financial and other sectors; if failed to do so, ensuring they are detected and reported by these sectors; and (iii) detecting and disrupting ML threats, sanctioning criminals, and recovering criminal assets. Immediate Outcomes refer to key goals in relation to (i) risk, policy, and coordination; (ii) international cooperation; (iii) AML supervision; (iv) preventive measures; (v) legal entities; (vi) financial intelligence; (vii) ML investigation and prosecution; (viii) confiscation; (ix) TF investigation and prosecution; (x) TF preventive measures and financial sanctions; and (xi) proliferation financial sanctions. See ibid 16.

72 FATF (n 27).

73 Ronald F Pol, 'Anti-Money Laundering Effectiveness: Assessing Outcomes or Ticking Boxes' (2018) 21(2) Journal of Money Laundering Control 215, 220.

74 FATF (n 70) 15.

75 The Wolfsberg Group, 'Statement on Effectiveness: Making AML/CTF Programmes More Effective' (December 2019) <www.wolfsberg-principles.com/sites/default/files/wb/pdfs/Effectiveness%201%20pager%20Wolfsberg%20Group%202019%20FINAL_Publication.pdf> accessed 31 December 2023.

on the exact meaning of "effectiveness" and the correct method of measuring it'.[76] That is to say that evaluating the effectiveness of an AML regime is a complicated process.

The same complexity is also valid for assessing the efficiency of an AML *modus operandi*. The FATF Methodology does not define the term efficiency,[77] and it appears only once throughout the document, where it furnishes assessors with guidance for technical compliance assessment concerning Recommendation 33. Recommendation 33 (i.e., Statistics) stipulates that '[c]ountries should maintain comprehensive statistics on matters relevant to the effectiveness and efficiency of their AML/CFT systems'.[78] As required by Recommendation 33, these statistics should incorporate numerical data on four areas, which comprise (i) STRs/SARs received and disseminated; (ii) ML/TF investigations, prosecutions, and convictions; as well as (iii) asset recovery practices (e.g., seizure and confiscation); and (iv) MLA or other international cooperation requests made and received.[79] In other words, although evaluating the effectiveness and/or efficiency of an AML system is not a straightforward process, such tangible indicators available in this context have been regarded as appropriate benchmarks to assess whether and to what extent an AML structure is fit for its purpose. Accordingly, in light of the defined outcomes determined by the FATF, the assessment of the effectiveness of the AML regimes embraced by Türkiye and the UK has been achieved by investigating whether and how these jurisdictions (i) exploit policy, coordination, and cooperation mechanisms to mitigate ML risks; (ii) prevent the financial and other sectors from misuse for ML; ensure proceeds of crime are detected and reported by these sectors; and (iii) detect and disrupt ML threats, sanction criminals, and recover criminal assets. Despite the criticism over the FATF Methodology, given that they are accepted as the universal criteria in this context, the study has exploited the aforementioned indicators (e.g., conviction and confiscation figures) to generate insights into the AML effectiveness and efficiency of Türkiye and the UK. Whilst this study predominantly investigates the AML effectiveness of Türkiye and the UK, it also provides insights into the efficiency of national AML regimes embraced by these jurisdictions (e.g., the period required for concluding an ML case at criminal courts). Importantly, the book reveals how effective and efficient the respective AML regimes have been in curbing certain predicate offences.

76 Miriam Goldby, 'Anti-Money Laundering Reporting Requirements Imposed by English Law: Measuring Effectiveness and Gauging the Need for Reform' (2013) 4 Journal of Business Law 367, 379.

77 Efficiency, in general terms, refers to 'the quality of achieving the largest amount of useful work using as little energy, fuel, effort, etc. as possible'. See Cambridge Dictionary, 'Efficiency' <https://dictionary.cambridge.org/dictionary/english/efficiency> accessed 31 December 2023.

78 FATF (n 39) Recommendation 33.

79 ibid.

In pursuing the aforementioned objectives, each methodology allows the authors to acknowledge the fundamental differences between two divergent legal families, namely civil law and common law, as Türkiye and the UK embrace, respectively. With these aims in mind, the researchers utilised three research methodologies: doctrinal (black letter law),[80] socio-legal (law in action),[81] and comparative legal analysis.[82] The doctrinal aspect of the methodology informs the book about the prevailing legal structure, whilst the socio-legal component allows investigating law in action, and the comparative approach enables identifying the best practices and solutions to the problems these jurisdictions face. Given the number of research methods, the locus of this qualitative study combining a multi-method research technique can be positioned within a larger body of studies fostering the dialogue between law and social sciences. More specifically, as Suchman and Mertz propose, it sits either within empirical legal studies (ELS) or new legal realism (NLR), as a study inspired by new legal empiricism,[83] with being closer to the latter due to its qualitative nature. Suchman and Mertz observe, amongst others, two salient differences between these two movements of new legal empiricism arising from the methodological variances and the lexical meaning disparities in terms of what the word 'legal' means for the followers of these two tendencies: 'a quantitative mindset remains deeply ingrained in the [ELS] movement's identity' and '[it] tends to highlight the top-down legal institutions of the state, whereas NLR tends to highlight the bottom-up normative contexts of civil society'.[84] McEvoy postulates that NLR scholarship has three striking features comprising its centre of attention on 'law in interaction', 'situated analysis', and 'consciousness manifest'.[85] According to McEvoy, the studies within the NLR realm focus on 'the interaction between people's experience of law, their ideas of the possible, and the legal actions they take'; the scholars of this movement direct their research interests on 'legal activity situated in particular contexts, where actors behave differently, rules mean different things, and causality operates differently depending on the circumstances in which people

80 As stated by Chaplin, black letter law 'is the term modern lawyers use to signify the law *as* law; to study black letter law is to study the text of the law "pure and simple," free of any extra-legal influences, free of any fictions of the law's origin'. See Sue Chaplin, '"Written in the Black Letter": The Gothic and/in the Rule of Law' (2005) 17(1) Law and Literature 47, 66. See also Michael Salter and Julie Mason, *Writing Law Dissertations: An Introduction and Guide to the Conduct of Legal Research* (Pearson 2007).

81 Roscoe Pound, 'Law in Books and Law in Action' (1910) 44 American Law Review 12. See also Salter and Mason (n 80) 128.

82 Hugh Collins, 'Methods and Aims of Comparative Contract Law' (1991) 11(3) Oxford Journal of Legal Studies 396. See also Michael Salter and Julie Mason (ibid).

83 Mark C Suchman and Elizabeth Mertz, 'Toward a New Legal Empiricism: Empirical Legal Studies and New Legal Realism' (2010) 6 Annual Review of Law and Social Science 555.

84 ibid 563–64.

85 Arthur F McEvoy, 'A New Realism for Legal Studies' (2005) 2005(2) Wisconsin Law Review 433.

find themselves' where the legal consciousness shapes the society.[86] Likewise, Shaffer posits that the focal point of NLR studies encompasses two behavioural characteristics of law as the scholars adopting this movement scrutinise, 'as empiricists – the world of facts, including material resources, social structures, and institutionalized practices, that explain how law operates; and as pragmatists – the context-shaping nature of law to address problems through reason'.[87] Given that this study examines the current relevant legal compositions of the two jurisdictions in order to discover the best practices in tackling ML and associated predicate crimes whilst evaluating their operational effectiveness in the social contexts they breathe, it sits in harmony with NLR.

As mentioned previously, this book endeavours to evaluate the effectiveness of each AML composition and to discover the underlying factors that generate discrepancies between the two jurisdictions' performance in impeding predicate crimes, thereby putting forward suggestions for reform in accordance with the research questions determined. Following this objective, the qualitative study is designed as desk-based research which has a number of limitations. For instance, interviewing the relevant authorities would make a significant contribution to the study, which would diminish the limitational concerns, as they would reflect law enforcement experiences and practices as well as operational challenges of principal stakeholders and LEAs involved in AML. However, the challenges they may encounter in carrying out their duties are hitherto available to some extent across the existing literature, including MERs of these jurisdictions, as has recently been conducted by the FATF. Moreover, along with the national risk assessments (NRAs) of these administrations,[88] the recent academic sources, such as the empirical work carried out by Basaranel and Turksen on Türkiye[89] and conducted by Savona and Riccardi relating to the other jurisdictions, including the UK,[90] further shed light on the hurdles they may confront. For instance, the UK Mutual Evaluation Report documents that the Scottish ML/predicate crime prosecution

86 ibid 441–42.

87 Gregory Shaffer, 'The New Legal Realist Approach to International Law' (2015) 28(2) Leiden Journal of International Law 189, 195.

88 It is necessary to note that the Turkish NRA is not publicly available. See HM Treasury and Home Office, 'National Risk Assessment of Money Laundering and Terrorist Financing 2017' (October 2017) <https://assets.publishing.service.gov.uk/government/uploads/system/uploads/attachment_data/file/655198/National_risk_assessment_of_money_laundering_and_terrorist_financing_2017_pdf_web.pdf> accessed 21 May 2023; HM Treasury and Home Office, 'National Risk Assessment of Money Laundering and Terrorist Financing 2020' (December 2020) <https://assets.publishing.service.gov.uk/government/uploads/system/uploads/attachment_data/file/945411/NRA_2020_v1.2_FOR_PUBLICATION.pdf> accessed 26 June 2023.

89 Basaranel and Turksen (n 67).

90 Ernesto Ugo Savona and Michele Riccardi, 'Assessing the Risk of Money Laundering: Research Challenges and Implications for Practitioners' (2019) 25(1) European Journal on Criminal Policy and Research 1.

rates are lower than the remaining British counterparts due to the unique legal framework and higher evidentiary threshold adopted therein, thereby rendering it arduous to prove criminal offences for the competent Scottish authorities.[91] Considering the limited time and available resources, as well as the difficulty associated, amongst others, with the COVID-19 pandemic in accessing LEA personnel for an interview in these jurisdictions, desk-based research was deemed to be the most suitable method. Furthermore, the previously mentioned research design does provide some advantages as it makes the data gathering process undemanding, and therefore less time-consuming in comparison to the field research, which in turn enables the researcher to conduct a more rigorous qualitative analysis of the primary sources and prior judicial decisions. Aspers and Corte describes qualitative research as 'an iterative process in which improved understanding to the scientific community is achieved by making new significant distinctions resulting from getting closer to the phenomenon studied'.[92] Accordingly, this desk-based research was designed as a qualitative study that revealed the examples of best practices performed by the two jurisdictions in tackling the phenomenon by repeating the identical evaluation criteria for both administrations, thereby unveiling any particular advantages or disadvantages of adopting one of the two divergent law disciplines.

In addition to explaining the research methodologies employed in this study, it is imperative to point out that method and methodology do not refer to the same meaning and should not be used interchangeably. Henn, Weinstein, and Foard remind us about this crucial distinction by stating that whilst method refers to a myriad of courses of action in gathering evidence about the social domain, methodology, on the other hand, stands for the research approach in its entirety.[93] Bearing this difference in mind, it is necessary also to note that the research methodologies utilised by the authors have some unique strengths and weaknesses. It is believed that utilising a combination of those approaches as the research methodology reinforces the validity of this study. Furthermore, there has been an eclectic argument on the academic position of the discipline of law as to whether it is a branch of knowledge akin to theology[94] by nature or analogous to the social sciences,[95] as well as whether it is

91 FATF, 'Anti-Money Laundering and Counter-Terrorist Financing Measures: United Kingdom – Mutual Evaluation Report' (December 2018) <www.fatf-gafi.org/media/fatf/documents/reports/mer4/MER-United-Kingdom-2018.pdf> accessed 18 January 2022.

92 Patrik Aspers and Ugo Corte, 'What Is Qualitative in Qualitative Research' (2019) 42(2) Qualitative Sociology 139, 155.

93 Matt Henn, Mark Weinstein and Nick Foard, *A Critical Introduction to Social Research* (2nd edn, Sage 2009) 10.

94 Geoffrey Samuel, 'Interdisciplinarity and the Authority Paradigm: Should Law Be Taken Seriously by Scientists and Social Scientists?' (2009) 36(4) Journal of Law and Society 431.

95 Geoffrey Samuel, 'Is Law Really A Social Science? A View from Comparative Law' (2008) 67(2) Cambridge Law Journal 288.

kindred of arts and humanities[96] or social sciences.[97] For instance, McCrudden argues that 'academic law sits uncomfortably somewhere between humanities and the social sciences in universities'.[98] Therefore, it is also believed that the use of a multimethod research approach consisting of doctrinal, socio-legal, and comparative research methodologies minimises locus concerns over the law as such a technique allows the researcher to scrutinise the legal phenomena from all relevant perspectives.

Although the aforementioned research methods have divergent standpoints and contextualisation mechanisms, the shared rationale of utilising them was to shed light on the areas of reform and compare the merits of suggestions put forward by others with regards to impeding predicate crimes. However, it requires the researcher to be vigilant in making suggestions for reform or transpose of any particular piece of law as such a transplantation process should be heeded for many reasons. Collins, for instance, reminds us that there are two common reservations about transplants from foreign legal doctrines.

Firstly, any particular law may not be useful for two distinct societies as they have distinctive social and economic structures. Secondly, a strand of law's transplantation into another body of law may result in failure as it may be well performing in regulating relevant social matters as a part of a unique set of legal concepts harnessed by a country.[99]

Kahn-Freund further notifies us that those transplantation reservations should not be limited to concerning the legal instruments as the same process may result in similar consequences when the subject is institutions due to the same social, cultural, and historical differences.[100] Accordingly, considering the two jurisdictions' discrete social, cultural, and economic backgrounds, any suggestions for legal reform, either statutory or institutional, were put forward diligently.

Reference List

Alldridge P, 'Money Laundering and Globalization' (2008) 35(4) Journal of Law and Society 437

Aspers P and Corte U, 'What Is Qualitative in Qualitative Research' (2019) 42(2) Qualitative Sociology 139

96 Paul Chynoweth, 'Legal Research' in Andrew Knight and Les Ruddock (eds), *Advanced Research Methods in the Built Environment* (Blackwell Publishing 2008).

97 Samuel (n 95).

98 Christopher McCrudden, 'Legal Research and the Social Sciences' (2006) 122 Law Quarterly Review 632.

99 Collins (n 82).

100 O Kahn-Freund, 'On Uses and Misuses of Comparative Law' (1974) 37(1) Modern Law Review 1.

Australian Government, 'Australian Transaction Reports and Analysis Centre (AUSTRAC)' <www.austrac.gov.au/about-us/austrac-overview> accessed 13 July 2023

Bardin G, 'Compliance and Anti-Money Laundering Regulation in France' (2002) 10(2) Journal of Financial Crime 135

Barone R, Masciandaro D and Schneider F, 'Corruption and Money Laundering: You Scratch My Back, I'll Scratch Yours' (2022) 73(1) Metroeconomica 318

Basaranel BU and Turksen U, *Counter-Terrorist Financing Law and Policy: An Analysis of Turkey* (Routledge 2019)

Bell R, 'Abolishing the Concept of "Predicate Offence"' (2003) 6(2) Journal of Money Laundering Control 137

Benson K, *Lawyers and the Proceeds of Crime: The Facilitation of Money Laundering and Its Control* (Routledge 2020)

Button M, Hock B and Shepherd D, *Economic Crime: From Conception to Response* (Routledge 2022)

Cambridge Dictionary, 'Efficiency' <https://dictionary.cambridge.org/dictionary/english/efficiency> accessed 31 December 2023

Cassella SD, 'Reverse Money Laundering' (2003) 7(1) Journal of Money Laundering Control 92

——— 'Illicit Finance and Money Laundering Trends in Eurasia' (2019) 22(2) Journal of Money Laundering Control 388

Chaplin S, '"Written in the Black Letter": The Gothic and/in the Rule of Law' (2005) 17(1) Law and Literature 47

Chynoweth P, 'Legal Research' in A Knight and L Ruddock (eds), *Advanced Research Methods in the Built Environment* (Blackwell Publishing 2008)

Collins H, 'Methods and Aims of Comparative Contract Law' (1991) 11(3) Oxford Journal of Legal Studies 396

Cornish DB and Clarke RV, 'Understanding Crime Displacement: An Application of Rational Choice Theory' (1987) 25(4) Criminology 933

Council of Europe, '46 Member States' <www.coe.int/en/web/portal/46-members-states> accessed 2 July 2023

Cox D, *An Introduction to Money Laundering Deterrence* (John Wiley & Sons 2015)

CTIF-FCI, 'Anti-Money Laundering and Countering the Financing of Terrorism System' <www.ctif-cfi.be/website/index.php?lang=en> accessed 22 May 2023

Egmont Group, 'Members by Region' <https://egmontgroup.org> accessed 13 July 2023

European Union, 'Country Profiles' <https://europa.eu/european-union/about-eu/countries_en> accessed 5 May 2023

FATF, 'Improving Global AML/CFT Compliance: Update On-Going Process' (February 2010) <www.fatf-gafi.org/countries/d-i/greece/documents/improvingglobalamlcftcomplianceupdateon-goingprocess-february2010.html> accessed 22 May 2023

——— 'Anti-Money Laundering and Counter-Terrorist Financing Measures – United Kingdom: Mutual Evaluation Report' (December 2018) <www.fatf-gafi.org/media/fatf/documents/reports/mer4/MER-United-Kingdom-2018.pdf> accessed 18 January 2023

——— 'International Standards on Combatting Money Laundering and the Financing of Terrorism & Proliferation: The FATF Recommendations' (Updated March 2022) <www.fatf-gafi.org/media/fatf/documents/recommendations/pdfs/FATF%20Recommendations%202012.pdf> accessed 26 June 2023

——— 'Jurisdictions Under Increased Monitoring' (March 2022) <www.fatf-gafi.org/publications/high-risk-and-other-monitored-jurisdictions/documents/increased-monitoring-march-2022.html#turkey> accessed 10 June 2023

——— 'How Much Money Is Laundered Per Year?' <www.fatf-gafi.org/faq/money-laundering/> accessed 21 May 2023

——— 'Outcomes of the Plenary Meeting of the FATF, Paris' (22–24 October 2014) <www.fatf-gafi.org/documents/news/plenary-outcomes-october-2014.html> accessed 22 May 2023

——— 'Methodology for Assessing Technical Compliance with the FATF Recommendations and the Effectiveness of AML/CTF Systems' (updated October 2021) <www.fatf-gafi.org/media/fatf/documents/methodology/FATF%20Methodology%2022%20Feb%202013.pdf> accessed 31 December 2023

——— 'FATF Members and Observers' <www.fatf-gafi.org/about/membersandobservers/> accessed 13 July 2023

——— 'An Effective System to Combat Money Laundering and Terrorist Financing' <www.fatf-gafi.org/publications/mutualevaluations/documents/effectiveness.html> accessed 22 August 2023

Ferwerda J and others, 'Estimating Money Laundering Flows with a Gravity Model-Based Simulation' (2020) 10(1) Scientific Reports <https://doi.org/10.1038/s41598-020-75653-x> accessed 11 July 2023

Financial Crimes Enforcement Network, 'FinCEN' <www.fincen.gov> accessed 13 July 2023

G20, 'Participants' <https://g20.org/en/about/Pages/Participants.aspx> accessed 5 May 2023

Global Financial Integrity, 'Illicit Financial Flows to and from 148 Developing Countries: 2006–2015' (January 2019) <https://gfintegrity.org/report/2019-iff-update/> accessed 21 May 2023

Goldby M, 'Anti-Money Laundering Reporting Requirements Imposed by English Law: Measuring Effectiveness and Gauging the Need for Reform' (2013) 4 Journal of Business Law 367

Goldsworth JG, Muller WH and Kälin CH, 'Belgium' in JG Goldsworth, WH Muller and CH Kälin (eds), *Anti-Money Laundering: International Law and Practice* (John Wiley & Sons 2012)

Government of Canada, 'Financial Transactions and Reports Analysis Centre (FINTRAC)' <www.fintrac-canafe.gc.ca/fintrac-canafe/1-eng> accessed 22 May 2023

Henn M, Weinstein M and Foard N, *A Critical Introduction to Social Research* (2nd edn, Sage 2009)

HL Deb 1 May 2018, vol 640, col 192

HM Treasury and Home Office, 'National Risk Assessment of Money Laundering and Terrorist Financing 2017' (October 2017) <https://assets.publishing.service.gov.uk/government/uploads/system/uploads/attachment_data/file/655198/National_risk_assessment_of_money_laundering_and_terrorist_financing_2017_pdf_web.pdf> accessed 21 May 2023

——— 'National Risk Assessment of Money Laundering and Terrorist Financing 2020' (December 2020) <https://assets.publishing.service.gov.uk/government/uploads/system/uploads/attachment_data/file/945411/NRA_2020_v1.2_FOR_PUBLICATION.pdf> accessed 26 June 2023

IMF, 'Factsheet: IMF and the Fight Against Money Laundering and the Financing of Terrorism' <www.imf.org/en/About/Factsheets/Sheets/2016/08/01/16/31/Fight-Against-Money-Laundering-the-Financing-of-Terrorism> accessed 13 July 2023

Jensen N, 'Creating an Environment in Australia Hostile to Money Laundering and Terrorism Financing: A Changing Role for AUSTRAC' (2008) 5(5) Macquarie Journal of Business Law 93

Kahn-Freund O, 'On Uses and Misuses of Comparative Law' (1974) 37(1) Modern Law Review 1

Law Commission, 'Money Laundering: Summary' (June 2019) <https://s3-eu-west-2.amazonaws.com/lawcom-prod-storage-11jsxou24uy7q/uploads/

2019/06/6.5612_LC_Anti-money-laundering-summary_v6.pdf> accessed 17 August 2023
Levi M, 'Making Sense of Professional Enablers' Involvement in Laundering Organized Crime Proceeds and of Their Regulation' (2020) 24(1) Trends in Organized Crime 96
——— and Gilmore W, 'Terrorist Finance, Money Laundering and the Rise and Rise of Mutual Evaluation: A New Paradigm for Crime Control?' in M Pieth (ed), *Financing Terrorism* (Springer 2002)
Levi M and Reuter P, 'Money Laundering' (2006) 34(1) Crime and Justice 289
McCrudden C, 'Legal Research and the Social Sciences' (2006) 122 Law Quarterly Review 632
McEvoy AF, 'A New Realism for Legal Studies' (2005) 2005(2) Wisconsin Law Review 433
Ministère de l'Économie, des Finances et de la Relance, 'TRACFIN' <www.economie.gouv.fr/tracfin> accessed 22 May 2023
Mugarura N, 'The Institutional Framework against Money Laundering and Its Underlying Predicate Crimes' (2011) 19(2) Journal of Financial Regulation and Compliance 174
NATO, 'NATO Member Countries' <www.nato.int/cps/en/natohq/nato_countries.htm> accessed 5 May 2023
OECD, *Money Laundering and Terrorist Financing Awareness Handbook for Tax Examiners and Tax Auditors* (OECD Publishing 2019) <www.oecd.org/tax/crime/money-laundering-and-terrorist-financing-awareness-handbook-for-tax-examiners-and-tax-auditors.pdf> accessed 1 February 2023
——— 'Our Global Reach: Member Countries' <www.oecd.org/about/members-and-partners/> accessed 11 July 2023
Pavlidis G, 'Financial Action Task Force and the Fight against Money Laundering and the Financing of Terrorism: Qua Vadimus?' (2020) 28(3) Journal of Financial Crime 765
Pieth M and Aiolfi G, *A Comparative Guide to Anti-Money Laundering: A Critical Analysis of Systems in Singapore, Switzerland, the UK and the USA* (Edward Elgar Publishing 2004)
Pol RF, 'Anti-Money Laundering Effectiveness: Assessing Outcomes or Ticking Boxes' (2018) 21(2) Journal of Money Laundering Control 215
Pound R, 'Law in Books and Law in Action' (1910) 44 American Law Review 12
Quirk PJ, 'Macroeconomic Implications of Money Laundering' (1996) International Monetary Fund Working Paper WP/96/66 <www.elibrary.imf.org/doc/IMF001/04385-9781451962123/04385-9781451962123/Other_formats/Source_PDF/04385-9781455295791.pdf> accessed 21 May 2023
Raza MS, Zhan Q and Rubab S, 'Role of Money Mules in Money Laundering and Financial Crimes: A Discussion Through Case Studies' (2020) 27(3) Journal of Financial Crime 911
Rossel L and others, 'The Implications of Making Tax Crimes a Predicate Crime for Money Laundering in the EU: Building a Legal Dataset of Tax Crimes and Money Laundering in the European Union' in B Unger, L Rossel and J Ferwerda (eds), *Combatting Fiscal Fraud and Empowering Regulators: Bringing Tax Money Back into the COFFERS* (OUP 2021)
Ryder N, 'The Financial Services Authority and Money Laundering: A Game of Cat and Mouse' (2008) 67(3) Cambridge Law Journal 635
——— *Money Laundering – An Endless Cycle? A Comparative Analysis of the Anti-Money Laundering Policies in the United States of America, the United Kingdom, Australia and Canada* (1st edn, Routledge 2012)
Salter M and Mason J, *Writing Law Dissertations: An Introduction and Guide to the Conduct of Legal Research* (Pearson 2007)

Samuel G, 'Is Law Really a Social Science? A View from Comparative Law' (2008) 67(2) Cambridge Law Journal 288

——— 'Interdisciplinarity and the Authority Paradigm: Should Law Be Taken Seriously by Scientists and Social Scientists?' (2009) 36(4) Journal of Law and Society 431

Savona EU and Riccardi M, 'Assessing the Risk of Money Laundering: Research Challenges and Implications for Practitioners' (2019) 25(1) European Journal on Criminal Policy and Research 1

Schneider F and Windischbauer U, 'Money Laundering: Some Facts' (2008) 26(3) European Journal of Law and Economics 387

Shaffer G, 'The New Legal Realist Approach to International Law' (2015) 28(2) Leiden Journal of International Law 189

Sharman JC, 'Power and Discourse in Policy Diffusion: Anti-Money Laundering in Developing States' (2008) 52(3) International Studies Quarterly 635

Simser JR, 'Canada's Financial Intelligence Unit: FINTRAC' (2020) 23(2) Journal of Money Laundering Control 297

Stokel-Walker C, 'Why the UK Is Losing Its Costly Battle Against Money Laundering' *Wired* (10 December 2018) <www.wired.co.uk/article/money-laundering-in-the-uk-russian-banks> accessed 22 May 2023

Stokes R, 'Virtual Money Laundering: The Case of Bitcoin and the Linden Dollar' (2012) 21(3) Information & Communications Technology Law 221

Suchman MC and Mertz E, 'Toward a New Legal Empiricism: Empirical Legal Studies and New Legal Realism' (2010) 6 Annual Review of Law and Social Science 555

Tax Justice Network, 'Financial Secrecy Index 2022: Turkey' <https://fsi.taxjustice.net> accessed 11 July 2023

——— 'Financial Secrecy Index 2022: United Kingdom' <https://fsi.taxjustice.net> accessed 11 July 2023

Toktas S and Selimoglu H, 'Smuggling and Trafficking in Turkey: An Analysis of EU-Turkey Cooperation in Combating Transnational Organized Crime' (2012) 14(1) Journal of Balkan and Near Eastern Studies 135

Transparency International, 'Corruption Perception Index – Countries: Turkey' <www.transparency.org/en/cpi/2021/index/tur> accessed 11 July 2023

——— 'Corruption Perception Index – Countries: United Kingdom' <www.transparency.org/en/cpi/2021/index/gbr> accessed 11 July 2023

Unger B, 'Can Money Laundering Decrease?' (2013) 41(5) Public Finance Review 658

United Nations, *World Economic Situation and Prospects 2022* (United Nations Publication 2022) <https://desapublications.un.org/file/728/download?_ga=2.182751270.1838915455.1661156885-1130433834.1661156885> accessed 17 August 2023

United Nations Convention Against Illicit Traffic in Narcotic Drugs and Psychotropic Substances 1988

UNODC, 'Money Laundering' <www.unodc.org/unodc/en/money-laundering/overview.html> accessed 26 June 2023

Whisker J and Lokanan ME, 'Anti-Money Laundering and Counter-Terrorist Financing Threats Posed by Mobile Money' (2019) 22(1) Journal of Money Laundering Control 158

The Wolfsberg Group, 'Statement on Effectiveness: Making AML/CTF Programmes More Effective' (December 2019) <www.wolfsberg-principles.com/sites/default/files/wb/pdfs/Effectiveness%201%20pager%20Wolfsberg%20Group%202019%20FINAL_Publication.pdf> accessed 31 December 2023

World Justice Project, 'WJP Rule of Law Index 2021: Turkey' <https://worldjusticeproject.org/rule-of-law-index/country/Turkey> accessed 17 August 2023

——— 'WJP Rule of Law Index 2021: United Kingdom' <https://worldjusticeproject.org/rule-of-law-index/country/2021/United%20Kingdom/> accessed 17 August 2023
Wronka C, 'Anti-Money Laundering Regimes: A Comparison Between Germany, Switzerland and the UK with A Focus on the Crypto Business' (2022) 25(3) Journal of Money Laundering Control 656

2 International AML Regime

2.1 Introduction

Over the last three decades, both national and international actors of the global financial world have been struggling to ensure the integrity and wellbeing of the worldwide economic composition by eliminating the risks posed by the illicit activities relating to the laundering of the proceeds of crime and associated predicate offences. These endeavours have been directed and supervised by pertinent global organisations, and jurisdictions have structured their unique AML systems in tandem with the minimum standards and rules set forth by them accordingly. However, despite such coordinated efforts, there remain divergences amongst AML approaches and experiences of states, the underlying reasons of which need to be investigated. Thus, the key objectives of this chapter consist of explaining the milestones of the evolution of current global AML framework, investigating the role of international AML organisations and their guidelines in composing nation-specific organisational AML structures, and identifying the potential deficiencies of those recommendations resulting in the structural AML heterogeneity across the world. By doing so, it aims to recognise the underlying causes responsible for the current global AML dissonance, present a deeper understanding of the concept of predicate crimes as to how they have developed in the global sphere, and put forward recommendations for a healthier international AML composition. In other words, in order to address the main aim presented in Chapter 1, this chapter establishes the global AML benchmarks and characteristics of such standards that result in different national AML regimes and the associated effectiveness in countering predicate crimes across the world in the first place. In this regard, firstly, the chapter sheds light on the creation or inclusion of each pertinent international organisation in the fight against ML from a historical perspective. Secondly, it identifies the instrumentalities utilised by them and how they undertake their responsibilities to establish a sounder AML framework. Finally, it concludes by proposing suggestions that would increase their effectiveness and enhance the harmony of the national AML compositions to an extent close to uniformity.

DOI: 10.4324/9781003466680-2

The considerably elevated volume of illegal proceeds derived from the international drug trade and associated concerns in the 1980s has triggered the impetus for establishing universal response mechanisms to combat ML.[1] The multidimensional nature of the phenomenon, threatening the financial integrity of the world as a whole, has motivated the UN and governments to create unique global organisational networks dedicated to tackling ML.[2] Accordingly, these initiatives have resulted in the establishment of such international bodies (e.g., the FATF) that strive to direct and coordinate the national AML efforts to prevent the misuse of the global financial ecosystem. While national actors endeavour to create their jurisdiction-specific AML structures in alignment with international rules and minimum standards determined by these international organisations, offenders continue to pose risks to the wellbeing of the global community as they develop new strategies to overcome prevailing AML measures and exploit nation-specific AML deficiencies to infiltrate the legitimate financial system.[3] As international AML standards come in the form of soft-law, they have not created worldwide uniformity. Consequently, the internal nuances and variances in jurisdiction-specific AML structures continue to offer exploitable avenues for perpetrators. In other words, a robust international AML composition depends on the harmonisation levels of national AML structures as to if and how they define ML and its predicates; which sanction mechanisms they make available to the relevant authorities; and how effectively they enforce the law. Correspondingly, the international actors of the AML realm endeavour to enhance the congruency of national AML components, synchronise and intensify the coordination across public and private stakeholders both nationally and internationally, and reinforce each link of the global AML chain.

Chronologically or in an evolutionary timeframe, it would be correct to group international AML efforts into three main areas consisting approximately of the periods of 1988–1995, 1996–2001, and from 2002 to the present. In other words, the global response to ML phenomena comprises primarily three surges of international actions. The initial international reaction, stimulated by the elevated levels of the transnational illicit drug trade, consisted of the gathering of the UN Convention against Illicit Traffic in Narcotic Drugs and Psychotropic Substances (i.e., the Vienna Convention

1 Eleni Tsingou, 'Global Financial Governance and the Developing Anti-Money Laundering Regime: What Lessons for International Political Economy' (2010) 47(6) International Politics 617.

2 Paul Allan Schott, World Bank and International Monetary Fund, *Reference Guide to Anti-Money Laundering and Combatting the Financing of Terrorism* (2nd edn, World Bank Publications 2006).

3 Fabian Teichmann, 'Recent Trends in Money Laundering' (2019) 73(2) Crime, Law, and Social Change 237.

1988), the establishment of the FATF and its first set of recommendations, the introduction of the first EU AML Directive (AMLD; 91/308/EEC); and the foundation of first FIUs. The mercurially taken steps were followed by a more mature upsurge of responses constituting the second wave, including the creation of the Egmont Group (1995), the FATF's 1996 revision to its recommendations, the initiation of the GPML (1997), and the inclusion of the IMF and the WB in the pertinent efforts (2000). Finally, the infamous 9/11 attacks have added a new dimension to the worldwide AML struggles and enlarged the functional scope of these international stakeholders to encompass CTF efforts,[4] which are two intertwined domains, isolation of which does not seem rational and practical.[5] Subsequently, all aforementioned global organisations reviewed and revised their roles, responsibilities, and authorities in the AML/CTF battle and reacted accordingly. However, it is necessary to state that this temporal categorisation of the global responses is not an attempt to provide a strict timeframe; rather, it helps to comprehend the milestones of the evolution of international AML efforts. The global financial ecosystem and its foremost actors continuously reform themselves to ensure harmony with the altering dynamics of the AML/CTF sphere and to develop responses against emerging risks, such as the novel concept of virtual assets.[6] The long-lasting battle between money launderers and the principal AML actors is likely to endure, unless some radical steps are taken. This chapter presents the evolution of international AML efforts, including its effects on the concept of predicate crimes, to identify the potential deficiencies relating to the current international AML regime/framework, and to put forward recommendations for a better AML composition accordingly. In other words, this chapter identifies the key underlying reasons for the diverse AML structures across jurisdictions.

2.2 International AML Framework

2.2.1 *The United Nations*

The recognition of the connection between the illicit international drug trade and other organised criminal activities, as well as the need for a cooperated global response in tackling the transnational dimension of such crimes in the 1980s, have motivated the UN to take responsibility for leading and coordinating nations' related efforts. The international AML efforts initiated by the

4 Nicholas Ridley and Dean C Alexander, 'Combatting Terrorist Financing in the First Decade of the Twenty-First Century' (2011) 15(1) Journal of Money Laundering Control 38.

5 As discussed previously, both illicit activities involve money or other assets with monetary value, where they both strive to disguise either the origin (ML) or target (TF) of resources. See Jayesh D'Souza, *Terrorist Financing, Money Laundering, and Tax Evasion: Examining the Performance of Financial Intelligence Units* (1st edn, CRC Press 2012).

6 See, for instance, Malcolm Campbell-Verduyn, 'Bitcoin, Crypto-Coins, and Global Anti-Money Laundering Governance' (2018) 69(2) Crime, Law, and Social Change 283.

UN in the 1980s constitute the basis for today's global response for ML threat and its underlying predicates. The Vienna Convention 1988 is the first example[7] of such a comprehensive initiative designed to deprive criminals of their proceeds of crime, thereby eliminating the principal incentive behind their illicit actions, albeit concerning only drug-related offences. Although there does not exist any explicit definition for ML or predicate crimes within the text of the Convention, the provisions of Article 3 of the Vienna Convention 1988 establish the core of how ML is defined today. It refers to the concealing and disguising practices of illegal proceeds in defining the relevant offence (Article 3(b)) whereby it prescribes the underlying criminal activities (i.e., predicate crimes) that could generate such illicit properties (Article 3(a)).[8] In other words, although it does not utilise the term ML or predicate crimes in stipulating those unlawful undertakings, it is the first international legal instrument that criminalises ML.[9]

A further crucial point put forward by the Vienna Convention 1988 is the concept of confiscation, which aims at depriving offenders of illicit gains and the instrumentalities utilised in committing the offence. Most importantly, it proscribes banks from denying disclosing financial or commercial records based on the grounds of 'bank secrecy' (Article 5(3)) and authorises competent authorities to confiscate illegal proceeds even though they have been transformed or converted into other forms (Article 5(6)(a)).[10] The remaining provisions of the Convention determine, *inter alia*, procedures relating to extradition (Article 6), mutual legal assistance (MLA; Article 7), transfer of proceedings (Article 8), other forms of cooperation and training (Article 9), international cooperation and assistance for transit states (Article 10), and controlled delivery (Article 11), each of which intensifies the global AML efforts as per the incentive fact behind the Convention.[11] Given that such powers and procedures constitute the backbone of current AML efforts, the Vienna Convention 1988 forms the initial milestone of the international legal instruments in the history of the AML efforts.

In 1997, based on the Vienna Convention 1988, in order to reinforce the MS' capabilities in combatting ML and to assist them regarding the use

7 It is necessary to note here that the previous two drug-related UN Conventions, namely the Single Convention on Narcotic Drugs 1961 (as amended by the 1972 Protocol) and the Convention on Psychotropic Substances 1971, were inadequate in combatting the international dimension of drug trafficking. The need to reinforce those Conventions was one of the underlying motivations for the Vienna Convention 1988. See United Nations Convention against Illicit Traffic in Narcotic Drugs and Psychotropic Substances 1988, preamble.

8 United Nations Convention Against Illicit Traffic in Narcotic Drugs and Psychotropic Substances 1988, art 3.

9 Norm Keith, 'Anti-Money Laundering: A Comparative Review of Legislative Development' (2018) 19(3) Business Law International 245.

10 United Nations Convention Against Illicit Traffic in Narcotic Drugs and Psychotropic Substances 1988, art 5.

11 ibid.

of confiscation powers, the Global Programme against Money Laundering (GPML) project was established by the UN.[12] In June 1998, the role of GPML was further augmented by the Political Declaration[13] and the Action Plan against Money Laundering as adopted by the General Assembly.[14] The Action Plan against Money Laundering aims to provide the beneficiary jurisdictions with the necessary training and expertise, enhance the international cooperation, as well as to assist them in creating a harmonious AML organisational structure with the requirements of the universal relevant legal instruments.[15] More specifically, it concentrates on three principal spheres of activities consisting of 'training, institution-building, and awareness-raising', 'research and analysis', and 'raising the effectiveness of law enforcement'.[16] For instance, within the scope of those activities, the GPML assists the beneficiary jurisdictions in establishing FIUs, develops web-based cooperation (i.e., IMOLIN) with other relevant international actors, such as the FATF and the Council of Europe (CoE), and provides LEAs with technical advice and thereby enhances their effectiveness and collaboration.[17] The International Money Laundering Information Network (IMoLIN) was established in 1998 by the UN on behalf of the world's major AML organisations.[18] It allows MS to access a secure electronic database of AML legal instruments, as hosted under the Anti-Money Laundering International Database (AMLID).[19]

Another cardinal manoeuvre undertaken by the UN relating to the AML realm is the United Nations Convention against Transnational Organized Crime (Palermo Convention) 2000. It aims to foster cooperation amongst the MS in preventing and battling transnational organised crime more effectively.[20] It is of utmost importance to state here that the Palermo Convention 2000, unlike the Vienna Convention 1988, overtly defines predicate crimes. The concept of predicate offence is defined as 'any offence as a result of which proceeds have been generated that may become the subject of an offence as defined in Article 6 of this Convention', where Article 6 prescribes the provisions for ML.[21] Article 6(2) of the Palermo Convention 2000 further determines the scope of predicate offences. It sets forth that the MS shall

12 UNODC, 'Global Programme Against Money Laundering' <www.unodc.org/pdf/gpml.pdf> accessed 5 June 2023.
13 UNGA A/RES/S-20/2 Political Declaration (21 October 1998).
14 IMOLIN, 'United Nations Global Programme Against Money Laundering' <www.imolin.org/imolin/gpml.html#whatis> accessed 5 June 2023.
15 UNODC, 'Global Programme Against Money Laundering' <www.unodc.org/unodc/en/money-laundering/global-programme-against-money-laundering/.html> accessed 2 July 2023.
16 IMOLIN (n 14).
17 ibid.
18 IMOLIN, 'About Us' <www.imolin.org/imolin/en/about_us.html> accessed 5 June 2023.
19 ibid.
20 United Nations Convention Against Transnational Organized Crime 2000, art 1.
21 ibid, arts 2(h) and 6.

consider 'the widest range of predicate offences' in determining the extent of underlying crimes for ML.[22] Furthermore, predicate crimes shall contain all serious offences,[23] as well as other crimes comprising participation in an organised criminal group (Article 5), corruption (Article 8), and obstruction of justice (Article 23).[24] Moreover, MS shall handle predicate offences equally regardless of the location, whether they have been committed at home or abroad,[25] albeit it puts forward some reservations relating to the principle of dual criminality. Additionally, considering the differences in the fundamental principles of the MS' domestic laws, Article 6(2)(e) provides flexibility to the MS in determining whether the ML offence as stipulated under Article 6(1) applies to the persons who committed the predicate crime or not.[26] The commission of an ML offence requires 'knowledge, intent or purpose' as the necessary elements, which may be inferred from 'objective factual circumstances'.[27] Lastly, the Palermo Convention 2000 requires the MS to establish the liability of legal persons, including criminal, civil, and administrative accountability, and to ensure effective, proportionate, and dissuasive sanctions available for them, where it shall be without prejudice to the criminal liability of the natural offenders.[28]

It is of equal significance to mention how the Palermo Convention 2000 defines the notion of 'proceeds of crime' as it directly affects the signatory jurisdictions' limitations of confiscation powers, as discussed concerning Türkiye and the UK in Chapters 3 and 4, respectively, as the two signatory administrations of the Convention. Under Article 2(e), 'proceeds of crime' is defined as 'any property derived from or obtained, directly or indirectly, through the commission of an offence' where the 'property' stands for the 'assets of every kind, whether corporeal or incorporeal, movable or immovable, tangible or intangible, and legal documents or instruments evidencing title to, or interest in, such assets'.[29] These provisions give insight into the boundaries of proceeds that could be confiscated in Türkiye and the UK, albeit having reservations regarding how those powers are utilised in practice, as discussed in the following chapters. Another crucial characteristic of the Palermo Convention 2000 that needs to be highlighted is the AML measures determined therein. It stipulates the establishment of a comprehensive AML organisational structure, including an FIU, employing robust KYC standards, record-keeping

22 ibid, art 6(2)(a).
23 Article 2(b) of the Palermo Convention 2000 stipulates that '[s]erious crime shall mean conduct constituting an offence punishable by a maximum deprivation of liberty of at least four years or a more serious penalty'.
24 United Nations Convention Against Transnational Organized Crime 2000, art 6(2)(b).
25 ibid, art 6(2)(c).
26 ibid, art 6(2)(e).
27 ibid, art 6(2)(f).
28 ibid, art 10.
29 ibid, arts 2(d) and 2(e).

practices, and an STR/SAR regime, which would deter and detect all forms of ML.[30] The remaining AML measures include (i) implementing practicable procedures to detect and monitor the cross-border movements of illegitimate cash and relevant transferable instruments; (ii) using supranational initiatives as a guideline in tackling ML; and (iii) at a supranational level, establishing close collaboration between the judiciary, LEAs, and financial regulatory authorities.[31]

Only one month after the Palermo Convention 2000 entered into force, the United Nations Convention against Corruption (Mexico Convention) 2003 was undertaken by the UN on 31 October 2003, whereby the close association between corruption and ML, *inter alia*, has been emphasised.[32] Mexico Convention 2003 promotes international cooperation for preventing and combatting corruption and confiscation more effectively, and to foster the integrity of public affairs and public property.[33] It provides a definition for predicate crimes as found in the Palermo Convention 2000,[34] suggesting that there had not been any alterations in the stance of global actors relating to the concept of predicate crimes (e.g., the exclusion of tax evasion). Under Article 23(1), the Mexico Convention 2003 provides the same provisions for a ML offence as those stipulated by Article 6(1) of the Palermo Convention 2000.[35] However, the scope of predicate crimes has been enlarged under this Convention as it refers to 'a comprehensive range of criminal offences'[36] rather than referring to serious offences as the Palermo Convention 2000 does. More specifically, the Mexico Convention 2003, in addition to the criminalisation of ML (Article 23), requires the MS to criminalise 'bribery of national public officials' (Article 15); 'bribery of foreign public officials and officials of public international organizations' (Article 16); 'embezzlement, misappropriation or other diversion of property by a public official' (Article 17); 'trading in influence' (Article 18); 'abuse of functions' (Article 19); 'illicit enrichment' (Article 20); 'bribery in private sector' (Article 21); 'embezzlement of property in the private sector' (Article 22); 'concealment' (Article 24); and 'obstruction of justice' (Article 25), where the participation and attempt in those offences are criminalised (Article 27) as well.[37] Given that some of the previously mentioned crimes had not fallen under the definition of serious crimes (i.e., they had not constituted predicate crimes) as determined by the Palermo Convention 2000, the Mexico Convention 2003 adopts a more comprehensive approach to the concept of predicate offences. For instance, 'bribery in the

30 ibid, art 7(1).
31 ibid, arts 7(2)–7(4).
32 United Nations Convention against Corruption 2003, preamble.
33 ibid, art 1.
34 ibid, arts 2(h) and 23.
35 ibid, art 23(1).
36 ibid, art 23(2)(b).
37 ibid, ch III.

private sector' (i.e., Article 21 of the Mexico Convention 2003) has been criminalised in Türkiye by the TCC 2004 (Article 252), which came into force on 1 June 2005.[38] The Mexico Convention 2003 envisages similar measures to combat ML that were put forward by the Palermo Convention 2000, such as the establishment of FIUs (Article 14(1)(b)). Nevertheless, it additionally emphasises the importance of beneficial owner identification and requires the MS to oblige FIs, including money remitters, to take specific measures relating to the electronic transfer of funds (e.g., adopting enhanced scrutiny on the originator of such transfers)[39] that had not been considered by the Palermo Convention 2000.

2.2.2 *The Financial Action Task Force*

The UN's Vienna Convention 1988, which constitutes the initial global reaction in response to the ML threat posed by the elevated levels of the illegal international drug trade, was followed by the Group of Seven (G-7) Paris Summit 1989 with a more extensive schedule beyond dealing in illicit drugs. The Summit participants determined, *inter alia*, to convene a financial action task force, which would oversee the wellbeing of the banking system and financial institutions to prevent ML and smooth the multilateral collaboration by harmonising the cross-national AML legal and regulatory structures.[40] Based on the Economic Declaration of the Paris Summit dated 16 July 1989, the Financial Action Task Force (FATF) was established originally by 16 members comprising the G-7 MS,[41] the European Commission (EC), and eight other countries, namely Austria, Australia, Belgium, Luxembourg, the Netherlands, Spain, Sweden, and Switzerland.[42] Following its inception in 1989, 11 additional members, including Türkiye, have attended the FATF during 1990–1991 plenary,[43] which may exemplify Türkiye's willingness to ensure its connectedness with the global financial *fora*, as it is one of the limited numbers of immediate applicants of this cardinal intergovernmental organisation. After accepting two more administrations during 1991–1992 plenary and three more jurisdictions in 1999–2000 to reach 32 participants, the FATF has expanded its membership to a current assembly of 39 members consisting

38 Law No 5237 (Turkish Criminal Code) 2004, art 252.

39 United Nations Convention Against Corruption 2003, art 14.

40 Paris G7 Summit Communique (16 July 1989). See also Liliya Gelemerova, 'On the Frontline Against Money-Laundering: The Regulatory Minefield' (2009) 52(1) Crime, Law and Social Change 33.

41 The G7 member states are Canada, France, Germany, Italy, Japan, the United Kingdom, and the United States. See Chiara Oldani and Jan Wouters, *The G7, Anti-Globalism and the Governance of Globalization* (Routledge 2018).

42 FATF, 'History of the FATF' <www.fatf-gafi.org/about/historyofthefatf/> accessed 8 June 2020.

43 FATF, 'FATF Members and Observers' <www.fatf-gafi.org/about/membersandobservers/> accessed 13 July 2023.

of 37 member jurisdictions as well as of two regional organisations in the last 20 years.[44] However, it is necessary to state that its jurisdiction is not limited to these members as it further incorporates a well-established global network of FATF-Style Regional Bodies (FSRBs),[45] and operates in close collaboration with other leading global organisations. More specifically, there exist nine FSRBs, which allows the FATF to reach 205 countries from all over the world.[46] Furthermore, the temporary status of the FATF has been abolished in April 2019 by the FATF Ministers, and revised as a permanent task force, eliminating the need for the specific decision taken by the Ministers to maintain its operations, thereby reinforcing its identity.[47]

The FATF's first concrete response to the ML phenomena was establishing a list of 40 recommendations in April 1990,[48] thereby introducing the fundamental requirements for the essential actors of the ML battle, such as FIs. The scope of the 1990 Recommendations was narrow as it was created to primarily address the predicate crime of international illicit drug trade and the use of banking system for ML. These recommendations did not prescribe due diligence procedures for KYC or give adequate deliberation to enhancing multilateral collaboration.[49] In 1996, in order to address those deficiencies, the FATF revised its 1990 Forty Recommendations, whereby the scope of predicate offences was extended beyond the illicit trafficking of drugs to encompass a broader spectrum of unlawful activities constituting 'serious offences' which generate illegal proceeds.[50] Furthermore, the reporting of suspicious transactions was made mandatory for the FIs, including non-bank entities, such as bureaux de change, and non-financial businesses were incorporated into the target audience of the recommendations.[51] The remaining amendments covered, *inter alia*, the refinement of customer identification requirements for

44 ibid.

45 The FSRBs consist of 'Asia/Pacific Group on Money Laundering (APG)'; 'Caribbean Financial Action Task Force (CFATF)'; 'Eurasian Group (EAG)'; 'Eastern and Southern Africa Anti-Money Laundering Group (ESAAMLG)'; 'Central Africa Anti-Money Laundering Group (GABAC)'; 'Financial Action Task Force of Latin America (GAFILAT)'; 'Inter Governmental Action Group against Money Laundering in West Africa (GIABA)'; 'Middle East and North Africa Financial Action Task Force (MENAFATF)'; and 'Committee of Experts on the Evaluation of Anti-Money Laundering Measures (MONEYVAL)'. See FATF, 'Countries' <www.fatf-gafi.org/countries/> accessed 8 June 2023.

46 ibid.

47 FATF, 'Financial Action Task Force – 30 Years' (2019) <www.fatf-gafi.org/media/fatf/documents/brochuresannualreports/FATF30-(1989-2019).pdf> accessed 8 June 2023.

48 FATF (n 42).

49 Mark Pieth and Gemma Aiolfi, *A Comparative Guide to Anti-Money Laundering: A Critical Analysis of Systems in Singapore, Switzerland, the UK and the USA* (Edward Elgar Publishing 2004).

50 FATF, 'Annual Report 1995–1996' (June 1996) <www.fatf-gafi.org/media/fatf/documents/reports/1995%201996%20ENG.pdf> accessed 15 July 2023.

51 ibid.

legal entities, the issues of shell corporations, transborder cash movements, and controlled delivery techniques.[52]

Whilst the initial tasks of the FATF were limited to examining and developing measures against ML, in order to address the emerging threats to the integrity of the international financial system, the FATF enriched its mission to incorporate efforts relating to CTF. More specifically, following the 9/11 terrorist attacks (2001), the FATF enlarged the scope of its activities to counter the associated TF risks whereby it created the Eight Special Recommendations on Terrorist Financing in October 2001, which were then expanded to Nine in October 2004.[53] In order to address the novel methods and techniques utilised by money launderers and counter the emerging trends in ML that the contemporaneous set of recommendations failed to respond, the FATF revised its Recommendations for the second time in June 2003. The 2003 revision of the standards introduced, amongst others, a new group of predicate offences and the inclusion of designated non-financial businesses and professions (DNFBPs) comprising casinos, real estate agents, dealers of precious metals/stones, accountants, lawyers, notaries and independent legal professionals, and trust and company service providers to the target audience of the recommendations.[54] Consequently, whilst the initial AML policies exclusively focused on drug-related financial offences and were concerned with banks only, the scope of predicate crimes and obliged entities has been enlarged to encompass numerous types of crime and copious actors from FIs and DNFBPs. However, this expansion was insufficient as it excluded, for instance, tax evasion from the notion of predicate offences, which obstructed the total homogeneity of the international AML system.[55] Despite its enormous magnitude and impact on the formal economy,[56] tax offences (e.g., tax fraud and evasion) were not considered predicate crimes for ML until the 2012 revision of the FATF Recommendations.

Following the 2008–2009 financial crisis, based on the shortcomings of the Recommendations detected during the third round of mutual evaluations, the FATF commenced a revision of its Recommendations in June 2009, thereby aimed at addressing the threats posed by evolving trends and techniques utilised by money launderers.[57] In February 2012, the revision process was completed by adopting the revised Recommendations, which further enlarged the

52 ibid.

53 FATF, 'FATF IX Special Recommendations' (October 2001) <www.fatf-gafi.org/media/fatf/documents/reports/FATF%20Standards%20-%20IX%20Special%20Recommendations%20and%20IN%20rc.pdf> accessed 8 June 2023.

54 FATF, 'Annual Report 2002–2003' (June 2003) <www.fatf-gafi.org/media/fatf/documents/reports/2002%202003%20ENG.pdf> accessed 9 June 2023.

55 Michael Levi and Peter Reuter, 'Money Laundering' (2006) 34(1) Crime and Justice 289.

56 See, for instance, European Commission, 'VAT Gap Report 2019 Figures' <https://ec.europa.eu/taxation_customs/business/vat/vat-gap_en> accessed 2 July 2023.

57 FATF, 'Annual Report 2011–2012' (September 2012) <www.fatf-gafi.org/media/fatf/documents/brochuresannualreports/FATF%20annual%20report%202011%202012%20website.pdf> accessed 10 June 2023.

scope of FATF's responsibility framework as the new mandate incorporated the task of combatting the proliferation financing (PF) regarding weapons of mass destruction.[58] The major revision points included, ***inter alia***, the introduction of a flexible RBA comprising proportionate measures (i.e., enhanced/simplified) as per the associated ML threats and the incorporation of tax crimes as the underlying predicate offences for ML.[59] Currently, the FATF envisages 21 types of offences that are designated categories of predicate crimes,[60] which may be seen in Table 2.1.

The FATF standards consisting of recommendations and interpretive notes have been recognised as essential minimum universal criteria for combating ML and other related threats.[61] The FATF utilises numerous control mechanisms and forms of soft power to ensure the jurisdictions implement the standards put forward. One of the available and well-known tools is the mutual evaluation report, whereby the FATF conducts periodical peer reviews of each member. Experts, not only from FATF members but also from other jurisdictions of the Global Network of FATF and FSRBs and FATF observer organisations, assess countries and territories based on the FATF Recommendations and FATF Assessment Methodology with regards to their 'effectiveness' and 'technical compliance'.[62] Based on the unique threats to which a jurisdiction is exposed, such as the prevalence of a particular type of predicate crimes, the FATF evaluates effectiveness of a country's AML structure.[63] In terms of assessing the state of technical compliance, the FATF investigates the legal instruments of a given jurisdiction within the AML legal framework.[64] In other words, the FATF assessors evaluate the effectiveness of 'law in the books' in engendering the envisioned outcomes (i.e., the law in action). However, it would be fair to argue here that the soundness of mutual evaluations depends on the trueness and sincerity of the information presented by the jurisdiction under assessment. That is not to say that jurisdictions are insincere in providing accurate data to the assessors, but it would be presumable to obtain distorted

58 FATF, 'International Standards on Combatting Money Laundering and the Financing of Terrorism & Proliferation: The FATF Recommendations' (Updated March 2022) <www.fatf-gafi.org/media/fatf/documents/recommendations/pdfs/FATF%20Recommendations%202012.pdf> accessed 26 June 2023. See Recommendation 7.

59 FATF (n 57). See also Colin King, Clive Walker and Jimmy Gurulé, *The Palgrave Handbook of Criminal and Terrorism Financing Law* (Palgrave Macmillan 2018).

60 FATF, 'Designated Categories of Offences' <www.fatf-gafi.org/glossary/d-i/> accessed 10 June 2023.

61 World Bank, *Combatting Money Laundering and the Financing of Terrorism: A Comprehensive Training Guide* (World Bank Publications 2009).

62 FATF, 'Mutual Evaluations' <www.fatf-gafi.org/publications/mutualevaluations/documents/more-about-mutual-evaluations.html> accessed 10 June 2023.

63 ibid.

64 ibid.

Table 2.1 Predicate crimes envisaged by the FATF.

Designated categories of offences	
Participation in an organised criminal group and racketeering	Environmental crime
Terrorism, including terrorist financing	Murder, grievous bodily injury
Trafficking in human beings and migrant smuggling	Kidnapping, illegal restraint, and hostage-taking
Sexual exploitation, including sexual exploitation of children	Robbery or theft
Illicit trafficking in narcotic drugs and psychotropic substances	Smuggling (including in relation to customs and excise duties and taxes)
Illicit arms trafficking	Tax crimes (related to direct taxes and indirect taxes)
Illicit trafficking in stolen and other goods	Extortion
Corruption and bribery	Forgery
Fraud	Piracy
Counterfeiting currency	Insider trading and market manipulation
Counterfeiting and piracy of products	

information on the number of, for instance, STR/SARs received[65] as the jurisdiction under assessment may seek to avoid being specified as non-compliant, albeit being dishonest.[66] Therefore, it would be appropriate for the FATF not to rely solely on the data provided; and to develop an evaluation methodology and a set of criteria independent from the information given, thereby enhancing the rigour of this assessment exercise.

The FATF has been undertaking its fourth cycle of mutual evaluations, suggesting that it is not practicable for the FATF to conduct such procedures frequently. However, the FATF utilises a further form of control mechanism, namely follow-up assessments, to continue its supervision of a given jurisdiction and thereby fill the gap between the mutual evaluations. The FATF considers the completion of a mutual evaluation on a given jurisdiction as the 'starting point' for the country or territory where it needs to initiate the

65 Information on STR reporting is one of the supporting indicators of the conclusions reached by the assessors relating to determining the compliance level of a given jurisdiction. See FATF, 'Methodology for Assessing Technical Compliance with the FATF Recommendations and the Effectiveness of AML/CTF Systems' (updated October 2021) 15 <www.fatf-gafi.org/media/fatf/documents/methodology/FATF%20Methodology%2022%20Feb%202013.pdf> accessed 31 December 2023.

66 See, for instance, Ioana Sorina Deleanu, 'Do Countries Consistently Engage in Misinforming the International Community About Their Efforts to Combat Money Laundering? Evidence Using Benford's Law' (2017) 12(1) PLOS One <https://doi.org/10.1371/journal.pone.0169632> accessed 13 July 2023; Joras Ferwerda, Ioana Sorina Deleanu and Brigitte Unger, 'Strategies to Avoid Blacklisting: The Case of Statistics on Money Laundering' (2019) 14(6) PLOS One <https://doi.org/10.1371/journal.pone.0218532> accessed 13 July 2023.

process in which the relevant deficiencies are eliminated. Although it is not a written rule, the FATF expects jurisdictions to address the weaknesses relating to the technical compliance within three years and those regarding the overall AML structure within five years, and it conducts a follow-up assessment for the latter to examine as to whether the priority actions from the MER were undertaken.[67] In other words, each type of assessment procedure is an ongoing process where the reciprocal communication between the FATF and the jurisdictions is not interrupted. Furthermore, the FATF provides all jurisdictions with various types of reports consisting of 'typologies reports', 'guidance and best practice reports', 'risk-based approach reports', and information for the private sector comprising 'risk and trends reports and guidance' and 'key issues and threats to the integrity of the financial system',[68] suggesting that there is constant information flow on evolving ML threats and on the best remedies to counter them. Therefore, ineffective implementation of 'legal, regulatory, and operational measures' for AML and the related threats or non-compliance of jurisdictions could be stemming from reasons other than the prevailing AML legal instruments as their congruency with the international AML legal texts is continuously examined and ensured within the auspices of the FATF observation. That is to say that the 'effectiveness' of jurisdictions is more likely to be determinant than their 'technical compliance' in determining the overall competency of the global financial system in tackling ML. However, it does not necessarily mean that there is no predicament relating to the prevailing legal instruments adopted by jurisdictions because differences in them constitute one of the cruces of the phenomenon exploited by offenders. Therefore, given the gravity and enormity of the ML problem, enhancing the precision of the current recommendations through more detailed explanations would be an appropriate approach for the FATF to obtain better transposition outcomes. Stipulating a uniform definition for predicate crimes and ML, for instance, would eliminate the concerns over technical compliance, thereby eradicating any issues relating to MLA or dual criminality and allowing jurisdictions to allot their scarce sources for increasing effectiveness. In alignment, the FATF would concentrate on the evaluations and programmes regarding the countries and territories' effectiveness, which is closely correlated with the level of expertise harnessed by law enforcement, judiciary, and FIs and DNFBPs, as they reflect the law in the books by their actions or inactions. That is to say that the flexibility provided by the FATF for jurisdictions in establishing definitions for predicate crimes may undermine the effectiveness of the global AML regime due to the national nuances across jurisdictions exploitable by money launderers. Adopting a more concrete definitional approach to ML and its underlying predicates, similar to the approach taken in defining

67 FATF (n 62).
68 ibid.

'murder' all over the world,[69] thereby ensuring the harmony amongst relevant legal instruments universally would undoubtedly reinforce the competency of global actors in the ML battle against the perpetrators. Hence, ensuring the universal technical uniformity, at least amongst those jurisdictions that desire to preserve their integrity with the global financial world, would equally strengthen all links of the AML chain and thereby hinder money launderers' aspiration to infiltrate the legitimate financial ecosystem.

The International Co-operation Review Group (ICRG) of the FATF continuously oversees the jurisdictions with strategic AML/CTF deficiencies, especially when they do not partake in an FSRB or do not agree on the publication of their MER results in due course.[70] Other circumstances under which the ICRG specially conducts a review process include the nomination of the jurisdiction by a FATF member or an FSRB, and unsatisfactory results relating to its mutual evaluation process.[71] In cases where the FATF determines that a jurisdiction is not compliant with the FATF standards, it applies to one of the 'sanctions' available as per the gravity of non-compliance. Depending on a given country or territory's prevailing AML structure as to whether it is sound enough to prevent criminal abuse of the financial ecosystem, it either declares the jurisdiction as a high-risk jurisdiction subject to a call for action (i.e., black list) or incorporates it into the 'grey list' of Jurisdictions under Increased Monitoring.[72] Although issuing a public warning about the risks emanating from the identified jurisdictions does not have a direct binding power on them, their decisions as to whether to collaborate with the FATF to address the recognised deficiencies determine the type of previously mentioned lists on which they will be included. In other words, jurisdictions under increased monitoring are countries or territories that have committed to eliminating the strategic deficiencies identified within agreed timeframes in collaboration with the FATF, and high-risk jurisdictions consist of those that do

69 The example here represents a more solid scenario where a person kills someone intentionally.

70 FATF, 'High-Risk and Other Monitored Jurisdictions' <www.fatf-gafi.org/publications/high-risk-and-other-monitored-jurisdictions/documents/increased-monitoring-june-2022.html> accessed 11 July 2023.

71 ibid. It is necessary to mention here which deficiencies make those MER outcomes unacceptable in preventing ML and its underlying predicates for the FATF: Having 20 or more Non-Compliant (NC) or Partially Compliant (PC) ratings for technical compliance or holding 3 or more NC/PC ratings on the Recommendations 3 (money laundering offence), 5 (terrorist financing offence), 6 (targeted financial sanctions related to terrorism and terrorist financing), 10 (customer due diligence), 11 (record-keeping), and 20 (reporting of suspicious transactions) make a jurisdiction incompetent concerning its mutual evaluation. Additionally, having a low or moderate level of effectiveness ratings for 9 or more of the 11 Immediate Outcomes (with a minimum of two lows) or holding a low level of effectiveness ratings for 6 or more of them render a jurisdiction inadequate concerning its AML composition. See ibid.

72 The FATF publicly lists those jurisdictions every four months (i.e., in February, June, and October). See ibid.

not actively work with the organisation.[73] The actions that the FATF calls for concerning the high-risk jurisdictions comprise the application of enhanced due diligence practices and countermeasures to be applied by all countries and territories, which would undoubtedly isolate those identified jurisdictions from the integrity of the global financial world. More specifically, Recommendation 19 (formerly Recommendation 21) requires FIs to apply enhanced due diligence measures in establishing business relationships with their counterparts from high-risk jurisdictions, including legal and natural persons, and to apply countermeasures regardless of any call by the FATF to do so.[74] Currently, there are two countries (i.e., Iran and the Democratic People's Republic of Korea) on the FATF's black list and 23 jurisdictions, including Türkiye, on the grey list.[75]

It is of utmost importance here to investigate the effectiveness of the FATF sanctions as to whether their soft nature is adequate in obligating the jurisdictions to comply with the FATF standards. It would be reasonable to postulate that the FATF's soft power is quite hard to compel countries and territories to ensure their congruency with the integrity of the global financial ecosystem as most of the FATF Recommendations are embedded in the UN legal instruments, such as UN Resolutions relating to terrorism (e.g., UNSCR 1267 or UNSCR 1373) or UN Conventions as discussed earlier. In other words, the close collaboration amongst the leading global organisations in the AML sphere eliminates the softness of the sanction mechanisms harnessed by the FATF. Furthermore, the soft characteristic of the FATF's sanction mechanisms is further augmented by enforcement at the national level. For example, the USA PATRIOT Act 2001[76] allows for significant financial penalties for jurisdictions (e.g., economic embargoes), which are not compliant with FATF Recommendations, as experienced, for instance, by Nauru.[77] Moreover, the stigma of failing to comply with the FATF standards and associated disgrace attached to ML further impose substantial reputational costs on such jurisdictions.[78]

73 ibid.

74 FATF (n 58) Recommendation 19.

75 As of 11 July 2022, jurisdictions under increased monitoring are Albania, Barbados, Burkina Faso, Cambodia, Cayman Islands, Gibraltar, Haiti, Jamaica, Jordan, Mali, Morocco, Myanmar, Nicaragua, Pakistan, Panama, Philippines, Senegal, South Sudan, Syria, Türkiye, Uganda, United Arab Emirates, and Yemen. See FATF (n 70).

76 For a more detailed discussion on PATRIOT Act and ML, see Michael Shapiro, 'The USA PATRIOT Act and Money Laundering' (2006) 123(7) The Banking Law Journal 629.

77 Katrin Eggenberger, 'When Is Blacklisting Effective? Stigma, Sanctions and Legitimacy: The Reputational and Financial Costs of Being Blacklisted' (2018) 25(4) Review of International Political Economy 483.

78 ibid. For a more detailed discussion on the impacts of blacklisting in general terms (e.g., as implemented by the OECD or the FATF) on jurisdictions, see Michael Jonsson and others, 'The Impact of Blacklists on External Deposits: One Size Does Not Fit All' (2022) 25(1) Journal of Money Laundering Control 4.

However, adopting a systematic change to the structure of the FATF that renders its recommendations and sanction mechanisms harder independent of the other leading competent international organisations would strengthen the FATF's identity and intensify its autonomous role in organising the global AML efforts. It would be reasonable to expect those jurisdiction-led sanction devices, such as the USA PATRIOT Act, may arouse concerns over the fairness of the punishments as the competent jurisdiction(s) may manipulate the use of those legal instruments as per their national interests.[79]

Before investigating the role of the Egmont Group in the global fight against ML, it is necessary to discuss the relationship between the FATF and the Organisation for Economic Cooperation and Development (OECD), as the FATF Secretariat is housed administratively at the OECD.[80] Although they share the same facilities, the FATF and the OECD are separate organisations with overlapping aims in tackling financial crime; the latter concentrates more specifically on economic crimes, such as corruption, tax fraud, and international bribery.[81] Furthermore, the OECD is one of the FATF Observer Organisations along with others, such as the IMF, the WB, and the Egmont Group.[82]

Lastly, in order to exemplify how the FSRBs operate within the global network of FATF, it would be appropriate to examine one of them briefly regarding its AML efforts. The MONEYVAL (i.e., the Committee of Experts on the Evaluation of Anti-Money Laundering Measures and the Financing of Terrorism) is one of the FSRBs that assesses and monitors the national authorities in terms of their compliance with the essential minimum global AML/CTF standards. This pan-European organisation operates under the auspices of the CoE, which consists of 46 MS, including Türkiye and the UK,[83] as an independent and permanent monitoring mechanism accountable directly to the Committee of Ministers.[84] MONEYVAL's responsibilities comprise evaluating a jurisdiction's AML composition as to whether it is harmonious with the principal relevant international standards and whether the principles embraced are put into practice effectively, thereby putting forward recommendations, if

79 Lorenzo Pasculli and Ben Stanford, 'Form and Flexibility: The Normalisation of "Magnitsky Sanctions" in the Face of the Rule of Law' (2022) 15(1) Hague Journal on the Rule of Law 109.

80 FATF, 'FATF Secretariat' <www.fatf-gafi.org/about/fatfsecretariat/> accessed 11 June 2023.

81 FATF, 'Organisation for Economic Cooperation and Development (OECD)' <www.fatf-gafi.org/pages/organisationforeconomiccooperationanddevelopmentoecd.html> accessed 11 June 2023.

82 FATF (n 43).

83 Council of Europe, '46 Member States' <www.coe.int/en/web/portal/46-members-states> accessed 2 July 2023.

84 Council of Europe, 'Committee of Experts on the Evaluation of Anti-Money Laundering Measures and the Financing of Terrorism' <www.coe.int/en/web/moneyval/> accessed 7 August 2023.

needed, to eliminate deficiencies detected within the AML structure.[85] Like any other FSRBs, it follows a similar procedure to that of the FATF conduct to undertake the tasks entrusted, as it utilises a peer review process of mutual evaluations and follow-up reports for executing the aforementioned purposes. Nevertheless, its authority covers evaluating the CoE MS, excluding the FATF members (Article 2.2a of the Statute) unless they request to continue to be assessed by MONEYVAL when they become members of the FATF (Article 2.2b of the Statute).[86] Therefore, considering the jurisdictional extent of MONEYVAL, it functions as a complementary organisation of the FATF, minimising the assessment coverage gaps the FATF is not authorised to evaluate, which contributes to the overall competency of the universal financial ecosystem. In other words, the FSRBs are crucial parts of the global network of AML/CTF assessment organisations, including the UN, the FATF, the IMF, the WB, and the EU, the close collaborators in the ML battle.

2.2.3 The Egmont Group of Financial Intelligence Units

Implementing an effective RBA, which constitutes one of the crucial elements of the contemporary AML *modus operandi*,[87] depends on the quality and effectiveness of the information and intelligence gathering and analysis capabilities which enable the financial sector to detect potential risks endangering the integrity of the global financial ecosystem. The ambiguous and secretive attributes of ML offences and the limited capabilities of LEAs in accessing the necessary financial data for identifying those crimes[88] have unveiled the need for establishing specialised agencies to access and process relevant information. In other words, the need for organising hubs that incorporate experts from finance and law enforcement domains who consolidate financial knowledge, analysis, intelligence, and investigation backgrounds, as per the nature of ML and associated predicates, has become more apparent. Furthermore, the success of the AML regimes both domestically and internationally requires the inclusion of the financial system to the conventional law enforcement practices[89] as the financial sector is at the forefront against ML where the placement stage of proceeds of crime takes place. Eventually, the recognition of

85 ibid.

86 Resolution CM/Res(2013)13 on the statute of the Committee of Experts on the Evaluation of Anti-Money Laundering Measures and the Financing of Terrorism (MONEYVAL), art 2.

87 Anna Simonova, 'The Risk-Based Approach to Anti-Money Laundering: Problems and Solutions' (2011) 14(4) Journal of Money Laundering Control 346.

88 George Pavlidis, 'Financial Information in the Context of Anti-Money Laundering: Broadening the Access of Law Enforcement and Facilitating Information Exchanges' (2020) 23(2) Journal of Money Laundering Control 369.

89 International Monetary Fund and World Bank, *Financial Intelligence Units: An Overview* (IMF Publication Services 2004) <www.imf.org/external/pubs/ft/FIU/fiu.pdf> accessed 23 June 2023.

these facts in the late 1980s resulted in the establishment of specific national agencies originally called 'disclosure receiving agencies' or 'financial information units'[90] to address the previously mentioned emergencies. Since then, the financial intelligence units' role in receiving, analysing, and disseminating financial intelligence nationally and internationally has been the backbone of the international AML efforts.

The establishment of the early FIUs could be considered as a response to the UN Vienna Convention's 1988 call for the development of structures that might simplify multilateral collaboration on combatting ML amongst the members of the global financial world. More specifically, on par with the universal expansion of ML threat and associated global responses, such as the establishment of 40 Recommendations by the FATF in 1990, the first few FIUs, such as FinCEN (the USA)[91] and AUSTRAC (Australia),[92] were established in the same era, just before or in the early 1990s. Although the FATF's 1990 Recommendations had not articulated the term FIU explicitly, it put forward the creation of such divisions to investigate ML cases. Recommendation 24, for instance, points out a 'national central agency' that receives (suspicious) currency transactions above a certain limit (see also other Recommendations, such as Recommendation 16, that refer to *competent authorities* to this end).[93] Accordingly, the prevalence of FIUs has progressively increased following the 1990 release of the FATF Recommendations, albeit gradually. On 9 June 1995, in order to discuss the role of FIUs and associated potential cooperation mechanisms, the jurisdictions with established specialised AML central agencies, including the UK, as well as representatives of eight international organisations and 11 other countries with no settled FIUs, gathered at the Egmont-Arenberg Palace in Brussels, Belgium.[94] Subsequently, the summit resulted in the inception of the Egmont Group by the meeting participants with established FIUs comprising Australia, Austria, Belgium, the USA, Luxembourg, the Netherlands, Norway, Monaco, Spain, the UK, Slovenia, Sweden, and France, the 'foundation cornerstones' of the organisation.[95] Following its foundation by 13 participants in 1995, the Egmont Group has expanded its member network to encompass 166 FIUs globally.[96]

90 Egmont Group, 'Annual Report June 2009 – July 2010' (2010) <https://egmontgroup.org/en/filedepot_download/1660/26> accessed 23 June 2023.

91 Financial Crimes Enforcement Network, 'FinCEN' <www.fincen.gov> accessed 13 July 2022.

92 Australian Government, 'Australian Transaction Reports and Analysis Centre (AUSTRAC)' <www.austrac.gov.au/about-us/austrac-overview> accessed 13 July 2022.

93 Recommendation 16 and 24. See FATF, 'The Forty Recommendations of the Financial Action Task Force on Money Laundering' (1990) <www.fatf-gafi.org/media/fatf/documents/recommendations/pdfs/FATF%20Recommendations%201990.pdf> accessed 4 July 2023.

94 Egmont Group (n 90).

95 ibid.

96 Egmont Group, 'About the Egmont Group' <https://egmontgroup.org/about/> accessed 2 July 2023.

Before investigating the role of the Egmont Group in the global fight against ML, it would be appropriate to examine its structural composition briefly. The Egmont Group's organisational structure consists of the Heads of Financial Intelligence Units (i.e., the governing body), the Egmont Committee (i.e., the advisory body addressing the administrative and operational issues of the network), the Egmont Group Secretariat, the Regional Groups, and the Working Groups (WGs), namely Technical Assistance and Training WG (TATWG); Membership, Support, and Compliance WG (MSCWG); Policy and Procedures WG (PPWG); and Information Exchange WG (IEWG).[97] It is worth particularly discussing the TATWG as it devotes itself to provide capacity enhancing activities through organising various training programmes, such as the Egmont AML/CTF Supervisory Course, as per the needs of FIUs identified.[98] Furthermore, it incorporates the Egmont Centre of FIU Excellence and Leadership (ECOFEL), which was created in 2018 and located within the auspices of the Egmont Group Secretariat in Canada, the 'operational arm' of the WG.[99] The point that needs to be stressed here is that it is a UK (and Switzerland)-funded initiative, which is another indicator of the UK's leading role in the universal ML combat. In more concrete terms, the Department for International Development of the UK has contributed a total of GBP 5,738,000 to the ECOFEL.[100]

The primary role of the Egmont Group in the global fight against ML and TF is to provide a secure communication platform for the member FIUs,[101] where they can interchange their expertise and financial intelligence as the global AML/CTF standards require.[102] Therefore, it would be fair to assert that the non-member jurisdictions of this informal forum for the FIUs may hinder the overall competency of the international financial ecosystem's financial intelligence exchanging ability, capacity development, and training activities. Considering the difference between the number of their associates regarding the FATF and the Egmont Group, eliminating this disassociation of the two organisations would help reinforce the current AML capacity of the global financial world. That is to say that unifying these two cardinal organisations

97 Egmont Group, 'Organization and Structure' <https://egmontgroup.org/about/organization-and-structure/> accessed 2 July 2023.

98 Egmont Group, 'Working Groups: Technical Assistance and Training Working Group (TATWG)' <https://egmontgroup.org/working-groups/tatwg/> accessed 2 July 2023.

99 Egmont Group (n 97).

100 Egmont Group, 'Egmont Group's Additional Voluntary Contributions Program' <https://egmontgroup.org/sites/default/files/filedepot/external/Egmont%20Group%27s%20Additional%20Voluntary%20Contributions%20Program.pdf> accessed 24 June 2023.

101 The secure communication platform, namely the Egmont Group Secure Web (ESW), provides an encrypted communication system for member FIUs to communicate securely amongst themselves, whereby they can request and share information on various matters, such as financial intelligence or typologies.

102 Egmont Group (n 96).

in one central global organisation would eradicate any discrepancy, increase the harmony of international efforts, and intensify the proficiency of the existing international AML structure. Consolidating the two enormous structures may be deemed impracticable, yet at least being an Egmont Group associate should be preconditioned by the FATF for accepting any jurisdiction into its Global Network to harmonise the separate but collateral struggles. It does not necessarily mean that the coordination and cooperation between the FATF and the Egmont Group are weak or inadequate. However, although the initial (1990) FATF Recommendations implicitly signified the inception of FIUs, it was not until the 2003 revision of the Recommendations[103] that the work of the Egmont Group was explicitly credited, and the creation of FIUs was stipulated. In other words, whilst the two organisations have vitally been the coordinators of the international AML efforts since their foundation, the explicit recognition of the Egmont Group within the FATF standards was actualised after the 9/11 attacks in 2003, which may give insight into the need for merging them.

It is necessary to examine how the Egmont Group describes FIUs; how the FATF Recommendations approaches them; which core functions they utilise; and how they differ in terms of their organisational structures as each model offers unique benefits and limitations. In alignment with the FATF Recommendations,[104] the Egmont Group defines an FIU as a national centre that receives and analyses STRs/SARs and other information relevant to ML, associated predicate offences, and TF and disseminates the results of that analysis to the competent authorities.[105] In other words, there is no difference between the leading global organisations' definitional approach to and expectations from these national agencies.

There are four types of FIU, namely judicial, law enforcement, administrative, and hybrid models,[106] each of which has distinct advantages and disadvantages relating to their composition and powers. The judicial type of FIUs (e.g., FIU-LUX (CRF) – the FIU of Luxembourg) are established within the judicial division of the administration wherein the aforementioned disclosures (i.e., STR/SARs and associated information) are received and processed.[107] That being the case, judiciary powers, such as seizing funds or freezing accounts,

103 Recommendation 26. See FATF, 'The Forty Recommendations' (June 2003) <www.fatf-gafi.org/media/fatf/documents/recommendations/pdfs/FATF%20Recommendations%202003.pdf> accessed 24 June 2023.

104 FATF (n 58) Recommendation 29.

105 Egmont Group, 'Financial Intelligence Units' <https://egmontgroup.org/about/financial-intelligence-units/> accessed 2 July 2023.

106 ibid.

107 La Justice Grand Duche de Luxembourg, 'Cellule de Renseignement Financier (CRF)' <https://justice.public.lu/fr/organisation-justice/crf.html> accessed 17 August 2023.

can be applied promptly when necessary.[108] In addition to allowing the swift application of judicial, investigative, and prosecution powers, adopting a judicial model of FIU also ensures a high degree of protection against potential political influence and intervention, provided that there is a strong separation of powers in that jurisdiction.[109] However, it may pose some disadvantages as well, such as communication problems with other types of FIUs in information exchange or focus issues relating to concentrating on investigations as opposed to prevention strategies.[110] The law enforcement model of FIUs (e.g., the UKFIU – see Chapter 6) operates as a part of or in close collaboration with LEAs, thereby harnessing the powers of those agencies that allow them, amongst others, to freeze transactions and seize assets.[111] Embracing a law enforcement type of FIU enables the use of existing law enforcement infrastructure, thereby allowing processing and sharing disclosures received with other LEAs swiftly along with the relevant criminal intelligence.[112] Nevertheless, it also brings along some disadvantages, including uncommon connection with obliged entities, autonomous operations independent of traditional LEAs, and similar to the judicial type of FIUs, concentrating on investigations rather than prevention strategies.[113] Administrative types of FIUs (e.g., MASAK in Türkiye – see Chapter 5), on the other hand, function as a 'buffer' between the obliged entities and enforcement authorities, including the judiciary, where the disclosures are received, analysed, and disseminated as a part of or under the supervision of an administrative body, often a ministry.[114] These models of FIUs facilitate neutral and technical analysis, smooth the information exchange with all types of FIUs, and encourage obliged entities to disclose their suspicions relating to illicit financial activities. Nonetheless, they inherently comprise limited legal powers and also lead to hindrance in the immediate use of law enforcement actions.[115] Lastly, hybrid FIUs (e.g., EFE – the FIU of Norway)[116] incorporate characteristics of the previously mentioned FIU models (e.g., having connections with both LEAs and the judiciary) and function as a 'disclosure intermediary'.[117] It would be apt to posit that the incentive behind adopting a hybrid model of FIU is to encompass the unique

108 Egmont Group (n 105).
109 World Bank, *Combatting Money Laundering and the Financing of Terrorism – A Comprehensive Training Guide: Workbook 4. Building an Effective Financial Intelligence Unit* (The World Bank 2009) <https://doi.org/10.1596/978-0-8213-7569-3> accessed 2 July 2023.
110 ibid.
111 International Monetary Fund and World Bank (n 89).
112 World Bank (n 109).
113 ibid.
114 Egmont Group (n 105).
115 World Bank (n 109).
116 Økokrim <www.okokrim.no/english.424311.no.html> accessed 17 August 2023.
117 Egmont Group (n 105).

advantages of all types of the aforementioned FIUs, thereby eliminating the disadvantages regarding their adoption. However, there exist only 19 jurisdictions around the world that embrace a hybrid model of FIU, either administrative/law enforcement (15) or judicial/law enforcement (4),[118] suggesting that the majority of countries and territories still maintain the type of FIU they operate, despite their drawbacks. Denmark, for instance, as one of the jurisdictions that utilise a hybrid FIU, is the highest ranked country in terms of the level of corruption,[119] which may give insight into its AML competency and thereby into the success of its FIU as a component of the AML composition. Ironically, however, Denmark is also the country where the biggest ML scandal in Europe was discovered, as the Estonian Branch of Danske Bank (the largest financial institution in Denmark) has failed to identify and prevent around EUR 200bn in suspicious money flows between 2007 and 2015.[120] It can be argued, therefore, that ranking high in such indexes is not enough; on the contrary, the suitability and effectiveness of overall AML composition, including the efficacy of FIU, determines the relevant outcomes. As the logic behind embracing a hybrid type of FIU is to maximise the expected outcomes, it can be stated that the Egmont Group, together with other key organisations, should promote or even stipulate an FIU arrangement incorporating comprehensive functions. However, the interpretive note to the FATF's Recommendation 29, in terms of the core mandate and functions, clarifies the minimum standards an FIU needs to have but sets forth that it 'does not prejudge a country's choice for a particular model, and applies equally to all of them'.[121] The flexibility in this end, as in defining predicate crimes, may be instrumental in the differences observed in the effectiveness of diverse FIUs across jurisdictions. Expecting identical FIU structure from each jurisdiction would be unreasonable as the nation-specific necessities differ amongst them, but enlarging the scope of the core mandate and functions or hardening them would unequivocally strengthen the current universal AML composition. In other words, considering the definition of FIUs and the essential FIU functions stated therein (i.e., receiving, analysing, and disseminating), the current international AML regime (or FIU structure/composition) needs to be revised

118 Egmont Group, 'Annual Report 2017/2018' (2018) 9 <https://egmontgroup.org/wp-content/uploads/2021/09/Egmont_Group_Annual_Report_2017-2018.pdf> accessed 2 July 2023.

119 Transparency International, 'Corruption Perception Index – Countries: Denmark' <www.transparency.org/en/cpi/2021/index/dnk> accessed 11 July 2023.

120 Elisabetta Bjerregaard and Tom Kirchmaier, 'The Danske Bank Money Laundering Scandal: A Case Study' (2019) <http://dx.doi.org/10.2139/ssrn.3446636> accessed 27 June 2023. See also Sean Curley, 'Danske Bank: The Story of Europe's Biggest Money Laundering Scandal' *News on Compliance* <https://newsoncompliance.com/danske-bank-the-story-of-europes-biggest-money-laundering-scandal/> accessed 27 June 2023.

121 FATF (n 58) Interpretive Note to Recommendation 29.

to encompass powers of judicial and law enforcement authorities. Assembling FIUs with representatives from all relevant components (i.e., law enforcement and judiciary), as well as experts and professionals from all related domains (i.e., financial forensic investigations, data analysis), would ensure the effective and timely use of those national centres in the AML battle.

As the primary focal point of the book is on predicate crimes, another critical consideration relating to the type of FIU adopted is the potential benefit of identifying predicate offences prospectively. The previously mentioned advantages regarding each type of FIU predominantly relate to their retrospective effectiveness in handling ML and associated predicates. As law enforcement and hybrid FIUs are authorised to utilise the criminal intelligence databases promptly, they are potentially more likely to predict and respond to ML threats and risks posed by their underlying predicates. Therefore, adopting such FIUs may help national authorities generate prospective risk assessments, as is the case regarding conventional crimes, thereby enhancing their effectiveness in the AML sphere. Considering these important advantages that the adoption of the hybrid type of FIUs brings along and the disadvantages posed by embracing the law enforcement model of FIUs discussed earlier, the FATF and the Egmont Group should consider promoting or stipulating their prevalence amongst the national FIUs. However, it is necessary to state that the Egmont Group correctly attaches importance to the operational independence and autonomy of an FIU rather than its type.[122] The FIU governance and organisational structure; budget and resources; the appointment and dismissal of FIU senior management and staff; the protection of information and information exchanges; and characteristics relating to accountability, integrity, transparency, and leadership constitute the main features of an operationally independent and autonomous FIU.[123] There is no doubt that operational independence and autonomy are essential characteristics of an FIU, but the advantages and disadvantages of the type of FIU adopted should not be neglected. Accordingly, Chapters 5 and 6 critically analyse the unique characteristics of FIU types adopted by Türkiye and the UK, respectively.

2.2.4 International Monetary Fund and the World Bank

The IMF and the WB[124] constitute additional principal international actors, which have taken part in the global fight against ML since 2000 when they

122 Egmont Group (n 118) 16.

123 Egmont Group, 'Understanding FIU Operational Independence and Autonomy' (October 2018) <https://egmontgroup.org/wp-content/uploads/2021/09/2018_Understanding_FIU_Operational_Independence_and_Autonomy.pdf> accessed 2 July 2023.

124 The IMF and the WB were established at the Bretton Woods conference in 1944. See the World Bank, 'The World Bank Group and the International Monetary Fund (IMF)' <www.worldbank.org/en/about/history/the-world-bank-group-and-the-imf> accessed 5 August 2023.

officially expanded their schedule to encompass AML efforts.[125] The essential functions of these bodies regarding the ML phenomena have been providing technical assistance, assessing national actors' compliance with the international AML principles, and developing action plans (e.g., the IMF's capacity development activities) against ML for the international community. Both organisations have observer status in the FATF,[126] and they acknowledge the FATF Recommendations as composing the international minimum standards for tackling ML and operate in close collaboration with the FATF, as well as with other pertinent global bodies, such as the UN, in structuring the international AML regime.[127] For instance, the revised FATF recommendations and assessment methodology were endorsed by the IMF Board in 2014, and the IMF staff have been actively participating in the mutual evaluations conducted by the FATF since then.[128] In alignment, the WB assists jurisdictions in undertaking NRAs, thereby helping compose a strategy to address vulnerabilities[129] as each jurisdiction is required to identify its nation-specific ML risks.[130] Furthermore, following the Asian financial crisis, these two organisations initiated a joint programme called the Financial Sector Assessment Programme (FSAP) in 1999,[131] whereby AML issues experienced by jurisdictions, amongst others, are addressed within the initiative.[132] More specifically, the FATF's Forty Recommendations is one of the assessment standards and tools of the FSAP in assessing the financial sector regulation and supervision.[133]

Following the incorporation of the AML policy into its programme in 2000, the IMF has further improved its response by generating permanent actions against ML. As an initial step, it recognised the FATF Recommendations as the appropriate international minimum standard for combatting ML in 2001 and supplemented its assessment criteria with those standards

125 IMF, 'Factsheet: IMF and the Fight Against Money Laundering and the Financing of Terrorism' <www.imf.org/en/About/Factsheets/Sheets/2016/08/01/16/31/Fight-Against-Money-Laundering-the-Financing-of-Terrorism> accessed 13 July 2022.

126 FATF (n 43).

127 For example, the representatives of the IMF and the WB attend the FATF working groups and plenary meetings as envisaged by the criteria for the FATF observers. See FATF, 'FATF Policy on Observers' <www.fatf-gafi.org/about/membersandobservers/fatfpolicyonobservers.html> accessed 5 August 2023.

128 IMF (n 125).

129 The World Bank, 'Financial Sector' <www.worldbank.org/en/topic/financialsector/overview#3> accessed 5 August 2020. See also Pierre-Laurent Chatain, 'The World Bank's Role in the Fight Against Money Laundering and Terrorist Financing' (2004) 6(3–4) International Law Forum (Hague, Netherlands) 190.

130 FATF (n 58) Recommendation 1.

131 The World Bank, 'Financial Sector Assessment Program (FSAP)' <www.worldbank.org/en/programs/financial-sector-assessment-program> accessed 5 August 2023.

132 IMF (n 125).

133 The World Bank, 'Financial Sector Assessment Program (FSAP): Assessment Standards & Tools' <www.worldbank.org/en/programs/financial-sector-assessment-program#2> accessed 5 August 2023.

in 2002, enlarging the operational framework of the organisation.[134] Ultimately, AML assessments and capacity development activities have become one of the regular duties of IMF since 2004, and the inclusion of AML issues in monitoring responsibilities relating to the observation of jurisdictions' financial integrity to the global monetary system has been mandated by its Executive Board since 2012.[135] The IMF monitoring consists of three main scales, namely country surveillance, region surveillance, and global surveillance.[136] The country level surveillance is of utmost importance to examine in the context of this book. Country surveillance is an ongoing consultation (i.e., Article IV consultations)[137] process in which an IMF team of economists visits a jurisdiction to assess its economic composition, including the AML organisational structure, thereby providing advice on the detected issues.[138] For instance, the IMF advised in its 2019 Article IV Consultation on Türkiye that the country should ensure compliance with pertinent UN Security Council Resolutions (UNSCRs),[139] reinforce border controls on cash flows, and intensify financial integrity safety relating to virtual assets.[140] Remarkably, similar to the FATF's follow-up assessment procedure, the Executive Board requires the IMF to conduct AML/CTF assessments approximately every five years whilst undertaking its FSAP mission.[141] A close look at the evolution process of the IMF's AML strategy reveals that the organisation has followed the global developments at the AML sphere, such as the 2012 revision of the FATF recommendations, in revising and structuring its current role in the ML battle. Additionally, it is worth noting that the IMF representatives actively participate in the FATF's revision procedures relating to recommendations and the assessment methodology.[142]

134 IMF, 'Review of the Fund's Strategy on Anti-Money Laundering and Combatting the Financing of Terrorism' (IMF Policy Paper, 20 February 2014) <www.imf.org/external/np/pp/eng/2014/022014a.pdf> accessed 5 August 2023.

135 IMF (n 125).

136 IMF, 'Surveillance' <www.imf.org/external/about/econsurv.htm> accessed 5 August 2023.

137 IMF, 'Articles of Agreement' <www.imf.org/external/pubs/ft/aa/pdf/aa.pdf> accessed 2 July 2023.

138 IMF (n 136).

139 These UNSCRs include UNSC Res 1267 (15 October 1999) UN Doc S/Res/1267 (i.e., the situation in Afghanistan); UNSC Res 1373 (28 September 2001) UN Doc S/Res/1373 (i.e., threats to international peace and security caused by terrorist acts); UNSC Res 1718 (14 October 2006) UN Doc S/Res/1718 (i.e., non-proliferation/Democratic People's Republic of Korea); and UNSC Res 2231 (20 July 2015) UN Doc S/Res/2231 (i.e., non-proliferation).

140 IMF, 'Turkey: 2019 Article IV Consultation-Press Release; Staff Report; and Statement by the Executive Director for Turkey' (IMF Country Report No 19/395, December 2019) <www.imf.org/en/Publications/CR/Issues/2019/12/26/Turkey-2019-Article-IV-Consultation-Press-Release-Staff-Report-and-Statement-by-the-48920> accessed 5 August 2023.

141 IMF (n 134).

142 ibid.

In tandem with the IMF's role in the international AML efforts, as a partner of the FSAP, the WB's AML mission includes providing technical assistance to jurisdictions in structuring/strengthening their AML regimes (e.g., conducting NRAs), revising their AML legal framework or establishing and bolstering FIUs.[143] The Financial Integrity unit of the WB provides jurisdictions with technical assistance to address illegal financial flows that diminish the transparency and integrity of their economic structures.[144] Furthermore, in a partnership with the UNODC, the Financial Integrity team has commenced a programme, namely the Stolen Asset Recovery Initiative (StAR), which contributes to the international AML efforts significantly. StAR endeavours to eradicate safe havens for corrupt funds, thereby preventing the laundering of the proceeds of corruption, and eventually, to recover stolen assets for public use.[145] As touched upon previously, the adoption of the Palermo Convention 2000 and the Mexico Convention 2003 has raised the importance of the issue of asset recovery; as such, in addition to the StAR's global network, numerous regional networks of asset recovery have been established since then. For instance, Türkiye and the UK are both members of the INTERPOL/StAR Global Focal Point Network and the Camden Asset Recovery Interagency Network (CARIN),[146] suggesting that the two jurisdictions sincerely aim to tackle laundering the proceeds of crime, including corruption, at all levels.

Lastly, it is necessary to discuss the potential outcomes of the assessment procedures that the IMF and the WB undertake on jurisdictions relating to their AML compositions. The IMF and the WB utilise various forms of soft power, suggesting that the jurisdictions may choose not to adopt their pertinent advice at the expense of being exposed to diverse sanctions, such as being destitute of technical and lending assistance. Other punitive actions they employ include, *inter alia*, terminating the relevant jurisdiction's voting and related rights and its eligibility to use the general resources of the organisation (see, for instance, sanctions against Zimbabwe as upheld by the Executive Board of the IMF in 2006).[147] Given the close collaboration between the FATF and these organisations and the effectiveness of the FATF's soft power mechanism, it is clear that the assessment procedures undertaken by the IMF and the WB are also crucial mechanisms for the global AML regime.

143 The World Bank (n 129).

144 The World Bank, 'Financial Integrity' <www.worldbank.org/en/topic/financialmarketintegrity> accessed 5 August 2023.

145 The World Bank and UNODC, 'Stolen Asset Recovery Initiative' <https://star.worldbank.org> accessed 5 August 2023.

146 Stolen Asset Recovery Initiative, 'International Partnerships on Asset Recovery: Overview and Global Directory of Networks' (2019) <https://star.worldbank.org/sites/star/files/networks-16-reduced-maps.pdf> accessed 5 August 2023.

147 IMF, 'Press Release: IMF Executive Board Upholds Sanctions Against Zimbabwe' (Press Release No 6/45, 8 March 2006) <www.imf.org/en/News/Articles/2015/09/14/01/49/pr0645> accessed 5 August 2023.

2.2.5 The European Union

The EU, another significant leader in the AML realm as a regional and supranational organisation, has introduced several legal instruments, generally in the form of directives, to counter financial crime, simultaneous with the global awareness of the risks emanating from laundering the proceeds of crime. Following the FATF's first set of recommendations, the EU's initial reaction was the introduction of the First AMLD (91/308/EEC) in 1991,[148] which aims to transpose the international standards and guidelines provided therein. In order to maintain its consistency with the dynamic global AML measures, the EU has steadily revised its AML legal framework since then. Currently, there exist six relevant Directives, the last of which (i.e., the Sixth AMLD (2018/1673/EU)) was published on 12 November 2018 and needs to be transposed by the EU MS into their national legal structures by 3 December 2020 (Article 13).[149] The novelties introduced by these Directives and the underlying reasons for their enactment are investigated in Chapter 4 when elucidating the evolution of the UK's, as a former EU member, AML legal framework. In general terms, the Directives have followed the revisions seen in the FATF Recommendations, suggesting that the prevailing AML regime adopted by the EU has mainly evolved based on and built upon the FATF's guidance. Furthermore, the timing and the frequency of enactment of the Directives give insight into the close collaboration and communication between the EU and other leading global AML actors. Equally important to note is that the EC, which represents the interests of the EU, and all EU MS are active members of the FATF[150] and the Egmont Group,[151] respectively, indicating the genuine intention and political will of the Union to counter ML and TF.

It is important to note that, on par with the enactment of each Directive, the scope of predicate crimes has consistently been enlarged. Whilst the focal point of predicate offences was initially confined to drug-related illegal activities, albeit additionally referring to organised crime and terrorism, within the First AMLD,[152] the Sixth AMLD expands it to encompass 22 types of predicate crimes.[153] More specifically, the initial narrow concept of

148 Council Directive 91/308/EEC of 10 June 1991 on prevention of the use of the financial system for the purpose of money laundering [1991] OJ L166/77.

149 Directive (EU) 2018/1673 of the European Parliament and of the Council of 23 October 2018 on combating money laundering by criminal law PE/30/2018/REV/1 [2018] OJ L284/22.

150 FATF (n 43).

151 Egmont Group, 'Members by Region' <https://egmontgroup.org> accessed 13 July 2023.

152 Council Directive 91/308/EEC of 10 June 1991 on prevention of the use of the financial system for the purpose of money laundering [1991] OJ L166/77.

153 The predicate crimes envisaged under Article 2 of the Sixth AMLD consist of participating in an organised criminal group and racketeering; terrorism; trafficking in human beings and migrant smuggling; sexual exploitation; illicit trafficking in narcotic drugs and psychotropic

predicate crimes was significantly magnified by the Second AMLD (Directive 2001/97/EC), from drug-related offences to all serious crimes.[154] The coverage of serious crimes, and thereby predicate offences, was further broadened by the ratification of Third AMLD (Directive 2005/60/EC), which explicitly urges the EU MS about terrorism-related criminal activities.[155] The Fourth AMLD (2015/849/EU) made an explicit reference to both direct and indirect tax crimes and enhanced the comprehensiveness of predicate offences to a greater extent.[156] The penultimate AMLD (2018/843/EU) brought along some amendments relating to the predicate crimes of terrorism and the activities of criminal organisations, which fundamentally provide more detailed provisions for these offences.[157] Notably, the last AMLD (Directive 2018/1673/EU) maximises the scope of predicate offences by acknowledging new crime types, such as environmental offences and cybercrime (see Article 2).[158] Furthermore, unlike the previous AMLDs, it explicitly mentions each crime type rather than using the general term of 'serious offences', which outlines borders for the concept of predicate crimes more clearly. However, it fails to define any predicate offences, a crucial and general shortcoming of the EU AMLDs that results in critical divergences concerning the implementation practices across the Union. The evolution process of the range of predicate crimes relating to the enactment of each Directive may be seen in Table 2.2.

---

substances; illicit arms trafficking; illicit trafficking in stolen goods and other goods; corruption; fraud; counterfeiting of currency; counterfeiting and piracy of products; environmental crime; murder and grievous bodily injury; kidnapping, illegal restraint and hostage-taking; robbery or theft; smuggling; tax crimes relating to both direct and indirect taxes; extortion; forgery; piracy; insider trading and market manipulation; and cybercrime.

154 Directive 2001/97/EC of the European Parliament and of the Council of 4 December 2001 amending Council Directive 91/308/EEC on prevention of the use of the financial system for the purpose of money laundering – Commission Declaration [2001] OJ L344/76.

155 Directive 2005/60/EC of the European Parliament and of the Council of 26 October 2005 on the prevention of the use of the financial system for the purpose of money laundering and terrorist financing (Text with EEA relevance) [2005] OJ L309/15.

156 Directive (EU) 2015/849 of the European Parliament and of the Council of 20 May 2015 on the prevention of the use of the financial system for the purposes of money laundering or terrorist financing, amending Regulation (EU) No 648/2012 of the European Parliament and of the Council, and repealing Directive 2005/60/EC of the European Parliament and of the Council and Commission Directive 2006/70/EC (Text with EEA relevance) [2015] OJ L141/73.

157 Directive (EU) 2018/843 of the European Parliament and of the Council of 30 May 2018 amending Directive (EU) 2015/849 on the prevention of the use of the financial system for the purposes of money laundering or terrorist financing and amending Directives 2009/138/EC and 2013/36/EU (Text with EEA relevance) PE/72/2017/REV/1 [2018] OJ L156/43.

158 Directive (EU) 2018/1673 of the European Parliament and of the Council of 23 October 2018 on combating money laundering by criminal law PE/30/2018/REV/1 [2018] OJ L284/22.

Table 2.2 Predicate crimes envisaged by each EU AMLD.

Number of predicate crimes envisaged	*First AMLD (91/308/EEC) (Drug-related offences)*	*Second AMLD (2001/97/EC) (All serious offences)*	*Third AMLD (2005/60/EC) (Expanding the scope of all serious offences)*	*Fourth AMLD (2015/849/EU) (Explicit reference to tax crimes)*	*Fifth AMLD (2018/843/EU) (Amendments relating to terrorism and the activities of criminal organisations)*	*Sixth AMLD (2018/1673/EU) (Introduction of new crimes as predicate offences)*
1	Drug-related offences (i.e., offences as defined in Article3(1) (a) of the Vienna Convention)[159]	Drug-related offences (i.e., offences as defined in Article3(1) (a) of the Vienna Convention)	Drug-related offences (i.e., offences as defined in Article3(1) (a) of the Vienna Convention)	Drug-related offences (i.e., offences as defined in Article3(1)(a) of the Vienna Convention)	Drug-related offences (i.e., offences as defined in Article3(1) (a) of the Vienna Convention)	Illicit trafficking in narcotic drugs and psychotropic substances
2		The activities of criminal organisations[160]	The activities of criminal organisations (no changes)	The activities of criminal organisations (no changes)	The activities of criminal organisations[161]	Participation in an organised criminal group and racketeering
3		Fraud	Fraud	Fraud	Fraud	Fraud
4		Corruption	Corruption	Corruption	Corruption	Corruption

(*Continued*)

159 In addition to drug-related offences, the First AMLD refers to other criminal activities, such as organised crime and terrorism, as predicate crimes by setting forth that: 'the Member States should, within the meaning of their legislation, extend the effects of the Directive to include the proceeds of such activities, to the extent that they are likely to result in laundering operations justifying sanctions on that basis'.

160 Concerning the activities of criminal organisations, the Second AMLD refers to 98/733/JHA, art 1. See 98/733/JHA: Joint action of 21 December 1998 adopted by the Council on the basis of Article K.3 of the Treaty on European Union, on making it a criminal offence to participate in a criminal organisation in the Member States of the European Union [1998] OJ L351/1.

161 Concerning the activities of criminal organisations, the Fifth AMLD refers to 2008/841/JHA, art 1(1). See Council Framework Decision 2008/841/JHA of 24 October 2008 on the fight against organised crime [2008] OJ L300/42.

Table 2.2 (Continued)

Number of predicate crimes envisaged	*First AMLD (91/308/EEC) (Drug-related offences)*	*Second AMLD (2001/97/EC) (All serious offences)*	*Third AMLD (2005/60/EC) (Expanding the scope of all serious offences)*	*Fourth AMLD (2015/849/EU) (Explicit reference to tax crimes)*	*Fifth AMLD (2018/843/EU) (Amendments relating to terrorism and the activities of criminal organisations)*	*Sixth AMLD (2018/1673/EU) (Introduction of new crimes as predicate offences)*
5		Any other serious offences[162]	**Terrorism**[163]	Terrorism (no changes)	Terrorism[164]	Terrorism
6			Any other serious offences[165]	**Tax crimes relating to direct and indirect taxes**	Tax crimes relating to direct and indirect taxes	Tax crimes relating to direct and indirect taxes
7				Any other serious offences (no changes)	Any other serious offences (no changes)	Illicit arms trafficking

(*Continued*)

162 Any other serious offence stands for at least 'an offence which may generate substantial proceeds, and which is punishable by a severe sentence of imprisonment in accordance with the penal law of the Member State' as determined under Article1(E) of Directive 2001/97/EC.

163 Concerning terrorism, the Third AMLD refers to Articles 1 to 4 of Framework Decision 2002/475/JHA, which determine the provisions for '[t]errorist offences and fundamental rights and principles'; '[o]ffences relating to a terrorist group'; '[o]ffences linked to terrorist activities'; and '[i]nciting, aiding or abetting, and attempting'. See Council Framework Decision of 13 June 2002 on combating terrorism [2002] OJ L164/3.

164 Concerning terrorism, the Fifth AMLD refers to Titles II and III of Directive (EU) 2017/541, which determine the provisions for '[t]errorist offences and offences related to a terrorist group' and '[o]ffences related to terrorist activities' and replaces the provisions of Council Framework Decision 2002/475/JHA. See Directive (EU) 2017/541 of the European Parliament and of the Council of 15 March 2017 on combating terrorism and replacing Council Framework Decision 2002/475/JHA and amending Council Decision 2005/671/JHA [2017] OJ L88/6.

165 Any other serious offences stand for 'all offences which are punishable by deprivation of liberty or a detention order for a maximum of more than one year or, as regards those States which have a minimum threshold for offences in their legal system, all offences punishable by deprivation of liberty or a detention order for a minimum of more than six months' as stipulated by the Directive 2005/60/EC, art (5)(F).

Table 2.2 (Continued)

Number of predicate crimes envisaged	*First AMLD (91/308/EEC) (Drug-related offences)*	*Second AMLD (2001/97/EC) (All serious offences)*	*Third AMLD (2005/60/EC) (Expanding the scope of all serious offences)*	*Fourth AMLD (2015/849/EU) (Explicit reference to tax crimes)*	*Fifth AMLD (2018/843/EU) (Amendments relating to terrorism and the activities of criminal organisations)*	*Sixth AMLD (2018/1673/EU) (Introduction of new crimes as predicate offences)*
8						Illicit trafficking in stolen goods and other goods
9						Trafficking in human beings and migrant smuggling
10						Counterfeiting of currency
11						Counterfeiting and piracy of products
12						Insider trading and market manipulation
13						Murder, grievous bodily injury
14						Kidnapping, illegal restraint and hostage-taking
15						Robbery or theft
16						Smuggling
17						Sexual exploitation
18						Extortion
19						Forgery
20						Piracy
21						**Environmental crime**
22						**Cybercrime**

Another crucial nuance that needs to be considered is the legal impact of the Directives on the EU MS as to whether those legal instruments provide any flexibility in structuring their national AML compositions. Article 288 of the Treaty on the Functioning of the European Union 2009 sets forth that '[a] directive shall be binding as to the result to be achieved upon each state to which it is addressed, but shall leave to the national authorities the choice of form and methods'.[166] As stipulated by the Directive, the EU MS are free to embrace a unique AML regime, suggesting that the national variations may impede the overall competency and/or harmonisation of the EU's AML composition. For instance, whilst some EU jurisdictions envisage harsher punishments for ML, others implement more lenient sanctions for the same criminal activity, as is evident in the imprisonment terms envisaged. Section 261 of the German Criminal Code (*Strafgesetzbuch – StGB*), for example, sets forth an incarceration period of three months to five years for money launderers,[167] whereas Article 648 *bis* of the Penal Code of Italy (*Codice Penale*) determines it from four to 12 years.[168] Furthermore, this polarity is more evident in non-EU MS' correspondent practices as whilst Türkiye, for example, envisages three to seven years,[169] the UK, on the other hand, sets forth an up to 14-year imprisonment term for ML.[170] In other words, as Turksen aptly observes, the harmonisation efforts of the EU devoted to creating a more consistent AML regime across the Union is far from generating a uniform AML legal framework.[171] Therefore, the EU Directives should outline the rules of desired national AML compositions through more detailed provisions to lessen the flexibility areas, thereby eliminating the significant variations in national AML practices. Alternatively, the EU should utilise different legal instruments, such as regulations or decisions,[172] to direct MS' AML efforts through binding and unifying legal instruments rather than setting ultimate goals only. That is not to say that the RBA, which the FATF Recommendations and the relevant EU Directives (excluding the first two) promote, should be withdrawn, and a 'rule-based'

166 Consolidated version of the Treaty on the Functioning of the European Union Part Six – Institutional and Financial Provisions Title I – Institutional Provisions Chapter 2 – Legal Acts of the Union, Adoption Procedures and Other Provisions Section 1 – The Legal Acts of the Union Article 288 (ex-Article 249 TEC) [2016] OJ C202/171.

167 German Criminal Code (Strafgesetzbuch – StGB), s 261.

168 Italian Criminal Code (Codice Penale), art 648 bis.

169 Law No 5237 (Turkish Criminal Code) 2004, art 282(1).

170 Proceeds of Crime Act 2002, s 334(1).

171 Umut Turksen, 'Implications of Anti-Money Laundering Law for Accountancy in the European Union – A Comparative Study' in Nicholas Ryder, Umut Turksen and Sabine Hassler (eds), *Fighting Financial Crime in the Global Economic Crisis* (1st edn, Routledge 2014) 107.

172 Article 288 of the Treaty on the Functioning of the European Union stipulates that '[a regulation] shall be binding in its entirety and directly applicable in all Member States'. It also envisages that '[a] decision shall be binding in its entirety', albeit binding only on those it specifies. See (n 166).

strategy should be embraced. Furthermore, this approach does not mean that all EU MS should adopt an identical organisational AML regime as each jurisdiction has unique dynamics, national variances, and nuances, and such a stipulation would contradict the founding principles of the Union. Yet, the RBA strategy would be more effective if the homogeneity of national AML legal instruments is increased, as a more harmonious AML regime throughout the Union would enhance its effectiveness in preventing the misuse of the financial system. As discussed, the EU AMLDs do not provide definitions for the predicate crimes specified. Nevertheless, unified definitions of the predicate offences would reinforce the AML regime, particularly regarding cross-border joint investigations, forum shopping, and similar issues/practices. However, establishing a more consistent AML structure is not adequate by itself. As Turksen rightly states, the harmony of the national legal instruments across the EU needs to be underpinned by robust coordination across public and private stakeholders for a reinforced AML composition.[173]

In order to increase the coherence amongst national AML legal frameworks and enhance the coordination between the relevant stakeholders, such as the FIUs, the EU modernised its regulatory framework in 2015.[174] In accordance with the FATF Recommendations, stipulating the risk assessment procedures for implementing an effective RBA,[175] and as the Fourth AMLD required,[176] the EC has started to conduct biennial supranational risk assessments since 2015. The first Supranational Risk Assessment Report (SNRA) was published on 26 June 2017,[177] and it was updated on 24 July 2019 by the publication of the second SNRA, whereby the relevant threats for the Union relating to the legal framework and the vulnerabilities stemming from the implementation have been identified.[178] It would be fair to claim that the Fourth AMLD has considerably reinforced the Union's AML composition, as it further

173 Turksen (n 171) 80.

174 European Commission, 'Anti-Money Laundering and Countering the Financing of Terrorism: 2015 Modernised Regulatory Framework' <https://ec.europa.eu/info/business-economy-euro/banking-and-finance/financial-supervision-and-risk-management/anti-money-laundering-and-counter-terrorist-financing_en> accessed 15 August 2023.

175 FATF (n 58) Recommendation 1.

176 Directive (EU) 2015/849, art 6(1).

177 European Commission, 'Report from the Commission to the European Parliament and the Council on the Assessment of the Risks of Money Laundering and Terrorist Financing Affecting the Internal Market and relating to Cross-Border Activities' COM (2017) 340 final <https://eur-lex.europa.eu/legal-content/EN/TXT/PDF/?uri=CELEX:52017DC0340> accessed 15 August 2023.

178 European Commission, 'Report from the Commission to the European Parliament and the Council on the Assessment of the Risks of Money Laundering and Terrorist Financing Affecting the Internal Market and relating to Cross-Border Activities' COM (2019) 370 final <https://ec.europa.eu/info/sites/info/files/supranational_risk_assessment_of_the_money_laundering_and_terrorist_financing_risks_affecting_the_union.pdf> accessed 15 August 2023.

introduced, *inter alia*, the mandate for identifying the high-risk third countries[179] and adopting the regulatory standards developed by the European Supervisory Authorities.[180] Accordingly, in order to protect the Union's financial ecosystem and ensure the proper functioning of the internal market, the EU periodically identifies such jurisdictions with strategic deficiencies in their AML regimes that pose significant threats to its economic integrity.[181] For instance, the EC has recently referred Austria, Belgium, and the Netherlands to the Court of Justice of the European Union, with an appeal for financial sanctions, for failing to fully comply with the Fourth AMLD as they have not thoroughly transposed it into their national law.[182]

Lastly, as an example of good practice, it would be appropriate to discuss FIU.net, a 'decentralised and sophisticated' communication network available to FIUs in the EU,[183] including the UK, albeit it has left the Union. Similar to the broader network of Egmont Secure Web (ESW), FIU.net provides a secure communication platform for the FIUs from the EU at a limited geographical level, where they can interchange their expertise and financial intelligence promptly and securely. The recognition of the need for a collaborative and Union-wide response to borderless ML phenomena and its underlying predicates has motivated the EU to internationalise the relevant intelligence efforts of its members. As an initial step, the FIUs of France, Italy, Luxembourg, and the UK joined the FIU of the Netherlands in 2002 based on the provisions of Council Decision 2000/642/JHA,[184] which considers the Egmont Group's worldwide network as an appropriate model,[185] constituting the genesis of today's FIU.net. Furthermore, FIU.net was incorporated into Europol in 2016,[186] suggesting that similar to the capabilities of hybrid or

179 Directive (EU) 2015/849, art 9.

180 Directive (EU) 2015/849, art 64.

181 See, for instance, Commission Delegated Regulation (EU) 2020/855 of 7 May 2020 amending Delegated Regulation (EU) 2016/1675 supplementing Directive (EU) 2015/849 of the European Parliament and of the Council, as regards adding the Bahamas, Barbados, Botswana, Cambodia, Ghana, Jamaica, Mauritius, Mongolia, Myanmar/Burma, Nicaragua, Panama and Zimbabwe to the table in point I of the Annex and deleting Bosnia-Herzegovina, Ethiopia, Guyana, Lao People's Democratic Republic, Sri Lanka and Tunisia from this table (Text with EEA relevance) [2020] OJ L195/1.

182 European Union Newsroom, 'Anti-Money Laundering: Commission Decides to Refer Austria, Belgium and the Netherlands to the Court of Justice of the EU for Failing to Fully Implement EU Anti-Money Laundering Rules' (2 July 2020) <https://europa.eu/newsroom/content/bekämpfung-von-geldwäsche-kommission-verklagt-österreich-belgien-und-die-niederlande-vor-dem_en> accessed 15 August 2023.

183 Europol, 'Financial Intelligence Units – FIU.net' <www.europol.europa.eu/about-europol/financial-intelligence-units-fiu-net> accessed 8 September 2023.

184 ibid.

185 Council Decision of 17 October 2000 concerning arrangements for cooperation between financial intelligence units of the Member States in respect of exchanging information (2000/642/JHA) [2000] OJ L271/4.

186 Europol (n 183).

law enforcement types of FIUs, the financial and criminal intelligence can be utilised simultaneously as the previously mentioned incorporation allows the use of opportunities available to Europol, the coordinator LEA of the EU. In other words, it can be argued that the EU has eliminated the deficiencies of its members relating to adopting a particular model of FIU that does not allow the utilisation of criminal intelligence promptly for financial matters. Therefore, in light of this example of good practice, the remaining jurisdictions of the global financial world, including Türkiye, should seek similar solutions to overcome the deficiencies relating to the type of FIU they operate to enhance their effectiveness in the AML sphere.

2.3 Conclusion

The FATF-orchestrated international AML efforts are firmly attached to and considerably supported by other international organisations, such as the UN, IMF, WB, and the EU. Whilst the FATF sets the minimum international standards and outlines the principal objectives and essential concepts for preventing the misuse of the legitimate financial system, others reflect those principles within their agendas and perform their responsibilities accordingly. The AML regimes are supervised and directed by these universal actors at international and regional levels. The jurisdictions that seek to establish and maintain their integrity with the global financial ecosystem harmonise their AML regimes in tandem with the international AML standards. However, there remain variations in the national AML regimes due to national differences, such as capacity constraints and inadequate resources,[187] and nation-specific nuances, such as the type of law discipline or FIU adopted. Furthermore, the sincerity of states in effectively carrying out the international guidelines and in collaborating with their cross-border counterparts remains to be another crucial determiner of the global success of the fight against ML and associated predicates.

The victory in the global AML battle incontrovertibly depends on the soundness of every single link of the international AML chain. However, substantial national variances in the legal compositions and enforcement practices across jurisdictions degenerate the overall competency of the universal AML ecosystem. Therefore, establishing worldwide uniformity in the AML regime seems to be the key to preventing offenders from infiltrating the legitimate financial system. As establishing a uniform AML composition globally is unpracticable, enhancing the harmony of legal instruments and enforcement practices as much as possible appears to be the most appropriate and feasible step to be taken. Currently, the international AML stakeholders follow a similar strategy, yet they should narrow the borders of flexibility for jurisdictions in composing their AML regimes to attain a more reinforced international AML structure.

187 Nankpan Moses Nanyun and Alireza Nasiri, 'Role of FATF on Financial Systems of Countries: Successes and Challenges' (2021) 24(2) Journal of Money Laundering Control 234.

The laundering methodologies utilised by offenders, like the emerging predicate crimes, have no limits and have been changing continuously.[188] In other words, today's AML rules may not be adequate tomorrow in preventing the phenomenon, which is dynamic and altering constantly. However, the evolution of the international AML regime betokens that the global actors have been developing and revising their responses retrospectively, as is evident in how the three waves of reactions have occurred. That being the case, developing prospective responses should be another consideration for each actor in the AML battle. For instance, in a scenario in which we cannot defeat the COVID-19 pandemic in a short period whereby movement and travel of persons may be limited, it would be rational to expect perpetrators to develop new ML typologies.[189] Therefore, considering the potential threats, the global AML bodies should improve the action plans they offer prospectively in providing technical assistance and necessary training activities to the relevant stakeholders, including law enforcement, judiciary, and the obliged entities.

This chapter has examined the roles of international AML organisations in the global fight against ML and its underlying predicates and highlighted the areas for reform in establishing a more precise response. The collaboration and the harmony amongst these bodies indicate that they are genuinely intent on eliminating the risks posed by their common adversary, ML. Nevertheless, these efforts would have no meaning unless they are underpinned by each link of the global AML chain. Inasmuch, the following chapters analyse the respective AML structures in Türkiye and the UK in order to establish how the two representatives of the financial world have composed their national regimes differently, albeit following identical international standards and principles. By doing so, this study sheds light on how those standards may generate diverse outcomes across the world, as demonstrated in terms of predicate crimes encountered by Türkiye and the UK, which would unveil the unique nuances responsible for the effectiveness or ineffectiveness of a given system.

Reference List

Australian Government, 'Australian Transaction Reports and Analysis Centre (AUSTRAC)' <www.austrac.gov.au/about-us/austrac-overview> accessed 13 July 2022

Bjerregaard E and Kirchmaier T, 'The Danske Bank Money Laundering Scandal: A Case Study' (2019) <http://dx.doi.org/10.2139/ssrn.3446636> accessed 27 June 2023

Campbell-Verduyn M, 'Bitcoin, Crypto-Coins, and Global Anti-Money Laundering Governance' (2018) 69(2) Crime, Law, and Social Change 283

188 He Ping, 'New Trends in Money Laundering from the Real World to Cyberspace' (2005) 8(1) Journal of Money Laundering Control 48; Fabian Teichmann, 'Recent Trends in Money Laundering and Terrorism Financing' (2019) 27(1) Journal of Financial Regulation and Compliance 2.

189 See, for instance, Christoph Wronka, 'Impact of COVID-19 on Financial Institutions: Navigating the Global Emerging Patterns of Financial Crime' (2022) 29(2) Journal of Financial Crime 476.

Chatain PL, 'The World Bank's Role in the Fight against Money Laundering and Terrorist Financing' (2004) 6(3–4) International Law Forum (Hague, Netherlands) 190

Council of Europe, '46 Member States' <www.coe.int/en/web/portal/46-members-states> accessed 2 July 2023

——— 'Committee of Experts on the Evaluation of Anti-Money Laundering Measures and the Financing of Terrorism' <www.coe.int/en/web/moneyval/> accessed 7 August 2023

Curley S, 'Danske Bank: The Story of Europe's Biggest Money Laundering Scandal' *News on Compliance* <https://newsoncompliance.com/danske-bank-the-story-of-europes-biggest-money-laundering-scandal/> accessed 27 June 2023

Deleanu IS, 'Do Countries Consistently Engage in Misinforming the International Community About Their Efforts to Combat Money Laundering? Evidence Using Benford's Law' (2017) 12(1) PLoS One <https://doi.org/10.1371/journal.pone.0169632> accessed 13 July 2023

D'Souza J, *Terrorist Financing, Money Laundering, and Tax Evasion: Examining the Performance of Financial Intelligence Units* (1st edn, CRC Press 2012)

Eggenberger K, 'When Is Blacklisting Effective? Stigma, Sanctions and Legitimacy: The Reputational and Financial Costs of Being Blacklisted' (2018) 25(4) Review of International Political Economy 483

Egmont Group, 'Annual Report June 2009 – July 2010' (2010) <https://egmontgroup.org/en/filedepot_download/1660/26> accessed 23 June 2023

——— 'Annual Report 2017/2018' (2018) <https://egmontgroup.org/wp-content/uploads/2021/09/Egmont_Group_Annual_Report_2017-2018.pdf> accessed 2 July 2023

——— 'Understanding FIU Operational Independence and Autonomy' (October 2018) <https://egmontgroup.org/wp-content/uploads/2021/09/2018_Understanding_FIU_Operational_Independence_and_Autonomy.pdf> accessed 2 July 2023

——— 'Egmont Group's Additional Voluntary Contributions Program' <https://egmontgroup.org/sites/default/files/filedepot/external/Egmont%20Group%27s%20Additional%20Voluntary%20Contributions%20Program.pdf> accessed 24 June 2023

——— 'About the Egmont Group' <https://egmontgroup.org/about/> accessed 2 July 2023

——— 'Financial Intelligence Units' <https://egmontgroup.org/about/financial-intelligence-units/> accessed 2 July 2023

——— 'Members by Region' <https://egmontgroup.org> accessed 13 July 2023

——— 'Organization and Structure' <https://egmontgroup.org/about/organization-and-structure/> accessed 2 July 2023

——— 'Working Groups: Technical Assistance and Training Working Group (TATWG)' <https://egmontgroup.org/working-groups/tatwg/> accessed 2 July 2023

European Commission, 'VAT Gap Report 2019 Figures' <https://ec.europa.eu/taxation_customs/business/vat/vat-gap_en> accessed 2 July 2023

——— 'Anti-Money Laundering and Countering the Financing of Terrorism: 2015 Modernised Regulatory Framework' <https://ec.europa.eu/info/business-economy-euro/banking-and-finance/financial-supervision-and-risk-management/anti-money-laundering-and-counter-terrorist-financing_en> accessed 15 August 2023

——— 'Report from the Commission to the European Parliament and the Council on the Assessment of the Risks of Money Laundering and Terrorist Financing Affecting the Internal Market and relating to Cross-Border Activities' COM (2017) 340 final <https://eur-lex.europa.eu/legal-content/EN/TXT/PDF/?uri=CELEX:52017DC0340> accessed 15 August 2023

——— 'Report from the Commission to the European Parliament and the Council on the Assessment of the Risks of Money Laundering and Terrorist Financing Affecting the Internal Market and relating to Cross-Border Activities' COM (2019) 370 final <https://ec.europa.eu/info/sites/info/files/supranational_risk_assessment_of_the_money_laundering_and_terrorist_financing_risks_affecting_the_union.pdf> accessed 15 August 2023

European Union Newsroom, 'Anti-Money Laundering: Commission Decides to Refer Austria, Belgium and the Netherlands to the Court of Justice of the EU for Failing to Fully Implement EU Anti-Money Laundering Rules' (2 July 2020) <https://europa.eu/newsroom/content/bekämpfung-von-geldwäsche-kommission-verklagt-österreich-belgien-und-die-niederlande-vor-dem_en> accessed 15 August 2023

Europol, 'Financial Intelligence Units – FIU.net' <www.europol.europa.eu/about-europol/financial-intelligence-units-fiu-net> accessed 8 September 2023

FATF, 'The Forty Recommendations of the Financial Action Task Force on Money Laundering' (1990) <www.fatf-gafi.org/media/fatf/documents/recommendations/pdfs/FATF%20Recommendations%201990.pdf> accessed 4 July 2023

——— 'Annual Report 1995–1996' (June 1996) <www.fatf-gafi.org/media/fatf/documents/reports/1995%201996%20ENG.pdf> accessed 15 July 2023

——— 'FATF IX Special Recommendations' (October 2001) <www.fatf-gafi.org/media/fatf/documents/reports/FATF%20Standards%20-%20IX%20Special%20Recommendations%20and%20IN%20rc.pdf> accessed 8 June 2023

——— 'Annual Report 2002–2003' (June 2003) <www.fatf-gafi.org/media/fatf/documents/reports/2002%202003%20ENG.pdf> accessed 9 June 2023

——— 'The Forty Recommendations' (June 2003) <www.fatf-gafi.org/media/fatf/documents/recommendations/pdfs/FATF%20Recommendations%202003.pdf> accessed 24 June 2023

——— 'Annual Report 2011–2012' (September 2012) <www.fatf-gafi.org/media/fatf/documents/brochuresannualreports/FATF%20annual%20report%202011%202012%20website.pdf> accessed 10 June 2023

——— 'Financial Action Task Force – 30 Years' (2019) <www.fatf-gafi.org/media/fatf/documents/brochuresannualreports/FATF30-(1989-2019).pdf> accessed 8 June 2023

——— 'Methodology for Assessing Technical Compliance with the FATF Recommendations and the Effectiveness of AML/CTF Systems' (updated October 2021) 15 <www.fatf-gafi.org/media/fatf/documents/methodology/FATF%20Methodology%2022%20Feb%202013.pdf> accessed 31 December 2023

——— 'International Standards on Combatting Money Laundering and the Financing of Terrorism & Proliferation: The FATF Recommendations' (Updated March 2022) <www.fatf-gafi.org/media/fatf/documents/recommendations/pdfs/FATF%20Recommendations%202012.pdf> accessed 26 June 2023

——— 'Countries' <www.fatf-gafi.org/countries/> accessed 8 June 2023

——— 'Designated Categories of Offences' <www.fatf-gafi.org/glossary/d-i/> accessed 10 June 2023

——— 'History of the FATF' <www.fatf-gafi.org/about/historyofthefatf/> accessed 8 June 2023

——— 'FATF Secretariat' <www.fatf-gafi.org/about/fatfsecretariat/> accessed 11 June 2023

——— 'High-Risk and Other Monitored Jurisdictions' <www.fatf-gafi.org/publications/high-risk-and-other-monitored-jurisdictions/documents/increased-monitoring-june-2022.html> accessed 11 July 2023

——— 'FATF Members and Observers' <www.fatf-gafi.org/about/membersandobservers/> accessed 13 July 2023

——— 'FATF Policy on Observers' <www.fatf-gafi.org/about/membersandobservers/fatfpolicyonobservers.html> accessed 5 August 2023
——— 'Mutual Evaluations' <www.fatf-gafi.org/publications/mutualevaluations/documents/more-about-mutual-evaluations.html> accessed 10 June 2023
——— 'Organisation for Economic Cooperation and Development (OECD)' <www.fatf-gafi.org/pages/organisationforeconomiccooperationanddevelopmentoecd.html> accessed 11 June 2020
Ferwerda J, Deleanu IS and Unger B, 'Strategies to Avoid Blacklisting: The Case of Statistics on Money Laundering' (2019) 14(6) PLOS One <https://doi.org/10.1371/journal.pone.0218532> accessed 13 July 2023
Financial Crimes Enforcement Network, 'FinCEN' <www.fincen.gov> accessed 13 July 2022
Gelemerova L, 'On the Frontline Against Money-Laundering: The Regulatory Minefield' (2009) 52(1) Crime, Law and Social Change 33
IMF, 'Press Release: IMF Executive Board Upholds Sanctions Against Zimbabwe' (Press Release No 6/45, 8 March 2006) <www.imf.org/en/News/Articles/2015/09/14/01/49/pr0645> accessed 5 August 2023
——— 'Review of the Fund's Strategy on Anti-Money Laundering and Combatting the Financing of Terrorism' (IMF Policy Paper, 20 February 2014) <www.imf.org/external/np/pp/eng/2014/022014a.pdf> accessed 5 August 2023
——— 'Turkey: 2019 Article IV Consultation-Press Release; Staff Report; and Statement by the Executive Director for Turkey' (IMF Country Report No 19/395, December 2019) <www.imf.org/en/Publications/CR/Issues/2019/12/26/Turkey-2019-Article-IV-Consultation-Press-Release-Staff-Report-and-Statement-by-the-48920> accessed 5 August 2023
——— 'Articles of Agreement' <www.imf.org/external/pubs/ft/aa/pdf/aa.pdf> accessed 2 July 2023
——— 'Factsheet: IMF and the Fight Against Money Laundering and the Financing of Terrorism' <www.imf.org/en/About/Factsheets/Sheets/2016/08/01/16/31/Fight-Against-Money-Laundering-the-Financing-of-Terrorism> accessed 13 July 2022
——— 'Surveillance' <www.imf.org/external/about/econsurv.htm> accessed 5 August 2023
IMOLIN, 'About Us' <www.imolin.org/imolin/en/about_us.html> accessed 5 June 2023
——— 'United Nations Global Programme Against Money Laundering' <www.imolin.org/imolin/gpml.html#whatis> accessed 5 June 2023
International Monetary Fund and World Bank, *Financial Intelligence Units: An Overview* (IMF Publication Services 2004) <www.imf.org/external/pubs/ft/FIU/fiu.pdf> accessed 23 June 2023
Jonsson M and others, 'The Impact of Blacklists on External Deposits: One Size Does Not Fit All' (2022) 25(1) Journal of Money Laundering Control 4
Keith N, 'Anti-Money Laundering: A Comparative Review of Legislative Development' (2018) 19(3) Business Law International 245
King C, Walker C and Gurulé J, *The Palgrave Handbook of Criminal and Terrorism Financing Law* (Palgrave Macmillan 2018)
La Justice Grand Duche de Luxembourg, 'Cellule de Renseignement Financier (CRF)' <https://justice.public.lu/fr/organisation-justice/crf.html> accessed 17 August 2023
Levi M and Reuter P, 'Money Laundering' (2006) 34(1) Crime and Justice 289
Nanyun NM and Nasiri A, 'Role of FATF on Financial Systems of Countries: Successes and Challenges' (2021) 24(2) Journal of Money Laundering Control 234
Økokrim <www.okokrim.no/english.424311.no.html> accessed 17 August 2023
Oldani C and Wouters J, *The G7, Anti-Globalism and the Governance of Globalization* (Routledge 2018)

Pasculli L and Stanford B, 'Form and Flexibility: The Normalisation of "Magnitsky Sanctions" in the Face of the Rule of Law' (2022) 15(1) Hague Journal on the Rule of Law 109
Pavlidis G, 'Financial Information in the Context of Anti-Money Laundering: Broadening the Access of Law Enforcement and Facilitating Information Exchanges' (2020) 23(2) Journal of Money Laundering Control 369
Pieth M and Aiolfi G, *A Comparative Guide to Anti-Money Laundering: A Critical Analysis of Systems in Singapore, Switzerland, the UK and the USA* (Edward Elgar Publishing 2004)
Ping H, 'New Trends in Money Laundering from the Real World to Cyberspace' (2005) 8(1) Journal of Money Laundering Control 48
Ridley N and Alexander DC, 'Combatting Terrorist Financing in the First Decade of the Twenty-First Century' (2011) 15(1) Journal of Money Laundering Control 38
Schott PA, World Bank and International Monetary Fund, *Reference Guide to Anti-Money Laundering and Combatting the Financing of Terrorism* (2nd edn, World Bank Publications 2006)
Shapiro M, 'The USA PATRIOT Act and Money Laundering' (2006) 123(7) The Banking Law Journal 629
Simonova A, 'The Risk-Based Approach to Anti-Money Laundering: Problems and Solutions' (2011) 14(4) Journal of Money Laundering Control 346
Stolen Asset Recovery Initiative, 'International Partnerships on Asset Recovery: Overview and Global Directory of Networks' (2019) <https://star.worldbank.org/sites/star/files/networks-16-reduced-maps.pdf> accessed 5 August 2023
Teichmann F, 'Recent Trends in Money Laundering' (2019) 73(2) Crime, Law, and Social Change 237
——— 'Recent Trends in Money Laundering and Terrorism Financing' (2019) 27(1) Journal of Financial Regulation and Compliance 2
Transparency International, 'Corruption Perception Index – Countries: Denmark' <www.transparency.org/en/cpi/2021/index/dnk> accessed 11 July 2023
Tsingou E, 'Global Financial Governance and the Developing Anti-Money Laundering Regime: What Lessons for International Political Economy' (2010) 47(6) International Politics 617
Turksen U, 'Implications of Anti-Money Laundering Law for Accountancy in the European Union – A Comparative Study' in N Ryder, U Turksen and S Hassler (eds), *Fighting Financial Crime in the Global Economic Crisis* (1st edn, Routledge 2014)
UNODC, 'Global Programme Against Money Laundering' <www.unodc.org/pdf/gpml.pdf> accessed 5 June 2023
——— 'Global Programme Against Money Laundering' <www.unodc.org/unodc/en/money-laundering/global-programme-against-money-laundering/.html> accessed 2 July 2023
The World Bank, *Combatting Money Laundering and the Financing of Terrorism: A Comprehensive Training Guide* (World Bank Publications 2009)
——— *Combatting Money Laundering and the Financing of Terrorism – A Comprehensive Training Guide: Workbook 4. Building an Effective Financial Intelligence Unit* (The World Bank 2009) <https://doi.org/10.1596/978-0-8213-7569-3> accessed 2 July 2023
——— 'Financial Integrity' <www.worldbank.org/en/topic/financialmarketintegrity> accessed 5 August 2023
——— 'Financial Sector' <www.worldbank.org/en/topic/financialsector/overview#3> accessed 5 August 2023
——— 'Financial Sector Assessment Program (FSAP)' <www.worldbank.org/en/programs/financial-sector-assessment-program> accessed 5 August 2023

——— 'Financial Sector Assessment Program (FSAP): Assessment Standards & Tools' <www.worldbank.org/en/programs/financial-sector-assessment-program#2> accessed 5 August 2023

——— 'The World Bank Group and the International Monetary Fund (IMF)' <www.worldbank.org/en/about/history/the-world-bank-group-and-the-imf> accessed 5 August 2023

——— and UNODC, 'Stolen Asset Recovery Initiative' <https://star.worldbank.org> accessed 5 August 2023

Wronka C, 'Impact of COVID-19 on Financial Institutions: Navigating the Global Emerging Patterns of Financial Crime' (2022) 29(2) Journal of Financial Crime 476

Legal Instruments

Commission Delegated Regulation (EU) 2020/855 of 7 May 2020 Amending Delegated Regulation (EU) 2016/1675 Supplementing Directive (EU) 2015/849 of the European Parliament and of the Council, as Regards Adding the Bahamas, Barbados, Botswana, Cambodia, Ghana, Jamaica, Mauritius, Mongolia, Myanmar/Burma, Nicaragua, Panama and Zimbabwe to the Table in Point I of the Annex and Deleting Bosnia-Herzegovina, Ethiopia, Guyana, Lao People's Democratic Republic, Sri Lanka and Tunisia from This Table (Text with EEA Relevance) [2020] OJ L195/1

Consolidated Version of the Treaty on the Functioning of the European Union Part Six – Institutional And Financial Provisions Title I – Institutional Provisions Chapter 2 – Legal Acts of the Union, Adoption Procedures and Other Provisions Section 1 – The Legal Acts of the Union Article 288 (ex-Article 249 TEC) [2016] OJ C202/171

Council Decision of 17 October 2000 Concerning Arrangements for Cooperation Between Financial Intelligence Units of the Member States in Respect of Exchanging Information (2000/642/JHA) [2000] OJ L271/4

Council Directive 91/308/EEC of 10 June 1991 on Prevention of the Use of the Financial System for the Purpose of Money Laundering [1991] OJ L166/77

Council Framework Decision 2008/841/JHA of 24 October 2008 on the Fight Against Organised Crime [2008] OJ L300/42

Council Framework Decision of 13 June 2002 on Combating Terrorism [2002] OJ L164/3

Directive (EU) 2015/849 of the European Parliament and of the Council of 20 May 2015 on the Prevention of the Use of the Financial System for the Purposes of Money Laundering or Terrorist Financing, Amending Regulation (EU) No 648/2012 of the European Parliament and of the Council, and Repealing Directive 2005/60/EC of the European Parliament and of the Council and Commission Directive 2006/70/EC (Text with EEA Relevance) [2015] OJ L141/73

Directive (EU) 2017/541 of the European Parliament and of the Council of 15 March 2017 on Combating Terrorism and Replacing Council Framework Decision 2002/475/JHA and Amending Council Decision 2005/671/JHA [2017] OJ L88/6

Directive (EU) 2018/1673 of the European Parliament and of the Council of 23 October 2018 on Combating Money Laundering by Criminal Law PE/30/2018/REV/1 [2018] OJ L284/22

Directive (EU) 2018/843 of the European Parliament and of the Council of 30 May 2018 Amending Directive (EU) 2015/849 on the Prevention of the Use of the Financial System for the Purposes of Money Laundering or Terrorist Financing and Amending Directives 2009/138/EC and 2013/36/EU (Text with EEA relevance) PE/72/2017/REV/1 [2018] OJ L156/43

Directive 2001/97/EC of the European Parliament and of the Council of 4 December 2001 Amending Council Directive 91/308/EEC on Prevention of the Use of the Financial System for the Purpose of Money Laundering -Commission Declaration [2001] OJ L344/76
Directive 2005/60/EC of the European Parliament and of the Council of 26 October 2005 on the Prevention of the Use of the Financial System for the Purpose of Money Laundering and Terrorist Financing (Text with EEA Relevance) [2005] OJ L309/15
German Criminal Code (Strafgesetzbuch – StGB)
Italian Criminal Code (Codice Penale)
Law No 5237 (Turkish Criminal Code) 2004
Paris G7 Summit Communique (16 July 1989)
Proceeds of Crime Act 2002
Resolution CM/Res(2013)13 on the Statute of the Committee of Experts on the Evaluation of Anti-Money Laundering Measures and the Financing of Terrorism (MONEYVAL)
UNGA A/RES/S-20/2 Political Declaration (21 October 1998)
United Nations Convention Against Corruption 2003
United Nations Convention Against Illicit Traffic in Narcotic Drugs and Psychotropic Substances 1988
United Nations Convention Against Transnational Organized Crime 2000
UNSC Res 1267 (15 October 1999) UN Doc S/Res/1267
UNSC Res 1373 (28 September 2001) UN Doc S/Res/1373
UNSC Res 1718 (14 October 2006) UN Doc S/Res/1718
UNSC Res 2231 (20 July 2015) UN Doc S/Res/2231
98/733/JHA: Joint Action of 21 December 1998 Adopted by the Council on the Basis of Article K.3 of the Treaty on European Union, on Making It a Criminal Offence to Participate in a Criminal Organisation in the Member States of the European Union [1998] OJ L351/1

3 Türkiye's Legal Framework Regarding AML and Its Predicates

3.1 Introduction

Türkiye, as any other integrated national component of the global financial ecosystem, has created/adopted a specific AML legal structure based on principal statutory instruments, which incorporate international minimum AML standards and rules (e.g., FATF Recommendations and the relevant UN Conventions). Nevertheless, as a natural consequence of considering nation-specific dynamics and unique needs in the ratification process,[1] as well as of the flexibility harnessed in this end, Türkiye's AML legal framework is not identical to that of any other jurisdictions, in particular, of the UK. Consequently, in order to clarify the divergent points of the two jurisdictions, this chapter aims to present the milestones of the development of Türkiye's present AML statutory framework and to point out the underlying reasons for the enactment of each constituent legal instrument. It also examines its congruency with the international minimum AML standards and rules, thereby identifying the potential deficiencies of the prevailing legal texts that may impede the overall AML competency of the country. By doing so, the chapter points out the underlying reasons for Türkiye's current successes or failures in the AML sphere and provides a detailed and critical understanding of the concept of predicate crimes as to how they have developed. It further strives to pinpoint the causes, if any, accountable for the prevalence of particular predicate offences stemming from the *jus scriptum*, thereby putting forward recommendations for a sounder national AML framework. By critically scrutinising the current AML framework in Türkiye, this chapter addresses the main research aim of demonstrating whether and how differences between the legal AML structures may impact the effectiveness in tackling and the prevalence of predicate crimes, thereby underlining the unique features of an optimum

1 For instance, in general terms, in cases where there is a conflict between national priorities and international legal instruments, national interests prevail. See Norman Mugarura, 'An Appraisal of United Nations and Other Money Laundering and Financing of Terrorism Counter-Measures' (2013) 16(3) Journal of Money Laundering Control 249.

DOI: 10.4324/9781003466680-3

AML regime. In order to achieve the previously mentioned purposes, firstly, it locates Türkiye within the global financial composition with regards to the international relevant organisations and legal instruments in terms of their effects on the country's AML composition. Secondly, it explains the country's legal framework, its evolution process, as well as particular statutes composing the frame of reference. After outlining Türkiye's key AML/CTF legislation, the chapter elucidates how this legal composition has developed concerning the underlying milestones. Finally, it scrutinises these principal statutory texts sequentially to present the incentives behind their enactment and to propose suggestions that would enhance their effectiveness.

In accordance and simultaneously with the global incentive behind creating a collaborative response mechanism against the noticeably extraordinary volume of illegal proceeds derived from the international drug trade and associated concerns in the 1980s,[2] Türkiye was suffering from the same problem in the corresponding period, the illicit drug enterprise. It has been one of the principal sources of income for the PKK,[3] a terrorist organisation established in Diyarbakir (Türkiye) in 1978,[4] and one of the significant problems in Türkiye, occupying the country's agenda over the last four decades. As the CTF component of AML/CTF efforts is beyond the scope of this book, and it has recently been studied in detail by academia,[5] this study does not investigate Türkiye's CTF regime and efforts. Yet it is worth emphasising that terrorism/TF is one of the greatest geneses of the problem in Türkiye, a persuasive example of why ML and TF are intertwined and cannot be isolated.[6] It is against this background that Türkiye, as a jurisdiction facing the then (and still) prevailing universal drug trafficking difficulty at the country level intensively, signed the Vienna Convention 1988[7] on 20 December 1988,

2 Richard Vogler and Shahrzad Fouladvand, 'The Convention Against Illicit Traffic in Narcotic Drugs and Psychotropic Substances 1988 and the Global War on Drugs' in Pierre Hauck and Sven Peterke (eds), *International Law and Transnational Organized Crime* (OUP 2016).

3 The PKK's annual income through drug smuggling is estimated to be USD 1.5bn. See TC İçişleri Bakanlığı AB ve Dış İlişkiler Dairesi Başkanlığı, 'Bakan Soylu Fransa'da Düzenlenen Terörizmin Finansmanı ile Mücadele Konferansına Katıldı' (26 April 2018) <www.icisleri.gov.tr/diab/bakan-soylu-fransada-duzenlenen-terorizmin-finansmani-ile-mucadele-konferansina-katildi> accessed 10 September 2023.

4 Mitchel P Roth, *Global Organized Crime: A 21st Century Approach* (Routledge 2017).

5 Burke U Basaranel and Umut Turksen, *Counter-Terrorist Financing Law and Policy: An Analysis of Turkey* (Routledge 2019).

6 For a more detailed discussion on the analogies and differences between ML and TF, see Tim Krieger and Daniel Meierrieks, 'Terrorist Financing and Money Laundering' (2011) <https://ssrn.com/abstract=1860069> accessed 15 July 2023.

7 United Nations Convention Against Illicit Traffic in Narcotic Drugs and Psychotropic Substances 1988.

on the same day as the UK.[8] It was, nonetheless, ratified by Türkiye on 16 January 1996,[9] the ratification of which founded the basis for Türkiye's first AML legal instrument, Law No 4208 on Prevention of Money Laundering. In fact, as a developing country, which is politically determined to maintain its integrity in the modern economic world, Türkiye has consistently played an active role in following the rules of the international financial system. In addition to the Vienna Convention 1988, Türkiye is a signatory to the Palermo Convention 2000[10] and the European Council Convention on Laundering, Search, Seizure and Confiscation of the Proceeds from Crime (Strasbourg Convention) 1990, which were ratified by Türkiye on 25 March 2003[11] and 6 October 2004,[12] respectively. Furthermore, Türkiye has been one of the 37 member jurisdictions of the FATF since 1991[13] and a member of the Egmont Group since 29 June 1998.[14] That is to say that Türkiye has been keen to ensure its congruency with the requirements of the modern financial world; and has continuously participated in the international AML efforts and revised its legal instruments accordingly.

In Türkiye, the range of AML legal instruments is quite broad, including, for instance, Banking Law No 5411 and Misdemeanours Law No 5326. This dispersed legislative composition results in fragmented AML regulation and enforcement practices. The current AML/CTF legal framework in Türkiye consists of seven core legal instruments,[15] including two statutes enacted by

8 United Nations Treaty Collection, 'Status of Treaties: 19. United Nations Convention Against Illicit Traffic in Narcotic Drugs and Psychotropic Substances' <https://treaties.un.org/pages/ViewDetails.aspx?src=TREATY&mtdsg_no=VI-19&chapter=6> accessed 4 July 2023.

9 Official Gazette No 22551 dated 11 February 1996, 'Karar Sayısı: 96/7801 – Milletlerarası Sözleşme' <www.resmigazete.gov.tr/arsiv/22551.pdf> accessed 10 September 2023.

10 United Nations Convention Against Transnational Organized Crime 2000.

11 United Nations Treaty Collection, 'Status of Treaties: 12. United Nations Convention Against Transnational Organized Crime' <https://treaties.un.org/Pages/ViewDetails.aspx?src=IND&mtdsg_no=XVIII-12&chapter=18> accessed 4 July 2023.

12 Council of Europe, 'Chart of Signatures and Ratifications of Treaty 141' <www.coe.int/en/web/conventions/full-list/-/conventions/treaty/141/signatures?p_auth=tV5pnJpN> accessed 4 July 2023.

13 FATF, 'FATF Members and Observers' <www.fatf-gafi.org/about/membersandobservers/> accessed 13 July 2023.

14 Egmont Group, 'Members by Region: Europe II' <https://egmontgroup.org/members-by-region/> accessed 4 July 2023.

15 The principal legislation included within the scope of this book comprises the legal instruments that the FATF referred to during its last Mutual Evaluation Report (MER) on Türkiye. The same approach will be adopted in the next chapter whilst determining the relevant legal instruments of the UK. See FATF, 'Anti-Money Laundering and Counter-Terrorist Financing Measures – Turkey: Mutual Evaluation Report' (December 2019) <www.fatf-gafi.org/media/fatf/documents/reports/mer4/Mutual-Evaluation-Report-Turkey-2019.pdf> accessed 18 January 2023.

the parliament, three regulations, one presidential decree, and MASAK regulatory publications.

- The two statutes are Law No 5549 on Prevention of Laundering Proceeds of Crime 2006; and Law No 6415 on the Prevention of the Financing of Terrorism 2013.
- The Presidential Decree is titled No. 1 on the Organisation of the Presidency 2018.
- The three relevant regulations are the Regulation on Measures Regarding Prevention of Laundering the Proceeds of Crime and Financing of Terrorism (ROM) 2008; Regulation on the Program of Compliance with Obligations of Anti-Money Laundering and Combating the Financing of Terrorism (ROC) 2008; and Regulation on the Procedures and Principles Regarding the Implementation of Law on the Prevention of the Financing of Terrorism (ROTF) 2013.
- In addition, the General Communiqués published by MASAK inform the AML/CTF legal framework in Türkiye.

The chapter presents (i) how the current AML legal framework has evolved; (ii) how this legal framework may empower or incapacitate the relevant competent authorities; and (iii) what essential areas of reform are needed to eliminate the obstacles hampering AML efforts. By doing so, this chapter aims to address the first and the last research questions mentioned in Chapter 1 previously. However, as the focal point of the book does not encompass the critique of CTF efforts, Law No 6415 and ROTF are not analysed in detail as the provisions therein concentrate primarily on TF.

3.2 The Development of the Current Legal Framework

Although a member of the FATF since 1991, Türkiye had failed to enact legislation criminalising ML and to take other essential preventive actions to comply with the FATF's prominent Forty Recommendations[16] until 1996. The underlying reason for this late reaction stemmed from the fact that Türkiye had failed to ratify the Vienna Convention 1988 until 1996, albeit Recommendation 1 (currently Recommendation 3)[17] of the FATF's first set of recommendations (1990) stipulated the immediate and full implementation

16 FATF, 'International Standards on Combatting Money Laundering and the Financing of Terrorism & Proliferation: The FATF Recommendations' (Updated March 2022) <www.fatf-gafi.org/media/fatf/documents/recommendations/pdfs/FATF%20Recommendations%202012.pdf> accessed 26 June 2023.

17 ibid.

of the Convention.[18] Correspondingly, Türkiye, as a noncompliant country, received an official letter from the FATF president, which was followed by a visit from the specialised FATF Commission in April 1996 to inform Türkiye about the potential sanctions in case it delayed or neglected the necessary steps to be taken.[19] Eventually, the FATF invoked Recommendation 21[20] by publishing a statement that warned FIs about the unsafe economic environment in Türkiye.[21] In response to these recommendations made by the FATF, on 19 November 1996, upon ratifying the Vienna Convention 1988, Türkiye criminalised ML by Law No 4208 on Prevention of Money Laundering, enactment of which also established the Turkish FIU, the Financial Crimes Investigation Board (*Mali Suçlar Araştırma Kurulu – MASAK*),[22] which became operational on 17 February 1997.[23]

Law No 4208 1996 was the sole principal AML legal instrument until 2005, when Law No 5237 (Turkish Criminal Code/TCC) came into force on 1 June 2005 and replaced its predecessor (i.e., Law No 765 (*former* TCC) 1926). With the adoption of the new criminal code, the AML legal framework has expanded as it introduced a new crime which can be/has been translated as 'laundering of assets acquired as a result of offence' under Article 282. However, referring to two distinct legal sources for handling the same criminal act precipitated difficulties for the judiciary and LEAs. In other words, provisions relating to ML offences had been regulated both by a special law (i.e., Law No 4208 1996, designed for confronting ML) and general law (i.e., TCC 2004, targeting all criminal activities, including ML). More importantly, considering the enactment date of Law No 4208 (19 November 1996) and the predicate crime types stated therein, it had been created considering and based on the provisions stated in the FATF's 1990 Recommendations, including its 1996 revision. However, the FATF revised its Recommendations for the second time in June 2003 and enlarged the scope of predicate crimes, obliged entities, and their obligations. That is to say that the need for a new legal instrument to

18 FATF, 'The Forty Recommendations of the Financial Action Task Force on Money Laundering' (1990) <www.fatf-gafi.org/media/fatf/documents/recommendations/pdfs/FATF%20Recommendations%201990.pdf> accessed 4 July 2023.

19 FATF, 'Annual Report 1995–1996' (June 1996) <www.fatf-gafi.org/media/fatf/documents/reports/1995%201996%20ENG.pdf> accessed 15 July 2023.

20 It corresponds to Recommendation 19, related to 'higher-risk countries', of the FATF's 2012-version of Recommendations. See FATF (n 16).

21 FATF, 'Annual Report 1996–1997' (June 1997) <www.fatf-gafi.org/media/fatf/documents/reports/1996%201997%20ENG.pdf> accessed 4 July 2023.

22 Official Gazette No 22822 dated 19 November 1996, 'Karaparanın Aklanmasının Önlenmesine, 2313 Sayılı Uyuşturucu Maddelerinin Murakabesi Hakkında Kanunda, 657 Sayılı Devlet Memurları Kanununda ve 178 Sayılı Maliye Bakanlığının Teşkilat ve Görevleri Hakkında Kanun Hükmünde Kararnamede Değişiklik Yapılmasına Dair Kanun' <www.resmigazete.gov.tr/arsiv/22822.pdf> accessed 4 July 2023.

23 Republic of Turkiye Ministry of Treasury and Finance, 'Duties and Powers' <https://en.hmb.gov.tr/fcib-duties-powers> accessed 4 July 2023.

address those developments seen in the AML realm had become more apparent, especially after 2003. Consequently, in order to enhance the capabilities of competent authorities regarding their AML practices and address the aforementioned advancements, Law No 5549 (i.e., Prevention of Laundering Proceeds of Crime Law) was enacted on 18 October 2006.[24]

Even though Law No 5549 2006, in tandem with the FATF's revised (2003) Recommendations, has, *inter alia*, outlined the obliged entities and obligations and enlarged the extent of those concepts, it has also referred to the enactment of particular regulations for determining the relevant principles and procedures in detail. Consequently, in 2008, taking their legal basis from Law No 5549 2006, two sets of regulations, namely ROM 2008 and ROC 2008, were introduced. The former regulation[25] has been legislated based on Article 27 of Law No 5549 2006.[26] Although the original version of Article 27 required for the enactment of these regulations six months after the Law No 5549 came into force, ROM was issued almost one and a half years later. Similarly, the latter regulation[27] was enacted based on Article 5 of Law No 5549 2006.[28] Likewise, its publication has been actualised approximately two years after the adoption of the pertinent law, albeit Article 27 required its enactment six months after Law No 5549 2006 came into force. Given the relatively late enactment of these regulations, the lack of necessary guidelines on handling ML and its predicates in the corresponding period have hindered the overall capacity of competent authorities, thereby worsening the country's financial integrity and subsequent status amongst the international community.

Another law regarding the AML/CTF legal framework of Türkiye is Law No 6415 on Prevention of the Financing of Terrorism, which was adopted

24 Official Gazette No 26323 dated 18 October 2006, 'Suç Gelirlerinin Aklanmasının Önlenmesi Hakkında Kanun' <www.resmigazete.gov.tr/eskiler/2006/10/20061018-1.htm> accessed 4 July 2023.

25 Official Gazette No 26751 dated 9 January 2008, 'Suç Gelirlerinin Aklanmasının ve Terörizmin Finansmanının Önlenmesine Dair Tedbirler Hakkında Yönetmelik' <www.resmigazete.gov.tr/eskiler/2008/01/20080109-4.htm> accessed 4 July 2023.

26 Article 27 of Law No 5549 stipulates that '[t]he principles and procedures relating to the subjects stated in the paragraph (d) and (e) of Article 2 and in Articles 3, 4, 6, 7, 11, 15, 16, 19 and 20 of this Law are arranged by the regulations which will be issued by the Council of Ministers within six months following the publication date of this Law'.

27 Official Gazette No 26999 dated 16 September 2008, 'Suç Gelirlerinin Aklanmasının ve Terörün Finansmanının Önlenmesine İlişkin Yükümlülüklere Uyum Programı Hakkında Yönetmelik' <www.resmigazete.gov.tr/eskiler/2008/09/20080916-1.htm> accessed 4 July 2023.

28 Article 5 of Law No 5549 sets forth that '[i]n the scope of necessary measures, the Ministry has the authority to determine obliged parties and implementation principles and procedures, including measures to assign an officer with necessary authority at the administrative level to ensure compliance with this Law and establish training, internal control and risk management systems by regarding the size of business and business volumes'.

by the GNAT on 7 February 2013.[29] It aims to determine the necessary principles and procedures for implementing the UN International Convention for the Suppression of Financing of Terrorism 1999,[30] as well as its Security Council Resolutions[31] dictating the official criminalisation of TF and regulation of asset freezing related to terrorism.[32] Similarly, ROTF 2013 was created to regulate principles and procedures regarding the effective administration of freezing of assets and effectually combatting terrorism and TF.[33]

Another piece of current legal instruments of Türkiye regarding ML and its predicates roots change in the management system of the country. Following the referendum, which was held on 16 April 2017, Türkiye officially shifted its administrative system from parliamentary to the new presidential executive policy on 24 June 2018.[34] In accordance with this governmental system change, Türkiye's state structure has been rebuilt by the publication of the first presidential decree.[35]

Whilst these laws and regulations constitute the current AML legal structure, MASAK periodically publishes regulatory instruments (i.e., General Communiqués) and guidelines to clarify principles and procedures outlined therein, thereby aiming to enhance relevant stakeholders' capabilities and compliance.[36] In other words, MASAK continuously observes the international developments in the AML sphere and endeavours to ensure that the

29 Official Gazette No 28561 dated 16 February 2013, 'Terörizmin Finansmanının Önlenmesi Hakkında Kanun' <www.resmigazete.gov.tr/eskiler/2013/02/20130216-3.htm> accessed 4 July 2023.

30 Türkiye signed this Convention on 27 September 2001 and ratified it on 28 June 2002. See United Nations Treaty Collection, 'Status of Treaties: 11. International Convention for the Suppression of the Financing of Terrorism' <https://treaties.un.org/pages/ViewDetails.aspx?src=IND&mtdsg_no=XVIII-11&chapter=18&clang=_en> accessed 4 July 2023.

31 Article 5 of Law No 6415 (2013) refers to Security Council Resolutions 1267 (1999), 1988 (2011), and 1989 (2011) to this end. These resolutions focus on the threat from those associated with the Taliban and Al-Qaida in Afghanistan.

32 UNGA A/RES/54/109 International Convention for the Suppression of the Financing of Terrorism (25 February 2000).

33 Article 19 of Law No 6415 stipulates that '[p]rocedures and principles regarding the application of this Law shall be regulated by a Regulation which will be prepared jointly by the Ministry of Justice, Ministry of Foreign Affairs, Ministry of Interior, and Ministry of Finance. The regulation shall be put into force within six months from the date this Law enters into force'.

34 TRT World, 'Erdogan to Be Sworn in on July 9 as Turkey's First Executive President' (*TRT World*, 4 July 2018) <www.trtworld.com/turkey/erdogan-to-be-sworn-in-on-july-9-as-turkey-s-first-executive-president-18662> accessed 4 July 2023.

35 Official Gazette No 30474 dated 10 July 2018, 'Cumhurbaşkanlığı Teşkilatı Hakkında Cumhurbaşkanlığı Kararnamesi (Kararname Numarası: 1)' <www.resmigazete.gov.tr/eskiler/2018/07/20180710-1.pdf> accessed 4 July 2023.

36 For instance, it published five guidelines in 2018 and 2019. These guidelines are 'Guideline Regarding the Obligations of Financial Institutions and Regulatory Compliance on AML/CFT (Factoring, Financial Leasing and Financing Companies)', 'The Principle of Reliance on Third Parties', 'Guidance on Transactions Against Erroneous Freezing Implementation and Application Procedures (False Positive)', 'Guidance for Those Who Hold Frozen Assets', and

country's existing AML regime maintains its harmony with the relevant global advancements and addresses the emerging issues accordingly.

After this brief discussion on the development of the current legal framework, it is appropriate to elaborate on these legal instruments, thereby evaluating whether they are fit for purpose and whether and how they may empower or incapacitate the relevant competent authorities responsible for AML and countering predicate crimes. Hereinafter, this chapter scrutinises the aforementioned legislation in chronological order.

3.3 AML Legal Instruments

3.3.1 Law No 4208 on the Prevention of Money Laundering 1996

Although most of the provisions of Law No 4208 1996 have been repealed by Law No 5549 2006 and currently are utilised merely to determine measures regarding controlled delivery,[37] it deserves consideration here as it is the first legal instrument that criminalised ML in Türkiye. In addition, an overview of this legal instrument allows us to identify the initial standpoint of the legal approaches to AML, the predicate crimes envisaged, and the penal provisions and sanctions determined accordingly.

A close reading of Law No 4208 1996 indicates that the term 'dirty money' had been adopted in specifying all the prerequisite economic advantages, whether it is money itself or any other means that have monetary value derived from relevant illegal activities stated therein, to commit the crime of ML.[38] It can also be argued that the laundering offence had been determined as a separate and independent crime, as identified as a 'money laundering offence'.[39] Furthermore, predicate crimes had been outlined and determined through a list-based approach comprising 29 types of predicate offences[40] under nine categories.[41] Table 3.1 demonstrates these predicate crimes.

'Guideline for Preventing Abuse of NPOs for Financing of Terrorism'. See Republic of Türkiye Ministry of Treasury and Finance, 'Guidelines' <https://en.hmb.gov.tr/fcib-guidelines> accessed 3 February 2023.

37 According to Article 26 of Law No 5549, Articles 1, 3–9, 12, 14, paragraphs (a), (b), (d), (e) of Article 2, the first and third paragraphs of article 15, the first and third paragraphs of article 13 of Law No 4208 dated 13/11/1996 are abolished and the second paragraph of Article 13 is amended as 'Ankara Criminal Court of Peace is authorised to give any decision on requests of foreign countries relating to the controlled delivery of assets derived from crime'. Therefore, Articles 2 (c), 10, 11, 13, and 15 of Law No 4208, which explain controlled delivery measures, are still in force. The law enforcement practice of controlled delivery takes its legal basis from the Vienna Convention 1988. See United Nations Convention against Illicit Traffic in Narcotic Drugs and Psychotropic Substances 1988, art 11.

38 Law No 4208 on the Prevention of Money Laundering 1996, art 2(a).

39 ibid, art 2(b).

40 Türkiye Bankalar Birliği, 'Karaparanın Aklanması ile Mücadelede Bankaların Yükümlülükleri' (December 2003) <www.tbb.org.tr/Dosyalar/Dosyalar/235_aralik2003.pdf> accessed 4 July 2023.

41 Law No 4208 on the Prevention of Money Laundering 1996, art 2(a).

Table 3.1 Predicate crimes envisaged by Law No 4208 on the Prevention of Money Laundering 1996.

Predicate crimes under list-based approach	
Trading and using of narcotic substances (*Uyuşturucu Madde Ticareti ve Kullanımı*)	Counterfeiting and using of the official stamp (*Devlet Mührünü Taklit ve Kullanma*)
Smuggling (*Gümrük Kaçakçılığı*)	Counterfeiting or using of official stamp and instruments (*Resmi Mühür ve Aletleri Taklit veya Kullanma*)
Trafficking of arms (*Silah Kaçakçılığı*)	Selling counterfeit goods (*Taklit İleri Taşıyan Şeyin Satılması*)
Trafficking of organs and tissues (*Organ ve Doku Kaçakçılığı*)	Forgery of official documents (*Resmi Belgede Sahtecilik*)
Illegal trafficking of historical works (*Tarihi Eser Kaçakçılığı*)	Forgery of private documents (*Hususi Belgede Sahtecilik*)
Crimes related to false invoice (*Sahte Fatura ile İlgili Suçlar*) (VUK 359/b)	Forgery of legitimacy documents (*Meşruiyet Belgelerinde Sahtecilik*)
Crimes against state identity (*Devletin Şahsiyetine Karşı Suçlar*)	Procuring, trafficking of women (*Fuhşa Teşvik, Kadın Ticareti*)
Deprivation of liberty (*Kişi Hürriyetinden Mahrumiyet*)	Robbery (*Yağma*)
Obtaining benefit by menace (*Tehdit ile Menfaat Temini*)	Plundering of bills (*Senedin Yağması*)
Smuggling of devastating, fatal tools or medicines (*Yıkıcı, Öldürücü Aletler veya Ecza Kaçakçılığı*)	Exploiting by intimidation (*Korkutarak Faydalanma*)
Forgery of money (*Paralarda Kalpazanlık*)	Abduction/kidnapping (*Adam kaldırma*)
Alteration through diminishing monetary value (*Para Değerini İndirerek Tağyir*)	Aggravated fraud (*Nitelikli Dolandırıcılık*)
Circulating counterfeit money (*Taklit Parayı Tedavüle Çıkartma*)	Fraudulent bankruptcy (*Hileli İflas*)
Counterfeiting and altering of valuable stamps (*Kıymetli Damgaların Taklit ve Tağyiri*)	Bribery (*Rüşvet*)
Forgery of transportation tickets (*Taşıma Biletlerinde Kalpazanlık*)	

Available sanctions for ML had included an imprisonment term of two to five years and an aggravated fine of one-fold of the amount of money laundered.[42] Therefore, considering the current sanction mechanism of Türkiye to

42 Article 7(1) of Law No 4208 1996 had set forth that: '[w]hoever commits money laundering offence shall be sentenced to imprisonment for from two years to up to five years and an also heavy fine of one-fold of the money laundered and all the property and assets in the scope of dirty money including the returns derived from them and in case the property and assets could not be seized, the corresponding value of them shall be subject to confiscation'.

this end (see below), it had provided more lenient sanctions initially. However, remarkably, the scope of aggravating circumstances of the crime had included the potential terrorism-related nature of the offence,[43] suggesting Türkiye's farsightedness in this regard, a clause signifying terrorism as a predicate crime, albeit not included within the previously mentioned list of predicate offences. Additional aggravated circumstances of the offence had included the use of violence, threat, or force of arms, as well as incorporated establishing an organisation for ML, including leading it or participating in the organisation and laundering as an enabler.[44] Lastly, the managers of corporate bodies had been determined as responsible for the ML offence, in cases where such bodies perpetrate those offences, whilst those entities had been subjected to punitive fines. Although Law No 4208 1996 had outlined the aforementioned framework of sanctions, it also referred to Article 165 of TCC 2004 as a supplementary regulation of the 'money laundering offence'. Article 165 stipulates that:

> [a]ny person who, without participation in the commission of the offence, sales, transfers, purchases, or accepts, property or other values of property, which was acquired through the commission of an offence, shall be sentenced to a penalty of imprisonment for a term of six months to three years and a judicial fine of up to ten thousand days.[45]

It is necessary to state that Article 165 is almost a *verbatim* copy of Article 282(2) of TCC 2004, whilst the latter stipulates an imprisonment term of two to five years. However, they address two different groups of offenders, albeit the difference between them is ethereal. Accordingly, those divergence points are examined subsequently in light of the legislative intent behind their enactment.

Law No 4208 1996 had determined only two sets of obligations, which constitute the integrity of measures in preventing ML:

a) Obligation to Submit Information and Documents; and
b) Obligation of Secrecy.[46]

43 Article 7(2) of Law No 4208 1996 had stipulated, amongst others, that if dirty money is derived from terrorism or the offence is committed to obtaining sources for terrorism, the term of imprisonment to be imposed on the perpetrator shall not be less than four years.

44 Article 7(3)(b) of Law No 4208 1996 had envisaged enablers as the officials or civil servants (due to their duties) and 'those who work at the bodies operating in accordance with Banks Act No 3182, Insurance Supervision Law No 7397, Law No 3326 on Financial Leasing, Law No 1567 Regarding the Protection of the Value of Turkish Currency, Capital Market Law No 2499, legislation on Money Lending Transactions and Principles and Procedures about Establishment, Operations and Liquidation of Special Finance Institutions'.

45 Law No 5237 (Turkish Criminal Code) 2004, art 165.

46 Law No 4208 on the Prevention of Money Laundering 1996, arts 5 and 6.

Given the late determination of comprehensive obligations and obliged entities,[47] the lack of in-depth legal tools for preventing ML and its predicates in the corresponding timeframe should have impaired the overall AML competency of the country. In addition, MASAK has published four General Communiqués to clarify the procedures and principles regarding the obligations mentioned in the Regulation, such as suspicious transaction reporting and appointment of compliance officer.[48] For instance, according to General Communiqué pertaining to customer identification dated 31 December 1997,[49] it was mandatory for the obliged parties to retain the records on customer identification for five years which has been extended to eight years under the current AML regime.[50]

Finally, it is worth reiterating that MASAK was created by this law, which also drew the general framework of its competencies, powers, and responsibilities. Articles 3 and 4 had, in particular, determined the duties and powers of the Presidency of MASAK and the Coordination Board for Combatting Financial Crimes, respectively.[51] The Coordination Board, which consists of representatives from MASAK, the Ministry of Finance, the Capital Markets Board, the Central Bank, and other state authorities, seeks to improve coordination among the relevant stakeholders in combatting financial crimes (see Chapter 5).

However, Law No 4208 1996 was abolished because of two primary concerns. Firstly, the 2004 revision of FATF's evaluation methodology has resulted in the acknowledgment of a need for a revised law as the FATF's new evaluator procedures emphasise the importance of measures regarding obligations. Accordingly, the need for a new legal instrument that comprehensively regulates obligations had become more apparent. Secondly and more importantly, regulation of the same criminal act by two discrete legal texts was problematic for the relevant stakeholders, as there were differences between the methodologies of how they handle those offences. In addition to the terminological

47 Obliged entities and obligations had been identified comprehensively after seven months of its publication by enacting the 'Regulation Regarding the Implementation of Law No 4208 on Prevention of Money Laundering'. See Official Gazette No 23037 dated 2 July 1997, 'Karaparanın Aklanmasının Önlenmesine Dair 4208 Sayılı Kanunun Uygulanmasına İlişkin Yönetmelik' <www.resmigazete.gov.tr/arsiv/23037.pdf> accessed 4 July 2023.

48 Republic of Türkiye Ministry of Treasury and Finance, 'Legal Framework of AML' <https://en.hmb.gov.tr/fcib-legal-framework-of-aml> accessed 4 July 2023.

49 MASAK General Communiqué No 1: Establishing the Principles and Procedures of Customer Identification. See also Official Gazette No 23217 dated 31 December 1997, 'Karaparanın Aklanmasının Önlenmesine Dair 4208 Sayılı Kanunun Uygulanmasına İlişkin Yönetmelikte Değişiklik Yapılması Hakkında Yönetmelik' <www.resmigazete.gov.tr/arsiv/23217.pdf> accessed 4 July 2023.

50 Regulation on Measures Regarding Prevention of Laundering Proceeds of Crime and Financing of Terrorism (ROM) 2008, art 46(1).

51 Law No 4208 on the Prevention of Money Laundering 1996, arts 3–4.

differences utilised by TCC 2004 and Law No 4208 1996, there were various major divergent points between the two legal instruments. More specifically, unlike Law No 4208 1996, which had embraced a list-based approach to predicate offences, TCC 2004 adopts a threshold approach for determining predicate crimes. Additionally, whilst Law No 4208 1996 had stipulated the framework of ML and associated sanctions differently, TCC 2004 determines the ML offence and penalties envisaged. Hence, in response to these concerns, Türkiye has published Law No 5549 2006 on the Prevention of Laundering Proceeds of Crime to eliminate the previously mentioned divergence points across the relevant legal instruments.

3.3.2 Law No 5237 (Turkish Criminal Code) 2004

Although the previous TCC (i.e., Law No 765 1926) had stipulated several criminal activities that could be regarded as ML offences (see Articles 296 or 512),[52] there were no specific provisions on this particular crime type therein. The amended criminal code of Türkiye, TCC 2004, filled this gap when it came into force on 1 June 2005.[53] Similar to Law No 4208 1996, it recognises ML as a separate and independent crime from its predicates. However, whilst predicate offences had been determined through a listing approach by Law No 4208 1996, TCC 2004 adopts a threshold approach in line with the FATF Recommendations.[54] Türkiye has significantly expanded the scope of predicate offences by adopting the threshold approach, whereby all offences punishable by a minimum penalty of more than six months imprisonment are considered predicate crimes. Under the title of 'Offences Against the Judicial Bodies or Court', Article 282 of the new criminal code recognises ML as 'Laundering of Assets Acquired from an Offence'. It is necessary to mention that the Turkish law does not concern merely with cash but also assets in general similar to the UK's AML legal regime that considers proceeds of crime as various assets, as explained in Chapter 4.

52 Law No 4208 had determined two prerequisites for an ML offence to be committed: the criminal act under consideration should not contravene Article 296 of Law No 765 (*Former* Turkish Criminal Code) 1926, and it should be one of the crimes listed through Article 2(a) of Law No 4208. Article 512 of Law No 765 (*Former* Turkish Criminal Code) 1926 was the provision that had determined penalties for 'buying or concealing property obtained through a felony'.

53 Official Gazette No 25611 dated 12 October 2004, 'Türk Ceza Kanunu' <www.resmigazete.gov.tr/eskiler/2004/10/20041012.htm> accessed 4 July 2023.

54 FATF (n 16) Recommendation 3.

Article 282(1), which was amended by Article 5 of the Law No 5918 on 26 June 2009,[55] provides that:

> [w]here a person conducts any act in relation to an asset, which has been acquired as a result of an offence which carries a minimum penalty of six months imprisonment, in order to transfer such asset abroad or to give the impression that such asset has been legitimately acquired and conceal the illegitimate source of such, shall be subject to a penalty of imprisonment for a term of three to seven years and a judicial fine of up to twenty thousand days.[56]

A close examination of this paragraph, as well as the terminology of the offence itself, suggests that the actualisation of the crime of 'laundering of assets acquired from an offence' depends on the perpetration of an underlying crime that requires a minimum penalty of six months imprisonment. The objective elements of the offence both include a prior crime that results in an illegal economic advantage, whether it is money itself or any other means that have monetary value derived from relevant illegal activities mentioned in the law, and acts aiming at transferring such pecuniary gains abroad or at disguising their illicit sources to render them ostensibly legal. It is necessary to clarify that the scope of 'illegal economic advantage' covers both tangible and intangible assets in Türkiye, as the international legal instruments that have been signed by the country determine the proceeds of crime by referring to both types of assets. For instance, the Palermo Convention 2000 defines 'proceeds of crime' as 'any property derived from or obtained, directly or indirectly, through the commission of an offence' where the 'property' stands for the 'assets of every kind, whether corporeal or incorporeal, movable or immovable, tangible or intangible, and legal documents or instruments evidencing title to, or interest in, such assets'.[57] Given that international treaties duly put into effect carry the force of law in Türkiye,[58] the previously mentioned provisions relating to the scope of proceeds of crime apply in Türkiye.

3.3.2.1 Defences

As mentioned earlier, ML has been determined as a crime that may be committed alternatively through the acts as described under Article 282(1). In order for this crime to be committed through the first route, which are the acts aiming at transferring such illicit economic gains abroad, the presence of ***dolus***

55 Official Gazette No 27283 dated 9 July 2009, 'Türk Ceza Kanunu ile Bazı Kanunlarda Değişiklik Yapılmasına Dair Kanun (Kanun No 5918)' <www.resmigazete.gov.tr/eskiler/2009/07/20090709-2.htm> accessed 4 July 2023.

56 Law No 5237 (Turkish Criminal Code) 2004, art 282(1).

57 United Nations Convention against Transnational Organized Crime 2000, arts 2(e) and 2(d).

58 Constitution of the Republic of Türkiye 1982, art 90(1).

generalis is sufficient. If the offender knows the illegitimate source of the assets to be transferred abroad, this general (i.e., basic) intent makes the perpetrator guilty in case the crime is committed. In terms of the second alternative for the commission of the crime, it requires a *dolus specialis*.[59] The specific intent of the criminal, which aims at disguising the relevant illegitimate sources to make them outwardly licit, is essential. The second alternative is determined as a *result crime*, which means the perpetration of the offence is independent of the various acts the offender has decided to utilise; the judicial authorities merely care for the result of the conduct. The punishment of a money launderer under Article 282 in Türkiye depends on these justifications, the details of which are elaborated in Chapter 4 compared to the UK's analogous approach.

It is also clear that TCC 2004 does not make any distinctions between the offences committed abroad or at home. In other words, it criminalises ML regardless of the location where the predicate crime is committed, a significant aspect of comparison, as examined in Chapter 4 regarding the UK's approach to crime abroad. Considering the transnational nature of these offences,[60] this empowers MLA efforts in Türkiye. However, it should be borne in mind that opening a criminal case in Türkiye depends on the 'dual criminality' principle, a policy that requires the criminalisation of the underlying activities in both jurisdictions.[61] Furthermore, Türkiye requires this principle for MLA requests of foreign jurisdictions, provisions of which are determined by Law No 6706 on the International Judicial Cooperation in Criminal Matters 2016.

3.3.2.2 Sanctions

It needs to be noted that the original version of Article 282(1) had envisaged the relevant sanctions for offences, which entail a minimum penalty of one-year imprisonment rather than a six-months incarceration term. As mentioned previously, whilst the FATF's initial AML priorities exclusively targeted drug-related financial offences, it has introduced a new group of predicate offences under its 2003 Revision to expand its scope to encompass a broader framework concentrating on all crimes, including terrorism, which generate ill-gotten gains. Correspondingly, Türkiye has gradually amended this provision to capture a myriad of predicate crimes by lowering the imprisonment threshold of underlying crimes. However, the inclusion of terrorism within the scope of predicate crimes has been actualised by enacting Law No 5549

59 For the legislative intention of Article 282 of Law No 5237, see Türkiye Büyük Millet Meclisi, 'Türk Ceza Kanunu Tasarısı ve Adalet Komisyonu Raporu (1/593)' <www.tbmm.gov.tr/sirasayi/donem22/yil01/ss664m.htm> accessed 4 July 2023.

60 Friedrich Schneider, 'The Financial Proceeds of Transnational Organized Crime All Over the World: Some New Empirical Facts' (2013) 33(1) The SAIS Review of International Affairs 91.

61 For a more detailed commentary on the double criminality principle, see Grainne Mullan, 'The Concept of Double Criminality in the Context of Extraterritorial Crimes' (1997) 1 Criminal Law Review 17.

2006, albeit Law No 4208 1996 had incorporated terrorism as an aggravating circumstance of the offence.

In terms of the penalties, TCC 2004 stipulates an imprisonment term, ranging from three to seven years, and a judicial fine of up to 20,000 days, reflecting how much harm the crime has caused.[62] It should be noted that the initial version of Article 282(1) had determined more lenient sanctions in terms of the incarceration term set forth, varying from two to five years, whilst the judicial fine had been the same. Therefore, Türkiye has taken a more acrimonious stand against the ML offence over time. Before proceeding any further, it is important to explain how the harm is measured in Türkiye, a crucial determiner of the sanctions to be levied within the specified ranges relating to their harshness. There exist seven factors that are considered by a judge in determining the basic penalty pertaining to a particular case, including ML and its underlying predicates. These elements comprise: (i) the manner in which the offence was committed; (ii) the means used to commit it; (iii) the time and place of the offence; (iv) the importance and value of the subject of the offence; (v) the gravity of the damage or danger; (vi) the degree of fault relating to the intent or recklessness; and (vii) the object and motives of the offender.[63] Furthermore, the personal and economic conditions of the person shall be taken into consideration by the judge in deciding the amount of the judicial fine, where it cannot be determined as less than five days and where it ranges from 20 to 100 TL per day,[64] which is approximately GBP 2.4–12.[65] In more concrete terms, the punitive fine ranges from 100 to 2,000,000 TL, which equals approximately GBP 12–240,000.[66] Furthermore, in cases where a legal entity is involved in the commission of this offence, it shall be subject to security measures specific to them.[67] TCC 2004 prohibits the imposition of penalties on legal entities and allows the application of security measures prescribed by law,[68] including ML and its underlying predicates. Article 60 of TCC 2004 determines the security measures relating to legal entities in this context, which comprise the revocation of the operational permit and confiscation. However, it is necessary to note that Law No 5326 (Misdemeanours Law) 2005[69] also envisages an administrative fine of TL 10,000–50,000,000, which equals approximately GBP 825–4,125,000.[70] In other words, the Turkish legal regime does not establish criminal liability of legal entities, a significant

62 Law No 5237 (Turkish Criminal Code) 2004, art 282(1).
63 Law No 5237 (Turkish Criminal Code) 2004, art 61(1).
64 Law No 5237 (Turkish Criminal Code) 2004, art 52.
65 The currency conversion was made on 29 May 2020. See Xe Currency Converter <www.xe.com/currencyconverter/convert/?Amount=100&From=TRY&To=GBP> accessed 29 May 2020.
66 ibid.
67 Law No 5237 (Turkish Criminal Code) 2004, art 282(5).
68 ibid, art 20(2).
69 Law No 5326 (Misdemeanours Law) 2005, art 43/A.
70 The currency conversion was made on 10 June 2021.

difference compared to the UK's legal framework. The effectiveness of these sanctions, whether they are lenient or harsh in terms of deterrence or fit for their purposes compared to the UK's sanction mechanism, is discussed in Chapter 7.

Based on Article 5 of Law No 5918, Article 282 of TCC 2004 was amended on 26 June 2009.[71] Before this amendment, there was no provision pertaining to perpetrators who, by being aware of its illegitimate nature, purchase, accept, keep, or use the assets acquired as a result of an offence entailing a minimum penalty of six months imprisonment. Although Law No 4208 1996 had referred to Article 165 of TCC 2004 as a supplementary regulation of the ML offence,[72] this legal gap was filled by the second paragraph of Article 282, which provides that:

> [a]ny person who, without participation in commission of the offence set out in the above-mentioned paragraph, purchases, accepts, keeps or uses this asset by being aware of its value and such nature shall be subject to a penalty of imprisonment for a term of two to five years.

A close reading of this paragraph reveals that the accusation of someone committing the relevant offence requires an acknowledgment element. That is to say that charging someone with the crime described in this article requires proving that the perpetrator has been aware of the illegitimate nature and the value of the asset under consideration. In other words, objective elements of the offence consist of two criteria:

a) Non-engagement in the commission of the crimes set out in the first paragraph; and
b) Awareness of the illicit nature of the monetary benefits subject to the activities determined in the paragraph.

Considering these facts, therefore, the wording of the paragraph makes it an arduous task for LEAs to uphold the relevant sanctions against the perpetrators, as the offenders may simply claim that they have not been aware of the illegitimate source of the assets.[73] The legislative intent indicates that this

71 Official Gazette No 27283 dated 9 July 2009 (n 55).

72 Article 165 (i.e., Purchasing or Accepting Property Acquired through the Commission of an Offence) sets forth that '[a]ny person who, without participation in the commission of the offence, sales, transfers, purchases, or accepts, property or other values of property which was acquired through the commission of an offence, shall be sentenced to a penalty of imprisonment for a term of six months to three years and a judicial fine of up to ten thousand days' (as amended on 26 June 2009 by Article 3 of Law No 5918).

73 This nuance constitutes another crucial point of comparison concerning the UK's analogous approach. Accordingly, how the UK regime deals with this group of offenders is investigated in Chapter 4, and the two jurisdictions' current mechanisms in this end are compared in Chapter 7.

particular offence has been determined as a criminal act that may be committed alternatively through the acts as described in the paragraph. In order for this crime to be committed, the presence of *dolus generalis* is not sufficient as it requires a *dolus directus*. In other words, the criminal's direct intent by being aware of the asset's illegitimate nature is essential. These features render it distinct from the crime determined under Article 165 as it can be perpetrated with oblique intention as well.[74] For this very reason, however, it can be argued that Article 165 of TCC 2004 functions as a supplementary/strengthening provision of Article 282. Owing to the fact that it may address the perpetrators who deny that they have been aware of the illicit nature of assets as Article 282 requires such conditions for imposing the relevant sanctions. Nevertheless, considering the penalties Article 165 and Article 282(2) envisage, these two articles need a revision to eliminate any exploitable points by perpetrators, which could be achieved probably by repealing the former and amending the latter to encompass those offenders as well. It is worth reiterating that whilst Article 165 stipulates an imprisonment term of six months to three years and a judicial fine of up to 10,000 days, Article 282(2), on the other hand, sets forth an incarceration term of two years to five years. This exploitable nuance comprising the intended difference of direct or oblique intention behind the determined sanctions may constitute a legal deficiency in Türkiye's AML composition as it can be manipulated effortlessly by offenders. It would be appropriate to hypothesise a concrete scenario here, which would present the ambiguity of the two articles, in which a customer buys a piece of art that has been acquired as a result of an underlying crime, such as theft. In cases where the customer claims that s/he has not been aware of the illicit nature of the product, it is not possible to impose the sanctions determined under Article 282(2), albeit (even if) s/he is well aware that the art piece was stolen. In such a scenario, although the culprit deserves harsher penalties, s/he may exploit the lacuna or incoherency in law without any struggle and relish the more lenient sanctions envisaged by Article 165. Consequently, s/he gets a penalty of imprisonment for a term of six months to three years and a judicial fine of up to 10,000 days, whereas s/he should have been sentenced to a penalty of imprisonment for a term of two to five years under the *lex lata*. Therefore, it would be apt to posit that this shadowy distinction needs to be eliminated by the *lex ferenda*.

The remaining paragraphs of the article describe the aggravating and mitigating circumstances that increase and decrease the relevant sanctions to be levied, respectively. Article 282(3) provides that '[w]here this offence is committed by a public officer or professional person in the course of his duty then the imprisonment penalty to be imposed shall be increased one half', a provision that addresses enablers. However, the sanctions determined for

74 For the legislative intention of Article 165 of Law No 5237, see Türkiye Büyük Millet Meclisi (n 59).

enablers under Law No 4208 1996 had been harsher as it had set forth an additional one-fold increase rather than a one-half increment. Therefore, TCC 2004 handles money launderers, who act on behalf of others, more leniently. Article 282(4), in alignment with Law No 4208 1996, stipulates that '[w]here this offence is conducted in the course of the activities of an organisation established for the purpose of committing an offence, the penalty to be imposed shall be doubled'. Nevertheless, there is a crucial difference between Law No 4208 1996 and TCC 2004 in determining sanctions for money launderers where legal entities are involved in such offences. Although the former law had impeached managers of legal entities and penalised them accordingly, the latter law does not articulate any natural persons responsible for ML offences perpetrated by legal entities. Article 282(5) sets forth in this end that legal entities shall be subject to security measures specific to them in cases where they involve in the commission of ML. The Turkish legal regime does not establish criminal liability of legal entities, but it would be appropriate to reconsider establishing such liability. Lastly, Article 282(6) stipulates that 'no penalty shall be imposed upon a person who directly enables the securing of financial assets, or who facilitates the securing of such assets, by informing the relevant authorities of the location of such before the commencement of a prosecution'; a provision that enables offenders to benefit from sincere confession, in alignment with the Turkish Civil Code 2001 regarding the protection of *goodwill*.[75]

TCC 2004 determines the legal rules regarding the confiscation of criminal assets through Articles 54, 55, 60, 64, 70, and 75. Article 54 and Article 55, in particular, determine the provisions of the confiscation of property[76] and the confiscation of gains,[77] respectively. Article 54(2) sets forth that '[w]here the property defined in paragraph one cannot be confiscated because it has been destroyed, given to another, consumed, or, for any other reason, an amount of money equal to the value of this particular property shall be confiscated'. Article 55(2) stipulates that '[w]here property and material gain which is subject to confiscation cannot be seized or provided to the authorities then value corresponding to such property and gains shall be confiscated'. It is necessary to underline the provisions of these paragraphs, as they allow LEAs to *confiscate the corresponding value of the property and material gain to be confiscated*, reinforcing competent authorities in recovering proceeds of crime. However, there exist strong safeguards the Turkish legal instruments put forward in balancing the property and other fundamental rights of the suspect or the accused, as discussed subsequently.

75 See for instance, Law No 4721 (Turkish Civil Code) 2001, arts 3 or 378.
76 Law No 5237 (Turkish Criminal Code) 2004, art 54.
77 ibid, art 55.

3.3.3 *Law No 5549 on the Prevention of Laundering Proceeds of Crime 2006*

As Law No 4208 1996 and TCC 2004 approached the phenomenon differently, Türkiye enacted Law No 5549 2006 to eliminate confusion faced by the competent authorities in tackling ML and its predicates. This law virtually abolished Law No 4208 1996, whereby consistent definitions for the ML offences were imbedded in the legal regime. For instance, Law No 5549 2006 states that '[t]he phrases "dirty money" and "dirty money laundering offence" in other legislation refer to "proceeds derived from crime" and "money laundering offence" respectively'.[78] There remains, however, a few provisions of Law No 4208 1996 in force, such as Articles 10 and 11, explaining provisions pertaining to controlled delivery,[79] as there are no contradictory relevant provisions in any other legal sources.[80]

In addition to consolidating terminologies across *jus scriptum*, Law No 5549 2006 adopts the identical definition for ML as stipulated by Article 282 of TCC 2004,[81] another unifying feature of the legal instrument. Furthermore, it has introduced fundamental changes, such as defining obliged entities and their obligations.[82] The comparative analysis of obliged entities as to whether they encompass more or less FIs and DNFBPs in Türkiye and the UK, is discussed in Chapter 7 with a specific reference to their obligations. Whilst the former regime under Law No 4208 1996 had described only two sets of obligations, the present law devotes a chapter for 'Obligations and Information Exchange' and determines exhaustive sets of obligations, including 'customer identification', 'suspicious transaction reports', and 'training, internal control and risk management systems and other measures'. As argued previously, this elaboration on obligations reflects the revision in FATF's evaluation methodology dated 27 February 2004, which prioritises the measures regarding obligations. For instance, the 2004-methodology set forth that '[t]he

78 Law No 5549 on the Prevention of Laundering Proceeds of Crime 2006, art 26(3).

79 Controlled delivery is an LEA *modus operandi* that seeks to determine offenders and catch them red-handed, determine and collect all evidence, and seize the contraband harbouring illegal goods (e.g., psychotropic substances) by allowing the transportation within the knowledge and under the control of the competent authorities. See also William C Gilmore, 'Police Co-Operation and the European Communities: Current Trends and Recent Developments' (1993) 19(4) Commonwealth Law Bulletin 1960.

80 See (n 37).

81 Law No 5549 on the Prevention of Laundering Proceeds of Crime 2006, art 2(g).

82 The obliged entities consist of those (i) who operate in the field of banking, insurance, individual pension, capital markets, money lending and other financial services, and postal service and transportation, lotteries, and bets; (ii) who deal with exchange, real estate, precious stones and metals, jewellery, all kinds of (transportation) vehicles, construction machines, historical artefacts, artworks, antiques or intermediaries in these operations; notaries, sports clubs, and freelance lawyers; and (iii) who operate in other fields determined by the President of the Republic. See Law No 5549 on the Prevention of Laundering Proceeds of Crime 2006, art 2(1)(d).

basic obligations under Recommendations 5, 10 and 13 should be set out in law or regulation',[83] referring to obligations on 'Customer Due Diligence and Record Keeping' and 'Reporting of Suspicious Transactions and Compliance'.

Another systematic innovation introduced by this law, compared to its predecessor, is the introduction of regulations on CTF. Whilst the former law had not contained any provisions about the prevention of TF, the current law presents measures pertaining to CTF in Articles 17, 18, and 19. Furthermore, although the provisions of Law No 5549 2006 regulating the duties and authorities of MASAK (i.e., Article 19) have been repealed,[84] and currently they are determined by Presidential Decree No. 1 on the Organisation of the Presidency 2018, it deserves to be considered here because it had considerably enlarged the framework of MASAK's responsibilities. More specifically, it had given additional powers to MASAK, which had expanded its scope to encompass gathering, receiving, analysing, and evaluating data and STRs relating to TF that the previous law had not envisaged. In other words, the functions and powers of MASAK had been reformed by this law. These included, amongst others, forwarding all serious suspicious cases to the Public Prosecutor's Office for further investigation.[85] It is necessary to state what makes a suspicious transaction 'serious' in Türkiye. Although there is no explicit definition or criteria for considering such transactions as serious, MASAK provides guidelines for the obliged entities in determining the seriousness of the suspicion. There exist two guidelines stipulating the circumstances where the obliged entities should file a 'suspicious transaction report with deferment request' based on the seriousness of the transaction.[86] For instance, understanding that the person or persons involved in the transaction are or may be related to crime as a result of checks from various databases or other sources enhances the seriousness of the suspicion, and as such, requires the obliged entities, including banks, to file their transaction reports accordingly.[87] MASAK conveys these 'serious' cases to the Public Prosecutor's Office.

Whilst the former legal regime had referred to both heavy fines and imprisonment for violation of obligations, the current legal framework stipulates

83 FATF, 'FATF Reference Document: Methodology for Assessing Compliance with the FATF 40 Recommendations and the FATF 9 Special Recommendations' (February 2004; updated as of February 2009) <www.fatf-gafi.org/media/fatf/documents/reports/methodology.pdf> accessed 4 July 2023.

84 Official Gazette No 30473 dated 9 July 2018, 'Anayasada Yapılan Değişikliklere Uyum Sağlanması Amacıyla Bazı Kanun ve Kanun Hükmünde Kararnamelerde Değişiklik Yapılması Hakkında Kanun Hükmünde Kararname' <www.resmigazete.gov.tr/eskiler/2018/07/20180709M3-1.pdf> accessed 4 July 2023.

85 Law No 5549 on the Prevention of Laundering Proceeds of Crime 2006, art 19.

86 MASAK, 'Şüpheli İşlem Bildirim Rehberi (Bankalar)' <www.procompliance.net/wp-content/uploads/2019/09/SIB_Rehberi_Bankalar_Icin_11092019.pdf> accessed 4 July 2023; MASAK, 'Şüpheli İşlem Bildirim Rehberi (Diğer Yükümlüler)' <https://ms.hmb.gov.tr/uploads/2020/11/SIB-REHBERI-DIGER-YUKUMLULER.pdf> accessed 4 July 2023.

87 ibid.

administrative or judicial penalties for liable persons for failure to comply with the obligations, depending on the type of the deficiency. In other words, Law No 5549 2006 imposes either administrative or judicial penalties for the liable persons for contravening the obligations, suggesting that it does not inflict both of them for the same failure. However, it is necessary to mention that the judicial penalties contain both an incarceration term and a judicial fine; therefore, the latter component of the sanction serves as administrative penalties simultaneously as they comprise fines only. More specifically, whilst it envisages administrative penalties for the violation of obligations relating to customer identification (Article 3), suspicious transaction reporting (Article 4(1)), training, internal control, control and risk management systems and other measures (Article 5), periodically reporting (Article 6), and electronic notification (Article 9/A),[88] it also stipulates judicial penalties for the violation of obligations concerning disclosing the process of STR (Article 4(2)), providing (Article 7), retaining, and submitting information and documents (Article 8), or for failure in declaring the transaction carried out on account of another person (Article 15).[89] Law No 5549 2006 classifies the gravity of violations, where it considers the latter group of breaches more aggravate and punishes them accordingly. Although it envisages imprisonment (judicial penalties) for some violations of AML obligations, it is the TCC 2004 that primarily regulates the criminal activities relating to ML. In other words, it has introduced administrative fines for failing to comply with particular essential obligations, such as customer identification and STR, that previously required imprisonment for violators of such responsibilities, an approach called 'dual separation' by MASAK.[90]

Article 17(1) of Law No 5549 2006 refers to Law No 5271 (Criminal Procedure Code – CPC) 2004 for the implementation of the seizure (*elkoyma*). It is important to clarify the differences between the concepts of seizure and confiscation as they are two distinct legal notions that stand for two different judicial procedures. The seizure is a type of (temporary and preventive) measure devoted to protecting the evidence relating to a particular crime.[91] More specifically, 'assets likely to be useful as means of proof or values of property that are subject to confiscation of goods or confiscation of gains shall be secured'.[92] Furthermore, 'in circumstances where the individual who holds the evidence refuses to surrender voluntarily, those assets may be seized (by force)'.[93] In other words, the seizure is defined as, in order to prevent crime or dangers, the process of removing the possessor's power of disposition over an asset despite his/her lack of consent, where it may be evidence of a crime or

88 Law No 5549 on the Prevention of Laundering Proceeds of Crime 2006, art 13.
89 ibid, art 14.
90 Republic of Türkiye Ministry of Treasury and Finance (n 48).
91 Law No 5271 (Criminal Procedure Code) 2004, pt four.
92 ibid, art 123(1).
93 ibid, art 123(2).

is subject to confiscation.[94] Therefore, it can be argued that the seizure constitutes the temporary form and the initial step of the confiscation. The confiscation (*müsadere*), on the other hand, is a type of security measure whereby the ownership of certain assets or gains related to a crime are transferred to the State, as determined under Chapter 3 of TCC 2004 titled 'Sanctions' and regulated under the title of 'Security Measures'.[95] In other words, the confiscation is a permanent version of the seizure, where the possession of the assets under consideration is handed over to the State permanently.

CPC 2004 comprises a solid legal framework for the use of seizure of the proceeds of crime. Accordingly, assets that belong to the suspect or the accused may be seized 'in cases where there are grounds for strong suspicion based on concrete evidence tending to show that the crime under investigation or prosecution has been committed and that they have been obtained from this crime'.[96] The assets that may be seized include (i) immovable goods; (ii) transport vehicles of land, sea, or air; (iii) all kinds of accounts in banks or other financial institutions; (iv) all kinds of rights and credits by real or juridical persons; (v) valuable documents; (vi) shares at the firm where s/he is a shareholder; (vii) contents of the rented safe; (viii) other assets belonging to him'.[97]

Although the use of confiscation is compulsory, as the close reading of Article 128(1) of CPC 2004 connotes, seizure of the assets prescribed by law depends on the concept of *strong grounds of suspicion based on concrete evidence*. Nevertheless, it also enables LEAs to seize these assets even in cases where they are possessed by third parties,[98] a provision that strengthens competent authorities in confiscating the illegal proceeds. Furthermore, the list-based approach to seizable assets may arouse concerns over Article 128(1) of TCC 2004 relating to its comprehensiveness as to whether it may be exploitable by offenders. However, it provides an exhaustive list as the last clause of the provision stipulates 'other assets belonging to him' may be seized, as well. Therefore, it can be inferred that seizure, and eventually confiscation, can encompass any proceeds of crime regardless of whether they are controlled by third parties or not.

It is essential to discuss here the safeguards to balance the property and other fundamental rights of the suspect or the accused, as it constitutes a crucial point of comparison concerning the UK's approach to this end, especially in light of the Unexplained Wealth Orders (UWOs). Firstly, it needs to be noted that although the right to property is guaranteed under the Turkish Constitution 1982, the exercise of the right to property shall not contravene public interest, and it may be limited by law because of an over-riding public interest.[99] Therefore, the execution of confiscation seeks, above all, the public

94 Regulation on the Judicial and Preventive Search 2005, art 4.
95 Law No 5237 (Turkish Criminal Code) 2004, arts 54 and 55.
96 Law No 5271 (Criminal Procedure Code) 2004, art 128(1).
97 ibid.
98 ibid.
99 Constitution of the Republic of Türkiye 1982, art 35.

interest. Crucially, the Turkish Constitution 1982 outlaws imposing general confiscation as a punishment.[100] In other words, the Turkish legal regime does not allow the confiscation of any asset unless proven to be related to a crime committed as determined under Articles 54 and 55 of TCC 2004, which envisage the provisions relating to specific confiscation concerning confiscation of property and gains, respectively. Accordingly, in order to understand the legal safeguards balancing the property and other fundamental rights of the suspect or the accused, the provisions of Articles 54 and 55 of TCC 2004 need to be examined in detail. Before scrutinising these Articles, it is necessary to state that the concept of confiscation is regulated as per the essential principles of legality, legitimate purpose, and proportionality, the principal safeguards of the suspect or the accused concerning confiscation or any other legal proceedings. Considering the legal principle that ***nullum crimen, nulla poena sine lege***,[101] both Law No 4721 (Turkish Civil Code) 2002[102] and, in particular, TCC 2004[103] explicitly stipulate that the law constitutes the basis for the judge to decide any judicial procedures. Accordingly, the regulations regarding confiscation are imbedded in Turkish legal instruments, including the Turkish Constitution 1982, demonstrating its congruency with the principle of legality. Additionally, the imposition of confiscation should be executed on the condition that 'the property does not belong to any third party acting in good faith',[104] indicating the legitimate purpose of the law. It is also provided that '[w]here the confiscation of property used in an offence would lead to more serious consequences than the offence itself and would be unfair, confiscation may not be ordered'.[105] These provisions provide judges discretionary power in deciding confiscation orders, denoting its harmony with the principle of proportionality. Furthermore, the execution of confiscation in Türkiye requires a finalised conviction judgement, as discussed later.

After outlining these principal safeguards, it is necessary to closely examine the provisions of Articles 54[106] and 55[107] of TCC 2004 to clarify the remaining

100 Constitution of the Republic of Türkiye 1982, art 38(10).

101 This maxim principally means that 'there must be no crime or punishment except in accordance with fixed, predetermined law'. See Aly Mokhtar, 'Nullum Crimen, Nulla Poena Sine Lege: Aspects and Prospects' (2005) 26(1) Statute Law Review 41.

102 Law No 4721 (Turkish Civil Code) 2001, art 1.

103 Law No 5237 (Turkish Criminal Code) 2004, art 2.

104 ibid, art 54(1).

105 Law No 5237 (Turkish Criminal Code) 2004, art 54(3).

106 Article 54(1) stipulates that: 'On the condition that the property does not belong to any third party acting in good faith, property that is used for committing an intentional offence or is allocated for the purpose of committing an offence, or property that has emerged as a result of an offence shall be confiscated. Property that is prepared for the purpose of committing a crime shall be confiscated, if it presents a danger to public security, public health, or public morality. In cases where there is a limited real right is established in favour of third parties acting in good faith on the properties, the confiscation decision is made on the condition that this right is reserved'.

107 Article 55(1) provides that: 'Material gain obtained through the commission of an offence or forming the subject of an offence or obtained for the commission of an offence and the economic earnings obtained as a result of its investment or conversion, shall be confiscated.

defences that perpetrators, including money launderers, may have intrinsically in protecting their legitimate assets against the execution of confiscation. As the close reading of these articles connotes (see footnotes 106 and 107), they do not allow confiscation of properties or gains held by offenders, including money launderers, unless proven that they are connected to the offence under consideration as per the circumstances of that connection as outlined within these provisions. Unlike the UK's approach to confiscation, LEAs in Türkiye cannot confiscate assets even in cases where the offenders cannot explain the (il)legitimate sources of their property or gains, constituting a crucial difference between the two legal regimes. It would be appropriate to underline here that the second clause of Article 54(1) allows the execution of confiscation of properties that pose risks to public security, public health, or public morality, regardless of whether they have been used in the commission of an offence or not. Although it is congruent with the core aim of security measures, protecting the public interest against the potential dangers, some experts criticise this clause based on the idea that it contradicts Article 38 of the Turkish Constitution 1982 as any crime has not come into existence.[108] More importantly, Article 54(1) protects the rights of *bona fide* third parties relating to the execution of confiscation. Article 55(1) prioritises returning the material gain to the victim of the offence and allows confiscation where that is not possible. These provisions explicitly indicate the legitimate purpose of the law concerning confiscation. Another crucial point that needs to be stated is that the judge can decide the confiscation of properties as determined under Article 54 of TCC 2004, regardless of whether or not the accused is guilty or convicted. In other words, even in circumstances where the accused does not have criminal liability under the TCC 2004, such as children and people with mental illnesses, or in cases where the decision of dismissal is given due to the statute of limitations, the judge can still decide the confiscation of properties. However, the decisions relating to the deferment of the announcement of the verdict (*Hükmün Açıklanmasının Geri Bırakılması*) given to the accused also encompass properties under consideration,[109] excluding the ones constituting crime by themselves as determined under Article 54(4), such as illicit drugs. Both Article 54(2) and Article 55(2) stipulate in harmony that in circumstances where the confiscation of properties or gains under consideration cannot be confiscated (e.g., they have been given to third parties), then the corresponding monetary value to such assets shall be confiscated. It would be right to state here that these provisions convey the message to the public that perpetrators will be deprived of the proceeds of their crimes in any case, targeting the incentive fact

---

Confiscation under this paragraph should only be ordered where it is impossible to return the material gain to the victim of the offence'.

108 Mahmut Koca, 'Türk Ceza Hukukunda Müsadere' *LEXPERA Blog* (27 May 2020) <https://blog.lexpera.com.tr/turk-ceza-hukukunda-musadere/#fn9> accessed 4 July 2023.

109 Ersan Sen, 'Temyiz İncelemesinde Müsadere Hakkında Verilebilecek Kararlar' *Hukuki Haber* (22 April 2020) <www.hukukihaber.net/temyiz-incelemesinde-musadere-hakkinda-verilebilecek-kararlar-makale,7743.html> accessed 4 July 2023.

behind committing financial crimes.[110] However, it is necessary to state that Article 55(3) stipulates that 'for the property within the scope of the article to be confiscated, the person who has subsequently obtained it must not benefit from the provisions concerning the protection of the goodwill', another provision that protects the *bona fide* third parties. Article 54(4) sets forth that any property the producing, possessing, using, transporting, purchasing, or selling of which constitutes a crime, such as counterfeit money or illicit drugs, shall be confiscated. Finally, Articles 54(5) and 54(6) stipulate that '[w]hen only a certain part of a property needs to be confiscated, then only that part shall be confiscated, if it is possible to do so without harming the whole, or if it is possible to separate that part of it' and '[w]here property is shared by more than one person, only the share of the person who has taken part in the crime shall be confiscated', respectively. In other words, there are strong safeguards for the execution of confiscation in Türkiye, which may explain its limited use when compared to the UK.

Securing a seizure decision requires obtaining a report, which indicates the monetary value of economic advantages the crime has catalysed, within three months at the latest, a period which may be extended for two months under certain circumstances upon request.[111] The judge is the only competent judicial authority for carrying out such robust action relating to seizure described by this article.[112] It is necessary to state that this authority used to belong to the aggravated felony courts, where the implementation of a seizure depended on a unanimous decision of judges in such courts. Furthermore, upon the opposition, the power to impose a confiscation order is still used to require a unanimous decision of the aggravated felony courts to render an injunction. That is to say that securing a seizure decision has been simplified in Türkiye, albeit the burden of obtaining the previously mentioned report remains a precondition of getting a seizure decision, which undoubtedly impedes the effectiveness of the confiscation powers of the country. In other words, getting a seizure decision, hence the implementation of an eventual confiscation in Türkiye, is a relatively burdensome process compared to the UK's analogous approach, as discussed later in Chapter 4.

Before proceeding any further, it is necessary to mention that Article 17 of Law No 5549 2006 regulates the circumstances relating to obtaining a seizure decision differently. Whilst Article 17(1) refers to Article 128 of CPC

110 For a more detailed discussion on the underlying reasons for committing financial crimes, see Petter Gottschalk, 'Theories of Financial Crime' (2010) 17(2) Journal of Financial Crime 210.

111 Law No 5271 (Criminal Procedure Code) 2004, art 128. Depending on the assets under consideration, it is necessary to get the relevant report within the specified period from one of these bodies: Banking Regulation and Supervision Agency, Capital Markets Board, MASAK, Undersecretariat of Treasury and Public Oversight, or Accounting and Auditing Standards Authority.

112 Law No 5271 (Criminal Procedure Code) 2004, art 128(9).

2004 for the implementation of seizure, Article 17(2), on the other hand, unlike the provisions stated therein, confers public prosecutors the authority to give a seizure order in circumstances where there is peril in delay. It further sets forth that in cases where the seizure decision has been executed based on such an order, it shall be submitted to the judge who has jurisdiction for this decision within 24 hours from the act of seizure; and it shall be decided by him/her whether it will be approved or not within a total of 48 hours starting from the implementation of seizure; otherwise, it shall be automatically void. Therefore, the provisions of Article 128 of CPC 2004 and Article 17 of Law No 5549 2006 regarding determining the authority who has power for the seizure decision need to be synchronised.

The provisions of Article 128(1) are (only) applicable to the offences determined under Article 128(2) of CPC 2004. In more concrete terms, it sets forth a detailed set of crime types, which may be interpreted as predicate offences and seen in Table 3.2.

Table 3.2 Predicate crimes envisaged by Law No 5271 (Criminal Procedure Code) 2004.

Law No 5271 (Criminal Procedure Code) 2004
'The following crimes as defined in the Turkish Criminal Code;
Genocide and crimes against humanity (Articles 76, 77, 78),
Smuggling migrants and human trading (Articles 79, 80), and (as *added on 24 November 2016 by Article 25 of Law No 6763*) trading organs or tissues (Article 91),
Theft (Articles 141, 142),
Robbery (Articles 148, 149),
Breach of trust (Article 155),
Fraud (Articles 157, 158),
Fraudulent bankruptcy (Article 161),
Producing and trading of narcotic or stimulating substances (Article 188),
Forgery of money (Article 197),
Establishing Organisation for the Purpose of Committing Crimes (Article 220(3)) (as *amended on 24 November 2016 by Article 25 of Law No 6763*),
Fraud during a tender (Article 235),
Fraud during the discharge of contractual obligations (Article 236),
Unlawful money lending (Article 241) (as *added on 24 November 2016 by Article 25 of Law No 6763*),
Embezzlement (Article 247),
Extortion (Article 250),
Bribery (Article 252),
Crimes against state security (Articles 302, 303, 304, 305, 306, 307, 308),
Crimes against the Constitutional order and crimes against the functioning of this system (Articles 309, 311, 312, 313, 314, 315, 316),
Crimes against state secrets and spying (Articles 328, 329, 330, 331, 333, 334, 335, 336, 337),
Smuggling weapons as defined in the Law on Firearms and Knives as well as Other Tools (Article 12),

(*Continued*)

Table 3.2 (Continued)

Embezzlement as defined in the Banking Law (Article 22/3 and 4),
Crimes as defined in Law on the Combating Smuggling that carry imprisonment as punishment,
Crimes as defined in Articles 68 and 74 of Law on the Protection of Cultural and Natural Values'.[113]

The remaining provisions of Article 128 of CPC 2004 determine the procedures as to how the assets can be seized.[114] In other words, Article 128 of CPC 2004 sets forth a comprehensive framework for the execution of seizure, which constitutes the first legal step of confiscation, as argued previously.

3.4 Regulations

3.4.1 Regulation on Measures Regarding Prevention of Laundering the Proceeds of Crime and Financing of Terrorism (ROM) 2008

On par with the diversifications in the financial activities conducted by criminals, the international financial standards have developed as well, which is evidenced by the revisions of the FATF methodology and recommendations. In response to these developments, taking its legal basis from Law No 5549 2006, ROM was put into force on 1 April 2008[115] to ensure Türkiye's compliance with the international legal instruments. For example, considering the

113 ibid, art 128(2).

114 More specifically, it sets forth that a decision on the seizure of an immovable good shall be enforced by taking a note in the title (Article 128(3)). In alignment, a decision on the seizure of transport vehicles operating on land, sea or air shall be enforced by taking a note in the title, where they are registered (Article 128(4)). A decision on the seizure of accounts at banks and other financial institutions shall be enforced by immediately informing the bank or financial institute by technical communication means. The related decision shall also be notified to the bank or financial institution separately. The interactions at the bank account, aimed to make the decision of seizure ineffective, which are conducted after the decision has been rendered, are void (Article 128(5)). A decision on the seizure of shares at a firm shall be enforced by notifying the administration of the related firm and the head of the commerce title by technical communication means immediately. The related decision shall also be notified to the related firm and to the directorate of the financial institution separately (Article 128(6)). A decision on the seizure of rights and credits shall be enforced by immediately notifying the related real or juridical person by technical communication means. The related decision shall also be notified to the real or juridical person separately (Article 128(7)). In cases where there are violations of the requirements of the decision on seizure, Article 289 of the Turkish Penal Code related to the 'misusing of the power of protection' shall apply (Article 128(8)). Seizure under the provision of this Article shall only be decided by the judge (Article 128(9)). Lastly, in cases where it is required to manage immovables, rights, and debts owed to one seized pursuant to this article, a trustee may be appointed to manage these assets (Article 128(10)).

115 Official Gazette No 26751 dated 9 January 2008 (n 25).

FATF's Forty Recommendations 2003, ROM 2008 introduced the concept of the *beneficial owner*.[116]

ROM 2008 may be regarded as the secondary legislation that provides a detailed set of measures related to provisions set out in Law No 5549 2006, as it has been drawn up based on Article 27 of the relevant law.[117] It strives to create a more hostile environment for the nefarious activities of ML/TF by regulating principles and procedures concerning obliged entities, their obligations, and other pertinent measures. It determines principles and procedures related, amongst others, to the STR and KYC standards, whereby it sets forth measures concerning, *inter alia*, the customer identification, identification of the beneficial owner, and relationships with risky countries whilst outlining the framework for the supervision of obligations.

Since ROM 2008 was enacted, it has been amended three times on 2 January 2010,[118] 10 June 2014,[119] and 18 March 2016.[120] By the first amendment, the scope of obliged entities has been enlarged to encompass, amongst others, independent audit institutions authorised to conduct an audit in financial markets. Arguably, the reason behind this amendment was to ensure harmonisation with the EU's Third AMLD (i.e., Directive 2005/60/EC), Article(2) of which had determined obliged entities.[121] The 2014 amendments introduced, amongst others, the 'identification of beneficial owners' and 'enhanced measures', which are of utmost importance in AML/CTF matters.[122] In advance of the second amendment, Türkiye had been criticised in its third-round MER conducted by the FATF regarding the aforementioned

116 It defines a beneficial owner as 'a natural person who ultimately controls or owns a natural person who carries out a transaction within an obliged entity or the natural persons, legal persons, or unincorporated organizations on whose behalf a transaction is being conducted within an obliged party'. See ROM 2008, Article 3(h).

117 Regulation on Measures Regarding Prevention of Laundering the Proceeds of Crime and Financing of Terrorism 2008, art 2.

118 Official Gazette No 27450 dated 2 January 2010, 'Suç Gelirlerinin Aklanmasının ve Terörün Finansmanının Önlenmesine Dair Tedbirler Hakkında Yönetmelikte Değişiklik Yapılmasına Dair Yönetmelik' <www.resmigazete.gov.tr/eskiler/2010/01/20100102-2.htm> accessed 4 July 2023.

119 Official Gazette No 29026 dated 10 June 2014, 'Aklama Suçu İncelemesi Hakkında Yönetmelik, Suç Gelirlerinin Aklanmasının ve Terörün Finansmanının Önlenmesine Dair Tedbirler Hakkında Yönetmelik ve Malî Suçlarla Mücadele Koordinasyon Kurulunun Çalışma Usul ve Esasları Hakkında Yönetmelikte Değişiklik Yapılmasına Dair Yönetmelik' <www.resmigazete.gov.tr/eskiler/2014/06/20140610-5.htm> accessed 4 July 2023.

120 Official Gazette No 29657 dated 18 March 2016, 'Suç Gelirlerinin Aklanmasının ve Terörün Finansmanının Önlenmesine Dair Tedbirler Hakkında Yönetmelikte Değişiklik Yapılmasına Dair Yönetmelik' <www.resmigazete.gov.tr/eskiler/2016/03/20160318-10.pdf> accessed 4 July 2023.

121 Directive 2005/60/EC of the European Parliament and of the Council of 26 October 2005 on the prevention of the use of the financial system for the purpose of money laundering and terrorist financing (Text with EEA relevance) [2005] OJ L309/15.

122 For a more detailed commentary on the concept of beneficial owners regarding the AML matter, see Paul Michael Gilmour, 'Lifting the Veil on Beneficial Ownership: Challenges of Implementing the UK's Registers of Beneficial Owners' (2020) 23(4) Journal of Money Laundering Control 717.

measures.[123] Accordingly, in response to this criticism, the country has amended these issues, albeit not promptly. The final amendment was mainly related to the scope of obliged entities; it has introduced new entities, such as electronic money institutions, in alignment with the relevant international developments (e.g., cryptocurrencies).[124]

3.4.2 *Regulation on the Program of Compliance With Obligations of Anti-Money Laundering and Combating the Financing of Terrorism (ROC) 2008*

ROC 2008[125] has been drawn up based on Article 5 of Law No 5549 2006.[126] It can be argued that the underlying incentives behind its enactment consist of addressing the advancements seen in the AML sphere and reflecting the requirements of international legal instruments, such as the FATF Recommendations and the AMLDs. It specifies a detailed set of principles and procedures for forming compliance programmes and appointment of compliance officers by obliged entities related to provisions stipulated in the aforementioned law.[127] ROC 2008 requires (i) banks (excluding the Central Bank of the Republic of Türkiye); (ii) development and investment banks; (iii) capital markets brokerage houses; (iv) insurance and pension companies, and (v) General Directorate of Post in relation to banking activities to develop a compliance programme and assign compliance officers as obliged entities.[128]

3.5 Presidential Decree No. 1 on the Organisation of the Presidency 2018

The most recent AML legal instrument was driven by the governmental change in the country. Presidential Decree No. 1 on the Organisation of the Presidency (the Decree) 2018[129] has redefined Türkiye's state and governance

123 FATF, 'Third Mutual Evaluation Report: Anti-Money Laundering and Combatting the Financing of Terrorism – Turkey' (February 2007) <www.fatf-gafi.org/media/fatf/documents/reports/mer/MER%20Turkey%20full.pdf> accessed 4 July 2023.

124 For a discussion on using cryptocurrencies for ML purposes, see Christoph Wronka, 'Money Laundering Through Cryptocurrencies: Analysis of the Phenomenon and Appropriate Prevention Measures' (2022) 25(1) Journal of Money Laundering Control 79.

125 Official Gazette No 26999 dated 16 September 2008 (n 27).

126 Regulation on the Program of Compliance with Obligations of Anti-Money Laundering and Combating the Financing of Terrorism (ROC) 2008, art 2.

127 ROC 2008 consists of four sections. The second section, namely Compliance Programme, amongst others, (i) clarifies obliged entities that are required to develop a compliance program; (ii) mandates developing an institutional policy by which institutional procedures are explicitly defined; (iii) stipulates establishing a risk management and a training policy; undertaking to monitor and control activities; assigning a compliance officer who is responsible for the execution of the compliance program; as well as annual and risk-based internal control activities.

128 Regulation on the Program of Compliance with Obligations of Anti-Money Laundering and Combating the Financing of Terrorism (ROC) 2008, arts 4 and 16.

129 Official Gazette No 30474 dated 10 July 2018 (n 35).

structure. Under Chapter 7 of the Decree, Article 217 sets forth the duties and powers of the Ministry of Treasury and Finance, such as determining principles and procedures for ML prevention.[130] It also governs the service units affiliated to the Ministry, including MASAK,[131] suggesting that the Decree has not altered the administrative nature of MASAK. Articles 231 and 232 define the duties and powers of MASAK and the Coordination Board for Combating Financial Crimes, respectively.[132] Remarkably, as per the provisions determined by Law No 5549 2006, in circumstances where serious ML/TF suspicion occurs, Article 231(e) of the Decree mandates MASAK to forward the cases to the competent Public Prosecutor's Office. In alignment with TCC 2004 and Law No 6706 2016, which refer to 'dual criminality',[133] the Decree alludes to the principle of reciprocity.[134] It authorises MASAK as the responsible body for answering information requests and allowing foreign competent authorities to conduct liability inspections on obliged entities whose main branches are located abroad. In other words, the Decree has considerably expanded the duties and powers of MASAK, which would indubitably reinforce the AML effectiveness of the country. However, notwithstanding such significant powers, it has not altered its administrative-type character. Therefore, the administrative nature of MASAK may intrinsically impede the abilities of this crucial organ compared to the UKFIU, which is a law enforcement type of FIU, as examined in the following chapters.

3.6 General Communiqués of MASAK

MASAK periodically publishes regulatory instruments and guidelines to clarify principles and procedures outlined in the relevant legislation, thereby creating a more antagonistic milieu for generating better outcomes. Currently, there are four General Communiqués in force, all of which are related to ROM 2008, namely General Communiqués No. 5, 7, 8, and 13.[135]

General Communiqué No. 5[136] explains principles and procedures for simplified due diligence as regulated by Article 26 of ROM 2008. General

130 Presidential Decree No 1 on the Organisation of the Presidency 2018, art 217.

131 ibid, art 219.

132 ibid. It is necessary to note that these Articles were amended on 7 August 2019. See Official Gazette No 30855 dated 7 August 2019, 'Bazı Cumhurbaşkanlığı Kararnamelerinde Değişiklik Yapılması Hakkında Cumhurbaşkanlığı Kararnamesi' <www.resmigazete.gov.tr/eskiler/2019/08/20190807-1.pdf> accessed 4 July 2023.

133 Dual criminality is a principle that entails the criminalisation of underlying activities in both jurisdictions. See Mullan (n 61).

134 Presidential Decree No 1 on the Organisation of the Presidency 2018, art 231(j).

135 Republic of Türkiye Ministry of Treasury and Finance, 'National Legislation' <https://en.hmb.gov.tr/fcib-national-legistation> accessed 4 July 2023.

136 Official Gazette No 26842 dated 9 April 2008, 'Mali Suçları Araştırma Kurulu Genel Tebliği' <www.resmigazete.gov.tr/eskiler/2008/04/20080409-8.htm> accessed 22 February 2023.

Communiqué No. 7[137] sets forth the principles regarding KYC standards. More precisely, it clarifies principles and procedures for ensuring that information of customers to whom the obliged parties have permanent business relationships is in harmony with ROM 2008. General Communiqué No. 8[138] had redetermined the due date for ensuring that obliged entities have adjusted the information about their (permanent) customers with whom they are in a permanent business relationship regarding customer identification in harmony with ROM 2008. Finally, General Communiqué No. 13[139] sets forth principles and procedures regarding the STR regime. It has been drawn up based on Articles 27 and 28 of ROM, which envisage provisions for STR and filling in STR forms and time limit for reporting, respectively. It introduces the web-based system called EMIS.ONLINE that enables sending STR forms electronically.[140] It determines reporting time for obliged parties as *ten workdays*, albeit stating that it should be reported 'immediately in cases where delay may cause inconveniences'.[141] Given that online ML transactions can be conducted in a matter of seconds by perpetrators,[142] the ten workdays period is an enormous time that may facilitate the commission of such unlawful conduct. Furthermore, it does not seem to be fit for purpose and may incapacitate the overall AML competency of the country.

3.7 Conclusion

As a member of the G20 and a candidate country for EU membership, Türkiye has composed its national AML statutory framework based on and following the minimum global AML standards set out by the FATF whilst ensuring its harmony with the international legal instruments, such as the relevant UN Conventions and EU AMLDs. Türkiye's progress in this end indicates its sincerity in maintaining its position within the international AML regime, albeit with slow and questionable effectiveness. However, there are significant variations between the national AML regimes adopted by Türkiye and the UK, such as LEA powers regarding, *inter alia*, the execution of confiscation due to the jurisdiction-specific nuances. These endogenous

137 Official Gazette No 27072 dated 2 December 2008, 'Mali Suçları Araştırma Kurulu Genel Tebliği' <www.resmigazete.gov.tr/eskiler/2008/12/20081202-5.htm> accessed 22 February 2023.

138 Official Gazette No 27239 dated 26 May 2009, 'Mali Suçları Araştırma Kurulu Genel Tebliği' <www.resmigazete.gov.tr/eskiler/2009/05/20090526-6.htm> accessed 4 July 2023.

139 Official Gazette No 29099 dated 25 August 2014, 'Mali Suçları Araştırma Kurulu Genel Tebliği' <www.resmigazete.gov.tr/eskiler/2014/08/20140825-5.htm> accessed 4 July 2023.

140 MASAK General Communiqué No 13, art 3(b).

141 ibid, art 5(1).

142 See, for instance, Christoph Wronka, '"Cyber-Laundering": The Change of Money Laundering in the Digital Age' (2022) 25(2) Journal of Money Laundering Control 330.

differences, in no uncertain terms, affect how Türkiye and the UK tackle the phenomenon, which is evident, for instance, in the prevalence of types of predicate offences and the value of assets confiscated in the two jurisdictions, as discussed subsequently.

The AML legal instruments of a country and the coherence amongst them undeniably constitute one of the strongest determiners of the success in the AML battle. Türkiye has established a consistent legal regime, albeit having some variances across *jus scriptum*, which would impede the effectiveness of the enforcement practices. Therefore, harmonisation of legal instruments by revising them to establish a uniform and more practical national AML legal framework appears to be one of the primary actions that is needed to deprive offenders of enjoying the illicit gains, which would eventually minimise the prevalence of predicate crimes. However, as creating a rigorous AML legal composition is not a remedy by itself, amending their provisions as per the national priorities, which would allow a more straightforward and swift process in addressing the phenomenon, seems to be the proper step to be taken.

The international framework of AML legal instruments has been amended several times in response to changing and evolving criminal activities so as to address the emerging typologies and necessities in the AML realm accordingly. Admittedly, generating prompt responses to the dynamic nature of the phenomenon at the national level depends on the timely transposition of up-to-date global legal texts. Nevertheless, the development of the national AML framework indicates that Türkiye's initial steps in establishing its domestic AML composition were not expeditious. That being the case, ratifying, transposing, and amending the relevant legal instruments on time, when necessary, should be another consideration for each national actor in the AML battle, including Türkiye. Therefore, considering the dynamic characteristic of the phenomenon, Türkiye should expedite the process it undertakes in aligning and ensuring the harmony of its national AML legal arsenal with the pertinent international structure.

This chapter has examined the development of Türkiye's current AML legal framework and highlighted the areas for reform in strengthening the components of the Turkish AML legal arsenal. Considering the harmony between the aforementioned essential legal instruments and pertinent international legal texts, Türkiye has achieved remarkable progress in bringing its national AML legal framework in line with the requirements of the global financial system. Nevertheless, this statutory foundation would be meaningless in contending with ML and its underlying predicates unless it is exercised effectively by the competent stakeholders, including LEAs, the FIU, and the judiciary, in close collaboration. Inasmuch, the following chapters analyse Türkiye's institutional AML structure (see Chapter 5) and its productivity (Chapters 7 and 8) regarding how the national AML actors tackle the phenomenon and whether the overall AML system is capable of generating intended outcomes.

Reference List

Basaranel BU and Turksen U, *Counter-Terrorist Financing Law and Policy: An Analysis of Turkey* (Routledge 2019)

Council of Europe, 'Chart of Signatures and Ratifications of Treaty 141' <www.coe.int/en/web/conventions/full-list/-/conventions/treaty/141/signatures?p_auth=tV5pnJpN> accessed 4 July 2023

Egmont Group, 'Members by Region: Europe II' <https://egmontgroup.org/members-by-region/> accessed 4 July 2023

FATF, 'The Forty Recommendations of the Financial Action Task Force on Money Laundering' (1990) <www.fatf-gafi.org/media/fatf/documents/recommendations/pdfs/FATF%20Recommendations%201990.pdf> accessed 4 July 2023

——— 'Annual Report 1995–1996' (June 1996) <www.fatf-gafi.org/media/fatf/documents/reports/1995%201996%20ENG.pdf> accessed 15 July 2023

——— 'Annual Report 1996–1997' (June 1997) <www.fatf-gafi.org/media/fatf/documents/reports/1996%201997%20ENG.pdf> accessed 4 July 2023

——— 'Third Mutual Evaluation Report: Anti-Money Laundering and Combatting the Financing of Terrorism – Turkey' (February 2007) <www.fatf-gafi.org/media/fatf/documents/reports/mer/MER%20Turkey%20full.pdf> accessed 4 July 2023

——— 'FATF Reference Document: Methodology for Assessing Compliance with the FATF 40 Recommendations and the FATF 9 Special Recommendations' (February 2004; updated as of February 2009) <www.fatf-gafi.org/media/fatf/documents/reports/methodology.pdf> accessed 4 July 2023

——— 'Anti-Money Laundering and Counter-Terrorist Financing Measures – Turkey: Mutual Evaluation Report' (December 2019) <www.fatf-gafi.org/media/fatf/documents/reports/mer4/Mutual-Evaluation-Report-Turkey-2019.pdf> accessed 18 January 2023

——— 'International Standards on Combatting Money Laundering and the Financing of Terrorism & Proliferation: The FATF Recommendations' (Updated March 2022) <www.fatf-gafi.org/media/fatf/documents/recommendations/pdfs/FATF%20Recommendations%202012.pdf> accessed 26 June 2023

——— 'FATF Members and Observers' <www.fatf-gafi.org/about/membersandobservers/> accessed 13 July 2023

Gilmore WC, 'Police Co-operation and the European Communities: Current Trends and Recent Developments' (1993) 19(4) Commonwealth Law Bulletin 1960

Gilmour PM, 'Lifting the Veil on Beneficial Ownership: Challenges of Implementing the UK's Registers of Beneficial Owners' (2020) 23(4) Journal of Money Laundering Control 717

Gottschalk P, 'Theories of Financial Crime' (2010) 17(2) Journal of Financial Crime 210

Koca M, 'Türk Ceza Hukukunda Müsadere' *LEXPERA Blog* (27 May 2020) <https://blog.lexpera.com.tr/turk-ceza-hukukunda-musadere/#fn9> accessed 4 July 2023

Krieger T and Meierrieks D, 'Terrorist Financing and Money Laundering' (2011) <https://ssrn.com/abstract=1860069> accessed 15 July 2023

MASAK, 'Şüpheli İşlem Bildirim Rehberi (Bankalar)' <www.procompliance.net/wp-content/uploads/2019/09/SIB_Rehberi_Bankalar_Icin_11092019.pdf> accessed 4 July 2023

——— 'Şüpheli İşlem Bildirim Rehberi (Diğer Yükümlüler)' <https://ms.hmb.gov.tr/uploads/2020/11/SIB-REHBERI-DIGER-YUKUMLULER.pdf> accessed 4 July 2023

Mokhtar A, 'Nullum Crimen, Nulla Poena Sine Lege: Aspects and Prospects' (2005) 26(1) Statute Law Review 41

Mugarura N, 'An Appraisal of United Nations and Other Money Laundering and Financing of Terrorism Counter-Measures' (2013) 16(3) Journal of Money Laundering Control 249

Mullan G, 'The Concept of Double Criminality in the Context of Extraterritorial Crimes' (1997) 1 Criminal Law Review 17

Official Gazette No 22551 dated 11 February 1996, 'Karar Sayısı: 96/7801 – Milletlerarası Sözleşme' <www.resmigazete.gov.tr/arsiv/22551.pdf> accessed 10 September 2023

Official Gazette No 22822 dated 19 November 1996, 'Karaparanın Aklanmasının Önlenmesine, 2313 Sayılı Uyuşturucu Maddelerinin Murakabesi Hakkında Kanunda, 657 Sayılı Devlet Memurları Kanununda ve 178 Sayılı Maliye Bakanlığının Teşkilat ve Görevleri Hakkında Kanun Hükmünde Kararnamede Değişiklik Yapılmasına Dair Kanun' <www.resmigazete.gov.tr/arsiv/22822.pdf> accessed 4 July 2023

Official Gazette No 23037 dated 2 July 1997, 'Karaparanın Aklanmasının Önlenmesine Dair 4208 Sayılı Kanunun Uygulanmasına İlişkin Yönetmelik' <www.resmigazete.gov.tr/arsiv/23037.pdf> accessed 4 July 2023

Official Gazette No 23217 dated 31 December 1997, 'Karaparanın Aklanmasının Önlenmesine Dair 4208 Sayılı Kanunun Uygulanmasına İlişkin Yönetmelikte Değişiklik Yapılması Hakkında Yönetmelik' <www.resmigazete.gov.tr/arsiv/23217.pdf> accessed 4 July 2023

Official Gazette No 25611 dated 12 October 2004, 'Türk Ceza Kanunu' <www.resmigazete.gov.tr/eskiler/2004/10/20041012.htm> accessed 4 July 2023

Official Gazette No 26323 dated 18 October 2006, 'Suç Gelirlerinin Aklanmasının Önlenmesi Hakkında Kanun' <www.resmigazete.gov.tr/eskiler/2006/10/20061018-1.htm> accessed 4 July 2023

Official Gazette No 26751 dated 9 January 2008, 'Suç Gelirlerinin Aklanmasının ve Terörizmin Finansmanının Önlenmesine Dair Tedbirler Hakkında Yönetmelik' <www.resmigazete.gov.tr/eskiler/2008/01/20080109-4.htm> accessed 4 July 2023

Official Gazette No 26842 dated 9 April 2008, 'Mali Suçları Araştırma Kurulu Genel Tebliği' <www.resmigazete.gov.tr/eskiler/2008/04/20080409-8.htm> accessed 22 February 2023

Official Gazette No 26999 dated 16 September 2008, 'Suç Gelirlerinin Aklanmasının ve Terörün Finansmanının Önlenmesine İlişkin Yükümlülüklere Uyum Programı Hakkında Yönetmelik' <www.resmigazete.gov.tr/eskiler/2008/09/20080916-1.htm> accessed 4 July 2023

Official Gazette No 27072 dated 2 December 2008, 'Mali Suçları Araştırma Kurulu Genel Tebliği' <www.resmigazete.gov.tr/eskiler/2008/12/20081202-5.htm> accessed 22 February 2023

Official Gazette No 27239 dated 26 May 2009, 'Mali Suçları Araştırma Kurulu Genel Tebliği' <www.resmigazete.gov.tr/eskiler/2009/05/20090526-6.htm> accessed 4 July 2023

Official Gazette No 27283 dated 9 July 2009, 'Türk Ceza Kanunu ile Bazı Kanunlarda Değişiklik Yapılmasına Dair Kanun (Kanun No 5918)' <www.resmigazete.gov.tr/eskiler/2009/07/20090709-2.htm> accessed 4 July 2023

Official Gazette No 27450 dated 2 January 2010, 'Suç Gelirlerinin Aklanmasının ve Terörün Finansmanının Önlenmesine Dair Tedbirler Hakkında Yönetmelikte Değişiklik Yapılmasına Dair Yönetmelik' <www.resmigazete.gov.tr/eskiler/2010/01/20100102-2.htm> accessed 4 July 2023

Official Gazette No 28561 dated 16 February 2013, 'Terörizmin Finansmanının Önlenmesi Hakkında Kanun' <www.resmigazete.gov.tr/eskiler/2013/02/20130216-3.htm> accessed 4 July 2023

Official Gazette No 29026 dated 10 June 2014, 'Aklama Suçu İncelemesi Hakkında Yönetmelik, Suç Gelirlerinin Aklanmasının ve Terörün Finansmanının Önlenmesine Dair Tedbirler Hakkında Yönetmelik ve Malî Suçlarla Mücadele Koordinasyon Kurulunun Çalışma Usul ve Esasları Hakkında Yönetmelikte Değişiklik Yapılmasına Dair Yönetmelik' <www.resmigazete.gov.tr/eskiler/2014/06/20140610-5.htm> accessed 4 July 2023

Official Gazette No 29099 dated 25 August 2014, 'Mali Suçları Araştırma Kurulu Genel Tebliği' <www.resmigazete.gov.tr/eskiler/2014/08/20140825-5.htm> accessed 4 July 2023

Official Gazette No 29657 dated 18 March 2016, 'Suç Gelirlerinin Aklanmasının ve Terörün Finansmanının Önlenmesine Dair Tedbirler Hakkında Yönetmelikte Değişiklik Yapılmasına Dair Yönetmelik' <www.resmigazete.gov.tr/eskiler/2016/03/20160318-10.pdf> accessed 4 July 2023

Official Gazette No 30473 dated 9 July 2018, 'Anayasada Yapılan Değişikliklere Uyum Sağlanması Amacıyla Bazı Kanun ve Kanun Hükmünde Kararnamelerde Değişiklik Yapılması Hakkında Kanun Hükmünde Kararname' <www.resmigazete.gov.tr/eskiler/2018/07/20180709M3-1.pdf> accessed 4 July 2023

Official Gazette No 30474 dated 10 July 2018, 'Cumhurbaşkanlığı Teşkilatı Hakkında Cumhurbaşkanlığı Kararnamesi (Kararname Numarası: 1)' <www.resmigazete.gov.tr/eskiler/2018/07/20180710-1.pdf> accessed 4 July 2023

Official Gazette No 30855 dated 7 August 2019, 'Bazı Cumhurbaşkanlığı Kararnamelerinde Değişiklik Yapılması Hakkında Cumhurbaşkanlığı Kararnamesi' <www.resmigazete.gov.tr/eskiler/2019/08/20190807-1.pdf> accessed 4 July 2023

Republic of Türkiye Ministry of Treasury and Finance, 'Guidelines' <https://en.hmb.gov.tr/fcib-guidelines> accessed 3 February 2023

——— 'Duties and Powers' <https://en.hmb.gov.tr/fcib-duties-powers> accessed 4 July 2023

——— 'Legal Framework of AML' <https://en.hmb.gov.tr/fcib-legal-framework-of-aml> accessed 4 July 2023

——— 'National Legislation' <https://en.hmb.gov.tr/fcib-national-legistation> accessed 4 July 2023

Roth MP, *Global Organized Crime: A 21st Century Approach* (Routledge 2017)

Schneider F, 'The Financial Proceeds of Transnational Organized Crime All Over the World: Some New Empirical Facts' (2013) 33(1) The SAIS Review of International Affairs 91

Sen E, 'Temyiz İncelemesinde Müsadere Hakkında Verilebilecek Kararlar' *Hukuki Haber* (22 April 2020) <www.hukukihaber.net/temyiz-incelemesinde-musadere-hakkinda-verilebilecek-kararlar-makale,7743.html> accessed 4 July 2023

TC İçişleri Bakanlığı AB ve Dış İlişkiler Dairesi Başkanlığı, 'Bakan Soylu Fransa'da Düzenlenen Terörizmin Finansmanı ile Mücadele Konferansına Katıldı' (26 April 2018) <www.icisleri.gov.tr/diab/bakan-soylu-fransada-duzenlenen-terorizmin-finansmani-ile-mucadele-konferansina-katildi> accessed 10 September 2023

TRT World, 'Erdogan to Be Sworn in on July 9 as Turkey's First Executive President' (*TRT World*, 4 July 2018) <www.trtworld.com/turkey/erdogan-to-be-sworn-in-on-july-9-as-turkey-s-first-executive-president-18662> accessed 4 July 2023

Türkiye Bankalar Birliği, 'Karaparanın Aklanması ile Mücadelede Bankaların Yükümlülükleri' (December 2003) <www.tbb.org.tr/Dosyalar/Dosyalar/235_aralik2003.pdf> accessed 4 July 2023

Türkiye Büyük Millet Meclisi, 'Türk Ceza Kanunu Tasarısı ve Adalet Komisyonu Raporu (1/593)' <www.tbmm.gov.tr/sirasayi/donem22/yil01/ss664m.htm> accessed 4 July 2023

United Nations Treaty Collection, 'Status of Treaties: 11. International Convention for the Suppression of the Financing of Terrorism' <https://treaties.un.org/pages/ViewDetails.aspx?src=IND&mtdsg_no=XVIII-11&chapter=18&clang=_en> accessed 4 July 2023

——— 'Status of Treaties: 12. United Nations Convention Against Transnational Organized Crime' <https://treaties.un.org/Pages/ViewDetails.aspx?src=IND&mtdsg_no=XVIII-12&chapter=18> accessed 4 July 2023

——— 'Status of Treaties: 19. United Nations Convention against Illicit Traffic in Narcotic Drugs and Psychotropic Substances' <https://treaties.un.org/pages/ViewDetails.aspx?src=TREATY&mtdsg_no=VI-19&chapter=6> accessed 4 July 2023

Vogler R and Fouladvand S, 'The Convention Against Illicit Traffic in Narcotic Drugs and Psychotropic Substances 1988 and the Global War on Drugs' in P Hauck and S Peterke (eds), *International Law and Transnational Organized Crime* (OUP 2016)

Wronka C, '"Cyber-Laundering": The Change of Money Laundering in the Digital Age' (2022) 25(2) Journal of Money Laundering Control 330

——— 'Money Laundering Through Cryptocurrencies: Analysis of the Phenomenon and Appropriate Prevention Measures' (2022) 25(1) Journal of Money Laundering Control 79

Xe Currency Converter <www.xe.com/currencyconverter/convert/?Amount=100&From=TRY&To=GBP> accessed 29 May 2023

Legal Instruments

Constitution of the Republic of Türkiye 1982

Directive 2005/60/EC of the European Parliament and of the Council of 26 October 2005 on the Prevention of the Use of the Financial System for the Purpose of Money Laundering and Terrorist Financing (Text with EEA Relevance) [2005] OJ L309/15

Law No 4208 on the Prevention of Money Laundering 1996

Law No 4721 (Turkish Civil Code) 2001

Law No 5237 (Turkish Criminal Code) 2004

Law No 5271 (Criminal Procedure Code) 2004

Law No 5326 (Misdemeanours Law) 2005

Law No 5549 on Prevention of Laundering Proceeds of Crime 2006

Law No 6415 on the Prevention of the Financing of Terrorism 2013

MASAK General Communiqué No 1: Establishing the Principles and Procedures of Customer Identification

MASAK General Communiqué No 13

Presidential Decree No 1 on the Organisation of the Presidency 2018

Regulation on the Judicial and Preventive Search 2005

Regulation on Measures Regarding Prevention of Laundering the Proceeds of Crime and Financing of Terrorism (ROM) 2008

Regulation on the Procedures and Principles Regarding the Implementation of Law on the Prevention of the Financing of Terrorism (ROTF) 2013

Regulation on the Program of Compliance with Obligations of Anti-Money Laundering and Combating the Financing of Terrorism (ROC) 2008

United Nations Convention Against Illicit Traffic in Narcotic Drugs and Psychotropic Substances 1988

United Nations Convention Against Transnational Organized Crime 2000

UNGA A/RES/54/109 International Convention for the Suppression of the Financing of Terrorism (25 February 2000)

4 The UK's Legal Framework Regarding AML and Its Predicates

4.1 Introduction

As one of the leading financial centres in the world,[1] the UK has a robust legal AML framework, which roots in the international treaties that determine the rules for the global financial ecosystem. The UK is a signatory jurisdiction to a myriad of international legal instruments collimating AML efforts worldwide. Similar to Türkiye, the UK signed the Vienna Convention 1988, the Strasbourg Convention 1990, and the Palermo Convention 2000, on 20 December 1988,[2] 8 November 1990,[3] and 14 December 2000,[4] respectively. Given that the Strasbourg Convention 1990 entered into force in the UK approximately 12 years before Türkiye,[5] it can be argued that the UK's AML legal structure is more mature. Moreover, the UK is a member of several international organisations, including the G7, the UN, the OECD, the IMF, and the World Bank, whereby it has spearheaded the rules on/provisions of AML regulations. Furthermore, the UK has been a member of the FATF since 1990,[6] as well as an observer of various groups and cooperator and supporter

1 Keith Stanton, 'The United Kingdom' in Sandra Booysen and Dora Neo (eds), *Can Banks Still Keep a Secret?* (CUP 2017).

2 United Nations Treaty Collection, 'Status of Treaties: 19. United Nations Convention against Illicit Traffic in Narcotic Drugs and Psychotropic Substances' <https://treaties.un.org/pages/ViewDetails.aspx?src=TREATY&mtdsg_no=VI-19&chapter=6> accessed 4 July 2023.

3 Council of Europe, 'Chart of Signatures and Ratifications of Treaty 141' <www.coe.int/en/web/conventions/full-list/-/conventions/treaty/141/signatures?p_auth=tV5pnJpN> accessed 4 July 2023.

4 United Nations Treaty Collection, 'Status of Treaties: 12. United Nations Convention Against Transnational Organized Crime' <https://treaties.un.org/Pages/ViewDetails.aspx?src=IND&mtdsg_no=XVIII-12&chapter=18> accessed 4 July 2023.

5 The provisions of the Convention came into force on 1 February 2005 in Türkiye, whereas on 1 September 1993 in the UK. See Council of Europe (n 3).

6 FATF, 'FATF Members and Observers' <www.fatf-gafi.org/about/membersandobservers/> accessed 13 July 2023. Additionally, it is crucial to state that the UK was one of the participants of the Paris Summit 1989, where the Financial Action Task Force convened under the French Presidency. Other participants were the USA, Japan, Germany, France, Italy, Canada, and the

DOI: 10.4324/9781003466680-4

of several task forces,[7] coordinating AML efforts at a regional level. It has also been a member of the Egmont Group since 1 January 1995.[8] Lastly, the UK is one of the administrations that funds international AML initiatives and supports capacity development in combating ML. For instance, it is one of the few jurisdictions that contribute to the Topical Trust Funds, a donor-funded enterprise launched by the IMF, providing technical assistance and staff training relating to the AML/CTF in many beneficiary countries all over the world.[9] In other words, its active and extensive participation in supervising, organising, and directing AML efforts at international and regional spheres is another indicator of the jurisdiction's maturity in the AML realm, in comparison to Türkiye.

After explaining the leading role of the UK within the global financial world and combatting financial crimes concerning its active participation in orchestrating the international AML endeavours, this chapter investigates the relevant legal composition of the jurisdiction, its evolution process, as well as specific principal statutes constituting the AML framework. As a starting point, it outlines the essential AML/CTF legal instruments adopted in the UK. Then, regarding the underlying global momentous advances, it examines the development process of the legal composition. Finally, it chronologically analyses principal legal instruments embraced in the jurisdiction to illustrate the intention behind their enactment and demonstrates their efficacy as to whether they are fit for purpose. By doing so, it aims to reveal similarities and differences in the legal approaches undertaken by Türkiye and the UK and their impacts on the notion of predicate crimes regarding their prevalence and the effectiveness in tackling such unlawful conduct. In other words, based on a similar strategy adopted in Chapter 3, this chapter aims to answer the first and last research questions, thereby addressing the main research aim of demonstrating whether and how differences between the legal AML structures may impact AML effectiveness regarding predicate crimes.

Commission of the European Committees. See Johannes Dumbacher, 'The Fight Against Money Laundering' (1995) 30(4) Inter Economics 177.

7 These groups and task forces include the Asia/Pacific Group on Money Laundering (APG), Eastern and Southern Africa Anti-Money Laundering Group (ESAAMLG), Middle East and North Africa Financial Action Task Force (MENAFATF), and Caribbean Financial Action Task Force (CFATF). See FATF, 'Asia/Pacific Group on Money Laundering (APG)' <www.fatf-gafi.org/pages/asiapacificgrouponmoneylaunderingapg.html> accessed 11 May 2023; FATF, 'Eastern and Southern Africa Anti-Money Laundering Group (ESAAMLG)' <www.fatf-gafi.org/pages/easternandsouthernafricaanti-moneylaunderinggroupesaamlg html> accessed 11 May 2023; FATF, 'Middle East and North Africa Financial Action Task Force (MENAFATF)' <www.fatf-gafi.org/pages/menafatf.html> accessed 11 May 2020; FATF, 'Caribbean Financial Action Task Force (CFATF)' <www.fatf-gafi.org/pages/caribbeanfinancialactiontaskforcecfatf.html> accessed 11 May 2023.

8 Egmont Group, 'Members by Region' <https://egmontgroup.org> accessed 13 July 2023.

9 IMF, 'Technical Assistance on AML/CTF' <www.imf.org/external/np/leg/amlcft/eng/aml3.htm> accessed 15 May 2023.

Similar to Türkiye's AML legal composition, the UK's corresponding set of legal instruments is quite comprehensive, but the principal legislation is selected based on the same point of reference that of Türkiye, which is the FATF's MER on the UK.[10] Having said that, the Sanctions and Anti-Money Laundering Act (SAMLA) 2018, which does not feature in the latest MER on the UK, is included in the analysis, as the underlying rationale for its enactment is to determine the legal AML structure of the jurisdiction for the post-Brexit era, whereby the UK's membership of the EU has ceased on 31 December 2020. Similarly, the most recent AML legal instrument, the Economic Crime (Transparency and Enforcement) Act 2022, is also included in the analysis. Accordingly, the current AML/CTF legal framework in the UK comprises eight legal instruments consisting of seven Acts and a Regulation: the Terrorism Act (TACT) 2000; the Anti-Terrorism, the Crime and Security Act (ATCSA) 2001; the Proceeds of Crime Act (POCA) 2002; the Serious Crime Act 2015; the Criminal Finances Act (CFA) 2017; the Sanctions and Anti-Money Laundering Act (SAMLA) 2018; the Economic Crime (Transparency and Enforcement) Act 2022; and the Money Laundering, Terrorist Financing and Transfer of Funds (Information on the Payer) Regulations (MLRs) 2017. With this legal framework in mind, this chapter begins by investigating how the current AML/CTF legal framework has evolved; how these particular legal instruments may empower or incapacitate the relevant competent authorities; and what key areas of reform are needed to eliminate the obstacles hampering AML/CTF efforts. However, as the focal point of the study does not encompass the critique of CTF efforts, the TACT 2000 and the ATCSA 2001 are not scrutinised as the provisions therein concentrate primarily on TF and other terrorism-related offences.

4.2 The Development of the Current Legal Framework

On par with the global recognition of the gravity of the drug-related ML problem, the UK's legal AML framework was initially created as a response to drug trafficking offences and the laundering of the associated illegal proceeds under the Drug Trafficking Offences Act (DTOA) 1986.[11] As a matter of fact, it was the failure in recovering approximately GBP 750,000 of drug trafficking proceeds in the prominent drug trafficking case codenamed Operation Julie (1978)[12] that triggered the government to enact this statute as the House of Lords (HL) did not deem it appropriate to deprive drug traffickers of the totality of illegal proceeds according to the existing legal instruments

10 FATF, 'Anti-Money Laundering and Counter-Terrorist Financing Measures: United Kingdom – Mutual Evaluation Report' (December 2018) <www.fatf-gafi.org/media/fatf/documents/reports/mer4/MER-United-Kingdom-2018.pdf> accessed 18 January 2022.

11 Drug Trafficking Offences Act 1986.

12 Lyn Ebenezer, *Operation Julie: The World's Greatest LSD Bust* (Y Lolfa Cyf 2010).

determining forfeiture procedures for the items used in the course of committing an offence.[13] Although the enactment of these provisions provided the competent authorities with significant powers relating to confiscation of assets, the confiscation of illegal proceeds derived from non-drug offences was not possible under them. Despite such shortcomings, the UK was ahead of other countries in addressing drug-related offences and the linked ML problem, as the global consensus on the issue was ensured by the Vienna Convention 1988. Therefore, it can be argued that the UK has been leading AML efforts since such initiatives started internationally.

Following the Vienna Convention 1988, the UK has transposed the provisions relating to MLA[14] under the Criminal Justice (International Co-operation) Act 1990[15] to ensure a unified response against ML by the international *fora*. It also provided relevant authorities with forfeiture powers, which allowed them to detain cash found at borders in cases where they believe it was derived from drug trafficking or would be used for such purposes.[16] In 1994, in order to consolidate the DTOA 1986 and particular provisions of the Criminal Justice (International Co-operation) Act 1990 relating to drug trafficking, the Drug Trafficking Act (DTA) 1994 was enacted.[17]

As the previously mentioned acts did not prescribe non-drug related offences and the associated ML crime, a similar failure encountered in Operation Julie was inevitable due to the then prevailing legal instruments. In response to eliminating the associated risks stemming from the scope of the relevant statutes, the UK has extended the confiscation powers to encompass non-drug indictable offences and specified summary offences by the enactment of the Criminal Justice Act 1988.[18] The Criminal Justice Act 1988 has been amended by the Criminal Justice Act 1993, which has enlarged the scope of ML offences and associated confiscation provisions,[19] and the POCA 1995, which has aligned relevant clauses with DTA 1994.[20] Given that the initial FATF Recommendations (1990) concentrated primarily on drug trafficking as a predicate crime, albeit referring to all or certain serious offences, as well,[21] the UK's providence in extending the scope of predicate crimes in 1988 is another indicator of its leading role within the AML realm. However,

13 Explanatory Notes to the Proceeds of Crime HC Bill (2001–02) [31].
14 United Nations Convention Against Illicit Traffic in Narcotic Drugs and Psychotropic Substances 1988, art 7.
15 Criminal Justice (International Co-operation) Act 1990.
16 ibid, pt 3.
17 Drug Trafficking Act 1994.
18 Criminal Justice Act 1988.
19 See, for instance, Criminal Justice Act 1993, s 29.
20 Proceeds of Crime Act 1995.
21 Recommendation 5. See FATF, 'The Forty Recommendations of the Financial Action Task Force on Money Laundering' (1990) <www.fatf-gafi.org/media/fatf/documents/recommendations/pdfs/FATF%20Recommendations%201990.pdf> accessed 4 July 2023.

considering the temporal differences relating to the enactment of the relevant statutes across all jurisdictions constituting the UK,[22] it had taken years for the UK to ensure a more progressive environment for ML on a UK-wide basis. That is to say, the lack of a single comprehensive legal instrument determining the provisions both for the proceeds of drugs and non-drugs related crime for the UK in its entirety was hindering the overall competency (and also efficacy) of the jurisdiction in combatting ML and its underlying predicates. Eventually, the need for such a legal instrument, which would consolidate the relevant legislation spread across the constituent jurisdictions, stimulated the competent authorities to address this deficiency. Following the recommendations put forward by the Performance and Innovation Unit of the Cabinet Office, which was entrusted with preparing a report examining the effectiveness of asset recovery practices and putting forward recommendations in this context, the POCA 2002 was enacted.[23]

Before explaining the novelties that POCA 2002 has introduced, it is necessary to discuss the measures taken at the EU level in the corresponding period and their impact on the UK's legal AML framework. In the aftermath of the FATF's 1990 Recommendations,[24] the first legislative reaction to ML given by the EU was the enactment of the First AMLD (91/308/EEC) on 10 June 1991.[25] The principal requirements introduced by the First AMLD included, amongst others, obligations on FIs relating to verifying the identity of their customers whilst initiating business relations with them (Article 3), record-keeping practices (Article 4), and the appointment of a responsible officer for reporting suspicious financial activities (Article 6).[26] The UK transposed these provisions into its national legal regime by the Money Laundering Regulations (MLRs) 1993.[27] In 1996, the FATF revised its Forty

22 For example, the corresponding legal instrument determining the predicate crimes of both drug and non-drug-related offences and the associated ML offences for Northern Ireland was the Criminal Justice (Confiscation) (Northern Ireland) Order 1990. See Criminal Justice (Confiscation) (Northern Ireland) Act 1990.

23 Cabinet Office, 'Recovering the Proceeds of Crime: A Performance and Innovation Unit Report' (June 2000) <https://webarchive.nationalarchives.gov.uk/+/http:/www.cabinetoffice.gov.uk/media/cabinetoffice/strategy/assets/crime.pdf> accessed 12 May 2023. See also Nicholas Ryder, 'To Confiscate or Not to Confiscate? A Comparative Analysis of the Confiscation of the Proceeds of Crime Legislation in the United States and United Kingdom' (2013) 8 Journal of Business Law 767.

24 FATF (n 21).

25 Council Directive 91/308/EEC of 10 June 1991 on prevention of the use of the financial system for the purpose of money laundering [1991] OJ L166/77. See also Colin Tyre, 'Anti-Money Laundering Legislation: Implementation of the FATF Forty Recommendations in the European Union' [2010] Journal of the Professional Lawyer 69.

26 ibid.

27 Explanatory Notes to the Money Laundering Regulations 1993. See also Commonwealth Secretariat, 'Money Laundering Regulations 1993 (United Kingdom)' (1994) 20(1) Commonwealth Law Bulletin 274.

Recommendations,[28] whereby it extended the list of predicate offences to encompass a wide range of unlawful conduct. As per the FATF's 1996 Recommendations, the First AMLD was amended by the enactment of the Second AMLD (2001/97/EC), whereby the scope of ML offences, predicate crimes, and obligated parties, amongst others, was enlarged.[29] The UK has realised its transposition into its domestic law by enacting MLRs 2003,[30] which also replaced its predecessors, namely MLRs 1993 and 2001.[31]

The introduction of POCA 2002 significantly augmented the AML capabilities of the relevant authorities as it simplified various procedures relating to confiscation, which used to constitute a burden for them prior to its enactment.[32] For instance, prior to POCA 2002, the judicial authorities had to prove that the proceeds under consideration were derived from a crime, where determining the type of offence was another critical issue as the relevant procedures were divergent between the drugs and non-drugs crimes. In general terms, the consolidation of discrete pieces of relevant legal instruments has been achieved by the enactment of POCA 2002, whereby the recovery of the proceeds of all types of crime has been simplified and extended civil forfeiture powers have been introduced. This robust legal instrument has been serving as the UK's primary AML legal instrument since its introduction whilst having been amended several times, including by the enactment of the Serious Organised Crime and Police Act 2005,[33] the Serious Crime Act 2007,[34] and the Serious Crime Act 2015.[35] The enactment of POCA 2002 also created the Assets Recovery Agency (ARA),[36] which had been established to generate an effective apparatus in recovering proceeds of crime in the UK. Nevertheless, it ceased to exist on 1 April 2008[37] due to its failure in meeting the expectations as it had cost around GBP 60 million, whilst in turn generated just over

28 FATF, 'The Forty Recommendations' (1996) <www.fatf-gafi.org/media/fatf/documents/recommendations/pdfs/FATF%20Recommendations%201996.pdf> accessed 13 May 2023.

29 Directive 2001/97/EC of the European Parliament and of the Council of 4 December 2001 amending Council Directive 91/308/EEC on prevention of the use of the financial system for the purpose of money laundering – Commission Declaration [2001] OJ L344/76, art 1.

30 Richard Alexander, 'The 2003 Money Laundering Regulations' (2005) 8(1) Journal of Money Laundering Control 75.

31 Explanatory Notes to the Money Laundering Regulations 2003.

32 Edward Rees, Richard Fisher and Richard Thomas, *Blackstone's Guide to the Proceeds of Crime Act 2002* (5th edn, OUP 2015).

33 See, for instance, Serious Organised Crime and Police Act 2005, ss 100 to 102. See also David Fitzpatrick, 'Crime Fighting in the Twenty-First Century?' (2006) 9(2) Journal of Money Laundering Control 129.

34 See, for instance, Serious Crime Act 2007, sch 8.

35 See, for instance, Serious Crime Act 2015, s 1.

36 Proceeds of Crime Act 2002 (as it was originally enacted), s 1.

37 UK Government, 'Assets Recovery Agency' <www.gov.uk/government/organisations/assets-recovery-agency> accessed 12 May 2023.

GBP 8 million until 2006.[38] Following its abolishment by the Serious Crime Act 2007, the functions of the ARA were transferred to the Serious Organised Crime Agency (SOCA).[39] However, the SOCA has been replaced by the National Crime Agency (NCA) by the enactment of the Crime and Courts Act 2013.[40] Given that such overhauling alterations to LEAs are likely to affect their operational aspects, those interventions experienced in a short period would have presumably negatively influenced their efficacy. Accordingly, the impact of those modifications is evaluated in Chapter 7 when comparing the two jurisdictions thematically, as LEAs in Türkiye have not encountered such shake-ups in the corresponding period.

In addition to the aforementioned amendments to the POCA 2002, it was also reinforced by the MLRs 2007, which gave effect to the Third AMLD (2005/60/EC) in the UK.[41] In more concrete terms, in the aftermath of the 9/11 terrorist attacks,[42] the FATF published its revised Forty Recommendations, whereby it combined them with Eight (later expanded to Nine) Special Recommendations on Terrorist Financing in 2003.[43] As per the FATF's 2003 Recommendations, the Third EU AMLD was enacted, whereby, *inter alia*, the procedures for CTF enhanced and simplified customer due diligence (CDD), and reporting obligations were determined.[44]

The perceived risks arose relating to the aforementioned terrorist attacks also and were primarily addressed by the Anti-Terrorism, Crime and Security Act (ATCSA) 2001,[45] the enactment of which, amongst others, enlarged the scope of responsibilities relating to the disclosure of information regarding TF as determined by the Terrorism Act 2000. In other words, whilst the provisions determined under POCA 2002 harness the relevant stakeholders with

38 BBC, 'Assets Recovery Agency "Failing"' *BBC News* (14 June 2006) <http://news.bbc.co.uk/1/hi/uk_politics/5077846.stm> accessed 12 May 2023.

39 Serious Crime Act 2007, sch 8. For a more detailed discussion on the SOCA, see Clive Harfield, 'SOCA: A Paradigm Shift in British Policing' (2006) 46(4) British Journal of Criminology 743. See also Peter Sproat, 'The Serious and Organised Crime Agency and the National Crime Squad: A Comparison of Their Output from Open-Source Materials' (2011) 21(3) Policing & Society 343.

40 Crime and Courts Act 2013, s 1.

41 Explanatory Notes to the Money Laundering Regulations 2007.

42 Gauri Sinha, 'AML-CTF: A Forced Marriage Post 9 11 and Its Effect on Financial Institutions' (2013) 16(2) Journal of Money Laundering Control 142.

43 FATF, 'FATF 40 Recommendations' (October 2003) <www.fatf-gafi.org/media/fatf/documents/FATF%20Standards%20-%2040%20Recommendations%20rc.pdf> accessed 13 May 2023.

44 Directive 2005/60/EC of the European Parliament and of the Council of 26 October 2005 on the prevention of the use of the financial system for the purpose of money laundering and terrorist financing (Text with EEA relevance) [2005] OJ L309/15. See also Angela Veng Mei Leong, 'Chasing Dirty Money: Domestic and International Measures against Money Laundering' (2007) 10(2) Journal of Money Laundering Control 140.

45 David Williams, 'Terrorism and the Law in the United Kingdom' (2003) 26(1) University of New South Wales Law Journal 179.

comprehensive powers in tackling ML and its underlying predicates, including terrorism, the UK devotes particular Acts for combatting TF. The Terrorism Act 2000 has been amended by the Terrorism Act 2000 and Proceeds of Crime Act 2002 (Amendment) Regulations 2007,[46] and the UK added several counter terrorism related instruments into its legal arsenal.[47] The Terrorism Act 2000 determines, amongst others, the relevant offences for the regulated sector, including failure to disclose (Section 21A) and tipping off (Section 21D), and the counter-terrorist powers of relevant stakeholders, such as arrest without a warrant (Section 41) and search of premises (Section 42) as amended by the previously mentioned legal instruments.[48] However, these legal instruments are not scrutinised here in detail as the provisions therein concentrate primarily on TF, which is beyond the scope of this book.

In February 2012, as per the international deficiencies detected during the third round of the mutual evaluation process, the FATF revised its Recommendations and introduced an RBA, thereby advising the application of proportional measures commensurate with the associated ML threats. It also enlarged the scope of predicate crimes to encompass tax crimes relating to both direct and indirect taxes (i.e., tax evasion).[49] Additionally, it has integrated the Nine Special Recommendations devoted to CTF efforts into the Forty Recommendations and obviated their discrete nature. The reflections of the FATF's 2012 Recommendations have been incorporated into the EU legislation by the Fourth AMLD (2015/849/EU).[50] As per the FATF's 2012 Recommendations, the Fourth AMLD, amongst others, reinforced the implementation of the RBA (Articles 6 to 8) and introduced tax crimes as a predicate offence (Article 3).[51] The UK has broadly mirrored the requirements

46 The Terrorism Act 2000 and Proceeds of Crime Act 2002 (Amendment) Regulations 2007.

47 These legal instruments include the Criminal Justice Act 2003, Prevention of Terrorism Act 2005, Terrorism Act 2006, Terrorism (United Nations Measures) Order 2006, Counter Terrorism Act 2008, Coroners and Justice Act 2009, Terrorism (United Nations Measures) Order 2009, Terrorist Asset-Freezing (Temporary Provisions) Act 2010, Crime and Courts Act 2013, Justice and Security Act 2013, Counter Terrorism and Security Act 2015, and Counter Terrorism and Border Security Act 2019.

48 Terrorism Act 2000.

49 FATF, 'International Standards on Combatting Money Laundering and the Financing of Terrorism & Proliferation: The FATF Recommendations' (Updated March 2022) <www.fatf-gafi.org/media/fatf/documents/recommendations/pdfs/FATF%20Recommendations%202012.pdf> accessed 26 June 2023.

50 Directive (EU) 2015/849 of the European Parliament and of the Council of 20 May 2015 on the prevention of the use of the financial system for the purposes of money laundering or terrorist financing, amending Regulation (EU) No 648/2012 of the European Parliament and of the Council, and repealing Directive 2005/60/EC of the European Parliament and of the Council and Commission Directive 2006/70/EC (Text with EEA relevance) [2015] OJ L141/73. See also Valsamis Mitsilegas and Niovi Vavoula, 'The Evolving EU Anti-Money Laundering Regime: Challenges for Fundamental Rights and the Rule of Law' (2016) 23(2) Maastricht Journal of European and Comparative Law 261.

51 ibid.

of the Fourth AMLD by the enactment of the Criminal Finances Act (CFA) 2017 as, for instance, it determines the corporate offences of failure to prevent the facilitation of tax evasion.[52] Scrutinising the relevant provisions of CFA 2017 is important as 'failure to prevent' composes an offence for relevant bodies due to the corporate criminal liability, which means in the UK, the elements of *mens rea* and *actus reus* apply to companies/legal persons as well. Another critical power established by the CFA 2017 is the UWOs, which have been available to LEAs since 31 January 2018.[53] UWOs obligate individuals suspected of possessing criminal property to explain the legal origins of the property, failure of which implies the property is criminal and thereby requires its recovery by the NCA.[54]

Another piece of a legal instrument that has reflected the necessities of the Fourth AMLD is the Money Laundering, Terrorist Financing and Transfer of Funds (Information on the Payer) Regulations 2017 (MLRs 2017).[55] The MLRs 2017 replaced the MLRs 2007 on 26 June 2017[56] and has been informing, alongside other legislation (i.e., POCA 2002), the current practice in combatting ML since then. The new set of regulations improved the AML regime by introducing, amongst others, a new concept of CDD procedures (Part 3), enhanced transparency of beneficial ownership (Part 5), and more practical sanctioning measures (Part 9).[57] The provisions of MLR 2017 have further been reinforced by the Money Laundering and Terrorist Financing (Amendment) Regulations 2019, which has transposed the obligations determined under the Fifth AMLD into the UK legal AML framework.[58] For instance, Section 14A of the MLR 2017 determines the provisions for crypto-asset exchange providers and custodian wallet providers as amended by the 2019 Regulations,[59] a recent matter of interest arisen within the AML realm following the novel technological developments.[60] The Fifth AMLD

52 Criminal Finances Act 2017, pt 3.

53 Home Office, 'Circular 003/2018: Unexplained Wealth Orders' (1 February 2018) <www.gov.uk/government/publications/circular-0032018-criminal-finances-act-unexplained-wealth-orders/circular-0032018-unexplained-wealth-orders> accessed 22 May 2023.

54 Peter Sproat, 'Unexplained Wealth Orders: An Explanation, Assessment and Set of Predictions' (2018) 82(3) Journal of Criminal Law 232.

55 Liz Campbell, 'Dirty Cash (Money Talks): 4AMLD and the Money Laundering Regulations 2017' (2018) 2 Criminal Law Review 102.

56 The Money Laundering, Terrorist Financing and Transfer of Funds (Information on the Payer) Regulations 2017, reg 1.

57 ibid. See also Sue Turner and Jonathan Bainbridge, 'An Anti-Money Laundering Timeline and the Relentless Regulatory Response' (2018) 82(3) Journal of Criminal Law 215.

58 Explanatory Notes to the Money Laundering and Terrorist Financing (Amendment) Regulations 2019.

59 The Money Laundering, Terrorist Financing and Transfer of Funds (Information on the Payer) Regulations 2017, reg 14A.

60 Sherena Sheng Huang, 'Crypto Assets Regulation in the UK: An Assessment of the Regulatory Effectiveness and Consistency' (2021) 29(3) Journal of Financial Regulation and Compliance 336.

(2018/843/EU) has extended the scope of the Fourth AMLD to include virtual currency exchange services and custodian wallet providers as obliged entities (Article (1)(1)(c)), and introduced more intensified regulations relating to, *inter alia*, access to information on beneficial ownership (see, for instance, Article (1)(15)(c)) and high-risk third countries (Article (1)(11)).[61] It is worth stating that by the Fifth AMLD, the EU gave effect to the FATF's updates and amendments, such as on virtual asset service providers, to its Recommendations 2012.[62]

However, the Fifth AMLD is not the last Directive of the EU as the Sixth AMLD (2018/1673/EU), which requires EU MS to transpose it into their national legal frameworks by 3 December 2020 (Article 13).[63] It determines minimum rules relating to the definition of criminal offences and sanctions associated with ML (Article (1)(1)), whereby it envisages, amongst others, the ML offence should be punishable by a maximum term of imprisonment of at least four years (Article (5)(2)).[64] As the UK has ceased to be an MS of the EU on 31 December 2020, thus there is no obligation to transpose the Sixth AMLD. In fact, the UK has decided to opt out from complying with the Sixth AMLD as the UK Government deemed that the prevailing British national legislation is largely compliant with the Directive's measures and that the relevant offences and penalties are already beyond what the Directive envisages.[65] Nevertheless, considering the provisions of POCA 2002, as discussed later, it can be argued that the UK Government is not wrong in its declaration regarding this decision.

As a legal preparation for the post-Brexit era, which officially started on 1 January 2021,[66] the UK has enacted SAMLA 2018 to ensure congruency and

61 Directive (EU) 2018/843 of the European Parliament and of the Council of 30 May 2018 amending Directive (EU) 2015/849 on the prevention of the use of the financial system for the purposes of money laundering or terrorist financing and amending Directives 2009/138/EC and 2013/36/EU (Text with EEA relevance) PE/72/2017/REV/1 [2018] OJ L156/43.

62 FATF, 'Information on Updates Made to the FATF Recommendations' <www.fatf-gafi.org/publications/fatfrecommendations/documents/fatf-recommendations.html#UPDATES> accessed 14 May 2023.

63 Directive (EU) 2018/1673 of the European Parliament and of the Council of 23 October 2018 on combating money laundering by criminal law PE/30/2018/REV/1 [2018] OJ L284/22.

64 ibid.

65 Letter from Rt Hon Ben Wallace MP (Minister of State for Security) to Sir William Cash MP (Chair of the European Scrutiny Committee) (11 September 2017) <http://europeanmemoranda.cabinetoffice.gov.uk/files/2017/10/2017-09-11_-_Security_Minister_to_ESC_Chair._Directive_on_countering_money_laundering_by_criminal_law_.pdf> accessed 1 December 2023; European Scrutiny Committee, 'EU Action Plan to Combat Money Laundering' (Thirteenth Report, HC 2019–21, 24 June 2020) <https://publications.parliament.uk/pa/cm5801/cmselect/cmeuleg/229-ix/22910.htm#footnote-041> accessed 1 December 2023.

66 UK Government, 'Brexit Transition: Time Is Running Out' <www.gov.uk/transition> accessed 7 December 2020.

integrity of the AML legal structure of the jurisdiction with the international financial world.[67] SAMLA 2018 empowers the UK government to impose sanctions or take necessary actions relating to the AML/CTF to ensure the jurisdiction's compliance with the international obligations (e.g., the UN obligations relating to TF) and harmony with the international standards (e.g., the FATF Recommendations).[68] In other words, as there will not be a legal obligation on the transposition of EU AMLDs into UK law as before,[69] the UK needs to follow global developments relating to the AML realm and take necessary steps unilaterally based on the SAMLA 2018.

Lastly, the recent Russian invasion of Ukraine prompted the UK Government to enact Economic Crime (Transparency and Enforcement) Act 2022, thereby targeting (Russian) oligarchs that own property/land or planning to do so in the UK.[70]

With this (recent) historical development of the current legal AML framework in mind, the rest of the chapter scrutinises previously mentioned principal legal instruments in chronological order. By doing so, it aims to investigate whether and to what extent they are fit for purpose, how their provisions diverge from Türkiye's corresponding legal framework, and how they may empower or undermine the functions of the AML authorities in the UK.

4.3 AML Legal Instruments

4.3.1 Proceeds of Crime Act 2002

In alignment with the initial international recognition of the phenomenon, the scope of the early AML legal instruments of the UK had been predominantly confined to drug-related offences.[71] Furthermore, although the UK was ahead of its time in addressing non-drug-related crimes and the associated ML problem, the relevant pieces of legislation were spread across the constituent jurisdictions. Eventually, on par with and in response to the developments in the AML sphere, the UK enacted POCA on 24 July 2002,[72] which came into force on 24 February 2003[73] as the primary statute orchestrating the UK's

67 Hugo D Lodge, *Blackstone's Guide to the Sanctions and Anti-Money Laundering Act 2018* (OUP 2020).

68 See, for instance, Sanctions and Anti-Money Laundering Act 2018, s 1.

69 Norman Mugarura, 'The Implications of Brexit for UK Anti-Money Laundering Regulations: Will the Fourth AML Directive Be Implemented or Be Binned?' (2018) 21(1) Journal of Money Laundering Control 5.

70 Home Office and others, 'News Story: New Measures to Tackle Corrupt Elites and Dirty Money Become Law' (15 March 2022) <www.gov.uk/government/news/new-measures-to-tackle-corrupt-elites-and-dirty-money-become-law> accessed 17 August 2023.

71 See, for instance, Drug Trafficking Act 1994.

72 Proceeds of Crime Act 2002, introduction.

73 The date indicates when Part 7 of POCA 2002, which is devoted to money laundering, came into force.

AML efforts. By the enactment of POCA 2002, the UK has consolidated not only the discrete relevant legal instruments but also the detached nature of pertinent predicate offences (i.e., drug- and non-drug-related crimes) into one inclusive statutory text. More importantly, its introduction has significantly expanded the scope of underlying predicates as it adopts an all-crimes approach, meaning that any crime generating illicit gains is regarded as a predicate crime in the UK regardless of its seriousness. Considering that Türkiye utilises a threshold approach to predicate offences, the UK's legal framework in this end is more likely to capture a broader group of such crimes compared to Türkiye. Furthermore, whilst several legal instruments constitute the Turkish AML regime, POCA 2002 serves as the fundamental statutory source for the UK's AML composition. Accordingly, it can be argued that the more integrated nature of the chief AML legislation and the absence of a threshold approach to predicate crimes may render the UK more effective in the fight against ML and associated predicates when compared to Türkiye.

It is necessary to state that POCA 2002, similar to Türkiye's pertinent legal structure, recognises ML as a separate and independent crime from its predicates. Sections 327 to 329 of POCA 2002 determine which activities constitute the principal ML offences in the UK. Accordingly, concealing, disguising, converting, transferring criminal property, or removing it from any constituent part of the UK embodies ML, where concealing or disguising refers to 'concealing or disguising its nature, source, location, disposition, movement or ownership or any rights with respect to it'.[74] ML offences also encompass relevant arrangement activities: 'a person commits an offence if he enters into or becomes concerned in an arrangement which he knows or suspects facilitates (by whatever means) the acquisition, retention, use or control of criminal property by or on behalf of another person'.[75] The last set of actions that constitute another form of primary ML offence consists of acquiring, using, or possessing criminal property.[76] By referring to these Sections, ML is defined as:

> an act which – (a) constitutes an offence under section 327, 328 or 329; (b) constitutes an attempt, conspiracy or incitement to commit an offence specified in paragraph (a); (c) constitutes aiding, abetting, counselling or procuring the commission of an offence specified in paragraph (a); or (d) would constitute an offence specified in paragraph (a), (b) or (c) if done in the United Kingdom.[77]

An examination of these provisions suggests that the actualisation of the ML offence depends on the knowledge or suspicion of the offender (i.e., it

74 Proceeds of Crime Act 2002, s 327(3).
75 ibid, s 328.
76 ibid, s 329.
77 ibid, s 340(11).

requires *mens rea*) that criminal property is involved. Therefore, similar to Türkiye's analogous legal arrangement, the burden of proving that the perpetrator has been aware of the illicit nature of the property under consideration is an essential prerequisite in the UK to charge someone with concerning ML offences. However, there exists a crucial difference between the two legal regimes. Whilst Türkiye requires ***grounds for strong suspicion based on concrete evidence*** for using seizure and eventual confiscation powers, the UK can utilise the relevant legal proceedings based on the ***circumstantial evidence*** inducing that the defendant had the necessary knowledge or suspicion. Furthermore, POCA 2002 harnesses the competent authorities with a myriad of investigatory powers, such as UWOs, which can further enhance the effectiveness of the jurisdiction's AML competency. In other words, although Türkiye and the UK define ML from a similar standpoint, the variety of legal powers, as well as the relatively undemanding proving onus of the pertinent offence, in the UK strengthens the existing AML structure of the administration.

It would be appropriate to express here how criminal property is defined under POCA 2002 and investigate whether it covers both tangible and intangible assets. POCA 2002 defines proceeds of crime as the property that constitutes a person's benefit from criminal activity or represents such a benefit regardless of whether wholly or partly and whether directly or indirectly, where the alleged offender knows or suspects that it embodies or represents such an advantage.[78] It should be interpreted as 'all property wherever situated and includes – (a) money; (b) all forms of property, real or personal, heritable or moveable; (c) things in action and other intangible or incorporeal property'.[79] In other words, Türkiye and the UK circumscribe the notion of proceeds of crime similarly, where they both include intangible assets within the scope of crime benefits and thereby assets that can be confiscated. Accordingly, the objective elements of the primary ML offences involve an underlying crime that generates or represents a benefit for the defendant, whether it is tangible or intangible in the form of criminal property. They further comprise acts aiming at subjecting such property to one of the prescribed activities as determined by Sections 327 to 329 of POCA 2002. That is to say that the two jurisdictions determine the framework of activities that constitute ML offence similarly.

4.3.1.1 Defences

Before proceeding forward, it is necessary to discuss the safeguards or defences to primary ML offences stipulated by Sections 327 to 329. First and foremost, the lack of necessary knowledge or suspicion that the property under consideration constitutes or represents a benefit from underlying criminal conduct

78 ibid, s 340(3).
79 ibid, s 340(9).

(i.e., predicate crimes) comprises a defence as it is one of the essential elements of the offence. Making an 'authorised disclosure',[80] such as submitting a SAR and thereby receiving an 'appropriate consent'[81] accordingly, or intending to make such disclosure but having a reasonable justification for failing to do so prevents one from being accused of committing the offence.[82] It is necessary to state that the NCA has to grant (or refuse to grant) appropriate consent within seven working days, a period called the notice period.[83] In cases where it fails to do so, this failure immunizes the reporters against primary ML offences correspondingly.[84] In circumstances where it refuses to grant consent within the notice period, this refusal triggers the moratorium period (i.e., a period of 31 days[85] in which the reporter has to suspend the relevant activity accordingly).[86] Upon application of the NCA, the moratorium period can be extended for additional (31-day) periods by the court, up to a maximum of 186 days.[87] Furthermore, acts done in the course of carrying out a function relating to the enforcement of any provision of POCA 2002 or any other enactment relating to criminal conduct or benefit from such conduct constitute a defence against primary ML offences.[88] In addition, knowing or, based on reasonable grounds, believing that the relevant criminal conduct occurred outside the UK and it was not illegal under the then prevailing criminal law of the pertinent jurisdiction when it occurred; and that it is not of a description by an order made by the Secretary of State comprise additional safeguards for these offences.[89] The last defence that these three Sections stipulate commonly concerns deposit-taking bodies. Accordingly, doing the act in operating an account maintained with it, and where the value of the criminal property under consideration is less than the threshold amount of GBP 250 (unless a higher amount is specified under Section 339A)[90] compose an additional defence for such bodies.[91] Lastly, Section 329 stipulates a further defence consisting of acquiring (Section329(a)), using, or having possession of the property for adequate consideration (Section 329(b)), where inadequate consideration stands for the significant difference between the value of the property and the

80 An authorised disclosure stands for disclosing, within the requisite timescales, to a constable, a customs officer, or a nominated officer by the alleged offender that property is criminal property as determined by Section 338. See Proceeds of Crime Act 2002, s 338.
81 Proceeds of Crime Act 2002, s 335.
82 ibid, ss 327(2)(a), 327(2)(b), 328(2)(a), 328(2)(b), 329(2)(a) and 329(2)(b).
83 ibid, s 335(5).
84 ibid, s 335(3).
85 ibid, s 335(6).
86 ibid, s 335(4).
87 ibid, s 336A(7).
88 ibid, ss 327(2)(c), 328(2)(c) and 329(2)(c).
89 ibid, ss 327(2A), 328(3) and 329(2A).
90 ibid, s 339A.
91 ibid, ss 327(2C), 328(5) and 329(2C).

consideration where the value of the former is higher.[92] For instance, in cases where a person buys a property that has criminal origins, such as a piece of artefact, for a suitable market price, it does not make the buyer guilty of this crime as s/he pays consideration sufficiently. However, Section 329(c) stipulates that in circumstances where there exists a proper consideration, knowing or suspecting that a provision, in terms of goods or services, may help another to carry out criminal conduct, such consideration is regarded as inadequate.[93] This last defence type constitutes another significant difference between Türkiye and the UK's AML legal regimes. Given that the Turkish TCC 2004 stipulates sanctions according to the intention of offenders,[94] which is onerous for competent authorities to identify correctly, the UK's approach in this end seems more appropriate as POCA 2002 does not make such a distinction between the two groups of offenders. Accordingly, adopting a similar approach by Turkish legal instruments needs to be considered.

Whilst the primary ML crimes pertain to all members of the jurisdiction as outlinedearlier, POCA 2002 further determines the failure of conducting certain activities within the scope of ML offence concerning the responsibilities of obliged entities (i.e., the secondary ML offences). More specifically, Sections 330 to 333D envisage what constitutes such particular offences for the legal and natural persons operating within and outside the regulated sector.[95] Criminal offences determined under Sections 330 to 333D of POCA 2002 consist mainly of 'failure to disclose' and 'tipping off' offences. Section 330 of POCA 2002 compels persons working in the regulated sector to disclose to a nominated officer their suspicion that occurred in the course of their business that another individual is involved in ML (i.e., it determines the reporting requirement).[96] Not complying with these provisions constitutes the 'failure to disclose' offence unless s/he has a reasonable excuse for not disclosing the required information; s/he is a professional legal adviser or relevant professional adviser and the information or the matter obtained in privileged

92 ibid, ss 329(3)(a) and 329(3)(b).

93 ibid, s 329(3)(c).

94 As may be recalled, the Turkish TCL (Law No 5237) creates a distinct but similar offence for the perpetrators who sell, transfer, purchase, or accept the criminal property. Whilst such conduct is criminalised both under money laundering (Article 282(2)) and the particular offence type (Article 165), the consideration devoted distinguishes the two groups of offenders. Whilst the former requires a direct intention, the latter determines this particular offence in a way that the oblique intention of the person accounts for a satisfactory condition for perpetrating it.

95 It is necessary to note that the regulated sector incorporates credit institutions (e.g., banks and building societies); financial institutions (e.g., money service businesses); accountants and tax advisers; independent legal professionals; trust or company service providers; estate agents; high value dealers; and gaming/leisure sector, including casinos. See Proceeds of Crime Act 2002, sch 9.

96 ibid s 330.

circumstances.[97] If such a person does not have the knowledge or suspicion that another person is engaged in ML and s/he has not been provided with the necessary training programme as is prescribed by the Secretary of State by order, then their failure to disclose does not constitute the relevant offence.[98] Likewise, knowing or, based on reasonable grounds, believing that the ML is occurring outside the UK and it is not illegitimate under the prevailing criminal law of the pertinent jurisdiction; and that it is not of a description by an order made by the Secretary of State comprise additional defences to this offence.[99] Similarly, in cases where the person is employed by, or is in partnership with, a previously mentioned adviser to provide them with assistance or support, where the relevant information or other matter comes to the person relating to such assistance or support, and where the information or the matter obtained in privileged circumstances, not making a disclosure does not comprise an offence.[100] Section 331 of POCA 2002 determines the failure to disclose offence for the nominated officers, such as money laundering reporting officers (MLROs), within the regulated sector. It envisages that such officers' failure to report disclosures they received under Section 330 of POCA 2002 to the NCA constitutes this particular offence.[101] Section 332 of POCA 2002 sets forth the legal framework for the nominated officers operating outside the regulated sector that constitutes a failure to disclose offence for them. Based on similar conditions outlined earlier, failing to report such disclosures to the NCA as soon as possible renders this group of nominated officers guilty.[102] Crucially, however, whilst Section 331 stipulates that the knowledge or suspicion based on reasonable grounds is a satisfactory condition for accusing someone of committing the particular offence,[103] Section 332, on the contrary, requires an actual knowledge or suspicion beyond reasonable grounds.[104] Therefore, it can be argued that POCA 2002 sets forth a more arduous set of obligations for the nominated officers operating in the regulated sector compared to their remaining (i.e., non-regulated) counterparts in reporting their suspicions. However, at the same time, it is debatable whether the ethereal difference of reasonable grounds can be identified practically and effectively, as the relevant defendants (i.e., the nominated officers from the non-regulated sector) may choose to deny their knowledge or suspicion straightforwardly.

Sections 333A to 333D, in general terms, create the offence of tipping off, which consists of the circumstances wherein making a disclosure likely to prejudice an ML investigation being carried out by competent authorities as

97 ibid s 330(6).
98 ibid s 330(7).
99 ibid s 330(7A).
100 ibid s 330.
101 ibid s 331.
102 ibid s 332.
103 ibid s 331(2).
104 ibid s 332(2).

determined by these Sections. However, the lack of necessary knowledge or suspicion that such a disclosure causes prejudice constitutes a defence as it is one of the essential elements of the offence.[105] In other words, the burden of proving the knowledge or suspicion also applies to these provisions, albeit it may be achieved based on circumstantial evidence. Furthermore, disclosures made by professional advisers to clients to dissuade them from engaging in an ML offence, as well as made to a person's client or customer to notify them of an application to extend the moratorium period, constitute additional defences to this end.[106] Lastly, although it is not regulated under ML offences, the offence of 'prejudicing an investigation' should also be examined here as it determines what constitutes an offence concerning investigations, *inter alia*, relating to ML. More specifically, making a disclosure of knowledge or suspicion likely to prejudice the investigation; falsifying, concealing, destroying, or otherwise disposing of relevant documents; or causing or permitting someone else to do so constitute the pertinent offence.[107] Although there exist similarities between how the tipping off offence and the offence of prejudicing an investigation are determined, it is necessary to outline the fundamental differences between those crimes. Whilst POCA 2002 distinguishes between the persons who operate in regulated- and non-regulated sectors in determining the tipping off offence, it sets forth a broader framework, encompassing both sectors, for prejudicing the investigation. More importantly, contrary to the tipping off offence, it does not require for the information to be disclosed to have been obtained in the course of business, suggesting that it is immaterial how such information is reached as determined under Section 342. Finally, as is the case relating to ML offences, the lack of knowledge or suspicion that disclosure (or the documents revealed) would prejudice an investigation constitutes the essential defence against this particular crime.[108]

4.3.1.2 Sanctions

POCA 2002 stipulates an imprisonment term as well as a judicial fine, where it is possible to impose one or both sanctions simultaneously. A person guilty of a primary ML offence, as determined under Sections 327 to 329, is liable '(a) on summary conviction, to imprisonment for a term not exceeding six months or to a fine not exceeding the statutory maximum or to both, or (b) on conviction on indictment, to imprisonment for a term not exceeding 14 years or to a fine or to both'.[109] In other words, POCA 2002 determines these primary ML offences as either-way offences, suggesting that defendants can be tried either

105 ibid ss 333D(3) and 333D(4).

106 ibid ss 333D(1A) and 333D(2). See also Andrew Haynes, 'Money Laundering: From Failure to Absurdity' (2008) 11(4) Journal of Money Laundering Control 303.

107 Proceeds of Crime Act 2002, ss 342(1) and 342(2).

108 ibid ss 342(3) and 342(6).

109 ibid s 334(1).

in Magistrates' Courts or in the Crown Court (see Chapter 6). It is worth reiterating that Türkiye's penal framework for this group of offenders comprises an imprisonment term of three to seven years and a judicial fine of up to 20,000 days, a form of monetary penalty as discussed in Chapter 3. However, even the aggravated circumstances (e.g., where the offender is a public officer) in Türkiye do not entail as severe penalties as envisaged by the UK's sanction mechanism. It can be argued that the UK's punitive provisions are more drastic, which unquestionably stands for another contributory factor to the better AML image of the jurisdiction.

In addition, a person guilty of a failure to disclose offence, as stipulated under Sections 330 to 332, is liable

> (a) on summary conviction, to imprisonment for a term not exceeding six months or to a fine not exceeding the statutory maximum or to both, or (b) on conviction on indictment, to imprisonment for a term not exceeding five years or to a fine or to both.[110]

In other words, similar to primary ML offences, POCA 2002 determines secondary ML crimes as either-way offences, meaning that they can also be tried in Magistrates' Courts or the Crown Court. It is worth reiterating that Türkiye envisages administrative penalties for the breach of obligations relating to STR and periodic reporting, where the fine envisaged is approximately GBP 480[111] (as of December 2020).[112] Hence, it can be argued that the UK's sanction framework for this group of offenders is also more severe compared to the analogous structure of Türkiye. The penalties for tipping off offences as determined under Sections 333A to 333D are more lenient than penalties envisaged for failure to disclose crimes. Accordingly, a person guilty of one of this group of offences is liable

> (a) on summary conviction to imprisonment for a term not exceeding three months, or to a fine not exceeding level 5 on the standard scale, or to both; (b) on conviction on indictment to imprisonment for a term not exceeding two years, or to a fine, or to both.[113]

As discussed previously, the violation of obligations concerning disclosing of STRs in Türkiye entails an imprisonment term of one to three years and a judicial fine of up to 5,000 days[114] (the maximum limit of judicial fine is between

110 ibid s 334(2).
111 Law No 5549 on the Prevention of Laundering Proceeds of Crime 2006, art 13(1).
112 The conversion was made on 9 December 2020. See Xe Currency Converter <www.xe.com/currencyconverter/convert/?Amount=100&From=TRY&To=GBP> accessed 9 December 2020.
113 Proceeds of Crime Act 2002, ss 333A(4) and 333A(5).
114 Law No 5549 on the Prevention of Laundering Proceeds of Crime 2006, art 14(1).

approximately GBP 9,570 and 47,845[115] as of December 2020).[116] Remarkably at the same time, whilst tipping off offence is considered more aggravating than the failure to disclose offence in Türkiye, the UK deems the graveness of these offences vice versa, as it stipulates more severe penalties for the latter. Therefore, this divergence point constitutes another difference between the two legal regimes relating to how Türkiye and the UK prioritise the importance of certain obligations. It can be argued that Türkiye's approach in this context seems more appropriate than the UK's strategy, as tipping off includes an active misconduct process rather than being passive relating to failing to fulfil an obligation. However, although the imprisonment term envisaged consists of extended periods in Türkiye, the UK's unlimited fine stipulated for this group of offenders may compensate for its relative leniency. Lastly, a person guilty of a prejudicing an investigation offence as determined under Section 342 of POCA is liable

> (a) on summary conviction, to imprisonment for a term not exceeding six months or to a fine not exceeding the statutory maximum or to both, or (b) on conviction on indictment, to imprisonment for a term not exceeding five years or to a fine or to both.[117]

It is worth clarifying that the statutory maxima consist of five levels, namely Level 1 (GBP 200), Level 2 (GBP 500), Level 3 (GBP 1,000), Level 4 (GBP 2,500), and Level 5 (unlimited for offences committed after 13 March 2015).[118] In other words, the fines envisaged for money launderers in the UK have no maximum limits as both primary and secondary ML offences entail a Level 5. However, it is necessary to note also that the maximum fine for Level 5 used to be GBP 5,000 for offences committed before the aforementioned date.[119] Therefore, although not promptly, the UK has aptly amended this deficiency as such a low maximum may not have any deterrence on the potential offenders. Considering the leniency of penalties determined in Türkiye for money launderers and the obliged entities, the UK's penal framework for such criminals is more likely to deter potential launderers and to ensure adherence to the STR obligations. For instance, the current amount of GBP 480 as the administrative fines relating to the reporting obligations in Türkiye would not serve as a significant deterrent, and it resembles a symbolic sanction given that the amount of money laundered may be 1,000 times more than that. Hence,

115 Article 52 of TCC 2004 stipulates that the judicial fine cannot be less than five days and ranges from 20 to 100 TL per day.

116 The conversion was made on 9 December 2020. See Xe Currency Converter (n 112).

117 Proceeds of Crime Act 2002, s 342(7).

118 Sentencing Council, 'Maximum Fines' <www.sentencingcouncil.org.uk/explanatory-material/magistrates-court/item/fines-and-financial-orders/approach-to-the-assessment-of-fines-2/9-maximum-fines/#> accessed 19 November 2023.

119 ibid.

revising the penalties for ML offences in Türkiye would strengthen the AML capacity of the AML regime.

The criminal liability of legal persons constitutes another crucial difference between the two AML legal regimes. As discussed previously, Turkish legal instruments do not envisage corporate liability for criminal activities and only set forth specific security measures, such as the revocation of license, for the ML offence of corporations. The UK, on the other hand, holds corporations criminally liable for offences that require the notion of *mens rea*, including ML, based on the identification principle, which requires prosecutors to prove that the natural person who has committed the offence is the 'directing mind and will' of the corporation.[120] In other words, criminal liability is attributable to corporations only in cases where the money launderers are qualified personnel – not any regular employee – of the corporation. Amongst many other cases, the leading case, *Tesco Supermarkets Ltd v Nattrass* [1972] AC 153 (HL), in this end[121] establishes the criteria for identifying the 'directing mind and will' of corporations:

> identifying those natural persons who by the Memorandum and Articles of Association or as a result of action taken by the directors, or by the company in general meeting pursuant to the Articles, are entrusted with the exercise of the powers of the company.[122]

Therefore, given that corporations are not held criminally liable for ML in Türkiye, this divergence point constitutes another strength of the UK's AML framework compared to Türkiye. Nevertheless, the current British legal regime does not set forth a strict liability for corporations relating to ML, a type of responsibility that does not require the mental element (i.e., *mens rea*).[123] As discussed later, the UK has established strict liability for legal entities regarding particular financial crimes (e.g., the failure to prevent tax evasion introduced by the CFA 2017). That is to say that enlarging the scope of strict liability for corporations to encompass ML would be an appropriate step for the UK as it would further reinforce its AML competency. Likewise, establishing criminal liability for legal persons relating to ML cases in Türkiye needs to be considered.

After investigating the scope of ML offences as determined under POCA 2002, it is necessary to scrutinise its approach to predicate crimes. POCA 2002 has significantly enlarged the focal point of underlying predicates by adopting an all-crimes approach, whereby predicate crimes are determined

120 Crown Prosecution Service, 'Corporate Prosecutions' para 12 <www.cps.gov.uk/legal-guidance/corporate-prosecutions> accessed 20 November 2023.

121 ibid para 20.

122 *Tesco Supermarkets Ltd v Nattrass* [1972] AC 153 (HL).

123 Crown Prosecution Service (n 120) para 18.

very comprehensively, without prescribing any imprisonment threshold in contrast with Türkiye. POCA 2002 refers to predicate crimes as either 'unlawful conduct'[124] or 'criminal conduct',[125] both of which refer to the same meaning and constitute a foundation for the ML offence regardless of their seriousness. Part 5 of POCA determines the provisions for civil recovery of the proceeds of unlawful conduct, one of the main routes for recovery of assets, as discussed subsequently, whereby it defines the meaning of the term under Section 241. Accordingly, it is defined as conduct that occurs in any constituent part of the UK if it is unlawful therein under the criminal law.[126] Furthermore, it also encompasses conduct that has been committed in a jurisdiction outside the UK, where the relevant activities are unlawful therein under the criminal law, and that had it occurred in a constituent of the UK, it would have been unlawful therein under the criminal law.[127] Moreover, the CFA 2017, as discussed later, concerning gross human rights abuses and violations,[128] brought along a new subsection under Section 241 that further extends the coverage of the unlawful conduct effective from 31 January 2018.[129] Correspondingly, it also extends to conduct that occurs in a jurisdiction outside the UK, that comprises, or is associated with, the commission of a gross human rights abuse or violation, and that had it occurred in a constituent of the UK, it would have been an offence therein triable under the criminal law on indictment only or either on indictment or summarily.[130]

Another term referred by POCA 2002 to predicate crimes is criminal conduct. Part 7 of POCA, where, amongst others, the principal and secondary ML offences are determined, utilises the term 'criminal conduct' in prescribing predicate crimes. Accordingly, it is conduct that constitutes an offence in the UK (England and Wales) or would constitute such an offence if it occurred therein.[131] The criminal conduct should be interpreted as an activity that constitutes (or would constitute) an offence in any part of the UK if it occurred there.[132] As the close reading of these provisions connotes, the UK does not consider the gravity of the conduct committed, nor does it make (any) distinction whether the offence was committed abroad or at home in determining predicate crimes. In other words, similar to Türkiye's locational approach to predicate crimes, it criminalises ML regardless of the location where the predicate crime is committed. However, it is necessary to state that there exist exceptions to this locational viewpoint: in cases where the person knows or believes on reasonable grounds that the predicate crime has been committed

124 Proceeds of Crime Act 2002, pt 5.
125 ibid pt 7.
126 ibid s 241(1).
127 ibid s 241(2).
128 ibid s 241A.
129 ibid s 241(2A).
130 ibid.
131 ibid s 76(1).
132 ibid s 340(2).

outside the UK; that it was not illegal under the criminal law then valid in that jurisdiction;[133] and that had it occurred in the UK, it would have been punishable by a maximum term of 12 months' imprisonment.[134] Given that Türkiye adopts a threshold perspective in prescribing which criminal activities constitute predicate crimes, the UK's all-offences strategy seems to create a more hostile environment for the perpetrators of those crimes. For example, counterfeiting valuable stamps[135] or trading as a public officer[136] constitute criminal offences entailing a maximum of six months imprisonment term in Türkiye as determined under TCC 2004. It would be reasonable to expect that such crimes may generate benefits for the perpetrators, which would naturally be considered proceeds of crime. As such, the threshold approach to predicate crimes as adopted by Türkiye[137] fails to encompass such crimes within the scope of ML cases. Therefore, embracing an all-crimes approach to predicate offences by Türkiye, as the UK does, would indubitably reinforce the jurisdiction's AML efforts as it would plug such exploitable gaps in the AML framework of the country.

Another essential distinction between the AML legal structures adopted by Türkiye and the UK is the power of recovery of criminal assets, as POCA 2002 does not confine that authority to the sole use of confiscation. Whilst the only (permanent) recovery of assets strategy relating to ML cases is confiscation in Türkiye, the UK can also use other means of recovery procedures in such cases where a conviction is not secured. These recovery powers consist of civil recovery[138] and taxation,[139] and the application of them, unlike confiscation, does not require a conviction. In other words, the UK's AML legal framework is more likely to deter criminals to a greater extent, as well as more likely to recover higher amounts of proceeds of crime, as there is a broad spectrum of recovery methods available for the competent authorities. For example, whilst HMRC has recovered GBP 7,947,889 based on refused DAML requests between April 2018 and March 2019,[140] there is no statement relating to recovered proceeds of crime in the annual reports provided by MoTF in

133 ibid ss 327(2A), 328(3) and 329(2A).

134 Explanatory Notes to the Proceeds of Crime Act 2002 (Money Laundering: Exceptions to Overseas Conduct Defence) Order 2006, SI 2006/1070.

135 Article 199(3) of Law No 5237 sets forth that any person who unknowingly receives a valuable counterfeit stamp, knowing it to be counterfeit, and circulates it shall be sentenced to a penalty of imprisonment for a term of one month to six months.

136 Article 259 of Law No 5237 stipulates that any public officer who, by taking advantage of the influence derived from his duty, attempts to sell goods or services to another shall be sentenced to a penalty of imprisonment for a term of up to six months or a judicial fine.

137 Crimes that are punishable by a minimum penalty of more than six months imprisonment qualify as predicate offences in Türkiye (See Chapter 3).

138 Proceeds of Crime Act 2002, pt 5.

139 ibid pt 6.

140 NCA, 'UK Financial Intelligence Unit Suspicious Activity Reports Annual Report 2019' (2019) <www.nationalcrimeagency.gov.uk/who-we-are/publications/390-sars-annual-report-2019/file> accessed 21 April 2023.

Türkiye, albeit indicating the amount deferred and seized.[141] It suggests either that the Turkish authorities have not been able to recover any crime benefits in the corresponding period[142] or that MASAK does not include those activities within the scope of annual reports. Furthermore, in addition to the previously stated amount obtained within the scope of civil and criminal investigations, HMRC has secured an additional GBP 6,088,723 and GBP 3,649,752 relating to the taxation powers and new CFA orders, such as UWOs or DOs, respectively.[143]

Another crucial factor impacting the varying levels of recovery turnovers is the incentive of LEAs in achieving such results in the proceedings. As discussed in the previous chapter, whilst confiscation secures the transfer of the ownership of proceeds of crime to the State in Türkiye, LEAs or any other operational units, such as MASAK, do not obtain any extra benefit from such procedures in fulfilling their duties. Despite criticism (e.g., amongst others, 'offenders seemingly buying their way out of prosecution'),[144] the competent stakeholders in the UK, on the other hand, are provided with incentives to pursue asset recovery, where none of the receipts are returned to the Treasury. More specifically, the UK introduced the Asset Recovery Incentivisation Scheme (ARIS) in 2006, a programme that envisages the division of net receipts from proceeds of crime between the Home Office and all operational partners that undertaken the associated asset recovery operations broadly on a 50/50 basis.[145] Furthermore, there is no obligation on how ARIS funds need to be used by receiving agencies, an essential incentivisation factor, suggesting that they can deploy them as per their priorities and decisions, such as investing in asset recovery practices or community projects.[146] For example, between April 2019 and March 2020, ARIS funds receiving agencies used GBP 67.1 million for such purposes, where the confiscation generated a turnover

141 See, for instance, the Annual Report provided by the MoTF, namely TC Hazine ve Maliye Bakanlığı, '2020 Yılı Faaliyet Raporu' (February 2021) <https://ms.hmb.gov.tr/uploads/2021/03/2020-HMB-Idare-Faaliyet-Raporu.pdf> accessed 9 February 2023.

142 It is necessary to mention that whilst MASAK publishes its annual reports on a calendar year basis, the UKFIU, on the other hand, publishes them as encompassing the period between April and the following year's March.

143 NCA (n 140).

144 Colin King, 'Asset Recovery: An Overview' in Colin King, Clive Walker and Jimmy Gurulé (eds), *The Palgrave Handbook of Criminal and Terrorism Financing Law* (Springer International Publishing 2018) 385.

145 Home Office, 'Asset Recovery Incentivisation Scheme Review' (February 2015) <http://data.parliament.uk/DepositedPapers/Files/DEP2015-0223/ARIS_Review_Report_unmarked.pdf> accessed 16 November 2023.

146 Home Office, 'Asset Recovery Statistical Bulletin 2014/15–2019/20' (September 2020) <https://assets.publishing.service.gov.uk/government/uploads/system/uploads/attachment_data/file/923194/asset-recovery-financial-years-2015-to-2020-hosb2320.pdf> accessed 31 October 2023.

of GBP 139 million in the same period.[147] That is to say that both motivation mechanisms and the productive recovery armoury considerably render British authorities more effective than their Turkish counterparts. Therefore, enhancing and diversifying the recovery powers of competent Turkish stakeholders, increasing the effective use of already available such authorities, and perhaps introducing incentive mechanisms for LEAs ought to be a priority for Türkiye.

Under POCA 2002, a confiscation order, which can only be made by the Crown Court,[148] constitutes the basis for confiscation procedures, whereby the recoverable amount of monetary value of the proceeds of crime is calculated,[149] and an equivalent sum is transferred to the State accordingly. It can be (and principally is) made in the sum of the benefit obtained from criminal conduct; or in cases where the defendant shows that the available amount is less than the benefit, in the sum of the available amount; and if there is no available amount, in the sum of a nominal amount.[150] It requires the convicted defendant to pay the amount determined immediately, or in cases where s/he shows that s/he cannot pay instantly, within a fixed period not exceeding six months, with an initial period of a maximum of three months.[151] It is worth reiterating here that the Turkish authorities primarily aim to confiscate criminal assets or gains themselves; in cases where it is not possible, then they seek to confiscate the value corresponding to such crime benefits. POCA 2002, on the other hand, regardless of the availability of such properties, allows British authorities to directly deprive (convicted) offenders of the crime benefits in terms of their monetary value. In other words, confiscation orders in the UK, unlike Türkiye's fundamentally *in rem* confiscation decisions, are in the form of *in personam*. This difference is of paramount importance as it facilitates a more straightforward and accelerated confiscation procedure for the British authorities, thereby enabling high levels of recovery, albeit raising some concerns (e.g., adverse impacts on offenders and their family members) simultaneously.[152] More importantly, a confiscation order is considered as an essential part of the sentencing procedure in the UK,[153] suggesting that the British judiciary aims at recovering any potential crime benefits in all cases in the first place. That is not to say that the Turkish courts do not seek to recover the proceeds of crime at all, but in the UK criminal asset recovery has become a reflex and

147 ibid.
148 Proceeds of Crime Act 2002, s 6.
149 ibid s 7.
150 ibid ss 7(1) and 7(2).
151 ibid ss 11(1), 11(3) and 11(5).
152 Craig Fletcher, 'Social Value or Social Harm? The Impact of the Proceeds of Crime Act 2002 Upon the Defendant and Their Families' in Katie Benson, Colin King and Clive Walker (eds), *Assets, Crimes and the State: Innovations in 21st Century Legal Responses* (Routledge 2020).
153 Crown Prosecution Service, 'Proceeds of Crime' <www.cps.gov.uk/crime-info/proceeds-crime> accessed 10 May 2023.

Table 4.1 The range of default sentences determined under Section 35 of POCA 2002.

Amount	*Maximum term*
GBP 10,000 or less	6 months
More than GBP 10,000 but no more than GBP 500,000	5 years
More than GBP 500,000 but no more than GBP 1 million	7 years
More than GBP 1 million	14 years

an entrenched part of the UK's sentencing practices. Therefore, adopting a similar approach, which also consolidates lifestyle provisions and UWOs, as discussed later, would substantially enhance the recovery capabilities of the Turkish authorities. In cases where an offender fails to pay the amount specified in the confiscation order, s/he has to serve a default imprisonment term of up to 14 years,[154] depending on the amount under consideration. Additionally, serving the default sentence does not eliminate the obligation for the offender to pay the outstanding amount,[155] which indubitably augments the productivity of confiscation orders in achieving a successful recovery. Table 4.1 indicates the default sentence terms regarding non-compliance with confiscation orders.

Another main route for recovery of assets in the UK is civil recovery, where the proceeds of crime can be recovered in civil proceedings in the High Court against property that is or represents property obtained through criminal conduct.[156] Remarkably, the court can decide the use of civil recovery 'on the balance of probabilities',[157] suggesting that it is a more straightforward procedure as the civil law standard of proof is sufficient in determining the utilisation of such a recovery method. Civil recovery, unlike confiscation, does not concern the guilt of the person who holds the property under consideration; instead, it seeks to recover the proceeds of unlawful conduct (i.e., recoverable property)[158] regardless of the possessor. In other words, whilst confiscation orders are *in personam*, civil recovery orders, on the other hand, are in the form of *in rem*. It can be applied, amongst others, in cases where LEAs deem that the evidence is not sufficient to secure a criminal conviction. Additional circumstances include: (i) where a conviction is obtained but a confiscation order is not made; and (ii) where the relevant court deems that civil recovery better serves the public interest than a confiscation order.[159] For instance, in cases where a defendant has fled the UK or where the UK courts cannot prosecute the offender as the offence has been committed abroad, utilising

154 Proceeds of Crime Act 2002, s 35.
155 Explanatory Notes to (Section 10 of) the Serious Crime Act 2015.
156 Proceeds of Crime Act 2002, s 240(1).
157 ibid s 241(3).
158 ibid s 304.
159 Crown Prosecution Service (n 153).

civil recovery better serves the public interest.[160] Competent authorities in the UK, such as SFO, FCA, HMRC, and the NCA,[161] recovered GBP 13 million in the 2020/2021 financial period through civil recovery.[162] It is necessary to state that civil recovery orders can be accompanied by provisional orders, such as property freezing orders[163] and interim receiving orders,[164] to prevent the disposition of the assets under consideration and allow time for LEAs to investigate them, respectively. Lastly, civil recovery powers have extraterritorial reach,[165] suggesting that the whereabouts of the asset under consideration are immaterial, whether in the UK or abroad. In such cases, where LEAs seek to apply civil recovery concerning proceeds of crime abroad, they carry out these procedures within the scope of MLA based on External Requests and Orders[166] as determined under Part 11 of POCA 2002.[167]

The recovery of cash,[168] recovery of listed assets,[169] and forfeiture of money held in bank and society building accounts[170] constitute other legal proceedings relating to civil recovery practices. LEAs are allowed to search any premises in cases where they have reasonable grounds for suspecting that they have present cash[171] above the minimum amount, which is the proceeds of or intended for use in crime,[172] where the minimum amount is more than GBP 1,000.[173] LEAs are also authorised to seize the cash based on the same justifications,[174] and where they maintain such suspicion, they are permitted to detain the cash seized for an initial period of 48 hours.[175] The detention period can be extended up to six months, and if an additional order is made,

160 ibid.

161 Proceeds of Crime Act 2002, s 316(1).

162 Home Office, 'Asset Recovery Statistical Bulletin: Financial Years Ending 2016 to 2021' (September 2021) <www.gov.uk/government/statistics/asset-recovery-statistical-bulletin-financial-years-ending-2016-to-2021/asset-recovery-statistical-bulletin-financial-years-ending-2016-to-2021> accessed 19 August 2023.

163 Property freezing orders proscribe anyone to whose property they apply in any way dealing with the property as determined by Section 254A of POCA 2002.

164 Interim receiving orders seek the detention, custody, or preservation of property, as well as the appointment of an interim receiver as determined by Section 246 of POCA 2002.

165 Proceeds of Crime Act 2002, ss 282A to 282F.

166 ibid s 444.

167 ibid pt 11.

168 ibid pt 5 (Chapter 3).

169 ibid pt 5 (Chapter 3A).

170 ibid pt 5 (Chapter 3B).

171 Cash stands for '(a) notes and coins in any currency, (b) postal orders, (c) cheques of any kind, including travellers' cheques, (d) bankers' drafts, (e) bearer bonds and bearer shares, (f) gaming vouchers, (g) fixed-value casino tokens, [and] (h) betting receipts' found at any place in the UK as determined by Section 289(6) of POCA 2002.

172 Proceeds of Crime Act 2002, s 289.

173 ibid s 303 and the Proceeds of Crime Act 2002 (Recovery of Cash in Summary Proceedings: Minimum Amount) Order 2006, SI 2006/1699.

174 Proceeds of Crime Act 2002, s 294.

175 ibid s 295.

up to two years beginning on the date of the first order.[176] Eventually, the cash detained can be forfeited without[177] or with the (magistrates') court order[178] as per the provisions determined under Sections 297A to 297G and Sections 298 to 300 of POCA 2002, respectively. In alignment with the aforementioned recovery procedures, listed assets can be recovered based on similar search, seizure, detention, and forfeiture practices relating to cash. Listed assets, which is a recent concept introduced by the CFA 2017 as discussed later, consist of precious metals, precious stones, watches, artistic works, face-value vouchers, and postage stamps. Lastly, in terms of the forfeiture of money held in bank and society building accounts, POCA 2002 extends the aforementioned powers to such financial statements. In cases where they have reasonable grounds for suspecting that money held in an account maintained with a bank or building society (whether in whole or part) is the proceeds of or intended for use in criminal conduct,[179] LEAs can apply to Magistrates' Courts to obtain an account freezing order (AFO). AFOs prohibit any person the order concerns from making withdrawals or payments from the relevant account.[180] However, amongst other exemptions, the order may allow the person to deal with his or her account to meet their reasonable living expenses; or to maintain any trade, business, profession, or occupation.[181] Regarding a frozen account in this context, a senior officer, based on the same justifications concerning suspicion as touched upon earlier, may give an account forfeiture notice (AFN) to the suspect without a court order relating to forfeiting money held in the account (whether in whole or part).[182] The AFN initiates an at least 30-days period starting from the next day it is given for the respondent for objecting to the proposed forfeiture if s/he has any objection[183] (anyone can make an objection relating to an AFN).[184] If there is no objection within the specified period (and the AFN has not lapsed), the money under consideration is forfeited accordingly.[185] However, receiving an objection lapses the AFN and, in such circumstances, forfeiture can only be achieved upon applying to Magistrates' Courts and obtaining a (consequential) forfeiture order (FO). Nevertheless, giving an AFN is not a prerequisite for applying for an FO for the authorities, as they can, whilst an account freezing order is in force, opt for doing so in the first place as well.[186] In other words, once LEAs in the UK have reasonable grounds for suspecting that there are cash or listed assets on the (relevant)

176 ibid s 295(2).
177 ibid ss 297A to 297G.
178 ibid ss 298 to 300.
179 ibid s 303Z1.
180 ibid s 303Z1(3).
181 ibid s 303Z5(3).
182 ibid s 303Z9.
183 ibid s 303Z9(5).
184 ibid s 303Z9(7).
185 ibid s 303Z9(6).
186 ibid s 303Z14.

premises that comprise recoverable property or that may be used for unlawful conduct, they can pursue the eventual recovery of them. Although both Turkish and British LEAs have similar powers in this end, the striking difference is that whilst the civil standard of proof is sufficient in the UK, it is not an adequate criterion in Türkiye for recovery of these assets. Türkiye principally requires a conviction to utilise a potential application of the recovery mechanism of confiscation relating to ML cases. Another noteworthy distinction stems from the fact that the British LEAs are more independent than their Turkish counterparts relating to undertaking functions within the scope of search, seizure, detention, and forfeiture powers in this context. Whilst LEAs in the UK conduct such activities autonomously, LEAs in Türkiye, on the other hand, (in circumstances where there is no peril in delay) operate based on the permission obtained from public prosecutors, as discussed previously. Therefore, establishing a civil recovery strategy and enhancing the independence of LEAs in this end in Türkiye would be an appropriate approach. This would further prevent criminals from engaging in criminality and impair their incentives to participate in ML schemes, as such an approach allows stripping away their crime benefits swiftly.

A more recent provision for recovery of assets introduced by POCA 2002, which does not require a conviction, is taxation (i.e., *in rem* legal proceedings). In cases where the NCA, based on reasonable grounds, suspects that a person or a company has income, profit, or assets obtained as a result of unlawful conduct,[187] it has authority to raise tax assessments as determined under Part 6 of POCA 2002. In such circumstances, the NCA may take the duty of undertaking revenue functions carried out by the Commissioners of Inland Revenue concerning a person or a company's tax responsibilities over a specified period.[188] Furthermore, the NCA is also permitted to exercise revenue functions relating to inheritance tax where the value transferred is attributable to (wholly or partially) criminal property[189] or where criminal property (in whole or part) is settled.[190] It is necessary to emphasise that the civil law standard of proof, unlike for civil recovery, is not sufficient to raise tax evaluations and a potential application of taxation. Crucially, however, it is immaterial for the NCA to identify the source of any income in taxation practices,[191] suggesting the underlying logical basis for creating this recovery method and preferring the utilisation of it rather than the civil recovery. The official website of the NCA provides an application form for LEAs, whereby it outlines criteria for referral relating to consideration of civil recovery and/or taxation.[192] Accordingly, recoverable property identified cannot be less than a value of GBP

187 ibid s 317.
188 ibid s 317(2).
189 ibid s 321.
190 ibid s 322.
191 ibid s 319.
192 NCA, 'Civil Recovery & Tax Referral Form' <www.nationalcrimeagency.gov.uk/who-we-are/publications/36-nca-civil-recovery-tax-referral-form> accessed 9 December 2023.

10,000, and assets acquired before 25 January 1998 cannot be subject to civil recovery, where taxation concerning assets obtained in the preceding 20-year period from the specified date is allowed.[193] Considering all recovery means as discussed until here, it can be argued that the UK has established suitable strategies for all possible investigatory means and measures entailing various evidential thresholds to implement a given recovery method. Therefore, establishing a similar recovery framework beyond confiscation would enhance the ability to reclaim the proceeds of crime in Türkiye, thereby establishing a more robust environment against criminals, including money launderers.

Before moving forward, it is necessary to state that Türkiye and the UK are both signatories of the European Convention on Human Rights (ECHR) 1950,[194] which, along with its protocols, stipulate the legal conditions relating to property rights among others.[195] As such, national recovery practices of these jurisdictions have to comply with the provisions of the Convention. In other words, courts in both administrations have to follow the requirements of ECHR 1950, and the relevant domestic legal instruments shall be construed as per the Convention, correspondingly. Article 1 of Protocol No. 1 to the Convention 1952 determines the legal framework for the 'protection of property'. It sets forth that:

> Every natural or legal person is entitled to the peaceful enjoyment of his possessions. No one shall be deprived of his possessions except in the public interest and subject to the conditions provided for by law and by the general principles of international law.
>
> The preceding provisions shall not, however, in any way impair the right of a State to enforce such laws as it deems necessary to control the use of property in accordance with the general interest or to secure the payment of taxes or other contributions or penalties.[196]

As the close examination of these provisions connotes, as a general rule, every person has the right to the 'peaceful enjoyment' of their possessions. Based on the condition that they are enjoyed through legal right, possessions incorporate shares, patents, licenses, leases, and welfare benefits; and peaceful enjoyment involves the right of access to the property.[197] Nevertheless, this general rule applies in cases where one of the two specific rules of 'deprivation of

193 ibid.
194 Council of Europe, 'Chart of Signatures and Ratifications of Treaty 005' <www.coe.int/en/web/conventions/full-list/-/conventions/treaty/005/signatures> accessed 23 December 2023.
195 European Convention on Human Rights 1950 (as amended by Protocols Nos 11, 14 and 15; supplemented by Protocols Nos 1, 4, 6–7, 12–13 and 16.
196 Protocol No 1 (1952) to the Convention for the Protection of Human Rights and Fundamental Freedoms 1950, art 1.
197 Council of Europe, 'Protocol No 1 to the Convention' <www.coe.int/en/web/echr-toolkit/protocole-1> accessed 4 July 2023.

property' and 'control of property' are not met based on a fair balance test (i.e., the deprivation or control must be reasonably proportionate).[198] As evident in Article 1(1), the deprivation can be executed if it is in the public interest and does not contravene the law and the general principles of international law (i.e., the first specific rule). Furthermore, the control must be conforming to laws, the general interest, or seek to secure the payment of taxes or penalties as determined under the second paragraph of the article. These rules constitute the legal basis for the European Court of Human Rights in trying relevant cases. Accordingly, recovery mechanisms and security measures, such as confiscation or the revocation of the operational permit, adopted by Türkiye and the UK must follow these legal safeguards; and it is evident that both jurisdictions have aspired to compose their laws in accordance with the ECHR 1950.

Before examining the investigatory powers that POCA 2002 grants, it is also of utmost importance to discuss the notion of lifestyle offences, which constitutes one of the crucial divergent points between Türkiye and the UK's confiscation capabilities. POCA 2002 stipulates that a defendant has a criminal lifestyle, *inter alia*, in cases where s/he commits one of the crimes, including ML,[199] specified in Schedule 2.[200] Accordingly, convictions for ML under Sections 327 and 328 automatically trigger the practice of the lifestyle assumptions as determined by Section 75 and Schedule 2 of POCA 2002, the use of which substantially strengthens the confiscation powers of the jurisdiction. The application of lifestyle assumptions allows the judiciary to consider any property transferred to the defendant, or any property held by the defendant, or any expenditure incurred by the defendant at any time within the last six years since conviction as the proceeds of crime.[201] As such, it is the defendant's responsibility to prove the contrary (i.e., those assets do not have any criminal origins) in cases where the lifestyle provisions are in force. It can be argued that POCA 2002 serves as an effective legal instrument that can deprive money launderers and certain predicate crime offenders with criminal lifestyles of their crime benefits, including ones prior to the crime under consideration. Given that Türkiye's confiscation powers are limited only to the offence before a relevant court, it would be correct to postulate that the UK's approach in this end substantially intensifies the AML competency of the jurisdiction. Hence, adopting a similar approach would create a better law enforcement ecosystem in Türkiye, which would deter potential offenders and relieve society as the offenders would not get away with their proceeds of crime.

198 ibid.

199 Proceeds of Crime Act 2002, s 75.

200 Other lifestyle offences comprise drug trafficking, directing terrorism, slavery, people trafficking, arms trafficking, counterfeiting, intellectual property, prostitution and child sex, blackmail, and inchoate offences as determined under Schedule (2) of POCA 2002.

201 Proceeds of Crime Act 2002, s 10.

It is necessary to state also that POCA 2002 allows for the *restraint* of assets, a legal procedure, which Türkiye refers to as *seizure* as discussed previously, utilised to prevent offenders disposing of the proceeds of crime during the criminal investigation before their (potential) convictions. In cases where there are reasonable grounds to suspect that an alleged offender under criminal investigation has benefited from criminal conduct, the Crown Court may make a restraint order (RO),[202] which prohibits a person from dealing with any 'realisable' assets held by him.[203] Additionally, the court can make an RO based on an application by a prosecutor as per the further provisions determined under Section 40 of POCA 2002. More specifically, ROs may be made only on an application by a prosecutor or an accredited financial investigator, as well as on an *ex parte* application to a judge in chambers.[204] ROs must include provisions relating to the legal aid payments and can incorporate other exceptions, such as relating to reasonable living expenses, as well.[205] They further may comprise stipulations permitting the detention of any property under consideration.[206] However, if the court believes that there has been undue delay in carrying the proceedings or application on or that the prosecutor does not intend to proceed, then it does not make the order.[207] Moreover, they (or anyone affected by the order) can also apply to discharge or vary an RO.[208] If the Crown Court denies making an RO or refuses to modify or expel it, then they may appeal to the Court of Appeal against such decision.[209] The Court of Appeal's decision in this end can further be appealed to the Supreme Court.[210] Accordingly, the property under consideration may be detained until there remains no further possibility of an appeal.[211] It is worth reiterating that whilst a seizure decision in Türkiye requires *strong grounds of suspicion based on concrete evidence*, *reasonable grounds to suspect* that the crime has benefited the defendant is sufficient in the UK. Whilst the Turkish AML legal framework stipulates the precondition of obtaining a report, which indicates the monetary value of economic advantages the crime has catalysed,[212] POCA 2002 or any other relevant British legal instruments do not set forth such an obligation. That is to say that obtaining a seizure order in the UK is a less demanding process, thereby minimising the risk of disposition of proceeds of crime

202 ibid s 40.
203 ibid s 41.
204 ibid s 42.
205 ibid s 41.
206 ibid s 41A.
207 ibid ss 40(7) and 40(8).
208 ibid s 42(3).
209 ibid s 43.
210 ibid s 44.
211 ibid s 44A(3).
212 Law No 5271 (Criminal Procedure Code) 2004, art 128(1).

before a potential confiscation, which undoubtedly intensifies the competency of AML efforts of the jurisdiction.

POCA 2002 harnesses the competent authorities with a myriad of investigatory powers, including production orders, search and seizure warrants, disclosure orders, UWOs, customer information orders, and account monitoring orders, which intensify the AML composition of the jurisdiction.[213] UWOs, in particular, are of utmost importance to be scrutinised here as they enable authorities to recover the relevant properties if the suspect cannot prove that they have been possessed by legitimate origins, as discussed later. Production orders obligate the person(s) subject to a prescribed investigation under Section 345 of POCA, including confiscation, civil recovery, and ML, to produce a specified material or give authorities access to it in the determined period stated in the order.[214] The default period stated in the production orders is seven days starting from the day on which the order is made, but the judge can determine a longer or shorter time frame if s/he deems it appropriate.[215] However, the authority of the production orders is debatable as the failure to comply with it does not constitute an offence; rather, it is regarded as a contempt of court.[216] Nevertheless, in cases where, amongst others, the relevant person(s) do not comply with a production order, and there are reasonable grounds for believing that the material under consideration is on the premises that authorities seek access to, they can apply to the court for a search and seizure warrant.[217] Search and seizure warrants empower authorities relating to numerous investigations, including ML, to enter and search the premises specified in the application for the warrant, and to seize and retain any material found therein in the context of the investigation for which the application is made.[218] Disclosure orders oblige the person(s) subject to a prescribed investigation under Section 357 of POCA, including the ones relating to ML, to answer questions, provide information, or produce documents specified in the notice.[219] It is necessary to mention that ML investigations have been recently included within the scope of disclosure orders by the enactment of the CFA 2017. If the pertinent person fails to comply with the requirements of the order, s/he becomes guilty of a summary offence, thereby s/he can be punished by an imprisonment term of fewer than or equal to six months, a maximum fine of level 5 on the standard scale, or both.[220] In cases where s/he, intentionally or recklessly, makes a false or misleading statement when in

213 Proceeds of Crime Act 2002, pt 8.
214 ibid s 345.
215 ibid s 345(5).
216 Explanatory Notes to the Proceeds of Crime Bill, para 495 <https://publications.parliament.uk/pa/ld200102/ldbills/057/en/02057x-j.htm> accessed 29 April 2023.
217 Proceeds of Crime Act 2002, s 352(6).
218 ibid s 352.
219 ibid s 357.
220 ibid s 359(2).

purported compliance with the order, it constitutes an either-way offence, which means s/he can be punished either on indictment by a maximum imprisonment term of two years, an unlimited fine, or both; or on summary conviction by a maximum imprisonment term of six months, a fine not exceeding the statutory maximum, or both.[221]

UWOs compel the person(s), who are subject to a prescribed investigation under Section 362A of POCA, to provide a statement explaining their interest in the property for which the order is made; how it is obtained concerning, in particular, how any costs incurred in the obtaining process were met; where the property is held; as well as setting out any other information specified in the order.[222] It is necessary to state also that UWOs are typically accompanied by interim freezing orders,[223] which are orders that proscribe the respondent to the UWO and any other person with interest in the property in question from in any means dealing with it.[224] Similar to disclosure orders made concerning ML investigations, UWOs are a recent legal measure introduced by the CFA 2017. Although it is a relatively new investigatory power launched on 31 January 2018, it covers any relevant properties regardless of whether they were obtained before or after 31 January 2018.[225] Therefore, it would be apt to posit that UWOs can be made concerning any assets, regardless of when they have come into possession of the person under consideration. However, it is necessary to note that there exist some requirements for making these orders. Firstly, the competent enforcement authority[226] must satisfy the relevant court that there are reasonable grounds for believing that the person under consideration holds the property, and the value of it exceeds £50,000.[227] Secondly, the pertinent court must also be satisfied that there is reasonable cause to suspect that the known sources of the relevant person's lawfully obtained income would not have been sufficient to acquire the property in question.[228] Lastly, the authorised court (i.e., the High Court in England and Wales) makes a UWO if it is satisfied either that the relevant individual is a PEP or that there are reasonable grounds for suspecting that s/he or a connected person with them is, or has been involved in serious crime regardless of the location where it is committed (i.e., within or outside the UK).[229] For instance, the first UWO of the UK, the *National Crime Agency*

221 ibid ss 359(3) and 359(4).
222 ibid s 362A(3).
223 Home Office (n 53).
224 Proceeds of Crime Act 2002, s 362J(3).
225 ibid s 362B(5)(b).
226 Section 362A(7) prescribes the relevant enforcement authority as the NCA, HMRC, the FCA, the Director of the SFO, or the Director of Public Prosecutions (concerning England and Wales) or the Director of Public Prosecutions for Northern Ireland (concerning Northern Ireland).
227 Proceeds of Crime Act 2002, s 362B(2).
228 ibid s 362B(3).
229 ibid s 362B(4).

v Hajiyeva [2018] EWHC 2534 (Admin), constitutes a successful example achieved in this end. The High Court denied the application of Zamira Hajiyeva, the wife of the former chairman of International Bank of Azerbaijan Jahangir Hajiyev, to discharge the UWO made concerning a property bought for GBP 11.5m.[230] The decision was made on the grounds, amongst others, that the proceeds of crime obtained as a result of Mr Hajiyev's, who is deemed as a PEP (paragraphs 41 to 54), various criminal activities, including serious fraud and embezzlement (paragraphs 58 and 84), had originated as the source for buying the property.[231]

Noncompliance with the requirements of a UWO within the specified period yields the presumption that the property under consideration is recoverable under any ensuing civil recovery procedures, where the person's intention to comply with it is considered sufficient for the (purported) compliance.[232] If the pertinent person, intentionally or recklessly, makes a false or misleading statement, s/he becomes guilty of an either-way offence, which means the offender can be punished either on indictment by an imprisonment term of fewer than two years, an unlimited fine, or both; or on summary conviction by an imprisonment term of fewer than 12 months, an unlimited fine, or both.[233] As the close reading of these provisions connotes, the standard of proof is relatively undemanding compared to that of the criminal standard, as it only requires reasonable grounds for suspicion. Furthermore, the burden of proof lies with the person that the UWO concerns, as s/he is responsible for proving that the property in question is not obtained as a result of unlawful conduct. Therefore, considering the enormous strength provided by these provisions, the AML legal arsenal of the UK comprises way more effective tools than its Turkish counterpart. However, it would not be unreasonable to assert that investing proceeds of crime into separate properties, the values of which do not exceed GBP 50,000 individually, would eliminate the risk of being exposed to a UWO, albeit it may not be practical. Hence, setting such a threshold may constitute an exploitable legal lacuna that needs to be reconsidered. Accordingly, amending the liminal value by focusing on the individual's total relevant wealth would be an appropriate step to be taken.

The effectiveness of UWOs remains questionable. They have been utilised only a few times, and only by the NCA,[234] suggesting that other enforcement

230 *National Crime Agency v Hajiyeva* [2018] EWHC 2534 (Admin).

231 ibid.

232 Proceeds of Crime Act 2002, s 362C(5).

233 ibid s 362E.

234 KYC360 News, '£1.5m Legal Bill Forces Rethink Over McMafia Wealth Orders' *KYC360 News* (14 July 2020) <www.riskscreen.com/kyc360/news/1-5m-legal-bill-forces-rethink-over-mcmafia-wealth-orders/> accessed 30 November 2023. See also Ali Shalchi and Steve Browning, 'Economic Crime (Transparency and Enforcement) Act 2022' (UK Parliament Research Briefing Paper No 9480, March 2022) 18 <https://researchbriefings.files.parliament.uk/documents/CBP-9486/CBP-9486.pdf> accessed 17 August 2023.

authorities, namely HMRC, the FCA, the SFO, and the CPS,[235] remain reluctant to exercise these legal powers. This reluctance may be stemming from the fact that the High Court recently decided a case relating to three UWOs, which were on three London properties worth GBP 80 million possessed by a Kazakh family, to the detriment of the NCA. The High Court granted the applications to discharge them in the case of *National Crime Agency v Baker* [2020] EWHC 822 (Admin), as it found the assumptions made by the NCA were unreliable (paragraphs 100, 167, 197, 209, and 215).[236] The decision was given on the grounds that the holding requirement (paragraphs 101 to 122, 169), the income requirement (paragraphs 126 to 138, 171, 207 to 210) and the PEP or serious crime requirement (paragraphs 140 to 153, 172, 215 and 216) have not been met.[237] The NCA consequently faced a legal bill of GBP 1.5 million following the decision by the Court of Appeal.[238] That is to say that although UWOs constitute a ground-breaking legal power, it appears that the competent LEAs of the UK need additional time for deploying them more effectively.

The last two significant pieces of investigatory powers available to competent British authorities consist of customer information orders and account monitoring orders. Customer information orders enable the relevant stakeholders to access information controlled by financial institutions, as those orders compel them to provide any pertinent customer information relating to the person(s) subject to a prescribed investigation under Section 363 of POCA, including confiscation, civil recovery, and ML.[239] Concerning an ML investigation, the order can be made based on the reasonable grounds for suspecting that the person under consideration has committed an ML offence.[240] If an FI fails to comply with the order; or intentionally or recklessly makes a false or misleading statement when in purported compliance with the order, it becomes guilty, whereby it faces, *inter alia*, an unlimited fine in each case.[241] Lastly, account monitoring orders compel the relevant FI(s) to provide account information (whether solely or jointly with another) for the specified period relating to the person(s) subject to a prescribed investigation under Section 370 of POCA, including confiscation, civil recovery, and ML.[242] As is the case in obtaining a customer information order, concerning a ML investigation, the order can be made based on the reasonable grounds for suspecting that the person under consideration has committed a ML offence.[243]

235 Proceeds of Crime Act 2002, s 362A(7).
236 *National Crime Agency v Baker* [2020] EWHC 822 (Admin).
237 ibid.
238 KYC360 News (n 234).
239 Proceeds of Crime Act 2002, s 363.
240 ibid s 365(4).
241 ibid, s 366.
242 ibid, s 370.
243 ibid, s 371(4).

4.3.1.3 Deferred Prosecution Agreements

Lastly, although it is not determined by POCA 2002, it would be appropriate to discuss the notion of DPAs, which is another legal power available to British authorities in enhancing the AML competency of the jurisdiction. The Crime and Courts Act 2013 makes both primary and secondary ML offences eligible for the use of such agreements[244] in cases where the (alleged) offenders are corporations, partnerships, or unincorporated associations.[245] A DPA requires offenders, amongst others, to pay a financial penalty and/or to compensate victims of the alleged offence,[246] where the breach of the agreement fails to suspend legal proceedings and results in a prosecution, which also brings about, amongst others, financial penalties. As such, it would be apt to posit that fulfilling the requirements of DPAs is a more desirable legal procedure for the alleged offenders than failing to do so. Despite many hurdles regarding DPA applications,[247] DPAs constitute another crucial apparatus for the UK in depriving non-individual alleged money launderers of proceeds of crime.[248] Such a process does not exist in Türkiye, and the breaching of AML regulations only results in confiscation and security measures (e.g., the revocation of the operational permit) for legal entities, as discussed previously.

4.3.2 Serious Crime Act 2015

In October 2013, in response to the threats posed by serious and organised crime, the UK released the Serious and Organised Crime Strategy, which aims, amongst others, to set out a plan of action relating to preventing people from taking part in such crime schemes.[249] Accordingly, the Serious Crime Act 2015 was enacted, *inter alia*, to amend the POCA 2002[250] and to give effect to the legislative proposals put forward in the aforementioned Strategy.[251]

Part 1 of the Serious Crime Act 2015 is of particular significance within the scope of this study as it provides provisions relating to the proceeds of crime, and thereby reinforces the relevant clauses of POCA 2002 concerning the

244 Crime and Courts Act 2013, sch 17, para 23.
245 ibid sch 17, para 4.
246 ibid sch 17, para 5.
247 Colin King and Nicholas Lord, 'Deferred Prosecution Agreements in England and Wales: Castles Made of Sand?' [2020] Public Law 307.
248 For a more detailed commentary on DPAs, see Colin King and Nicholas Lord, *Negotiated Justice and Corporate Crime: The Legitimacy of Civil Recovery Orders and Deferred Prosecution Agreements* (Palgrave Pivot 2018).
249 HM Government, 'Serious and Organised Crime Strategy' (October 2013) <https://assets.publishing.service.gov.uk/government/uploads/system/uploads/attachment_data/file/248645/Serious_and_Organised_Crime_Strategy.pdf> accessed 30 November 2023.
250 Serious Crime Act 2015, introduction.
251 UK Government, 'Serious Crime Act 2015 – Fact Sheet: Overview of the Act' <https://assets.publishing.service.gov.uk/government/uploads/system/uploads/attachment_data/file/415943/Serious_Crime_Act_Overview.pdf> accessed 30 November 2023.

confiscation practices.[252] It introduces new provisions relating to the defendant's interest in the criminal property.[253] By doing so, it ensures the disruption of such assets even in circumstances where they are held by other people, such as other family members. It also aims to secure a more successful application of recovery of assets by setting forth an immediate payment of confiscation orders liability[254] and by increasing the imprisonment terms relating to the failure to do so.[255] It stipulates a reporting requirement for the applicants of ROs, whereby obligating them to inform the court of the progress of the investigation[256] and thereby seeks to execute those orders more swiftly. Furthermore, it also requires courts, in securing compliance with confiscation orders, to consider imposing travel bans that prohibit defendants to leave the UK.[257]

In addition to the reinforcement of the confiscation powers as discussed earlier, the Serious Crime Act 2015 introduced amendments relating to disclosures, investigations, cooperation, and enforcement, which further intensify the overall AML competency of the jurisdiction. More specifically, it exempts good faith authorised disclosures made concerning the suspicion of ML from civil liability.[258] Given that it would not be unreasonable to expect that the lack of such an amendment would cause client losses for the FIs and businesses, the Act has aptly addressed this loophole. Furthermore, it enlarges the scope of investigative powers by allowing the competent authorities to trace any relevant property available for satisfying a confiscation order[259] whilst increasing international cooperation through the extended interest regarding criminal assets.[260] Lastly, in terms of amendments made concerning enforcement practices, Section 40 of the Serious Crime Act 2015 sets forth the provisions relating to confiscation orders determined by Magistrates' Courts, whereby it prescribes, amongst others, the upper limit of those orders as GBP 10,000 for such courts.[261]

4.3.3 Criminal Finances Act 2017

Following the enactment of POCA 2002 in the UK, the international financial world witnessed significant developments (e.g., the inclusion of new predicate crimes). The Third (2005/60/EC) and Fourth (2015/849/EU) AMLDs,

252 Serious Crime Act 2015, pt 1. See also Jonathan Fisher, 'Part 1 of the Serious Crime Act 2015: Strengthening the Restraint and Confiscation Regime' (2015) 10 Criminal Law Review 754.
253 Serious Crime Act 2015, ss 1 to 4.
254 ibid s 5.
255 ibid s 10.
256 ibid s 11.
257 See, for instance, ibid s 7.
258 ibid s 37.
259 ibid s 38.
260 ibid s 39.
261 ibid s 40.

which have introduced terrorism and tax crimes as predicate offences, respectively, are the two examples of legal instruments that aim to address such global financial developments (i.e., the revision of the FATF Recommendations) at the EU level. On par with the previously mentioned developments, CFA 2017 was enacted,[262] amongst others, to amend the POCA 2002, thereby extending its scope to encompass terrorism-related property and create new corporate offences relating to the facilitation of tax evasion.[263] Most of the powers that POCA 2002 makes available for LEAs today, such as UWOs and interim freezing orders, originate from the CFA 2017, as discussed previously.

Part 1 of CFA 2017 provides provisions relating to the proceeds of crime, whereby it introduces new investigatory powers and strengthens the capabilities within the scope of ML, civil recovery, and enforcement powers.[264] It is worth reiterating that UWOs require any person suspected of possessing criminal property to explain the (legitimate) origins of such property, where failing to do so results in the assumption that the property has illegitimate connections and as such triggers the use of civil recovery powers accordingly.[265] In addition to UWOs, CFA 2017 has also enlarged the scope of disclosure orders, which were previously available for confiscation investigations under POCA 2002, to encompass ML investigations.[266] Another crucial reform is the power to extend the moratorium period (up to a maximum of six months in certain circumstances), which had been confined only to a 31-day timeframe under POCA 2002 hitherto.[267] Given that an unrenewable moratorium period was insufficient for developing evidence in some circumstances, such as complex cases or cases with overseas connections, the CFA 2017 has substantially eliminated this hurdle by introducing the moratorium extension powers. For instance, the UKFIU considers the renewable moratorium period, in conjunction with AFOs, as one of the most significant reasons for the considerable increase in proceeds of crime restrained since the introduction of CFA 2017 as it has resulted in denying of more than three times higher funds to criminals through DAML.[268] In addition to the ability to extend the moratorium period, CFA 2017 further amends the SAR regime by allowing the sharing of

262 For a more detailed commentary on the CFA 2017, see Jonathan Fisher and Anita Clifford, *The Criminal Finances Act 2017* (Informa Law 2018).

263 Criminal Finances Act 2017, introduction.

264 ibid pt 1. See also Nicola Padfield, 'The Criminal Finances Act 2017' (2017) 7 Criminal Law Review 505.

265 Criminal Finances Act 2017, s 1.

266 ibid s 7.

267 ibid s 10.

268 Moratorium extensions allowed the competent British authorities to deny GBP 51,362,549 to criminals between April 2019 and March 2020. See NCA, 'UK Financial Intelligence Unit Suspicious Activity Reports Annual Report 2020' (April 2020) 6 <www.nationalcrimeagency.gov.uk/who-we-are/publications/480-sars-annual-report-2020/file> accessed 24 February 2023.

information within the regulated sector and thereby submitting joint disclosures[269] (i.e., Super SARs).[270] A further paramount amendment the CFA 2017 has brought about is the provisions relating to the improvement of civil recovery powers. It sets forth, *inter alia*, the concept of listed assets and extends the use of these powers to the HMRC[271] and FCA,[272] two vital components of the British institutional AML framework (see Chapter 6). It is worth reiterating that civil recovery powers allow competent authorities to disrupt (illicit) assets regardless of a criminal investigation. Therefore, considering these cardinal provisions stipulated by the CFA 2017 relating to the proceeds of crime, it has considerably reinforced the jurisdiction's AML competency compared to (m) any national AML legal structures, including Türkiye.

Part 2 of CFA 2017 extends AML and associated powers relating to the recovery of assets to apply to CTF investigations.[273] Part 3 of the Act, *inter alia*, creates new corporate offences relating to the failure to prevent the facilitation of tax evasion. More specifically, it creates strict (criminal) liability for corporate bodies and partnerships[274] for failing to prevent the facilitation of tax evasion relating to both UK[275] and foreign taxes,[276] which had not raised any liability for them hitherto. Lastly, Part 4 of CFA 2017, in conjunction with Schedule 5 of the Act, introduces minor and consequential amendments to the relevant legal instruments, including POCA 2002.

4.3.4 Sanctions and Anti-Money Laundering Act 2018

Another AML legal instrument crucial to examine here is the SAMLA 2018. It was enacted, *inter alia*, to make provisions relating to AML and CTF as per the FATF Recommendations, thereby ensuring the legal harmony and integrity of the jurisdiction with the international financial world.[277] The primary incentive behind the enactment of SAMLA 2018 was to smooth the UK's leaving process from the EU and to take the necessary legal steps before 1 January 2021, when the UK left the EU.[278] During its EU membership, the UK did not need such a legal instrument because the obligations stipulated at the international level, such as the relevant UN resolutions and/or the FATF Recommendations, have had an autonomous and direct effect on the jurisdiction's legal framework. The

269 Criminal Finances Act 2017, s 11.
270 Law Commission, 'Anti-Money Laundering: The SARS Regime Consultation Paper' (Consultation Paper No 236, 20 July 2018) <www.cicm.com/wp-content/uploads/2018/09/Anti-Money-Laundering-the-SARS-Regime-Consultation-paper.pdf> accessed 30 November 2023.
271 Criminal Finances Act 2017, s 19.
272 ibid s 20.
273 See, for instance, ibid s 41.
274 ibid s 44.
275 ibid s 45.
276 ibid s 46.
277 Sanctions and Anti-Money Laundering Act 2018, introduction. See also Lodge (n 67).
278 UK Government (n 66).

EU transposes all sanctions adopted by the UN into its legal framework, which binds all MS to implement them entirely (see Chapter 2). The EU AMLDs have always ensured that the EU MS comply with the FATF Recommendations. The withdrawal of the UK from the EU has rendered the enactment of SAMLA 2018, the first legal instrument devoted to the post-Brexit era that has completed its passage through the UK Parliament,[279] inevitable, indicating the high level of importance given by the UK government to AML/CTF matters. The then Foreign Secretary of the UK, Boris Johnson, explained the necessity of SAMLA 2018, amongst others, in the following words:

> [SAMLA 2018] will also provide us with the power to amend and update anti-money laundering and counter-terrorist finance legislation, allowing the Government to keep pace with changing international standards and practices, and help to protect the UK from money laundering and terrorist financing.[280]

Part 2 of the Act is devoted to AML, whereby the legal rules regarding the AML/CTF, reporting obligations, and beneficial ownership requirements are provided. It allows an appropriate Minister to make provisions relating, amongst others, to enabling or facilitating the detection, investigation, and prevention of ML and the implementation of the FATF Standards.[281] It also obligates the Secretary of State to publish three reports annually explaining, amongst others, the progress made during the period towards setting up a register of beneficial owners of overseas entities.[282] Lastly, it compels the Secretary of State to assist the governments of the UK Overseas Territories in establishing their transparent, publicly accessible registries for beneficial ownership of companies registered therein,[283] suggesting the extent of the British AML framework will reach those jurisdictions, as well.[284] It can be argued that the UK is keen to ensure the harmony of its organisational AML structure with the exigencies of the global financial world and has prepared itself for the post-Brexit area accordingly. However, it is an early phase to make a clear judgement whether this legislative preparation will be effective in addressing ML and its underlying predicates.

279 UK Government, 'News Story: Sanctions and Anti-Money Laundering Act Receives Royal Assent' (24 May 2018) <www.gov.uk/government/news/sanctions-and-anti-money-laundering-act-receives-royal-assent> accessed 3 December 2023.

280 ibid.

281 Sanctions and Anti-Money Laundering Act 2018, s 49.

282 ibid s 50.

283 ibid s 51.

284 For a more detailed discussion on the impacts of SAMLA 2018 on the UK overseas territories, see John Hatchard, 'Money Laundering, Public Beneficial Ownership Registers and the British Overseas Territories: The Impacts of the Sanctions and Money Laundering Act 2018 (UK)' (2018) 30(1) Denning Law Journal 185.

4.3.5 Economic Crime (Transparency and Enforcement) Act 2022

As an urgent response to the invasion of Ukraine by Russia, the UK enacted Economic Crime (Transparency and Enforcement) Act 2022 in March 2022,[285] thereby further reinforcing its AML legal framework. Part 1 of the Act has created a public register of beneficial owners of overseas entities. It requires non-UK entities who want to buy, sell, or transfer land in the UK to identify their beneficial owners, register with the Companies House, and update such information annually.[286] Furthermore, the registration requirement applies retrospectively to land under consideration whose transaction was made on or after 1 January 1999 (in England and Wales).[287]

Part 2 of the Act has extended the scope of UWOs introduced by the CFA 2017 to encompass 'responsible officers' (e.g., the director of an entity that owns the property).[288] It also created an alternative test to the income requirement for granting a UWO, thereby enabling courts, ***based on reasonable grounds for suspecting that the property has been obtained through unlawful conduct***, to impose a UWO.[289] Furthermore, it introduced new powers to extend the period for an additional 126 days for which interim freezing order has effect so that the enforcement authorities can review material provided in response to a UWO and act accordingly.[290] Lastly, Part 3 stipulates sanctions for failing to comply with and the breach of obligations introduced under the Act, and Part 4 provides general provisions (e.g., determines the extent of the Act) in this context. In other words, Economic Crime (Transparency and Enforcement) Act 2022, which primarily addresses (Russian) oligarchs that own property in the UK,[291] has further strengthened the scope of the AML legal framework of the jurisdiction.

4.3.6 The Money Laundering, Terrorist Financing and Transfer of Funds (Information on the Payer) Regulations 2017 (MLRs)

As discussed previously, the FATF has introduced a more flexible set of measures under its 2012 Revision,[292] whereby it recommended the use of proportionate and effective regulatory and operational procedures based on the level of perceived risks (i.e., RBA). Subsequently, in order to ensure the congruency of the relevant EU legal instruments with the international standards as set out by the FATF, the Fourth AMLD (i.e., 2015/849/EU) was enacted on 20

285 Shalchi and Browning (n 234).
286 Economic Crime (Transparency and Enforcement) Act 2022, s 7.
287 ibid ss 9(10) and 41(6).
288 ibid s 45(7).
289 ibid ss 47 and 48.
290 ibid ss 49–50.
291 Home Office and others (n 70).
292 These measures include, amongst others, simplified due diligence (SDD) and enhanced due diligence (EDD).

May 2015.[293] Eventually, the UK, as an EU MS in the corresponding period, has realised its transposition into its national legal framework by enacting the 2017 MLRs to comply with EU requirements and thereby with the FATF's revised recommendations. The 2017 MLRs came into force on 26 June 2017[294] and replaced their predecessor, namely the MLRs 2007. The 2017 MLRs are the corresponding legal instrument of the UK determining the relevant policies, principles, and procedures relating to obligated parties that of Türkiye's three discrete regulations, namely ROM 2008, ROC 2008, and ROTF 2013, as discussed previously. However, there are disparities between the two jurisdictions' correspondent legal instruments in prescribing pertinent frameworks and measures, such as the differences in the scope of obliged parties, KYC standards, identification of the beneficial owner, and record-keeping practices. Given that those dissimilarities may affect the overall AML competency of a given jurisdiction, the differences between the AML structures of Türkiye and the UK are investigated subsequently (see Chapter 7).

Compared to the 2007 MLRs, the 2017 MLRs determine a more rigorous requirement framework relating to preventing and detecting threats associated with ML and TF for the obliged entities, requiring them to take the appropriate measures proportionate to the volume and nature of the business. For such purposes, the 2017 MLRs obligate them to establish systems and control mechanisms to detect, evaluate, manage, and mitigate risks based on an RBA. In alignment, as per the size and nature of the profession, they are obliged to conduct thorough risk evaluations in each phase of their business based on the policies developed. For instance, establishing a business relationship, carrying out an occasional transaction exceeding EUR 1,000, suspecting ML or TF, or doubting the veracity or adequacy of identification or verification documents previously obtained require them to apply CDD measures.[295] Although the 2017 MLRs determine the scope of obliged entities similar to their predecessor,[296] the legal instrument exempts persons, amongst others, whose total annual turnover relating to the financial activity does not exceed the threshold of GBP 100,000,[297] which had earlier been GBP 64,000 under the 2007 MLRs.[298] Therefore, the new set of regulations appears to be focusing on a relatively narrower group of relevant financial transactions. Nevertheless, the comprehensiveness of the UK's legal framework compared to Türkiye

293 Directive (EU) 2015/849 (n 50).

294 The Money Laundering, Terrorist Financing and Transfer of Funds (Information on the Payer) Regulations 2017, SI 2017/692, reg 1.

295 ibid reg 27(1).

296 Obliged entities under 2017 MLRs comprise credit institutions, financial institutions; auditors, insolvency practitioners, external accountants, and tax advisers; independent legal professionals; trust or company service providers; estate agents; high-value dealers; and casinos. See ibid reg 8(2).

297 ibid reg 15(3).

298 The Money Laundering Regulations 2007, SI 2007/2157, sch 2(1)(a).

is also evident here, as Türkiye obligates a more restricted group of persons as the obliged entities in its national AML legal framework. Yet, given that there is no threshold limit set in terms of annual turnover in determining the obligated entities in Türkiye, the UK's approach to this end may result in the oversight of certain ML offences committed by persons whose annual turnover remains below the threshold.

Another salient difference observed in the 2017 MLRs is the introduction of more stringent rules relating to exercising an RBA. Although the 2007 MLRs also set forth the requirement of risk-sensitive basis evaluation in CDD practices,[299] the 2017 MLRs devote a chapter for risk assessment and controls, whereby it stipulates a detailed set of regulations in this context.[300] Accordingly, the 2017 MLRs place more rigid regulations in conducting an appropriate level of CDD within the scope of KYC standards. For example, whilst the 2007 MLRs put forward certain circumstances where a relevant person is not required to apply CDD measures relating to the simplified CDD,[301] the 2017 MLRs allow the application of the simplified CDD based only on risk assessments.[302] In terms of enhanced CDD, the approach towards the PEPs constitutes a remarkable divergence point, as the 2017 MLRs, unlike the former set of regulations,[303] are not confined as applying only to foreign PEPs.[304] Furthermore, in alignment with the relevant international developments in cryptocurrencies, the 2017 MLRs put in place new regulations on electronic money, such as the obligation of appointment of central contact points,[305] while the 2007 MLRs had regulated the concept relating only to SDD.[306] Lastly, they also create an additional criminal offence, whereby recklessly providing false or misleading information whilst being in purported compliance with a requirement imposed by the 2017 MLRs is criminalised within the scope of information offences.[307]

Before concluding this section, it is necessary to mention that the provisions of the 2017 MLRs have further been reinforced by the Money Laundering and Terrorist Financing (Amendment) Regulations 2019, which transposes the obligations determined under the Fifth AMLD into the UK legal AML framework. The 2019 (Amendment) MLRs, which came into force

299 ibid SI 2007/2157, reg 7.
300 The Money Laundering, Terrorist Financing and Transfer of Funds (Information on the Payer) Regulations 2017, SI 2017/692, ch 2.
301 The Money Laundering Regulations 2007, SI 2007/2157, reg 13(1).
302 The Money Laundering, Terrorist Financing and Transfer of Funds (Information on the Payer) Regulations 2017, SI 2017/692, reg 37.
303 The Money Laundering Regulations 2007, SI 2007/2157, reg 14(5).
304 The Money Laundering, Terrorist Financing and Transfer of Funds (Information on the Payer) Regulations 2017, SI 2017/692, reg 35.
305 ibid reg 22.
306 The Money Laundering Regulations 2007, SI 2007/2157, reg 13(7)(d).
307 The Money Laundering, Terrorist Financing and Transfer of Funds (Information on the Payer) Regulations 2017, SI 2017/692, reg 88.

on 10 January 2020,[308] amongst others, enlarged the scope of the regulated sector by incorporating letting agents, art market participants, crypto-asset exchange providers, and custodian wallet providers.[309] For instance, letting agents, which rent out property valued at 10,000 euros or more for a minimum of one calendar month,[310] and those in the art market who deal in the sales, purchases, and storage of works of art with a value of 10,000 euros or more[311] have become obliged entities accordingly. The 2019 (amendment) MLRs also introduced, *inter alia*, new requirements relating to enhanced and simplified CDD measures. For example, under the revised 2017 MLRs, electronic money products amounting to 150 euros or less can be exempt from CDD, a threshold which was previously 250 euros.[312] It can be stated that in response to global developments seen in the AML domain, such as the prevalence of cryptocurrencies,[313] the UK has adjusted its national AML framework to address a broad range of illegal financial activities.

Lastly, the 2017 MLRs, as amended by the 2019 (amendment) MLRs,[314] task three statutory supervisory authorities, namely the FCA, the HMRC, and the Gambling Commission, with AML supervisory responsibilities.[315] In addition, the 2017 MLRs oblige 22 legal and accountancy professional body supervisors, such as the Law Society, to supervise the AML compliance of their members operating in the legal and accountancy sectors.[316] Whilst these 25 AML supervisors endeavour to ensure that obliged entities abide by the AML legal framework, three more professional body supervisors, namely CILEx Regulation, Bar Standards Board, and Solicitors Regulation Authority, are entrusted with delegated regulatory functions.[317] Furthermore, as discussed in

308 The amendments relating to CDD within the scope of anonymous prepaid cards (Part 3 of the 2017 MLRs) and the additional part (Part 5A of the 2017 MLRs) regulating the bank account portal came into force on 10 July 2020 and 10 September 2020, respectively. Nevertheless, (as of 17 December 2020), the latter group of amendments has not been applied to the 2017 MLRs. See the Money Laundering and Terrorist Financing (Amendment) Regulations 2019, SI 2019/1511, reg 1.

309 The Money Laundering and Terrorist Financing (Amendment) Regulations 2019, SI 2019/1511, reg 4.

310 ibid reg 4(4).

311 ibid reg 4(6).

312 ibid reg 5(5)(a)(ii).

313 Chad Albrecht and others, 'The Use of Cryptocurrencies in the Money Laundering Process' (2019) 22(2) Journal of Money Laundering Control 210.

314 The enactment of 2019 (amendment) MLRs introduced AML supervisory responsibilities for the FCA concerning crypto asset service providers. Similarly, HMRC became the AML supervisor for letting agents and art market participants.

315 The Money Laundering, Terrorist Financing and Transfer of Funds (Information on the Payer) Regulations 2017, SI 2017/692, reg 7.

316 ibid SI 2017/692, reg 7 and sch 1.

317 HM Treasury, 'Review of the UK's AML/CTF Regulatory and Supervisory Regime' (June 2022) 43 <https://assets.publishing.service.gov.uk/government/uploads/system/uploads/attachment_data/file/1085407/MLRs_Review_Report_-_2.5_for_publication.pdf> accessed 31 December 2023.

Chapter 6 in detail, the Office for Professional Body Anti-Money Laundering Supervision (OPBAS), which operates under the auspices of the FCA, oversees all these professional body supervisors.[318] The 2017 MLRs also oblige HM Treasury to ask all AML supervisors to provide information on their supervisory activity[319] and publish a consolidated review of this information.[320] In other words, as correctly observed by Button, Hock, and Shepherd, the UK has established a multi-layered AML supervisory mechanism that obliges a plethora of AML regulators and supervisors to monitor and ensure the AML compliance of obliged entities.[321] Given the monopolised AML supervisory responsibility of MASAK in Türkiye, this comprehensive AML regulatory and supervisory armada established in the UK suggests that the UK attaches more importance to AML supervision of obliged entities than Türkiye. Whilst that is not to say that Türkiye does not ascribe sufficient consideration to AML oversight, its relatively limited organisational structure in this context may explain the insufficient contribution of particular obliged entities, such as accountants,[322] to the AML efforts of the jurisdiction. Accordingly, Chapter 6 examines these UK AML authorities in detail, thereby underlining their function in the fight against ML and its underlying predicates. However, the discussion excludes the Gambling Commission as Türkiye does not incorporate a corresponding institution because gambling (whether online or land-based) is prohibited therein (see Chapter 7).

4.4 Conclusion

As a member of several international organisations, including the G7, the UN, and the OECD, to name a few, the UK has always been one of the foremost financial centres in the world that spearhead the international AML standards. Its providence in addressing the phenomenon has always been evident, such as enlarging the scope of predicate crimes in 1988 before the FATF's first set of (i.e., 1990) recommendations. However, this judiciousness has not been able to remedy the ongoing global ML problem or the associated predicate crimes, suggesting that there remain certain lacunas that need to be filled and amended

318 FCA, 'Office for Professional Body Anti-Money Laundering Supervision (OPBAS)' <www.fca.org.uk/opbas> accessed 31 December 2022.

319 The Money Laundering, Terrorist Financing and Transfer of Funds (Information on the Payer) Regulations 2017, SI 2017/692, reg 51.

320 See, for example, HM Treasury, 'Anti-Money Laundering and Countering the Financing of Terrorism: Supervision Report 2020–22' (December 2022) <https://assets.publishing.service.gov.uk/government/uploads/system/uploads/attachment_data/file/1125446/Supervision_report_final_draft_-_signed.pdf> accessed 31 December 2023.

321 Mark Button, Branislav Hock and David Shepherd, *Economic Crime: From Conception to Response* (Routledge 2022) 228.

322 For example, whilst Turkish accountants and tax advisers did not submit a single STR, notaries and independent audit institutions submitted only seven STRs to MASAK in 2020. See Ch 7.

accordingly. These exploitable gaps and differences across the national AML legal structures, such as the approaches to predicate crimes or the criminal liability of corporations, undoubtedly constitute invaluable opportunities for the perpetrators of ML and predicate crimes. Therefore, increasing its effectiveness and maintaining its leading position in the universal AML sphere must be one of the priorities for the UK.

As ML and transnational predicate crimes require a collective response internationally, the congruency of the national AML regimes with the international AML instruments is essential. The EU membership of the UK has always ensured that the harmony and integrity of its AML framework are congruent with the necessities of the regional and global financial *fora*, such as the relevant UN Conventions and EU AMLDs. Nevertheless, henceforward, similar to Türkiye, the UK has to be more engaged in amending its domestic laws as per the international AML legislation as it has left the EU. Nevertheless, the current state of affairs of the British AML legal composition indicates that the UK will maintain its preeminent status by setting AML standards that go beyond the requirements of minimum international standards.

The current British AML framework offers a myriad of tools, such as UWOs and lifestyle provisions, in dealing with ML and predicate crimes effectively. Furthermore, it also makes available a variety of asset recovery measures that can be utilised depending on the evidence and offender (i.e., natural or legal person). In other words, AML legal instruments of the UK, particularly POCA 2002, propose adjustable leverages for LEAs to utilise, which leaves (almost) no room for offenders of the financial crimes to benefit from such dirty profits. An existence of a mere suspicion is sufficient for LEAs to disrupt illicit money flows and recover the proceeds, including all crime benefits. For example, once LEAs in the UK suspect that a legal or natural person enjoys the proceeds of crime, they can opt to apply either for confiscation, or a DPA (in cases where the alleged offenders are not natural persons), or taxation, or civil recovery by pulling the leverages accordingly. These investigatory and recovery powers render the competent British authorities seemingly way more advantageous than their Turkish counterparts. Additionally, the incentivisation programmes, such as ARIS, may further motivate them to deprive offenders of their illegal gains. Nevertheless, this supposedly favourable statutory composition alone cannot prove the productivity of the two jurisdictions. Therefore, their institutional structures need to be examined, as well. Accordingly, how Türkiye and the UK compose their institutional AML frameworks and whether the responsible stakeholders effectively reflect their domestic legal compositions in this context are discussed in Chapters 5 and 6, respectively.

This chapter has inquired into the evolution of the UK's prevailing AML legal framework and presented its strong characteristics compared to (m)any other jurisdictions, including Türkiye. It has also provided insight into current problems and (potential) deficiencies of the British response mechanism that can be exploited by money launderers and offenders of the associated predicate crimes, such as the reluctance seen in the application of UWOs. By doing so, it has highlighted the areas for reform relating to reinforcing the British AML composition. In light of the prodigious potency of the aforementioned principal legal instruments, it can be argued that the UK harnesses its AML components with an array of tools. However, given that the mere examination of the statutory texts would not be sufficient to comprehend the effectiveness of the British AML composition, the institutional components of the AML structure and their real-life experiences in this context need to be analysed as well. Accordingly, Chapter 6 investigates the constituent stakeholders of the British AML structure, thereby outlining their effectiveness and responsibilities to this end. By doing so, this study aims to highlight the organisational differences between the Turkish and British AML frameworks, thereby generating opportunities to understand the underlying reasons that account for the prevalence of particular and distinct predicate crimes in the two jurisdictions.

Reference List

Albrecht C and others, 'The Use of Cryptocurrencies in the Money Laundering Process' (2019) 22(2) Journal of Money Laundering Control 210

Alexander R, 'The 2003 Money Laundering Regulations' (2005) 8(1) Journal of Money Laundering Control 75

BBC, 'Assets Recovery Agency "Failing"' *BBC News* (14 June 2006) <http://news.bbc.co.uk/1/hi/uk_politics/5077846.stm> accessed 12 May 2023

Button M, Hock B and Shepherd D, *Economic Crime: From Conception to Response* (Routledge 2022)

Cabinet Office, 'Recovering the Proceeds of Crime: A Performance and Innovation Unit Report' (June 2000) <https://webarchive.nationalarchives.gov.uk/+/http:/www.cabinetoffice.gov.uk/media/cabinetoffice/strategy/assets/crime.pdf> accessed 12 May 2023

Campbell L, 'Dirty Cash (Money Talks): 4AMLD and the Money Laundering Regulations 2017' (2018) 2 Criminal Law Review 102

Commonwealth Secretariat, 'Money Laundering Regulations 1993 (United Kingdom)' (1994) 20(1) Commonwealth Law Bulletin 274

Council of Europe, 'Chart of Signatures and Ratifications of Treaty 005' <www.coe.int/en/web/conventions/full-list/-/conventions/treaty/005/signatures> accessed 23 December 2023

——— 'Chart of Signatures and Ratifications of Treaty 141' <www.coe.int/en/web/conventions/full-list/-/conventions/treaty/141/signatures?p_auth=tV5pnJpN> accessed 4 July 2023

——— 'Protocol No 1 to the Convention' <www.coe.int/en/web/echr-toolkit/protocole-1> accessed 4 July 2023

Crown Prosecution Service, 'Proceeds of Crime' <www.cps.gov.uk/crime-info/proceeds-crime> accessed 10 May 2023

——— 'Corporate Prosecutions' para 12 <www.cps.gov.uk/legal-guidance/corporate-prosecutions> accessed 20 November 2023

Dumbacher J, 'The Fight Against Money Laundering' (1995) 30(4) Inter Economics 177

Ebenezer L, *Operation Julie: The World's Greatest LSD Bust* (Y Lolfa Cyf 2010)

Egmont Group, 'Members by Region' <https://egmontgroup.org> accessed 13 July 2023

European Scrutiny Committee, 'EU Action Plan to Combat Money Laundering' (Thirteenth Report, HC 2019–21, 24 June 2020) <https://publications.parliament.uk/

pa/cm5801/cmselect/cmeuleg/229-ix/22910.htm#footnote-041> accessed 1 December 2023

FATF, 'The Forty Recommendations of the Financial Action Task Force on Money Laundering' (1990) <www.fatf-gafi.org/media/fatf/documents/recommendations/pdfs/FATF%20Recommendations%201990.pdf> accessed 4 July 2023

——— 'The Forty Recommendations' (1996) <www.fatf-gafi.org/media/fatf/documents/recommendations/pdfs/FATF%20Recommendations%201996.pdf> accessed 13 May 2023

——— 'FATF 40 Recommendations' (October 2003) <www.fatf-gafi.org/media/fatf/documents/FATF%20Standards%20-%2040%20Recommendations%20rc.pdf> accessed 13 May 2023

——— 'Anti-Money Laundering and Counter-Terrorist Financing Measures: United Kingdom – Mutual Evaluation Report' (December 2018) <www.fatf-gafi.org/media/fatf/documents/reports/mer4/MER-United-Kingdom-2018.pdf> accessed 18 January 2022

——— 'International Standards on Combatting Money Laundering and the Financing of Terrorism & Proliferation: The FATF Recommendations' (Updated March 2022) <www.fatf-gafi.org/media/fatf/documents/recommendations/pdfs/FATF%20Recommendations%202012.pdf> accessed 26 June 2023

——— 'Middle East and North Africa Financial Action Task Force (MENAFATF)' <www.fatf-gafi.org/pages/menafatf.html> accessed 11 May 2020

——— 'Asia/Pacific Group on Money Laundering (APG)' <www.fatf-gafi.org/pages/asiapacificgrouponmoneylaunderingapg.html> accessed 11 May 2023

——— 'Caribbean Financial Action Task Force (CFATF)' <www.fatf-gafi.org/pages/caribbeanfinancialactiontaskforcecfatf.html> accessed 11 May 2023

——— 'Eastern and Southern Africa Anti-Money Laundering Group (ESAAMLG)' <www.fatf-gafi.org/pages/easternandsouthernafricaanti-moneylaunderinggroupesaamlg.html> accessed 11 May 2023

——— 'Information on Updates Made to the FATF Recommendations' <www.fatf-gafi.org/publications/fatfrecommendations/documents/fatf-recommendations.html#UPDATES> accessed 14 May 2023

——— 'FATF Members and Observers' <www.fatf-gafi.org/about/membersandobservers/> accessed 13 July 2023

FCA, 'Office for Professional Body Anti-Money Laundering Supervision (OPBAS)' <www.fca.org.uk/opbas> accessed 31 December 2022

Fisher J, 'Part 1 of the Serious Crime Act 2015: Strengthening the Restraint and Confiscation Regime' (2015) 10 Criminal Law Review 754

——— and Clifford A, *The Criminal Finances Act 2017* (Informa Law 2018)

Fitzpatrick D, 'Crime Fighting in the Twenty-First Century?' (2006) 9(2) Journal of Money Laundering Control 129

Fletcher C, 'Social Value or Social Harm? The Impact of the Proceeds of Crime Act 2002 Upon the Defendant and Their Families' in K Benson, C King and C Walker (eds), *Assets, Crimes and the State: Innovations in 21st Century Legal Responses* (Routledge 2020)

Harfield C, 'SOCA: A Paradigm Shift in British Policing' (2006) 46(4) British Journal of Criminology 743

Hatchard J, 'Money Laundering, Public Beneficial Ownership Registers and the British Overseas Territories: The Impacts of the Sanctions and Money Laundering Act 2018 (UK)' (2018) 30(1) Denning Law Journal 185

Haynes A, 'Money Laundering: From Failure to Absurdity' (2008) 11(4) Journal of Money Laundering Control 303

HM Government, 'Serious and Organised Crime Strategy' (October 2013) <https://assets.publishing.service.gov.uk/government/uploads/system/uploads/attachment_data/file/248645/Serious_and_Organised_Crime_Strategy.pdf> accessed 30 November 2023

HM Treasury, 'Review of the UK's AML/CTF Regulatory and Supervisory Regime' (June 2022) <https://assets.publishing.service.gov.uk/government/uploads/system/uploads/attachment_data/file/1085407/MLRs_Review_Report_-_2.5_for_publication.pdf> accessed 31 December 2023

——— 'Anti-Money Laundering and Countering the Financing of Terrorism: Supervision Report 2020–22' (December 2022) <https://assets.publishing.service.gov.uk/government/uploads/system/uploads/attachment_data/file/1125446/Supervision_report_final_draft_-_signed.pdf> accessed 31 December 2023

Home Office, 'Asset Recovery Incentivisation Scheme Review' (February 2015) <http://data.parliament.uk/DepositedPapers/Files/DEP2015-0223/ARIS_Review_Report_unmarked.pdf> accessed 16 November 2023

——— 'Circular 003/2018: Unexplained Wealth Orders' (1 February 2018) <www.gov.uk/government/publications/circular-0032018-criminal-finances-act-unexplained-wealth-orders/circular-0032018-unexplained-wealth-orders> accessed 22 May 2023

——— 'Asset Recovery Statistical Bulletin 2014/15–2019/20' (September 2020) <https://assets.publishing.service.gov.uk/government/uploads/system/uploads/attachment_data/file/923194/asset-recovery-financial-years-2015-to-2020-hosb2320.pdf> accessed 31 October 2023

——— 'Asset Recovery Statistical Bulletin: Financial Years Ending 2016 to 2021' (September 2021) <www.gov.uk/government/statistics/asset-recovery-statistical-bulletin-financial-years-ending-2016-to-2021/asset-recovery-statistical-bulletin-financial-years-ending-2016-to-2021> accessed 19 August 2023

Home Office and others, 'News Story: New Measures to Tackle Corrupt Elites and Dirty Money Become Law' (15 March 2022) <www.gov.uk/government/news/new-measures-to-tackle-corrupt-elites-and-dirty-money-become-law> accessed 17 August 2023

Huang SS, 'Crypto Assets Regulation in the UK: An Assessment of the Regulatory Effectiveness and Consistency' (2021) 29(3) Journal of Financial Regulation and Compliance 336

IMF, 'Technical Assistance on AML/CTF' <www.imf.org/external/np/leg/amlcft/eng/aml3.htm> accessed 15 May 2023

King C, 'Asset Recovery: An Overview' in C King, C Walker and J Gurulé (eds), *The Palgrave Handbook of Criminal and Terrorism Financing Law* (Springer International Publishing 2018)

——— and Lord N, 'Deferred Prosecution Agreements in England and Wales: Castles Made of Sand?' [2020] Public Law 307

——— and Lord N, *Negotiated Justice and Corporate Crime: The Legitimacy of Civil Recovery Orders and Deferred Prosecution Agreements* (Palgrave Pivot 2018)

KYC360 News, '£1.5m Legal Bill Forces Rethink Over McMafia Wealth Orders' *KYC360 News* (14 July 2020) <www.riskscreen.com/kyc360/news/1-5m-legal-bill-forces-rethink-over-mcmafia-wealth-orders/> accessed 30 November 2023

Law Commission, 'Anti-Money Laundering: The SARS Regime Consultation Paper' (Consultation Paper No 236, 20 July 2018) <www.cicm.com/wp-content/uploads/2018/09/Anti-Money-Laundering-the-SARS-Regime-Consultation-paper.pdf> accessed 30 November 2023

Leong AVM, 'Chasing Dirty Money: Domestic and International Measures Against Money Laundering' (2007) 10(2) Journal of Money Laundering Control 140

Letter from Rt Hon Ben Wallace MP (Minister of State for Security) to Sir William Cash MP (Chair of the European Scrutiny Committee) (11 September 2017) <http://europeanmemoranda.cabinetoffice.gov.uk/files/2017/10/2017-09-11_-_Security_Minister_to_ESC_Chair._Directive_on_countering_money_laundering_by_criminal_law_.pdf> accessed 1 December 2023

Lodge HD, *Blackstone's Guide to the Sanctions and Anti-Money Laundering Act 2018* (OUP 2020)
Mitsilegas V and Vavoula N, 'The Evolving EU Anti-Money Laundering Regime: Challenges for Fundamental Rights and the Rule of Law' (2016) 23(2) Maastricht Journal of European and Comparative Law 261
Mugarura N, 'The Implications of Brexit for UK Anti-Money Laundering Regulations: Will the Fourth AML Directive Be Implemented or Be Binned?' (2018) 21(1) Journal of Money Laundering Control 5
NCA, 'UK Financial Intelligence Unit Suspicious Activity Reports Annual Report 2019' (2019) <www.nationalcrimeagency.gov.uk/who-we-are/publications/390-sars-annual-report-2019/file> accessed 21 April 2023
——— 'UK Financial Intelligence Unit Suspicious Activity Reports Annual Report 2020' (April 2020) <www.nationalcrimeagency.gov.uk/who-we-are/publications/480-sars-annual-report-2020/file> accessed 24 February 2023
——— 'Civil Recovery & Tax Referral Form' <www.nationalcrimeagency.gov.uk/who-we-are/publications/36-nca-civil-recovery-tax-referral-form> accessed 9 December 2023
Padfield N, 'The Criminal Finances Act 2017' (2017) 7 Criminal Law Review 505
Rees E, Fisher R and Thomas R, *Blackstone's Guide to the Proceeds of Crime Act 2002* (5th edn, OUP 2015)
Ryder N, 'To Confiscate or Not to Confiscate? A Comparative Analysis of the Confiscation of the Proceeds of Crime Legislation in the United States and United Kingdom' (2013) 8 Journal of Business Law 767
Sentencing Council, 'Maximum Fines' <www.sentencingcouncil.org.uk/explanatory-material/magistrates-court/item/fines-and-financial-orders/approach-to-the-assessment-of-fines-2/9-maximum-fines/#> accessed 19 November 2023
Shalchi A and Browning S, 'Economic Crime (Transparency and Enforcement) Act 2022' (UK Parliament Research Briefing Paper No 9480, March 2022) <https://researchbriefings.files.parliament.uk/documents/CBP-9486/CBP-9486.pdf> accessed 17 August 2023
Sinha G, 'AML-CTF: A Forced Marriage Post 9 11 and Its Effect on Financial Institutions' (2013) 16(2) Journal of Money Laundering Control 142
Sproat P, 'The Serious and Organised Crime Agency and the National Crime Squad: A Comparison of Their Output from Open-Source Materials' (2011) 21(3) Policing & Society 343
——— 'Unexplained Wealth Orders: An Explanation, Assessment and Set of Predictions' (2018) 82(3) Journal of Criminal Law 232
Stanton K, 'The United Kingdom' in S Booysen and D Neo (eds), *Can Banks Still Keep a Secret?* (CUP 2017)
TC Hazine ve Maliye Bakanlığı, '2020 Yılı Faaliyet Raporu' (February 2021) <https://ms.hmb.gov.tr/uploads/2021/03/2020-HMB-Idare-Faaliyet-Raporu.pdf> accessed 9 February 2023
Turner S and Bainbridge J, 'An Anti-Money Laundering Timeline and the Relentless Regulatory Response' (2018) 82(3) Journal of Criminal Law 215
Tyre C, 'Anti-Money Laundering Legislation: Implementation of the FATF Forty Recommendations in the European Union' (2010) Journal of the Professional Lawyer 69
UK Government, 'News Story: Sanctions and Anti-Money Laundering Act Receives Royal Assent' (24 May 2018) <www.gov.uk/government/news/sanctions-and-anti-money-laundering-act-receives-royal-assent> accessed 3 December 2023
——— 'Brexit Transition: Time Is Running Out' <www.gov.uk/transition> accessed 7 December 2020

——— 'Assets Recovery Agency' <www.gov.uk/government/organisations/assets-recovery-agency> accessed 12 May 2023

——— 'Serious Crime Act 2015 – Fact Sheet: Overview of the Act' <https://assets.publishing.service.gov.uk/government/uploads/system/uploads/attachment_data/file/415943/Serious_Crime_Act_Overview.pdf> accessed 30 November 2023

United Nations Treaty Collection, 'Status of Treaties: 12. United Nations Convention Against Transnational Organized Crime' <https://treaties.un.org/Pages/ViewDetails.aspx?src=IND&mtdsg_no=XVIII-12&chapter=18> accessed 4 July 2023

——— 'Status of Treaties: 19. United Nations Convention Against Illicit Traffic in Narcotic Drugs and Psychotropic Substances' <https://treaties.un.org/pages/ViewDetails.aspx?src=TREATY&mtdsg_no=VI-19&chapter=6> accessed 4 July 2023

Williams D, 'Terrorism and the Law in the United Kingdom' (2003) 26(1) University of New South Wales Law Journal 179

Xe Currency Converter <www.xe.com/currencyconverter/convert/?Amount=100&From=TRY&To=GBP> accessed 9 December 2020

Legal Instruments

International

United Nations Convention Against Illicit Traffic in Narcotic Drugs and Psychotropic Substances 1988

EU

Council Directive 91/308/EEC of 10 June 1991 on Prevention of the Use of the Financial System for the Purpose of Money Laundering [1991] OJ L166/77

Directive 2001/97/EC of the European Parliament and of the Council of 4 December 2001 Amending Council Directive 91/308/EEC on Prevention of the Use of the Financial System for the Purpose of Money Laundering – Commission Declaration [2001] OJ L344/76

Directive 2005/60/EC of the European Parliament and of the Council of 26 October 2005 on the Prevention of the Use of the Financial System for the Purpose of Money Laundering and Terrorist Financing (Text with EEA Relevance) [2005] OJ L309/15

Directive (EU) 2015/849 of the European Parliament and of the Council of 20 May 2015 on the Prevention of the Use of the Financial System for the Purposes of Money Laundering or Terrorist Financing, Amending Regulation (EU) No 648/2012 of the European Parliament and of the Council, and Repealing Directive 2005/60/EC of the European Parliament and of the Council and Commission Directive 2006/70/EC (Text with EEA relevance) [2015] OJ L141/73

Directive (EU) 2018/843 of the European Parliament and of the Council of 30 May 2018 Amending Directive (EU) 2015/849 on the Prevention of the Use of the Financial System for the Purposes of Money Laundering or Terrorist Financing and Amending Directives 2009/138/EC and 2013/36/EU (Text with EEA relevance) PE/72/2017/REV/1 [2018] OJ L156/43

Directive (EU) 2018/1673 of the European Parliament and of the Council of 23 October 2018 on Combating Money Laundering by Criminal Law PE/30/2018/REV/1 [2018] OJ L284/22

European Convention on Human Rights 1950 (as amended by Protocols Nos. 11, 14 and 15; Supplemented by Protocols Nos. 1, 4, 6, 7, 12, 13 and 16

Protocol No 1 (1952) to the Convention for the Protection of Human Rights and Fundamental Freedoms 1950

Türkiye

Law No 5237 (Turkish Criminal Code) 2004
Law No 5271 (Criminal Procedure Code) 2004
Law No 5549 on the Prevention of Laundering Proceeds of Crime 2006

United Kingdom

Coroners and Justice Act 2009
Counter Terrorism Act 2008
Counter Terrorism and Border Security Act 2019
Counter Terrorism and Security Act 2015
Crime and Courts Act 2013
Criminal Finances Act 2017
Criminal Justice Act 1988
Criminal Justice Act 1993
Criminal Justice Act 2003
Criminal Justice (Confiscation) (Northern Ireland) Act 1990
Criminal Justice (International Co-operation) Act 1990
Drug Trafficking Act 1994
Drug Trafficking Offences Act 1986
Economic Crime (Transparency and Enforcement) Act 2022
Explanatory Notes to the Money Laundering Regulations 1993
Explanatory Notes to the Money Laundering Regulations 2003
Explanatory Notes to the Money Laundering Regulations 2007
Explanatory Notes to the Money Laundering and Terrorist Financing (Amendment) Regulations 2019
Explanatory Notes to the Proceeds of Crime Act 2002 (Money Laundering: Exceptions to Overseas Conduct Defence) Order 2006, SI 2006/1070
Explanatory Notes to the Proceeds of Crime HC Bill (2001–02) [31]
Explanatory Notes to the Serious Crime Act 2015
Justice and Security Act 2013
The Money Laundering and Terrorist Financing (Amendment) Regulations 2019, SI 2019/1511
The Money Laundering Regulations 2007, SI 2007/2157
The Money Laundering, Terrorist Financing and Transfer of Funds (Information on the Payer) Regulations 2017, SI 2017/692
Prevention of Terrorism Act 2005
Proceeds of Crime Act 1995
Proceeds of Crime Act 2002
Proceeds of Crime Act 2002 (Recovery of Cash in Summary Proceedings: Minimum Amount) Order 2006, SI 2006/1699
Sanctions and Anti-Money Laundering Act 2018
Serious Crime Act 2007
Serious Crime Act 2015
Serious Organised Crime and Police Act 2005
Terrorism Act 2000
The Terrorism Act 2000 and Proceeds of Crime Act 2002 (Amendment) Regulations 2007
Terrorism Act 2006
Terrorism (United Nations Measures) Order 2006
Terrorism (United Nations Measures) Order 2009
Terrorist Asset-Freezing (Temporary Provisions) Act 2010

Cases (United Kingdom)

National Crime Agency v Baker [2020] EWHC 822 (Admin)
National Crime Agency v Hajiyeva [2018] EWHC 2534 (Admin)
Tesco Supermarkets Ltd v Nattrass [1972] AC 153 (HL)

5 The Institutional AML Composition of Türkiye

5.1 Introduction

Having outlined the respective AML legal frameworks of the two jurisdictions in Chapters 3 and 4, it is imperative to look at the essential differences between the Turkish and British institutional AML frameworks. Although Türkiye and the UK have established their organisational AML structures according to the international minimum standards, there remain characteristics peculiar to them associated with unique socio-legal and political backgrounds. For example, whilst Türkiye adopts an administrative type of FIU, the UK embraces a law enforcement model of FIU. Each type of these FIUs has unique advantages and disadvantages in tackling ML and its underlying predicates. Therefore, exploring fundamental divergence points of the two systems and the underlying mechanisms that account for such differences may help us understand how those latent features generate diverse AML outcomes for Türkiye and the UK, as evident in the prevalence of dissimilar types of predicate crimes.

Türkiye, as a monist legal jurisdiction,[1] espouses civil law jurisprudence. This characteristic constitutes one of the essential contrasts compared to the UK's legislative and judicial processes. The law tradition adopted (i.e., civil law and common law) signifies, amongst others, the sources where laws originate and how judges operate in a given jurisdiction. As discussed in the next chapter, the UK is a common law jurisdiction with a dualist legal system,[2] suggesting that the legal precedent binds courts in concluding current cases and that international legal instruments need to be implemented by national legislation for effectuation. Court judgements in the UK constitute one of the sources of law, whereas, in Türkiye, they do not play an active role in establishing the legal (AML) framework. In Türkiye, the authority to make laws belongs to the Grand National Assembly of Türkiye (GNAT), along with the executive legal powers vested in the president, as discussed later. Adopting

1 Paul Gragl, *Legal Monism: Law, Philosophy, and Politics* (OUP 2018).
2 John Wheeler and MyiLibrary, *Essentials of the English Legal System* (2nd edn, Pearson Longman 2006).

DOI: 10.4324/9781003466680-5

a monist legal system provides Türkiye with an accelerated response mechanism for harmonising the domestic legal (AML) framework with the international AML instruments as they enter into force automatically once they are signed.[3] However, being a civil law jurisdiction may diversify court decisions, including ML and predicate crime cases, across the judicature contrast with common-law territories as judges therein follow previous judgements given by the higher courts.[4]

The operational dimension of tackling ML and its predicates is incumbent on LEAs and the FIU of the jurisdiction. Whilst LEAs undertake preventive measures autonomously against the commission of any crime, including ML and associated predicates, as an entrenched practice of their conventional course of action, when a crime occurs, they perform as judicial security forces under the supervision of public prosecutors. Whilst the General Command of Gendarmerie (GCG) and the General Directorate of Security (GDS) have specific departments (i.e., KOMs) for combatting smuggling and organised crime, the Coast Guard Command (CGC) and the Customs Enforcement (CE) do not have such units dedicated to counter ML and its underlying predicates as well developed as KOMs of the GCG and the GDS. Considering the most prevalent predicate crimes in Türkiye (i.e., drug trafficking, migrant smuggling, human trafficking, and fuel smuggling, as identified in the NRA),[5] as well as the transnational and functional aspects of those crimes, this institutional choice, at least to some extent, appears to be unaccommodating. In other words, this organisational preference may be accountable, at least partly, for the prevalence of the previously mentioned predicate offence types. For example, the CE prevented the smuggling of approximately 17 tons of fuel and 8.8 tons of illicit drugs in 2019, 79 kg of which is cocaine as caught at a seaport in Istanbul following simultaneous intelligence exchanging with British LEAs.[6] The CGC intervened in 1,761 irregular migration incidents in 2019 (624 in 2020) concerning 60,802 (20,380 in 2020) migrants, and thereby caught 80 smugglers/traffickers (53 in 2020).[7] These figures suggest that the CGC and the CE would benefit from well-developed/dedicated specific units to counter the associated ML problem with these and alike predicate offences.

3 Constitution of the Republic of Türkiye 1982, art 90(5).

4 Neil Duxbury, *The Nature and Authority of Precedent* (CUP 2008).

5 FATF, 'Anti-Money Laundering and Counter-Terrorist Financing Measures – Turkey: Mutual Evaluation Report' (December 2019) para 88 <www.fatf-gafi.org/media/fatf/documents/reports/mer4/Mutual-Evaluation-Report-Turkey-2019.pdf> accessed 18 January 2023.

6 TC Ticaret Bakanlığı Gümrükler Muhafaza Genel Müdürlüğü, '2019 Faaliyet Raporu' (2020) 15 <https://muhafaza.ticaret.gov.tr/data/5d31b1ee13b876092c062161/faaliyet%20raporu_2019%20(1).pdf> accessed 7 January 2021.

7 TC İçişleri Bakanlığı Sahil Güvenlik Komutanlığı, 'Düzensiz Göç İstatistikleri: 2019–2020 Yılları Tüm Denizlere Ait Kıyaslamalı Düzensiz Göç İstatistikleri' <www.sg.gov.tr/duzensiz-goc-istatistikleri> accessed 7 January 2021.

The Turkish FIU, MASAK, operates as a central administrative hub between the financial sector and the aforementioned authorities, thereby receiving suspicious activity transactions which may be forwarded to the prosecution authorities. Its administrative character intrinsically deprives this pivotal unit of law enforcement and judicial powers, thereby rendering the communication, collaboration, and cooperation procedures between all AML components extremely significant. However, as discussed later, whilst LEAs of Türkiye are organisationally dispersed across the country, MASAK operates from a single centre and does not have any affiliated units, the creation of which would facilitate such interconnections between those authorities. Interestingly, the Coordination Board for Combatting Financial Crimes (CBCFC) does not have any representatives of the GCG and the CGC, two critical LEAs of the jurisdiction, in combatting the phenomenon. Therefore, it is necessary to examine whether and how these institutional compositions mentioned earlier may impact the fight against ML and its predicates in Türkiye.

This chapter begins by explaining the judicial composition of Türkiye by focusing particularly on the criminal courts which have the competence to hear ML and associated predicate crime cases. It also investigates whether and what qualifications judges hold sitting in judgement at those judicial institutions, as well as their *modus operandi* relating, amongst others, to their independence. The chapter then examines the legal sources of the jurisdiction and the hierarchy between them. It also outlines the working principles of the Turkish legislative body and the law-making process in Türkiye. In doing so, it aims to highlight how long enacting a particular AML legal instrument may take, thereby giving insight into whether Türkiye can keep pace with the international developments in the AML sphere and address them promptly. The discussion then turns to the institutional structures of the Turkish LEAs and the FIU. It analyses if and to what extent the LEAs in Türkiye have structured their AML units; how they operate individually and jointly (e.g., JITs); how these organisational arrangements may enhance or diminish their effectiveness; and what particular areas require reform to reinforce the current AML/CTF exercises. Likewise, through the same lenses, it analyses how MASAK performs; whether and how it has created PPPs; how this type of FIU contributes to or stands in the way of the effectiveness; and what constitutes an obstacle for this FIU in carrying out its AML functions. By investigating such disparities, this chapter addresses the main research aim of demonstrating whether and how differences between the institutional AML structures may impact the effectiveness in tackling and the prevalence of predicate crimes, thereby underlining the unique features of an optimum AML regime. In other words, this chapter aims to address the last two research questions, in particular, exploring (i) how an institutional AML structure may affect the prevalence of certain types of predicate crimes; and (ii) the areas in need of reform to ensure optimum AML effectiveness in addressing such offences. Accordingly, it investigates whether the role of the current institutional AML structure of Türkiye contributes to its effectiveness in tackling the highest-risk predicate crimes (e.g., illicit drug trafficking as identified in the NRA).[8]

5.2 Judicial Composition of Türkiye

The legal rules in Türkiye innately consist of codified legal instruments as it is a civil law jurisdiction. In other words, prior judicial decisions neither constitute the essential source of law nor bind courts or judges in deciding subsequent cases. However, it is necessary to underline that the legal precedent, in unequivocal terms, provides guidance for the judiciary. Article 1 of Turkish Civil Code 2001, for instance, sets forth, *inter alia*, that 'the judge benefits from scientific opinions and judicial decisions when making decisions'.[9] Nevertheless, as the close examination of this clause connotes, the wording of the provision does not obligate the judiciary to adhere to the case law; rather, as a recommendation, it envisages that the precedence, as well as scientific facts, may be taken into consideration in the decision-making process in the interest of consistency and justice. As a predictable consequence of the non-binding nature of preceding judicial decisions, the judicial outcomes on the same or similar matters, such as on ML cases, may diversify across the spectrum of courts. For that very reason, however, it needs to be mentioned that the higher courts are empowered to deliver final judgements in such disputes between courts. More specifically, the Constitution of the Turkish Republic (hereinafter the Constitution) 1982 envisages the judicial power as one of the principal organs of Türkiye, whereby it determines the higher courts through Articles 146 to 158. The higher courts in Türkiye are:

a) *Anayasa Mahkemesi* (the Constitutional Court/Articles 146 to 153);
b) *Yargıtay* (the High Court of Appeals/Article 154);
c) *Danıştay* (the Council of State/Article 155); and
d) *Uyuşmazlık Mahkemesi* (the Court of General Disputes/Article 158).[10]

The High Court of Appeals is 'the last instance for revising decisions and judgements given by judicial courts and which are not referred by law to other judicial authority; [i]t is also the first and last instance for handling particular cases prescribed by law'.[11] In alignment, the Council of State is 'the last instance for revising decisions and judgements given by administrative courts and which are not referred by law to other administrative courts; [i]t is also the first and last instance for handling particular cases prescribed by law'.[12] Finally,

8 FATF (n 5) para 88.
9 Law No 4721 (Turkish Civil Code) 2001, art 1.
10 Constitution of the Republic of Türkiye 1982.
11 ibid art 154(1).
12 ibid art 155(1).

'[t]he Court of General Disputes is authorised to absolutely resolve the dispute between the judicial and administrative judicial authorities concerning their jurisdiction and decisions'.[13] Therefore, these provisions enable higher courts for reviewing any decisional conflicts of the relevant courts so as to ensure the judicial harmonisation. Furthermore, it should be noted that the High Court of Appeals and the Council of State's decisions on the unification of (conflicting) judgements do mandate judges to comply with, as an exception for the non-obligatory disposition of case law in Türkiye. More specifically, 'the decisions on the unification of judgements bind the Court of Appeal's General Assembly, its chambers and the courts of justice on similar legal matters'.[14] Likewise, the Council of State's chambers and boards, administrative courts, and the administration shall comply with such decisions of the Council of State.[15] Finally, it needs to be also emphasised that the Constitutional Court is characterised as *primus inter pares* as the Constitution sets forth:

> If a court which is ruling a case considers that the provisions of the law or the Presidential Decree to be applied are unconstitutional, or if it is convinced of the gravity of a claim of unconstitutionality alleged by one of the parties, then it shall postpone the consideration of the case until the Constitutional Court decides on this issue.[16]

After this brief introduction to the higher courts of the jurisdiction, it is appropriate to outline the full range of courts and the hierarchy between them to elaborate on and express the courts dealing with ML cases and the predicate crimes, and to investigate whether and how they differentiate in handling those offences. The judicial organs in Türkiye can be classified into four categories as comprising:

a) The Constitutional Court;
b) Civil and criminal courts;
c) Administrative courts; and
d) Courts of dispute.

Additionally, civil, criminal, and administrative courts are categorised as three instances of courts. Whilst civil and criminal courts constitute the first instance judicial courts,[17] regional courts of appeal, on the other hand, compose the second instance courts of the jurisdiction in this context.[18] Similarly, admin-

13 ibid art 158(1).
14 Law No 2797 on the High Court of Appeals 1983, art 45(5).
15 Law No 2575 on the Council of State 1982, art 40(4).
16 Constitution of the Republic of Türkiye 1982, art 152(1).
17 Law No 5235 on the Establishment, Duties, and Jurisdiction of First Instance Courts and Regional Courts of Appeal 2004, art 2.
18 ibid art 3.

istrative and tax courts are determined as the first instance courts, whereas regional courts of appeal are dedicated as the second instance administrative courts.[19] Lastly, Articles 154(1) and 155(1) of the Constitution 1982 authorise the High Court of Appeal and the Council of State as the last instance courts in judicial and administrative matters, respectively. Therefore, the courts in Türkiye can be classified into three instances as comprising:

a) *Hukuk ve Ceza Mahkemeleri/İdare ve Vergi Mahkemeleri* (Civil and Criminal Courts/Administrative and Tax Courts – i.e., courts of the first instance);
b) *Bölge Adliye Mahkemeleri* (Regional Courts of Appeal – i.e., courts of the second instance); and
c) *Yargıtay ve Danıştay* (The High Court of Appeal and the Council of State – i.e., the last instance courts).

Finally, it is necessary to provide more information on the criminal courts as they are responsible for dealing with ML as well as underlying predicate crime cases. It should be noted that Article 10 of Law No 5235 2004 envisages the establishment of *Sulh Ceza Hakimliği* (the Criminal Judgeship of Peace),[20] albeit not being a court. Accordingly, the criminal courts in Türkiye are divided into three categories as:

a) *Asliye Ceza Mahkemeleri* (Criminal Courts of General Jurisdiction);
b) *Ağır Ceza Mahkemeleri* (Aggravated Felony Courts); and
c) *İhtisas Mahkemeleri* (Specialised Criminal Courts).[21]

The duties of the Criminal Courts of General Jurisdiction consist, with reservation of the circumstances where the judgeships and courts are specifically prescribed by law, of 'handling the cases and proceedings which do not fall under the jurisdiction of criminal judgeships of peace and aggravated felony courts'.[22] The duties of Aggravated Felony Courts comprise, with reservation of the circumstances specially prescribed by law, handling criminal cases stipulated in TCC 2004 and Law No 3713 on the Fight against Terrorism 1991 and crimes which entail aggravated life imprisonment, life imprisonment, and imprisonment of more than ten years.[23] The relevant criminal offences envisaged in the TCC 2004 include robbery (*yağma*) (Article 148); extortion (*irtikap*) (Articles 250(1) and 250(2)); forgery of official documents (*resmi*

19 Law No 2577 on the Procedure of Administrative Justice 1982, art 45.
20 Law No 5235 on the Establishment, Duties, and Jurisdiction of First Instance Courts and Regional Courts of Appeal 2004, art 10.
21 ibid art 8.
22 ibid art 11.
23 ibid art 12.

belgede sahtecilik) (Article 204(2)); aggravated fraud (*nitelikli dolandırıcılık*) (Article 158); and fraudulent bankruptcy (*hileli iflas*) (Article (161)) as well as the criminal offences determined in Chapters Four to Seven of Part Four of Second Volume of Turkish Criminal Code, excluding Articles 318, 319, 323,[24] 324, 325, and 332.[25] Considering these crimes, dealing with particular predicate offences, such as robbery, extortion, and fraudulent bankruptcy, fall under the jurisdiction of Aggravated Felony Courts. Nevertheless, given the myriad range of predicate crimes, it can be stated that the underlying predicate offences are heard generally before Criminal Courts of General Jurisdiction. The specialised courts referred to as other courts under Article 8 of Law No 5235 2004 include, amongst others, juvenile courts, juvenile heavy penal courts,[26] civil and criminal courts of intellectual and industrial property rights,[27] and debt enforcement courts.[28] Therefore, in circumstances where the offenders of ML crimes or its predicates are juveniles, these cases are heard before the relevant specialised courts. Finally, court hearings are held publicly, with reservation of the circumstances where an open session can endanger the public morals or security and the situations where the trial is of juveniles;[29] and all court decisions must be written and include the legal base and justification for the judgement.[30]

Additionally, it is necessary to provide the structure of the Criminal Courts of General Jurisdiction and Aggravated Felony Courts and explain whether and what the required qualifications for the judges of these courts are. Law No 5235 2004 determines the establishment of the criminal courts whereby it envisages, amongst others, the geographic location they shall be established and the number of judges they shall be composed of. It sets forth that 'criminal courts shall be established in each provincial centre and in the districts designated in accordance with the regional geographic conditions and workload, by the Ministry of Justice (MoJ) upon the positive opinion of the (High) Council of Judges and Prosecutors'.[31] In other words, there is no locational difference regarding the establishment of these courts. However, whilst the

24 Official Gazette No 30145 dated 5 August 2017, 'Hakimler ve Savcılar Kurulu Birinci Dairesinin Kararı (Karar No: 1069)' <www.resmigazete.gov.tr/eskiler/2017/08/20170805-2.pdf> accessed 12 January 2023.

25 Law No 5235 on the Establishment, Duties, and Jurisdiction of First Instance Courts and Regional Courts of Appeal 2004, art 12.

26 Law No 5395 on the Juvenile Protection 2005, art 25.

27 Law No 6769 (Industrial Property Law) 2016, art 156(1). In alignment, Article 76 of Law No 5846 (Intellectual and Artistic Works Law) 1951 refers to Article 156 of Law No 6769 (Industrial Property Law) 2016.

28 These courts handle the cases regarding the offences prescribed under Articles 331 to 345 of Law No 2004 (Debt Enforcement and Bankruptcy Code) 1932.

29 Constitution of the Republic of Türkiye 1982, arts 141(1) and 141(2).

30 ibid art 141(3).

31 Law No 5235 on the Establishment, Duties, and Jurisdiction of First Instance Courts and Regional Courts of Appeal 2004, art 9(1).

Criminal Courts of General Jurisdiction shall have a single judge,[32] Aggravated Felony Courts shall have one president and adequate number of members and assemble with one president and two members.[33] Furthermore, it needs to be noted that the Aggravated Felony Courts give their decisions through deliberations on a majority of votes basis. Understanding the decision and judgement procedures followed by these courts requires the examination CPC 2004, which determines, *inter alia*, the decision and judgement procedures. It stipulates that only those judges who are going to participate in the decision and the judgement shall be present at the deliberations.[34] The president shall lead the deliberations.[35] Regarding the procedure for collecting votes, the presiding judge, starting from the most junior judge, shall collect them separately and declare his vote at the end (Article 229(1)). Any of the judges, including the president, cannot abstain from voting on any subject or problem, by stating being in the minority (Article 229(2)). In circumstances where the votes diverge, then the majority is achieved by adding the most unfavourable vote against the accused to the vote, which is closest to this opinion (Article 229(3)).[36] In light of these judgement procedures adopted in the two courts and considering the limited experience levels of judges sitting in first instance courts, authorising Aggravated Felony Courts rather than Criminal Courts of General Jurisdiction for hearing ML cases would be an appropriate approach.[37]

Given the close correlation between respect for the rule of law and judicial independence, which are prerequisites for democracy,[38] another significant point to be underlined about the decision and judgement *modus operandi* is the independence of judges. This crucial necessity ensuring the independence and impartiality of judges in concluding the cases they hear is guaranteed by the Constitution. The Constitution 1982 stipulates that judges shall be independent in carrying out their duties; they shall adjudicate following the Constitution, laws, and their conviction conforming to the legal instruments (Article 138(1)). Further, it proscribes any authority or individual from giving orders or instructions to courts or judges concerning the use of judicial power via any means (Article 138(2)). Article 138(3) outlaws asking questions, holding debates, or making statements in the Legislative Assembly concerning the use of judicial power relating to a case under trial. Finally, Article

32 ibid art 9(2).
33 ibid art 9(3).
34 Law No 5271 (Criminal Procedure Code) 2004, art 227(1).
35 ibid art 228.
36 ibid art 229.
37 Türkiye recently assigned certain Criminal Courts of General Jurisdiction as specialised money laundering courts on 24 June 2021. However, the impacts of this institutional amendment are yet to be seen. See Official Gazette No 31522 dated 25 June 2021, 'Hakimler ve Savcılar Kurulu Birinci Dairesinin Kararı – Karar No: 485' <www.resmigazete.gov.tr/eskiler/2021/06/20210625-15.pdf> accessed 28 May 2023.
38 BC Smith, *The Rule of Law and Judicial Independence* (1st edn, Routledge 2017).

138(4) mandates any authorities to comply with court decisions without any alteration or adjournment of their execution.[39] Article 139 determines the security of tenure of judges and public prosecutors by setting forth, amongst others, that they cannot be dismissed or retired unless they request so before the age specified by the Constitution, which is the age of 65,[40] and they cannot be deprived of any of their status-related rights, even as a consequence of the abolishment of a court or a post.[41] In other words, there remains no external influence in theory that may affect the outcomes of court hearings, including ML and the underlying predicate crime cases, as the legal instruments, including the Constitution, secure the independence of judges.

It is also necessary to discuss how a court's duty is determined. Regardless of the aggravating or mitigating circumstances, the upper limit of the penalty of the criminal offence prescribed in the law determines the relevant court's duty.[42] Therefore, whilst predicate crimes that entail more than ten years imprisonment fall under the jurisdiction of Aggravated Felony Courts, the trial of the majority of those crimes is the responsibility of the Criminal Courts of General Jurisdiction. Accordingly, hearing ML cases falls under the jurisdiction of the Criminal Courts of General Jurisdiction as the upper limit of the penalty envisaged is seven years.[43]

In terms of eligibility of judges to be assigned to the aforementioned courts and the first instance administrative courts, they need to carry the prescribed qualifications upon accomplishing the candidature process.[44] More precisely, 'the (High) Council of Judges and Prosecutors shall decide on accepting trainees to the profession who pass the written and oral exam at the end of the pre-service training, provided that they have no obstacle to acceptance'.[45] The working place of judicial judiciary professionals, as well as working place and posts of the administrative judiciary professionals shall be determined by the (High) Council of Judges and Prosecutors by casting lots, taking into consideration the needs of the judicial and the administrative judiciary and as well as trainees' family status.[46] In other words, judges can be assigned to the first instance courts regardless of their legal experience. Nonetheless, it needs to be mentioned that the second instance courts require some qualifications for the judges and prosecutors to be appointed. More specifically, legal professionals shall be in the first category and have not lost the necessary qualifications

39 Constitution of the Republic of Türkiye 1982, art 138.
40 ibid art 140.
41 ibid art 139.
42 Law No 5235 on the Establishment, Duties, and Jurisdiction of First Instance Courts and Regional Courts of Appeal 2004, art 14.
43 Law No 5237 (Turkish Criminal Code) 2004, art 282(1). See (n 790).
44 Law No 2802 on Judges and Public Prosecutors 1983, arts 7 to 14.
45 ibid art 13(1).
46 ibid art 13(2).

for being selected for the first category[47] to qualify for the assignment to the Regional Courts of Appeal as the president or heads of chambers.[48] Similarly, they shall be designated at least for the first category and have not lost the necessary qualifications for being selected for the first category to qualify for being appointed as a chamber member.[49] Finally, this appointment is made by the (High) Council of Judges and Prosecutors from amongst the judges and prosecutors of judicial jurisdiction.[50] Likewise, the chief public prosecutor of the Regional Court of Appeal to be appointed shall be a judge or prosecutor of judicial jurisdiction, be at the first category, and have not lost the necessary qualifications for being selected for the first category.[51] For this assignment, a public prosecutor shall be a judge or prosecutor of the same jurisdiction with at least an eight-year *de facto* judicial experience as a judge and/or a prosecutor.[52] Similarly, this appointment is made by the (High) Council of Judges and Prosecutors from amongst the aforementioned judges and prosecutors.[53] In other words, the current appointment mechanism appears to be fit for its purpose, albeit having some limitations. The most salient drawback is that the judiciary does not have a specific strategy in appointing judges and prosecutors, which would allow them to develop subject-specific expertise in ML and associated predicate crime cases. Considering the sophisticated nature of such legal proceedings, originating a nomination policy would admittedly increase the identification of intricate ML schemes, thereby enhancing the recovery figures of proceeds of the crime.

Given that 'justice delayed is justice denied',[54] before scrutinising the legal sources of the jurisdiction and explaining the hierarchy between them, it is appropriate to express the workload of the judges, as it may affect the success rate in handling criminal offences, including ML and its predicates. As the average time required for concluding a criminal case has exponentially increased following the coup attempt in 2016 (i.e., less than eight months before 2016 and consistently more than nine months after 2016),[55] the necessary period for deciding an ML or the underlying predicate crime case has increased for

47 Being selected for the first category requires the judges and prosecutors, *inter alia*, to serve as a judge and/or a prosecutor at least for ten years. See Law No 2802 on Judges and Public Prosecutors 1983, art 32.

48 Law No 5235 on the Establishment, Duties, and Jurisdiction of First Instance Courts and Regional Courts of Appeal 2004, art 43.

49 ibid.

50 ibid.

51 ibid art 44.

52 ibid.

53 ibid.

54 Stefan Voigt, 'Determinants of Judicial Efficiency: A Survey' (2016) 42(2) European Journal of Law and Economics 183.

55 TC Adalet Bakanlığı Adli Sicil ve İstatistik Genel Müdürlüğü, 'Adli İstatistikler 2019' (2020) 31 <https://adlisicil.adalet.gov.tr/Resimler/SayfaDokuman/1062020170359HizmeteOzel-2019-baskı-İSA.pdf> accessed 15 January 2023.

the judiciary correspondingly. Nevertheless, it needs to be noted that Türkiye has aptly raised the number of judges and prosecutors over time. According to the most recent available data, there were 10,274 judges in the criminal, civil, and administrative courts in 2019.[56] The number of cases brought to courts was almost 7.7 million in the same period, 758 of which were ML lawsuits with 326 convictions in the end, and the number of litigations per judge was 747.[57] More specifically, as of the end of 2019, there were 20,629 judiciary personnel in Türkiye, consisting of 14,064 judges and 6,565 public prosecutors, suggesting that the average of judges per 100,000 people is 16.9, whereas the prosecutor average is 7.9.[58] According to a 2020 CoE report, the number of professional judges per 100,000 inhabitants was 15.6 in Türkiye in 2018,[59] indicating a continuous increase in this context in recent years. Furthermore, the MoJ has initiated a programme called *Yargıda Hedef Süre* as of 1 January 2019: accordingly, the parties of a relevant case, including the defendants, plaintiffs, complainants, advocates, and those who suffer from crime, are notified of the trial and investigation conclusion periods.[60] Within the scope of the initiative, for 1,438 types of cases and 220 investigative crime types, including ML and underlying predicate crimes, the target period has been envisaged.[61] Accordingly, the maximum conclusion period for all criminal cases is determined as ten to 13 months. For instance, according to the project, the Chief Public Prosecutor's Office should conclude the investigation of a robbery offence, a predicate crime, in three months.[62] In alignment, the Constitution 1982 tasks the judiciary with minimising both the required period and the expenditure for concluding trials.[63] In other words, the judiciary of Türkiye endeavours to conclude all cases in an optimum period. Given that ML and its predicates deteriorate the economy,[64] the integrity of the

56 Ministry of Justice General Directorate of Judicial Record and Statistics, 'Judicial Statistics 2019' (August 2020) 9 <https://adlisicil.adalet.gov.tr/Resimler/SayfaDokuman/1092020162733adalet_ist-2019.pdf> accessed 1 February 2023.

57 ibid 97, 111.

58 TC Adalet Bakanlığı Strateji Geliştirme Başkanlığı, '2019 Yılı Bakanlık Faaliyet Raporu' (Şubat 2020) 12 <https://sgb.adalet.gov.tr/Resimler/Dokuman/16720201409152019%20Yılı%20Bakanlık%20Faaliyet%20Raporu.pdf> accessed 15 January 2023.

59 Council of Europe, 'European Judicial Systems CEPEJ Evaluation Report: 2020 Evaluation Cycle (2018 Data)' (September 2020) 46 <https://rm.coe.int/evaluation-report-part-1-english/16809fc058> accessed 19 August 2023.

60 ibid.

61 TC Adalet Bakanlığı Basın ve Halkla İlişkiler Müşavirliği, 'Yargıda Yeni Dönem' (2 January 2019) <https://basin.adalet.gov.tr/yargida-yeni-donem> accessed 15 January 2023.

62 ibid.

63 Constitution of the Republic of Türkiye 1982, art 141(4).

64 Vito Tanzi, 'Macroeconomic Implications of Money Laundering' in Ernesto U Savona (ed), *Responding to Money Laundering: International Perspectives* (1st edn, Routledge 1997); Sisira Dharmasri Jayasekara, 'Deficient Regimes of Anti-Money Laundering and Countering the Financing of Terrorism: An Analysis of Short Term Economic Implications' (2020) 23(3) Journal of Money Laundering Control 663.

criminal justice system, and diminish public confidence in the state,[65] concluding relevant trials as soon as possible enables compensating people who suffer from those illicit financial activities in a shorter period, thereby reinforcing the AML ecosystem. Lastly, given that the financial resources allocated to the judicial system can affect judicial efficiency, it is necessary to examine such expenditures. According to the same CoE report mentioned earlier, Türkiye had an approximately 0.22% judicial system budget as a percentage of GDP, which equalled roughly 18 euros per inhabitant in 2018,[66] considerably lower than the budget for the UK judiciary, as discussed later.

5.3 Legal Sources of Türkiye and the Hierarchy Between Them

The interpretation of the legal sources and the hierarchy between them requires a close reading of the Constitution 1982, which is the primary legal source. It sets forth that 'the Constitutional provisions are the essential rules of law binding legislative, executive and judicial bodies, administrative authorities and other organisations and individuals; [l]aws cannot be against the Constitution'.[67]

International treaties duly put into effect follow the Constitution in the hierarchical pyramid as they carry the force of law.[68] In cases where there are disputes between the provisions of international treaties, which were duly put into effect, and the national laws regarding the fundamental rights and freedoms, the international treaty provisions shall be taken as a basis for such circumstances.[69] Therefore, if the international treaties do not contain any provisions regarding the fundamental rights and freedoms (e.g., the right to liberty),[70] the national laws are considered a basis for such situations. It needs also to be emphasised that Articles 17 to 40 of the Constitution guarantee fundamental human rights. Although the implications of international AML legal instruments may arouse concerns over the violations of fundamental rights and freedoms, such as the exchanging of information between FIUs and the use of confiscation powers[71] regarding AML efforts of the jurisdictions, they do not regulate fundamental rights and freedoms. Accordingly, Türkiye

65 Brigitte Unger and Elena Madalina Busuioc, *The Scale and Impacts of Money Laundering* (Edward Elgar Publishing 2007); Joras Ferwerda, 'The Effects of Money Laundering' in Brigitte Unger and Daan van der Linde (eds), *Research Handbook on Money Laundering* (Edward Elgar Publishing 2013).

66 Council of Europe (n 59) 21.

67 Constitution of the Republic of Türkiye 1982, art 11.

68 ibid art 90(5).

69 ibid.

70 The Universal Declaration of Human Rights (UN General Assembly Resolution 217 A) and European Convention on Human Rights (as amended by Protocols Nos 11, 14–15; supplemented by Protocols Nos 1, 4, 6, 7, 12–13, 16).

71 Valsamis Mitsilegas and Niovi Vavoula, 'The Evolving EU Anti-Money Laundering Regime: Challenges for Fundamental Rights and the Rule of Law' (2016) 23(2) Maastricht Journal of European and Comparative Law 261.

holds national laws superior to international treaties in these instances. Hence, the ratification of such international legal instruments should be heeded so as to comply with the global financial system.

The (national) laws follow international agreements duly put into effect in the hierarchical pyramid. The Preamble of the Constitution states, *inter alia*, that:

> [t]he separation of powers does not imply an order of precedence among the organs of State but reflects a civilised division of labour and mode of cooperation restricted to the exercise of specific State powers, and that supremacy is vested solely in the Constitution and the laws.[72]

As the close examination of this paragraph connotes, the supremacy of the Constitution is shared with the laws. However, considering the previously mentioned articles of the Constitution, which determines the hierarchy between itself, the international agreements, and the national laws, their superiority should be interpreted, respectively.

The Constitution had envisaged the *Kanun Hükmünde Kararnameler* (Decrees Having Force of Law/Article 91) and *Tüzükler* (Regulations/Article 115), both of which enacted by the Council of Ministers, as well as *Yönetmelikler* (Bylaws/Article 124) as other legal instruments partaking in the following steps of the hierarchy of norms. However, the Constitution has been considerably modified by the enactment of Law No 6771.[73] Consequently, Articles 91 and 115 of the Constitution have been repealed, and Article 124 has been amended by Article 16 of Law No 6771. Accordingly, the president, the ministries, and public corporate bodies may issue bylaws to ensure the implementation of laws and presidential decrees relating to their jurisdiction as long as they are not contrary to these laws and decrees.[74] Finally, there remain regulations still in force as the temporary provisions of the Constitution stipulate that the decrees and regulations, as well as bylaws and other regulatory procedures legislated by the Prime Minister and the Council of Ministers maintain their validity unless they are nullified.[75] Therefore, the legal instruments of the Republic constituting the national legal hierarchy can be listed by superiority as follows:

a) The Constitution;
b) International treaties duly put into effect;[76]

72 Constitution of the Republic of Türkiye 1982, preamble.

73 Official Gazette No 29976 dated 11 February 2017, 'Türkiye Cumhuriyeti Anayasasında Değişiklik Yapılmasına Dair Kanun (Kanun No 6771)' <www.resmigazete.gov.tr/eskiler/2017/02/20170211-1.htm> accessed 21 January 2023.

74 Constitution of the Republic of Türkiye 1982, art 124(1).

75 ibid temporary art 21(F).

76 In cases where international treaties contain provisions on fundamental rights and freedoms, they are superior to national laws.

c) The national laws (statutes);
d) Presidential Decrees;
e) Regulations; and
f) Bylaws.

The GNAT, founded in the capital of Türkiye, Ankara, on 23 April 1920, is the sole authority in making laws based on the Constitution. The Constitution authorises GNAT as a unicameral legislature by stating that 'legislative authority, on behalf of the Turkish Nation, belongs to the Grand National Assembly of Türkiye; [t]his authority cannot be delegated'.[77] In other words, the entrenched body of legal instruments in Türkiye is predicated solely on GNAT's legislative decisions. However, it needs to be noted as an exception that the president also carries legislative powers, such as issuing presidential decrees,[78] as mentioned previously. Although there is no set time frame for enacting a legal instrument, GNAT made 23 legal instruments in March 2021 alone,[79] evidencing its ability to enact laws swiftly. Furthermore, it is worth noting that the ratified legal instruments come into effect only when they are published in the Official Gazette unless otherwise prescribed by the provisions of the enacted legislative documents. In other words, the Turkish legislation procedure is capable of addressing any international legislative AML amendments swiftly.

5.4 Competent Authorities of Türkiye

Finally, before investigating the UK's corresponding disposition, it is appropriate to examine the essential competent Turkish authorities responsible for tackling ML and its underlying predicates. Although the institutional framework for AML/CTF encompasses a broad range of ministries and institutions, such as Ministry of Trade or Banking Regulation and Supervision Agency, the responsibilities of Ministry of Justice (MoJ), Ministry of Interior (MoI), as well as Ministry of Treasury and Finance (MoTF) are of utmost importance to be elaborated within the scope of this study. More specifically, the role of public prosecutors, the GCG, the CGC, the GDS, and the FIU (i.e., MASAK) are analysed with regard to the organisational AML structure of the country.

Articles 38 to 64 of Presidential Decree No. 1 on the Organisation of the Presidency (Decree No. 1) are devoted to the MoJ, whereby its responsibilities and authorities are determined under Article 38. Accordingly, they include,

77 Constitution of the Republic of Türkiye 1982, art 7.

78 The Constitution of the Republic of Türkiye 1982 determines the duties and powers of the President. See Constitution of the Republic of Türkiye 1982, art 104.

79 Türkiye Büyük Millet Meclisi, 'Kanun Sorgu Sonuçları: Mart 2021' <www.tbmm.gov.tr/develop/owa/kanunlar_sd.sorgu_yonlendirme?Kanun_no=&k_Baslangic_Tarihi=01/03/2021&k_Bitis_Tarihi=31/03/2021&r_Baslangic_Tarihi=&r_Bitis_Tarihi=&sorgu_kelime=> accessed 12 April 2023.

inter alia, establishing and organising the courts and other judiciary institutions and carrying out inspections on their administrative duties (Article 38(1)(a)); carrying out services related to keeping criminal records (Article 38(1)(ç)); undertaking procedures regarding foreign countries in matters related to judicial services (Article 38(1)(d)); and examining the legislative drafts sent by the ministries as to whether they comply with the Turkish Legal System and legislation technique and to provide opinions on these issues (Article 38(1)(f)).[80] Furthermore, carrying out legal procedures with cross-border characteristics (e.g., reciprocity or dual criminality) constitute other critical duties of the Ministry that may affect the country's overall AML efforts.

5.4.1 Law Enforcement Agencies of Türkiye

Türkiye has four LEAs consisting of the General Command of Gendarmerie (GCG), the Coast Guard Command (CGC), the General Directorate of Security (GDS), and the Customs Enforcement (CE). Whilst the CE undertakes its activities under the Ministry of Trade (MoT), the remaining LEAs of the jurisdiction, namely the GCG,[81] the CGC,[82] and the GDS,[83] operate under the auspices of the MoI. Although the CE is a component of the country's organisational AML structure as its duties include combatting smuggling activities,[84] it has no specialised AML unit. In cases where a smuggling incident is detected, upon the first necessary intervention, the CE reports these cases to the relevant judicial LEA and conducts relevant activities in collaboration with the GDS, the GCG, and the CGG as directed by the public prosecutor.[85] The CE carries out its activities at a total of 203 border gates comprising 30 land crossings, eight railway crossings, 101 seaports, and 64 airports.[86] For example, the drug amount seized by the CE at the previously mentioned border gates in 2018, 2019, and 2020 is equivalent to the market value of more than 1 billion TL for each year,[87] which is equal approximately

80 Presidential Decree No 1 on the Organisation of the Presidency 2018, art 38.

81 Law No 2803 on the Organisation, Duties and Powers of the Gendarmerie 1983, art 4.

82 Law No 2692 on the Coast Guard Command 1982, art 2(2).

83 Law No 3201 on the Security Organisation 1937, art 1.

84 TC Ticaret Bakanlığı Gümrükler Muhafaza Genel Müdürlüğü, 'Muhafaza Memurunun Görev, Yetki ve Sorumlulukları' <https://muhafaza.ticaret.gov.tr/gumruk-muhafaza/muhafaza-memuru> accessed 14 January 2023.

85 ibid.

86 TC Ticaret Bakanlığı, 'Ticaret Bakanlığı 2019 Yılı Faaliyet Raporu' (2020) 24 <https://ticaret.gov.tr/data/5e58fdaa13b8764dec3bf81d/TICARET_BAKANLIGI_2019YILI_FAALIYET_RAPORU.pdf> accessed 14 January 2021.

87 TC Ticaret Bakanlığı, 'Türlerine Göre Uyuşturucu Madde Yakalamaları' (December 2020) <https://ticaret.gov.tr/data/5d76399213b8768ba06eaf49/4-Turlerine%20Gore%20Uyusturucu%20Madde%20Yakalamalari.pdf> accessed 14 January 2021.

to GBP 100 million as of January 2021.[88] The monetary value of these illicit assets gives insight into the potential total amount for the proceeds of crime to be laundered. Therefore, Türkiye would benefit from establishing specialised AML units within the CE.

In terms of the remaining LEAs of the jurisdiction, whilst the GDS is responsible for conducting policing in urban areas, the GCG maintains law and order in rural areas,[89] and the CGC carries out policing activities throughout the country's coasts.[90] The primary duties of these authorities, amongst others, include preventing the commission of any offence; and, if committed, capturing the criminals,[91] including money launderers and the offenders of underlying predicate crimes. Their judicial duties start when a crime occurs, and they execute their responsibilities as judicial security forces (*adli kolluk*) on behalf of and following the guidance given by the public prosecutors. More specifically, carrying out interactions concerning the investigation shall be achieved according to the orders and directions of the public prosecutor, primarily by the judicial security forces, and they shall execute these orders on the judicial duties.[92] It is worth underlining here that although LEAs in Türkiye act on behalf of public prosecutors, this does not clash with the separation of powers, nor does it breach the principle of *nemo judex in causa sua*.[93] LEAs in Türkiye do not operate autonomously in prosecutorial matters but rather obey orders given by prosecutors. Therefore, the knowledge and experience of public prosecutors in dealing with ML cases and the relevant predicate crimes become more prominent as they direct LEAs to trail the offenders or the illicit monetary assets. It does not necessarily mean that the public prosecutors do not have essential expertise. That is to say that their specific investigation plans are imperative in setting the direction for LEAs as their sole responsibility, as judicial security forces, is to execute what they order. Therefore, establishing specialised bureaus within the offices of chief public prosecutors, and assigning prosecutors whose principal responsibility is to investigate laundering of proceeds of crime cases would be an appropriate approach. Türkiye has been implementing such a procedure for investigating domestic violence cases.[94]

88 The currency conversion was made on 14 January 2021. See Xe Currency Converter <www.xe.com> accessed 14 January 2021.

89 Law No 2803 on the Organisation, Duties and Powers of the Gendarmerie 1983, art 10.

90 Law No 2692 on the Coast Guard Command 1982, art 4(A).

91 Law No 2803 on the Organisation, Duties and Powers of the Gendarmerie 1983, art 7; Law No 2692 on the Coast Guard Command 1982, art 4; and Law No 2559 on the Powers and Duties of Police 1934, art 2.

92 Law No 5271 (Criminal Procedure Code) 2004, art 164(2).

93 This bedrock principle means that no one should be the judge in his/her own case. See Georg Schwarzenberger, 'The Nemo Judex in Sua Causa Maxim in International Judicial Practice' (1972) 1(4) Anglo-American Law Review 482.

94 See TC Adalet Bakanlığı, 'Genelge No 154/1 Ailenin Korunması ve Kadına Karşı Şiddetin Önlenmesine Dair Kanunun Uygulanması' <https://cigm.adalet.gov.tr/Resimler/SayfaDokuman/18220201432351541-nolu-genelge.pdf> accessed 1 July 2023.

Articles 164 to 169 of CPC 2004 are devoted to judicial security forces,[95] albeit there exists a regulation that envisages, ***inter alia***, their duties in detail. The Judicial Security Forces Regulation, enacted based on Article 167 of TCC 2004,[96] determines the duties of LEAs as the judicial security forces and sets forth the judicial procedures for them. It regulates, amongst others, their working principles, training procedures, and relations with other service units and envisages the qualifications of such forces.[97] Public prosecutors primarily assign judicial security forces to undertake investigation proceedings.[98] Judicial law enforcement officers, in line with the orders and instructions of the public prosecutor, carry out judicial duties without delay.[99] Judicial law enforcement officers shall immediately notify the public prosecutor's office and the highest-ranking law enforcement officer of denunciations or complaints relating to a crime they received, the incidents they have intervened in, the persons captured, and the measures taken.[100] Subsequently, they shall begin the investigation procedures in line with the order of the relevant public prosecutor.[101] Public prosecutors give their orders to judicial security forces in written format unless there is a peril in delay.[102] In cases where the orders are in a verbal format, they shall, if possible, convert them into written form as soon as possible and notify the relevant law enforcement forces through the fastest communication mean available.[103] Otherwise, they shall prepare the written form to be taken by the pertinent law enforcement forces; however, judicial security forces execute what the verbal order requires without waiting for the order to be written.[104] In cases where the judicial security forces catch someone red-handed, or there is a peril in delay, and in circumstances where they cannot access the public prosecutor, or the width of the incident exceeds the workforce of the public prosecutor, the criminal judge of peace may also direct

95 Judicial security forces comprise law enforcement personnel that is determined under (i) Criminal Procedure Law No 5271 2004; (ii) Articles 8, 9, and 12 of Law No 3201 on the Security Organisation 1937; (iii) Article 7 of Law No 2803 on the Organisation, Duties and Powers of the Gendarmerie 1983; (iv) Article 8 of the Decree-Law No 485 on the Establishment and Duties of the Undersecretariat of Customs 1993; (v) Article 4 of the Law No 2692 on the Coast Guard Command 1982; (vi) as well as commander, chief, officer, and other officers assigned per the appointment procedure they are subject to, to carry out the investigation procedures specified in the Regulation on the Duties and Powers of the Gendarmerie Organisation, which was enacted by the Council of Ministers Decision (83/7362) dated 3 November 1983. See Judicial Security Forces Regulation 2005, art 3.

96 Judicial Security Forces Regulation 2005, art 2.

97 ibid art 1.

98 ibid art 6(1).

99 ibid.

100 ibid art 6(2).

101 ibid.

102 ibid art 6(6).

103 ibid.

104 ibid.

the investigation process.[105] In these instances, judicial security forces take the measures ordered and carry out the investigation process accordingly.[106] Judicial security forces, in accordance with the orders of the public prosecutor and as per the provisions of the relevant law, are obliged to collect, protect, and present all evidence in favour or against the suspect, and present them to the public prosecutor by an investigation report to ensure the investigation of the material truth and secure a fair trial.[107] In cases where it is identified that there has been unlawful evidence obtained, this issue shall be included in the investigation report.[108] Judicial security forces shall carry out other investigation activities with the same rigour.[109] In other words, there exists no room for LEAs to act in bias, bolstering the principle of *nemo judex in causa sua*, as touched upon earlier.

Concerning institutional AML structures of LEAs, the GCG and the GDS have specific departments, duties of which also include tackling ML and its predicates. Considering the most prevalent predicate crimes,[110] both the GCG and the GDS have established their dedicated specialised units. For example, in 2019, the GCG intervened in 10,954 illicit drug trafficking cases and thereby captured 17,562 suspects accordingly.[111] However, it is necessary to note that Türkiye administratively consists of 81 cities and 922 districts,[112] each of which hosts both gendarmerie command and directorate of security, either provincial or district, respectively. Furthermore, Türkiye has a land area of 780,043 square kilometres,[113] with a population of approximately 83.2 million people (as of 31 December 2019).[114] It is the responsibility of the GCG to ensure the security and safety of 93% of the land area and 21% of the population.[115] Moreover, the relevant district LEAs also have additional law enforcement stations.

105 ibid art 6(7).
106 ibid.
107 ibid art 6(8).
108 ibid.
109 ibid.
110 The most significant predicate crimes in Türkiye consist of drug trafficking, migrant smuggling, human trafficking, and fuel smuggling, as identified in the NRA. See FATF (n 5) para 88.
111 TC İçişleri Bakanlığı Jandarma Genel Komutanlığı, '2019 Yılı Faaliyet Raporu' (January 2020) 25 <www.jandarma.gov.tr/kurumlar/jandarma.gov.tr/Duyurular/guncel/JGNKLIGI-2019-YILI-FAALIYET-RAPORU.pdf> accessed 12 February 2023.
112 TC İçişleri Bakanlığı, 'Türkiye Mülki İdare Bölümleri Envanteri' <www.e-icisleri.gov.tr/Anasayfa/MulkiIdariBolumleri.aspx> accessed 12 February 2023.
113 TC Millî Savunma Bakanlığı Harita Genel Müdürlüğü, 'İl ve İlçe Yüzölçümleri' <www.harita.gov.tr/il-ve-ilce-yuzolcumleri> accessed 12 February 2023.
114 TURKSTAT, 'The Results of Address Based Population Registration System, 2019' <https://data.tuik.gov.tr/Bulten/Index?p=The-Results-of-Address-Based-Population-Registration-System-2019-33705&dil=2> accessed 12 February 2023.
115 TC İçişleri Bakanlığı Jandarma Genel Komutanlığı, 'Jandarma Sorumluluk Alanları ve Korunan Tesisler' <www.jandarma.gov.tr/jandarma-tarafindan-korunan-tesisler> accessed 12 February 2023.

For instance, currently, the GCG has 1,135 gendarmerie stations.[116] In other words, although the GCG and the GDS have specific departments, it does not seem possible to assign specialists to each LEA throughout the country, unlike the UK's practice (see Chapter 6).

The Department of Public Order (*Asayiş Başkanlığı*) is the principal stakeholder of the GCG in tackling ML and its predicates as it incorporates, *inter alia*, the Anti-Smuggling and Organised Crime Department (*Kaçakçılık ve Organize Suçlarla Mücadele Başkanlığı*/KOM), the Anti-Cyber-Crime Department (*Siber Suçlarla Mücadele Daire Başkanlığı*), the Anti-Smuggling Migrants and Human Trading (*Göçmen Kaçakçılığı ve İnsan Ticaretiyle Mücadele*), and the Counterterrorism Department,[117] each of which has a specific role in ML (and TF) investigations. Although the GCG cannot appoint specialists to each LEA throughout the country, these departments coordinate and supervise the relevant activities of each LEA through the chain of command and provide additional assistance, training, and support. Additionally, all provincial gendarmerie commands have the previously mentioned competent units, such as the Anti-Smuggling and Organised Crime (KOM), at the branch office level. Each district and its affiliated gendarmerie station commands have corresponding sub-level units or responsible personnel conducting relevant AML activities. Furthermore, the activities of all units beginning from the lowest up to the highest level are evaluated periodically through daily, weekly, monthly, and yearly evaluations. For instance, as an entrenched assessment procedure of the gendarmerie *modus operandi*, each provincial gendarmerie command sets up monthly evaluation meetings whereby they evaluate the performance of their affiliated units. The performance indicators comprise, *inter alia*, how many crimes district gendarmerie commands have intervened in, how many suspects they have captured and referred to the judicial authorities, or what they have seized through their relevant actions, including operations within the scope of AML, in a given month.[118] As an illustration, the official website of the GCG provides monthly statistics on all crimes, including ML and its predicates, as performance indicators of the affiliated LEAs. For instance, in terms of smuggling and organised crime, data from December 2020 indicates that from 1–31 December 2020, a total of 2,496 incidents, including 914 smuggling, 174 financial, 1,379 drugs, and 29 organised crime occurred in the GCG's responsibility area; and the number of suspects caught in this period is 4,042.[119] Nevertheless, there were only two

116 TC İçişleri Bakanlığı Jandarma Genel Komutanlığı, '2020 Yılı Performans Programı' 4 <www.jandarma.gov.tr/kurumlar/jandarma.gov.tr/Duyurular/guncel/JGnKligi-2020-Yili-Performans-Programi.pdf> accessed 12 February 2023.

117 TC İçişleri Bakanlığı Jandarma Genel Komutanlığı, 'Asayiş Başkanlığı' <www.jandarma.gov.tr/asayis> accessed 12 February 2023.

118 Personal experience.

119 TC İçişleri Bakanlığı Jandarma Genel Komutanlığı, '2020 Aralık Ayı Verileri' <www.jandarma.gov.tr/2020-aralik-ayi-verileri> accessed 15 February 2023.

incidents in the same period relating to ML out of 2,303 incidents.[120] Therefore, it would be fair to conclude either that the GCG personnel, by detecting a high number of predicate crimes, effectively prevented the occurrence of the ML offence or that they were not productive in identifying ML cases. Additionally, it is worth mentioning that the aforementioned statistics do not cover figures on irregular migration (i.e., the smuggling of migrants and human trading). In December 2020, the GCG personnel intervened in 1,268 irregular migration incidents, whereby they detected 6,421 irregular migrants and captured 100 suspects organising immigrant smugglings. They also acted on three cases relating to human trading and rescued four victims and caught 11 human traders accordingly.[121] It is necessary to underline these aggregates as they may give insight into the effectiveness levels of the GCG personnel in tackling ML and its underlying predicates. However, reports provided by the GCG do not contain any information on asset recovery figures, a significant component of the competency indicators concerning the fight against ML that needs to be addressed accordingly.

Similar to the GCG, the institutional structure of GDS contains several departments designated for tackling ML and the underlying predicate crimes. However, whilst the relevant service units of the GCG serve under the auspices of the Department of Public Order, the GDS has structured them as individual departments. The competent departments of the GDS include the Department of Anti-Smuggling and Organised Crime (*Kaçakçılık ve Organize Suçlarla Mücadele Başkanlığı*/KOM), the Department of Combatting Narcotic Crimes (*Narkotik Suçlarla Mücadele Daire Başkanlığı*), the Department of Combatting Cyber Crimes (*Siber Suçlarla Mücadele Daire Başkanlığı*), the Department of Combatting Smuggling of Migrants and Border Gates (*Göçmen Kaçakçılığı ile Mücadele ve Hudut Kapıları Daire Başkanlığı*), the Department of INTERPOL-Europol, and the Counterterrorism Department.[122] Given the riskiest predicate crimes as identified in the NRA,[123] the focus and establishment of these departments correspond to the volume and number of predicate crimes in these areas. Nevertheless, similar to the GCG's organisation concerning the AML efforts, the Bureau of Combatting Proceeds of Crime (*Suç Gelirleri ile Mücadele Büro Amirliği*) is attached to the GDS's

120 TC İçişleri Bakanlığı Jandarma Genel Komutanlığı, '2020 Aralık Ayı Verileri (KOM-1)' <www.jandarma.gov.tr/kurumlar/jandarma.gov.tr/Veriler/2020/Aralik-2020-Asayis-Verileri.xlsx> accessed 15 February 2023.

121 TC İçişleri Bakanlığı Jandarma Genel Komutanlığı, '2020 Aralık Ayı Verileri (GÖÇMEN)' <www.jandarma.gov.tr/kurumlar/jandarma.gov.tr/Veriler/2020/Aralik-2020-Asayis-Verileri.xlsx> accessed 15 February 2023.

122 TC İçişleri Bakanlığı Emniyet Genel Müdürlüğü, 'Daire Başkanlıkları' <www.egm.gov.tr/daire-baskanliklari> accessed 17 February 2023.

123 These crimes include drug trafficking, migrant smuggling, human trafficking, and fuel smuggling. See FATF (n 5).

Department of Public Order (*Asayiş Daire Başkanlığı*).[124] For instance, as a result of an operation carried out by a Bureau of Combatting Proceeds of Crime in a relatively small city of Türkiye, Şanlıurfa, the court has concluded that 12 suspects have committed the offence of laundering the proceeds of crime. Subsequently, the relevant court has ordered the seizure of ten immovable properties, 31 vehicles, and the bank accounts of 34 real and two legal persons. Consequently, these assets, which equal approximately 4 million TL (approximately GBP 400,000 as of January 2021), were seized, and 15 suspects were arrested accordingly in March 2020.[125] From a broader perspective, the GDS personnel undertook 29 operations against ML/TF in 2019, whereby they captured 155 suspects; and applied seizure procedures in 671 incidents, thereby seized 125 million TL (GBP 12.5 million) accordingly.[126] Nevertheless, similar to reports provided by the GCG, the GDS's bulletins do not include any data on asset recovery figures.

Before proceeding any further, it is necessary to discuss the Department of INTERPOL-Europol as it operates as the National Bureau[127] of the country in coordinating international cooperation in criminal matters, including ML and its underlying predicates. The participation of Türkiye in the global fight against transnational illegal schemes dates back to the early years of the Republic since it became a member of the INTERPOL in 1930 by the Decree bearing the signature of Atatürk, the founder of modern Türkiye.[128] Türkiye has continuously expanded its international collaboration over time, and in 2005, the competent department of the GDS became the Department of INTERPOL-Europol-SIRENE[129] following the cooperation agreement between Türkiye and the European Union Agency for Law Enforcement Cooperation (Europol) dated 18 May 2004.[130] Additionally, Türkiye has been a participant in the international Anti-Money Laundering Operational Network

124 TC İçişleri Bakanlığı Emniyet Genel Müdürlüğü Asayiş Daire Başkanlığı, 'Suç Gelirleri ile Mücadele' <www.asayis.pol.tr/sucgelirleri> accessed 17 February 2023.

125 TC İçişleri Bakanlığı Emniyet Genel Müdürlüğü Asayiş Daire Başkanlığı, 'Suç Gelirleri ile Mücadele Şanlıurfa' (13 March 2020) <www.asayis.pol.tr/13032020-oto-hirsizligi-suc-gelirleri-ile-mucadele-sanliurfa> accessed 17 February 2023.

126 TC İçişleri Bakanlığı Emniyet Genel Müdürlüğü, 'Kaçakçılık ve Organize Suçlarla Mücadele 2019 Raporu' (September 2020) 93–94 <www.egm.gov.tr/kurumlar/egm.gov.tr/IcSite/kom/YAYINLARIMIZ/TÜRKÇE/2019-RAPORU-TR.pdf> accessed 17 February 2023.

127 TC İçişleri Bakanlığı Emniyet Genel Müdürlüğü, 'Interpol-Europol Dairesi Başkanlığı' <www.egm.gov.tr/interpol/hakkimizda> accessed 17 February 2023.

128 Decree No 8761 dated 8 January 1930 <www.egm.gov.tr/kurumlar/egm.gov.tr/IcSite/interpol/Tarihçe/Kararname.PNG> accessed 1 July 2022.

129 Official Gazette No 25747 dated 6 March 2005, 'Bakanlar Kurulu Kararı (Karar No 2005/8496)' <www.resmigazete.gov.tr/eskiler/2005/03/20050306-1.htm> accessed 18 February 2023.

130 Official Gazette No 25523 dated 15 July 2004, 'Türkiye Cumhuriyeti ve Avrupa Polis Teşkilatı Arasında İşbirliğine İlişkin Anlaşma' <www.resmigazete.gov.tr/eskiler/2004/07/20040715.htm#7> accessed 18 February 2023.

(AMON), an initiative operating under the auspices of Europol and aiming at establishing an informal network amongst national AML units of LEAs, since 27 January 2012.[131] It would be appropriate to mention meanwhile that the UK partakes in the steering group of the initiative.[132] Furthermore, Türkiye has been one of the non-EU member jurisdictions with liaison officers at Europol[133] since 21 March 2016.[134] The Department of INTERPOL-Europol of the GDS, as a *strategic* partner of Europol,[135] consists of seven subunits.[136] The duties of the Department of INTERPOL-Europol include, amongst others, ensuring the necessary contact and coordination between relevant domestic and foreign units to effectively combat all kinds of international crimes, carrying out proceedings regarding foreigners who commit crimes in the country, and concerning Turkish citizens who commit crimes abroad or who committed crimes in the country and fled abroad, and relating to persons who commit crimes against the jurisdiction overseas.[137] For instance, during an operation undertaken in collaboration with Europol, Turkish LEAs contributed to the arrest of 47 suspects for labour exploitation and the identification/ protection of 275 victims in 2016 within the scope of preventing trafficking in human beings and facilitation of irregular migration.[138]

AMON is not the only international network devoted to AML efforts supported by Europol. FIU.net, which was incorporated into Europol in

131 Europol, 'International Anti-Money Laundering Operational Network (AMON) Launched' (30 January 2012) <www.europol.europa.eu/newsroom/news/international-anti-money-laundering-operational-network-amon-launched> accessed 21 February 2023.

132 Europol, 'Anti-Money Laundering Experts Call for More International Cooperation' (7 June 2019) <www.europol.europa.eu/newsroom/news/anti-money-laundering-experts-call-for-more-international-cooperation> accessed 21 February 2023.

133 Europol, 'Partners and Agreements' <www.europol.europa.eu/partners-agreements> accessed 21 February 2023.

134 Europol, 'Turkey and Europol Sign Liaison Agreement' (21 March 2016) <www.europol.europa.eu/newsroom/news/turkey-and-europol-sign-liaison-agreement> accessed 21 February 2023.

135 Europol, 'Strategic Agreements' <www.europol.europa.eu/partners-agreements/strategic-agreements> accessed 21 February 2023.

136 These units include International Anti-Smuggling Branch Office, International Anti-Terrorism Branch Office, International Public Security Branch Office, International Legal Aid Branch Office, Strategy Development and Support Branch Office, International Communication and Information Technologies Branch Office, Europol-SIRENE Branch Office, and Presidential Administrative Office. See TC İçişleri Bakanlığı Emniyet Genel Müdürlüğü, 'Interpol-Europol Dairesi Başkanlığı: Organizasyon Şeması' <www.egm.gov.tr/interpol/birimlerimiz> accessed 21 February 2023.

137 TC İçişleri Bakanlığı Emniyet Genel Müdürlüğü, 'Interpol-Europol Dairesi Başkanlığı: Tarihçe' <www.egm.gov.tr/interpol/tarihce> accessed 21 February 2023.

138 Europol, 'International Operation CICONIA ALBA Kicks off to Crack Down on Organised Crime' (20 June 2016) <www.europol.europa.eu/newsroom/news/international-operation-ciconia-alba-kicks-to-crack-down-organised-crime> accessed 21 February 2023.

January 2016,[139] and European Financial and Economic Crime Centre (EFECC), an integral component of Europol that operates as the central repository on EU criminal intelligence, including ML cases,[140] are additional initiatives performing within the Europol. FIU.net, similar to its global counterpart, Egmont Group, endeavours to conglomerate and organise national AML efforts of the EU MS at the Union level.[141] EFECC primarily aims to provide the EU MS with a 'pan-European platform' in tackling financial and economic crime.[142] That is to say that although Türkiye has established a close collaboration with Europol regarding AML efforts, its cooperation cannot be absolute intrinsically as it is not an organic part of the EU. Therefore, it would be an appropriate approach for Türkiye to reinforce the Department of INTERPOL-Europol, thereby intensifying its international participation in the fight against ML and its underlying predicates, which would also benefit the EU, as well as the global AML realm.

Although the GDS has a dedicated unit for combatting ML, the fight against organised crime, smuggling, financial crimes, and ML has primarily been undertaken by KOM since 1981[143] as the principal department of the GDS in this context. Therefore, KOM constitutes the core unit of the GDS, coordinating and confronting AML efforts of the LEA. The GDS KOM has affiliated divisions as KOM Branch Directorates in 78 provincial directorates of security and KOM Group Chief Offices in 44 district police departments.[144] It further incorporates the Directorate of Combatting Financial Crimes, the Directorate of Combating Smuggling Crimes, and the Directorate of Combating Organised Crime located in the remaining three big provinces of Türkiye, namely in Ankara, Istanbul, and Izmir.[145] KOM conducted 29 operations in 2019 and captured 155 suspects within the scope of AML (and CTF) efforts, as mentioned previously.[146] Furthermore, it embodies the Turkish International Academy Against Drugs and Organised Crime (TADOC) – an in-service training academy that organises national, regional, and international specialist training in the fight against smuggling, economic, and organised crime – which was established on 26 January 2000 in cooperation with

139 Europol, 'Europol Joins Forces With EU FIUs to Fight Terrorist Financing and Money Laundering' (28 January 2016) <www.europol.europa.eu/about-europol/financial-intelligence-units-fiu-net#fndtn-tabs-0-bottom-1> accessed 23 February 2023.

140 Europol, 'European Financial and Economic Crime Centre (EFECC)' <www.europol.europa.eu/about-europol/european-financial-and-economic-crime-centre-efecc> accessed 23 February 2023.

141 Europol (n 139).

142 Europol (n 140).

143 TC İçişleri Bakanlığı Emniyet Genel Müdürlüğü, 'Kaçakçılık ve Organize Suçlarla Mücadele Dairesi Başkanlığı: Tarihçe ve Tanıtım' <www.egm.gov.tr/kom/baskanligimiz-tarihce-ve-tanitim> accessed 23 February 2023.

144 ibid.

145 ibid.

146 TC İçişleri Bakanlığı Emniyet Genel Müdürlüğü (n 126).

UNODC.[147] Considering the significance of specialised personnel in combatting ML and its predicates, TADOC's training organisations are of utmost importance. It has organised 137 national and 35 international training programmes, and approximately 4,500 personnel have attended those activities,[148] an indicator of the LEAs' development efforts regarding the country's AML competency. The education programmes organised by KOM in coordination with TADOC include 'expertise in combatting the proceeds of crime', 'financial crime investigations', and 'combatting money laundering and financing of terrorism'.[149] The official website of the GDS provides further statistical information on their activities. For example, in 2019, the GDS KOM conducted 11,389 operations regarding combatting smuggling and 563 operations concerning battling organised crime and smuggling of weapons and ammunition, and 17,995 and 3,987 suspects were caught in these operations, respectively.[150] Nevertheless, there is no available data that indicate asset recovery figures neither in the GDS reports nor in the GCG bulletins, which render any evaluation far from comprehending the actual effectiveness of a given LEA.

5.4.2 Turkish Financial Intelligence Unit – MASAK (Mali Suçları Araştırma Kurulu)

The limited access of LEAs to the relevant data on financial activities and their limited capacity for analysing financial information[151] render it inevitable to establish FIUs. Considering these necessities and the globally threatening nature of these crimes, the Egmont Group exhorts the global financial world to create national FIUs to gather, analyse, and disseminate such data and provide inter-state information exchange in combatting ML and its predicates.[152] In alignment with the Egmont Group's call for setting up national FIUs, also the FATF recommends instituting these cardinal actors.[153] It is worth reiterating here that both organisations define FIU as 'a national centre for the receipt and analysis of: (a) suspicious transaction reports; and (b) other information relevant to money laundering, associated predicate offences and

147 TC İçişleri Bakanlığı Emniyet Genel Müdürlüğü, '2019 Faaliyet Raporu' (2020) 22 <www.egm.gov.tr//kurumlar/egm.gov.tr/IcSite/strateji/Planlama/2019-IDARE-FAALIYET-RAPORU.pdf> accessed 24 February 2023.

148 ibid.

149 TC İçişleri Bakanlığı Emniyet Genel Müdürlüğü (n 126) 95.

150 TC İçişleri Bakanlığı Emniyet Genel Müdürlüğü (n 147) 20.

151 Barry Rider, 'Intelligent Investigations: The Use and Misuse of Intelligence – A Personal Perspective' (2013) 20(3) Journal of Financial Crime 293.

152 Egmont Group, 'Financial Intelligence Units' <https://egmontgroup.org/about/financial-intelligence-units/> accessed 2 July 2023.

153 FATF, 'International Standards on Combatting Money Laundering and the Financing of Terrorism & Proliferation: The FATF Recommendations' (Updated March 2022) Recommendation 29 <www.fatf-gafi.org/media/fatf/documents/recommendations/pdfs/FATF%20Recommendations%202012.pdf> accessed 26 June 2023.

terrorist financing, and for the dissemination of the results of that analysis'.[154] In response to these concerns, Türkiye established its national FIU, MASAK, in Ankara on 19 November 1996 by enacting Law No 4208 1996, and this pivotal structure became operational on 17 February 1997.[155] MASAK operates under the auspices of the MoTF.[156] As examined in Chapter 2, there are four types of FIUs with unique advantages and disadvantages. It is necessary to discuss the administrative model of FIUs as Türkiye embraces such a model. The Egmont Group defines this particular type of FIU as 'a centralized, independent, administrative authority, that receives and processes financial sector information and transmits disclosures to judicial or law enforcement authorities for prosecution'.[157]

Considering its centralised position within the MoTF, MASAK is an administrative model of FIU operating independently as a 'buffer' between the financial sector and the forces of law and order, as per the Egmont Group's definition. Given that other FIU types operate as a part of judicial or LEAs, MASAK's relationships with such authorities are intrinsically limited. More specifically, its centralised organisational structure arguably diminishes MASAK's collaboration with those authorities due to distant and timely communication issues as they adopt a dispersed organisational structure across the country. Moreover, its inferior bureaucratic position and limited enforcement powers within the Turkish administrative hierarchy as a sub-unit of the MoTF is another significant matter to be considered. In other words, its administrative status inherently poses various drawbacks that impede its authorities compared to its counterparts.[158] For instance, MASAK personnel cannot instruct competent authorities to carry out confiscation procedures. Therefore, organisationally restructuring MASAK and establishing regional offices throughout the country would intensify the cooperation with the previously mentioned LEAs, thereby increasing the overall AML competency. It is worth emphasising that Presidential Decree No. 1 2018 enables the MoTF to establish additional offices affiliated with MASAK.[159] Adopting an administrative type of FIU may provide some unique advantages as it may encourage obliged entities to submit STRs to an administrative authority rather than to an LEA or judicial authority unless there is clear evidence of unusual economic activities.

154 Egmont Group (n 152) and FATF (n 153).

155 MASAK, 'Görev ve Yetkiler' <https://masak.hmb.gov.tr/gorev-ve-yetkiler> accessed 25 February 2023.

156 ibid.

157 Egmont Group (n 152).

158 Sisira Dharmasri Jayasekara, 'Administrative Model of Financial Intelligence Units: An Analysis of Effectiveness of the AML/CTF Regime' (2022) 25(3) Journal of Money Laundering Control 511; Fabio A Siena, 'The European Anti-Money Laundering Framework – At a Turning Point? The Role of Financial Intelligence Units' (2022) 13(2) New Journal of European Criminal Law 216.

159 Presidential Decree No 1 on the Organisation of the Presidency 2018, art 231(6).

In Chapter 7, the validity of this assumption as to whether the type of FIU embraced affects the disclosure tendencies of obliged entities is examined.

The duties of MASAK can be grouped into six essential responsibilities consisting of 'analysis and evaluation', 'examination', 'liability audit', 'external affairs', 'data collecting', and 'administrative sanctions'.[160] More specifically, MASAK's powers and responsibilities, amongst others, include: (a) contributing to the plan, programme, policy, and strategy preparation and development processes to prevent ML and financing of terrorism, ensuring coordination among institutions and organisations, including risk assessment studies at the national level; (b) conducting legislative studies related to its field of activity; (c) monitoring developments within the scope of revealing and preventing laundering proceeds of crime, financing terrorism and risks to economic security, developing measures, undertaking analysis, research, and examination activities; (d) collecting data within the scope of preventing laundering proceeds of crime and the financing of terrorism, receiving, analysing and recording suspicious transaction reports, generating intelligence, informing the relevant units about the intelligence and analysis results produced when necessary.[161] Whilst undertaking these duties/responsibilities, in cases where a serious suspicion of ML/TF occurs, MASAK has to refer the matter to the relevant public prosecutor and file a criminal complaint to the chief public prosecutor's office accordingly.[162] MASAK is also required to analyse and examine issues relating to ML/TF conveyed by the judiciary.[163] It is also authorised to request intelligence and ask LEAs to conduct examination and research in their field of duty when necessary, thereby cooperating and exchanging information with them to prevent ML/TF.[164] However, it is necessary to state that annual reports of MASAK do not have any evidence regarding whether it has applied for this power so far, albeit the GDS (11,640) and the GCG (10,973) requested analysis of data on 22,613 suspects in 2019 alone.[165] In other words, these powers and responsibilities endeavour to compensate for the disadvantages associated with being an administrative model of FIU. As the close examination of Article 231 connotes, in addition to its essential FIU functions, MASAK also undertakes regulatory, supervisory, and educational roles. MASAK has the power to assign supervisory tasks to other competent authorities[166] to conduct liability audits over obliged entities. For example, in 2018 and 2019, 59 and 17 such compliance inspections have been concluded

160 MASAK, 'Faaliyet Raporu 2019' (2020) 7 <https://ms.hmb.gov.tr/uploads/sites/12/2021/01/FAALIYET_RAPORU_2019-FINAL-1.pdf> accessed 25 February 2023.

161 Presidential Decree No 1 on the Organisation of the Presidency 2018, art 231.

162 ibid.

163 ibid.

164 ibid.

165 MASAK (n 160) 34.

166 These competent authorities include, amongst others, Banking Regulation and Supervisory Agency (BRSA) and Capital Market Board (CMB). See Presidential Decree No 1 on the Organisation of the Presidency 2018, art 231.

respectively by and on behalf of MASAK.[167] Furthermore, within the scope of educational activities, MASAK provides the relevant stakeholders with typologies produced based on the new laundering methods emerging in the global financial systems, including tax evasion techniques.[168] It also organises training activities addressing all responsible components of the national AML structure, including the judiciary, LEAs, and obliged entities, such as banks and real estate agencies. For example, a total of 788 LEA and the judiciary personnel and 106 DNFBP employees, consisting amongst others of notaries and accountants, attended such programmes organised by MASAK in 2019.[169] In other words, MASAK actively seeks to reinforce the cooperation and collaboration between obliged entities and AML authorities. FIs, by that means, can be made aware of red flags and take necessary measures to prevent associated risks. Accordingly, public prosecutors and LEAs direct their efforts to deprive offenders of the proceeds of crime by seizing and confiscating illicit assets.

With a total of 225 personnel, MASAK's organisational structure consists of six departments, namely department for strategic analysis, department for operational analysis, department for liability control, department for external affairs, department for special sanctions, and department for human resources and strategy.[170] It is necessary to note that although the number of dedicated staff of MASAK has gradually increased in recent years (e.g., 232 in 2015, 243 in 2016, and 262 in 2017),[171] its workload has escalated far faster (e.g., 369 requests from the judiciary and LEAs in 2015, 6,336 in 2016, and 26,977 in 2017).[172] Furthermore, the same exponential increase is apparent in the STRs submitted by obliged entities to MASAK. For instance, whilst MASAK received 74,221 STRs in 2015, it has almost tripled by reaching 222,743 in 2018, with a slight decrease in 2019 (203,786).[173] Yet, MASAK recently changed its organisational structure on 20 January 2020 (from 12 to six departments), thereby decreasing its number of staff significantly (i.e., 267 in 2018 and 225 in 2019) whilst its workload remains about the same (e.g., 22,939 requests from the judiciary and LEAs in 2018 and 22,128 in 2019).[174] The decreased personnel capacity of MASAK may be associated with the recent structural modification, but the increased workload may impede the overall AML competency of the jurisdiction. For example, as touched upon previously, whilst 59 obliged entities were inspected in 2018, in 2019, on the other hand, just 17 AML compliance inspections were conducted (almost 75% decrease), which may be due to the inadequate number of personnel.

167 MASAK (n 160) 18.
168 MASAK, 'Tipolojiler' <https://masak.hmb.gov.tr/tipolojiler> accessed 25 February 2023.
169 MASAK (n 160) 57.
170 ibid 8–9.
171 MASAK, 'Faaliyet Raporu 2018' (2019) 10 <https://ms.hmb.gov.tr/uploads/sites/12/2021/01/2018_FAALIYET-RAPORU-v7-1.pdf> accessed 1 July 2023.
172 ibid 19.
173 MASAK (n 160) 23.
174 ibid 8–9, 18.

Another salient issue that needs to be highlighted here is the STR gathering process of MASAK, as it may constitute an additional drawback for the Turkish AML competency. MASAK predominantly receives STRs via EMIS. ONLINE (*Entegre Mali İstihbarat Sistemi/*Integrated Financial Intelligence System),[175] a web-based system that enables sending STR forms electronically, similar to its British counterpart NCA SAR Online System (see Chapter 6). Although MASAK is provided with these STRs preponderantly through electronic means (99.7%), there remain some obliged entities, such as dealers of precious metals, that submit their STRs by mail.[176] Therefore, considering the meteoric nature of ML offences,[177] non-electronic STR submission may hinder the overall efficacy of the country's AML system.

MASAK provides statistics for its yearly activities on its official website through annual reports. It further makes available the indicators for how it performed for a given year by setting goals within those reports. The benchmarks determined as good performance comprise: the number of STRs received, the number of obliged entities inspected regarding liability audit, the number of training and workshops held with relevant stakeholders, the number of obliged entities that sent STRs, and the number of strategic analysis studies made based on mass data and STRs.[178] It is necessary to note that the last two criteria have replaced 'the completion period of the analysis and evaluation studies on the requests submitted by the judicial authorities within the scope of Law No 5549' and 'the number of data types collected', which were former performance indicators for MASAK.[179] Given that these standards set aptly by MASAK for its self-performance evaluation are paramount in ensuring the wellbeing of an AML system, it can be argued that MASAK is eager to improve its capacity. However, this improvement depends on whether it meets the standards and generates intended outcomes. For instance, the only criterion met was the number of STRs received in 2019.[180] Nonetheless, it does not cover any information indicating whether and how many persons have been convicted of ML or the underlying predicate crimes, nor does it include data on the recovery figures. This trend could be stemming from two facts; either the judiciary does not provide feedback to MASAK on the judicial outcomes, which means that the communication between the courts and the Turkish FIU is not adequate, or there have been no convictions or confiscations following the STRs. Therefore, either the communication between these

175 MASAK, 'EMIS Online' <https://masak.hmb.gov.tr/emis-online> accessed 26 February 2023.
176 MASAK (n 171) 23.
177 Paul Michael Gilmour, 'Re-Examining the Anti-Money Laundering Framework: A Legal Critique and New Approach to Combatting Money Laundering' (2022) 30(1) Journal of Financial Crime 35.
178 MASAK (n 160) 60–64.
179 MASAK (n 171) 62–66.
180 MASAK (n 160) 65.

authorities or the judicial outcomes concerning perpetrators of ML and its predicates should be strengthened.

Annual reports published by MASAK also give insight into its connections with other competent authorities. MASAK carries out its activities with close collaboration with the judiciary and LEAs in bidirectional information flow. Whilst the aforementioned authorities request reports from the Turkish FIU, MASAK informs these authorities and any other relevant institutions spontaneously in cases where it encounters issues that fall into their fields of responsibility. For instance, MASAK shared information with 15 institutions (18 in 2018) about 106,917 people in 2019 (214,987 in 2018), the majority of which with LEAs (i.e., on 22,613 people with GDS and GCG combined (177,572 in 2018)) and judicial authorities (i.e., on 82,215 people (6,217 in 2018)).[181] However, the vast majority of the data flow is within the scope of CTF activities (i.e., about 100,513/106,917 people in 2019 and 208,817/214,987 in 2018),[182] suggesting that the analysis of ML and its predicates is inadequate compared to the TF inquiry. Nevertheless, it is worth reiterating that MASAK's cooperation with LEAs and the judiciary is not limited to the information exchange as it also provides training activities in this context. For example, in 2019, a total of 788 personnel from MoJ, MoI, and MoTF (1,209 personnel in 2018) attended such educatory programmes organised by MASAK,[183] which indicates the collaboration between the LEAs and the Turkish FIU in enhancing the judicial security forces' knowledge of required AML practices.

MASAK is also responsible for ensuring coordination amongst relevant authorities in preparing the NRAs as per the FATF's specific guidance.[184] In order to prepare its NRA, Türkiye launched an initiative called 'National Risk Assessment Project' based on the Prime Ministry Circular No. 2016/22; and MASAK coordinated relevant activities with the 'Project Steering Committee' created based on the same circular.[185] Admittedly, preparing the NRA is imperative to identify state-specific risks as it enables the implementation of an RBA, thereby helping countries prioritise their limited resources and allocate them efficiently. However, it needs to be stated that the 2018 NRA is Türkiye's first-ever report in assessing and understanding its national risks and is not publicly available. Hence, although it is a considerable step to compose an

181 ibid 34 and MASAK (n 171) 34.
182 ibid 35 and 35, respectively.
183 ibid 57 and 57, respectively.
184 FATF, 'FATF Guidance: National Money Laundering and Terrorist Financing Risk Assessment' (February 2013) <www.fatf-gafi.org/media/fatf/content/images/National_ML_TF_Risk_Assessment.pdf> accessed 27 February 2023.
185 Official Gazette No 29864 dated 21 October 2016, 'Genelge 2016/22: Mali Eylem Görev Gücü (FATF) IV. Tur Değerlendirmesi Hazırlıkları ve Ulusal Risk Değerlendirmesi Çalışmaları' <www.resmigazete.gov.tr/eskiler/2016/10/20161021-2-1.pdf> accessed 27 February 2023.

NRA, its non-transparent nature cannot benefit all stakeholders partaking in the national AML efforts.

Whilst the Egmont Group enables FIUs to exchange information through the ESW system,[186] MASAK signs bilateral Memoranda of Understanding (MoU) with its foreign counterparts to ensure rapid and effective information flow internationally.[187] The last two MoUs were signed with Ecuador and Uzbekistan FIUs in 2018, and the number of MoUs signed has reached 52 jurisdictions, including the UK.[188] Furthermore, MASAK implements this MoU signing exercise with domestic relevant authorities, including all LEAs and supervisory authorities, albeit not being legally prescribed. It is necessary to express also that national authorities have adopted a joint protocol to secure a more comprehensive collaboration in this context. These MoUs and protocols enable relevant stakeholders, particularly MASAK, to access public and private sector databases electronically regarding their economic activities. For example, MASAK has direct access, amongst others, to the GDS's database[189] and financial transactions data of all banks in Türkiye.[190] More specifically, MASAK has online access to a total of 51 data types from 14 institutions and an offline data repository that aggregates 120 data types from another eight institutions, electronically held by all public institutions and organisations.[191]

Regarding international collaboration enterprises, MASAK is a member of the CARIN,[192] an informal network of law enforcement and judiciary personnel from 54 jurisdictions established to ensure the denial of criminal proceedings to offenders.[193] It is also necessary to note that the UK is one of the nine members of the organisation that constitute its Steering Group,[194] another

186 Egmont Group, 'Organization and Structure' <https://egmontgroup.org/about/organization-and-structure/> accessed 2 July 2023.

187 Presidential Decree No 1 on the Organisation of the Presidency 2018, art 231(5).

188 MASAK (n 160) 52.

189 Council of Europe, 'iPROCEEDS: Güneydoğu Avrupa Ülkelerinde ve Türkiye'de Siber Suçlardan Gelir Elde Edilmesi ile Mücadele Projesi' (Mayıs 2017) 12 <https://rm.coe.int/3156-25-guide-interagency-international-cooperationprotocolturkey-tr/16807be2e3> accessed 27 February 2023.

190 MASAK (n 171) 60.

191 Council of Europe, 'iPROCEEDS Report: Advisory Mission and Workshop on Online Fraud and Other Cybercrime Reporting Mechanisms' (March 2017) 9 <https://rm.coe.int/3156-26-iproceeds-report-reporting-mechanisms-turkey/16807be380> accessed 27 February 2023.

192 Camden Asset Recovery Inter-Agency Network, 'The History, Statement of Intent, Membership and Functioning of CARIN' (2015) 15 <https://6205d188-5e8e-4e98-976e-0b39bbb814e3.filesusr.com/ugd/d54f05_4ccdfc507cb44d3588354132a68af289.pdf> accessed 27 February 2023.

193 Camden Asset Recovery Inter-Agency Network, 'Recovering Criminal Assets' <www.carin.network> accessed 27 February 2023.

194 Camden Asset Recovery Inter-Agency Network, 'CARIN Steering Group 2018' <https://6205d188-5e8e-4e98-976e-0b39bbb814e3.filesusr.com/ugd/d54f05_81361c6d39794f0fa47160c78760cbbf.pdf> accessed 27 February 2023.

example of the UK's leading position in this context. CARIN endeavours to achieve four strategic goals: reinforcing cooperation between members and international partners, improving information exchange between members, developing CARIN as a centre of excellence, and influencing policy concerning criminal asset recovery.[195] MASAK also takes part in *iPROCEEDS*, a joint project of the EU and the CoE targeting crime proceeds on the internet in South-Eastern Europe (i.e., Albania, Bosnia and Herzegovina, Montenegro, North Macedonia, Serbia, and Kosovo) and Türkiye.[196] In other words, partaking in such JITs allows MASAK to tackle the transnational aspect of the phenomenon effectively.

Lastly, PPPs have proven to be a significant catalyser for countering ML and its underlying predicates.[197] The TBB-MASAK Working Group constitutes one of the examples of PPPs in Türkiye in this context. The Banks Association of Türkiye and MASAK have initiated this PPP to evaluate banks relating to the implementation of AML standards, thereby devising opinions and planning future activities that would improve such transactions and intensify cooperation between the two organisations.[198] For example, it has published several academic studies to nurture the financial sector in the fight against ML.[199] Although it endeavours to secure better outcomes against the phenomenon, unlike the UK's practice (e.g., Joint Money Laundering Intelligence Task Force – JMLIT), it does not devise an integrated mechanism incorporating the private sector into the investigation process. That is to say that the private sector in Türkiye cannot actively participate in and contribute to the destruction of ML and TF as their sole contribution remains as submitting STRs to MASAK. Therefore, establishing novel PPPs that bring together, *inter alia*, FIs and other obliged entities, supervisory authorities, and LEAs, thereby providing opportunities for the private sector to exchange information with one another effectively, would unquestionably reinforce the AML competency of the jurisdiction.

195 Camden Asset Recovery Inter-Agency Network, 'CARIN Strategic Plan: Actions for 2018–2021' <https://6205d188-5e8e-4e98-976e-0b39bbb814e3.filesusr.com/ugd/d54f05_36d2d08c83d0441da3198ecd4aee3c92.pdf> accessed 27 February 2023.

196 Council of Europe, 'iPROCEEDS – Targeting Crime Proceeds on the Internet in South Eastern Europe and Turkey' <www.coe.int/en/web/cybercrime/iproceeds> accessed 27 February 2023.

197 As discussed in the next chapter, Joint Money Laundering Intelligence Task Force (JMLIT), the most prominent PPP in the UK in this context, has contributed to more than 500 LEA investigations, thereby securing more than 130 ML arrests and the denial of over GBP 13 million since its inception in 2015.

198 Türkiye Bankalar Birliği, 'TBB-MASAK Çalışma Grubu' <www.tbb.org.tr/tr/hakkimizda/kurumsal/calisma-gruplari/surekli-calisma-gruplari/tbb-masak-calisma-grubu/223> accessed 27 February 2023.

199 See, for instance, TBB-MASAK Çalışma Grubu, 'Para Aklama Riskinin Yönetimi ve Türk Bankacılık Sisteminde Uygulama Kılavuzu' (2007) 60 Bankacılar Dergisi 58.

5.4.3 The Coordination Board for Combatting Financial Crimes

Finally, the Coordination Board,[200] which consists of representatives from competent state authorities, seeks to improve coordination and cooperation amongst the relevant stakeholders in tackling ML/TF, thereby determining implementation strategies, taking guiding decisions, and evaluating draft legislation in this context. The CBCFC meets at least twice a year, where representatives of (any other) institutions and organisations may be invited to seek their opinions and information when necessary.[201] Remarkably, however, whilst the GDS and the CE are the (permanent) members of the CBCFC, the remaining two LEAs of the jurisdiction, the GCG and the CGC, are not represented at the Coordination Board, albeit having significant AML/CTF roles. This controversial organisational structure of the CBCFC does not correspond to its primary objective of enhancing coordination amongst all relevant AML actors. Therefore, restructuring the CBCFC and including all essential components of the AML battle would bolster the cooperation/collaboration amongst the institutions.

5.5 Conclusion

As a civil law jurisdiction, Türkiye has established its (AML) legal arsenal on codified statutory instruments where case law is not binding for the judiciary to conclude subsequent cases. Although Türkiye recently designated some courts for hearing ML cases, the judicial composition of the jurisdiction does not comprise specific courts dealing only with ML. The gravity of predicate offences determines which courts hold the hearings. Whilst Criminal Courts of General Jurisdiction try relatively minor predicate crime cases, Aggravated Felony Courts adjudicate more significant trials, such as extortion, where the decision process requires a more deliberate procedure. Generally, hearings of ML litigations fall under the jurisdiction of Criminal Courts of General Jurisdiction, which suggests that Türkiye considers such cases less serious than most predicate crimes. However, in reality, it may be the intricate and obscure characteristics of the criminal conduct (ML) that render it ostensibly trivial compared to such crimes. It can be argued therefore that the gravity and impact of the ML offences may have been underestimated compared to the UK, where ML attracts longer terms of imprisonment than predicate crimes.

200 Under the leadership of the Deputy Minister of Treasury and Finance, its representatives comprise the Deputy President of the National Intelligence Agency, General Manager of Financial Markets and Foreign Exchange, President of Tax Audit Board, President of Financial Crimes Investigation Board, General Manager of Criminal Affairs of the Ministry of Justice, General Director of Research and Security Affairs of Ministry of Foreign Affairs, General Directorate of Customs Enforcement of the Ministry, Deputy President of the Banking Regulation and Supervision Agency, and Deputy General Manager of the General Directorate of Security. See Presidential Decree No 1 on the Organisation of the Presidency 2018, art 232.

201 ibid.

Lastly, Türkiye has consistently increased its workforce in the judiciary and ensured an average of 17 judges per 100,000 people; yet this figure is still less than the standard secured by the CoE-member jurisdictions (22 judges per 100,000 people).[202] Therefore, increasing the number of judges and considering the designation of Aggravated Felony Courts for concluding ML cases would be an appropriate approach for Türkiye's judicial *modus operandi*.

As a unicameral legislature, the GNAT, except for certain occasions, constitutes the single source that has established the entrenched body of national (AML) legal instruments in Türkiye. Additionally, unlike the UK's dualist legal system, Türkiye has adopted a monist legal system whereby international treaties are directly applicable in Turkish law. Accordingly, the Constitution 1982 sits at the highest level of the hierarchy of norms and is followed by international treaties duly put into effect in the hierarchical pyramid. The power to propose laws belongs to members of the parliament, and legislation adopted by the GNAT is subject to the presidential review before promulgation, suggesting the origins of the legislative process as well as the period as to how long an enactment procedure may take. In other words, the current law-making methodology of Türkiye seems to be punctual and efficient in addressing global legislative developments seen in the AML sphere, suggesting that the jurisdiction can keep pace with such harmonic alterations.

Türkiye has four LEAs consisting of the GCG, the CGC, the GDS, and the CE. Whilst the GCG and the GSD have specific departments (KOMs), the CE and the CGC do not have such dedicated units for combatting the phenomenon. That is to say that tackling ML and its predicates does not appear to be occupying equally high positions at each LEA's agendas. More precisely, it seems that the primarily responsible LEAs are the GCG and the GDS in the AML battle. Paradoxically at the same time, whilst the CE and the GDS represent their institutions at the CBCFC, the GCG and the CGC are not permanent members of the Coordination Board, and they attend such meetings only if the CBCFC invites them. Accordingly, restructuring the CBCFC, thereby including all essential AML actors, would undoubtedly reinforce the current cooperation mechanism. Furthermore, embodying the Department of INTERPOL-Europol and TADOC renders the GDS as the principal LEA for the international aspect of the fight against ML and its underlying predicates. Establishing these unique centres comprising personnel from all LEAs would equally integrate them in the AML regime, thereby ensuring the development of the same levels of expertise for each LEA. LEA personnel act as judicial security forces relating to judicial matters under the direction of public prosecutors, a critical point that renders the AML expertise harnessed by public prosecutors' imperative. It is worth reiterating that this praxis does not clash with the separation of powers, nor does it breach the principle of *nemo judex in causa sua*, as LEAs do not operate autonomously in prosecutorial matters.

202 TC Adalet Bakanlığı Strateji Geliştirme Başkanlığı (n 58) 12.

Yet, considering the prominence of public prosecutors in these legal proceedings, establishing specialised bureaus within the offices of chief public prosecutors, and assigning prosecutors whose principal responsibility is to investigate laundering of proceeds of crime cases would be a significant step to be taken. LEAs set up periodic meetings whereby the performance of their affiliated units relating to their responsibilities, including AML practices, are assessed, suggesting the importance devoted by LEAs to tackling the predicament. However, it is not possible to evaluate the effectiveness of a given LEA relating to the AML domain accurately, as none of their (annual) reports provide data on the recovery or conviction figures. Accordingly, addressing this deficiency would present a clear understanding of the current state of affairs of the Turkish LEAs relating to their AML efforts.

Unlike the UK's practice in this end, Türkiye has embraced an administrative type of FIU that is intrinsically devoid of crucial (law enforcement and judicial) powers, such as asset recovery or confiscation. This characteristic renders it more significant for MASAK to establish robust communication and collaboration with LEAs and the judiciary. However, its centralised organisational structure arguably diminishes such cooperation opportunities as those authorities adopt a dispersed organisational structure throughout the jurisdiction. Accordingly, establishing additional offices across the country affiliated with MASAK would secure a more prompt and collective response mechanism addressing associated risks and deficiencies. MASAK recently went under structural changes, halving its dedicated departments and decreasing its personnel capacity correspondingly. Although this is an early stage for evaluating the consequences of this modification, given the increasing workload of MASAK, such attenuations may impede its existing competency and efficiency.

PPPs have proven to be effective in securing better outcomes against financial crimes. Although MASAK participates in such alliances, they are far from generating the intended results as their functional structures do not incorporate the private sector into the exchange of information or investigation process. It renders the STR submissions as the only manifest contribution of the private sector in tackling money launderers and terrorism financiers. Even though MASAK receives STRs predominantly through electronic means, some obliged entities, such as dealers of precious metals, still submit their STRs by mail, suggesting that it cannot compete with particular ML incidents, at least on certain occasions. That being the case, raising its personnel capacity and ensuring the online STR submission opportunity for all obliged entities would intensify the productivity of MASAK. Although MASAK has established standards for its self-evaluation of effectiveness (which is an outstanding practice), the criteria determined do not include some crucial performance indicators, such as the number of persons convicted of ML(TF) or the asset recovery figures. Accordingly, incorporating such KPIs for self-assessment would benefit the AML efforts of the jurisdiction. The NRA which is prepared by the coordination of MASAK is not publicly available. Providing such information publicly would enhance the transparency and understanding of the emerging threats relating to ML, thereby allowing the relevant stakeholders to conduct better risk-based AML practices.

This chapter has examined the Turkish institutional AML composition. It has also inquired into the legal sources of jurisdiction and the hierarchy between them, thereby shedding light on the law-making processes and the necessary period for enacting a particular legal instrument in Türkiye. It has further investigated the Turkish FIU as well as the LEAs of the country. In doing so, it has provided insight into current difficulties and exploitable deficiencies of the Turkish AML *modus operandi*, thereby highlighting the areas for reform that would improve them. The continuous increase in the judge workforce, the division of (legal) labour between the criminal courts relating to hearing predicate crime cases according to their gravity, and initiatives started in this context aiming at concluding such cases in specified periods (e.g., *Yargıda Hedef Süre*) are noteworthy developments devoted to enhancing the promptness of the associated judicial outcomes. The legal sources and the monist characteristic of the jurisdiction clarify the hierarchy between statutory instruments and accelerate the law-making process, thereby facilitating harmonising of the national AML legal framework with its international counterparts. In light of these facets, the Turkish legislative and judicial institutional composition complements the efforts in tackling ML and associated predicate crimes. Nevertheless, this cannot be said for the institutional structure of LEAs and the FIU in Türkiye. Whilst the GDS and the GCG are entrusted with the same (AML) duties regarding different responsibility areas of rural and urban landscapes, the GDS's institutional structure, including TADOC and the Department of Interpol-Europol, renders it more at the crux of the national AML efforts. Furthermore, Turkish LEAs do not have specific and well-developed departments devoted only to tackling ML and its predicates; on the contrary, they are, by and large, subunits of departments dealing with smuggling and organised crimes. More importantly, the most prevalent predicate crimes in Türkiye[203] and the inherent transnational commission methodologies of such offences[204] imply that the roles of the CGC and the CE are extremely important. These facts become more salient given that MASAK is an administrative type of FIU devoid of law enforcement or judicial powers. Although participating in PPPs and JITs by MASAK is of significant importance, these initiatives would be more meaningful when they are strengthened. More specifically, novel PPPs (e.g., JMLIT), which require the private sector to actively participate in the fight against ML and its underlying predicates, should be created. In addition, assigning liaison officers to the most critical countries partaking in the aforementioned international predicate crime schemes would further reinforce the Turkish AML competency regarding JITs.

203 These crimes comprise drug trafficking, migrant smuggling, human trafficking, and fuel smuggling. See FATF (n 5).

204 Mangai Natarajan, *International and Transnational Crime and Justice* (CUP 2019).

Reference List

Camden Asset Recovery Inter-Agency Network, 'The History, Statement of Intent, Membership and Functioning of CARIN' (2015) <https://6205d188-5e8e-4e98-976e-0b39bbb814e3.filesusr.com/ugd/d54f05_4ccdfc507cb44d3588354132a68af289.pdf> accessed 27 February 2023

——— 'CARIN Steering Group 2018' <https://6205d188-5e8e-4e98-976e-0b39bbb814e3.filesusr.com/ugd/d54f05_81361c6d39794f0fa47160c78760cbbf.pdf> accessed 27 February 2023

——— 'CARIN Strategic Plan: Actions for 2018–2021' <https://6205d188-5e8e-4e98-976e-0b39bbb814e3.filesusr.com/ugd/d54f05_36d2d08c83d0441da3198ecd4aee3c92.pdf> accessed 27 February 2023

——— 'Recovering Criminal Assets' <www.carin.network> accessed 27 February 2023

Council of Europe, 'iPROCEEDS Report: Advisory Mission and Workshop on Online Fraud and Other Cybercrime Reporting Mechanisms' (March 2017) <https://rm.coe.int/3156-26-iproceeds-report-reporting-mechanisms-turkey/16807be380> accessed 27 February 2023

——— 'iPROCEEDS: Güneydoğu Avrupa Ülkelerinde ve Türkiye'de Siber Suçlardan Gelir Elde Edilmesi ile Mücadele Projesi' (Mayıs 2017) <https://rm.coe.int/3156-25-guide-interagency-international-cooperationprotocolturkey-tr/16807be2e3> accessed 27 February 2023

——— 'iPROCEEDS – Targeting Crime Proceeds on the Internet in South Eastern Europe and Turkey' <www.coe.int/en/web/cybercrime/iproceeds> accessed 27 February 2023

——— 'European Judicial Systems CEPEJ Evaluation Report: 2020 Evaluation Cycle (2018 Data)' (September 2020) <https://rm.coe.int/evaluation-report-part-1-english/16809fc058> accessed 19 August 2023

Duxbury N, *The Nature and Authority of Precedent* (CUP 2008)

Egmont Group, 'Financial Intelligence Units' <https://egmontgroup.org/about/financial-intelligence-units/> accessed 2 July 2023

——— 'Organization and Structure' <https://egmontgroup.org/about/organization-and-structure/> accessed 2 July 2023

Europol, 'International Anti-Money Laundering Operational Network (AMON) Launched' (30 January 2012) <www.europol.europa.eu/newsroom/news/international-anti-money-laundering-operational-network-amon-launched> accessed 21 February 2023

——— 'Europol Joins Forces With EU FIUs to Fight Terrorist Financing and Money Laundering' (28 January 2016) <www.europol.europa.eu/about-europol/financial-intelligence-units-fiu-net#fndtn-tabs-0-bottom-1> accessed 1 July 2023

——— 'Turkey and Europol Sign Liaison Agreement' (21 March 2016) <www.europol.europa.eu/newsroom/news/turkey-and-europol-sign-liaison-agreement> accessed 21 February 2023

——— 'International Operation CICONIA ALBA Kicks off to Crack Down on Organised Crime' (20 June 2016) <www.europol.europa.eu/newsroom/news/international-operation-ciconia-alba-kicks-to-crack-down-organised-crime> accessed 21 February 2023

——— 'Anti-Money Laundering Experts Call for More International Cooperation' (7 June 2019) <www.europol.europa.eu/newsroom/news/anti-money-laundering-experts-call-for-more-international-cooperation> accessed 21 February 2023

——— 'Partners and Agreements' <www.europol.europa.eu/partners-agreements> accessed 21 February 2023

——— 'Strategic Agreements' <www.europol.europa.eu/partners-agreements/strategic-agreements> accessed 21 February 2023

——— 'European Financial and Economic Crime Centre (EFECC)' <www.europol.europa.eu/about-europol/european-financial-and-economic-crime-centre-efecc> accessed 23 February 2023

FATF, 'FATF Guidance: National Money Laundering and Terrorist Financing Risk Assessment' (February 2013) <www.fatf-gafi.org/media/fatf/content/images/National_ML_TF_Risk_Assessment.pdf> accessed 27 February 2023

——— 'Anti-Money Laundering and Counter-Terrorist Financing Measures – Turkey: Mutual Evaluation Report' (December 2019) <www.fatf-gafi.org/media/fatf/documents/reports/mer4/Mutual-Evaluation-Report-Turkey-2019.pdf> accessed 18 January 2023

——— 'International Standards on Combatting Money Laundering and the Financing of Terrorism & Proliferation: The FATF Recommendations' (Updated March 2022) <www.fatf-gafi.org/media/fatf/documents/recommendations/pdfs/FATF%20Recommendations%202012.pdf> accessed 26 June 2023

Ferwerda J, 'The Effects of Money Laundering' in B Unger and D van der Linde (eds), *Research Handbook on Money Laundering* (Edward Elgar Publishing 2013)

Gilmour PM, 'Re-Examining the Anti-Money Laundering Framework: A Legal Critique and New Approach to Combatting Money Laundering' (2022) 30(1) Journal of Financial Crime 35

Gragl P, *Legal Monism: Law, Philosophy, and Politics* (OUP 2018)

Jayasekara SD, 'Deficient Regimes of Anti-Money Laundering and Countering the Financing of Terrorism: An Analysis of Short Term Economic Implications' (2020) 23(3) Journal of Money Laundering Control 663

——— 'Administrative Model of Financial Intelligence Units: An Analysis of Effectiveness of the AML/CTF Regime' (2022) 25(3) Journal of Money Laundering Control 511

MASAK, 'Faaliyet Raporu 2018' (2019) <https://ms.hmb.gov.tr/uploads/sites/12/2021/01/2018_FAALIYET-RAPORU-v7-1.pdf> accessed 1 July 2023

——— 'Faaliyet Raporu 2019' (2020) <https://ms.hmb.gov.tr/uploads/sites/12/2021/01/FAALIYET_RAPORU_2019-FINAL-1.pdf> accessed 25 February 2023

——— 'Görev ve Yetkiler' <https://masak.hmb.gov.tr/gorev-ve-yetkiler> accessed 25 February 2023

——— 'Tipolojiler' <https://masak.hmb.gov.tr/tipolojiler> accessed 25 February 2023

——— 'EMIS Online' <https://masak.hmb.gov.tr/emis-online> accessed 26 February 2023

Ministry of Justice General Directorate of Judicial Record and Statistics, 'Judicial Statistics 2019' (August 2020) <https://adlisicil.adalet.gov.tr/Resimler/SayfaDokuman/1092020162733adalet_ist-2019.pdf> accessed 1 February 2023

Mitsilegas V and Vavoula N, 'The Evolving EU Anti-Money Laundering Regime: Challenges for Fundamental Rights and the Rule of Law' (2016) 23(2) Maastricht Journal of European and Comparative Law 261

Natarajan M, *International and Transnational Crime and Justice* (CUP 2019)

Rider B, 'Intelligent Investigations: The Use and Misuse of Intelligence – A Personal Perspective' (2013) 20(3) Journal of Financial Crime 293

Schwarzenberger G, 'The Nemo Judex in Sua Causa Maxim in International Judicial Practice' (1972) 1(4) Anglo-American Law Review 482

Siena FA, 'The European Anti-Money Laundering Framework – At a Turning Point? The Role of Financial Intelligence Units' (2022) 13(2) New Journal of European Criminal Law 216

Smith BC, *The Rule of Law and Judicial Independence* (1st edn, Routledge 2017)

Tanzi V, 'Macroeconomic Implications of Money Laundering' in EU Savona (ed), *Responding to Money Laundering: International Perspectives* (1st edn, Routledge 1997)

TBB-MASAK Çalışma Grubu, 'Para Aklama Riskinin Yönetimi ve Türk Bankacılık Sisteminde Uygulama Kılavuzu' (2007) 60 Bankacılar Dergisi 58

TC Adalet Bakanlığı Adli Sicil ve İstatistik Genel Müdürlüğü, 'Adli İstatistikler 2019' (2020) <https://adlisicil.adalet.gov.tr/Resimler/SayfaDokuman/1062020170359HizmeteOzel-2019-baskı-İSA.pdf> accessed 15 January 2023

TC Adalet Bakanlığı Basın ve Halkla İlişkiler Müşavirliği, 'Yargıda Yeni Dönem' (2 January 2019) <https://basin.adalet.gov.tr/yargida-yeni-donem> accessed 15 January 2023

TC Adalet Bakanlığı Strateji Geliştirme Başkanlığı, '2019 Yılı Bakanlık Faaliyet Raporu' (Şubat 2020) <https://sgb.adalet.gov.tr/Resimler/Dokuman/16720201409152019%20Yılı%20Bakanlık%20Faaliyet%20Raporu.pdf> accessed 15 January 2023

TC İçişleri Bakanlığı, 'Türkiye Mülki İdare Bölümleri Envanteri' <www.e-icisleri.gov.tr/Anasayfa/MulkiIdariBolumleri.aspx> accessed 12 February 2023

TC İçişleri Bakanlığı Emniyet Genel Müdürlüğü, '2019 Faaliyet Raporu' (2020) <www.egm.gov.tr//kurumlar/egm.gov.tr/IcSite/strateji/Planlama/2019-IDARE-FAALIYET-RAPORU.pdf> accessed 24 February 2023

——— 'Kaçakçılık ve Organize Suçlarla Mücadele 2019 Raporu' (September 2020) <www.egm.gov.tr/kurumlar/egm.gov.tr/IcSite/kom/YAYINLARIMIZ/TÜRKÇE/2019-RAPORU-TR.pdf> accessed 17 February 2023

——— 'Daire Başkanlıkları' <www.egm.gov.tr/daire-baskanliklari> accessed 17 February 2023

——— 'Interpol-Europol Dairesi Başkanlığı' <www.egm.gov.tr/interpol/hakkimizda> accessed 17 February 2023

——— 'Interpol-Europol Dairesi Başkanlığı: Organizasyon Şeması' <www.egm.gov.tr/interpol/birimlerimiz> accessed 21 February 2023

——— 'Interpol-Europol Dairesi Başkanlığı: Tarihçe' <www.egm.gov.tr/interpol/tarihce> accessed 21 February 2023

——— 'Kaçakçılık ve Organize Suçlarla Mücadele Dairesi Başkanlığı: Tarihçe ve Tanıtım' <www.egm.gov.tr/kom/baskanligimiz-tarihce-ve-tanitim> accessed 23 February 2023

TC İçişleri Bakanlığı Emniyet Genel Müdürlüğü Asayiş Daire Başkanlığı, 'Suç Gelirleri ile Mücadele Şanlıurfa' (13 March 2020) <www.asayis.pol.tr/13032020-oto-hirsizligi-suc-gelirleri-ile-mucadele-sanliurfa> accessed 17 February 2023

——— 'Suç Gelirleri ile Mücadele' <www.asayis.pol.tr/sucgelirleri> accessed 17 February 2023

TC İçişleri Bakanlığı Jandarma Genel Komutanlığı, '2019 Yılı Faaliyet Raporu' (January 2020) <www.jandarma.gov.tr/kurumlar/jandarma.gov.tr/Duyurular/guncel/JGNKLIGI-2019-YILI-FAALIYET-RAPORU.pdf> accessed 12 February 2023

——— '2020 Aralık Ayı Verileri' <www.jandarma.gov.tr/2020-aralik-ayi-verileri> accessed 15 February 2023

——— '2020 Aralık Ayı Verileri (GÖÇMEN)' <www.jandarma.gov.tr/kurumlar/jandarma.gov.tr/Veriler/2020/Aralik-2020-Asayis-Verileri.xlsx> accessed 15 February 2023

——— '2020 Aralık Ayı Verileri (KOM-1)' <www.jandarma.gov.tr/kurumlar/jandarma.gov.tr/Veriler/2020/Aralik-2020-Asayis-Verileri.xlsx> accessed 15 February 2023

——— '2020 Yılı Performans Programı' <www.jandarma.gov.tr/kurumlar/jandarma.gov.tr/Duyurular/guncel/JGnKligi-2020-Yili-Performans-Programi.pdf> accessed 12 February 2023

——— 'Asayiş Başkanlığı' <www.jandarma.gov.tr/asayis> accessed 12 February 2023

——— 'Jandarma Sorumluluk Alanları ve Korunan Tesisler' <www.jandarma.gov.tr/jandarma-tarafindan-korunan-tesisler> accessed 12 February 2023

TC İçişleri Bakanlığı Sahil Güvenlik Komutanlığı, 'Düzensiz Göç İstatistikleri: 2019–2020 Yılları Tüm Denizlere Ait Kıyaslamalı Düzensiz Göç İstatistikleri' <www.sg.gov.tr/duzensiz-goc-istatistikleri> accessed 7 January 2023

TC Millî Savunma Bakanlığı Harita Genel Müdürlüğü, 'İl ve İlçe Yüzölçümleri' <www.harita.gov.tr/il-ve-ilce-yuzolcumleri> accessed 12 February 2023

TC Ticaret Bakanlığı, 'Ticaret Bakanlığı 2019 Yılı Faaliyet Raporu' (2020) <https://ticaret.gov.tr/data/5e58fdaa13b8764dec3bf81d/TICARET_BAKANLIGI_2019YILI_FAALIYET_RAPORU.pdf> accessed 14 January 2023

——— 'Türlerine Göre Uyuşturucu Madde Yakalamaları' (December 2020) <https://ticaret.gov.tr/data/5d76399213b8768ba06eaf49/4-Turlerine%20Gore%20Uyusturucu%20Madde%20Yakalamalari.pdf> accessed 14 January 2023

TC Ticaret Bakanlığı Gümrükler Muhafaza Genel Müdürlüğü, '2019 Faaliyet Raporu' (2020) <https://muhafaza.ticaret.gov.tr/data/5d31b1ee13b876092c062161/faaliyet%20raporu_2019%20(1).pdf> accessed 7 January 2023

——— 'Muhafaza Memurunun Görev, Yetki ve Sorumlulukları' <https://muhafaza.ticaret.gov.tr/gumruk-muhafaza/muhafaza-memuru> accessed 14 January 2023

Türkiye Bankalar Birliği, 'TBB-MASAK Çalışma Grubu' <www.tbb.org.tr/tr/hakkimizda/kurumsal/calisma-gruplari/surekli-calisma-gruplari/tbb-masak-calisma-grubu/223> accessed 27 February 2023

Türkiye Büyük Millet Meclisi, 'Kanun Sorgu Sonuçları: Mart 2021' <www.tbmm.gov.tr/develop/owa/kanunlar_sd.sorgu_yonlendirme?Kanun_no=&k_Baslangic_Tarihi=01/03/2021&k_Bitis_Tarihi=31/03/2021&r_Baslangic_Tarihi=&r_Bitis_Tarihi=&sorgu_kelime=> accessed 12 April 2023

TURKSTAT, 'The Results of Address Based Population Registration System, 2019' <https://data.tuik.gov.tr/Bulten/Index?p=The-Results-of-Address-Based-Population-Registration-System-2019-33705&dil=2> accessed 12 February 2023

Unger B and Busuioc EM, *The Scale and Impacts of Money Laundering* (Edward Elgar Publishing 2007)

Voigt S, 'Determinants of Judicial Efficiency: A Survey' (2016) 42(2) European Journal of Law and Economics 183

Wheeler J and MyiLibrary, *Essentials of the English Legal System* (2nd edn, Pearson Longman 2006)

Xe Currency Converter <www.xe.com> accessed 14 January 2021

Legal Instruments

Türkiye

Constitution of the Republic of Türkiye 1982
Decree No 8761 dated 8 January 1930 <www.egm.gov.tr/kurumlar/egm.gov.tr/IcSite/interpol/Tarihçe/Kararname.PNG> accessed 1 July 2023
Judicial Security Forces Regulation 2005
Law No 2559 on the Powers and Duties of Police 1934
Law No 2575 on the Council of State 1982
Law No 2577 on the Procedure of Administrative Justice 1982
Law No 2692 on the Coast Guard Command 1982
Law No 2797 on the High Court of Appeals 1983
Law No 2802 on Judges and Public Prosecutors 1983
Law No 2803 on the Organisation, Duties and Powers of the Gendarmerie 1983
Law No 3201 on the Security Organisation 1937

Law No 4721 (Turkish Civil Code) 2001
Law No 5235 on the Establishment, Duties, and Jurisdiction of First Instance Courts and Regional Courts of Appeal 2004
Law No 5237 (Turkish Criminal Code) 2004
Law No 5271 (Criminal Procedure Code) 2004
Law No 5395 on the Juvenile Protection 2005
Official Gazette No 25523 dated 15 July 2004, 'Türkiye Cumhuriyeti ve Avrupa Polis Teşkilatı Arasında İşbirliğine İlişkin Anlaşma' <www.resmigazete.gov.tr/eskiler/2004/07/20040715.htm#7> accessed 18 February 2023
Official Gazette No 25747 dated 6 March 2005, 'Bakanlar Kurulu Kararı (Karar No 2005/8496)' <www.resmigazete.gov.tr/eskiler/2005/03/20050306-1.htm> accessed 18 February 2023
Official Gazette No 29864 dated 21 October 2016, 'Genelge 2016/22: Mali Eylem Görev Gücü (FATF) IV. Tur Değerlendirmesi Hazırlıkları ve Ulusal Risk Değerlendirmesi Çalışmaları' <www.resmigazete.gov.tr/eskiler/2016/10/20161021-2-1.pdf> accessed 27 February 2023
Official Gazette No 29976 dated 11 February 2017, 'Türkiye Cumhuriyeti Anayasasında Değişiklik Yapılmasına Dair Kanun (Kanun No 6771)' <www.resmigazete.gov.tr/eskiler/2017/02/20170211-1.htm> accessed 21 January 2023
Official Gazette No 30145 dated 5 August 2017, 'Hakimler ve Savcılar Kurulu Birinci Dairesinin Kararı (Karar No 1069)' <www.resmigazete.gov.tr/eskiler/2017/08/20170805-2.pdf> accessed 12 January 2023
Official Gazette No 31522 dated 25 June 2021, 'Hakimler ve Savcılar Kurulu Birinci Dairesinin Kararı – Karar No 485' <www.resmigazete.gov.tr/eskiler/2021/06/20210625-15.pdf> accessed 28 May 2023
Presidential Decree No 1 on the Organisation of the Presidency 2018
TC Adalet Bakanlığı, 'Genelge No 154/1 Ailenin Korunması ve Kadına Karşı Şiddetin Önlenmesine Dair Kanunun Uygulanması' <https://cigm.adalet.gov.tr/Resimler/SayfaDokuman/18220201432351541-nolu-genelge.pdf> accessed 1 July 2023

6 The Institutional AML Composition of the UK

6.1 Introduction

After examining how Türkiye has structured its institutional AML framework in light of international standards and its unique law enforcement traditions and priorities, it is crucial to analyse how the UK has organised its institutional AML composition. Investigating such divergence points associated with historical, geographical, cultural, socio-legal, and political differences between the two AML regimes constitutes a solid ground for identifying underlying reasons for the diverse AML experience and success of Türkiye and the UK. In doing so, this chapter explains the unique institutional characteristics of the UK's AML structure, thereby identifying the key features responsible, at least partly, for the differentiation of the most prevalent predicate offence types from those found in Türkiye.

As a natural consequence of being a dualist state with a common law tradition,[1] the UK's legislative and judicial *modus operandi* significantly differ from such principles adopted in Türkiye. Amongst other characteristics, the sources of laws, the enactment process of legal instruments, and the experience of competent judges responsible for hearing ML and associated predicate crime cases may influence the AML effectiveness and enforcement practices of a jurisdiction. The previous chapter explained, *inter alia*, that the legal precedent does not constitute an essential source of law and does not bind courts in concluding present cases in Türkiye, suggesting that court verdicts may diversify across the judicature. It was also argued that ML and the vast majority of predicate crime lawsuits fall under the jurisdiction of Criminal Courts of General Jurisdiction, implying that newly graduated judges with limited experience may be in charge of trying these complex ML and organised crime cases. In addition to these contextual and remarkable differences between the two countries, the UK's law-making procedure enables the active participation of and consultation with the public in ratifying legislation in contrast with Türkiye,

1 Jacqueline Martin, *English Legal System* (8th edn, Hodder Education Group 2016).

DOI: 10.4324/9781003466680-6

implicating that the principal AML stakeholders may have a say in forming the UK's AML legal framework. However, the UK's judicial structure does not comprise any specialist court dedicated to dealing with ML, the introduction of which would strengthen the AML competency of the jurisdiction.

The operational AML armada in the UK, beyond its conventional LEAs, consists of a broad range of organisations with specific enforcement, investigative, and prosecution powers. The most striking divergence point of the institutional AML structure of the UK is that *each* mainstream police force, including local and regional units, incorporates financial forensics experts and specialist economic crime teams.[2] Furthermore, whilst these forces tackle relatively less serious predicate crimes, such as cash smuggling, several agencies are dedicated to confronting more complex and sophisticated predicate offences, such as fraud and tax evasion. More importantly, each component of the UK's institutional structure, the NCA, HMRC, and the SFO, to name a few, deal predominantly with specific types of predicate crimes and the associated ML problem, suggesting that each institution can develop crime-specific expertise to this end. In other words, given that tackling ML is not incumbent only on the conventional LEAs in contrast with Türkiye, the law enforcement strategy for tackling ML adopted in the UK gives reasonable grounds for expecting a more productive AML effectiveness. However, it is necessary to analyse whether this ostensibly advantageous organisational structure generates more effective AML outcomes and, if so, whether this would potentially benefit the Turkish AML framework.

The UKFIU operates under the auspices of the NCA, the core LEA established for tackling serious and organised crime, including ML. The UKFIU can utilise already existing law enforcement infrastructure, thereby processing and sharing the disclosures received (i.e., SARs) with other LEAs swiftly in company with the relevant intelligence, a crucial difference compared to MASAK. However, in contrast with MASAK, the UKFIU is not the sole authority in receiving, analysing, and disseminating financial intelligence in the UK. As discussed later, several other competent authorities harness similar functions whereby they process such intelligence as per their organisation-specific priorities. In other words, whilst being obligated to undertake the very same responsibilities as stipulated by the FATF Recommendations, FIUs of the two jurisdictions have been provided with divergent powers owing to the flexibility bestowed on administrations in this context. Therefore, it is of utmost importance to investigate whether and how this unique approach, which renders the UKFIU to share its exclusiveness in the financial intelligence domain, may impact the overall AML competency of the UK.

Firstly, the chapter examines the judicial composition of the UK with a specific focus on the criminal courts and investigates the qualifications of the

2 HM Government and UK Finance, 'Economic Crime Plan 2019–22' (July 2019) <https://assets.publishing.service.gov.uk/government/uploads/system/uploads/attachment_data/file/816215/2019-22_Economic_Crime_Plan.pdf> accessed 31 March 2023.

judiciary responsible for hearing ML and associated predicate crime cases. It also delves deeper into the workload of judges and the completion period of a relevant criminal case, as these may give insight to the judicial efficiency. It then explores the legal sources of the jurisdiction, elucidates the hierarchy between them, and explains the law-making process for codified (AML) legal instruments. In doing so, it endeavours to underline how being a dualist State with common law discipline may diversify the UK's AML response compared to Türkiye regarding legislative and juridical procedures. The chapter then analyses the UK's competent AML authorities, their legal (investigative, enforcement, prosecution) powers, and operational capabilities. By doing so, it seeks to identify the strength and weaknesses of the organisational UK AML composition, thereby shedding light on the areas in need of reform. Analysing the impact of such distinctive features addresses the main research aim of demonstrating whether and how differences between the institutional AML structures may impact the effectiveness in tackling and the prevalence of predicate crimes, thereby underlining the unique characteristics of an optimum AML regime.

This chapter aims to address the last two research questions, in particular, investigating (i) how an institutional AML structure may affect the prevalence of certain types of predicate crimes; and (ii) the areas in need of reform to ensure optimum AML effectiveness in addressing such offences. Accordingly, it investigates whether the role of the current institutional AML structure of the UK contributes to the effectiveness in tackling highest-risk predicate crimes (e.g., fraud and tax offences as identified in the NRA).[3] Additionally, it puts forward suggestions that would impede the prevalence of such crimes, thereby increasing the effectiveness of the organisational AML framework.

6.2 Judicial Composition of the UK

The judiciary in the UK diversifies across the jurisdiction, as England and Wales embrace the same judicial structure, whereas Scotland adopts another, and Northern Ireland utilises a third legal system. The criminal, civil, and family courts and tribunals are affiliated administratively to the Her Majesty's Courts and Tribunals Service (HMCTS) in England and Wales.[4] Moreover, whilst

3 HM Treasury and Home Office, 'National Risk Assessment of Money Laundering and Terrorist Financing 2020' (December 2020) <https://assets.publishing.service.gov.uk/government/uploads/system/uploads/attachment_data/file/945411/NRA_2020_v1.2_FOR_PUBLICATION.pdf> accessed 26 June 2023.

4 HM Courts & Tribunals Service, 'About Us' <www.gov.uk/government/organisations/hm-courts-and-tribunals-service/about> accessed 31 March 2023. Courts and tribunals in Scotland are connected to the Scottish Courts and Tribunals Service (SCTS); and the courts and tribunals in the Northern Ireland to the Northern Ireland Courts and Tribunals Service (NICTS). See Scottish Courts and Tribunals, 'About the Scottish Courts and Tribunals Service' <www.scotcourts.gov.uk/about-the-scottish-court-service> accessed 31 March 2023; Department of Justice, 'Courts and Tribunals' <www.justice-ni.gov.uk/topics/courts-and-tribunals> accessed 31 March 2023.

England, Wales, and Northern Ireland adopt common law doctrine, Scotland embraces a hybrid system,[5] which encapsulates common law and civil law principles. Consequently, the formation of the courts varies across these legal systems as the countries comprising the UK have their own autonomous legal systems and structures. However, it needs to be noted that the Supreme Court carries the judicial authority throughout the jurisdiction as the final court of appeal for hearing civil and criminal cases in the UK, except for criminal cases from Scotland,[6] an exemption for each country's autonomy as regards its legal composition. Therefore, hearing relevant ML or its underlying predicate crimes cases (i.e., appeals made either by the prosecution or the defence) as the last instance court in the UK is the responsibility of the Supreme Court. However, the Supreme Court accepts such cases provided that the appellant court certifies that a point of law of general public importance is involved in the decision and that the point of law is one which ought to be considered by the Supreme Court.[7] For example, on 22 April 2015, concerning an appeal from the England and Wales Court of Appeal (EWCA) in 2013, where the appellant court certified such importance by referring to criminal property, the UK Supreme Court concluded the *R v GH (Respondent)* [2015] UKSC 24 case as per Section 328(1) of POCA 2002 concerning ML.[8] The Supreme Court consists of 12 judges, hears cases by five, seven, or nine judges and determines them either by unanimity or a simple majority.[9] The Supreme Court judgements, similar to its predecessor (i.e., the Appellate Committee of the House of Lords), bind all inferior courts and mandate judges to comply with them.[10]

Before considering the courts that deal with ML and its underlying predicate crime cases in the UK, it is necessary to outline the whole set of courts and the hierarchy between them, thereby investigating whether and how they differentiate in handling those offences. There are five jurisdictions in England and Wales consisting of criminal, civil, family, military, and tribunal; and the competent court and the judges for dealing with the relevant cases vary accordingly.[11] Given the scope of the book, the analysis excludes family courts, military courts, tribunals, and the judicial organs in Scotland and Northern Ireland. The judicial organs in England and Wales can be classified into nine categories:

5 Thomas Mackay Cooper, 'The Common and the Civil Law. A Scot's View' (1950) 63(3) Harvard Law Review 468.

6 The Supreme Court, 'Role of the Supreme Court' <www.supremecourt.uk/about/role-of-the-supreme-court.html> accessed 31 March 2023.

7 Criminal Appeal Act 1968, s 33.

8 *R v GH (Respondent)* [2015] UKSC 24 [4].

9 Chris Hanretty, *A Court of Specialists: Judicial Behaviour on the UK Supreme Court* (OUP 2020).

10 Stephen R Wilson and others, *English Legal System* (4th edn, OUP 2020) 181.

11 Courts and Tribunals Judiciary, 'Jurisdictions' <www.judiciary.uk/about-the-judiciary/the-justice-system/jurisdictions/> accessed 31 March 2021.

a) The Supreme Court;
b) The Court of Appeal;
c) Divisional Courts (i.e., Chancery, Queen's Bench and Family Divisions of the High Court);
d) The High Court;
e) The Crown Court;
f) Magistrates' Courts;
g) County Courts;
h) Family Courts; and
i) Tribunals.

There exist three instances of courts that have jurisdiction over criminal and civil matters. The first instance criminal courts of England and Wales consist of Magistrates' Courts, the Crown Court, and youth courts, where a youth court is a specialised Magistrates' Court handling cases for people aged 10 to 17.[12] Civil courts of the first instance, on the other hand, are composed of County Courts and the High Court.[13] Although the High Court is responsible for trying more serious and complicated civil and family cases as the first instance court, it also hears appeals from previously mentioned criminal and civil first instance courts as a second instance court. Therefore, the High Court is one of the competent courts that deal with ML and its underlying predicate offence cases as its Divisional Courts hear appeals from the first instance courts, including criminal courts.[14] Lastly, the Supreme Court constitutes the last instance court as the final court of appeal in the UK. Therefore, the British criminal and civil courts can be listed as follows:

a) Magistrates' Courts (including youth courts), the Crown Court,[15] and the County Courts – (i.e., courts of the first instance);
b) The High Court (i.e., Divisional Courts of the High Court)[16] and the Court of Appeal – (i.e., courts of the second instance); and,
c) The Supreme Court – (i.e., the last instance court).

The High Court, one of the two Senior Courts of England and Wales, comprises three divisions, including the Queen's Bench Division, the Chancery Division, and the Family Division.[17] The Queen's Bench Division, which

12 UK Government, 'Criminal Courts' <www.gov.uk/courts> accessed 31 March 2023.
13 Courts and Tribunals Judiciary, 'County Court' <www.judiciary.uk/you-and-the-judiciary/going-to-court/county-court/> accessed 31 March 2023.
14 Martin (n 1) 28.
15 The Crown Court also acts as a second instance court regarding appeals against a Magistrates' Court's conviction or sentence decision.
16 It is also a court of the first instance for complex civil and family cases.
17 Courts and Tribunals Judiciary, 'High Court' <www.judiciary.uk/you-and-the-judiciary/going-to-court/high-court/> accessed 31 March 2023.

comprises 73 High Court Judges led by a president,[18] incorporates various specialist courts, such as Commercial Courts.[19] It has both civil and criminal jurisdiction and hears civil cases relating to contracts, such as breach of a contract, and the trials relating to tort law (i.e., civil wrongs, such as defamation of character and libel).[20] In other words, it tries civil cases that exceed the workforce of the County Courts in terms of their complexity or expenses. More importantly, it hears the most serious criminal cases, including predicate offences, such as robbery, in the Crown Court through its judges who travel around the jurisdiction for these purposes within the scope of its criminal jurisdiction.[21] Parenthetically, England and Wales consist of six geographical regions (i.e., circuits) in terms of practicing law, namely North West, North East, Midlands, South East, South West, and Wales, comprising the areas for the aforementioned judicial travel of the High Court Judges.[22] The Chancery Division of the High Court, which comprises 18 High Court Judges led by the Chancellor of the High Court, embodies three specialist courts, namely Insolvency and Companies, Patents, and Intellectual Property Enterprise Courts.[23] Lastly, the Family Division is authorised to hear all cases as the first instance court relating to children and tries trials as the second instance court regarding appeals from the Family Courts.[24] Therefore, as the only division with criminal jurisdiction, the qualifications of judges sitting in the Queen's Bench Division are of utmost importance regarding ML and predicate crime cases, as discussed subsequently. This institutional structure suggests that these judges, unlike their Turkish counterparts, can develop expertise in dealing with certain predicate offences as they are responsible for hearing the most serious criminal cases. That is not to say that judges in Türkiye cannot increase their competence, but the UK's judicial structure seems to actively promote such development. However, the UK does not devote a specialised court for

18 Courts and Tribunals Judiciary, 'High Court: Queen's Bench Division' <www.judiciary.uk/you-and-the-judiciary/going-to-court/high-court/queens-bench-division/work/> accessed 31 March 2023.

19 These specialist courts are Commercial, Technology and Construction, Admiralty, Administrative (including the Planning Court), and Circuit Commercial Courts. See Courts and Tribunals Judiciary, 'Courts of the Queen's Bench Division' <www.judiciary.uk/you-and-the-judiciary/going-to-court/high-court/queens-bench-division/courts-of-the-queens-bench-division/> accessed 31 March 2023.

20 Courts and Tribunals Judiciary (n 18).

21 ibid.

22 Judicial Office, 'The Judicial System of England and Wales: A Visitor's Guide' 11 <www.judiciary.uk/wp-content/uploads/2016/05/international-visitors-guide-10a.pdf> accessed 31 March 2023.

23 Courts and Tribunals Judiciary, 'High Court: The Chancery Division' <www.judiciary.uk/you-and-the-judiciary/going-to-court/high-court/the-chancery-division/work/> accessed 31 March 2023.

24 Courts and Tribunals Judiciary, 'High Court: Family' <www.judiciary.uk/you-and-the-judiciary/going-to-court/high-court/family2/> accessed 31 March 2023.

hearing ML cases and associated predicate crime cases, suggesting that the UK would benefit from establishing such courts.

The Court of Appeal comprises two divisions, namely the Criminal Division and the Civil Division.[25] Whilst the Civil Division hears appeals relating to civil cases, including the family domain, the Criminal Division tries appeals against criminal convictions and sentences.[26] Therefore, appeals against convictions or sentences relating to ML and associated predicate crime cases are heard before the Criminal Division of the Court of Appeal. Putting forward an appeal, regardless of their situation (i.e., whether or not they pleaded guilty), as a prerequisite, requires offenders to apply for obtaining permission to do so, which is then reviewed and determined by a judge.[27] The Criminal Division of the Court of Appeal determines these appeals against conviction and sentence within the criminal jurisdiction from the Crown Court and hears them in the presence of a bench comprising three Lord or Lady Justices, whereby it concludes them either by unanimity or by a majority.[28] Lastly, judgements given by the Court of Appeal, similar to the decisions of the Supreme Court, constitute the legal precedent that must be adhered to by courts in all subsequent cases.[29]

After outlining the full range of courts of England and Wales, it is necessary to provide the structure of the criminal courts and explain the qualifications of the judges sitting in these courts as they are responsible for dealing with ML and underlying predicate crime cases. As mentioned previously, regardless of the seriousness of a crime or the prescribed sentence envisaged for it, Magistrates' Courts are the starting point of any criminal case in England and Wales. Magistrates' Courts pass serious cases on to the Crown Court as committal hearings were abolished on 28 May 2013 in order to accelerate the British justice process.[30] Magistrates' Courts hear cases either by a District Judge (Magistrates' Courts) or two or three magistrates (i.e., Justices of the Peace).[31] They do not incorporate a jury and commit alleged offender(s) for trial by jury for any indictable offence accordingly.[32] In other words, they

25 Courts and Tribunals Judiciary, 'The Court of Appeal' <www.judiciary.uk/you-and-the-judiciary/going-to-court/court-of-appeal-home/> accessed 1 April 2023.

26 Courts and Tribunals Judiciary, 'The History of the Court of Appeal' <www.judiciary.uk/you-and-the-judiciary/going-to-court/court-of-appeal-home/coa-sub/> accessed 1 April 2023.

27 UK Government, 'Appeal a Crown Court Decision' <www.gov.uk/appeal-against-crown-court-verdict> accessed 1 April 2023.

28 Peter Hungerford-Welch, *Criminal Procedure and Sentencing* (9th edn, Routledge 2019).

29 Martin (n 1).

30 Ministry of Justice, 'Faster Justice as Unnecessary Committal Hearings Are Abolished' (*Press Release*, 28 May 2013) <www.gov.uk/government/news/faster-justice-as-unneccessary-committal-hearings-are-abolished> accessed 1 April 2023.

31 The Criminal Procedure Rules 2020, SI 2020/759, Rule 24.1.

32 Magistrates' Court Act 1980, s 6.

mainly hear less serious criminal cases, also known as summary offences,[33] such as common assault with insignificant injury or minor criminal damage, as the first instance criminal courts. Their jurisdiction also covers more serious crimes (i.e., either-way offences, offences that can also be tried in the Crown Court),[34] such as burglary and drug-related crimes, which are also examples of predicate offences. Nevertheless, Magistrates' Courts do not have jurisdiction over the most serious criminal cases (i.e., indictable-only offences), such as murder, rape, and robbery, and refer such cases to the Crown Court. Therefore, concerning ML and its underlying predicates, the seriousness of the predicate crimes determines the relevant competent court, and thereby their handling process, in the UK. It can be concluded that the UK and Türkiye embrace a similar approach to determining the appropriate court, which considers the seriousness of the criminal offence. Another similarity between the UK and Türkiye in determining the competent court is the upper limit of the penalty to be levied. More specifically, Magistrates' Courts can impose one or a combination of the following penalties: a ban, a fine, a community or prison sentence, where the prison sentence cannot exceed six months or be more than 12 months in total for two or more crimes.[35] As discussed previously, one of the criteria in determining the duties of relevant criminal courts in Türkiye, similar to the UK's exercise, is the maximum imprisonment term a court can impose, albeit the specified threshold is way higher (i.e., ten years).

The Crown Court is responsible for hearing indictable only crimes, either-way offences consigned by a Magistrates' Court for trial or sentencing, as well as appeals against a Magistrates' Court conviction or sentence.[36] Although all criminal cases start in Magistrates' Courts, it is the Crown Court that is responsible for hearing ML and (the vast majority of) predicate crime cases as they constitute serious offences[37] that fall under the jurisdiction of the Crown Court. The Crown Court follows a three-tier system, whereby cases, according to their nature, are allocated to different Crown Court centres, namely first-tier, second-tier, and third-tier centres.[38] Whilst first-tier centres deal with criminal and High Court civil cases, second-tier and third-tier centres deal only with Crown Court criminal cases.[39] Whilst criminal cases are handled by Circuit Judges and recorders in all types of centres, also High Court Judges hear cases in first-tier and second-tier centres.[40] Furthermore, all crime types heard in the Crown Court are categorised into three classes

33 ibid s 2.
34 ibid.
35 ibid s 32.
36 The Criminal Procedure Rules 2020, SI 2020/759, Rule 25.1.
37 Explanatory Notes to the Serious Crime Act 2015.
38 Courts and Tribunals Judiciary, 'Crown Court' <www.judiciary.uk/you-and-the-judiciary/going-to-court/crown-court/> accessed 6 April 2023.
39 ibid.
40 ibid.

of offences depending on their seriousness. More specifically, whilst Class 1 incorporates the most serious crimes (e.g., murder), Class 2 comprises predominantly sexual crimes (e.g., rape), whereas Class 3 includes all other criminal offences, including predicate crimes (e.g., burglary).[41] Accordingly, whilst Class 1 offences are ordinarily tried by a High Court Judge, Class 2 crimes, under the jurisdiction of the Presiding Judge, are heard by a Circuit Judge, and Class 3 cases are determined by a Circuit Judge or recorder.[42] In contrast with the Magistrates' Courts, the Crown Court incorporates a jury, which is in charge of deciding whether the suspect is guilty or not.[43] However, it is necessary to state that juries cannot find defendants guilty in the absence of (satisfactory) evidence as judges have the judicial power to instruct them to acquit the accused in such circumstances.[44] Other members of the Crown Court consist of one of the previously mentioned relevant judges, who is responsible for determining the sentence to be levied, and the solicitor of the defendant if s/he has one.[45] In circumstances where the Crown Court hears an appeal against a Magistrates' Court's decision, magistrates (i.e., ordinarily two but no more than four) may also sit in the Crown Court with a judge (i.e., usually a Circuit Judge).[46] Whilst Magistrates' Courts can impose the aforementioned punishments, Crown Courts, on the other hand, can charge heavier penalties, including life sentences, as they handle more serious criminal cases. Upon obtaining the necessary permission, the verdicts of the Crown Court (i.e., the conviction, sentence, or both decisions) can be appealed to the Criminal Division of the Court of Appeal, as touched upon previously.

It is important to investigate the eligibility of judges who are authorised to determine criminal cases in the aforementioned criminal courts and express the qualifications they need to carry to be assigned. The Lord Chief Justice is responsible for the training of the judiciary, including the fee paid and salaried judges, magistrates, and legal advisors.[47] Magistrates' Courts hear the relevant trials either by a District Judge or a panel of two or three magistrates, depending on the seriousness of the criminal matter. Magistrates are the volunteer members of local inhabitants aged between 18 and 74, who need to possess specific merits (rather than holding formal qualifications or legal training), such as good character, social awareness, and sound judgement, to serve in the

41 Ministry of Justice, 'Guide to Criminal Court Statistics' (Updated 24 September 2020) 7 <https://assets.publishing.service.gov.uk/government/uploads/system/uploads/attachment_data/file/920481/A_Guide_to_Criminal_Court_Statistics.pdf> accessed 6 April 2023.
42 ibid.
43 UK Government, 'Criminal Courts: Crown Court' <www.gov.uk/courts/crown-court> accessed 6 April 2023.
44 Gary Slapper and David Kelly, *The English Legal System* (18th edn, Routledge 2017) 546–47.
45 ibid.
46 Ministry of Justice (n 41).
47 Constitutional Reform Act 2005, s 7.

relevant courts of England and Wales.[48] Anyone who has these qualifications can be appointed as a magistrate, following a compulsory training programme that harnesses them with the necessary knowledge.[49] They carry out their duties as part-time law administers without being paid, and they are expected to serve at least five years before giving up their assignments whilst sitting at least 13 full or 26 half-days annually.[50] Lastly, legal advisors (i.e., Justices' Clerks) assist them in Magistrates' Courts concerning legal procedures, practices, and points of law.[51] District Judges, on the other hand, are legal professionals who have specific statutory qualifications. In more concrete terms, they need to have a five-year right of audience (i.e., the judicial appointment eligibility),[52] which means 'the right of a lawyer to appear and speak as an advocate for a party in a case in the court – in relation to all proceedings in any part of the Supreme Court, or all proceedings in county courts or magistrates' courts'.[53] Another frequently required qualification is the existence of a minimum of two years (i.e., 30 days' sittings) experience of serving as a Deputy District Judge, who is appointed from amongst the legal professionals experienced in criminal law and procedure.[54] In other words, considering ML and its underlying predicates, magistrates, in particular, do not play a critical role in the fight against the phenomenon directly. However, their contribution to the British judicial system is substantial, as most (criminal) cases (i.e., more than 95%) are handled by them,[55] allowing higher courts to devote their energy to more critical trials, such as ML. As discussed in Chapter 5 in detail, Criminal Courts of General Jurisdiction, in addition to relatively less serious criminal cases, try ML and the vast majority of predicate crime trials, which indubitably impair the efficiency of the Turkish judiciary in tackling phenomenon. Therefore, similar to the UK, decreasing the workload of the competent Turkish courts responsible for hearing ML and associated predicate crime cases would be an appropriate step to be taken.

The legal professionals who can sit in the Crown Court comprise High Court Judges, Circuit Judges, and recorders, as well as magistrates in specific

48 UK Government, 'Become a Magistrate' <www.gov.uk/become-magistrate/can-you-be-a-magistrate> accessed 24 August 2023.

49 ibid.

50 ibid.

51 ibid.

52 Courts Act 2003, s 22.

53 Courts and Tribunals Judiciary, 'District judge (Magistrates' Courts)' <www.judiciary.uk/about-the-judiciary/who-are-the-judiciary/judicial-roles/judges/district-judge-mags-ct/> accessed 6 April 2023.

54 ibid.

55 Courts and Tribunals Judiciary, 'The Justice System' <www.judiciary.uk/about-the-judiciary/the-justice-system/jurisdictions/criminal-jurisdiction/> accessed 6 April 2023. See also Berni Bell and Christian Dadomo, 'Magistrates Courts and the 2003 Reforms of the Criminal Justice System' (2006) 14(4) European Journal of Crime, Criminal Law, and Criminal Justice 339.

circumstances. Recorders have to hold a qualification of at least seven years of a solicitor or barrister experience and attend a training programme comprising an induction course in which they are supervised by a Circuit Judge for one week and periodical in-service training running on two days triennially.[56] They are appointed for five years by the Queen, which is then extended for an additional five years by the Lord Chancellor unless they fail to serve successfully, where they are required to sit for 30 days annually.[57] Circuit Judges, on the other hand, are appointed from amongst lawyers who have at least ten years of experience (of the right of audience, as discussed previously) with additional practical knowledge (in terms of serving either full time as District Judges on civil cases or part time as recorders on criminal cases).[58] Furthermore, some Circuit Judges get specialised in certain civil jurisdictions, such as mercantile cases,[59] which allow them to develop expertise in determining those cases accordingly. However, there does not exist a crime-specific specialisation approach, the adoption of which would generate expert judges in hearing criminal cases relating to ML and its predicates, thereby resulting in a more effective judicial AML competency. Considering the qualifications of the legal professionals sitting in the Crown Court, it can be argued that embracing such a policy would not demand significant shifts in the current system in securing expert judges in hearing the relevant cases. For instance, lawyers who have advocated for their defendants relating to ML or its underlying predicates (for at least ten years) would become specialist judges for hearing those cases as the current legal infrastructure seems suitable for such an approach. Finally, as the last group of legal professionals who can sit in the Crown Court, High Court Judges are appointed from amongst the Circuit Judges or candidates who have at least two years of experience or carry the necessary conditions for the judicial appointment eligibility on a seven-year basis, respectively.[60] In other words, given the qualifications of relevant legal professionals dealing with ML and its underlying predicate crime cases, the overall competency of the judicial composition of the UK seems to be fit for purpose. However, there remain opportunities for developing the current pertinent structure, such as recruiting crime-specific lawyers as competent judges for hearing the previously mentioned cases or establishing specialised relevant courts analogous to youth courts. Nevertheless, a 2016 Home Affairs Committee report highlighted that

56 Courts and Tribunals Judiciary, 'Judicial Roles: Recorder' <www.judiciary.uk/about-the-judiciary/who-are-the-judiciary/judicial-roles/judges/recorder/> accessed 8 April 2023.

57 ibid.

58 Courts and Tribunals Judiciary, 'Judicial Roles: Circuit Judge' <www.judiciary.uk/about-the-judiciary/who-are-the-judiciary/judicial-roles/judges/ciruit-judge/> accessed 8 April 2023.

59 ibid.

60 Courts and Tribunals Judiciary, 'Judicial Roles: High Court Judges' <www.judiciary.uk/about-the-judiciary/who-are-the-judiciary/judicial-roles/judges/high-court-judges/> accessed 8 April 2023.

neither judges nor prosecutors seem eager to develop expertise in this context as they consider asset recovery and proceeds of crime (i.e., tackling ML) 'a very niche area of law',[61] confirming the aptness of these suggestions.

Before examining the legal sources of the UK and investigating the hierarchy between them, it is appropriate to inquire into the workload of judges as it may affect the success of the jurisdiction in dealing with criminal offences efficaciously, including ML and associated predicate crimes. According to a 2020 CoE report, the number of professional judges per 100,000 inhabitants was 3.1 in the UK (i.e., England and Wales – it was 3.7 in Scotland and 3.6 in Northern Ireland) in 2018, way below the ratio in Türkiye (i.e., 15.6 in 2018).[62] However, the UK had approximately 0.25% judicial system budget as a percentage of GDP in 2018.[63] Whilst this ratio is similar to the corresponding budget in Türkiye (i.e., 0.22%, as touched upon previously), it equalled roughly 75 euros per inhabitant in 2018,[64] around four times higher than the budget reserved for the judiciary in Türkiye. The annual average of the number of magistrates and judges serving in England and Wales between 1 April 2019 and 31 March 2020 was 13,177 and 3,174, respectively.[65] In this period, whilst Magistrates' Courts received 1.5 million cases where the median waiting time from offence to completion of a case was 161 days, the Crown Court received 104,000 cases.[66] More recently, between 1 February 2020 and 1 February 2021, Magistrates' Courts received 1,207,690 cases (i.e., approximately 92,900 cases per month) and concluded 1,111,547 proceedings (i.e., around 85,504 lawsuits monthly); and as of 1 February 2021, they have 412,494 trials to be determined.[67] In the same period, the Crown Court received 108,180 cases (i.e., approximately 8,322 cases per month) and completed 89,472 judicial proceedings (i.e., around 6,882 proceedings monthly), and as of 1 February 2021, it has 57,625 'outstanding cases' that have yet to be concluded.[68] Another significant point that needs to be investigated here

61 Home Affairs Committee, 'Collecting Proceeds of Crime' (HC 2015–16) para 29 <https://publications.parliament.uk/pa/cm201617/cmselect/cmhaff/25/2505.htm#_idTextAnchor009> accessed 8 April 2023.

62 Council of Europe, 'European Judicial Systems CEPEJ Evaluation Report: 2020 Evaluation Cycle (2018 Data)' (September 2020) 46 <https://rm.coe.int/evaluation-report-part-1-english/16809fc058> accessed 19 August 2023.

63 ibid 21.

64 ibid.

65 Georgina Sturge, 'Court Statistics for England and Wales' (UK Parliament Research Briefing Paper No 8372, 22 December 2020) 25 <https://commonslibrary.parliament.uk/research-briefings/cbp-8372/> accessed 10 April 2023.

66 ibid.

67 HM Courts & Tribunals Service, 'Statistical Data Set: HMCTS Management Information – February 2020 to February 2021' (8 April 2021) <https://assets.publishing.service.gov.uk/government/uploads/system/uploads/attachment_data/file/976398/20210327_HMCTS_raw_data_for_Feb20_to_Feb21.csv/preview> accessed 10 April 2023.

68 ibid.

is the completion period of a trial, particularly in the Crown Court, as the primary court in dealing with ML and associated predicate crimes. According to the quarterly criminal court statistics of the Ministry of Justice, from October to December 2020 (i.e., Q4 2020), cases before the Crown Court remained as 'outstanding' on average (i.e., mean) 196 days with a median of 125 days.[69] These figures suggest that although having a low judge ratio per 100,000 inhabitants, the UK has ensured a more accelerated judicial process for concluding criminal cases, including ML and its underlying predicates, compared to Türkiye. Admittedly, this may be considered another strength of the UK's AML framework. Therefore, although Türkiye has determined to conclude all criminal cases in ten to 13 months (see Chapter 5), targeting shorter periods and allocating more financial resources to the judiciary would help create a more hostile environment for offenders, including money launderers.

6.3 Legal Sources of the UK and the Hierarchy Between Them

Compared with the history of the (modern) Turkish legal system, the British legal framework can be identified as atavistic as its evolution dates back to ancient times and the accumulation of the UK's legal instruments roots in the feudal background of the jurisdiction. In advance of the establishment of the King's Court (i.e., *Curia Regis*), there had been no judicial uniformity across the kingdom as each feudal territory used to resolve relevant disputes according to the local customs and norms.[70] In order to ensure that the judicial outcomes on the same or similar matters do not diversify across the realm, the previously mentioned court, whose verdicts composed the (initial) common obligatory legal ground for the entire administration, had been established.[71] In other words, although the King's Court does not exist today, as a common law jurisdiction, the legal precedent constitutes one of the essential sources of law for the UK that binds courts and judges in concluding subsequent cases as per the principle of *stare decisis*.[72] That is not to say that the prior judicial decisions do not affect determining current lawsuits in Türkiye at all; but, unlike common law jurisdictions, they do not comprise the essential basis of the law. Additionally, having examined the AML legal frameworks of Türkiye and the

69 Ministry of Justice, 'National Statistics – Criminal Court Statistics Quarterly: October to December 2020' (Published 25 March 2021) <www.gov.uk/government/statistics/criminal-court-statistics-quarterly-october-to-december-2020/criminal-court-statistics-quarterly-october-to-december-2020> accessed 10 April 2023.

70 Joseph Dainow, 'The Civil Law and the Common Law: Some Points of Comparison' (1967) 15(3) The American Journal of Comparative Law 419.

71 ibid.

72 Wilson and others (n 10) 179. See also Rupert Cross and James William Harris, *Precedent in English Law* (4th edn, OUP 1991).

UK, a noteworthy difference between them that needs to be highlighted here is that whilst Turkish codified legal instruments prescribe more general principles, the UK's legislation provides a more detailed codification. Therefore, the binding nature of the legal precedent and the thoroughly codified legal instruments render court decisions, including ML and predicate crime verdicts, more consistent in and across the UK than Türkiye, thereby enhancing the UK's judicial AML effectiveness and efficiency.

In addition to the common law made up of legal precedents established by the courts, the principal legal sources of the UK comprise statutes enacted by the UK Parliament, international legal instruments, and until recently, the EU law. However, it is necessary to state that as the UK is a dualist State, international legal instruments do not give any domestic legal effect by ratification unless they are incorporated into national legislation by Acts of Parliament or other secondary legislation.[73] Similarly, although the European Communities Act 1972 had ensured that the EU legal instruments gained direct effect in the UK, the EU law (except for the retained EU law) is no longer directly applicable as the UK is not an EU member anymore.[74] Lastly, in contrast to Türkiye, the UK does not have a wholly codified constitution, which can be found in a single text, albeit substantial parts of it made up of various written legal instruments (i.e., statutes).[75] Therefore, case law (i.e., common law) and enacted law constitute legal sources of the jurisdiction. Considering that the judiciary must comply with both the legislation and the legal precedent in concluding cases before them, common law, as a source of law, is not a level of hierarchy intrinsically. The two origins of law complement each other as the legal precedent bases for the judgements of courts, where the judiciary also interprets and has to comply with codified legal instruments in establishing the legal precedent. Nevertheless, given that as a general rule, the courts cannot overrule enacted law,[76] the codified legal instruments of the UK sit at the highest level of the *hierarchy of norms* as the Parliament is the supreme authority for the enactment, amendment, and repeal of laws as well as ratifying international agreements. In other words, codified legal instruments are superior to the legal precedent.[77]

Legal instruments that comprise legislation can be classified into two categories as consisting of primary and secondary legislation. The primary legislation encompasses the principal laws (e.g., Acts enacted by the UK Parliament) and Prerogative Orders, which are specific legal instruments created either by

73 European Scrutiny Committee, 'The EU Bill and Parliamentary Sovereignty' (Tenth Report, HC, 24 December 2010) para 10 <https://publications.parliament.uk/pa/cm201011/cmselect/cmeuleg/633/63304.htm> accessed 12 April 2023.

74 European Union (Withdrawal Act) 2018, ss 2 to 7.

75 UK Parliament, 'Parliament's Authority' <www.parliament.uk/about/how/role/sovereignty/> accessed 12 April 2023.

76 ibid.

77 Martin (n 1) 39.

the Crown or the Privy Council[78] under the royal prerogative.[79] It is necessary to state that in parallel with the diversification of the judiciary across the jurisdiction, the geographical extent of each legal text diverges, correspondingly. However, legislation enacted by the UK Parliament, including AML legal instruments, apply to the UK in its entirety as they deal with matters of general public interest. The secondary legislation includes legal instruments created predominantly for detailing the primary legislation, thereby ensuring their effective implementation in practical terms. It consists primarily of Statutory Instruments (e.g., Orders, Regulations, and Rules), Statutory Rules and Orders, and Church Instruments, each of which has an equal legislative force.[80] Lastly, By-Laws constitute the last group of codified legal instruments, which can be legislated by local authorities or particular public bodies to regulate their jurisdictions.[81] Accordingly, the legal instruments of the UK constituting the national legal hierarchy can be listed by superiority as follows:

a) The Constitution;[82]
b) Statutes enacted by the UK Parliament;[83]
c) Statutory Instruments, Statutory Rules and Orders, and Church Instruments;
d) By-Laws; and
e) Case Law (i.e., common law and jurisprudence).

In terms of legislative power, as the primary legislature, the UK Parliament is the sole authority in making laws that apply in all constituent countries. It is crucial to explain the unique aspects of the law-making process of the jurisdiction and the period it may take to enact a particular legal instrument, which would give insight into whether the UK can address international AML developments promptly. The need for enacting new laws arises from many reasons, including addressing an emergent issue, such as AML/CTF matters, and the revision of case law made by the judiciary,[84] another example that clarifies the place of common law in the legal hierarchy. Whilst there are three kinds of

78 The Privy Council refers to 'the mechanism through which interdepartmental agreement is reached on those items of Government business which, for historical or other reasons, fall to Ministers as Privy Counsellors rather than as Departmental Ministers'. See, The Privy Council Office <https://privycouncil.independent.gov.uk> accessed 14 April 2023.

79 UK Legislation, 'Understanding Legislation' <www.legislation.gov.uk/understanding-legislation> accessed 14 April 2023.

80 ibid.

81 ibid.

82 It is worth reiterating that although the British Constitution does not consist only of codified legal rules, both common law and legislated legal instruments must comply with it.

83 Given that the UK requires domestic legal action to implement international obligations, international legal instruments do not have superiority over national legislation by themselves.

84 UK Parliament, 'Why Are New Laws Needed?' <www.parliament.uk/about/how/laws/new-laws/> accessed 17 April 2023.

Bills,[85] it is necessary to explain the enactment process of Public Bills as the relevant AML legislation originates from Public Bills (e.g., POCA 2002) and concerns the general population.[86]

In order for a Public Bill to be enacted, it rotates in the Parliament through many phases before being sent to the Monarch for royal assent.[87] Before this formal introduction, a Bill can be published as a Draft Bill, which allows the members of both chambers to scrutinise its provisions, a procedure called 'pre-legislative scrutiny'.[88] This scrutinisation process is undertaken either by select committees in one of the Houses or a joint committee composed of members of those chambers.[89] The most striking difference of the legislative process in the UK in comparison to Türkiye is the public consultation. The Government can consult the public opinion through White and Green Papers, whereby the community debates on the matter and declares their standpoint, albeit not compulsory.[90] For example, the UK Government recently opened a public consultation regarding changes to bodies granted investigatory and other powers under the POCA 2002,[91] suggesting that all AML actors intrinsically have a say in establishing the pertinent legal framework. Therefore, given that the public is actively involved in the law-making process in the UK, British legal instruments, including AML legislation, are more likely to be effective in ensuring public trust and addressing society's needs. That is not to say that the Turkish AML legal structure is ineffective, but obtaining, for instance, opinions of the obliged entities in such a process would undoubtedly intensify the rigour of the Turkish AML legal armada.

The passage of a Bill through Parliament before becoming an Act comprises five stages of legislation in each House, consisting of the first reading, second reading, committee stage, report stage, and third reading.[92] Although there is no set time frame for passing a Bill, considering the usual intervals between

85 These are Public Bills, including Private Members' Bills, Private Bills, and Hybrid Bills. See UK Parliament, 'What Is a Bill?' <www.parliament.uk/about/how/laws/bills/> accessed 17 April 2023.

86 UK Parliament, 'Public Bills' <www.parliament.uk/about/how/laws/bills/public/> accessed 17 April 2023.

87 For a more detailed discussion on the procedural legislative process, see Cabinet Office, 'Guide to Making Legislation' (2022) <https://assets.publishing.service.gov.uk/government/uploads/system/uploads/attachment_data/file/645652/Guide_to_Making_Legislation_Jul_2017.pdf> accessed 29 June 2023.

88 UK Parliament (n 84).

89 UK Parliament, 'What Is a Draft Bill?' <www.parliament.uk/about/how/laws/draft/> accessed 17 April 2023.

90 ibid.

91 Home Office, 'Government Consultation: Changes to Bodies Granted Investigatory and Other Powers Under the Proceeds of Crime Act 2002' (January 2021) <https://assets.publishing.service.gov.uk/government/uploads/system/uploads/attachment_data/file/956309/AFI_Order_Consultation_V8.pdf> accessed 28 May 2023.

92 Cabinet Office (n 87).

the parliamentary stages, it ordinarily takes approximately a minimum of three months.[93] However, in some cases, such as regarding international agreements (e.g., UN Conventions concerning AML/CTF matters), the Parliament can apply for fast-track procedures for legislation, whereby enacting a legal instrument in a few days.[94] It is also necessary to state that Acts come into effect from midnight at the start of the day of the Royal Assent unless otherwise prescribed by a commencement order.[95] In light of these legislation stages, it would be apt to posit that there are no undue inhibitors in the British legislative system, suggesting that it can promptly respond to AML developments.

6.4 Competent Authorities of the UK

Similar to its Turkish counterpart, the UK's AML/CTF framework consists of a myriad of authorities, including ministerial departments, such as Home Office and HM Treasury (HMT); non-ministerial departments, such as HM Revenue and Customs (HMRC), National Crime Agency (NCA), and Serious Fraud Office (SFO); other public bodies, such as Financial Conduct Authority (FCA); and the conventional LEAs (i.e., the police). However, except for the prevailing Turkish LEAs, there is no specialised operational agency in Türkiye entrusted with combatting ML and its underlying predicates. In other words, apart from FIUs, whilst tackling ML is the responsibility of mainstream LEAs in Türkiye, there are numerous institutions in charge of preventing ML in the UK, each of which is dedicated to investigating particular aspects of the phenomenon as discussed subsequently. Additionally, whilst MASAK serves as the national hub for receiving and analysing financial intelligence in Türkiye, HMRC, NCA, SFO, FCA, and the police, along with the UKFIU, gather and analyse such data in the UK, thereby investigating and prosecuting[96] ML cases. For example, the FCA commenced a criminal prosecution against National Westminster Bank Plc under the 2007 MLRs on 16 March 2021, albeit it was the first-ever application of such powers by the organisation.[97] Therefore, this organisational structure suggests that the responsibility of tackling predicate offences is relinquished to a broad range of agencies with specific expertise and legal powers. Considering the sophisticated nature of

93 ibid.

94 Constitution Committee, 'Fast-Track Legislation: Constitutional Implications and Safeguards' (HL, 17 June 2009) para 22 <https://publications.parliament.uk/pa/ld200809/ldselect/ldconst/116/11604.htm#note4> accessed 20 April 2023.

95 UK Parliament, 'Royal Assent' <www.parliament.uk/about/how/laws/passage-bill/commons/coms-royal-assent/> accessed 20 April 2023.

96 The prosecution authority for money laundering cases belongs, amongst others, to the Crown Prosecution Service (CPS), SFO, and the FCA.

97 Financial Conduct Authority, 'FCA Starts Criminal Proceedings Against NatWest Plc' (*Press Release*, 16 March 2021) <www.fca.org.uk/news/press-releases/fca-starts-criminal-proceedings-against-natwest-plc> accessed 13 April 2023.

various predicate offences and associated ML schemes,[98] the UK's approach to institutional AML structure appears to be more effective as it fosters the development of expertise. The remaining part of this chapter investigates the role and operational capabilities of the principal AML agencies and examines their particular contribution to the national AML response.

6.4.1 Law Enforcement Agencies of the UK

6.4.1.1 Police Forces

The policing network, which comprises 43 local police forces (in England and Wales),[99] constitutes a vital part of the British national response to the ML threat at a regional and local level. The most striking difference regarding the organisational characteristics of these conventional LEAs compared to their Turkish counterparts is that *each* police force in the UK incorporates specialist economic crime teams.[100] Nevertheless, since there are dedicated national agencies responsible for investigating specific types of predicate crimes and associated ML (e.g., arising from tax offences), the mainstream police forces deal with relatively less complex predicate offences, such as cash smuggling. However, it is necessary to state that specialist economic crime teams of the Metropolitan Police Service and the City of London Police are more advanced than the remaining police forces as they deal with more complex predicate offences.[101] The prevalence of organised crime groups, the transportation network connected with risky jurisdictions, and extensive cash-based business transactions render the jurisdiction of these police forces more vulnerable to ML and associated threats.[102] Accordingly, the Economic Crime Department of the City of London Police is designated as the principal LEA for preventing and investigating economic crime, particularly fraud.[103] It hosts the National Fraud Intelligence Bureau (NFIB) and Action Fraud, the UK's national fraud

98 Ping He, 'A Typological Study on Money Laundering' (2010) 13(1) Journal of Money Laundering Control 15.

99 POLICE.UK, 'UK Police Forces' <www.police.uk/pu/contact-the-police/uk-police-forces/> accessed 13 April 2023.

100 See, for example, the Serious Economic Crime Unit of Kent Police, which includes, amongst others, the Proactive Money Laundering Team. Kent Police, 'Progression Opportunities' <www.kent.police.uk/police-forces/kent-police/areas/kent-police/c/careers/police-officers/new-investigate-first/progression-opportunities/> accessed 13 April 2023.

101 HM Government and UK Finance (n 2).

102 Matt Hopkins and Nikki Shelton, 'Identifying Money Laundering Risk in the United Kingdom: Observations from National Risk Assessments and a Proposed Alternative Methodology (2018) 25(1) European Journal on Criminal Policy and Research 63.

103 The Economic Crime Department of the City of London Police has been the National Lead Force for Fraud since 2008. See Home Office, 'National Lead Force for Fraud' <www.gov.uk/government/publications/national-lead-force-for-fraud/national-lead-force-for-fraud> accessed 14 April 2023.

and cybercrime reporting centre.[104] For example, the City of London Police has ensured the confiscation of criminal assets equivalent to approximately GBP 5.5 million and secured the conviction of 155 individuals on fraud charges in 2019/2020.[105] Similarly, an investigation led by the Proactive Money Laundering Team of the Metropolitan Police Service denied approximately GBP 450,000 to an offender in December 2020, which resulted in the perpetrator's imprisonment under Section 329 of POCA 2002.[106] These figures may shed light on the effectiveness of mainstream police forces regarding the fight against ML and its underlying predicates in the UK. Although it is impossible to assign specialist economic crime teams to each mainstream LEA in Türkiye (see Chapter 5), appointing such units to each LEA operating in higher-risk ML cities would be an appropriate approach for Türkiye.

6.4.1.2 Regional Organised Crime Units

ROCUs, as 'the primary interface' between police forces and the NCA,[107] are additional components of the policing network that harness a comprehensive specialist policing toolkit addressing serious and organised crime. The UK Government's Serious and Organised Crime Strategy 2018 determines ML and, amongst others, particular predicate crimes, such as bribery, corruption, fraud, and human trafficking, as the main categories of serious offences.[108] Accordingly, involving in (i.e., planning, coordinating, and committing) such crimes, whether individually or collectively and/or as part of international criminal organisations, constitutes a serious and organised crime in the UK.[109] In close collaboration with the NCA, ROCUs lead the operational response to serious and organised crime, including ML and its underlying predicates, at the regional level and support police forces within their regions in this context. In circumstances where the complexity of ML and associated predicate

104 ActionFraud, 'Who Are the National Fraud Intelligence Bureau?' <www.actionfraud.police.uk/what-is-national-fraud-intelligence-bureau> accessed 14 April 2023.

105 City of London Police, 'Annual Report 2019/2020' (2020) 29 <www.cityoflondon.police.uk/SysSiteAssets/media/downloads/city-of-london/about-us/annual-report-2019-final.pdf> accessed 14 April 2023.

106 Metropolitan Police, 'Man Jailed After Money Laundering Team Investigation' (18 February 2021) <https://news.met.police.uk/news/man-jailed-after-money-laundering-team-investigation-421551> accessed 14 April 2023.

107 Home Office, 'The Strategic Policing Requirement' (March 2015) 14 <https://assets.publishing.service.gov.uk/government/uploads/system/uploads/attachment_data/file/417116/The_Strategic_Policing_Requirement.pdf> accessed 14 April 2023.

108 HM Government, 'Serious and Organised Crime Strategy' (November 2018) <https://assets.publishing.service.gov.uk/government/uploads/system/uploads/attachment_data/file/752850/SOC-2018-web.pdf> accessed 14 April 2023. See also NCA, 'Annual Plan 2022–2023' (August 2022) <www.nationalcrimeagency.gov.uk/who-we-are/publications/594-nca-annual-plan-2022-23/file> accessed 17 August 2023.

109 ibid.

crimes exceed the investigatory capabilities of police forces, ROCUs take over the investigation of such cases unless they do not require the involvement of a dedicated national agency, such as the NCA. They operate as regional police units since their creation in 2009, and there are nine ROCUs across England and Wales that encompass all police forces (except for the Metropolitan Police Service and the City of London Police)[110] in this ROCU network.[111] Furthermore, all ROCUs incorporate Regional Asset Recovery Teams (RARTs) and Asset Recovery Enforcement (ACE) Teams that significantly contribute to the overall amount recovered in proceeds of crime in the UK.[112] For instance, ACE Teams confiscated more than GBP 36.5m between April 2018 and March 2019.[113] It is worth reiterating here that the GDS personnel undertook 29 operations against ML/TF in 2019, whereby they captured 155 suspects; and applied seizure procedures in 671 incidents, and thereby seized 125 million TL (approximately GBP 10.25m as of June 2021) as discussed in Chapter 5 previously. More recently, the ROCU of the Eastern Region Special Operations Unit (ERSOU)[114] secured the confiscation of approximately GBP 2.25m, as well as the compensation of GBP 1.3m for victims, in 2020.[115] By the deployment of specialist policing capabilities to (local) police forces within, *inter alia*, the scope of AML efforts, ROCUs serve similar to the KOM branches of the GCG in this regard. However, considering the aforementioned confiscation figures secured in the UK, ROCUs' contribution to the fight against ML and the associated predicate crimes is more visible and impressive than KOMs in Türkiye. Therefore, the confiscation efforts devoted by the competent Turkish authorities to asset recovery need to be reinforced accordingly.

110 Although the Metropolitan Police Service and the City of London Police are not part of any of the nine ROCUs, along with the British Transport Police, they harness ROCU functions and other specialist capabilities as discussed above.

111 HMICFRS, 'Regional Organised Crime Units: An Inspection of the Effectiveness of the Regional Organised Crime Units' (February 2021) <www.justiceinspectorates.gov.uk/hmicfrs/publication-html/regional-organised-crime-units-effectiveness/> accessed 14 April 2023.

112 Home Office, 'Asset Recovery Action Plan' (July 2019) <https://assets.publishing.service.gov.uk/government/uploads/system/uploads/attachment_data/file/815900/20190709_Asset_Recovery_Action_Plan_FINAL_Clean.pdf> accessed 14 April 2023.

113 ibid 6.

114 ERSOU consists of Bedfordshire, Cambridgeshire, Essex, Hertfordshire, Kent, Norfolk, and Sussex Police Forces. See Eastern Region Special Operations Unit <https://ersou.police.uk> accessed 14 April 2023.

115 Eastern Region Special Operations Unit, 'Region's Criminals Forced to Repay £2.25m in 2020' <https://ersou.police.uk/news/2020/12/17/region's-criminals-forced-to-repay-£2.25m-in-2020/> accessed 15 April 2023.

6.4.1.3 National Crime Agency

The NCA was established by the Crime and Courts Act 2013.[116] It leads and coordinates national efforts against serious and organised crime, including ML and predicate crimes.[117] It also hosts the National Economic Crime Centre (NECC) and the UKFIU. Accordingly, it is appropriate to scrutinise its organisational structure, powers, and capabilities to understand the disposition of the UKFIU.[118] The NCA's organisational structure consists of three principal directorates, namely the NECC, Operations, and Capabilities, which conduct their activities as affiliated to the Director-General of the NCA.[119] The Directorate of Operations incorporates Intelligence, Investigations, and Threat Leadership subdirectories and the Directorate of Capabilities embodies the Chief Financial Officer, Director of Strategy, and the Director of Digital Data and Technology.[120] The NCA Board also incorporates non-executive members and sub-committees,[121] which provide external expertise and advice relating to criminal matters and policing practices and contribute to the rigour of the activities held by the agency. In other words, the organisational composition of the NCA appears to be well established to encompass a wide range of capabilities, thereby developing an authoritative view of the threat for all competent authorities that allows dealing with (serious and organised) criminal activities, including ML and predicate crimes.

The serious and organised crime schemes addressed (specifically) by the NCA encompass the most harmful predicate crimes, such as drug trafficking and human trafficking, and the ML offence.[122] The criminal asset denial, as well as the relevant legal powers harnessed in this end (i.e., confiscation,

116 Crime and Courts Act 2013, pt 1.

117 It is a non-ministerial, operationally independent government department overseen by the Home Secretary with officers who harness the operational powers of a police constable, an immigration officer, and a customs officer and general customs official, authorities that render the agency a core LEA in this end. See NCA, 'Governance and Transparency' <www.nationalcrimeagency.gov.uk/who-we-are/governance-and-transparency> accessed 16 April 2023. See also Christopher Recker, 'The National Crime Agency: A Critical Analysis of Its Potential Impact on the UK's Financial Crime Policy' in Nicholas Ryder, Jon Tucker and Umut Turksen (eds), *The Financial Crisis and White-Collar Crime – Legislative and Policy Responses: A Critical Assessment* (Routledge 2017).

118 It is necessary to state that although the NCA is the FIU of the UK, the UKFIU was discussed in a separate section in detail subsequently.

119 NCA, 'NCA Senior Leadership Structure' (January 2021) <https://nationalcrimeagency.gov.uk/accessibility-text/493-nca-senior-leadership-structure-january-2021-text-version/file> accessed 16 April 2023.

120 ibid.

121 See, for instance, NCA, 'Audit and Risk Assurance Committee' <www.nationalcrimeagency.gov.uk/who-we-are/publications/108-nca-audit-risk-assurance-committee-terms-of-reference/file> accessed 16 April 2023.

122 NCA, 'What We Investigate' <www.nationalcrimeagency.gov.uk/what-we-do/crime-threats> accessed 17 April 2023.

civil recovery, taxation, UWOs, to name a few), constitute the nucleus of the NCA's response to ML and its underlying predicates. The NCA considers the criminal asset denial as an operational tactic, which is utilised primarily for disrupting serious and organised criminals rather than recovering the proceeds of crime in the first place.[123] That is not to say that it does not attach importance to the recovery practices, but the NCA prioritises the recovery of assets as per the magnitude of the disruption.[124] In order to ensure a more successful criminal asset recovery, the NCA devotes a centre, namely Proceeds of Crime Centre, which is dedicated to accrediting and monitoring the financial investigators in the UK, as well as to providing training in financial investigation and the application of recovery powers as determined by POCA 2002.[125] The NCA also hosts the Joint Financial Analysis Centre (JFAC), which pieces together, amongst others, the analysis and intelligence capabilities of the four crucial LEAs in this context, namely the NCA, HMRC, the FCA, and the SFO.[126] Although it was created originally to address the Panama Papers leak in 2016,[127] JFAC maintains its activities to provide the competent British authorities with financial analysis and intelligence in the fight against economic crime,[128] including ML and predicate crimes. Furthermore, besides liaising with Europol and INTERPOL,[129] the NCA has established an international network of (more than 150) liaison officers that operate abroad in higher-risk jurisdictions, including Türkiye, complementing the UK's international cooperation efforts.[130] In contrast with MASAK's solitary position regarding producing financial intelligence in Türkiye, the UKFIU's analysis and intelligence capacity have been augmented by various LEAs, which indubitably provide competent British authorities with more substantial amounts of such intelligence. Given that these more advanced capabilities are strongly associated

123 NCA, 'Criminal Asset Denial' <www.nationalcrimeagency.gov.uk/what-we-do/how-we-work/investigating-and-disrupting-the-highest-risk-serious-and-organised-criminals/criminal-asset-denial> accessed 17 April 2023.

124 ibid.

125 NCA, 'Contact the Proceeds of Crime Centre' <www.nationalcrimeagency.gov.uk/contact-us/13-proceeds-of-crime-centre> accessed 17 April 2023.

126 HMRC, 'Taskforce Launches Criminal and Civil Investigations into Panama Papers' (8 November 2016) <www.gov.uk/government/news/taskforce-launches-criminal-and-civil-investigations-into-panama-papers> accessed 17 April 2023.

127 Carmina FS Del Mundo, 'How Countries Seek to Strengthen Anti-Money Laundering Laws in Response to the Panama Papers, and the Ethical Implications of Incentivizing Whistleblowers' (2019) 40(1) Northwestern Journal of International Law and Business 87.

128 HMRC (n 126).

129 NCA, 'Intelligence: Enhancing the Picture of Serious Organised Crime Affecting the UK' <www.nationalcrimeagency.gov.uk/what-we-do/how-we-work/intelligence-enhancing-the-picture-of-serious-organised-crime-affecting-the-uk> accessed 17 April 2023.

130 NCA, 'International Network' <www.nationalcrimeagency.gov.uk/what-we-do/how-we-work/providing-specialist-capabilities-for-law-enforcement/international-network> accessed 31 May 2023.

with being a law enforcement type of FIU, revising the administrative role of MASAK in Türkiye would similarly reinforce the Turkish AML competency.

Whilst the NCA is the national response to serious and organised crime in the UK, the NECC constitutes the operational dimension of such response by assembling each component of the AML battle, including LEAs, justice agencies, and the public and private sectors. As a multi-agency centre, which aims to ensure a coordinated and well-implemented appropriate criminal, civil, and regulatory action against the phenomenon, it brings together officers/representatives from the NCA, SFO, FCA, City of London Police, HMRC, Home Office, and the CPS.[131] Furthermore, it incorporates JMLIT, a PPP enabling sharing of information between LEAs and the financial sector relating to AML,[132] aiming at advancing intelligence-sharing methods and increasing the effectiveness of financial data gathered through a wide range of diverse sources with a specific focus on ML. The task force was initiated as a pilot programme in 2015 by the alliance of the Home Office, the NCA, the City of London Police, the British Bankers' Association (BBA), and other financial institutions[133] and was made permanent in 2016.[134] It collaborates with the key AML LEAs, namely the NCA, SFO, HMRC, City of London Police, and the Metropolitan Police Service, more than 40 financial institutions, the FCA, and Cifas,[135] a non-profit fraud prevention membership organisation.[136] In other words, both the NECC and JMLIT constitute significant networks amongst all AML stakeholders enabling them to share intelligence instantaneously and uninterruptedly, thereby rendering it possible to address the phenomenon uniformly and promptly. For example, between April 2019 and March 2020, the NCA, as a direct result of the NECC and JMLIT support, *inter alia*, secured the arrest of 56 money launderers and restrained or seized approximately GBP 3.5m in funds,[137] which are indicators of the effectiveness of the AML regime in the UK. From a broader perspective, JMLIT has directly contributed to more than 130 arrests and the seizure or restraint of approximately GBP 13m since its inception.[138] In light of these figures, estab-

131 NCA, 'National Economic Crime Centre' <www.nationalcrimeagency.gov.uk/what-we-do/national-economic-crime-centre> accessed 31 May 2023.

132 ibid.

133 Home Office and others, 'Anti-Money Laundering Taskforce Unveiled' (25 February 2015) <www.gov.uk/government/news/anti-money-laundering-taskforce-unveiled> accessed 17 April 2023.

134 Ben Scott and Mark McGoldrick, 'Financial Intelligence and Financial Investigation: Opportunities and Challenges' (2018) 13(3) Journal of Policing, Intelligence and Counterterrorism 301.

135 ibid.

136 Cifas, 'What Is Cifas?' <www.cifas.org.uk/about-cifas/what-is-cifas> accessed 17 April 2023.

137 NCA, 'Annual Report and Accounts 2019–20' (July 2020) 22 <www.nationalcrimeagency.gov.uk/who-we-are/publications/467-national-crime-agency-annual-report-and-accounts-2019-20/file> accessed 17 April 2023.

138 NCA (n 131).

lishing such a PPP in Türkiye should be one of the priorities of the Turkish authorities, including MASAK. Additionally, JMLIT has been accepted as an example of best practice by the international financial world,[139] suggesting that other jurisdictions, including Türkiye, would benefit from such an intelligence sharing platform.

Lastly, the NCA manages the Joint Asset Recovery Database (JARD), an operational database where competent (AML) authorities harnessed with asset recovery powers (e.g., the police, the CPS, and the SFO) provide entries, *inter alia*, on the proceeds of crime they recovered.[140] Accordingly, the system enables strong coordination amongst the institutional components of the UK's AML framework, thereby undertaking a more effective fight against the predicament as it provides simultaneous information on the responsible agency for the recovery and the level of enforcement.[141] In other words, it also serves as a supervisory mechanism, whereby the responsible LEAs are overseen regarding their effectiveness in fulfilling their responsibilities concerning recovering criminal proceeds. Although JARD is a restricted system inaccessible by the public, Home Office publishes annual bulletins on asset recovery secured through the relevant powers available under POCA 2002 and based on data stored on the system. For example, according to the last available bulletin, LEAs collected approximately GBP 139m and around GBP 69m against confiscation orders and forfeitures, respectively, between April 2019 and March 2020.[142] However, it is necessary to state that it is an elusive target to identify the underlying predicate crimes for such recovery sums, as JARD offers insight into figures on ML rather than making such a categorisation.[143] Nevertheless, considering the functionality of the database and its efficacy evident in these figures, developing a similar asset recovery system, which allows maintaining simultaneous coordination amongst the competent AML authorities in Türkiye, would reinforce the Turkish AML competency.

139 FATF, 'Anti-Money Laundering and Counter-Terrorist Financing Measures: United Kingdom – Mutual Evaluation Report' (December 2018) <www.fatf-gafi.org/media/fatf/documents/reports/mer4/MER-United-Kingdom-2018.pdf> accessed 18 January 2022.

140 Home Affairs Committee, 'Proceeds of Crime: Government Response to the Committee's Fifth Report of Session 2016–17' (HC, 15 November 2016) <https://publications.parliament.uk/pa/cm201617/cmselect/cmhaff/805/80504.htm#_idTextAnchor011> accessed 17 April 2023.

141 College of Policing, 'Effective Financial Investigation' <www.app.college.police.uk/app-content/investigations/investigative-strategies/financial-investigation-2/effective-financial-investigation/#updating-jard> accessed 17 April 2023.

142 Home Office, 'Asset Recovery Statistical Bulletin 2014/15–2019/20' (September 2020) <https://assets.publishing.service.gov.uk/government/uploads/system/uploads/attachment_data/file/923194/asset-recovery-financial-years-2015-to-2020-hosb2320.pdf> accessed 31 October 2023.

143 Yulia Chistyakova, Davis S Wall and Stefano Bonino, 'The Back-Door Governance of Crime: Confiscating Criminal Assets in the UK' (2019) 27(4) European Journal on Criminal Policy and Research 495.

6.4.1.4 *Serious Fraud Office*

The SFO was created as a response to serious and complex fraud under the Criminal Justice Act (CJA) 1987.[144] The scope of the Director of the SFO's investigative powers[145] has been expanded to encompass the pre-investigation process of foreign bribery and corruption cases by the enactment of the Criminal Justice and Immigration Act 2008.[146] Accordingly, the SFO, as a crucial member of the NECC, operates as a specialist LEA that investigates serious and complex fraud, bribery, corruption, and connected ML cases. Additionally, as a prosecuting authority and a part of the UK's criminal justice system, it prosecutes such legal proceedings, thereby recovering the illegal proceeds obtained by offenders involved in such crime schemes.[147] For instance, between April 2019 and March 2020, the SFO obtained 11 confiscation orders, which equals more than GBP 13m, and secured three DPAs, including the one with Airbus SE, where the company agreed to pay EUR 991m (approximately GBP 860m) in the UK and EUR 3.6bn (GBP 3.13bn as of April 2021) globally.[148] In other words, the UK has established an effective crime-specific investigation and prosecution LEA, which indubitably enhances the overall AML competency in tackling these particular predicate crimes and the associated ML problem, as evidenced by these figures. Therefore, considering the sophisticated nature of these predicate crimes (i.e., fraud) and the linked ML predicament,[149] Türkiye would benefit from creating an analogous specialist authority dedicated to investigating such cases.

6.4.1.5 *HM Revenue and Customs*

As the UK's tax and customs authority, HMRC possesses similar investigation powers that are conferred to other LEAs for tackling fiscal fraud, such as fraudulent tax evasion. More specifically, within the scope of its criminal investigation powers, it can utilise production orders and search warrants, and can make arrests and undertake a subsequent search of suspects and premises,

144 Criminal Justice Act 1987, s 1.
145 These investigatory powers, amongst others, oblige persons to answer questions, produce documents, and allow the SFO to search premises. The Director of the SFO, based on reasonable grounds, may investigate any criminal act suspected of involving a connection to serious and complex fraud, bribery, or corruption. See, Criminal Justice Act 1987, ss 2 and 2A.
146 Criminal Justice and Immigration Act 2008, s 59.
147 Serious Fraud Office, 'About Us' <www.sfo.gov.uk/about-us/> accessed 15 April 2023.
148 Serious Fraud Office, 'Annual Report, 2019–2020' (2020) <www.sfo.gov.uk/download/annual-report-2019-2020/> accessed 15 April 2023.
149 Rosalind Wright, 'Fraud After Roskill: A View from the Serious Fraud Office' (2003) 11(1) Journal of Financial Crime 10.

and finally recover proceeds of crime in this context.[150] Similarly, it harnesses several civil authorities to investigate tax-related predicate offences (e.g., tax fraud). These civil powers include, amongst others, obtaining information and documents from taxpayers and third parties and inspecting business premises to check the tax position of the taxpayer where the application of them requires approval from the First-tier Tribunal.[151] These civil powers have further been reinforced by the Finance Act 2021, which introduces a new measure called Financial Institution Notice that does not require obtaining the independent tribunal's approval in requesting such information and documents from FIs.[152] Furthermore, HMRC is an AML supervisory body that supervises several business sector participants, including, *inter alia*, money service businesses, high-value dealers, estate agency businesses, and art market participants.[153] Thus, HMRC, as a key member of the NECC, constitutes a significant component of the British institutional AML arsenal that addresses tax-related predicate offences and the ML conundrum. For example, between April 2019 and March 2020, HMRC made 1,958 supervisory interventions within the scope of AML efforts, thereby recovering approximately GBP 167m in proceeds of crime and securing 31 convictions for ML offences.[154] Lastly, HMRC has a network of international Fiscal Crime Liaison Officers, which prevented a loss of approximately GBP 596m and helped the arrest of more than 200 criminals globally in the same period.[155] That is to say that adopting a similar approach, which allows developing expertise in tackling particular predicate offences, would undoubtedly reinforce the AML effectiveness of the relevant Turkish institutional composition.

6.4.1.6 Financial Conduct Authority

As an AML supervisor for FIs and a regulatory body of the financial sector and financial advisers,[156] the FCA incorporates a broad range of criminal, civil, and regulatory enforcement powers, such as suspending or prohibiting individuals and firms from undertaking regulated activities, as in the case of market

150 HMRC, 'Guidance: HMRC's Criminal Investigation Powers and Safeguards' (Updated 13 July 2021) <www.gov.uk/government/publications/criminal-investigation/criminal-investigation> accessed 12 February 2023.

151 Finance Act 2008, sch 36.

152 Finance Act 2021, s 126.

153 HMRC, 'Guidance: Who Needs to Register for Money Laundering Supervision' (Updated 21 May 2020) <www.gov.uk/guidance/money-laundering-regulations-who-needs-to-register> accessed 15 April 2023.

154 HMRC, 'Annual Report and Accounts 2019 to 2020' (November 2020) 34 <https://assets.publishing.service.gov.uk/government/uploads/system/uploads/attachment_data/file/932874/HMRC_Annual_Report_and_Accounts_2019_to_2020__Print_.pdf> accessed 15 April 2023.

155 ibid.

156 See, for instance, Financial Services and Market Act 2000, s 1L.

abuse,[157] albeit not being an LEA. Additionally, similar to the SFO, as a part of the UK's criminal justice system, it prosecutes, amongst other criminal offences, cases relating to a breach of the MLRs (i.e., ML offences).[158] Furthermore, it hosts the Office for Professional Body Anti-Money Laundering Supervision (OPBAS), which supervises 25 professional body supervisors overseeing the legal and accountancy sectors, such as the Institute of Chartered Accountants in England and Wales (ICAEW), regarding the requirements of the 2017 MLRs.[159] It is worth underlining that the UK has established a supervisory mechanism for the supervision of the AML supervisors, which demonstrates the importance given to the AML by the UK. For example, since its creation in 2018, OPBAS has improved, amongst others, the application of RBA and intelligence and information sharing practices utilised by the professional body supervisors.[160] Similarly, between April 2019 and March 2020, the FCA conducted 65 ML investigations and imposed a total of 15 financial penalties, which equals approximately GBP 224m.[161] In other words, the FCA, along with the OPBAS, significantly contributes to the AML battle undertaken by the UK. That is to say, the fact that lawyers were included as obliged entities recently and the limited STRs from accountants (see Chapter 7) may explain the small amount of asset recovery secured in Türkiye. Therefore, revising the current regulation and supervision mechanisms in these sectors would undeniably enhance the effectiveness of the Turkish institutional AML framework.

6.4.2 The UK Financial Intelligence Unit

The UKFIU became operational on 1 January 1995.[162] It operates under the auspices of the NCA and exploits the financial intelligence submitted through the SAR regime as the responsible national authority in this context.[163] Section 10 of the Crime and Courts Act 2013 equips NCA person-

157 FCA, 'Enforcement' <www.fca.org.uk/about/enforcement> accessed 16 April 2023.
158 FCA, 'Enforcement Guide: Prosecution of Criminal Offences' <www.handbook.fca.org.uk/handbook/EG/12.pdf> accessed 16 April 2023.
159 FCA, 'Office for Professional Body Anti-Money Laundering Supervision (OPBAS)' <www.fca.org.uk/opbas> accessed 31 December 2022.
160 OPBAS, 'Anti-Money Laundering Supervision by the Legal and Accountancy Professional Body Supervisors: Progress and Themes from 2019' (March 2020) <www.fca.org.uk/publication/opbas/supervisory-report-progress-themes-2019.pdf> accessed 25 February 2023. See also HM Treasury, 'Anti-Money Laundering and Counter-Terrorist Financing: Supervision Report 2019–20' (November 2021) 4 <https://assets.publishing.service.gov.uk/government/uploads/system/uploads/attachment_data/file/1034539/HMT_Supervision_Report_19-20.pdf> accessed 20 August 2023.
161 FCA, 'Annual Report and Accounts 2019/20' (September 2020) 12 <www.fca.org.uk/publication/annual-reports/annual-report-2019-20.pdf#page=12> accessed 16 April 2023.
162 Egmont Group, 'UK Financial Intelligence Unit (NCA)' <https://egmontgroup.org/en/content/united-kingdom-uk-financial-intelligence-unit> accessed 20 April 2023.
163 NCA, 'Financial Intelligence' <www.ukciu.gov.uk/(0trxse55xsqtci45n3hq3c45)/Information/Info.aspx> accessed 20 April 2023.

nel, thereby the UKFIU staff, with various powers and privileges, which considerably increase the UKFIU's authorities in contrast with its Turkish counterpart. More specifically, the General Director (i.e., the chief of the NCA) may harness any NCA officers, including the UKFIU personnel, with one or more of the powers held by a constable, an HMRC officer, a general customs official, and an immigration officer.[164] In other words, on a par with the Egmont Group's definition for the law enforcement type of FIUs, the UKFIU implements AML measures as a part of an LEA, suggesting that its collaboration with LEAs and the judiciary is intrinsically more enhanced than its administrative model Turkish counterpart. However, it is crucial to state that the UKFIU does not function as the sole competent authority in processing intelligence relating to ML and its underlying predicates, whereas MASAK sits alone at the apex of the financial intelligence network in Türkiye. Therefore, the shared authority in gathering, analysing, and disseminating financial intelligence aggravates the UKFIU's ascendancy regarding directing the jurisdiction's AML efforts. Accordingly, the FATF regarded the UKFIU's effectiveness as deficient and the SAR regime questionable due to its limited role in carrying out financial data exploitation in the last MER.[165] Additionally, given that it operates under the auspices of the NCA, the NCA may utilise the UKFIU as per its agency-specific priorities rather than the national high-risk predicate crime threats and the associated ML problem. However, this distribution of responsibilities may also help the relevant competent authorities to develop expertise in utilising a particular type of financial intelligence to create a more hostile environment for the offenders and diminish the associated risks. For example, the SFO's Intelligence Unit directs its intelligence efforts to analyse and disseminate financial intelligence relating to specific predicate crimes comprising serious or complex fraud, bribery, corruption, and associated ML offences.[166] Therefore, reviewing the UKFIU's position within the financial intelligence realm, rendering it as the core authority, and bolstering the coordination amongst all financial intelligence services would be an appropriate approach to enhance the overall AML competency of the jurisdiction.

According to the World Bank Group, obliged entities in jurisdictions adopting a law enforcement type of FIU are more likely to be reluctant to make SARs compared to those operating in countries embracing an administrative model of FIU.[167] However, a comparison of SARs/STRs the UKFIU and MASAK receive annually does not confirm this view since the UKFIU gets twice as many disclosures compared to MASAK relating to unusual financial activities from obliged entities periodically (see Chapter 7). In other words, having a

164 Crime and Courts Act 2013, s 10.

165 FATF (n 139) 6.

166 Serious Fraud Office (n 147).

167 The World Bank Group, 'Role of the Financial Intelligence Units' <https://pubdocs.worldbank.org/en/834721427730119379/AML-Module-2.pdf> accessed 20 April 2023.

law enforcement natured FIU does not appear to affect the tendency of disclosures by obliged entities in the UK negatively. In addition to the substantial variation in the number of obliged entities, one crucial distinction between the two reporting regimes that may account for this difference is that even private individuals are equally required to engage in the SARs regime in the UK as the obliged entities and DNFBPs. For example, private individuals submitted 82 SARs to the UKFIU between April 2019 and March 2020.[168] That is not to say that their submissions constitute such a difference, yet it suggests the comprehensiveness of the reporting regime and indicates the willingness of reporters in the UK. Accordingly, the UKFIU received approximately half a million SARs annually each year since 2018 (i.e., 463,938 in 2018,[169] 478,437 in 2019,[170] and remarkably, 573,085 in 2020).[171] The same exponential increase in the workload is also apparent in the DAML requests[172] submitted by obliged entities to the UKFIU. For example, whilst it received approximately 35,000 DAML SARs in 2018, DAML requests submitted to the UKFIU increased by around 80%, reaching almost 62,000 in 2019.[173] However, although the workload of the UKFIU has increased rapidly, the number of its dedicated staff remains relatively inadequate (in numbers). As of April 2019, 118 personnel were operating within the UKFIU, with an almost 50% increase compared to the previous year (i.e., 80 personnel in March 2018).[174] Given that the UKFIU operates with a personnel capacity of half of MASAK's workforce numerically whilst dealing with a workload of more than twice of MASAK,[175] the UKFIU suffers from insufficient staff, albeit harnessing advanced (AI) technologies. Therefore, enhancing the UKFIU's personnel capacity would fortify the overall competency of the jurisdiction's AML efforts. The functionality of obtaining a DAML encourages obligated persons to make more requests from the NCA, thereby intensifying the relationship between the UKFIU and the

168 NCA, 'UK Financial Intelligence Unit Suspicious Activity Reports Annual Report 2020' (April 2020) 21 <www.nationalcrimeagency.gov.uk/who-we-are/publications/480-sars-annual-report-2020/file> accessed 24 February 2023.

169 NCA, 'Suspicious Activity Reports (SARs) Annual Report 2018' (2018) 3 <www.nationalcrimeagency.gov.uk/who-we-are/publications/256-2018-sars-annual-report/file> accessed 21 April 2023.

170 NCA, 'UK Financial Intelligence Unit Suspicious Activity Reports Annual Report 2019' (2019) 4 <www.nationalcrimeagency.gov.uk/who-we-are/publications/390-sars-annual-report-2019/file> accessed 21 April 2023.

171 NCA (n 168) 4.

172 DAML is a type of SAR where reporters seek defence against principal ML offences (See Chapter 4).

173 ibid.

174 NCA (n 170) 2.

175 It is necessary to state here that the number of disclosures (i.e., STRs/SARs) is not the only indicator of the workload of a given jurisdiction. Additional factors, such as the higher number of banks and the volume of transactions, and overseas territories, to name a few, render the workload of the UKFIU greater than MASAK.

obliged entities and increasing the asset recovery opportunities. As a result of the DAML requests, the UK deprived criminals of approximately GBP 170m in 2019,[176] suggesting a more tangible indicator of how such a system would benefit Türkiye. Therefore, introducing a similar *modus operandi* in Türkiye should be considered by the relevant Turkish stakeholders.

The UKFIU receives SARs, including DAML and DATF (i.e., Defence Against Terrorism Financing) SARs, via SAR Online,[177] a web-based system that enables sending SAR forms electronically. Although the UKFIU receives these SARs preponderantly through electronic means, similar to MASAK, it also allows the regulated sector to submit their reports by mail.[178] Therefore, the UKFIU is not immune from the criticism made concerning the non-electronic SAR submission on MASAK before, as it may hinder the overall effectiveness of the jurisdiction's AML system given the rapid characteristics of the perpetration of ML offences.

6.4.3 Crown Prosecution Service

The CPS is the principal prosecution authority in England and Wales responsible for prosecuting criminal cases, including ML and its underlying predicates, investigated by the police and other investigative organisations,[179] such as the NCA. It comprises, amongst others, three Central Casework Divisions dedicated to prosecuting the most complex criminal cases, such as fraud.[180] More importantly, it devotes a division, namely CPS Proceeds of Crime (CPSPOC), for restraint, enforcement, and asset recovery proceedings (i.e., confiscation and civil recovery) flowing from other AML components of the jurisdiction, such as the NCA, HMRC, ROCUs, and the police.[181] As a part of CPS Asset Recovery Strategy 2014, *all* prosecutors are provided with training on the proceeds of crime legal framework, including ML, where the training programme

176 NCA (n 168) 4.

177 NCA, 'SAR Online Portal' <www.ukciu.gov.uk/(py0zn2f23wsy1145xsccytmo)/saronline.aspx> accessed 21 April 2023.

178 NCA, 'Submitting a Suspicious Activity Report (SAR)' <www.ukciu.gov.uk/(0trxse55xsqtci45n3hq3c45)/Information/info.aspx?InfoSection=Submission> accessed 21 April 2023.

179 Crown Prosecution Service, 'About CPS' <www.cps.gov.uk/about-cps> accessed 10 May 2023.

180 The Central Casework Divisions consist of International Justice and Organised Crime Division, Special Crime and Counter-Terrorism Division, and Specialist Fraud Division. See Crown Prosecution Service, 'CPS Central Casework Divisions' <www.cps.gov.uk/about-cps/cps-areas-cps-direct-cps-central-casework-divisions-and-cps-proceeds-crime> accessed 10 May 2023.

181 Crown Prosecution Service, 'Proceeds of Crime' <www.cps.gov.uk/crime-info/proceeds-crime> accessed 10 May 2023.

is more focused and envisaged for prosecutors who serve in CPSPOC.[182] In other words, besides providing all LEAs with specialist personnel experts in AML, the UK's AML regime ensures that all prosecutors are trained in AML matters, a substantial difference compared to the Turkish AML composition. However, it is necessary to state that whilst the CPS provides prosecution guidance to prosecutors relating to a myriad of criminal offences, it does not devote specific guidance regarding ML,[183] the introduction of which would benefit them and increase the consistency of decisions given in this context.

6.5 Conclusion

The judicial composition of the UK and the division of jurisdictions between the courts allow the competent courts and the judiciary responsible for hearing ML and predicate crime cases to devote more time and energy for determining such cases. More specifically, Magistrates' Courts serve as a legal filter by handling and, where appropriate, concluding most of the criminal cases, thereby preventing higher courts from being overwhelmed by excessive workload, which would deteriorate the judicial efficiency. Such separation of the juridical workload renders the UK's judicial structure more effective than its Turkish counterpart, as Criminal Courts of General Jurisdiction in Türkiye, unlike the Crown Court in the UK, hear the vast majority of criminal lawsuits, along with ML and predicate crime cases. Accordingly, the UK has ensured a more accelerated judgement process where the completion period of a trial in the Crown Court[184] takes around six months, approximately half the period in Türkiye. Furthermore, given that the legal professionals consist of legal practitioners (e.g., barristers, solicitors) with at least five to ten years of experience and additional practical knowledge, the most 'inexperienced' judge eligible for trying ML cases in the UK is intrinsically more experienced than their Turkish counterparts. Last but not least, the UK's AML regime ensures that *all* prosecutors are trained in AML matters, which indubitably increases the accuracy of the AML legal proceedings. However, notwithstanding this relatively more fitting for purpose judicial arrangement, the judicial composition of the jurisdiction does not comprise specific courts dealing only with ML and underlying predicate crime cases, the introduction of which would enhance its AML competency.

As a common law jurisdiction, the UK's AML legal arsenal originates both from codified legal instruments and the preceding judicial decisions given in this context. The binding nature of the legal precedent and in detail codified

182 Crown Prosecution Service, 'CPS Asset Recovery Strategy' (June 2014) 10 <www.cps.gov.uk/sites/default/files/documents/publications/cps_asset_recovery_strategy_2014.pdf> accessed 10 May 2023.

183 Crown Prosecution Service, 'Prosecution Guidance' <www.cps.gov.uk/prosecution-guidance> accessed 10 May 2023.

184 The Crown Court is the primary court in dealing with ML and associated predicate crimes.

legal texts render court decisions on (AML and predicate crime) litigations more homogenous across the jurisdiction, thereby reinforcing the British AML effectiveness. The UK Parliament constitutes the principal source of the British AML legislation. The most striking divergence point of the law-making process in the UK is the pre-legislative scrutiny and public consultation procedures, which allow the community to participate actively in the codification process. It undoubtedly enables better societal ownership, trust, and arguably better compliance with the laws. Accordingly, the opinions of all AML stakeholders, such as obliged entities, constitute a basis for the prevailing AML legal framework at least partially. Therefore, the UK's AML legal instruments are likely to be more effective. In other words, the British law-making methodology derives, at least partially, from the direct contribution of the AML stakeholders, thereby allowing them to intensify the rigour of the legal framework based on their real-life AML experiences. This feature undoubtedly constitutes a good example as to how to ensure the law in the books better addresses the deficiencies observed in the law in action.

The institutional AML structure, beyond the mainstream police forces, consists of a broad range of organisations with investigative, enforcement, and prosecution powers, along with the UKFIU. Additionally, each agency dedicates itself to tackling particular aspects of the conundrum. This organisational structure enables the competent authorities to develop expertise in dealing with sophisticated and complex predicate crime types, such as fraud and tax offences, and the associated ML problem. Furthermore, the NCA orchestrates intelligence and operational efforts devoted by these institutions by mustering their representatives in the JFAC and the NECC, thereby providing strong and synchronised cooperation and coordination mechanism. The asset recovery sits at the heart of the AML efforts, and databases accessible to *all* AML institutions in this end, such as JARD, further intensify the connection amongst these authorities, thereby enhancing the proceeds of crime recovered. This vehement interagency network is not limited to national borders. The international network of liaison officers established by the NCA and such a network of Fiscal Crime Liaison Officers organised by the HMRC allows uninterrupted communication and exchange of intelligence between the UK AML organisational armada and their representatives operating abroad in higher-risk jurisdictions regarding ML and its underlying predicates, thereby reinforcing JIT capabilities of the jurisdiction. Moreover, this interconnected system ensures the active participation of the private sector in the fight against the phenomenon through a successful PPP, namely JMLIT. The supervisory mechanism introduced for the supervision of the AML supervisors (i.e., OPBAS) enhances the AML integrity of the legal and accountancy sectors, manifesting the importance attached to the gatekeepers.[185] Along with these

185 Katie Benson, 'Money Laundering, Anti-Money Laundering and the Legal Profession' in Colin King, Clive Walker and Jimmy Gurulé (eds), *The Palgrave Handbook of Criminal and Terrorism Financing Law* (Springer 2018).

specialised organisations and ingenious initiatives, *each* conventional police force, including ROCUs, incorporates specialist economic crime teams. In other words, whilst tackling predicate offences and the associated ML is relinquished to the mainstream LEAs in Türkiye (except for the FIU), the institutional AML structure in the UK comprises a broad range of agencies with specific expertise, legal powers, innovative tools, and networks.

The UKFIU harnesses legal powers available to LEAs as it operates under the auspices of the core LEA of the jurisdiction (i.e., the NCA). Consequently, the communication and collaboration opportunities for exploiting the financial intelligence submitted through the SAR regime with the remaining components of the national institutional AML structure are intrinsically superior to MASAK. However, it shares its authority in gathering, analysing, and disseminating financial intelligence with several LEAs, rendering its effectiveness questionable as the central AML unit. Additionally, whilst it deals with twice as much workload as MASAK undertakes, it runs with half as much workforce as MASAK possesses, suggesting that the UK does not prioritise the UKFIU's role in this context. In other words, these facts connote that the NCA may utilise the UKFIU as per its agency-specific priorities rather than the national high-risk predicate crime threats and the associated ML problem. Lastly, similar to MASAK, it receives a minor proportion of SARs through the mail, impeding its AML response for particular occasions. Therefore, revising the role of the UKFIU, enhancing its personnel capacity, and ensuring SAR submission through electronic means available for everyone would strengthen the British institutional AML composition.

This chapter has investigated the cornerstones and unique characteristics of the institutional AML framework of the UK. The separation of less serious criminal cases from the overall criminal cases at the early stages of the judicial process, the experience of competent judges responsible for hearing ML and its underlying predicates, and the binding nature of the legal precedent coupled with thoroughly codified legal instruments generate accelerated and consistent judicial outcomes. Public consultations allow for meaningful debate about the suitability, societal acceptance, and potential (in)effectiveness of proposed AML legal instruments based on their real-life experiences from key stakeholders. The AML-wise and well-equipped LEAs; liaison officers abroad; national and international networks; the supervision of supervisory agencies; and PPPs that enable active participation of the private sector are the remarkable features of the UK's institutional AML armada. Orchestrated by the NCA, each competent authority has crime-specific responsibilities and operational priorities congruent with the highest risk predicate crimes identified in the NRA. In other words, the UK's AML *modus operandi* harbours a wide range of organisations with various legal powers tailored to address the most sophisticated predicate offences, thereby enabling expertise development, albeit rendering the role of the UKFIU questionable. However, the next chapter thematically compares the actual effectiveness of this arguably promising AML structure and the AML framework embraced by Türkiye, thereby revealing which adoption would be more fit for purpose and why.

Reference List

ActionFraud, 'Who Are the National Fraud Intelligence Bureau?' <www.actionfraud.police.uk/what-is-national-fraud-intelligence-bureau> accessed 14 April 2023

Bell B and Dadomo C, 'Magistrates Courts and the 2003 Reforms of the Criminal Justice System' (2006) 14(4) European Journal of Crime, Criminal Law, and Criminal Justice 339

Benson K, 'Money Laundering, Anti-Money Laundering and the Legal Profession' in C King, C Walker and J Gurulé (eds), *The Palgrave Handbook of Criminal and Terrorism Financing Law* (Springer 2018)

Cabinet Office, 'Guide to Making Legislation' (2022) <https://assets.publishing.service.gov.uk/government/uploads/system/uploads/attachment_data/file/645652/Guide_to_Making_Legislation_Jul_2017.pdf> accessed 29 June 2023

Chistyakova Y, Wall DS and Bonino S, 'The Back-Door Governance of Crime: Confiscating Criminal Assets in the UK' (2019) 27(4) European Journal on Criminal Policy and Research 495

Cifas, 'What Is Cifas?' <www.cifas.org.uk/about-cifas/what-is-cifas> accessed 17 April 2023

City of London Police, 'Annual Report 2019/2020' (2020) <www.cityoflondon.police.uk/SysSiteAssets/media/downloads/city-of-london/about-us/annual-report-2019-final.pdf> accessed 14 April 2023

College of Policing, 'Effective Financial Investigation' <www.app.college.police.uk/app-content/investigations/investigative-strategies/financial-investigation-2/effective-financial-investigation/#updating-jard> accessed 17 April 2023

Constitution Committee, 'Fast-track Legislation: Constitutional Implications and Safeguards' (HL, 17 June 2009, para 22) <https://publications.parliament.uk/pa/ld200809/ldselect/ldconst/116/11604.htm#note4> accessed 20 April 2023

Cooper TM, 'The Common and the Civil Law: A Scot's View' (1950) 63(3) Harvard Law Review 468

Council of Europe, 'European Judicial Systems CEPEJ Evaluation Report: 2020 Evaluation Cycle (2018 Data)' (September 2020) <https://rm.coe.int/evaluation-report-part-1-english/16809fc058> accessed 19 August 2023

Courts and Tribunals Judiciary, 'County Court' <www.judiciary.uk/you-and-the-judiciary/going-to-court/county-court/> accessed 31 March 2023

——— 'Courts of the Queen's Bench Division' <www.judiciary.uk/you-and-the-judiciary/going-to-court/high-court/queens-bench-division/courts-of-the-queens-bench-division/> accessed 31 March 2023

——— 'High Court' <www.judiciary.uk/you-and-the-judiciary/going-to-court/high-court/> accessed 31 March 2023

——— 'Crown Court' <www.judiciary.uk/you-and-the-judiciary/going-to-court/crown-court/> accessed 6 April 2023

——— 'District judge (Magistrates' Courts)' <www.judiciary.uk/about-the-judiciary/who-are-the-judiciary/judicial-roles/judges/district-judge-mags-ct/> accessed 6 April 2023

——— 'High Court: The Chancery Division' <www.judiciary.uk/you-and-the-judiciary/going-to-court/high-court/the-chancery-division/work/> accessed 31 March 2023

——— 'High Court: Family' <www.judiciary.uk/you-and-the-judiciary/going-to-court/high-court/family2/> accessed 31 March 2023

——— 'High Court: Queen's Bench Division' <www.judiciary.uk/you-and-the-judiciary/going-to-court/high-court/queens-bench-division/work/> accessed 31 March 2023

——— 'Jurisdictions' <www.judiciary.uk/about-the-judiciary/the-justice-system/jurisdictions/> accessed 31 March 2023

——— 'The History of the Court of Appeal' <www.judiciary.uk/you-and-the-judiciary/going-to-court/court-of-appeal-home/coa-sub/> accessed 1 April 2023

——— 'The Court of Appeal' <www.judiciary.uk/you-and-the-judiciary/going-to-court/court-of-appeal-home/> accessed 1 April 2023

——— 'Judicial Roles: Circuit Judge' <www.judiciary.uk/about-the-judiciary/who-are-the-judiciary/judicial-roles/judges/ciruit-judge/> accessed 8 April 2023

——— 'Judicial Roles: High Court Judges' <www.judiciary.uk/about-the-judiciary/who-are-the-judiciary/judicial-roles/judges/high-court-judges/> accessed 8 April 2023

——— 'Judicial Roles: Recorder' <www.judiciary.uk/about-the-judiciary/who-are-the-judiciary/judicial-roles/judges/recorder/> accessed 8 April 2023

——— 'The Justice System' <www.judiciary.uk/about-the-judiciary/the-justice-system/jurisdictions/criminal-jurisdiction/> accessed 6 April 2023

Cross R and Harris JW, *Precedent in English Law* (4th edn, OUP 1991)

Crown Prosecution Service, 'CPS Asset Recovery Strategy' (June 2014) <www.cps.gov.uk/sites/default/files/documents/publications/cps_asset_recovery_strategy_2014.pdf> accessed 10 May 2023

——— 'About CPS' <www.cps.gov.uk/about-cps> accessed 10 May 2023

——— 'CPS Central Casework Divisions' <www.cps.gov.uk/about-cps/cps-areas-cps-direct-cps-central-casework-divisions-and-cps-proceeds-crime> accessed 10 May 2023

——— 'Proceeds of Crime' <www.cps.gov.uk/crime-info/proceeds-crime> accessed 10 May 2023

——— 'Prosecution Guidance' <www.cps.gov.uk/prosecution-guidance> accessed 10 May 2023

Dainow J, 'The Civil Law and the Common Law: Some Points of Comparison' (1967) 15(3) The American Journal of Comparative Law 419

Del Mundo CFS, 'How Countries Seek to Strengthen Anti-Money Laundering Laws in Response to the Panama Papers, and the Ethical Implications of Incentivizing Whistleblowers' (2019) 40(1) Northwestern Journal of International Law and Business 87

Department of Justice, 'Courts and Tribunals' <www.justice-ni.gov.uk/topics/courts-and-tribunals> accessed 31 March 2023

Eastern Region Special Operations Unit <https://ersou.police.uk> accessed 14 April 2023

——— 'Region's Criminals Forced to Repay £2.25m in 2020' <https://ersou.police.uk/news/2020/12/17/region's-criminals-forced-to-repay-£2.25m-in-2020/> accessed 15 April 2023

Egmont Group, 'UK Financial Intelligence Unit (NCA)' <https://egmontgroup.org/en/content/united-kingdom-uk-financial-intelligence-unit> accessed 20 April 2023

European Scrutiny Committee, 'The EU Bill and Parliamentary Sovereignty (Tenth Report, HC, 24 December 2010) <https://publications.parliament.uk/pa/cm201011/cmselect/cmeuleg/633/63304.htm> accessed 12 April 2023

FATF, 'Anti-Money Laundering and Counter-Terrorist Financing Measures: United Kingdom – Mutual Evaluation Report' (December 2018) <www.fatf-gafi.org/media/fatf/documents/reports/mer4/MER-United-Kingdom-2018.pdf> accessed 18 January 2022

FCA, 'Annual Report and Accounts 2019/20' (September 2020) <www.fca.org.uk/publication/annual-reports/annual-report-2019-20.pdf#page=12> accessed 16 April 2023

——— 'FCA Starts Criminal Proceedings Against NatWest Plc' (*Press Release*, 16 March 2021) <www.fca.org.uk/news/press-releases/fca-starts-criminal-proceedings-against-natwest-plc> accessed 13 April 2023

——— 'Enforcement' <www.fca.org.uk/about/enforcement> accessed 16 April 2023

——— 'Enforcement Guide: Prosecution of Criminal Offences' <www.handbook.fca.org.uk/handbook/EG/12.pdf> accessed 16 April 2023

——— 'Office for Professional Body Anti-Money Laundering Supervision (OPBAS)' <www.fca.org.uk/opbas> accessed 31 December 2022

Hanretty C, *A Court of Specialists: Judicial Behaviour on the UK Supreme Court* (OUP 2020)

He P, 'A Typological Study on Money Laundering' (2010) 13(1) Journal of Money Laundering Control 15

HM Courts & Tribunals Service, 'Statistical Data Set: HMCTS Management Information – February 2020 to February 2021' (8 April 2021) <https://assets.publishing.service.gov.uk/government/uploads/system/uploads/attachment_data/file/976398/20210327_HMCTS_raw_data_for_Feb20_to_Feb21.csv/preview> accessed 10 April 2023

——— 'About Us' <www.gov.uk/government/organisations/hm-courts-and-tribunals-service/about> accessed 31 March 2023

HM Government, 'Serious and Organised Crime Strategy' (November 2018) <https://assets.publishing.service.gov.uk/government/uploads/system/uploads/attachment_data/file/752850/SOC-2018-web.pdf> accessed 14 April 2023

HM Government and UK Finance, 'Economic Crime Plan 2019–22' (July 2019) <https://assets.publishing.service.gov.uk/government/uploads/system/uploads/attachment_data/file/816215/2019-22_Economic_Crime_Plan.pdf> accessed 31 March 2023

HM Treasury, 'Anti-Money Laundering and Counter-Terrorist Financing: Supervision Report 2019–20' (November 2021) <https://assets.publishing.service.gov.uk/government/uploads/system/uploads/attachment_data/file/1034539/HMT_Supervision_Report_19-20.pdf> accessed 20 August 2023

HM Treasury and Home Office, 'National Risk Assessment of Money Laundering and Terrorist Financing 2020' (December 2020) <https://assets.publishing.service.gov.uk/government/uploads/system/uploads/attachment_data/file/945411/NRA_2020_v1.2_FOR_PUBLICATION.pdf> accessed 26 June 2023

HMICFRS, 'Regional Organised Crime Units: An Inspection of the Effectiveness of the Regional Organised Crime Units' (February 2021) <www.justiceinspectorates.gov.uk/hmicfrs/publication-html/regional-organised-crime-units-effectiveness/> accessed 14 April 2023

HMRC, 'Taskforce Launches Criminal and Civil Investigations into Panama Papers' (8 November 2016) <www.gov.uk/government/news/taskforce-launches-criminal-and-civil-investigations-into-panama-papers> accessed 17 April 2023

——— 'Guidance: Who Needs to Register for Money Laundering Supervision' (updated 21 May 2020) <www.gov.uk/guidance/money-laundering-regulations-who-needs-to-register> accessed 15 April 2023

——— 'Annual Report and Accounts 2019 to 2020' (November 2020) <https://assets.publishing.service.gov.uk/government/uploads/system/uploads/attachment_data/file/932874/HMRC_Annual_Report_and_Accounts_2019_to_2020__Print_.pdf> accessed 15 April 2023

——— 'Guidance: HMRC's Criminal Investigation Powers and Safeguards' (Updated 13 July 2021) <www.gov.uk/government/publications/criminal-investigation/criminal-investigation> accessed 12 February 2023

Home Affairs Committee, 'Collecting Proceeds of Crime' (HC 2015–16) <https://publications.parliament.uk/pa/cm201617/cmselect/cmhaff/25/2505.htm#_idTextAnchor009> accessed 8 April 2023

——— 'Proceeds of Crime: Government response to the Committee's Fifth Report of Session 2016–17' (HC, 15 November 2016) <https://publications.parliament.uk/pa/cm201617/cmselect/cmhaff/805/80504.htm#_idTextAnchor011> accessed 17 April 2023

Home Office, 'The Strategic Policing Requirement' (March 2015) <https://assets.publishing.service.gov.uk/government/uploads/system/uploads/attachment_data/file/417116/The_Strategic_Policing_Requirement.pdf> accessed 14 April 2023

——— 'Asset Recovery Action Plan' (July 2019) <https://assets.publishing.service.gov.uk/government/uploads/system/uploads/attachment_data/file/815900/20190709_Asset_Recovery_Action_Plan_FINAL_Clean.pdf> accessed 14 April 2023

——— 'Asset Recovery Statistical Bulletin 2014/15–2019/20' (September 2020) <https://assets.publishing.service.gov.uk/government/uploads/system/uploads/attachment_data/file/923194/asset-recovery-financial-years-2015-to-2020-hosb2320.pdf> accessed 31 October 2023

——— 'Government Consultation: Changes to Bodies Granted Investigatory and Other Powers Under the Proceeds of Crime Act 2002' (January 2021) <https://assets.publishing.service.gov.uk/government/uploads/system/uploads/attachment_data/file/956309/AFI_Order_Consultation_V8.pdf> accessed 28 May 2023

——— 'National Lead Force for Fraud' <www.gov.uk/government/publications/national-lead-force-for-fraud/national-lead-force-for-fraud> accessed 14 April 2023

Home Office and others, 'Anti-Money Laundering Taskforce Unveiled' (25 February 2015) <www.gov.uk/government/news/anti-money-laundering-taskforce-unveiled> accessed 17 April 2023

Hopkins M and Shelton N, 'Identifying Money Laundering Risk in the United Kingdom: Observations from National Risk Assessments and a Proposed Alternative Methodology' (2018) 25(1) European Journal on Criminal Policy and Research 63

Hungerford-Welch P, *Criminal Procedure and Sentencing* (9th edn, Routledge 2019)

Judicial Office, 'The Judicial System of England and Wales: A Visitor's Guide' <www.judiciary.uk/wp-content/uploads/2016/05/international-visitors-guide-10a.pdf> accessed 31 March 2023

Kent Police, 'Progression Opportunities' <www.kent.police.uk/police-forces/kent-police/areas/kent-police/c/careers/police-officers/new-investigate-first/progression-opportunities/> accessed 13 April 2023

Martin J, *English Legal System* (8th edn, Hodder Education Group 2016)

Metropolitan Police, 'Man Jailed After Money Laundering Team Investigation' (18 February 2021) <https://news.met.police.uk/news/man-jailed-after-money-laundering-team-investigation-421551> accessed 14 April 2023

Ministry of Justice, 'Faster Justice as Unnecessary Committal Hearings Are Abolished' (*Press Release*, 28 May 2013) <www.gov.uk/government/news/faster-justice-as-unneccessary-committal-hearings-are-abolished> accessed 1 April 2023

——— 'Guide to Criminal Court Statistics' (Updated 24 September 2020) <https://assets.publishing.service.gov.uk/government/uploads/system/uploads/attachment_data/file/920481/A_Guide_to_Criminal_Court_Statistics.pdf> accessed 6 April 2023

——— 'National Statistics – Criminal Court Statistics Quarterly: October to December 2020' (Published 25 March 2021) <www.gov.uk/government/statistics/criminal-court-statistics-quarterly-october-to-december-2020/criminal-court-statistics-quarterly-october-to-december-2020> accessed 10 April 2023

NCA, 'Suspicious Activity Reports (SARs) Annual Report 2018' (2018) <www.nationalcrimeagency.gov.uk/who-we-are/publications/256-2018-sars-annual-report/file> accessed 21 April 2023

——— 'UK Financial Intelligence Unit Suspicious Activity Reports Annual Report 2019' (2019) <www.nationalcrimeagency.gov.uk/who-we-are/publications/390-sars-annual-report-2019/file> accessed 21 April 2023

——— 'UK Financial Intelligence Unit Suspicious Activity Reports Annual Report 2020' (April 2020) <www.nationalcrimeagency.gov.uk/who-we-are/publications/480-sars-annual-report-2020/file> accessed 24 February 2023

——— 'Annual Report and Accounts 2019–20' (July 2020) <www.nationalcrimeagency.gov.uk/who-we-are/publications/467-national-crime-agency-annual-report-and-accounts-2019-20/file> accessed 17 April 2023

——— 'NCA Senior Leadership Structure' (January 2021) <https://nationalcrimeagency.gov.uk/accessibility-text/493-nca-senior-leadership-structure-january-2021-text-version/file> accessed 16 April 2023

——— 'Annual Plan 2022–2023' (August 2022) <www.nationalcrimeagency.gov.uk/who-we-are/publications/594-nca-annual-plan-2022-23/file> accessed 17 August 2023

——— 'Audit and Risk Assurance Committee' <www.nationalcrimeagency.gov.uk/who-we-are/publications/108-nca-audit-risk-assurance-committee-terms-of-reference/file> accessed 16 April 2023

——— 'Governance and Transparency' <www.nationalcrimeagency.gov.uk/who-we-are/governance-and-transparency> accessed 16 April 2023

——— 'Contact the Proceeds of Crime Centre' <www.nationalcrimeagency.gov.uk/contact-us/13-proceeds-of-crime-centre> accessed 17 April 2023

——— 'Criminal Asset Denial' <www.nationalcrimeagency.gov.uk/what-we-do/how-we-work/investigating-and-disrupting-the-highest-risk-serious-and-organised-criminals/criminal-asset-denial> accessed 17 April 2023

——— 'Financial Intelligence' <www.ukciu.gov.uk/(0trxse55xsqtci45n3hq3c45)/Information/Info.aspx> accessed 20 April 2023

——— 'Intelligence: Enhancing the Picture of Serious Organised Crime Affecting the UK' <www.nationalcrimeagency.gov.uk/what-we-do/how-we-work/intelligence-enhancing-the-picture-of-serious-organised-crime-affecting-the-uk> accessed 17 April 2023

——— 'International Network' <www.nationalcrimeagency.gov.uk/what-we-do/how-we-work/providing-specialist-capabilities-for-law-enforcement/international-network> accessed 31 May 2023

——— 'National Economic Crime Centre' <www.nationalcrimeagency.gov.uk/what-we-do/national-economic-crime-centre> accessed 31 May 2023

——— 'SAR Online Portal' <www.ukciu.gov.uk/(py0zn2f23wsy1145xsccytmo)/saronline.aspx> accessed 21 April 2023

——— 'Submitting a Suspicious Activity Report (SAR)' <www.ukciu.gov.uk/(0trxse55xsqtci45n3hq3c45)/Information/info.aspx?InfoSection=Submission> accessed 21 April 2023

——— 'What We Investigate' <www.nationalcrimeagency.gov.uk/what-we-do/crime-threats> accessed 17 April 2023

OPBAS, 'Anti-Money Laundering Supervision by the Legal and Accountancy Professional Body Supervisors: Progress and Themes from 2019' (March 2020) <www.fca.org.uk/publication/opbas/supervisory-report-progress-themes-2019.pdf> accessed 25 February 2023

POLICE.UK, 'UK Police Forces' <www.police.uk/pu/contact-the-police/uk-police-forces/> accessed 13 April 2023

The Privy Council Office <https://privycouncil.independent.gov.uk> accessed 14 April 2023

Recker C, 'The National Crime Agency: A Critical Analysis of Its Potential Impact on the UK's Financial Crime Policy' in N Ryder, J Tucker and U Turksen (eds), *The Financial Crisis and White-Collar Crime – Legislative and Policy Responses: A Critical Assessment* (Routledge 2017)

Scott B and McGoldrick M, 'Financial Intelligence and Financial Investigation: Opportunities and Challenges' (2018) 13(3) Journal of Policing, Intelligence and Counterterrorism 301

Scottish Courts and Tribunals, 'About the Scottish Courts and Tribunals Service' <www.scotcourts.gov.uk/about-the-scottish-court-service> accessed 31 March 2023

Serious Fraud Office, 'Annual Report, 2019–2020' (2020) <www.sfo.gov.uk/download/annual-report-2019-2020/> accessed 15 April 2023

——— 'About Us' <www.sfo.gov.uk/about-us/> accessed 15 April 2023
Slapper G and Kelly D, *The English Legal System* (18th edn, Routledge 2017)
Sturge G, 'Court Statistics for England and Wales' (UK Parliament Research Briefing Paper No 8372, 22 December 2020) <https://commonslibrary.parliament.uk/research-briefings/cbp-8372/> accessed 10 April 2023
The Supreme Court, 'Role of the Supreme Court' <www.supremecourt.uk/about/role-of-the-supreme-court.html> accessed 31 March 2023
UK Government, 'Criminal Courts' <www.gov.uk/courts> accessed 31 March 2023
——— 'Appeal a Crown Court Decision' <www.gov.uk/appeal-against-crown-court-verdict> accessed 1 April 2023
——— 'Criminal Courts: Crown Court' <www.gov.uk/courts/crown-court> accessed 6 April 2023
——— 'Become a Magistrate' <www.gov.uk/become-magistrate/can-you-be-a-magistrate> accessed 24 August 2023
UK Legislation, 'Understanding Legislation' <www.legislation.gov.uk/understanding-legislation> accessed 14 April 2023
UK Parliament, 'Parliament's Authority' <www.parliament.uk/about/how/role/sovereignty/> accessed 12 April 2023
——— 'Public Bills' <www.parliament.uk/about/how/laws/bills/public/> accessed 17 April 2023
——— 'What Is a Bill?' <www.parliament.uk/about/how/laws/bills/> accessed 17 April 2023
——— 'What Is a Draft Bill?' <www.parliament.uk/about/how/laws/draft/> accessed 17 April 2023
——— 'Why Are New Laws Needed?' <www.parliament.uk/about/how/laws/new-laws/> accessed 17 April 2023
——— 'Royal Assent' <www.parliament.uk/about/how/laws/passage-bill/commons/coms-royal-assent/> accessed 20 April 2023
Wilson SR and others, *English Legal System* (4th edn, OUP 2020)
The World Bank Group, 'Role of the Financial Intelligence Units' <https://pubdocs.worldbank.org/en/834721427730119379/AML-Module-2.pdf> accessed 20 April 2023
Wright R, 'Fraud After Roskill: A View from the Serious Fraud Office' (2003) 11(1) Journal of Financial Crime 10

Legal Instruments

Constitutional Reform Act 2005
Courts Act 2003
Crime and Courts Act 2013
Criminal Appeal Act 1968
Criminal Justice Act 1987
Criminal Justice and Immigration Act 2008
The Criminal Procedure Rules 2020, SI 2020/759
European Union (Withdrawal Act) 2018
Explanatory Notes to the Serious Crime Act 2015
Finance Act 2008
Finance Act 2021
Financial Services and Market Act 2000
Magistrates' Court Act 1980

Cases

R v GH (Respondent) [2015] UKSC 24 [4]

7 Thematic Comparison of Obliged Entities – Obligations and Performance Indicators

7.1 Introduction

Having presented the structural differences between the legal and institutional AML frameworks of Türkiye and the UK, it is necessary to explore the practical/operational implications of these fundamental divergence points. Accordingly, from a broader AML perspective, this chapter addresses the main aim of this book by demonstrating whether and how differences between the legal and institutional AML structures may impact the effectiveness in tackling and the prevalence of predicate crimes, thereby underlining the unique features of an optimum AML regime. This is done by (i) evaluating the appropriateness of these respective AML structures; (ii) examining their suitability for intended aims; and (iii) critically analysing how AML laws operate in action in these jurisdictions. Case law, official statistics, and reports are examined to identify and critique the existing conditions regarding the AML efforts in practice. Therefore, based on such examples and evidence of law in practice, this chapter aims to reveal how heterogeneities between the two AML regimes impact the overall AML outcomes of a given jurisdiction, thereby preparing a sound ground for understanding their potential effects on the prevalence of predicate crimes, as discussed in Chapter 8.

FIs and DNFBPs, as obliged entities, are envisaged or expected to be a source of financial intelligence (e.g., suspicious transaction/activity reports-SARs/STRs) so that illicit financial transactions can be identified, and investigations can be instigated.[1] However, jurisdictions do not act uniformly in designating financial and non-financial businesses and professions as obliged entities, resulting in national differences regarding the scope of such entities and what information comes from whom. That being the case, the comprehensiveness of the ambit of obliged entities is one of the most significant themes that require a close examination regarding the AML compositions of Türkiye and

1 Chat Le Nguyen, 'Preventing the Use of Financial Institutions for Money Laundering and the Implications for Financial Privacy' (2018) 21(1) Journal of Money Laundering Control 47.

DOI: 10.4324/9781003466680-7

the UK. Additionally, dissimilarities in the AML obligations, such as KYC standards, record-keeping practices, and reporting (i.e., making STRs/SARs), imposed on obliged entities further impact the AML outcomes generated in Türkiye and the UK. For example, given that SARs/STRs trigger the AML *modus operandi* in most cases,[2] the unique characteristics of the two AML regimes (e.g., the threshold envisaged for suspicion) deserve thorough scrutiny, thereby rendering the obligations as another theme of the chapter.

Although evaluating the effectiveness and/or efficiency of an AML system is not a straightforward process, activities undertaken by the AML components of a given jurisdiction provide insights into the effectiveness of such a composition. In other words, tangible indicators available in this context, *inter alia*, the number of STRs/SARs reported by obliged entities to FIUs, the number of prosecutions/convictions secured, and the asset recovery figures, allow assessing whether and to what extent an AML structure is fit for its purpose. Accordingly, analysing the two AML frameworks based on such discernible benchmarks contributes to understanding the current state of affairs in Türkiye and the UK, thereby identifying obstacles, if any, accounting for the unsatisfactory AML outcomes in those jurisdictions. Therefore, such performance indicators constitute additional comparison theme of this chapter.

The complexity of ML and its underlying predicates and sophisticated methods developed by money launderers necessitate the creation of innovative mechanisms to counter them effectively. In order to address the intricate nature of the conundrum, the UK has introduced a plethora of novel strategies, such as the notion of Super SARs, the foundation of OPBAS, and the creation of PPPs (e.g., JMLIT), to name a few, indicating the inventive AML approach of the jurisdiction. Therefore, it is necessary to examine the function of these unconventional AML methods, thereby identifying whether adopting similar initiatives would reinforce the Turkish AML effectiveness. Accordingly, the penultimate section of this chapter takes a closer look at these examples of best practices.

Given that the inclusion or exclusion of particular sectors within the scope of obliged entities has a direct impact on the AML efforts of a given jurisdiction, this chapter begins by investigating the ambit of obliged entities as determined in Türkiye and the UK, thereby revealing which jurisdiction adopts a more comprehensive framework in this context. It then examines the obligations imposed on obliged entities to identify any significant differences between the two AML compositions, which may contribute to or stand in the way of ensuring an effective AML *modus operandi*. In this regard, the chapter compares the two AML regimes relating to the implementation of KYC standards, record-keeping practices, and the STR/SAR mechanisms. In doing so, it aims to discover whether such divergence points may be effective in generating varying

2 Ping He, 'The Suspicious Transactions Reporting System' (2005) 8(3) Journal of Money Laundering Control 252.

degrees of observable AML outcomes for Türkiye and the UK. Accordingly, it compares the number of STRs/SARs reported by obliged entities to FIUs, the volume of cases disseminated by FIUs to competent authorities for further legal action (e.g., prosecution), the number of prosecutions/convictions secured and the associated judicial outcomes, including the severity of sanctions, and the asset recovery figures achieved by the two administrations. The analysis also is supported by court decisions from Türkiye and the UK where appropriate to demonstrate the heterogeneities between the judiciary in civil law and common law jurisdictions. After providing insights into the AML effectiveness and efficiency of Türkiye and the UK, the chapter concludes by outlining examples of best practices from both jurisdictions. In doing so, it also highlights areas that require reform and puts forward solutions that would reinforce the prevailing AML practices. In other words, by observing how competent authorities practice AML laws, this chapter aims to address all three research questions. Whilst the core focus of the research questions is to identify the impacts of legal and institutional AML differences on the prevalence of predicate crimes, thereby putting forward recommendations for an optimum AML composition, this chapter investigates the effects of such divergence points on the overall AML outcomes. Accordingly, this general snapshot provides a solid basis for the next chapter that undertakes a predicate-crime-specific evaluation.

7.2 Obliged Entities

FATF Recommendations stipulate that states are expected to establish legal obligations for FIs and DNFBPs to identify and assess ML/TF and PF risks and respond to them effectively.[3] In other words, obliged entities consist of FIs and DNFBPs. Recommendations 22 and 23 state that the DNFBPs include casinos, real estate agents, dealers in precious metals and precious stones, lawyers, notaries, other independent legal professions and accountants, and trust and company service providers.[4] However, jurisdictions designate varying categories of financial and non-financial businesses and professions as obliged entities,[5] suggesting national preferences adopted in this context may affect the AML capacity of a given jurisdiction. For example, lawyers had not been regarded as DNFBPs in Türkiye until recently, and they have been subject to FATF Recommendations only since 31 December 2020.[6] Table 7.1 indicates the obliged entities in Türkiye and the UK.

3 FATF, 'International Standards on Combatting Money Laundering and the Financing of Terrorism & Proliferation: The FATF Recommendations' (Updated March 2022) Recommendation 1 <www.fatf-gafi.org/media/fatf/documents/recommendations/pdfs/FATF%20Recommendations%202012.pdf> accessed 26 June 2023.

4 ibid.

5 Michael Levi, Peter Reuter and Terence Halliday, 'Can the AML System Be Evaluated without Better Data?' (2017) 69(2) Crime, Law, and Social Change 307.

6 Official Gazette No 31351 dated 31 December 2020, 'Kitle İmha Silahlarının Yayılmasının Finansmanının Önlenmesine İlişkin Kanun' <www.resmigazete.gov.tr/eskiler/2020/12/20201231M5-19.htm> accessed 2 June 2023.

Table 7.1 Obliged entities in Türkiye and the UK.

Obliged entities	
Türkiye[7]	*United Kingdom*[8]
Banks; Nonbank institutions with the authority to issue bank cards or credit cards;	Credit institutions (e.g., banks and building societies);
Authorised establishments specified in the foreign exchange legislation; Financing and factoring companies; Capital Market Brokerage Houses and portfolio management companies; Precious metals brokerage firms; Investment partnerships; Insurance, reinsurance and pension companies, and insurance and reinsurance brokers; Financial leasing companies; Savings finance companies; Institutions furnishing settlement and custody services within the framework of capital markets legislation;	Financial institutions (e.g., money service businesses);
Freelance lawyers;[9] Certified general accountants, certified public accountants and sworn-in certified public accountants operating without being attached to an employer; Independent audit institutions authorised to conduct audit in financial markets;	Auditors, insolvency practitioners, external accountants, and tax advisors;
Notaries;	Independent legal professionals (e.g., notaries);
Persons who buy and sell immovables for trading purposes, including intermediaries of these transactions;	Estate agents and letting agents;

(*Continued*)

7 Law No 5549 on the Prevention of Laundering Proceeds of Crime 2006, art 2(1)(d); Regulation on Measures Regarding Prevention of Laundering Proceeds of Crime and Financing of Terrorism (ROM) 2008, art 4(1).

8 The Money Laundering, Terrorist Financing and Transfer of Funds (Information on the Payer) Regulations 2017, SI 2017/692 reg 8; Companies House, 'What an Obliged Entity Is?' <www.gov.uk/guidance/report-a-discrepancy-about-a-beneficial-owner-on-the-psc-register-by-an-obliged-entity> accessed 22 June 2023.

9 Freelance lawyers are considered obliged entities in cases where their functions are limited to (i) the realisation of financial transactions relating to the trading of immovables; (ii) the establishment and abolishment of limited real rights; (iii) the establishment, amalgamation, administration, transfer, and liquidation of companies, foundations, and associations; and where (iv) management of the bank, securities, and all kinds of accounts and assets in these accounts.

Table 7.1 (Continued)

Obliged entities	
Türkiye	*United Kingdom*
Dealers of precious metals, stones, and jewellery, including intermediaries;	High-value dealers (i.e., persons trading goods in cash amounting to 10,000 euros or more);
Directorate General of Turkish State Mint pertaining only to its activities of minting gold coins;	
Dealers of any kinds of sea, air, and land transportation vehicles inclusive of construction machines, including intermediaries;	
Persons who operate in lottery and betting fields, including Turkish National Lottery Administration, Turkish Jockey Club and Football Pools Organisation Directorate;	Casinos (i.e., gambling services);
Dealers and auctioneers of historical artefacts, antiques, and works of art;	Art market participants (e.g., art dealers in galleries, auction houses, and freeports);
Crypto asset service providers;	Crypto asset exchange providers;
Payment service providers and electronic money institutions;	Custodian wallet providers;
Assets management companies;	Trust or company service providers.
Borsa Istanbul AS pertaining only to its custody service relating to Precious Metals and Precious Stones;	
PTT Corporate (Company of Post and Telegraph Organisation) and cargo companies; and	–
Sports clubs.	

The close examination of the scope of obliged entities in the two jurisdictions connotes that although Türkiye and the UK require similar FIs and DNFBPs to comply with AML legal instruments, there are differences between these sectors. The first striking dissimilarity is that the AML legal regime in Türkiye does not designate letting agents as obliged entities. However, rental income constitutes one of the specific indicators of ML through real estate transactions, whereby offenders seek to legitimise illicit funds.[10] Another remarkable

10 Brigitte Unger and Johan den Hertog, 'Water Always Finds Its Way: Identifying New Forms of Money Laundering' (2012) 57(3) Crime, Law and Social Change 287; Cécile Remeur, 'Understanding Money Laundering through Real Estate Transactions' (European Parliamentary Research Service, February 2019) <www.europarl.europa.eu/cmsdata/161094/7%20-%2001%20EPRS_Understanding%20money%20laundering%20through%20real%20estate%20transactions.pdf> accessed 26 October 2023.

diversity relates to the monetary threshold (i.e., 10,000 euros or more) in determining which professions constitute high-value dealers. Türkiye does not set such a threshold for the corresponding set of businesses/professions, suggesting that the AML framework envisaged in this end is more comprehensive. An additional heterogeneity emerging from the table is that the UK does not consider persons who work in the postal service (and cargo/transportation fields) DNFBPs. Although their vulnerability to ML was reported previously, it relates only to the suspicious cash deposits at Post Office branches,[11] not concerning mailing services. Cargo companies in Türkiye relating to mailing services made a total of 3,115 STRs between 2016 and 2020,[12] suggesting the volume of suspicious transactions the UK authorities fail to exploit, as they are not included within the scope of DNFBPs. Given that it is not an uncommon practice for offenders to undertake drug smuggling and move illicit money around, one of the most common predicate crimes in Türkiye and the UK, via mail, the UK would benefit from including them within the scope of DNFBPs. For example, a recent GDS operation in Türkiye ensured the detention of four suspects who sent illicit drugs via cargo companies and the seizure of approximately 115 kg heroin accordingly.[13] Sports clubs constitute another divergence point relating to the scope of DNFBPs as determined in the two jurisdictions. However, it is necessary to state that whilst they are regarded as DNFBPs in Türkiye, there has not been a single STR made by them (at least) between 2016 and 2020,[14] suggesting the inactive participation of particular obliged entities in the AML efforts. Lastly, it is worth mentioning that casinos are prohibited in Türkiye.[15] With these differences in the two AML regimes in mind, it is necessary to examine the obligations envisaged for FIs and DNFBPs in Türkiye and the UK, thereby detecting whether and how they differentiate in addressing their legal duties.

11 HM Treasury and Home Office, 'National Risk Assessment of Money Laundering and Terrorist Financing 2020' (December 2020) <https://assets.publishing.service.gov.uk/government/uploads/system/uploads/attachment_data/file/945411/NRA_2020_v1.2_FOR_PUBLICATION.pdf> accessed 26 June 2023.

12 MASAK, 'Faaliyet Raporu 2020' (2021) 20 <https://ms.hmb.gov.tr/uploads/sites/12/2021/09/Faaliyet-Raporu-2020.pdf> accessed 18 January 2023.

13 Editorial, 'Kargoyla Uyuşturucu Taşıyan Sanıkların 22,5 Yıla Kadar Hapsi İstendi' *TRTHaber* (Türkiye, 14 January 2021) <www.trthaber.com/haber/turkiye/kargoyla-uyusturucu-tasiyan-saniklarin-225-yila-kadar-hapsi-istendi-547276.html> accessed 19 October 2023.

14 MASAK (n 12) 20.

15 Law No 5237 (Turkish Criminal Code) 2004, art 228. It is necessary to note that TCC 2004 prohibits any form of gambling, whether online or land-based, such as casinos.

7.3 Obligations

The core requirements[16] on FIs and DNFBPs put forward by the FATF consist of CDD, also known as KYC standards[17] (Recommendation 10), record-keeping (Recommendation 11), and reporting of suspicious transactions (Recommendation 20).[18] Whilst ROM 2008 stipulates these requirements thoroughly in Türkiye, the 2017 MLRs determine the relevant policies, principles, and procedures concerning obliged entities in the UK. However, there exist differences in the incorporation of these recommendations and the sanctions for non-compliance, suggesting that such discrepancies may impact the AML efforts. It is, therefore, necessary to examine how these obligations differ in Türkiye and the UK, thereby assessing their potential effects on the national AML outcomes.

7.3.1 Know Your Customer Standards

The FATF Recommendation 10 states that FIs need to take CDD measures on a risk-based approach (RBA) when (i) establishing business relations; (ii) carrying out occasional transactions (e.g., above the designated threshold envisaged); (iii) there is a suspicion of ML/TF; and when (iv) they have doubts about the veracity or adequacy of customer identification data obtained previously.[19] These CDD measures consist of (i) identifying and verifying (the identity of) the customer; (ii) identifying and taking reasonable measures to verify the beneficial owner; (iii) understanding the essential characteristics (i.e., the purpose and intended nature) of the business relationship to be established; and (iv) maintaining continuous due diligence during the relationship.[20] In other words, CDD procedures aim to ensure the identification, verification, and confirmation of the identity of customers and beneficial owners, where jurisdictions follow differing methods in addressing those goals,[21] suggesting the origin of national disparities in this context. Table 7.2 indicates the circumstances where FIs need to take CDD measures in Türkiye and the UK.

16 According to the FATF, Recommendations 3 (i.e., ML offence), 5 (i.e., TF offence), 6 (i.e., targeted financial sanctions for TF), 10, 11, and 20 constitute the 'Big Six Recommendations' as *vital building blocks* of any AML/CTF regime. See FATF, 'Report on the State of Effectiveness and Compliance with the FATF Standards' (April 2022) 10 <www.fatf-gafi.org/media/fatf/documents/recommendations/Report-on-the-State-of-Effectiveness-Compliance-with-FATF-Standards.pdf> accessed 17 August 2023.

17 FATF, 'FATF Guidance: Anti-Money Laundering and Terrorist Financing Measures and Financial Inclusion – With a Supplement on Customer Due Diligence' (November 2017) <www.fatf-gafi.org/media/fatf/content/images/Updated-2017-FATF-2013-Guidance.pdf> accessed 19 October 2023.

18 FATF (n 3).

19 ibid.

20 ibid.

21 Pavel M Shust and Victor Dostov, 'Implementing Innovative Customer Due Diligence: Proposal for Universal Model' (2020) 23(4) Journal of Money Laundering Control 871.

Table 7.2 Circumstances requiring CDD in Türkiye and the UK.

Customer due diligence	
Türkiye[22]	*United Kingdom*[23]
Regardless of the monetary amount when establishing a permanent business relationship	(If the obliged person) establishes a business relationship
When the amount of a single transaction or the total amount of multiple linked transactions is equal to or more than 75,000 TL (i.e., as of 22 October 2021, approximately 6,700 euros)	(If the obliged person) carries out an occasional transaction that amounts to 15,000 euros or more, whether the transaction is executed in a single operation or in several operations which appear to be linked
When the amount of a single transaction or the total amount of multiple linked transactions is equal to or more than 7,500 TL (i.e., as of 22 October 2021, approximately 670 euros) in wire transfer	(If the obliged person) carries out an occasional transaction that amounts to a transfer of funds exceeding 1,000 euros
Regardless of the monetary amount in cases requiring STR submission	(If the obliged person) suspects ML or TF
Regardless of the monetary amount in cases where there is suspicion about the adequacy and the accuracy of previously acquired identification information	(If the obliged person) doubts the veracity or adequacy of documents or information previously obtained for the identification/verification purposes

This table indicates that although there are differences regarding the wording of relevant provisions in Türkiye and the UK, they both reflect the spirit of Recommendation 10. The only material difference relates to the thresholds envisaged for occasional transactions, including wire transfers, where such margins are lower within the Turkish AML legal framework. That being the case, it is more likely for the Turkish obliged entities to take CDD measures more frequently. However, it is necessary to state that whilst ROM 2008 sets forth these measures as equally applying to all obliged entities, including DNFBPs, the 2017 MLRs, as per Recommendation 22,[24] stipulate them differently for particular sectors, such as high-value dealers and casinos, regarding

22 Regulation on Measures Regarding Prevention of Laundering Proceeds of Crime and Financing of Terrorism (ROM) 2008, art 5(1).

23 The Money Laundering, Terrorist Financing and Transfer of Funds (Information on the Payer) Regulations 2017, SI 2017/692 reg 27.

24 Recommendation 22 (FATF Recommendations) puts forward a detailed set of circumstances for each DNFBP sector (e.g., real estate agents, dealers in precious metals) regarding when to apply CDD measures. See FATF (n 3).

the monetary thresholds specified.[25] Therefore, it can be argued that whilst the UK has determined the essential CDD measures on an RBA as recommended by the FATF, Türkiye has failed to set forth particular CDD measures for DNFBPs commensurate with the risks identified. Considering the compliance costs to the obliged entities[26] and the advantages of implementing an RBA as it allows devoting AML efforts proportionate to the risks, adopting an RBA in dictating the fundamental CDD measures would be an appropriate approach for Türkiye.

In line with the principle of RBA, considering the types of customers (e.g., residency status), geographic factors, and particular products, services, transactions, or delivery channels (e.g., anonymous transactions), the FATF recommends jurisdictions to implement enhanced or simplified CDD measures where appropriate as per the risks identified.[27] In broad terms, enhanced CDD measures require obliged entities to obtain additional information on the customer/beneficial owner, update such information more frequently, obtain the approval of senior management in onboarding customers, and undertake rigorous monitoring of the business relationship established. Simplified CDD measures, on the other hand, envisage, amongst others, less frequent customer identification updates and a reduced degree of the ongoing monitoring process.[28] In light of these recommendations, the comparison of the AML provisions set forth by Türkiye and the UK indicates that whilst both jurisdictions regard similar risk factors (e.g., types of customers, sectors, and geographical origins) as entailing an enhanced CDD, PEPs do not necessitate such CDD measures in Türkiye.[29] However, the FATF recommends jurisdictions to require obliged entities to take enhanced CDD measures in doing business with foreign PEPs, their family members, or close associates.[30] Therefore, it can be claimed that the CDD obligations in the UK are more comprehensive than those in Türkiye, and the Turkish AML legislation fails to comply with the FATF Recommendations entirely in this context. The FATF's recent update on the jurisdictions under increased monitoring, whereby Türkiye's position has been updated as one of such jurisdictions due to the strategic deficiencies

25 For example, according to Regulation 27(3) of the Money Laundering, Terrorist Financing and Transfer of Funds (Information on the Payer) Regulations 2017, a high-value dealer must take CDD measures when carrying out an occasional transaction in cash that amounts to 10,000 euros or more, including multiple linked transactions.

26 LexisNexis Risk Solutions, 'Cutting the Costs of AML Compliance' (June 2021) <www.oxfordeconomics.com/recent-releases/Cutting-the-costs-of-AML-compliance> accessed 23 October 2023. See also Jackie Harvey, 'An Evaluation of Money Laundering Policies' (2005) 8(4) Journal of Money Laundering Control 339.

27 FATF (n 3) Interpretive Note to Recommendation 10.

28 ibid.

29 Regulation on Measures Regarding Prevention of Laundering Proceeds of Crime and Financing of Terrorism (ROM) 2008, art 26/A; and the Money Laundering, Terrorist Financing and Transfer of Funds (Information on the Payer) Regulations 2017, SI 2017/692 reg 33.

30 FATF (n 3) Recommendation 12.

identified relating, amongst others, to the limited up-to-date beneficial ownership information,[31] a CDD matter, corroborates this fact. It should be borne in mind that the world has witnessed serious ML cases, where (non-domestic) PEPs, along with their family members and close associates, abused the well-being of the global financial system,[32] suggesting the need for the application of enhanced CDD measures.

Lastly, as Koker observes, the FATF's CDD recommendations appear to be focusing on procedures rather than the substance of the process: the notion of CDD does not merely refer to the identification and verification of customer/beneficial owner identities, and such procedures, in a more comprehensive manner, need to be utilised for customer profiling purposes.[33] As a remarkable example, a recent court decision from Türkiye dated 24 September 2020 (Decision No: 2020/939) given by *İstanbul Bölge Adliye Mahkemesi 13. Hukuk Dairesi* indicates that the court decided on the dismissal of an appeal, where the appellant claimed that the bank did not comply with KYC standards, based, amongst others, on the grounds that 'the bank that opens the account is not responsible for questioning the *reliability* of the customer opening the account'.[34] That is to say that whilst undertaking a box-ticking approach may eliminate the risks associated with noncompliance for obliged entities, as evident in the court decision, it remains questionable whether such *modus operandi* can ensure an effective AML framework. Therefore, it can be argued that the FATF Recommendations, and thereby international and (supra)national AML legal instruments, need to concentrate more on the quintessence of the measures rather than the formal compliance.

7.3.2 Record-Keeping Practices

Another requirement that addresses FIs put forward by the FATF is the record-keeping, whereby FIs need to maintain all records on transactions and information obtained through the CDD measures for at least five years and make

31 FATF, 'Jurisdictions Under Increased Monitoring' (October 2021) <www.fatf-gafi.org/publications/high-risk-and-other-monitored-jurisdictions/documents/increased-monitoring-october-2021.html#turkey> accessed 24 May 2023.

32 Theodore S Greenberg and others, *Politically Exposed Persons: A Guide on Preventive Measures for the Banking Sector* (World Bank Publications 2010).

33 Louis de Koker, 'The FATF's Customer Identification Framework: Fit for Purpose?' (2014) 17(3) Journal of Money Laundering Control 281.

34 İstanbul Bölge Adliye Mahkemesi 13. Hukuk Dairesi, Alacak Davası (Esas No 2019/89 Esas), Decision No 2020/939 dated 24 September 2020 <http://emsal.uyap.gov.tr/BilgiBankasiIstemciWeb/GelismisDokumanAraServlet?dokumanTurleriString=UYAP,&aranan=Müşteri%20Tanı%20kara%20para&aramaG=sdsorRxP&baslangic=20&son=40&dokumanTuruAdi=UYAP&fromSonucSayfasindan=TRUE&sonucSayfasi=yeniTasarim/adaletAramaSonuc.jsp&sirala=1&mevzuatAdi=null&mevzuatNo=null&mevzuatMadde=null> accessed 15 October 2023.

them available for the competent domestic authorities.[35] The retention period, which aims to enable FIs to comply swiftly with information requests from the competent authorities, starts after the termination of the business relationship, or in the case of an occasional transaction, after the date of the last occasional transaction.[36] These record-keeping duties apply to DNFBPs as well (Recommendation 22). Accordingly, FIs and DNFBPs adhere to the obligation of record-keeping not only to ensure an adequate audit trail concerning ML/TF investigations but to prove that they have complied with their regulatory obligations.[37]

Comparison of the record-keeping obligations under the AML regimes of Türkiye and the UK indicates that whilst obliged entities shall keep the records specified at least for eight years in Türkiye,[38] such entities must retain them at least for five years in the UK.[39] Additionally, the record-keeping obligation in Türkiye entails retaining internal and external suspicion reports, including documents attached to such disclosures, as well as records explaining the reasons why compliance officers have not submitted STRs based on such suspicion disclosures.[40] Therefore, the prolonged retention period and the comprehensive documentation framework determined in Türkiye provide competent authorities with the ability to obtain ML/TF evidence from a more comprehensive source of documents and for a more extensive timespan. However, it is not evident whether these relatively expedient investigative authorities constitute a remarkable advantage therein. If not, concerning the complying costs, as touched upon previously, stipulating shorter record-keeping requirement periods (i.e., five years) would lessen the burden of obliged entities in Türkiye.

*7.3.3 **Reporting (Suspicious Transaction/Activity Reports)***

The suspicious activity/transaction reporting (SAR/STR) regime has been considered as the backbone of AML efforts.[41] The primary purpose of a SAR/STR *modus operandi* is to reduce the profits of perpetrating an ML offence and facilitating the detection of its underlying predicates, thereby deterring offenders and minimising associated crimes.[42] Both Türkiye and the UK have deter-

35 FATF (n 3) Recommendation 11.

36 ibid.

37 Dennis Cox, *Handbook of Anti-Money Laundering* (John Wiley & Sons Incorporated 2014) 271.

38 Law No 5549 on the Prevention of Laundering Proceeds of Crime 2006, art 8; and Regulation on Measures Regarding Prevention of Laundering Proceeds of Crime and Financing of Terrorism (ROM) 2008, art 46(1).

39 The Money Laundering, Terrorist Financing and Transfer of Funds (Information on the Payer) Regulations 2017, SI 2017/692 reg 40.

40 Regulation on Measures Regarding Prevention of Laundering Proceeds of Crime and Financing of Terrorism (ROM) 2008, art 46(2).

41 Gauri Sinha, 'To Suspect or Not to Suspect: Analysing the Pressure on Banks to Be "Policemen"' (2014) 15(1) Journal of Banking Regulation 75.

42 David Chaikin, 'How Effective are Suspicious Transaction Reporting Systems?' (2009) 12(3) Journal of Money Laundering Control 238.

mined their national legal framework for reporting suspicious transactions/ activities in line with the spirit of FATF's Recommendation 20, which sets forth:

> If a financial institution suspects or has reasonable grounds to suspect that funds are the proceeds of a criminal activity, or are related to terrorist financing, it should be required, by law, to report promptly its suspicions to the financial intelligence unit (FIU).[43]

The close examination of SAR/STR regimes under the two AML legal frameworks demonstrates that the most salient difference is the time limit envisaged for the reporting obligation. As discussed in Chapter 4, obliged entities in the UK must report their suspicions to the NCA (i.e., the UKFIU) 'as soon as is practicable' after such suspicions occur.[44] However, ROM 2008 envisages a period of ten workdays starting from the date suspicion materialised for obliged entities to report their suspicions to MASAK.[45] Therefore, given the rapid nature of ML offences, it can be argued that the period of ten workdays relating to fulfilling the reporting obligation constitutes the most crucial problem, representing a legal lacuna concerning the Turkish STR regime. With this important difference in mind, it is necessary to examine the number of SARs/ STRs the UKFIU and MASAK receive annually.

Table 7.3 demonstrates that except for the slight decrease in the number of STRs submitted in Türkiye in 2019, the number of STRs/SARs in Türkiye and the UK has continually increased over time. However, the table indicates also that the number of SARs submitted to the UKFIU by obliged entities in the UK is consistently at least two times higher than the STRs submitted to MASAK in any given year. This remarkable difference stems from various factors, including but not limited to the AML legal frameworks of the two jurisdictions (e.g., sanctions envisaged and the scope of obliged entities), the institutional AML structures adopted by Türkiye and the UK (i.e., administrative type of FIU and law enforcement model of FIU dichotomy), and external factors, such as the (reporting) culture and the volume of transactions actualised therein. It is worth reiterating that whilst a failure to disclose (i.e., reporting SARs) results in criminal consequences for the obliged entities in the UK, the violation of complying with the STR submission obligation entails only administrative penalties (which is less than GBP 500) in Türkiye, as discussed in Chapters 3 and 4 previously. Additionally, given that the unique notion of DAML (as well as DATF), whereby obliged entities seek 'appropriate consent' from the UKFIU, provides criminal immunity for obliged entities in the UK, it serves as another booster for making such a substantial number of SARs. Furthermore, the threshold of suspicion set forth for making STRs/SARs by the national AML legal frameworks of Türkiye and the UK contributes to such a differentiation

43 FATF (n 3).
44 Proceeds of Crime Act 2002, ss 330–32.
45 ROM 2008, art 28(2).

Table 7.3 The number of STRs/SARs received by MASAK and the UKFIU.

Suspicious transaction/activity reports received by MASAK and the UKFIU (2016–2020)							
FIU		*2016*	*2017*	*2018*	*2019*	*2020*	*Total*
MASAK[46]	**AML**	**92,079**	**138,365**	**195,604**	**188,924**	**235,544**	**850,516**
	CTF	40,491	38,046	27,139	14,862	1,987	122,525
	Total	132,570	176,411	222,743	203,786	237,531	973,041
UKFIU	**AML**	**634,113**[47]		**463,938**[48]	**478,437**[49]	**573,085**[50]	**2,149,573**
	CTF	2,026		2,688	1,908	1,897	8,519
	Total[51]	634,113		463,938	478,437	573,085	2,149,573

46 MASAK (n 12) 19. It is necessary to note that MASAK recently published its 2021 Annual Report in April 2022. However, the statistics available therein do not make any difference to the argument of this study. See MASAK, 'Faaliyet Raporu 2021' (2022) <https://ms.hmb.gov.tr/uploads/sites/12/2022/03/Faaliyet-Raporu-2021.pdf> accessed 18 April 2023.

47 NCA, 'Suspicious Activity Reports (SARs) – Annual Report 2017' (2017) <www.nationalcrimeagency.gov.uk/who-we-are/publications/112-suspicious-activity-reports-annual-report-2017/file> accessed 12 October 2023.

48 NCA, 'Suspicious Activity Reports (SARs) Annual Report 2018' (2018) <www.nationalcrimeagency.gov.uk/who-we-are/publications/256-2018-sars-annual-report/file> accessed 21 April 2023.

49 NCA, 'UK Financial Intelligence Unit Suspicious Activity Reports Annual Report 2019' (2019) <www.nationalcrimeagency.gov.uk/who-we-are/publications/390-sars-annual-report-2019/file> accessed 21 April 2023.

50 NCA, 'UK Financial Intelligence Unit Suspicious Activity Reports Annual Report 2020' (April 2020) <www.nationalcrimeagency.gov.uk/who-we-are/publications/480-sars-annual-report-2020/file> accessed 24 February 2023.

51 As the UKFIU identifies and disseminates the CTF-related SARs from amongst all SARs received, the 'total' row indicates the same aggregates as the 'AML' row.

between the disclosure figures of obliged entities. Although both national AML legislation stipulate similar provisions for obliged entities to make disclosures (e.g., the requirement of reasonable grounds for suspicion), court decisions from Türkiye and the UK indicate that the judiciary in these jurisdictions can take a heterogeneous approach in evaluating such a threshold. For example, although POCA 2002 requires obliged entities' knowledge, suspicion, or ***reasonable grounds for knowing or suspecting*** that there is a risk of ML/TF incident relating to their transactions in submitting SARs, case law has proffered a lower threshold. In the case of *Regina v Da Silva*, Longmore LJ expressed his views on the concept of suspicion as follows:

> It seems to us that the essential element in the word 'suspect' and its affiliates, in this context, is that the defendant must think that there is a possibility, which is more than fanciful, that the relevant facts exist. A vague feeling of unease would not suffice. But the statute does not require the suspicion to be 'clear' or 'firmly grounded and targeted on specific facts' or based upon 'reasonable grounds'. To require the prosecution to satisfy such criteria as to the strength of the suspicion would, in our view, be putting a gloss on the section.[52]

As the close reading of this Court of Appeal judgement connotes, the concept of suspicion is a subjective matter, which does not entail well-grounded facts in establishing such a notion. However, it is necessary to note that the judgement was made within the scope of Section 93(1)(a) of the Criminal Justice Act 1988 (i.e., assisting another to retain the benefit of criminal conduct), which has been repealed by the enactment of POCA 2002. Nevertheless, more recent cases concerning POCA 2002 still refer to the aforementioned judgement given the importance of the rationales it puts forward relating to the notion of suspicion, an outstanding example illustrating how the judiciary conventionally operates in common law jurisdictions. For instance, in the case of *Shah v HSBC Private Bank Ltd*[53] and *Parvizi v Barclays Bank Plc*,[54] the High Court, referring to the *Regina v Da Silva* judgement, maintained the judicial standpoint concerning establishing suspicion in making SARs. On the other hand, court decisions from Türkiye demonstrate that the Turkish judiciary does not impose penalties on obliged entities for failing to submit STRs to MASAK. For example, although a recent court proceeding (Decision No: 2020/497–30 October 2020) at *İstanbul 13. Asliye Ticaret Mahkemesi* found that the bank failed to make an STR (involving a suspicious transaction amounting to USD 30,000) and notify the Turkish FIU, MASAK, it did not charge or sanction bank officials with penalties stipulated by Law No 5549 2006 (i.e., Article 14).[55] Therefore, the criminal sanctions envisaged for breaching disclosure obligations and the low subjective threshold of suspicion

52 *Regina v Da Silva* [2006] EWCA Crim 1654 [2007] 1 WLR 303 [16].

53 *Shah v HSBC Private Bank Ltd* [2012] EWHC 1283 [2012] 5 WLUK 503 (QB) [67].

54 *Parvizi v Barclays Bank Plc* [2014] EWHC B2 (QB) [2014] 5 WLUK 725 [4] [5].

55 İstanbul 13. Asliye Ticaret Mahkemesi, Tazminat Davası (Bankacılık İşlemlerinden Kaynaklanan) (Esas No 2019/438 Esas), Decision No 2020/497 dated 30 October 2020 <http://

established in the UK lead to elevated reporting figures made by obliged entities therein.[56] In other words, the high number of SARs shall not necessarily be regarded as an indicator of greater sensitivity to ML and its underlying predicates in the UK compared to Türkiye. Additionally, these facts rather than the type of FIU adopted seem to be more likely to affect the disclosure tendencies of the obliged entities operating in the UK. Consequently, the pervasive culture of 'box-ticking'[57] and defensive over-reporting amongst obliged entities, particularly bank professionals, inevitably impairs how the UKFIU operates due to the associated scarcity of resources devoted to overwhelming SARs, leading to an eventual failure to detect actual ML incidents.[58] Whilst overreporting slows down the screening process at an FIU intrinsically,[59] the sheer number of SARs in the UK raises concerns over the effectiveness of the UKFIU whether it can address them promptly and efficiently. It is worth noting that according to a Europol report, the UK alone accounted for 36% of all STRs/SARs filed in the EU with almost 2.5m disclosures between 2006 and 2014,[60] indicating the huge workload for the UKFIU.

That being the case, the enormous disparity between the number of SARs filed in the UK compared with STRs filed in Türkiye also brings about concerns over the quality of such disclosures. It has been argued that the prodigious number of SARs in the UK stems from the fact that the UK AML regime attaches weight to quantity rather than the quality of SARs.[61] However, as Ryder aptly posits, this overreporting reflex of obliged entities in the UK creates 'a needle-in-the-haystack' problem.[62] In other words, the high number of SARs/STRs hinders rather than promotes the AML efforts, given the ratio of false positives (i.e., approximately 95%),[63] an indicator of the qual-

---

emsal.uyap.gov.tr/BilgiBankasiIstemciWeb/GelismisDokumanAraServlet> accessed 13 October 2023.

56 Peter Burrell, Rita Mitchell and David Savell, 'A Troubling Bank Balance – Competing Duties for Banks When Making Suspicious Activity Reports' (2012) 129(6) Banking Law Journal 542.

57 Sinha (n 41).

58 Igho L Dabor, 'Crying Wolf: An Examination of the UK's Suspicious Activity Report Regime' (2019) 40(4) Company Lawyer 107.

59 Lucia dalla Pellegrina and others, 'Organized Crime, Suspicious Transaction Reporting and Anti-Money Laundering Regulation' (2020) 54(12) Regional Studies 1761.

60 Europol, 'From Suspicion to Action – Converting Financial Intelligence into Greater Operational Impact' (September 2017) 10 <www.europol.europa.eu/publications-documents/suspicion-to-action-converting-financial-intelligence-greater-operational-impact> accessed 5 November 2023.

61 Sabrina Fiona Preller, 'Comparing AML Legislation of the UK, Switzerland and Germany' (2008) 11(3) Journal of Money Laundering Control 234.

62 Nicholas Ryder, 'The Financial Services Authority and Money Laundering: A Game of Cat and Mouse' (2008) 67(3) Cambridge Law Journal 635, 652. See also XiaoTong Loh, 'Suspicious Activity Reports (SARs) Regime: Reforming Institutional Culture' (2021) 24(3) Journal of Money Laundering Control 514.

63 Sanne Wass, 'Banks' Suspicious Activity Report Ramp-Up Is Inefficient, Warn Industry Figures' *S&P Global Market Intelligence* (27 February 2020) <www.spglobal.com/marketintelligence/en/news-insights/latest-news-headlines/banks-suspicious-activity-report-ramp-up-is-inefficient-warn-industry-figures-57265800> accessed 27 October 2023.

ity of such disclosures. For example, whilst the relatively modest penalties for not reporting and its sporadic execution give rise to sparse but qualitatively better unusual transaction reports (i.e., STRs/SARs) in the Netherlands, the harsh sanction mechanism produces vice versa figures in the US.[64] Therefore, the best way to evaluate the quality of the two STR/SAR regimes would be to compare the qualitative outcomes they generate, such as the percentage of SARs/STRs forwarded by MASAK and the UKFIU to prosecuting authorities and the associated conviction and confiscation figures. Accordingly, those measures are examined in a separate section later.

Considering that SARs/STRs submitted by banks constitute the most substantial proportion of such reports in Türkiye and the UK and that enablers (e.g., lawyers and accountants) have attracted an increasing policy discourse,[65] it is worth examining the SARs/STRs practices of these particular FIs and DNFBPs. As of March 2021, there were 54 banks (with 11,194 affiliated branch offices) operating in Türkiye,[66] whereas the number of financial services, including banks, operational in the UK is approximately 300,[67] equivalent to a sixfold the volume concerning FIs functional in Türkiye. Additionally, there is a substantial difference between the volume and number of trading/ transactions in the two jurisdictions where consolidated assets of banks are equal to EUR 621.5 billion in Türkiye and EUR 11,223.7 billion in the UK.[68] In terms of the accountancy profession, there are approximately 115,000 professional accountants in Türkiye[69] and 326,000 in the UK.[70] In light of these figures, Table 7.4 demonstrates the number of SARs/STRs made by these (see the first three rows) and other sectors.

64 Unger and den Hertog (n 10).

65 Ilaria Zavoli and Colin King, 'The Challenges of Implementing Anti-Money Laundering Regulation: An Empirical Analysis' (2021) 84(4) Modern Law Review 740; Michael Levi, Hans Nelen and Francien Lankhorst, 'Lawyers as Crime Facilitators in Europe: An Introduction and Overview' (2005) 42(2–3) Crime, Law, and Social Change 117.

66 Türkiye Bankalar Birliği, 'Faaliyet Raporu 2020–2021' (Mayıs 2021) <www.tbb.org.tr/Content/Upload/Dokuman/7773/Faaliyet_Raporu_2020-2021.pdf> accessed 13 October 2023; European Banking Federation, 'Turkey's Banking Sector: Facts & Figures' <www.ebf.eu/turkey/> accessed 19 May 2022.

67 UK Finance, 'Our Members' <www.ukfinance.org.uk/membership/find-a-member> accessed 13 October 2021.

68 TheBanks.eu, 'Compare Countries by Banking Sector' <https://thebanks.eu/compare-countries-by-banking-sector#ref_4> accessed 19 May 2022. See also Türkiye Cumhuriyeti Merkez Bankası, 'Markets Data' <www.tcmb.gov.tr/wps/wcm/connect/EN/TCMB+EN/Main+Menu/Statistics/Markets+Data/> accessed 19 May 2023; UK Finance, 'UK Payment Markets Summary 2021' (June 2021) <www.ukfinance.org.uk/sites/default/files/uploads/SUMMARY-UK-Payment-Markets-2021-FINAL.pdf> accessed 19 May 2023; Bank of England, 'Payment and Settlement Statistics' <www.bankofengland.co.uk/payment-and-settlement/payment-and-settlement-statistics> accessed 19 May 2023.

69 TÜRMOB (Union of Chambers of Certified Public Accountants of Türkiye), 'Üye İstatistikleri' <www.turmob.org.tr/istatistikler/c8172e63-2bef-4919-a863-86e403bfdf0a/meslek-mensubu-dagilim-tablosu-(sm-smmm)> accessed 20 October 2023.

70 Oxford Economics, 'The Accountancy Profession in the UK and Ireland' (November 2018) <www.ccab.org.uk/wp-content/uploads/2020/06/The-Accountancy-Profession-in-the-UK-and-Ireland.pdf> accessed 20 October 2023.

Table 7.4 Summary of STRs/SARs reporting by sector.

Summary of SARs/STRs[71] reporting by sector	*2016 and 2017*		*2018*		*2019*		*2020*		*Total*	
	Türkiye	*UK[72]*	*Türkiye*	*UK[73]*	*Türkiye*	*UK[74]*	*Türkiye*	*UK[75]*	*Türkiye*	*UK*
Banks	276,082	525,361	195,803	371,522	174,764	383,733	182,828	432,316	**829,477**	**1,712,932**
Accountants and tax advisers	14	6,693	1	5,140	1	5,055	0	5,347	**16**	**22,235**
Independent legal professionals[76] (e.g., notaries)	5	4,878	0	2,660	2	2,774	7	3,006	**14**	**13,318**
Credit institution – building societies	NA	22,323	NA	19,640	NA	21,714	NA	30,579	**NA**	**94,256**
Credit institution – others	NA	19,326	NA	13,678	NA	10,203	NA	8,080	**NA**	**51,287**
Financial institution – MSBs	4,085	16,704	13,796	21,198	19,225	18,940	46,840	17,701	**83,946**	**74,543**
Financial institution – others[77]	18,753	23,675	8,075	21,446	7,224	24,911	5,461	58,930	**39,513**	**128,962**
Trust or company service providers	1	112	2	53	3	23	3	31	**9**	**219**
Estate agents	NA	766	NA	710	NA	635	NA	861	**NA**	**2,972**
High value dealers[78]	88	265	95	249	85	481	105	370	**373**	**1,365**
Gaming (including casinos)/leisure	4	2,223	5	2,154	64	4,163	262	5,150	**335**	**13,690**
Cargo companies	1,538	–	948	–	270	–	359	–	**3,115**	–
Others	8,411	–	4,018	–	2,148	–	1,666	–	**16,243**	–
Not under MLRs	NA	11,787	NA	5,488	NA	5,805	NA	10,714	**NA**	**33,794**
Total	**308,981**	**634,113**	**222,743**	**463,938**	**203,786**	**478,437**	**237,531**	**573,085**	**973,041**	**2,149,573**

71 MASAK (n 12).
72 NCA (n 47).
73 NCA (n 48).
74 NCA (n 49).
75 NCA (n 50).
76 Regarding Türkiye, these sums consist of STRs submitted by notaries and independent audit institutions authorised to audit financial markets.
77 Regarding Türkiye, FI – others include factoring companies; insurance, reinsurance/pension companies; insurance and reinsurance brokers; financing companies; Capital Market Brokerage Houses and portfolio management companies; financial leasing companies; investment partnerships; and precious metals brokerage firms.
78 Concerning Türkiye, STRs submitted by dealers of precious metals, stones, and jewellery, including intermediaries and dealers of any kinds of the sea, air, and land vehicles, inclusive of construction machines, including intermediaries, are grouped as high-value dealers.

The number of SARs/STRs submitted by banks is proportionate to their aggregates operating in Türkiye and the UK. However, there is a stark difference between the reporting figures of legal professionals and accountants, suggesting that the disclosure culture is not prevalent in these professions in Türkiye. One possible explanation for these inadequate STR sums in Türkiye might be frequent tax amnesties and similar initiatives,[79] as such strategies may undermine efforts devoted by legal professionals and accountants and diminish their trust in the rule of law and the criminal justice system.[80] Other reasons seem to be including the fear of losing clients, losing the confidence of their clients, and the lack of trust and confidence in the STR ***modus operandi***,[81] which are crucial factors strongly associated with the independence of those professionals.[82] Equally important, as reported by MASAK, there is a lack of awareness amongst the majority of accounting and auditing professionals operating in Türkiye (i.e., certified general accountants, certified public accountants, and sworn-in certified public accountants) concerning obligations stipulated under the AML/CTF legal regime.[83] The AML supervisory mechanisms created for these professions in Türkiye and the UK indubitably constitute another distinguishing feature responsible for dissimilar SAR/STR figures. The Turkish (AML) legal instruments do not set forth any provisions, which authorise a supervisory body for supervising, monitoring, supporting, and advising its members on AML requirements, as all these responsibilities are incumbent only on MASAK. For example, as far as accountants are concerned, although they operate under the auspices of TÜRMOB, a self-regulatory body setting professional standards for its members,[84] TÜRMOB does not have any supervisory duty for AML compliance. Its AML efforts are limited to providing its members with AML training activities and educational materials, such as a series of case studies prepared

79 Gelir İdaresi Başkanlığı, 'Varlık Barışı' <www.gib.gov.tr/node/146992> accessed 20 October 2023.

80 Umut Turksen, 'Implications of Anti-Money Laundering Law for Accountancy in the European Union – A Comparative Study' in Nicholas Ryder, Umut Turksen and Sabine Hassler (eds), *Fighting Financial Crime in the Global Economic Crisis* (1st edn, Routledge 2014).

81 ibid. See also Umut Turksen, Ismail U Misirlioglu and Osman Yukselturk, 'Anti-Money Laundering Law of Turkey and the EU: An Example of Convergence?' (2011) 14(3) Journal of Money Laundering Control 279.

82 Prem Sikka and Hugh Willmott, 'The Power of "Independence": Defending and Extending the Jurisdiction of Accounting in the United Kingdom' (1995) 20(6) Accounting, Organizations and Society 547.

83 MASAK, 'Serbest Muhasebeci Mali Müşavirler ve Yeminli Mali Müşavirler Sektör Araştırma Raporu' (February 2021) <https://ms.hmb.gov.tr/uploads/sites/12/2021/03/SMMM-YMM-SEKTOR-ARASTIRMA-RAPORU.pdf> accessed 21 October 2023.

84 TÜRMOB, 'TÜRMOB Hakkında' <https://turmob.org.tr/Kurumsal/TURMOB-Hakkinda> accessed 21 October 2023.

by IFAC and ICAEW.[85] On the other hand, the institutional AML structure of the UK has established a professional supervisory mechanism – conducted by OPBAS – for the legal services and accountancy sectors (see Chapter 6). That is to say that MASAK's monopolised supervisory authority inherently may fail to supervise all FIs and DNFBPs effectively, thereby diminishing the optimum contribution of the legal and accountancy sectors in the AML efforts. Therefore, as Yukselturk and others aptly posit, introducing legal provisions that harness TÜRMOB with AML functions (e.g., supervising and reporting) and authorising it as an AML supervisory body for accountants would increase the AML effectiveness of the aforementioned professionals.[86] For the legal services sector, a similar supervisory role can be conferred to the Union of Turkish Bar Associations.[87] Nevertheless, it is necessary to inquire into whether there are additional factors in force, such as the sanctions levied by courts, which generate different levels of AML outcomes for Türkiye and the UK relating to the AML efforts devoted by obliged entities. Accordingly, in what follows, the chapter examines the effects of such characteristics in detail.

7.4 Insights Into the Enforcement Effectiveness

Evaluating the quality of an STR/SAR regime in general and assessing the effectiveness of any AML enforcement regime in particular is not a straightforward task.[88] However, there exist particular parameters that can help form an opinion of the efficacy of such procedures. These can include for example, the volume of STRs/SARs received by FIUs, the number of cases disseminated by FIUs to competent authorities, such as LEAs or the prosecutor's office, for further investigation,[89] the number of prosecutions/convictions, and the asset recovery figures.[90] Accordingly, it is necessary to examine the relevant data from Türkiye and the UK to generate insights into the AML effectiveness of the two jurisdictions. Table 7.5 presents the number of files/cases examined by MASAK and the UKFIU and referral outcomes of such inspections annually.

85 TÜRMOB, 'Karaparanın Aklanmasının Önlenmesi/Örnek Olay-1' <www.turmob.org.tr/haberler/32366455-c7d8-4402-a213-d3df03f7f60c/karaparanin-aklanmasinin-onlenmesi-ornek-olay-1> accessed 21 October 2023.

86 Osman Yukselturk, İsmail Misirlioglu, and Umut Turksen, 'Check the Weather Before You Hang the Laundry! Accounting Turkish Progress in Anti-Money Laundering Mechanisms' (Society of Legal Scholars Annual Conference, Southampton, September 2010) <https://eprints.kingston.ac.uk/id/eprint/35430/> accessed 21 October 2021.

87 Union of Turkish Bar Associations <www.barobirlik.org.tr> accessed 7 December 2023.

88 Ronald F Pol, 'Anti-Money Laundering: The World's Least Effective Policy Experiment? Together, We Can Fix It' (2020) 3(1) Policy Design and Practice 73.

89 Corina-Narcisa (Bodescu) Cotoc and others, 'Efficiency of Money Laundering Countermeasures: Case Studies from European Union Member States' (2021) 9(6) Risks 120.

90 Jackie Harvey, 'Just How Effective Is Money Laundering Legislation?' (2008) 21(3) Security Journal 189.

Table 7.5 Annual case completion achieved by MASAK[91] and the UKFIU.

	2016		*2017*		*2018*		*2019*		*2020*	
	MASAK	*UKFIU*	*MASAK*	*UKFIU*	*MASAK*	*UKFIU*	*MASAK*	*UKFIU*	*MASAK*	*UKFIU*
Number of files opened for examination[92]	84	NA	87	NA	89	NA	29	NA	46	NA
Number of files examined	20	NA	38	NA	75	NA	70	NA	46	NA
Number of people mentioned in the files examined	1,431	NA	1,775	NA	3,554	NA	3,112	NA	2,613	NA
Number of persons reported for prosecution	145	NA	203	NA	279	NA	220	NA	187	NA

Table 7.5 illustrates that following a steady annual performance, the volume of files opened for further examination by MASAK decreased dramatically in 2019 when MASAK significantly reduced its members of staff, as touched upon in Chapter 5 previously, suggesting the correlation between the personnel count and the associated capacity. However, the same reduction is not evident concerning the number of files examined. The most significant fact the table signifies is that MASAK has contributed to the prosecution and probably to the conviction of at least 1,034 offenders out of almost 12,500 suspects between 2016 and 2020. Whilst the relevant data concerning the UK is not available, the Internal Revenue Service (IRS), a USA agency that undertakes criminal investigation on behalf of FinCEN (i.e., the FIU of the USA), initiated 856, 838, and 1,050 investigations on ML and referred 780, 745, and 934 suspects to prosecuting authorities, whereby secured the sentencing of 508, 379, and 383 offenders in 2019, 2020, and 2021, respectively.[93] These figures provide a degree of insight into the performance of MASAK in comparison to another leading jurisdiction in AML. The overall prosecution and conviction sums produced by the two criminal justice systems between 2016 and 2020 are as follows:

91 MASAK (n 12) 27–28.

92 The number of files opened for examination does not stand for all files investigated in a given year. For instance, MASAK has analysed more than 75,000 cases since 2016 and opened approximately 350 investigation files, as it is believed that a more detailed examination was necessary for those instances.

93 Internal Revenue Service: Criminal Investigation, 'Annual Report 2021' (2021) 48 <www.irs.gov/pub/irs-pdf/p3583.pdf> accessed 3 June 2023.

Table 7.6 Money laundering cases and the associated judicial outcomes.

ML cases and the judicial outcomes[94]	*2016*		*2017*		*2018*		*2019*		*2020*	
	Türkiye[95]	*UK*	*Türkiye*[96]	*UK*	*Türkiye*[97]	*UK*	*Türkiye*[98]	*UK*	*Türkiye*[99]	*UK*
ML cases	**880**	**1,998**	**1,406**	**1,906**	**894**	**1,503**	**758**	**1,342**	**805**	**1,294**
Sentenced	**62** **(7%)**	**1,411** **(70%)**	**114** **(8%)**	**1,341** **(70%)**	**156** **(17%)**	**1,073** **(71%)**	**326** **(43%)**	**1,042** **(78%)**	**89** **(11%)**	**836** **(65%)**
Imprisonment	*17* *(27%)*	*511* *(36%)*	*31* *(27%)*	*462* *(34%)*	*56* *(36%)*	*362* *(34%)*	*91* *(28%)*	*353* *(34%)*	*25* *(28%)*	*299* *(36%)*
Fine	*16*	*44*	*26*	*33*	*43*	*29*	*80*	*26*	*20*	*13*
Suspended sentence	*0*	*549*	*0*	*579*	*1*	*429*	*3*	*433*	*0*	*384*
Security measures	*15*	--	*27*	--	*25*	--	*80*	--	*16*	--
Other imprisonment sentence decisions	*14*	*0*	*30*	*0*	*31*	*0*	*72*	*0*	*28*	*0*
Acquittal decisions	**68** **(8%)**	**563** **(28%)**	**53** **(4%)**	**559** **(29%)**	**266** **(30%)**	**409** **(27%)**	**256** **(34%)**	**298** **(22%)**	**197** **(24%)**	**476** **(37%)**

94 The relevant data concerning the UK was extracted from Criminal Justice System Outcomes by Offence 2010 to 2020. Additionally, some judicial outcomes, such as community sentence decisions, were not included in the table as there is no corresponding sentence within the relevant Turkish sentencing framework. Therefore, the aggregates for sentencing outcomes concerning the UK columns will not represent the exact number of sentence decisions. Ministry of Justice, 'Criminal Justice System Statistics: Outcomes by Offence 2010 to 2020' (May 2021) <https://assets.publishing.service.gov.uk/government/uploads/system/uploads/attachment_data/file/987715/outcomes-by-offence-2020.xlsx> accessed 2 November 2023.

95 Ministry of Justice General Directorate of Judicial Record and Statistics, 'Judicial Statistics 2016' (November 2017) 99, 113, 122, 131, 140, 149, 158, 167 <https://adlisicil.adalet.gov.tr/Resimler/SayfaDokuman/2082019114041Adalet_ist_2016.pdf> accessed 28 October 2023.

96 Ministry of Justice General Directorate of Judicial Record and Statistics, 'Judicial Statistics 2017' (August 2018) 97, 111, 120, 129, 138, 147, 156, 165 <https://adlisicil.adalet.gov.tr/Resimler/SayfaDokuman/2082019114010Adalet_ist_2017.pdf> accessed 28 October 2023.

97 Ministry of Justice General Directorate of Judicial Record and Statistics, 'Judicial Statistics 2018' (August 2019) 97, 111, 120, 129, 138, 147, 156, 165 <https://adlisicil.adalet.gov.tr/Resimler/SayfaDokuman/1792019103654adalet_ist_2018.pdf> accessed 28 October 2023.

98 Ministry of Justice General Directorate of Judicial Record and Statistics, 'Judicial Statistics 2019' (August 2020) 97, 111, 120, 129, 138, 147, 156, 165 <https://adlisicil.adalet.gov.tr/Resimler/SayfaDokuman/1092020162733adalet_ist-2019.pdf> accessed 1 February 2023.

99 Ministry of Justice General Directorate of Judicial Record and Statistics, 'Judicial Statistics 2020' (September 2021) 97, 111, 120, 129, 138, 147, 156, 165 <https://adlisicil.adalet.gov.tr/Resimler/SayfaDokuman/1692021162011adalet_ist-2020.pdf> accessed 1 February 2023.

Table 7.6 indicates that the number of ML cases filed at the criminal courts in Türkiye has fluctuated, except for the sharp increase observed in 2017, with slight variances over time and a minimum case volume of 758 in 2019. The sheer growth in 2017 can be attributable to the aftermath of the coup attempt in 2016, after which MASAK has immediately concentrated primarily on the terrorists and their finances, as touched upon in Chapters 3 and 5. It is worth reiterating that terrorism and TF are (also) predicate crimes in Türkiye, thereby contributing to the volume of ML cases. As a corroborative statistic, whilst acquittal decisions made in 2016 and 2017 constituted less than 10% of all ML cases (i.e., approximately 8% and 3%, respectively), such judicial outcomes were equivalent to approximately 30% of all ML lawsuits in each following year (i.e., around 30%, 34%, and 24%, respectively), supporting the argument put forward. The table also demonstrates that except for 2019, when such decisions amounted to almost half of all ML cases (i.e., 43%), the number of judicial outcomes where a sentence decision was made accounted for roughly 10% of all ML cases annually. Of those court verdicts where the decision was a sentence, approximately 30% involved imprisonment (i.e., around 27%, 27%, 36%, 28%, and 28% in respective years) consistently. In other words, almost one-third of all ML suspects (i.e., 220 offenders) were sentenced to an imprisonment term in Türkiye between 2016 and 2020. It is necessary to state also that an additional 175 offenders were incarcerated for other offences, such as robbery, albeit their trials were within the ambit of ML, which render the total imprisonment rate 53%. The figures on the incarceration for other crimes suggest that the identification and gathering of evidence necessary to ensure an effective ML prosecution are not always conducted effectively in Türkiye. The remaining judicial outcomes included the imposition of judicial and administrative fines with similar figures to imprisonment sums, suspensions of imprisonment decisions, and the application of security measures. It is burdensome, if not impossible, to regard these figures as the direct results of STRs made by obliged entities since there does not exist such integrated/interconnected data provided by the judiciary, LEAs, and MASAK in this context. However, given that the STR regime constitutes the most significant source of financial intelligence for LEAs, including Türkiye,[100] it can be argued that the total of approximately 850,000 STRs (see Table 7.3) yielded roughly 1,000 ML cases (see Table 7.5) and around 400 imprisonments (see Table 7.6) between 2016 and 2020.

The statistics from the UK indicate that the number of ML cases handled at the courts has slightly decreased annually, with a maximum case volume of 1,998 in 2016 and a minimum of 1,294 in 2020. However, the ML caseload has been consistently higher in the UK than in Türkiye (e.g., 2.27 times in 2016 and 1.6 times in 2020) each year. Table 7.6 shows that the number of judicial outcomes where the result was a sentence decision[101] accounted for approximately 71% of all ML cases yearly, equalling to the sevenfold of

100 Neil J Jensen, 'Technology and Intelligence' (2005) 8(3) Journal of Money Laundering Control 227.

101 Sentence decisions comprise imprisonment, fine, suspended sentence, security measures, and other imprisonment sentence decisions. See Table 7.6.

such decisions given in Türkiye, suggesting the higher competence of ML sentencing procedures followed in the UK. Of the sentences passed in the UK, the imprisonment amounted to 35% on average consistently, which is slightly higher than the standard observed in Türkiye (i.e., 30%). Nevertheless, given the low ratio of sentences concerning ML cases (i.e., 10% of all ML cases annually) in Türkiye, the close aggregates relating to the incarceration figures of the two jurisdictions can be deceptive. A careful comparison of imprisonment sums in Türkiye and the UK reveals that whilst they present similar custody percentages, the number of offenders sentenced to an imprisonment term in the UK is four to 30 times higher than in Türkiye in any given year. For example, whilst 220 suspects were found guilty and sent to prison in Türkiye between 2016 and 2020, the analogous imprisonment percentages resulted in the custody of 1,987 offenders in the UK, almost nine times more than in Türkiye. Therefore, it can be contended that the Turkish Criminal Justice System handles money launderers more leniently than the UK. However, it is essential to note that acquittal decisions in the UK were consistently and, except for 2019, significantly higher than such judicial outcomes observed in Türkiye. This can be attributable to the proportionality of the caseloads of the two jurisdictions as, except for 2016 and 2017 when the Turkish judiciary predominantly held ML cases concerning the terrorists behind the coup attempt faced therein, the acquittal percentages were not far from each other. Additionally, it is worth underlining here that in contrast with Türkiye, there are no offenders who were incarcerated for other offences as a result of ML trials, suggesting the accuracy of the detection and collection of evidence process required for ensuring an effective ML prosecution in the UK. Although the number of persons reported by the UKFIU for prosecution is not available (see Table 7.5), it can be argued that approximately 2 million SARs (see Table 7.3) yielded roughly 8,000 ML cases and around 2,000 imprisonments (see Table 7.6) in the UK between 2016 and 2020. Nevertheless, drawing such a conclusion, where a direct cause and effect relationship between SARs and judicial proceedings is established, needs to be heeded. For instance, Gold and Levi remind us that there are too many instances where such disclosures follow arrests rather than securing the detention of offenders,[102] suggesting that it is not a straightforward process to establish such a causative correlation. Lastly, it should be borne in mind that the data within this table cannot be a precise snapshot of the yearly judicial AML *modus operandi* of the two jurisdictions, as not all cases are concluded within a calendar year.

It is worth mentioning again that the Turkish legal regime differentiates between offenders who deal with criminal proceedings (e.g., purchasing, accepting) by being aware (Article 282/2 of TCC 2004) and unaware (Article 165 of TCC 2004) of the illegitimate sources of such assets (see Chapter 3). Therefore, it is crucial to inquire into the judicial handling process of the second group of offenders, who are not regarded as money

102 Michael Gold and Michael Levi, *Money Laundering in the UK: An Appraisal of Suspicion-Based Reporting* (Police Foundation & University of Wales 1994).

launderers in Türkiye, thereby rendering the provided table (i.e., Table 7.6) more meaningful. A minor amendment to the TCC 2004, which eliminates the intentional differences these two groups of criminals entertain (i.e., direct and oblique intention), would result in higher figures for ML cases and the associated judicial outcomes in Türkiye. It is clear that almost identical wording of Articles 165 and 282(2) of TCC 2004 makes it a burdensome task for LEAs and the judiciary to uphold the appropriate sanctions against the perpetrators,[103] as identifying whether offenders are aware of the illegitimate sources of the assets under consideration is challenging. For example, a recent court decision on the unification of judgements made by the High Court of Appeal (i.e., *Yargıtay*) vacated the decision given by a first instance court in favour of Article 165, which was ruled as per Article 282 of TCC 2004,[104] indicating the ethereal difference between the two offences. Table 7.7 demonstrates judicial outcomes on offenders who have been prosecuted under Article 165 of TCC 2004 (i.e., purchasing or accepting property acquired through the commission of an offence), suggesting that an additional almost 80,000 offenders could have been judged as ML suspects between 2016 and 2020.

Table 7.7 Criminal cases under Article 165 of TCC 2004 and the judicial outcomes.

Article 165 of TCC 2004	*2016*[105]	*2017*[106]	*2018*[107]	*2019*[108]	*2020*[109]
Cases	**15,622**	**15,456**	**17,850**	**19,183**	**10,182**
Sentenced	9,302	8,970	12,238	11,780	5,050
Imprisonment	**1,918**	**1,761**	**2,532**	**2,553**	**1,083**
Fine	3,646	3,490	4,542	4,414	1,998
Suspended sentence	542	522	676	719	287
Security measures	1,213	1,263	1,797	1,779	720
Other imprisonment sentence decisions	1,983	1,934	2,691	2,315	962
Acquittal decisions	7,315	6,092	6,792	6,509	2,300

103 Ersan Sen, 'Kara Para Aklama Suçunda Soruşturma Ne Zaman Başlar?' *Ersan Sen Hukuk ve Danışmanlık* (9 May 2022) <https://sen.av.tr/tr/makale/kara-para-aklama-sucunda-sorusturma-ne-zaman-baslar> accessed 31 July 2023.

104 Yargıtay 16. Ceza Dairesi, İçtihat Metni (Esas No 2020/7564 Esas), Decision No 2021/4553 dated 30 June 2021 <https://karararama.yargitay.gov.tr/YargitayBilgiBankasiIstemciWeb/pf/sorgula.xhtml> accessed 10 November 2023.

105 Ministry of Justice General Directorate of Judicial Record and Statistics (n 95) 95, 109, 118, 127, 136, 145, 154, 163.

106 Ministry of Justice General Directorate of Judicial Record and Statistics (n 96) 93, 107, 116, 125, 134, 143, 152, 161.

107 Ministry of Justice General Directorate of Judicial Record and Statistics (n 97) 93, 107, 116, 125, 134, 143, 152, 161.

108 Ministry of Justice General Directorate of Judicial Record and Statistics (n 98) 93, 107, 116, 125, 134, 143, 152, 161.

109 Ministry of Justice General Directorate of Judicial Record and Statistics (n 99) 93, 107, 116, 125, 134, 143, 152, 161.

Before examining the asset recovery capabilities of the two jurisdictions, it is necessary to inquire into the judicial treatment of legal persons as ML suspects/offenders, as the criminal liability of legal entities constitutes one of the most significant differences between the two (AML) legal regimes. The Turkish legal instruments do not allow sanctioning of legal persons unless there is a prosecution or conviction of a natural person. Therefore, given that the legal entities in Türkiye are not criminally liable under the Turkish (AML) legal framework, it is worth investigating their involvement in the ML cases, thereby identifying whether the current sanctions mechanism envisaged for them is fit for its purpose. The statistics on the judicial outcomes from Türkiye indicates that 15 offenders were legal persons relating to ML cases filed at the criminal courts between 2016 and 2020 (i.e., 2 in 2016,[110] 6 in 2017,[111] 5 in 2018,[112] and 2 in 2020).[113] However, only one court decision was rendered regarding legal entities in that period.[114] Although the OECD points out that the sanctioning mechanism envisaged for legal entities in Türkiye is insufficient to be effective, proportionate, and dissuasive,[115] it is necessary to note that there has not been a single legal entity prosecuted for ML under criminal law in the corresponding period in the UK.[116] As discussed in Chapter 6 previously, the criminal prosecution (commenced by the FCA) against National Westminster Bank Plc under the 2007 MLRs on 16 March 2021 constitutes the first-ever application of such powers in the UK.[117] National Westminster Bank Plc pleaded guilty to the charges on 7 October 2021.[118] Nevertheless, alternative legal powers to the criminal prosecution of legal entities in this context, such as DPAs, which can be applied, amongst others, to predicate ML offences, explain the underlying reasons for the lack of such prosecutions therein. For example, SFO has recently secured two DPAs amounting to approximately GBP 2.5m, comprising disgorgement of profits and a financial penalty, with two

110 Ministry of Justice General Directorate of Judicial Record and Statistics (n 95) 99.

111 Ministry of Justice General Directorate of Judicial Record and Statistics (n 96) 97.

112 Ministry of Justice General Directorate of Judicial Record and Statistics (n 97) 97.

113 Ministry of Justice General Directorate of Judicial Record and Statistics (n 99) 97.

114 Ministry of Justice General Directorate of Judicial Record and Statistics (n 97) 183.

115 OECD, 'Turkey's Foreign Bribery Enforcement Framework Needs to Be Urgently Strengthened and Corporate Liability Legislation Reformed' <www.oecd.org/corruption/turkey-s-foreign-bribery-enforcement-framework-needs-to-be-urgently-strengthened-and-corporate-liability-legislation-reformed.htm> accessed 8 November 2023.

116 The pertinent data concerning the UK was extracted from Criminal Justice System Outcomes by Offence 2010 to 2020. See Ministry of Justice (n 94).

117 Financial Conduct Authority, 'NatWest Plc Pleads Guilty in Criminal Proceedings' (3 November 2021) <www.fca.org.uk/news/press-releases/natwest-plc-pleads-guilty-criminal-proceedings> accessed 19 November 2023.

118 ibid.

UK-based companies for bribery offences under the Bribery Act 2010.[119] Similarly, DPAs have been frequently used as enforcement and sanctioning mechanisms against British banks (e.g., HSBC, Standard Chartered, Barclays, and Lloyds Bank) for ML originating from the OFAC-sanctioned countries (e.g., Iran) by the US prosecution authorities at the international sphere even before their first-ever application in the UK,[120] suggesting the UK's dilatoriness and probably reluctance in this end. Whilst it is beyond the scope of this study to discuss the proportionality of DPAs as to whether they are conducive to justice or can fully address the sanctions deserved, it remains a philosophical and academic debate to be settled,[121] which would constitute the core interest of another academic study. Yet, given that they have been applied only against wealthy companies, such as Rolls-Royce and Airbus SE,[122] it would be an unrealistic expectation to overcome the phenomenon without changing the mindset regarding such organisations as 'too big to jail'.[123]

Asset recovery (e.g., confiscation) has been considered one of the performance indicators of an effective AML regime.[124] One might expect that the frequent/overhauling alterations to the principal asset recovery authority of a jurisdiction experienced in a short period negatively influence the operational efficacy of such an agency. Whilst it has been the case for the UK (e.g., ARA, SOCA, and NCA), those modifications do not seem to have impacted the UK LEAs adversely when compared to their Turkish counterparts who have not encountered such shake-ups. Table 7.8 provides the asset recovery figures of LEAs operating in the two jurisdictions regarding confiscation of criminal assets.

119 Serious Fraud Office, 'SFO Secures Two DPAs with Companies for Bribery Act Offences' (20 July 2021) <www.sfo.gov.uk/2021/07/20/sfo-secures-two-dpas-with-companies-for-bribery-act-offences/> accessed 19 November 2023.

120 OECD, 'Illicit Financial Flows from Developing Countries: Measuring OECD Responses' (2014) <www.oecd.org/corruption/Illicit_Financial_Flows_from_Developing_Countries.pdf> accessed 30 November 2023.

121 Oliver Charles and Umut Turksen, 'Deferred Prosecution Agreements: A Soft Touch?' in Dan Jasinski, Amber Phillips and Ed Johnston (eds), *Organised Crime, Financial Crime, and Criminal Justice: Theoretical Concepts and Challenges* (Routledge 2023).

122 Serious Fraud Office, 'Deferred Prosecution Agreements' <www.sfo.gov.uk/publications/guidance-policy-and-protocols/guidance-for-corporates/deferred-prosecution-agreements/> accessed 19 November 2021.

123 Nicholas Ryder, '"Too Scared to Prosecute and Too Scared to Jail?" A Critical and Comparative Analysis of Enforcement of Financial Crime Legislation Against Corporations in the USA and the UK' (2018) 82(3) Journal of Criminal Law (Hertford) 245; Patrick Hardouin, 'Too Big to Fail, Too Big to Jail: Restoring Liability a Lesson from HSBC Case' (2017) 24(4) Journal of Financial Crime 513.

124 Peter Alldridge, *Money Laundering Law Forfeiture, Confiscation, Civil Recovery, Criminal Laundering, and Taxation of the Proceeds of Crime* (1st edn, Oregon Hart Publishing 2003).

Table 7.8 Confiscation figures in relation to the money laundering offence.

Confiscation figures (ML)	*2016*		*2017*		*2018*		*2019*		*2020*	
	Türkiye[125]	*UK*	*Türkiye*[126]	*UK*	*Türkiye*[127]	*UK*	*Türkiye*	*UK*	*Türkiye*	*UK*
Number of files[128]	**4**	**6,000**	**3**	**5,500**	**4**	**5,000**	**NA**	**4,400**	**NA**	**4000**
TL	*874,035*		*326,500*		*5,019,761*		NA		NA	
(GBP)	**(66,455)**		**(24,825)**		**(381,664)**					
USD	*142,196*		*2,000,000*		–		*NA*		*NA*	
(GBP)	**(103,859)**		**(1,460,773)**							
EUR	*34,935*		–		–		*NA*		*NA*	
(GBP)	**(29,505)**									

(*Continued*)

125 FATF, 'Anti-Money Laundering and Counter-Terrorist Financing Measures – Turkey: Mutual Evaluation Report' (December 2019) 64 <www.fatf-gafi.org/media/fatf/documents/reports/mer4/Mutual-Evaluation-Report-Turkey-2019.pdf> accessed 18 January 2023. There are not publicly available and integrated data on ML cases and associated confiscation figures in Türkiye. Therefore, the relevant statistics were extracted from the FATF's Mutual Evaluation Report (MER) on Türkiye. Thus, such information concerning Türkiye is limited to three years, as provided by the MER.

126 ibid.

127 ibid.

128 The relevant data concerning the UK stands for the 'Volume of Confiscation Orders Impositions' and are in approximate volumes. However, it is essential to note that the number of confiscation orders includes other offences, such as forgery, and thus more than the number of ML cases in Table 4.1. See Home Office, 'Asset Recovery Statistical Bulletin: Financial Years Ending 2016 to 2021' (September 2021) <www.gov.uk/government/statistics/asset-recovery-statistical-bulletin-financial-years-ending-2016-to-2021/asset-recovery-statistical-bulletin-financial-years-ending-2016-to-2021> accessed 19 August 2023.

Table 7.8 (Continued)

Confiscation figures (ML)	*2016*		*2017*		*2018*		*2019*		*2020*	
	Türkiye	*UK*	*Türkiye*	*UK*	*Türkiye*	*UK*	*Türkiye*	*UK*	*Türkiye*	*UK*
Total[129] (GBP)	**0.2m**	**207m[130]**	**1.49m**	**161m[131]**	**0.38m**	**142m[132]**	**NA**	**167m[133]**	**NA**	**139m[134]**
Gold (14)	–		–		2,387.56		NA		NA	
Gold (22)	–		–		2,731		NA		NA	
Jewellery	–		–		80		NA		NA	
Immovable	–		–		1		NA		NA	
Vehicle	10		–		5		NA		NA	
Instrumentality	2		2		--		NA		NA	

129 The currency conversions were made on 31 October 2021. See Xe Currency Converter <www.xe.com/currencyconverter/> accessed 31 October 2023.

130 Home Office, 'Asset Recovery Statistical Bulletin 2014/15–2019/20' (September 2020) 6 <https://assets.publishing.service.gov.uk/government/uploads/system/uploads/attachment_data/file/923194/asset-recovery-financial-years-2015-to-2020-hosb2320.pdf> accessed 31 October 2023.

131 ibid.

132 ibid.

133 ibid.

134 ibid.

Before making any comparisons between the figures presented in the table, it is worth reiterating that whilst confiscation primarily aims to recover (material) criminal assets or gains in Türkiye, regardless of the availability of such properties, confiscation seeks to deprive offenders of the crime benefits monetarily in the UK. In other words, whilst confiscation decisions are fundamentally in the form of *in rem* in Türkiye, confiscation orders in the UK are *in personam*, explaining the variety of items confiscated in the former. That being the case, it is not practicable to compare asset recovery figures of the two jurisdictions, as the monetary values of the vehicles/instrumentalities confiscated in Türkiye are unknown. Additionally, whilst confiscation is the only asset recovery means in Türkiye, it should be borne in mind that asset recovery methods in the UK include additional instruments, such as civil recovery and taxation, albeit the table indicates the criminal confiscation sums. For instance, whilst confiscation ensured the recovery of GBP 207m in 2016 (GBP 161m in 2017) in the UK, the whole set of asset recovery tools, including but not limited to civil recovery and taxation, secured the recovery of GBP 321.72m in 2016 (GBP 483.64m in 2017).[135] Yet, the preceding table is capable of illuminating the enormous divergence points of the two AML mechanisms relating to asset recovery practices. The first remarkable aspect is that although the number of ML cases filed at the criminal courts in Türkiye on average is approximately 950 per year (see Table 7.6), the volume of court files where the decision included confiscation is consistently less than five (i.e., 0.5%) annually. These low figures could be stemming from the fact that, unlike the UK's approach to asset recovery, the Turkish legal regime does not allow the confiscation of properties or gains offenders hold unless proven that such proceeds are associated with the offence under consideration. Correspondingly, confiscation decisions in Türkiye could secure the recovery of only minimal proportions of what asset recovery practices ensured in the UK per annum. These sums also confirm the argument made in previous chapters (i.e., Chapters 3 and 4) that, unlike the UK's sentencing *modus operandi*, asset recovery has not become an imbedded part of the sentencing practices of the Turkish courts. Consequently, although there is a steady decrease in the value of asset recovery sums through confiscation in the UK, it has consistently ensured the denial of at least approximately GBP 140m proceeds of crime to offenders annually. This overall downward trend can be attributable to the enactment of CFA 2017, whereby civil recovery powers have been reinforced (e.g., the introduction of UWOs), which enabled LEAs to opt for the most appropriate recovery means commensurate with the prevailing circumstances, as discussed in Chapter 4.

135 FATF, 'Anti-Money Laundering and Counter-Terrorist Financing Measures: United Kingdom – Mutual Evaluation Report' (December 2018) 74 <www.fatf-gafi.org/media/fatf/documents/reports/mer4/MER-United-Kingdom-2018.pdf> accessed 18 January 2022.

7.5 Sanctions

Sanctions envisaged for violation of legal rules have conventionally been considered one of the cornerstones of crime prevention strategies.[136] Therefore, it is necessary to compare sanctions levied on money launderers in Türkiye and the UK. Accordingly, Table 7.9 demonstrates available statistics on the average custodial sentence length and the monetary penalties imposed on money launderers in the two jurisdictions.

Whilst the relevant data from Türkiye are limited, the available statistics show that Türkiye imposes roughly two times longer imprisonment sentences for money launderers than the UK. Whilst the analogous imprisonment percentages result in the custody of the more money launderers in the UK (i.e., approximately ninefold of Türkiye's incarceration figures in this context), the Turkish Criminal Justice System levies longer terms when it comes to confinement of persons. Given that the Turkish AML legal instruments envisage shorter imprisonment terms (i.e., three to seven years) than its British counterpart (i.e., up to 14 years), these unprecedented statistics are worth emphasising. For instance, money launderers were sentenced to an average of 74, 66, and 75 months for ML in 2019, 2020, and 2021, respectively, in

Table 7.9 Sanctions imposed on money launderers in Türkiye[137] and the UK.[138]

	2016		*2017*		*2018*		*2019*		*2020*	
	Türkiye	*UK*	*Türkiye*	*UK*	*Türkiye*	*UK*	*Türkiye*	*UK*	*Türkiye*	*UK*
Average custodial sentence length (months)	40	23.9	65	25.3	NA	27.0	NA	31.8	NA	30.9
Average fine (GBP)	NA	309	NA	276	NA	206	NA	249	NA	1,273

136 David M Kennedy, *Deterrence and Crime Prevention: Reconsidering the Prospect of Sanction* (Routledge 2009).

137 FATF (n 125) 61. Given that there is no publicly available data on the average time of incarceration imposed for ML offences in Türkiye, the relevant statistics were extracted from the FATF's MER on Türkiye. Consequently, such figures regarding Türkiye are limited to two years, as provided by the MER.

138 The relevant data concerning the UK was extracted from Criminal Justice System Outcomes by Offence 2010 to 2020. See Ministry of Justice (n 94).

the USA (a common-law jurisdiction),[139] crystallising the relative shortness of the sentences given in the UK. As illustrated in Table 7.6 earlier, whilst criminal courts in Türkiye have imposed (administrative and judicial) fines on 185 offenders within the ambit of ML cases, the judiciary in the UK has levied such penalties on 145 money launderers between 2016 and 2020. Although the monetary aggregates of fines imposed in Türkiye are not available, the average fine figures in the UK indicate that they are just GBP 260 on average annually, excluding 2020, which makes the average approximately GBP 460 per year, suggesting that they are not astronomic sums. Therefore, considering the shorter imprisonment sentences and the modest fines levied on money launderers in the UK, it can be argued that the sanctions envisaged for such offenders in Türkiye are more deterrent than the UK's sanctioning mechanism.

7.6 Examples of Best Practices

Amongst many other unique AML characteristics, such as UWOs and lifestyle provisions, innovative approaches to the SAR regime constitute additional strengths of the UK's AML composition. The notion of Super SARs that allows the sharing of information within the regulated sector voluntarily and thereby submitting joint disclosures to the NCA, as discussed in Chapter 4, represents such a novel example. However, it is necessary to note that this private-private information-sharing mechanism has not been exploited effectively, if any, yet.[140] Having said that, the public-private partnership established between the financial sector and LEAs in this context, namely JMLIT, has been regarded as an example of best practice regionally[141] and internationally,[142] albeit its structure has been criticised for being too restrictive.[143] This secure and permanent information-sharing platform offers a regular forum that brings together FIs and competent authorities, thereby enabling LEAs to access sensitive information (e.g., Personal Current Accounts)[144] and FIs to get informed on emerging ML threats/tactical intelligence.[145] The participants of JMLIT meet every week, thereby concentrating on particular cases that pose higher ML risks,[146] indicating its risk-based and more focused approach, as well as the close collaboration

139 Internal Revenue Service: Criminal Investigation (n 93) 48. It is necessary to note that a violation of 18 USC §1956 can result in a sentence of up to 20 years in prison.
140 Rafael Pontes and others, 'Anti-Money Laundering in the United Kingdom: New Directions for a More Effective Regime' (2022) 25(2) Journal of Money Laundering Control 401.
141 Europol (n 60) 10.
142 FATF (n 135) para 9.
143 Nicholas Ryder, 'Cryptoassets, Social Media Platforms and Defence Against Terrorism Financing Suspicious Activity Reports: A Step into the Regulatory Unknown' (2020) 8 Journal of Business Law 668.
144 FATF (n 135) para 115.
145 NCA, 'Joint Money Laundering Intelligence Taskforce' <www.nationalcrimeagency.gov.uk/what-we-do/national-economic-crime-centre> accessed 1 November 2023.
146 Nick Kochan, 'Banks Engage in Anti-Money-Laundering Fight' *The Banker* (1 April 2016) <www.thebanker.com/Banking-Regulation-Risk/Management-Strategy/Banks-engage-in-anti-money-laundering-fight?ct=true> accessed 1 November 2023.

between the AML stakeholders in the UK. Furthermore, its voluntary information sharing feature enabled the swift identification of the transaction records of the terrorists involved in the London Bridge terrorist attack in 2017,[147] suggesting its effectiveness relating to the CTF efforts along with the AML practices. Therefore, this more concise and relatively more successful SAR mechanism raises doubts about the effectiveness of the prevailing STR/SAR regimes adopted by most jurisdictions around the world. As a corroborative observation, Levi and others posit that the introduction of JMLIT has been based upon the enthusiasm to generate discernible AML effects proportionate to costs devoted by obliged entities to compliance requirements,[148] suggesting that the traditional SAR mechanism does not produce such observable AML outcomes. For example, JMLIT has supported at least 750 ML investigations, whereby it has ensured the denial of GBP 56m in proceeds of crime to offenders and the conviction of 210 money launderers since its inception.[149] That being the case, remodelling the conventional STR/SAR mechanisms would help increase the overall effectiveness of any given reporting system, including Türkiye and the UK.

7.7 Conclusion

The flexibility provided by the FATF Recommendations has resulted in designating varying categories of FIs and DNFBPs as obliged entities in Türkiye and the UK. In addition, it has given rise to crucial divergence points regarding obligations imposed on the regulated sector and the sanctions envisaged for non-compliance with the AML requirements between the two jurisdictions. Whilst both administrations regard similar risk factors as determinants for KYC standards (i.e., implementing an enhanced or simplified CDD), the CDD measures determined in Türkiye manifest some deficiencies, such as the exclusion of PEPs and the limited implementation of the RBA. In terms of record-keeping obligations, the prolonged retention period and the comprehensive documentation framework determined beyond FATF Recommendations in Türkiye seem to be increasing the burden of obliged entities to be shouldered gratuitously. As far as the SAR/STR regimes under the two AML legal frameworks are concerned, the most salient difference pertains to the time limit of ten workdays envisaged for the reporting obligation in Türkiye, unfit for the rapid nature of ML offences. Furthermore, although national AML legal instruments of Türkiye and the UK set forth similar provisions

147 Dominic O'Neill, 'Privacy Fears Slow Spread of UK-Style Data-Sharing to Combat Money Laundering' *Euromoney* (29 August 2019) <www.euromoney.com/article/b1gxtdng8xn576/privacy-fears-slow-spread-of-uk-style-data-sharing-to-combat-money-laundering> accessed 1 November 2023.

148 Levi, Reuter and Halliday (n 5).

149 Nick J Maxwell, 'Five Years of Growth in Public-Private Financial Information-Sharing Partnerships to Tackle Crime' (Future of Financial Intelligence Sharing (FFIS) Research Programme, August 2020) 19 <www.future-fis.com/uploads/3/7/9/4/3794525/five_years_of_growth_of_public-private_partnerships_to_fight_financial_crime_-_18_aug_2020.pdf> accessed 5 November 2023.

for obliged entities regarding the threshold of suspicion in making STRs/SARs, the judiciary in the UK acknowledges a lower threshold as established by the case law. The lack of awareness of the AML obligations and the lack of trust and confidence in the STR regime amongst particular obliged entities, such as the accounting and auditing professionals, curtail the proliferation of disclosure culture, thereby resulting in lower STR figures in Türkiye. Last but not least, the unique institutional AML structure adopted by Türkiye, such as the monopolised AML supervisory mechanism, which is incumbent only on MASAK, further contributes to the contrast between how the AML law operates in action in Türkiye and the UK.

The outcomes generated by the two AML regimes, *inter alia*, the volume of cases disseminated by FIUs to competent authorities for further legal action instigated by or based on STRs/SARs received, the number of prosecutions/convictions secured, and the asset recovery figures, give insights into the effectiveness and efficiency of the AML compositions. Although the annual number of files opened for further examination by the UKFIU is not available, such data from Türkiye indicate the correlation between the personnel count and the associated capacity, as MASAK's performance in this end decreased significantly when the Turkish FIU reduced its members of staff in 2019. That being the case, recruiting more expert personnel would increase its efficiency in this context. Concerning the overall prosecution/conviction figures, whilst sentencing decisions present similar incarceration rates, imprisonment decisions given in Türkiye are significantly lower than the UK regarding the number of total ML cases, suggesting the difficulty of securing custody sentences in the former. However, it is necessary to state that notwithstanding the shorter incarceration terms envisaged for money launderers in Türkiye than in the UK, imprisonment sentences imposed on such offenders demonstrate that the Turkish courts impose longer periods on this group of criminals. Furthermore, given that a significant proportion of ML trials result in the incarceration of offenders for other crimes in Türkiye, the identification and gathering of evidence necessary to ensure an effective ML prosecution gestate problems therein. One potential reason for this ineffectiveness is the almost identical wording of Articles 165 and 282(2) of TCC 2004, constituting an ethereal difference for LEAs and the judiciary to identify and thereby aggravating the effective upholding of the appropriate legal procedures. Therefore, as argued in previous chapters, addressing the elusive nature of these provisions would help increase the AML effectiveness of the jurisdiction. The lack of criminal liability established for legal persons in Türkiye and the associated alternative legal powers to the criminal prosecution, such as the DPAs, render the Turkish AML legal regime less productive than its British counterpart concerning the judicial treatment of legal entities. That being the case, introducing effective, proportionate, and dissuasive sanctions for legal entities in Türkiye would enhance the deterrence effect of the Turkish sanctioning mechanism in this context, thereby reinforcing its AML effectiveness.

The dichotomy between *in rem* (Türkiye) and *in personam* (UK) confiscation decisions constitutes a significant diversity between the two AML regimes, affecting the asset recovery practices of the two jurisdictions. Given that the Turkish legal regime allows the confiscation of properties or gains offenders hold when only proven that such proceeds are associated with the offence under consideration, *in rem* confiscation orders further reduce the effectiveness of asset recovery practices undertaken in Türkiye compared to the UK. Considering the nature of the ML offence, where money launderers layer criminal proceedings through a plethora of transactions and investments as an ingrained part of the laundering process (i.e., layering), making connections between the ML offence and the criminal profits gets an even more arduous task for LEAs and the judiciary. The scarcity of confiscation decisions given by the Turkish courts confirms that asset recovery has not become a reflex and an entrenched part of the sentencing *modus operandi* of the Turkish courts, corroborating the previously mentioned hurdles. Consequently, as the only asset recovery means in Türkiye, the criminal confiscation cannot generate similar recovery figures to the British asset recovery arsenal, which further includes civil recovery and taxation. Therefore, introducing additional recovery powers, such as UWOs, would increase the AML competency of the Turkish judiciary and LEAs. Lastly, the active inclusion of the private sector in the AML efforts through the JMLIT and the division of labour in supervising obliged entities in the UK (e.g., OPBAS) are the outstanding characteristics of the British AML regime that reinforce the integrity of the AML components of the jurisdiction. Considering the substantial contribution of these novel strategies adopted in the UK to the fight against the phenomenon, adopting similar ingenious initiatives by Türkiye would certainly ensure a more integrated national AML composition.

In light of concrete evidence provided by the competent AML authorities of the two jurisdictions, this chapter has explored and compared the AML outcomes (i.e., the law in action) generated by the AML compositions (i.e., the law in the books and the institutional frameworks) adopted in Türkiye and the UK. The narrow scope of obliged entities (e.g., the exclusion of letting agencies and the recent inclusion of lawyers), the unaccommodating application of particular obligations (e.g., the ten workdays envisaged for making an STR), and the gratuitous burden of certain complying costs beyond the FATF Recommendations (e.g., the eight-year retention period) constitute the cardinal AML deficiencies for Türkiye regarding obliged entities and their obligations. The reduction of MASAK's personnel count, the cryptic nature of particular provisions (i.e., the almost indistinguishable wording of Articles 165 and 282(2) of TCC 2004), and the associated hurdles in securing sufficient evidence required for achieving effective ML prosecutions impede the AML effectiveness of the jurisdiction. The lack of criminal liability established for legal persons, the sole asset recovery means of criminal confiscation, the requirement for establishing a direct connection between the offence under consideration and the criminal proceedings to order confiscation, and *in rem* characteristics of such verdicts are additional reasons for the relatively limited AML effectiveness of Türkiye. Lastly, the absence of PPPs (e.g., JMLIT) that enable the active participation of the private sector in the fight against ML, the monopolised supervisory responsibility of MASAK, and the associated difficulties constitute additional underlying weaknesses of the Turkish AML regime compared to its British counterpart. Therefore, addressing these issues and reforming the law as far as possible would enhance the AML competency of Türkiye. Although particular amendments would not be feasible or in harmony with the legal traditions of Türkiye (e.g., the introduction of criminal liability for legal entities), practicable steps, such as establishing PPPs, would indubitably ensure an enhanced Turkish AML effectiveness. This chapter has inquired into the real-life impacts of structural differences of the two AML regimes on the overall AML outcomes. The following chapter provides critical inquiries into the core point of interest of the book, which is how these divergence points affect the AML effectiveness of Türkiye and the UK concerning tackling the most prevalent predicate crimes for both jurisdictions, tax crimes and drug-related offences.

Reference List

Alldridge P, *Money Laundering Law Forfeiture, Confiscation, Civil Recovery, Criminal Laundering, and Taxation of the Proceeds of Crime* (1st edn, Oregon Hart Publishing 2003)

Bank of England, 'Payment and Settlement Statistics' <www.bankofengland.co.uk/payment-and-settlement/payment-and-settlement-statistics> accessed 19 May 2023

TheBanks.eu, 'Compare Countries by Banking Sector' <https://thebanks.eu/compare-countries-by-banking-sector#ref_4> accessed 19 May 2023

Burrell P, Mitchell R and Savell D, 'A Troubling Bank Balance – Competing Duties for Banks When Making Suspicious Activity Reports' (2012) 129(6) Banking Law Journal 542

Chaikin D, 'How Effective are Suspicious Transaction Reporting Systems?' (2009) 12(3) Journal of Money Laundering Control 238

Charles O and Turksen U, 'Deferred Prosecution Agreements: A Soft Touch?' in D Jasinski, A Phillips and E Johnston (eds), *Organised Crime, Financial Crime, and Criminal Justice: Theoretical Concepts and Challenges* (Routledge 2023)

Companies House, 'What an Obliged Entity Is?' <www.gov.uk/guidance/report-a-discrepancy-about-a-beneficial-owner-on-the-psc-register-by-an-obliged-entity> accessed 22 June 2023

Cotoc CN and others, 'Efficiency of Money Laundering Countermeasures: Case Studies from European Union Member States' (2021) 9(6) Risks 120

Cox D, *Handbook of Anti-Money Laundering* (John Wiley & Sons Incorporated 2014)

Dabor IL, 'Crying Wolf: An Examination of the UK's Suspicious Activity Report Regime' (2019) 40(4) Company Lawyer 107

dalla Pellegrina L and others, 'Organized Crime, Suspicious Transaction Reporting and Anti-Money Laundering Regulation' (2020) 54(12) Regional Studies 1761

de Koker L, 'The FATF's Customer Identification Framework: Fit for Purpose?' (2014) 17(3) Journal of Money Laundering Control 281

Editorial, 'Kargoyla Uyuşturucu Taşıyan Sanıkların 22,5 Yıla Kadar Hapsi İstendi' *TRTHaber* (Türkiye, 14 January 2021) <www.trthaber.com/haber/turkiye/

kargoyla-uyusturucu-tasiyan-saniklarin-225-yila-kadar-hapsi-istendi-547276.html> accessed 19 October 2023
European Banking Federation, 'Turkey's Banking Sector: Facts & Figures' <www.ebf.eu/turkey/> accessed 19 May 2023
Europol, 'From Suspicion to Action – Converting Financial Intelligence into Greater Operational Impact' (September 2017) <www.europol.europa.eu/publications-documents/suspicion-to-action-converting-financial-intelligence-greater-operational-impact> accessed 5 November 2023
FATF, 'FATF Guidance: Anti-Money Laundering and Terrorist Financing Measures and Financial Inclusion – with a Supplement on Customer Due Diligence' (November 2017) <www.fatf-gafi.org/media/fatf/content/images/Updated-2017-FATF-2013-Guidance.pdf> accessed 19 October 2023
——— 'Anti-Money Laundering and Counter-Terrorist Financing Measures: United Kingdom – Mutual Evaluation Report' (December 2018) <www.fatf-gafi.org/media/fatf/documents/reports/mer4/MER-United-Kingdom-2018.pdf> accessed 18 January 2022
——— 'Anti-Money Laundering and Counter-Terrorist Financing Measures – Turkey: Mutual Evaluation Report' (December 2019) <www.fatf-gafi.org/media/fatf/documents/reports/mer4/Mutual-Evaluation-Report-Turkey-2019.pdf> accessed 18 January 2023
——— 'Jurisdictions Under Increased Monitoring' (October 2021) <www.fatf-gafi.org/publications/high-risk-and-other-monitored-jurisdictions/documents/increased-monitoring-october-2021.html#turkey> accessed 24 May 2023
——— 'International Standards on Combatting Money Laundering and the Financing of Terrorism & Proliferation: The FATF Recommendations' (Updated March 2022) <www.fatf-gafi.org/media/fatf/documents/recommendations/pdfs/FATF%20Recommendations%202012.pdf> accessed 26 June 2023
——— 'Report on the State of Effectiveness and Compliance with the FATF Standards' (April 2022) <www.fatf-gafi.org/media/fatf/documents/recommendations/Report-on-the-State-of-Effectiveness-Compliance-with-FATF-Standards.pdf> accessed 17 August 2023
Financial Conduct Authority, 'NatWest Plc Pleads Guilty in Criminal Proceedings' (3 November 2021) <www.fca.org.uk/news/press-releases/natwest-plc-pleads-guilty-criminal-proceedings> accessed 19 November 2023
Gelir İdaresi Başkanlığı, 'Varlık Barışı' <www.gib.gov.tr/node/146992> accessed 20 October 2023
Gold M and Levi M, *Money Laundering in the UK: An Appraisal of Suspicion-Based Reporting* (Police Foundation & University of Wales 1994)
Greenberg TS and others, *Politically Exposed Persons: A Guide on Preventive Measures for the Banking Sector* (World Bank Publications 2010)
Hardouin P, 'Too Big to Fail, too Big to Jail: Restoring Liability a Lesson from HSBC Case' (2017) 24(4) Journal of Financial Crime 513
Harvey J, 'An Evaluation of Money Laundering Policies' (2005) 8(4) Journal of Money Laundering Control 339
——— 'Just How Effective Is Money Laundering Legislation?' (2008) 21(3) Security Journal 189
He P, 'The Suspicious Transactions Reporting System' (2005) 8(3) Journal of Money Laundering Control 252
HM Treasury and Home Office, 'National Risk Assessment of Money Laundering and Terrorist Financing 2020' (December 2020) <https://assets.publishing.service.gov.uk/government/uploads/system/uploads/attachment_data/file/945411/NRA_2020_v1.2_FOR_PUBLICATION.pdf> accessed 26 June 2023
Home Office, 'Asset Recovery Statistical Bulletin 2014/15–2019/20' (September 2020) <https://assets.publishing.service.gov.uk/government/uploads/system/uploads/

attachment_data/file/923194/asset-recovery-financial-years-2015-to-2020-hosb2320.pdf> accessed 31 October 2023

——— 'Asset Recovery Statistical Bulletin: Financial Years Ending 2016 to 2021' (September 2021) <www.gov.uk/government/statistics/asset-recovery-statistical-bulletin-financial-years-ending-2016-to-2021/asset-recovery-statistical-bulletin-financial-years-ending-2016-to-2021> accessed 19 August 2023

Internal Revenue Service: Criminal Investigation, 'Annual Report 2021' (2021) <www.irs.gov/pub/irs-pdf/p3583.pdf> accessed 3 June 2023

Jensen NJ, 'Technology and Intelligence' (2005) 8(3) Journal of Money Laundering Control 227

Kennedy DM, *Deterrence and Crime Prevention: Reconsidering the Prospect of Sanction* (Routledge 2009)

Kochan N, 'Banks Engage in Anti-Money-Laundering Fight' *The Banker* (1 April 2016) <www.thebanker.com/Banking-Regulation-Risk/Management-Strategy/Banks-engage-in-anti-money-laundering-fight?ct=true> accessed 1 November 2023

Le Nguyen C, 'Preventing the Use of Financial Institutions for Money Laundering and the Implications for Financial Privacy' (2018) 21(1) Journal of Money Laundering Control 47

Levi M, Nelen H and Lankhorst F, 'Lawyers as Crime Facilitators in Europe: An Introduction and Overview' (2005) 42(2–3) Crime, Law, and Social Change 117

Levi M, Reuter P and Halliday T, 'Can the AML System Be Evaluated without Better Data?' (2017) 69(2) Crime, Law, and Social Change 307

LexisNexis Risk Solutions, 'Cutting the Costs of AML Compliance' (June 2021) <www.oxfordeconomics.com/recent-releases/Cutting-the-costs-of-AML-compliance> accessed 23 October 2023

Loh X, 'Suspicious Activity Reports (SARs) Regime: Reforming Institutional Culture' (2021) 24(3) Journal of Money Laundering Control 514

MASAK, 'Faaliyet Raporu 2020' (2021) <https://ms.hmb.gov.tr/uploads/sites/12/2021/09/Faaliyet-Raporu-2020.pdf> accessed 18 January 2023

——— 'Serbest Muhasebeci Mali Müşavirler ve Yeminli Mali Müşavirler Sektör Araştırma Raporu' (February 2021) <https://ms.hmb.gov.tr/uploads/sites/12/2021/03/SMMM-YMM-SEKTOR-ARASTIRMA-RAPORU.pdf> accessed 21 October 2023

——— 'Faaliyet Raporu 2021' (2022) <https://ms.hmb.gov.tr/uploads/sites/12/2022/03/Faaliyet-Raporu-2021.pdf> accessed 18 April 2023

Maxwell NJ, 'Five Years of Growth in Public-Private Financial Information-Sharing Partnerships to Tackle Crime' (Future of Financial Intelligence Sharing (FFIS) Research Programme, August 2020) <www.future-fis.com/uploads/3/7/9/4/3794525/five_years_of_growth_of_public-private_partnerships_to_fight_financial_crime_-_18_aug_2020.pdf> accessed 5 November 2023

Ministry of Justice, 'Criminal Justice System Statistics: Outcomes by Offence 2010 to 2020' (May 2021) <https://assets.publishing.service.gov.uk/government/uploads/system/uploads/attachment_data/file/987715/outcomes-by-offence-2020.xlsx> accessed 2 November 2023

Ministry of Justice General Directorate of Judicial Record and Statistics, 'Judicial Statistics 2016' (November 2017) <https://adlisicil.adalet.gov.tr/Resimler/SayfaDokuman/2082019114041Adalet_ist_2016.pdf> accessed 28 October 2023

——— 'Judicial Statistics 2017' (August 2018) <https://adlisicil.adalet.gov.tr/Resimler/SayfaDokuman/2082019114010Adalet_ist_2017.pdf> accessed 28 October 2023

——— 'Judicial Statistics 2018' (August 2019) <https://adlisicil.adalet.gov.tr/Resimler/SayfaDokuman/1792019103654adalet_ist_2018.pdf> accessed 28 October 2023

——— 'Judicial Statistics 2019' (August 2020) <https://adlisicil.adalet.gov.tr/Resimler/SayfaDokuman/1092020162733adalet_ist-2019.pdf> accessed 1 February 2023

——— 'Judicial Statistics 2020' (September 2021) <https://adlisicil.adalet.gov.tr/Resimler/SayfaDokuman/1692021162011adalet_ist-2020.pdf> accessed 1 February 2023
NCA, 'Suspicious Activity Reports (SARs) – Annual Report 2017' (2017) <www.nationalcrimeagency.gov.uk/who-we-are/publications/112-suspicious-activity-reports-annual-report-2017/file> accessed 12 October 2023
——— 'Suspicious Activity Reports (SARs) Annual Report 2018' (2018) <www.nationalcrimeagency.gov.uk/who-we-are/publications/256-2018-sars-annual-report/file> accessed 21 April 2023
——— 'UK Financial Intelligence Unit Suspicious Activity Reports Annual Report 2019' (2019) <www.nationalcrimeagency.gov.uk/who-we-are/publications/390-sars-annual-report-2019/file> accessed 21 April 2023
——— 'UK Financial Intelligence Unit Suspicious Activity Reports Annual Report 2020' (April 2020) <www.nationalcrimeagency.gov.uk/who-we-are/publications/480-sars-annual-report-2020/file> accessed 24 February 2023
——— 'Joint Money Laundering Intelligence Taskforce' <www.nationalcrimeagency.gov.uk/what-we-do/national-economic-crime-centre> accessed 1 November 2023
OECD, 'Illicit Financial Flows from Developing Countries: Measuring OECD Responses' (2014) <www.oecd.org/corruption/Illicit_Financial_Flows_from_Developing_Countries.pdf> accessed 30 November 2023
——— 'Turkey's Foreign Bribery Enforcement Framework Needs to Be Urgently Strengthened and Corporate Liability Legislation Reformed' <www.oecd.org/corruption/turkey-s-foreign-bribery-enforcement-framework-needs-to-be-urgently-strengthened-and-corporate-liability-legislation-reformed.htm> accessed 8 November 2023
O'Neill D, 'Privacy Fears Slow Spread of UK-Style Data-Sharing to Combat Money Laundering' *Euromoney* (29 August 2019) <www.euromoney.com/article/b1gxtdng8xn576/privacy-fears-slow-spread-of-uk-style-data-sharing-to-combat-money-laundering> accessed 1 November 2023
Oxford Economics, 'The Accountancy Profession in the UK and Ireland' (November 2018) <www.ccab.org.uk/wp-content/uploads/2020/06/The-Accountancy-Profession-in-the-UK-and-Ireland.pdf> accessed 20 October 2023
Pol RF, 'Anti-Money Laundering: The World's Least Effective Policy Experiment? Together, We Can Fix It' (2020) 3(1) Policy Design and Practice 73
Pontes R and others, 'Anti-Money Laundering in the United Kingdom: New Directions for a More Effective Regime' (2022) 25(2) Journal of Money Laundering Control 401
Preller SF, 'Comparing AML Legislation of the UK, Switzerland and Germany' (2008) 11(3) Journal of Money Laundering Control 234
Remeur C, 'Understanding Money Laundering Through Real Estate Transactions' (European Parliamentary Research Service, February 2019) <www.europarl.europa.eu/cmsdata/161094/7%20-%2001%20EPRS_Understanding%20money%20laundering%20through%20real%20estate%20transactions.pdf> accessed 26 October 2023
Ryder N, '"Too Scared to Prosecute and Too Scared to Jail?" A Critical and Comparative Analysis of Enforcement of Financial Crime Legislation Against Corporations in the USA and the UK' (2018) 82(3) Journal of Criminal Law (Hertford) 245
——— 'Cryptoassets, Social Media Platforms and Defence Against Terrorism Financing Suspicious Activity Reports: A Step into the Regulatory Unknown' (2020) 8 Journal of Business Law 668
Sen E, 'Kara Para Aklama Suçunda Soruşturma Ne Zaman Başlar?' *Ersan Sen Hukuk ve Danışmanlık* (9 May 2022) <https://sen.av.tr/tr/makale/kara-para-aklama-sucunda-sorusturma-ne-zaman-baslar> accessed 31 July 2023
Serious Fraud Office, 'SFO Secures Two DPAs with Companies for Bribery Act Offences' (20 July 2021) <www.sfo.gov.uk/2021/07/20/sfo-secures-two-dpas-with-companies-for-bribery-act-offences/> accessed 19 November 2023

——— 'Deferred Prosecution Agreements' <www.sfo.gov.uk/publications/guidance-policy-and-protocols/guidance-for-corporates/deferred-prosecution-agreements/> accessed 19 November 2023
Shust PM and Dostov V, 'Implementing Innovative Customer Due Diligence: Proposal for Universal Model' (2020) 23(4) Journal of Money Laundering Control 871
Sikka P and Willmott H, 'The Power of "Independence": Defending and Extending the Jurisdiction of Accounting in the United Kingdom' (1995) 20(6) Accounting, Organizations and Society 547
Sinha G, 'To Suspect or Not to Suspect: Analysing the Pressure on Banks to Be "Policemen"' (2014) 15(1) Journal of Banking Regulation 75
Turksen U, 'Implications of Anti-Money Laundering Law for Accountancy in the European Union – A Comparative Study' in N Ryder, U Turksen and S Hassler (eds), *Fighting Financial Crime in the Global Economic Crisis* (1st edn, Routledge 2014)
——— Misirlioglu IU and Yukselturk O, 'Anti-Money Laundering Law of Turkey and the EU: An Example of Convergence?' (2011) 14(3) Journal of Money Laundering Control 279
Türkiye Bankalar Birliği, 'Faaliyet Raporu 2020–2021' (Mayıs 2021) <www.tbb.org.tr/Content/Upload/Dokuman/7773/Faaliyet_Raporu_2020-2021.pdf> accessed 13 October 2023
Türkiye Cumhuriyeti Merkez Bankası, 'Markets Data' <www.tcmb.gov.tr/wps/wcm/connect/EN/TCMB+EN/Main+Menu/Statistics/Markets+Data/> accessed 19 May 2023
TÜRMOB, 'Üye İstatistikleri' <www.turmob.org.tr/istatistikler/c8172e63-2bef-4919-a863-86e403bfdf0a/meslek-mensubu-dagilim-tablosu-(sm-smmm)> accessed 20 October 2023
——— 'Karaparanın Aklanmasının Önlenmesi/Örnek Olay-1' <www.turmob.org.tr/haberler/32366455-c7d8-4402-a213-d3df03f7f60c/karaparanin-aklanmasinin-onlenmesi-ornek-olay-1> accessed 21 October 2023
——— 'TÜRMOB Hakkında' <https://turmob.org.tr/Kurumsal/TURMOB-Hakkinda> accessed 21 October 2023
UK Finance, 'UK Payment Markets Summary 2021' (June 2021) <www.ukfinance.org.uk/sites/default/files/uploads/SUMMARY-UK-Payment-Markets-2021-FINAL.pdf> accessed 19 May 2023
——— 'Our Members' <www.ukfinance.org.uk/membership/find-a-member> accessed 13 October 2023
Unger B and Hertog J, 'Water Always Finds Its Way: Identifying New Forms of Money Laundering' (2012) 57(3) Crime, Law and Social Change 287
Union of Turkish Bar Associations <www.barobirlik.org.tr> accessed 7 December 2023
Wass S, 'Banks' Suspicious Activity Report Ramp-Up Is Inefficient, Warn Industry Figures' *S&P Global Market Intelligence* (27 February 2020) <www.spglobal.com/marketintelligence/en/news-insights/latest-news-headlines/banks-suspicious-activity-report-ramp-up-is-inefficient-warn-industry-figures-57265800> accessed 27 October 2023
Xe Currency Converter <www.xe.com/currencyconverter/> accessed 31 October 2023
Yukselturk O, Misirlioglu I and Turksen U, 'Check the Weather Before You Hang the Laundry! Accounting Turkish Progress in Anti-Money Laundering Mechanisms' (Society of Legal Scholars Annual Conference, Southampton, September 2010) <https://eprints.kingston.ac.uk/id/eprint/35430/> accessed 21 October 2023
Zavoli I and King C, 'The Challenges of Implementing Anti-Money Laundering Regulation: An Empirical Analysis' (2021) 84(4) Modern Law Review 740

Legal Instruments

Türkiye

Law No 5237 (Turkish Criminal Code) 2004
Law No 5549 on the Prevention of Laundering Proceeds of Crime 2006
Official Gazette No 31351 dated 31 December 2020, 'Kitle İmha Silahlarının Yayılmasının Finansmanının Önlenmesine İlişkin Kanun' <www.resmigazete.gov.tr/eskiler/2020/12/20201231M5-19.htm> accessed 2 June 2023
Regulation on Measures Regarding Prevention of Laundering Proceeds of Crime and Financing of Terrorism (ROM) 2008

United Kingdom

The Money Laundering, Terrorist Financing and Transfer of Funds (Information on the Payer) Regulations 2017, SI 2017/692
Proceeds of Crime Act 2002

Cases (Türkiye)

İstanbul Bölge Adliye Mahkemesi 13. Hukuk Dairesi, Alacak Davası (Esas No 2019/89 Esas), Decision No 2020/939 dated 24 September 2020 <http://emsal.uyap.gov.tr/BilgiBankasiIstemciWeb/GelismisDokumanAraServlet?dokumanTurleriString=UYAP,&aranan=Müşteri%20Tanı%20kara%20para&aramaG=sdsorRxP&baslangic=20&son=40&dokumanTuruAdi=UYAP&fromSonucSayfasindan=TRUE&sonucSayfasi=yeniTasarim/adaletAramaSonuc.jsp&sirala=1&mevzuatAdi=null&mevzuatNo=null&mevzuatMadde=null> accessed 15 October 2023
İstanbul 13. Asliye Ticaret Mahkemesi, Tazminat Davası (Bankacılık İşlemlerinden Kaynaklanan) (Esas No 2019/438 Esas), Decision No 2020/497 dated 30 October 2020 <http://emsal.uyap.gov.tr/BilgiBankasiIstemciWeb/GelismisDokumanAraServlet> accessed 13 October 2023
Yargıtay 16. Ceza Dairesi, İçtihat Metni (Esas No 2020/7564 Esas), Decision No 2021/4553 dated 30 June 2021 <https://karararama.yargitay.gov.tr/YargitayBilgiBankasiIstemciWeb/pf/sorgula.xhtml> accessed 10 November 2023

Cases (United Kingdom)

Parvizi v Barclays Bank Plc [2014] EWHC B2 (QB) [2014] 5 WLUK 725 [4] [5]
Regina v Da Silva [2006] EWCA Crim 1654 [2007] 1 WLR 303 [16]
Shah v HSBC Private Bank Ltd [2012] EWHC 1283 [2012] 5 WLUK 503 (QB) [67]

8 Efficacy of AML Structures on Predicate Crimes – Case Studies of Drug Trafficking and Tax Crimes

8.1 Introduction

After examining how the differences between the legal and institutional AML frameworks of Türkiye and the UK impact their overall AML effectiveness, it is essential to inquire into the focal point of the study and to investigate if and how such divergence points affect the fight against and the prevalence of two of the most pressing predicate crimes, namely drug trafficking and tax crimes. Accordingly, this chapter aims to indicate if and to what extent unique characteristics of a national AML structure impact the prevalence of and the AML effectiveness in tackling predicate crimes and put forward tentative solutions that would reinforce the prevailing AML regimes adopted by Türkiye and the UK in this end. In doing so, it aims to address all three areas of inquiry, thereby achieving the main aim of the book presented in Chapter 1.[1] In the confines of this book it would be impossible to scrutinise such effects on all predicate crimes; therefore, it is necessary to focus on predicate crimes that constitute the highest-risk threat both for Türkiye and the UK.

Mutual Evaluation Reports (MERs) conducted by the FATF on Türkiye and the UK,[2] as well as National Risk Assessments (NRAs)[3] and annual FIU

1 For the main research aim and research questions, see Section 1.2.

2 FATF, 'Anti-Money Laundering and Counter-Terrorist Financing Measures – Turkey: Mutual Evaluation Report' (December 2019) <www.fatf-gafi.org/media/fatf/documents/reports/mer4/Mutual-Evaluation-Report-Turkey-2019.pdf> accessed 18 January 2023; FATF, 'Anti-Money Laundering and Counter-Terrorist Financing Measures: United Kingdom – Mutual Evaluation Report' (December 2018) <www.fatf-gafi.org/media/fatf/documents/reports/mer4/MER-United-Kingdom-2018.pdf> accessed 18 January 2022.

3 HM Treasury and Home Office, 'National Risk Assessment of Money Laundering and Terrorist Financing 2020' (December 2020) <https://assets.publishing.service.gov.uk/government/uploads/system/uploads/attachment_data/file/945411/NRA_2020_v1.2_FOR_PUBLICATION.pdf> accessed 26 June 2023.

DOI: 10.4324/9781003466680-8

reports[4] compiled by national authorities from these jurisdictions, signify, amongst others, drug-related offences and tax evasion/fraud as the most prevalent and riskiest predicate crimes. Additionally, as reported by EUROPOL, of those criminal networks active across the EU whose main activity is ML, illicit drug trafficking (49%) and fraud (33%), including tax fraud, constitute the most prevalent predicate offences,[5] suggesting the relevance of the predicament for the two EU-neighbouring jurisdictions. Moreover, given that drug-related offences and tax evasion/fraud can be regarded as the representatives of two distinct crime categories,[6] investigating the role of national AML structures in addressing these crimes would help us understand whether and how they affect the prevalence of each predicate crime differently. Furthermore, whilst drug-related offences are the first recognised predicate crimes globally,[7] tax evasion/fraud is one of the last officially approved underlying predicates of ML, as discussed in Chapter 2 previously. Given that jurisdictions, including Türkiye and the UK, apply the same set of AML frameworks for addressing each predicate crime regardless of its nature, examining the effectiveness of such structures on discrete offences provides an opportunity for observing their appropriateness in controlling divergent illegal activities.

Based on discernible evidence from Türkiye and the UK (e.g., the number of STRs/SARs reported by obliged entities to FIUs, the number of prosecutions/convictions secured, and the asset recovery figures), this chapter examines whether and how the unique characteristics of each AML regime influence the prevalence of and the AML effectiveness in tackling these two particular predicate crimes. It also investigates whether introducing legal and institutional AML amendments has reinforced the AML competency of the two jurisdictions regarding the effectiveness in tackling predicate crimes. By doing so, the chapter identifies principal AML deficiencies in these jurisdictions and recommends solutions for minimising/eliminating specific risks

4 See, for instance, MASAK, 'Faaliyet Raporu 2020' (2021) <https://ms.hmb.gov.tr/uploads/sites/12/2021/09/Faaliyet-Raporu-2020.pdf> accessed 18 January 2023; NCA, 'UK Financial Intelligence Unit Suspicious Activity Reports Annual Report 2020' (April 2020) 12 <www.nationalcrimeagency.gov.uk/who-we-are/publications/480-sars-annual-report-2020/file> accessed 24 February 2023.

5 Europol, 'European Union Serious and Organised Crime Threat Assessment (EU SOCTA 2021) – A Corrupting Influence: The Infiltration and Undermining of Europe's Economy and Society by Organised Crime' (2021) 28 <www.europol.europa.eu/cms/sites/default/files/documents/socta2021_1.pdf> accessed 16 February 2023.

6 Although the extent of financial crime is vague, drug-related offences are regarded as conventional/violent crimes, whereas tax evasion/fraud is considered a financial/white-collar crime in this chapter. For a more detailed discussion on financial crimes see Nicholas Ryder, ***Financial Crimes in the 21st Century: Law and Policy*** (Edward Elgar Publishing 2011).

7 United Nations Convention against Illicit Traffic in Narcotic Drugs and Psychotropic Substances 1988.

accounting for high-level drug-related offences and tax crimes. Following a similar approach adopted in the previous chapter, in light of official statistics and reports, this is done (i) by examining the suitability of the two AML frameworks in controlling these particular predicate crimes and (ii) by critically analysing whether these AML regimes in practice address them effectively. This crime-specific analysis provides insights into how a national AML structure may be effective in addressing particular predicate crimes but ineffective in countering others, thereby indicating the functionality of AML frameworks and the significance of national preferences in this end on predicate offences. In other words, whilst this chapter focuses only on drug-related offences and tax evasion/fraud, it highlights areas that require improvement/amendment to ensure an optimum AML structure concerning tackling all predicate crimes regardless of their nature effectively. The analysis reveals that the heterogeneities between the national AML structures do impact the prevalence of predicate crimes and the AML effectiveness in tackling such offences. The chapter also concludes that the legal AML amendments addressing predicate crimes cannot be functional for enhancing AML effectiveness without being supported by institutional modifications.

8.2 Illicit Drug Trafficking

Illicit drug trafficking was the essential stimulator for the initiation of international AML efforts (e.g., the establishment of the FATF) as the first recognised predicate crime category, and it has been sitting at the heart of the global policy on countering organised crime for decades.[8] For instance, the United Nations dedicated an International Day against Drug Abuse and Illicit Trafficking (i.e., 26 June each year) in 1987, expressing its determination to tackle the problem in international solidarity.[9] The volume of proceeds of crime generated by illegal drug trafficking and the threat to the legitimate economy posed by associated ML render jurisdictions (including Türkiye and the UK) exposed to this phenomenon more vulnerable.[10] As the two components of the Balkan Route, which is one of the most prominent (drug) trafficking routes in the world,[11] drug trafficking poses a high-level threat both for Türkiye and

8 UNODC, 'Organized Crime' <www.unodc.org/unodc/en/organized-crime/intro.html> accessed 8 March 2023.

9 UNGA A/RES/42/112 (7 December 1987).

10 Petrus C van Duyne and Michael Levi, *Drugs and Money: Managing the Drug Trade and Crime Money in Europe* (Routledge 2005).

11 Roger Lewis, 'Drugs, War and Crime in the Post-Soviet Balkans' in Vincenzo Ruggiero, Nigel South and Ian R Taylor (eds), *The New European Criminology: Crime and Social Order in Europe* (Routledge 1998).

the UK.[12] Whilst Türkiye is an essential transit country between the source and the other Balkan Route jurisdictions, the UK is a final destination as one of the four leading markets, along with Germany, France, and Italy, in Western and Central Europe.[13] For example, concerning five years encompassing 2015 and 2019, the UK and Türkiye respectively seized similar quantities of amphetamine-type stimulants of 70,866 kg and 63,448 kg, thereby occupying the fifth and sixth place in the world ranking in this regard, respectively,[14] indicating the prevalence of the drug problem faced by these jurisdictions. Remarkably, Türkiye ensured the most substantial proportion of heroin and morphine seizure (i.e., 62%) across all Europe in 2019, whilst the UK was one of the leading Central and Western European jurisdictions that seized the largest heroin and morphine quantities therein in the same year.[15] Likewise, following the USA (26%), Türkiye was the second jurisdiction that made the most substantial quantities of ecstasy seizure (15%) concerning the amount of ecstasy seized globally in 2019.[16] The European Monitoring Centre for Drugs and Drug Addiction (EMCDDA) reports that Türkiye's annual ecstasy (i.e., MDMA tablets) seizures in 2017, 2018, and 2019 exceeded the total amounts reported in the EU.[17] Furthermore, as reported by the UNODC, Türkiye con-

12 It is necessary to note that the UK is one of the biggest (narcotic) drugs consumers in Europe. See Jenn Selby, 'UK Is the Largest Consumer of Cocaine in Europe, National Crime Agency Says' *Inews* (16 May 2020) <https://inews.co.uk/news/uk-largest-consumer-cocaine-europe-national-crime-agency-428521> accessed 8 March 2023; Dame Carol Black, 'Review of Drugs: Summary (Accessible Version)' (Home Office Independent Report, February 2020) <www.gov.uk/government/publications/review-of-drugs-phase-one-report/review-of-drugs-summary> accessed 8 March 2023; Home Office and others, 'United Kingdom Drug Situation 2019: Focal Point Annual Report' (Updated 31 March 2021) <www.gov.uk/government/publications/united-kingdom-drug-situation-focal-point-annual-report/united-kingdom-drug-situation-focal-point-annual-report-2019> accessed 4 April 2023.

13 UNODC, 'Drug Money: The Illicit Proceeds of Opiates Trafficked on the Balkan Route' (2015) <www.unodc.org/documents/rpanc/Publications/other_publications/Balkan_route_web.pdf> accessed 18 January 2022; EMCDDA, 'EU Drug Market: Methamphetamine' (2022) <www.emcdda.europa.eu/publications/eu-drug-markets/methamphetamine_en> accessed 19 May 2023.

14 UNODC, *World Drug Report 2021 – Statistical Annex: Seizures of Illicit Drugs by Region and High-Ranking Countries* (United Nations Publication, June 2021) <https://dataunodc.un.org/data/drugs/Global%20Seizures> accessed 18 January 2023.

15 UNODC, *World Drug Report 2021 – Drug Market Trends: Cannabis Opioids* (United Nations Publication, June 2021) 90 <www.unodc.org/res/wdr2021/field/WDR21_Booklet_3.pdf> accessed 18 January 2023.

16 UNODC, *World Drug Report 2021 – Drug Market Trends: Cocaine Amphetamine-Type Stimulants* (United Nations Publication, June 2021) 76 <www.unodc.org/res/wdr2021/field/WDR21_Booklet_4.pdf> accessed 18 January 2023.

17 EMCDDA, *European Drug Report 2021: Trends and Developments* (Publications Office of the European Union 2021) 24 <www.emcdda.europa.eu/system/files/publications/13838/TDAT21001ENN.pdf> accessed 18 January 2023.

sistently seizes more heroin than any other European country.[18] Last but not least, it has been well documented that both Türkiye and the UK have suffered from narco-terrorism[19] as the PKK (*Parteya Karkeran Kurdistan* – Kurdistan Workers' Party) and the IRA (Irish Republican Army) exploit(ed) illicit drug trafficking for financing their operations.[20] In accordance with this observable and high-level prevalence of this crime, both Türkiye[21] and the UK[22] identify illicit drug trafficking as one of the most serious predicate crimes that pose a high ML threat. Therefore, such facts render it inevitable to investigate and also illustrate the appropriateness of concentrating on drug-related offences as the underlying predicates of ML in examining the impacts of AML regimes on the prevalence of predicate crimes.

Before investigating the developments and subsequent impacts of AML regimes on illicit drug trafficking as a predicate crime in Türkiye and the UK, it is necessary to briefly outline which activities constitute a 'drugs offence' in these jurisdictions. Türkiye regulates the production, supply, and possession of (illicit) drugs under three principal legal instruments: Law No 2313 on the Control of Narcotic Drugs 1933, Law No 3298 on the Narcotic Drugs 1986, and TCC 2004. In general terms, Law No 2313 on the Control of Narcotic Drugs 1933 sets forth provisions that govern the cultivation, importation, exportation, and sale of narcotic and psychotropic substances.[23] Similarly, Law No 3298 on the Narcotic Drugs 1986 stipulates the legal rules on planting, controlling, collecting, utilising, disposing of, purchasing, and selling, amongst others, opium poppy and coca.[24] Although both legal instruments envisage

18 UNODC, *World Drug Report 2021 – Covid-19 and Drugs: Impact Outlook* (United Nations Publication, June 2021) 41 <www.unodc.org/res/wdr2021/field/WDR21_Booklet_5.pdf> accessed 18 January 2023.

19 Coined by Peruvian President Fernando Belaunde Terry in 1982 (see, John E Thomas, 'Narco-Terrorism: Could the Legislative and Prosecutorial Responses Threaten Our Civil Liberties?' (2009) 66(4) Washington and Lee Law Review 1881, 1886), narco-terrorism fundamentally refers to the link between the narcotics trade and terrorist organisations. For a more detailed discussion see, Emma Björnehed, 'Narco-Terrorism: The Merger of the War on Drugs and the War on Terror' (2004) 6(3–4) Global Crime 305.

20 Burke U Basaranel and Umut Turksen, *Counter-Terrorist Financing Law and Policy: An Analysis of Turkey* (Routledge 2019); Frank Cilluffo, 'The Threat Posed from the Convergence of Organized Crime, Drug Trafficking, and Terrorism' (Testimony of the Deputy Director, Global Organized Crime Program and the Director of Counterterrorism Task Force, Centre for Strategic and International Studies to the US House Committee on the Judiciary Subcommittee on Crime, 13 December 2000) <http://csis-website-prod.s3.amazonaws.com/s3fs-public/legacy_files/files/attachments/ts001213_cilluffo.pdf> accessed 18 January 2023; Colin P Clarke, 'Drugs and Thugs: Funding Terrorism Through Narcotics Trafficking' (2016) 9(3) Journal of Strategic Security 1.

21 FATF (n 2) 32.

22 HM Treasury and Home Office (n 3) 28.

23 Law No 2313 on the Control of Narcotic Drugs 1933, arts 1–20.

24 Law No 3298 on the Narcotic Drugs 1986, arts 1–3.

penalties for offenders who breach the relevant provisions stipulated therein (see, for instance, Article 23 of Law No 2313 1933 and Article 4 of Law No 3298 1986), the core legal text that criminalises illicit drug trafficking is the TCC 2004. Accordingly, unlicensed or illegal (i) manufacture, importation, or exportation of narcotics or psychotropic substances;[25] and (ii) domestically selling, offering for sale, shipping, transporting, storing, purchasing, accepting, possessing narcotics or psychotropic substances, and giving such substances to others constitute illicit drug trafficking under the TCC 2004.[26] Additionally, without obtaining official permission, subjecting precursors and chemicals[27] to the previously mentioned activities (e.g., producing, importing, exporting, etc.) entails similar penalties,[28] as discussed later. Even though Türkiye does not categorise such drugs and stimulants explicitly in determining the severity of the sanctions, in circumstances where the offence concerns heroin, cocaine, morphine, synthetic cannabinoids, and its derivatives, or base morphine, the penalties envisaged are increased by one half.[29] This approach is similar to the UK's classification of narcotics and psychotropic substances into three groups as per their envisioned harms, as discussed later.

What constitutes illicit drug trafficking in the UK requires the examination of POCA 2002. Before addressing such an inquiry, it is necessary to state that the core legal instrument that regulates the production, supply, and possession of drugs in the UK is the Misuse of Drugs Act (MDA) 1971. It refers to the term 'controlled drugs' in framing substances that can be the subject of illicit drug trafficking and classifies them into three groups, namely Class A, Class B, and Class C drugs,[30] with Class A drugs, such as cocaine, being the most harmful drugs.[31] Accordingly, POCA 2002 determines drug trafficking by referring to the MDA 1971, and by the same token by referring to the Customs and Excise Management Act (CEMA) 1979, Criminal Justice (International Co-operation) Act 1990, and the Psychoactive Substances Act

25 Law No 5237 (Turkish Criminal Code) 2004, art 188(1).

26 ibid art 188(3).

27 Precursors and chemicals refer to any substances used in producing narcotics or psychotropic substances, albeit not having a narcotic or psychotropic effect. For a detailed explanation, see International Narcotics Control Board, *Precursors and Chemicals Frequently Used in the Illicit Manufacture of Narcotic Drugs and Psychotropic Substances* (Report of the International Narcotics Control Board for 2020 on the Implementation of Article 12 of the United Nations Convention Against Illicit Traffic in Narcotic Drugs and Psychotropic Substances of 1988, January 2021) <www.incb.org/documents/PRECURSORS/TECHNICAL_REPORTS/2020/AR_with_Annexes/Precursors_with_annex_E_eBook_final_rev.pdf> accessed 28 January 2023.

28 Law No 5237 (Turkish Criminal Code) 2004, art 188(7).

29 ibid art 188(4).

30 Misuse of Drugs Act 1971, s 2.

31 ibid sch 2.

2016.[32] In light of the relevant provisions of these legal instruments, illicit drug trafficking is defined by POCA 2002[33] as: (i) unlawful production or supply of controlled drugs;[34] possession of controlled drugs with intent to supply;[35] permitting certain activities (e.g., producing, supplying, etc.) relating to controlled drugs;[36] assisting in or inducing the commission of such offences outside the UK provided that they are punishable under the pertinent corresponding law;[37] (ii) importation[38] and exportation of such goods,[39] including the associated fraudulent evasion relating to customs and excise;[40] and (iii) manufacturing or supplying of such substances,[41] using a ship for trafficking controlled drugs illicitly.[42] In other words, both Türkiye and the UK provide a comprehensive definition for illicit drug trafficking, which considers various aspects of the phenomenon. However, it is worth reiterating that POCA 2002 regards illicit drug trafficking as a criminal lifestyle offence,[43] the commission of which substantially strengthens the confiscation powers of the jurisdiction automatically (see Chapter 4), which renders the UK more effective than Türkiye regarding criminal asset denial, at least theoretically. That is to say that although both jurisdictions adopt a similar definitional approach to illicit drug trafficking, the extant AML legislation in its entirety enables LEAs in the UK to be more effective than their Turkish counterparts regarding the application of legal tools, such as confiscation. Therefore, adopting a similar approach to the UK, which can increase the effectiveness of law in practice, would help Türkiye reach a more enhanced AML effectiveness. Accordingly, Türkiye recently introduced a national strategy document to increase its effectiveness in countering ML/TF and implementing confiscation in July 2021.[44] However, because there have been no statistics related to the outcome of this strategy, it is impossible to evaluate its success or impact on AML effectiveness.

32 ibid sch 2.
33 ibid.
34 Misuse of Drugs Act 1971, s 4.
35 ibid s 5(3).
36 ibid s 8.
37 ibid s 20.
38 Customs and Excise Management Act 1979, ss 50(2) and 50(3).
39 ibid s 68(2).
40 ibid s 170.
41 Criminal Justice (International Co-operation) Act 1990, s 12.
42 ibid s 19.
43 Proceeds of Crime Act 2002, sch 2.
44 Official Gazette No 31544 dated 17 July 2021, 'Genelge 2021/16: Türkiye'de Suç Gelirlerinin Aklanması ve Terörizmin Finansmanı ile Mücadele ve Müsadere Uygulamalarında Etkinliğin Arttırılması Strateji Belgesi (2021–2025)' <www.resmigazete.gov.tr/eskiler/2021/07/20210717-10.pdf> accessed 10 June 2023.

In response to this high-level threat posed by illegal drugs trade, Türkiye has produced national anti-drug trafficking strategies and action plans since 2006. National Policy and Strategy Document on Counteracting Addictive Substance and Substance Addiction 2006–2012[45] and Action Plan for Implementing National Policy and Strategy Document on Counteracting Addictive Substance and Substance Addiction 2007–2009[46] constitute the first-ever national strategy and action plan of Türkiye in this context. However, as the primary concern of these policies was health-related issues, none of them addressed the ML aspect of the predicament by regarding drug trafficking as a predicate crime in the first place. In order to create a more effective tackling mechanism regarding the drug-related conundrum, based on the Prime Ministerial Circular 2014/19, Türkiye established the High Council of Combatting Drugs (*Uyuşturucu ile Mücadele Yüksek Kurulu*), which encompasses eight ministries, including the Ministry of Justice, Ministry of Interior, and the then Ministry of Customs and Trade, in 2014.[47] Thereby, all AML components of the jurisdiction, excluding MASAK, have come together under the auspices of this council. Later, this exclusion was eliminated by designating the president of MASAK as a member of the Anti-Drug Council, a subunit of the High Council of Combatting Drugs, in April 2016.[48] Consequently, the following policy documents (e.g., Anti-Drug Emergency Action Plan 2015) adopted a more holistic and multidisciplinary approach and aimed at, *inter alia*, preventing illegal drug trafficking, thereby tackling the associated ML problem.[49] Nevertheless, the current national strategy paper (i.e., National Strategy Document and Action Plan on Combatting Drugs 2018–2023) does not make any explicit reference to ML, albeit articulating the prevention of access to the proceeds of drug trafficking by monitoring the financial dimension of drugs as one

45 TC İçişleri Bakanlığı, *Bağımlılık Yapıcı Maddeler ve Bağımlılıkla Mücadelede Ulusal Politika ve Strateji Belgesi 2006–2012* (TC İçişleri Bakanlığı 2006).

46 TC İçişleri Bakanlığı, *Bağımlılık Yapıcı Maddeler ve Bağımlılıkla Mücadelede Ulusal Politika ve Strateji Belgesinin Uygulanması İçin Eylem Planı 2007–2009* (TC İçişleri Bakanlığı 2007).

47 Official Gazette No 29174 dated 13 November 2014, 'Genelge 2014/19: Uyuşturucu ile Mücadele' <www.resmigazete.gov.tr/eskiler/2014/11/20141113-13.htm> accessed 19 January 2023.

48 TC İçişleri Bakanlığı, 'Türkiye Cumhuriyeti Uyuşturucu ile Mücadele Yüksek Kurulu Ulusal Uyuşturucu ile Mücadele Eylem Planı 2016–2018' <www.narkotik.pol.tr/kurumlar/narkotik.pol.tr/Arsiv/TUBIM/Documents/EYLEM%20PLANI_2016-2018_TR.pdf> accessed 19 January 2023.

49 TC İçişleri Bakanlığı, 'Ulusal Uyuşturucu ile Mücadele Strateji Belgesi' (2015) 4 <www.narkotik.pol.tr/kurumlar/narkotik.pol.tr/Arsiv/TUBIM/Documents/1-STRATEJİ%20BELGESİ_EYLEM%20PLANI_İL%20KURULLARI_2015_TR.pdf> accessed 19 January 2023.

of the policy objectives.[50] This policy objective stipulates three particular action plans: (i) providing training by MASAK to LEA personnel and sharing financial information simultaneously in centrally planned operations; (ii) establishing a separate unit within MASAK regarding the identification of the proceeds of drug trafficking crime; and (iii) by exploiting technological developments, carrying out studies for the detection and continuous control of illegal cultivation areas.[51] Accordingly, MASAK has trained at least 275 LEA personnel,[52] and LEAs (the GCG in particular) have incrementally incorporated the use of technology (e.g., Unmanned Aerial Vehicles) for detecting and eradicating illegal drug cultivation areas[53] since the introduction of the national strategy document specified. However, a separate unit within MASAK dedicated to tackling the proceeds of illicit drug trafficking has not been established yet, the creation of which would reinforce the AML effectiveness of the jurisdiction in this context.

In line with the national strategy documents and action plans on combatting drugs, Türkiye has made notable amendments to its pertinent legal and institutional framework over the years to address illicit drug trafficking more effectively, thereby addressing the associated ML problem. In its AML legal framework, Türkiye increased the severity of penalties envisaged for illicit drug trafficking in the same year with the previously mentioned Prime Ministerial Circular 2014/19. More specifically, whilst the original version of the pertinent article (i.e., Article 188(1) of TCC 2004) stipulated an imprisonment term of at least ten years for (international) illicit drug traffickers,[54] it currently sets forth a sentence of 20 to 30 years in prison for such offenders.[55] Additionally, the imprisonment sentences envisaged for this group of offenders whose activities remain domestically have been amended accordingly as entailing a term of not less than ten years, which had been between five and 15 years

50 TC Başbakanlık, 'Ulusal Uyuşturucu ile Mücadele Ulusal Strateji Belgesi ve Eylem Planı 2018–2023' (2018) 66 <https://hsgm.saglik.gov.tr/depo/birimler/tutun-mucadele-bagimlilik-db/haberler/uyusturucu_eylem_plani/2018-2023_Uyusturucu_ile_Mucadele_Ulusal_Strateji_Belgesi_ve_Eylem_Plani.pdf> accessed 19 January 2023.

51 ibid.

52 Turkish National Police Counter Narcotics Department, 'Turkish Drug Report: Trends and Developments' (2021) 52 <www.narkotik.pol.tr/kurumlar/narkotik.pol.tr/TUBİM/2021-TURKISH-DRUG-REPORT.pdf> accessed 24 January 2023.

53 TC İçişleri Bakanlığı Jandarma Genel Komutanlığı, '2020 Yılı Faaliyet Raporu' (January 2021) <www.jandarma.gov.tr/kurumlar/jandarma.gov.tr/Duyurular/subat-2021/JANDARMA-GENEL-KOMUTANLIGI-2020-YILI-FAALIYET-RAPORU.pdf> accessed 9 February 2023.

54 Illicit drug traffickers stand for offenders who, without a license or contrary to an existing license, produce, import, or export narcotics or psychotropic substances as determined by Art 188 of TCC 2004.

55 Law No 5237 (Turkish Criminal Code) 2004, art 188(1).

previously.[56] Moreover, the minimum imprisonment term envisaged for offenders involved in the trafficking of any substances used in the production of narcotics or psychotropic substances, albeit not having a narcotic or psychotropic effect by itself (i.e., precursors), has been doubled from four to eight years.[57] It is necessary to state that each offence category also entails a maximum judicial fine of 20,000 days[58] (i.e., up to TL 2 m,[59] which is approximately GBP 107,750 as of 17 February 2022).[60] However, the maximum sentences envisaged for drug-related offences in the UK include a life sentence and/or an unlimited fine for the supply, production, and importation of Class A drugs (e.g., cocaine),[61] suggesting a more deterrent legal ecosystem for potential illicit drug traffickers.

Before investigating recent institutional AML amendments and their impacts on illicit drug trafficking and the associated ML, it is worth reiterating that Türkiye, in collaboration with the UNODC, established TADOC in 2000 as a response to the predicament.[62] Türkiye also created the Turkish Monitoring Centre for Drugs and Drug Addiction (TUBIM) to be an integral part of the EMCDDA and its information exchange network of REITOX in October 2002.[63] Since its establishment, TADOC has organised 610 international and 1,715 domestic training programmes whereby it provided 11,488 foreign and 56,949 national LEA personnel with, amongst others, countering illicit drug trafficking and ML training.[64] Whilst TADOC has no operational function as an academy, it has established multilateral partnerships with, *inter alia*, UNODC, NCA, FBI, and the US Drug Enforcement Agency, thereby following emerging international issues in this context and maintaining an up

56 Law No 5237 (Turkish Criminal Code) 2004, art 188(3). However, in cases where the person to whom narcotics or psychotropic substances are delivered or sold is a juvenile, the imprisonment sentence to be imposed cannot be less than 15 years.

57 Law No 5237 (Turkish Criminal Code) 2004, art 188(7). These substances consist of the substances whose importation requires permission from the authorities.

58 ibid arts 188(1), 188(3), and 188(7). For an explanation regarding how the judicial fine is calculated, see Chapter 3.

59 ibid art 52.

60 Xe Currency Converter <www.xe.com/currencyconverter/convert/?Amount=2000000&From=TRY&To=GBP> accessed 17 February 2023.

61 Sentencing Council, 'Drug Offences' <www.sentencingcouncil.org.uk/outlines/drug-offences/> accessed 17 February 2023.

62 See Chapter 5.

63 EMCDDA, 'Turkish National Focal Point' <www.emcdda.europa.eu/about/partners/reitox/turkey_en> accessed 17 February 2022; EGM Narkotik Suçlarla Mücadele Daire Başkanlığı, 'Hakkımızda' <www.narkotik.pol.tr/narkotik-suclarla-mucadele-daire-baskanligi-hakkinda> accessed 17 February 2023.

64 KOM Anti-Smuggling and Organized Crime Department, 'Turkish International Academy Against Drugs and Organized Crime Bulletin 2019–2020' (2020) 2, 7, 17 <www.egm.gov.tr/kurumlar/egm.gov.tr/IcSite/tadoc/2019_20_BulletinENGLISH.pdf> accessed 17 February 2023.

to date training programme for LEAs.[65] That is to say that Türkiye's national counter-narcotics and associated AML efforts precede the introduction of pertinent strategy documents and action plans.[66] However, if we accept such documents and action plans as a milestone, the establishment of the Bureau of Combatting Proceeds of Crime (*Suç Gelirleri ile Mücadele Büro Amirliği*) within the GDS Counter Narcotics Department[67] and the creation of Counter Narcotics Training Academy (*Narkotik Suçlarla Mücadele Eğitim Akademisi/ NEA*) in 2018,[68] as well as the institution of Narcotics Crime Department (*Narkotik Suçlarla Mücadele Dairesi*) and NARKOKIMs (*Narkotik Kısım Amirlikleri*) within the CE in the same year,[69] constitute the essential institutional amendments addressing this particular predicate crime. It is necessary to note that the aforementioned Bureaus of Combatting Proceeds of Crime are not the bureaus that serve under the auspices of the GDS's Department of Public Order (*Asayiş Daire Başkanlığı*) discussed in Chapter 5 previously, albeit being called by the same name. These are new units created within the GDS Counter Narcotics Department recently. It is worth underlining that all these institutional amendments followed the introduction of the National Strategy Document and Action Plan on Combatting Drugs 2018–2023, suggesting that Türkiye is sincere in its efforts to tackle illicit drug trafficking and the associated ML problem as a priority. Although Türkiye envisaged creating a dedicated unit within MASAK to deal with the identification of the proceeds of drug trafficking crime by 2018, it has not been formed yet (as of September 2022).[70] After this brief outline on the legal and institutional AML amendments addressing illicit drug trafficking, it is necessary to examine its affects, if any, on the prevalence of this predicate crime. As a starting point, Table 8.1 illustrates the number of illicit drug trafficking incidents identified by LEAs in Türkiye and the UK, as well as the offenders involved in those crimes.

65 ibid 10.

66 For a more detailed discussion on the evolution of the national drug policy in Türkiye, see Philip Robins, 'Public Policy Making in Turkey: Faltering Attempts to Generate a National Drugs Policy' (2009) 37(2) Policy and Politics 289.

67 Turkish National Police Counter Narcotics Department (n 52) 52.

68 EGM Narkotik Suçlarla Mücadele Daire Başkanlığı, 'Narkotik Suçlarla Mücadele Eğitim Akademisi: Our Organization' <www.narkotik.pol.tr/nea/kurulusumuz> accessed 23 January 2023.

69 TC Ticaret Bakanlığı, '2018 Faaliyet Raporu' (2019) 3 <https://muhafaza.ticaret.gov.tr/data/5d31b1ee13b876092c062161/2018%20FALİYET%20RAPORU.pdf> accessed 20 January 2023.

70 TC Başbakanlık (n 50).

Table 8.1 The number of illicit drug trafficking incidents identified by LEAs and offenders involved in those crimes.

Years	*Türkiye*		*United Kingdom*[71]	
	Incidents	*Suspects*	*Incidents*	*Suspects*
2011[72]	8,895	21,597	31,316	NA
2012[73]	11,397	27,125	29,746	NA
2013[74]	13,840	31,183	29,348	NA
2014[75]	14,072	30,841	27,368	NA
2015[76]	15,438	31,673	26,072	NA
2016[77]	15,831	28,333	25,953	NA
2017[78]	23,424	45,056	27,121	NA
2018[79]	29,842	52,125	30,453	NA
2019[80]	29,668	60,380	34,504	NA
2020[81]	30,341	59,186	42,461	NA
Total	**192,748**	**387,499**	**304,342**	**NA**

71 Office for National Statistics, 'Crime in England and Wales: Appendix Tables – Table A4' (November 2021) <www.ons.gov.uk/file?uri=%2fpeoplepopulationandcommunity%2fcrimeandjustice%2fdatasets%2fcrimeinenglandandwalesappendixtables%2fyearendingjune2021/appendixtablejun21final.xlsx> accessed 24 January 2023.

72 EGM KOM Daire Başkanlığı, 'EMCDDA Türkiye Ulusal Raporu: Yeni Gelişmeler, Trendler, Seçilmiş Konular' (2013) 126–27 <www.narkotik.pol.tr/kurumlar/narkotik.pol.tr/Arsiv/TUBIM/Documents/TURKIYE%20UYUSTURUCU%20RAPORU%202013.pdf> accessed 24 January 2023.

73 ibid.

74 EGM KOM Daire Başkanlığı, 'EMCDDA Türkiye Ulusal Raporu: Yeni Gelişmeler, Trendler, Seçilmiş Konular' (2014) 101–2 <www.narkotik.pol.tr/kurumlar/narkotik.pol.tr/Arsiv/TUBIM/Documents/TURKIYE%20UYUSTURUCU%20RAPORU%202014.pdf> accessed 24 January 2023.

75 Turkish National Police Counter Narcotics Department, '2015 Turkish National Drug Report' (2017) 8 <www.narkotik.pol.tr/kurumlar/narkotik.pol.tr/Arsiv/TUBIM/Documents/2015%20TURKISH%20NATIONAL%20DRUG%20REPORT.pdf> accessed 24 January 2023.

76 Turkish National Police Counter Narcotics Department, '2016 Turkish National Drug Report' (2017) 7 <www.narkotik.pol.tr/kurumlar/narkotik.pol.tr/Arsiv/TUBIM/Documents/2016%20TURKISH%20NATIONAL%20DRUG%20REPORT.pdf> accessed 24 January 2023.

77 Turkish National Police Counter Narcotics Department, '2017 Turkish National Drug Report' (2017) 7 <www.narkotik.pol.tr/kurumlar/narkotik.pol.tr/Arsiv/TUBIM/Documents/2017%20TURKISH%20NATIONAL%20DRUG%20REPORT.pdf> accessed 24 January 2023.

78 Turkish National Police Counter Narcotics Department, '2018 Turkish National Drug Report' (2018) 11 <www.narkotik.pol.tr/kurumlar/narkotik.pol.tr/TUBİM/Ulusal%20Yayınlar/2018-Turkish-Drug-Report.pdf> accessed 24 January 2023.

79 Turkish National Police Counter Narcotics Department, 'Turkish Drug Report 2019' (2019) 30<www.narkotik.pol.tr/kurumlar/narkotik.pol.tr/TUBİM/Ulusal%20Yayınlar/2019-TURKISH-DRUG-REPORT_30122019.pdf> accessed 24 January 2023.

80 Turkish National Police Counter Narcotics Department, 'Turkish Drug Report: Trends and Developments' (2020) 36 <www.narkotik.pol.tr/kurumlar/narkotik.pol.tr/TUBİM/Uluslar-Arasi-Yayinlar/2020uyusturucuraporuENG.pdf> accessed 24 January 2023.

81 Turkish National Police Counter Narcotics Department (n 52) 30.

The preceding table demonstrates that, regarding illicit drug trafficking as identified by the national LEAs of Türkiye and the UK, the number of incidents identified in the UK has been consistently higher than in Türkiye in any given year, with relatively closer sums in the second half of the last decade. Whilst the relevant offences have invariably increased over time in Türkiye, such an increase is more evident between 2018 and 2020, when Turkish LEAs identified approximately 30,000 drug trafficking cases each year. This remarkable difference can be attributable to the institutional AML amendments, such as NARKOKIMS, introduced in 2018. Additionally, it is worth emphasising that the first significant rise in the number of incidents happened in 2017 (i.e., approximately 48% compared to the previous year), following the inclusion of the president of MASAK as a member of the Anti-Drug Council. However, such observable impact is not evident regarding the amendments to AML laws associated with the predicate crime of illicit drug trafficking, as the considerable increase in imprisonment sentence terms in this context in 2014 seems to have no such effects. Therefore, it can be argued that the institutional AML amendments concerning predicate crimes have been more functional than the legal AML amendments in Türkiye in reinforcing the national AML effectiveness. In other words, procedural amendments that have impacted how the law operates in practice seem to be more effective than the sole revision of the law in the books. Given the practical contribution of such institutional modifications to the AML law in action, such as the increased training capabilities of LEAs in educating expert personnel (e.g., the establishment of the NEA) and the enlargement of the identification network of such crimes (e.g., the inclusion of NARKOKIMs), this consequence is not surprising. That is to say that the AML legal amendments addressing predicate crimes cannot be functional for enhancing AML effectiveness without being supported by institutional modifications. Therefore, Türkiye would benefit from more profound legal AML amendments, similar to the UK's UWOs and lifestyle provisions,[82] as the introduction of heavier penalties does not seem to have generated noticeable AML outcomes by itself. Nevertheless, under the prevailing legal regime, Turkish LEAs cannot confiscate any assets of an illicit drug trafficker unless it is proven that the assets under consideration have been acquired through the criminal proceeds obtained from this particular crime, as discussed previously.

Having said that, it is necessary to mention that the data given in Table 8.1 cannot be regarded as the direct indicator of the AML effectiveness of Türkiye

82 NCA, 'NCA Secures First Serious Organised Crime Unexplained Wealth Order for Property Worth £10 Million' (*Press Release*, 25 March 2022) <www.nationalcrimeagency.gov.uk/news/nca-secures-first-serious-organised-crime-unexplained-wealth-order-for-property-worth-10-million> accessed 4 April 2023; Ali Shalchi, 'Unexplained Wealth Orders' (UK Parliament Research Briefing Paper No 9098, February 2022) <https://researchbriefings.files.parliament.uk/documents/CBP-9098/CBP-9098.pdf> accessed 4 April 2023.

as drug-related offences do not trigger an ML investigation automatically therein. For instance, as documented by the FATF, based on the Turkish NRA data, LEAs in Türkiye conducted 234,390 illicit drug trafficking investigations between 2013 and 2018. However, approximately only 1 in every 2,000 this particular predicate offence investigations resulted in an ML investigation[83] (see Table 8.2). Although such data are not available for the UK, the relevant statistics from Türkiye indicate that the high level of LEA intervention in drug trafficking activities does not necessarily mean an enhanced AML effectiveness. Accordingly, this dimension of the phenomenon as to whether intervening in more illicit drug trafficking incidents signifies an increased AML effectiveness requires a closer examination of associated confiscation figures secured in Türkiye. However, not coincidentally, such information that establishes a direct link between illicit drug trafficking and the associated ML has been available since 2019 (see, for instance, Turkish Drug Report 2020), following the introduction of the relevant national policy paper and additional institutional AML components in 2018.[84] That is not to say that the Turkish LEAs had not been securing the confiscation of criminal proceeds acquired through illicit drug trafficking and the prosecution of the associated money launderers prior to 2019, but such integrated data have only become available since then. Therefore, it is necessary to inquire into the last two national drug reports, which integrate all relevant operational data provided by all Turkish LEAs into a single document, to form an opinion of the Turkish AML effectiveness regarding the predicate crime of illicit drug trafficking.

Table 8.2 The number of illicit drug trafficking and the associated money laundering investigations.

Years	*Türkiye*[85]		*United Kingdom*	
	Drug trafficking investigations	*Associated ML files*	*Drug trafficking investigations*	*Associated ML files*
2013	31,308	25	NA	NA
2014	34,431	21	NA	NA
2015	37,090	19	NA	NA
2016	33,203	26	NA	NA
2017	45,614	18	NA	NA
2018	52,744	19	NA	NA
Total	**234,390**	**128**	**NA**	**NA**

83 FATF (n 2) 56.
84 TC Başbakanlık (n 50).
85 FATF (n 2) 56.

The investigations regarding laundering proceeds of illicit drug trafficking made by the GDS narcotics units ensured the denial of around 111.5 million TL (as of 31 December 2020) in cash in foreign currencies and gold, which equalled approximately GBP 10 million then, and 282 vehicles in 2020.[86] Such investigations undertaken by the GDS secured the confiscation of around GBP 1.46 million (as of 31 December 2019)[87] in cash in several currencies and gold and 407 vehicles in 2019.[88] The GCG KOM led 14 investigations (12 in 2019) within the scope of tackling proceeds of crime generated by illicit drug trafficking and ensured the prosecution of 34 suspects (20 suspects in 2019) and the confiscation of 1,147,665 TL (40,879 TL and EUR 3,504 in 2019), which equalled approximately GBP 115,000, in 2020.[89] The CE-led investigations undertaken in this context yielded the confiscation of 72 trucks, 15 cars/minibuses, and three buses (39 TIRs, 29 automobiles, and nine buses in 2019) in the same year.[90] However, the CGC could only involve in nine operations addressing illicit drug trafficking, eight of which were joint operations with the previously mentioned LEAs, whereby it seized, amongst others, approximately 1.5 kg cannabis and 29 kg cocaine.[91] Considering the geographical composition of Türkiye as a peninsula with a coastline of 8,484 km,[92] the contribution of the CGC to the fight against the phenomenon needs to be increased. The CGC is aware of its weaknesses in combatting smuggling and organised crimes,[93] corroborating the recommendations made in Chapter 5 relating to reinforcing its capacity in this context and establishing specialised AML units.

In addition to these domestic/national operations, JITs established with international counterparts, including the UK, generated 'the largest anti-narcotics and money laundering operation in Türkiye's history'[94] (i.e., Operation Swamp) in 2020. Within the scope of Operation Swamp, which aimed specifically at tackling the proceeds of illicit drug trafficking, 81 suspects were detained, and approximately 18 tons of cocaine, 30 tons of cannabis, 5 tons of base morphine, and 0.2 tons of heroin were seized worldwide

86 Turkish National Police Counter Narcotics Department (n 52) 53.

87 All conversions were made via Xe currency converter according to the currency rates provided for the relevant dates. See Xe Currency Converter, 'Historical Rate Tables' <www.xe.com/currencytables/?from=TRY&date=2019-12-31#table-section> accessed 20 January 2023.

88 Turkish National Police Counter Narcotics Department (n 80) 36.

89 Turkish National Police Counter Narcotics Department (n 52) 53.

90 ibid.

91 Sahil Güvenlik Komutanlığı, '2020 Yılı İdare Faaliyet Raporu' (2021) 41, 58 <www.sg.gov.tr/kurumlar/sg.gov.tr/komutanlik/yayinlar/2020-Yili-Idare-Faaliyet-Raporu.pdf> accessed 20 January 2023.

92 ibid 12.

93 ibid 61.

94 TRT World, 'Turkey Carries Out Its Largest-Ever Narcotics Operation, Arrests Dozens' (*TRT World*, 30 June 2020) <www.trtworld.com/turkey/turkey-carries-out-its-largest-ever-narcotics-operation-arrests-dozens-37750> accessed 20 January 2023.

(i.e., in Belgium, Brazil, Ecuador, France, the Netherlands, Italy and Peru).[95] Additionally, the operation secured the confiscation of approximately at least 2 billion TL[96] (i.e., around GBP 110 million as of January 2022).[97] It is noticeable that each LEA is actively seeking international JIT opportunities. For example, the CE, in collaboration with the Northern Macedonian authorities, interrupted the transit of over one tone of precursors shipped from China to Northern Macedonia, thereby securing the prosecution of two suspects, as well as the seizure of the substances that constitute the raw material of amphetamine and methamphetamine.[98] Concerning a more recent international operation, in cooperation with the Spanish and Guinean counterparts, the GDS KOM secured the seizure of 528 kg of cocaine and the detention of ten suspects behind the illicit drug trafficking scheme at the Guinean offshore.[99] Although there is no available data that allows a comparison of confiscations made in the two jurisdictions concerning ML deriving from illicit drug trafficking, recent statistics from Türkiye, Operation Swamp, in particular, are promising. For instance, the UK imposed a total of 2,600 confiscation orders concerning all offences (i.e., not only drug-related crimes) in 2020–2021, the value of which corresponds to GBP 139 m,[100] where Operation Swamp alone yielded the confiscation of GBP 110 m in Türkiye, as touched upon earlier. Given that illicit drug trafficking-related asset confiscation orders constituted 51% of the volume and 16% of the value of all asset confiscation orders made in the UK in 2018 and 2019,[101] the data from the 2020–2021 financial year can help estimate the proportion of confiscation orders made within the scope of this particular predicate crime. Therefore, it can be argued that AML amendments addressing deficiencies regarding how the law operates in action can be functional in controlling underlying predicate crimes, thereby reinforcing the overall AML effectiveness of a given jurisdiction.

95 Turkish National Police Counter Narcotics Department (n 52) 53; EMCDDA, 'EU Drug Market: Cocaine' (2022) <www.emcdda.europa.eu/publications/eu-drug-markets/cocaine_en> accessed 19 May 2023.

96 ibid.

97 Xe Currency Converter <www.xe.com/currencyconverter/convert/?Amount=2000000000&From=TRY&To=GBP> accessed 20 January 2023.

98 GMGM, 'Gümrük Muhafazadan Avrupa'da Ses Getiren Uluslararası Uyuşturucu Operasyonu' (7 February 2022) <https://muhafaza.ticaret.gov.tr/haberler/kacakcilikla-mucadele/gumruk-muhafazadan-avrupada-ses-getiren-uluslararasi-uyusturucu-operasyonu> accessed 7 February 2023.

99 EGM, '07.02.2022 Tarihli Basın Açıklaması' (7 February 2022) <www.egm.gov.tr/07022022-tarihli-basin-aciklamasi> accessed 7 February 2023.

100 Home Office, 'Asset Recovery Statistical Bulletin: Financial Years Ending 2016 to 2021' (September 2021) <www.gov.uk/government/statistics/asset-recovery-statistical-bulletin-financial-years-ending-2016-to-2021/asset-recovery-statistical-bulletin-financial-years-ending-2016-to-2021> accessed 19 August 2023.

101 HM Treasury and Home Office (n 3) 28.

8.3 Tax Offences

Tax offences are an international problem which damage the public budgets globally. Amongst many other scandals, Lux Leaks,[102] Swiss Leaks,[103] the Panama Papers,[104] and the Pandora Papers,[105] to name a few, have documented the complexity, magnitude, and extensiveness of the problem at a global scale.[106] The Tax Justice Network estimates that the universal tax loss was USD 483 bn in 2021, including Türkiye and the UK that lost approximately USD 1.65 bn (0.2% of GDP) and USD 52 bn (1.9% of GDP) due to abusive tax practices (e.g., tax avoidance, evasion, and fraud),[107] respectively.[108] Although tax evasion has not been identified as a critical threat generating significant proceeds of crime in the Turkish NRA,[109] approximately 40% of STRs sent by obliged entities to MASAK were related to tax-related offences in 2020,[110] evidencing the prevalence of this crime. Whilst such statistics are not available in the UKFIU annual reports,[111] the UK's NRA 2020 indicates that tax evasion, along with fraud, constitutes the most substantial proportion of criminal proceeds in

102 Matthew Caruana Galizia and others, 'Explore the Documents: Luxembourg Leaks Database' (*ICIJ*, 5 November 2014) <www.icij.org/investigations/luxembourg-leaks/explore-documents-luxembourg-leaks-database/> accessed 6 February 2022.

103 Gerard Ryle and others, 'About This Project: Swiss Leaks' (*ICIJ*, 8 February 2015) <www.icij.org/investigations/swiss-leaks/about-project-swiss-leaks/> accessed 6 February 2022.

104 Will Fitzgibbon and Michael Hudson, 'Five Years Later, Panama Papers Still Having a Big Impact' (*ICIJ*, 3 April 2021) <www.icij.org/investigations/panama-papers/five-years-later-panama-papers-still-having-a-big-impact/> accessed 6 February 2022.

105 ICIJ, 'Offshore Havens and Hidden Riches of World Leaders and Billionaires Exposed in Unprecedented Leak' (*ICIJ*, 3 October 2021) <www.icij.org/investigations/pandora-papers/global-investigation-tax-havens-offshore/> accessed 6 February 2022.

106 Umut Turksen and Adam Abukari, 'OECD's Global Principles and EU's Tax Crime Measures' (2021) 28(2) Journal of Financial Crime 406.

107 This chapter does not distinguish between tax evasion and its specific form of tax fraud, and the chapter refers to any criminal tax practice as tax evasion. The difference between tax avoidance and criminal forms of tax noncompliance (i.e., tax evasion and tax fraud) is explained below. See OECD, 'Glossary of Tax Terms' <www.oecd.org/ctp/glossaryoftax-terms.htm#T> accessed 2 February 2023.

108 Tax Justice Network, 'The State of Tax Justice 2021' (November 2021) 6, 24, 26 <https://taxjustice.net/wp-content/uploads/2021/11/State_of_Tax_Justice_Report_2021_ENGLISH.pdf> accessed 9 February 2023.

109 Whilst the Turkish NRA is not publicly accessible, the last MER conducted by the FATF on Türkiye documents that the riskiest predicate crimes posing a high ML threat in the Turkish NRA are drug trafficking, migrant smuggling, human trafficking, and fuel smuggling. See FATF (n 2) 32.

110 MASAK (n 4) 21. Please note that the percentage shows the distribution among selected STRs.

111 The UKFIU does not keep statistics on SAR reporting by predicate offence, as it adopts an all-crimes approach, as discussed in Chapter 4 previously.

the UK.[112] For instance, HMRC estimated that the tax gap resulting from *tax evasion* was GBP 5.5 bn in 2019–2020.[113] Earlier estimates indicated that whilst the level of the tax gap was 11.1% of the GDP in Türkiye (i.e., USD 89.3 bn), it was 3.2% of the GDP (i.e., USD 92.8 bn) in the UK in 2015,[114] evidencing the seriousness of the problem faced by these jurisdictions, as well as the difficulty in estimating its volume accurately. Suffice it to say that tax evasion has been a predicate crime for ML in Türkiye since 1996[115] and since 1993 in the UK[116] long before there was an international obligation/recommendation to do so, evidencing the foresight exercised by these jurisdictions.

Tax offences have long been considered as some of the most sizeable sources of ML.[117] However, as discussed in Chapters 2 and 4, the inclusion of tax crimes in the scope of predicate offences is a relatively recent AML reform following the 2012 revision of the FATF Recommendations and, concerning the EU, the subsequent enactment of the Fourth AMLD (i.e., Directive (EU) 2015/849).[118] Accordingly, the differences between the national AML structures may be more manifest in addressing these particular predicate crimes as each jurisdiction shows progress at varying paces in aligning their national compositions with the international standards. For example, as documented by PROTAX project, some EU MS had not completed the transposition of the Fourth AMLD, thereby failing to designate tax offences as predicate crimes

112 HM Treasury and Home Office (n 3) 27.

113 HMRC, 'Measuring Tax Gaps 2021 Edition – Tax Gap Estimates for 2019 to 2020' (September2021)<www.gov.uk/government/statistics/measuring-tax-gaps/measuring-tax-gaps-2021-edition-tax-gap-estimates-for-2019-to-2020> accessed 1 February 2023.

114 Konrad Raczkowski and Bogdan Mroz, 'The Tax Gap in the Global Economy' (2018) 21(4) Journal of Money Laundering Control 567, 570.

115 Law No 4208 on the Prevention of Money Laundering 1996, art 2(1). Please note that although this article has been repealed (see Chapter 3), the threshold approach to predicate crimes has not changed the status of tax offences as predicate crimes in Türkiye.

116 Criminal Justice Act 1988, s 93A(7) (as amended by Criminal Justice Act 1993, ss 29–31). The current legal instrument is POCA 2002.

117 OECD, 'Money Laundering Awareness Handbook for Tax Examiners and Tax Auditors' (2009) <www.oecd.org/ctp/crime/money-laundering-awareness-handbook-for-tax-examiners-and-tax-auditors.pdf> accessed 6 February 2023.

118 Directive (EU) 2015/849 of the European Parliament and of the Council of 20 May 2015 on the prevention of the use of the financial system for the purposes of money laundering or terrorist financing, amending Regulation (EU) No 648/2012 of the European Parliament and of the Council, and repealing Directive 2005/60/EC of the European Parliament and of the Council and Commission Directive 2006/70/EC (Text with EEA relevance) [2015] OJ L 141/73. For a more detailed discussion on the underlying reasons why it took so long for tax offences to be considered a predicate crime, see Lucia Rossel and others, 'The Implications of Making Tax Crimes a Predicate Crime for Money Laundering in the EU: Building a Legal Dataset of Tax Crimes and Money Laundering in the European Union' in Brigitte Unger, Lucia Rossel and Joras Ferwerda (eds), *Combatting Fiscal Fraud and Empowering Regulators: Bringing Tax Money Back into the COFFERS* (OUP 2021).

until recently.[119] This shows that despite the harmonisation as well as unification of many rules creating the EU's Single Market, the EU MS are far from achieving a homogenous set of AML regulations across the EU, albeit transposing the same Directives.[120] That being the case, examining the unique AML frameworks adopted by Türkiye and the UK as the two non-EU MS can help us understand how divergence points between the AML structures may contribute to or stand in the way of tackling the predicate crime of tax offences.

Before investigating the impact of AML structures of Türkiye and the UK on tax offences, it is necessary to crystallise the difference between the notions of tax avoidance and tax evasion, including tax fraud, albeit the dividing line between them is blurry.[121] Whilst there is no uniform legal definition of these phenomena at the international level, tax avoidance generally refers to bending the rules of the tax system in a way that contradicts the spirit, but not the letter, of the fiscal body of laws, thereby obtaining a tax advantage.[122] On the other hand, tax evasion stands for illegal and deliberate tax arrangements or dishonest acts, whereby taxpayers seek to reduce or disregard their tax liability in breach of the legal provisions.[123] In other words, whilst both concepts may constitute a tax non-compliance,[124] tax evasion/fraud embodies a predicate crime as one of the designated categories of offences as recommended by the FATF.[125] Therefore, this section focuses on the criminal aspect of tax

119 Umut Turksen and others, 'Case Studies of Tax Crimes in the European Union' (787098 PROTAX EU H2020 Project D1.2, October 2018) <https://protaxwebtoolkit.eu/index.php/2021/04/23/case-studies-of-tax-crimes-in-the-eu/> accessed 12 February 2022.

120 Lucia Rossel, Brigitte Unger and Joras Ferwerda, 'Shedding Light Inside the Black Box of Implementation: Tax Crimes as a Predicate Crime for Money Laundering' (2021) 16 Regulation & Governance <https://doi.org/10.1111/rego.12407> accessed 3 February 2022; Umut Turksen, 'Implications of Anti-Money Laundering Law for Accountancy in the European Union – A Comparative Study' in Nicholas Ryder, Umut Turksen and Sabine Hassler (eds), *Fighting Financial Crime in the Global Economic Crisis* (1st edn, Routledge 2014) 107.

121 Peter Alldridge, 'Tax Avoidance, Tax Evasion, Money Laundering and the Problem of "Offshore"' in S Rose-Ackerman and P Lagunes (eds), *Greed, Corruption, and the Modern State* (Edward Elgar Publishing 2015).

122 OECD (n 107).

123 ibid.

124 Antony Seely, 'Tax Avoidance and Tax Evasion' (UK Parliament Research Briefing Paper No 7948, November 2021) <https://researchbriefings.files.parliament.uk/documents/CBP-7948/CBP-7948.pdf> accessed 6 February 2023; Valerie Braithwaite, *Taxing Democracy: Understanding Tax Avoidance and Evasion* (Routledge 2003).

125 See the FATF Recommendations (i.e., Recommendation 3, Interpretive Note to Recommendation 3, and the definition of the 'Designated Categories of Offences'). FATF, 'International Standards on Combatting Money Laundering and the Financing of Terrorism & Proliferation: The FATF Recommendations' (Updated March 2022) <www.fatf-gafi.org/media/fatf/documents/recommendations/pdfs/FATF%20Recommendations%202012.pdf> accessed 26 June 2023.

non-compliance, rather than tax avoidance or aggressive tax planning,[126] as to whether and how the AML structures/reforms may affect the prevalence of such predicate offences.

Given that Türkiye and the UK are two of the founding 20 members of the OECD[127] and that the OECD's Ten Global Principles (TGPs) for fighting tax crimes can serve as international minimum standards in countering tax offences,[128] comparing the two AML frameworks against such benchmarks provides a sound comparison. The TGPs comprise (i) criminalisation of tax offences; (ii) devising effective strategy addressing tax crimes; (iii) effective and adequate resources and powers for LEAs; (iv) an organisational structure with defined responsibilities; (v) designating tax crimes as predicate offences for ML; (vi) domestic and international inter-agency cooperation; and (vii) protection of fundamental rights of tax offenders.[129] In line with the TGPs (see Principle 1), Law No 213 (Tax Procedure Law – TPL) 1961, as the core legal instrument regulating the fiscal domain in Türkiye, sets forth provisions for the procedures and main rules of all tax laws and establishes tax offences and associated penalties. Accordingly, (i) manipulating account and accounting records in commercial books and records; (ii) falsifying or concealing commercial books, records, and documents, as well as preparing or using misleading documents; (iii) suppressing the commercial books, records, and documents wholly or partially, or preparing or using forged copies of such documents; (iv) producing unauthorised documents; and (v) interfering with the payment recording devices in this context are criminalised under the TPL 1961.[130] In other words, any dishonest, deliberate, and deceptive tax practice that results in a decrease in the tax base constitutes tax evasion in Türkiye. Whilst manipulating, falsifying, or concealing commercial books, records, and documents, or formulating or using misleading documents entail an imprisonment term of 18 months to three years,[131] suppressing such materials, or producing or utilising forged copies thereof entail three to five years in prison.[132] Similarly, interfering with the payment recording devices in a way that prevents the recording of financial documents or information of sales on the device or that changes or deletes such records entails an imprisonment term

126 Christina HJI Panayi, *Advanced Issues in International and European Tax Law* (Hart Publishing 2015).

127 OECD, 'List of OECD Member Countries – Ratification of the Convention on the OECD' <www.oecd.org/about/document/ratification-oecd-convention.htm> accessed 8 March 2023.

128 Umut Turksen, *Countering Tax Crime in the European Union: Benchmarking the OECD's Ten Global Principles* (Hart Publishing 2021) 3.

129 OECD, *Fighting Tax Crime – The Ten Global Principles* (2nd edn, OECD Publishing 2021) <www.oecd-ilibrary.org/sites/006a6512-en/index.html?itemId=/content/publication/006a6512-en> accessed 14 February 2023.

130 Law No 213 (Tax Procedure Law) 1961, art 359.

131 ibid art 359(a).

132 ibid art 359(b).

of three to five years.[133] Lastly, producing or using unauthorised documents (i.e., documents produced by persons who do not have an agreement with the Ministry of Finance for doing so) necessitates two to five years in prison.[134] In addition to these imprisonment sentences, TPL 1961 imposes a monetary penalty of threefold of the tax loss caused by such activities on tax evaders.[135] However, unlike the UK's tax regime, as discussed later, Türkiye does not establish an offence that criminalises the failure of corporations to prevent the criminal facilitation of tax evasion,[136] which is the most remarkable difference between the two legal (AML) frameworks regarding this particular predicate crime.

Concerning the UK's pertinent legal framework, tax evasion constitutes a criminal offence both at common law[137] and statutory legal instruments (e.g., CFA 2017). The common-law offence of cheating the public revenue,[138] fraudulent evasion of income tax,[139] fraudulent evasion of Value Added Tax (VAT),[140] providing false documents or information to HMRC,[141] fraudulent evasion of duty,[142] and the (corporate) criminal offence of the failure to prevent the UK[143] or foreign[144] tax evasion[145] are the principal offences in this context.[146] In other

133 ibid art 359(ç).
134 ibid art 359(c).
135 ibid art 344(2).
136 It is worth reiterating here that, as a general rule, Türkiye does not attribute criminal liability to legal entities (see Chapter 3). On the other hand, the failure to prevent tax evasion, as introduced by the CFA 2017, constitutes a strict liability offence for corporations in the UK (see Chapter 4).
137 *R v Hudson* [1956] 2 QB 252; *R v Mavji* [1987] 84 Cr App R 34; *R v Mulligan* [1990] BTC 135. For a more detailed discussion on the scope of the common law offence of cheating the public revenue, see David Omerod, 'Cheating the Public Revenue' [1998] Criminal Law Review 627; Graham McBain, 'Modernising the Common Law Offence of Cheating the Public Revenue' (2015) 8(1) Journal of Politics and Law 40.
138 The common law offence of Cheating the Public Revenue was defined in *R v Less* [1993] (unreported case) as: 'The common law offence of cheating the public revenue does not necessarily require a false representation either by words or conduct. Cheating can include any form of fraudulent conduct which results in diverting money from the revenue and in depriving the revenue of the money to which it is entitled'. The Times, 30 March 1993 (See Omerod (n 137) 74). It is worth noting also that the Theft Act 1968 (s 32(1)(a)) has expressly preserved this offence.
139 Taxes Management Act (TMA) 1970, s 106A.
140 Value Added Tax Act (VATA) 1994, s 72.
141 Customs and Excise Management Act 1979, s 167.
142 ibid s 170.
143 Criminal Finances Act 2017, s 45.
144 ibid s 46.
145 Jonathan Fisher and Anita Clifford, *The Criminal Finances Act 2017* (Informa Law 2018) 73–86.
146 See also Karen Harrison and Nicholas Ryder, 'The Avoidance and Evasion of Tax' in Karen Harrison and Nicholas Ryder (eds), *The Law Relating to Financial Crime in the United Kingdom* (2nd edn, Routledge 2016).

words, unlike Türkiye's pertinent legal composition, tax evasion is stipulated across various legal instruments in the UK. However, a close examination of these provisions reveals that each legal norm (i.e., common-law or statutory legislation), in defining tax offences, essentially underlines deceitful and deliberate (***knowingly concerned***)[147] tax practices that aim to cheat tax authorities. That is to say that both legal regimes adopted in Türkiye and the UK, apart from the UK's novel concept of the failure to prevent the facilitation of tax evasion, set forth similar legal frameworks in determining what constitutes tax evasion therein. However, the penalties envisaged for tax evaders in the UK include, at least in theory, life imprisonment (under common law),[148] albeit statutory penalties stipulate a maximum imprisonment term of seven years, indicating the increased severity of penal framework in this end compared to Türkiye. Arguably, these relatively stiffer criminal sanctions adopted in the UK may render the jurisdiction, apart from its overseas territories, less attractive for tax offenders than Türkiye. Whilst Türkiye and the UK have criminalised tax offences and designated them as predicate crimes for ML as per the spirit of the FATF Recommendations[149] and the TGPs,[150] these nuances between the two regimes cannot demonstrate whether and to what extent they impact the tax evasion-related ML problem differently. Therefore, after this brief outline, it is necessary to examine the national AML ***modus operandi*** of the two jurisdictions and investigate their impacts on this particular predicate crime.

In response to the associated ML threat deriving from tax evasion, in alignment with the TGPs (see Principle 2),[151] Türkiye and the UK have placed comprehensive national strategies and action plans addressing this challenge.[152] The Turkish Ministry of Treasury and Finance Strategic Plan 2019–2023 stipulates

147 See TMA 1970, s 106A; VATA 1994, s 72; CEMA 1979, ss 167 and 170; CFA 2017 ss 45–46.

148 Sentencing Council, 'Revenue Fraud' <www.sentencingcouncil.org.uk/offences/magistrates-court/item/revenue-fraud/> accessed 5 February 2023.

149 FATF (n 125). It is worth reiterating that the UK also implemented/complied with the EU AML Directives until Brexit.

150 OECD (n 129) TGPs 1, 7.

151 ibid.

152 TC Hazine ve Maliye Bakanlığı GIB, 'Kayıt Dışı Ekonomiyle Mücadele Stratejisi Eylem Planı (2019–2021)' (2019) <www.gib.gov.tr/sites/default/files/fileadmin/user_upload/Kayit_Disi_Ekonomiyle_Mucadele_Stratejisi_Eylem_Plani_2019_2021.pdf> accessed 9 February 2023; HM Treasury and HMRC, 'Tackling Tax Avoidance, Evasion, and Other Forms of Non-Compliance' (March 2019) <https://assets.publishing.service.gov.uk/government/uploads/system/uploads/attachment_data/file/785551/tackling_tax_avoidance_evasion_and_other_forms_of_non-compliance_web.pdf> accessed 9 February 2023; HM Treasury and Home Office, 'Economic Crime Plan, 2019 to 2022' (Policy Paper, updated 4 May 2021) <www.gov.uk/government/publications/economic-crime-plan-2019-to-2022/economic-crime-plan-2019-to-2022-accessible-version> accessed 9 February 2023.

tackling the informal economy and reducing financial crimes by undertaking tax inspections, thereby 'increasing efficiency in the fight against money laundering and financing of terrorism' as one of the policy objectives.[153] As per this policy objective, Türkiye established the General Directorate of Risk Analysis within the auspices of the MoTF on 18 April 2020[154] to ensure an RBA to prevent tax evasion. Its duties include, amongst others, investigating tax loss and evasion and unregistered economic activities and preventing them by carrying out risk analysis and evaluation studies, as well as by ensuring coordination with relevant public institutions and organisations.[155] As a performance indicator, the MoTF proclaims that this institutional amendment contributed by 20% to reach a success rate of 89% concerning the objective of tackling the informal economy and reducing financial crimes in 2020,[156] suggesting the functionality of AML reforms in addressing predicate crimes. However, it is necessary to inquire into evidential indicators, such as the prosecution/conviction figures of tax offenders and the associated money launderers, to assess the observable effectiveness of the tax enforcement ecosystem in Türkiye and the UK.

Before such an assessment, it is necessary to briefly contour the essential authorities that supervise taxpayers' compliance with fiscal regulations in Türkiye. The Directorate of Tax Inspection Board (*Vergi Denetim Kurulu Başkanlığı/VDK*), which operates under the auspices of the MoTF,[157] is the principal organisation designated for and dedicated to conducting tax crime investigations, thereby ensuring the tax compliance of taxpayers. Its organisational structure comprises, amongst others, Tax Evasion Audit Departments[158] established in the riskiest cities regarding the volume of tax evasion threats, such as Istanbul and Ankara.[159] Accordingly, its duties consist of, *inter alia*,

153 TC Hazine ve Maliye Bakanlığı, 'TC Hazine ve Maliye Bakanlığı 2019–2023 Stratejik Planı' 12 <https://ms.hmb.gov.tr/uploads/2020/03/2019-2023-Maliye-Bakanlığı-Stratejik-Planı_Basılacak-Versiyon.28.02.2020.pdf> accessed 9 February 2023.

154 Official Gazette No 31103 dated 18 April 2020, 'Cumhurbaşkanlığı Kararnamesi (Kararname No 60)' <www.resmigazete.gov.tr/eskiler/2020/04/20200418-1.pdf> accessed 9 February 2023.

155 Presidential Decree No 1 on the Organisation of the Presidency 2018, arts 222(1)(a) and 222(1)(b).

156 TC Hazine ve Maliye Bakanlığı, '2020 Yılı Faaliyet Raporu' (February 2021) 119 <https://ms.hmb.gov.tr/uploads/2021/03/2020-HMB-Idare-Faaliyet-Raporu.pdf> accessed 9 February 2023.

157 TC Hazine ve Maliye Bakanlığı, 'Vergi Denetim Kurulu Başkanlığı' <www.hmb.gov.tr/vergi-denetim-kurulu-baskanligi> accessed 7 February 2023.

158 Presidential Decree No 1 on the Organisation of the Presidency 2018, art 228(2).

159 Vergi Denetim Kurulu Başkanlığı, 'Faaliyet Raporu 2018' (2019) 91 <https://ms.hmb.gov.tr/uploads/2019/04/VDK-2018-Birim-Faaliyet-Raporu-1102019-002.pdf> accessed 7 February 2023.

conducting tax inspections within the scope of tax legislation,[160] conducting research on emerging tax evasion and tax avoidance methods to identify and prevent them effectively,[161] and conducting investigations on the ML aspect of the predicament.[162] However, as tax auditors/inspectors do not have similar criminal investigation powers to conventional LEAs of the jurisdiction, they shall notify the Directorate of the potential criminal acts detected to be forwarded to the competent authorities,[163] signifying an indirect intervention process. Similarly, in circumstances where such acts constitute tax evasion (i.e., falling within the scope of Article 359 of TPL 1961), they shall prepare tax crime reports[164] and notify the Public Prosecutor's Office of the offence accordingly.[165] On the other hand, in cases where public prosecutors get informed of potential tax evasion through other means, they cannot initiate a criminal case without a confirmation from the tax authority who verifies such suspicions based on their tax inspections and analysis.[166] In other words, the initiation of a criminal case regarding tax offences in Türkiye invariably predicates upon the *obiter dictum* of tax officials. It is worth underlining this unconventional legal practice for Türkiye as it is a unique approach for prosecuting tax crimes (i.e., public prosecutors can initiate a criminal case autonomously concerning any other crime). Given the complexity of tax offences and the technical expertise required for identifying such crimes, this mechanism constitutes a legal filter whereby unqualifying cases are excluded from further judicial action at the very early stages of the process, thereby increasing the efficiency of judicial procedures.[167] Lastly, it is worth reiterating that the president of VDK is one of the permanent members of the CBCFC,[168] as discussed in Chapter 5 previously.

160 Presidential Decree No 1 on the Organisation of the Presidency 2018, art 228(4)(a).
161 ibid art 228(4)(g).
162 Tax Audit Board Regulation 2021, art 36(ç).
163 ibid art 38(1).
164 ibid art 54.
165 Law No 213 (Tax Procedure Law) 1961, art 367(1).
166 ibid arts 367(2) and 367(3).
167 It is worth noting that, regarding a lawsuit opened based on the grounds, amongst others, that obtaining the opinion of tax authorities in initiating a criminal case nullifies the independence of courts (Article 138 of the Constitution 1982), the Constitutional Court concluded that seeking the *obiter dictum* of tax officials is not against the Constitution. According to the Constitutional Court, this procedure helps prosecution authorities decide as per statutes and the spirit of the law. See the Constitutional Court decision dated 10 February 2011 (*Esas No* 2009/89, *Karar No* 2011/40): Anayasa Mahkemesi, *Anayasa Mahkemesi Kararlar Dergisi* (Sayı: 49, 1. Cilt, Anayasa Mahkemesi Yayınları 2012) 63–72 <https://anayasa.gov.tr/media/4890/kararlar_dergisi_49_1.pdf> accessed 21 February 2023.
168 Presidential Decree No 1 on the Organisation of the Presidency 2018, art 232(2).

It is also necessary to state that the Directorate of Tax Inspection Board undertakes its inspections in coordination with the Revenue Administration (*Gelir İdaresi Başkanlığı/GIB*),[169] an affiliated unit to the MoTF[170] that governs the taxation domain in Türkiye as the tax administration of the jurisdiction. It also has an essential role in tackling tax evasion as its duties include, amongst others, taking necessary measures to prevent tax loss and evasion.[171] However, similar to the Tax Inspection Board, the powers granted to GIB do not comprise authorities that LEAs harness intrinsically, suggesting that tackling tax evasion regarding legal proceedings is predominantly incumbent on (KOM units of) the conventional LEAs of the jurisdiction. Within the scope of tackling tax crimes, similar to VDK, the core operational function of GIB is to conduct inspections on liable taxpayers to ensure their compliance with the fiscal legislation. For example, GIB personnel inspected 3,061 taxpayers in 2020, thereby identified a base difference of 3,259,240,971 TL (approximately GBP 178 m) and a tax difference of 101,734,020 TL (around GBP 5.5 m) and levied a tax of 66,658,208 TL (roughly GBP 3.6 m)[172] accordingly.[173] Likewise, VDK personnel audited 47,597 taxpayers in 2020, thereby detecting a base difference of approximately TL 328.32 bn (around GBP 17.93 bn) and levying a tax of roughly TL 24.92 bn (approximately GBP 1.36 bn).[174] Whilst these statistics suggest the magnitude of the problem prevalent in Türkiye, there are no available data that indicate whether any non-compliant tax practices identified by GIB or VDK personnel resulted in or yielded to a subsequent ML investigation or conviction.

Having outlined the duties and legal powers of tax authorities in Türkiye, it is necessary to underline the essential differences between these fiscal agencies and the HMRC, the UK's tax enforcement authority. First and foremost, whilst HMRC harnesses criminal and civil investigation powers that can be applied autonomously, tackling tax offences in Türkiye necessitates an integrated operational approach established between LEAs and the tax authorities at each phase of the intervention process as directed by public prosecutors. It is worth reiterating that HMRC, within the scope of its criminal investigation

169 ibid art 228(4)(ç).
170 Revenue Administration <www.gib.gov.tr/en> accessed 7 February 2023.
171 Presidential Decree No 4 2018, art 137(h).
172 Xe Currency Converter <www.xe.com/currencyconverter/convert/?Amount=66658208&From=TRY&To=GBP> accessed 7 February 2023.
173 Gelir İdaresi Başkanlığı, '2020 Faaliyet Raporu' (February 2021) 102–3 <www.gib.gov.tr/sites/default/files/fileadmin/faaliyetraporlari/2020/2020_faaliyet_raporu.pdf> accessed 7 February 2023.
174 TC Hazine ve Maliye Bakanlığı (n 156) 68–70.

powers,[175] can apply for production orders, apply for and execute search warrants, make arrests, (in case of an arrest) undertake a subsequent search of suspects and premises,[176] and recover criminal assets.[177] Furthermore, regarding serious tax offences,[178] HMRC can even be granted, by the Home Secretary and a Judicial Commissioner, to administer the intrusive surveillance powers (e.g., the interception of communications)[179] provided that they do not contradict the spirit of ECHR and the Regulation of Investigatory Powers Act 2000.[180] However, the investigation powers bestowed on tax authorities in Türkiye are limited to applying for and executing search warrants[181] and obtaining information,[182] suggesting that the use of other similar powers (e.g., arrest) requires the involvement of LEAs. More importantly, from an AML perspective, whilst HMRC has direct access to data held by the UKFIU concerning administrating and assessing taxes, tax authorities in Türkiye can exploit such information if and when MASAK utilises its ability to share information spontaneously in this context.[183] This procedure is not different concerning accessing FIU data relating to investigating tax offences. Whilst HMRC also has direct access to such data in this regard, MASAK has no obligation to share information with LEAs and the tax authorities, albeit having the ability to do so spontaneously.[184] Given that having access to FIU data (i.e., STRs/SARs) by tax authorities increases the effectiveness in countering tax

175 Criminal investigation powers are available only for authorised personnel operating under the auspices of HMRC's Fraud Investigation Service (FIS) and Risk and Intelligence Service (RIS). See HMRC, 'Guidance: HMRC's Criminal Investigation Powers and Safeguards' (Updated 13 July 2021) <www.gov.uk/government/publications/criminal-investigation/criminal-investigation> accessed 12 February 2023; HMRC, 'Counter Fraud in HMRC' <https://fraudinvestigationjobs.hmrc.gov.uk/criminal-justice-in-hmrc/overview/> accessed 12 February 2023.

176 Police and Criminal Evidence Act (PACE) 1984, ss 8(7) and 114; HMRC (n 175).

177 See, for example, Proceeds of Crime Act (POCA) 2002, s 2A(2)(f); HMRC (n 175).

178 Serious Crime Act 2007, sch 1. Serious Crime Act 2007 stipulates serious tax offences as comprising fraudulent evasion of duty, fraudulent evasion of VAT, fraudulent evasion of income tax, tax credit fraud, the common law offence of cheating the public revenue, and the failure to prevent the facilitation of UK tax evasion offences or foreign tax evasion offences.

179 Investigatory Powers Act 2016, s 18(1)(f).

180 HMRC (n 175).

181 Law No 213 (Tax Procedure Law) 1961, art 142.

182 ibid arts 148–49.

183 OECD, *Effective Inter-Agency Co-Operation in Fighting Tax Crimes and Other Financial Crimes* (3rd edn, OECD Publishing 2017) 100 <www.oecd.org/tax/crime/effective-inter-agency-co-operation-in-fighting-tax-crimes-and-other-financial-crimes-third-edition.pdf> accessed 14 February 2023.

184 ibid 103. It is necessary to note that MASAK shares information with the CE in this context only when requested (see ibid 107). Additionally, MASAK has direct access to information held by the tax administration (see ibid 72).

crimes,[185] establishing a more straightforward information-sharing mechanism between MASAK and the VDK/GIB would help increase the (associated) AML effectiveness of Türkiye. Additionally, whilst pertinent information that would benefit tax authorities regarding administrating taxes identified during an investigation by LEAs or public prosecutors is shared with tax administrations only when requested in Türkiye, such officials can communicate relevant information to HMRC spontaneously in the UK.[186] However, it is necessary to note that in cases where such information signifies a potential tax crime, LEAs and public prosecutors in Türkiye and the UK can share it with tax authorities spontaneously, albeit not having an obligation to do so.[187] In other words, the effective enforcement of tax laws, or from a broader perspective, tackling tax evasion, requires the active involvement of LEAs and MASAK intrinsically in Türkiye, corroborating the importance of devising an effective mechanism for inter-agency cooperation domestically, as envisaged by the TGPs (Principle 8). HMRC, equipped with comprehensive law enforcement tools for carrying out legal proceedings and investigating associated ML, can undertake such activities for the most part singlehandedly, albeit passing criminal cases to the CPS for potential prosecution.[188] Accordingly, whilst Türkiye predominantly exploits JITs in countering tax offences,[189] the UK benefits from its relatively more independent tax (enforcement) authority and inter-agency centre of intelligence, namely NECC, whose members include HMRC, as discussed in Chapter 6 previously. Therefore, this relatively limited set of legal powers that tax inspectors/auditors possess in Türkiye[190] renders it crucial to investigate the information flows between competent authorities and how Turkish LEAs are involved in the national efforts addressing tax crimes. Table 8.3 summarises the abilities of competent authorities in accessing inter-agency tax-related (and non-tax-related) information.

185 OECD, 'Improving Co-operation Between Tax and Anti-Money Laundering Authorities: Access by Tax Administrations to Information Held by Financial Intelligence Units for Criminal and Civil Purposes' (September 2015) 14 <www.oecd.org/ctp/crime/report-improving-cooperation-between-tax-anti-money-laundering-authorities.pdf> accessed 12 February 2023.

186 ibid 89.

187 ibid 91 and 92.

188 HMRC, 'Guidance: HMRC's Criminal Investigation Policy' (Updated 13 July 2021) <www.gov.uk/government/publications/criminal-investigation/hmrc-criminal-investigation-policy> accessed 12 February 2023.

189 See, for instance, GMGM, '2020 Faaliyet Raporu' (2021) 34–37 <https://muhafaza.ticaret.gov.tr/data/5d31b1ee13b876092c062161/faaliyet%20raporu%202020.pdf> accessed 9 February 2023.

190 Comparing the investigation powers granted to tax enforcement authorities in Türkiye and the UK based on the criteria provided by the OECD indicates the relatively limited set of legal powers tax inspectors/auditors possess in Türkiye. See OECD, 'Tax Crime Investigation Maturity Model' (2020) <www.oecd.org/tax/crime/tax-crime-investigation-maturity-model.pdf> accessed 12 February 2022.

Table 8.3 The information flow between competent AML authorities in Türkiye and the UK.[191]

Türkiye — Agency providing data	*Agency receiving data*: *VDK/GIB*	*LEAs investigating crimes other than tax offences*	*MASAK*	*Public Prosecutors investigating crimes other than tax offences*
VDK/GIB[192]	x	Permitted[193]	Direct access	Obliged
LEAs investigating crimes other than tax offences	Permitted[196]	x	Permitted	Obliged
MASAK	Permitted	Permitted[199]	x	Obliged
Public Prosecutors investigating crimes other than tax offences	–	–	–	x

UK — Agency providing data	*Agency receiving data*: *HMRC*	*LEAs investigating crimes other than tax offences*	*UKFIU*	*CPS*
HMRC	x	Permitted[194]	Obliged[195]	Permitted
LEAs	Permitted	x	Obliged[197]	Permitted[198]
UKFIU	Direct access	Direct access	x	Permitted[200]
CPS	–	–	–	x

191 The table has been prepared based on the inspiration relating to the work of the OECD (n 183).

192 Although the VDK and the GIB are separate units with different primary responsibilities, they are considered combined authority for the purposes of this chapter. It is necessary to note that both agencies have direct access to relevant data held by each other in countering tax evasion.

193 Whilst tax officials may have discretion in notifying LEAs of the potential criminal acts relating to non-tax-offences, they are obliged to provide the CE with relevant data relating to customs activities.

194 HMRC can notify the police or the CPS of the information it obtains relating to suspected non-tax offences, but it is not under an obligation to do so.

195 As discussed in Chapter 6, HMRC is an AML supervisory body that supervises particular business sectors, such as high-value dealers. In cases where it identifies potential ML practices undertaken by these sectors, it is obliged to inform the UKFIU accordingly.

196 Whilst LEAs may have discretion in providing information to tax authorities spontaneously, the CE is obliged to share information relevant to determining civil tax liabilities spontaneously. However, the CE may exercise discretion in providing information to tax crime investigators.

197 In cases where the police obtain information on a potential ML activity, they have to report it to the UKFIU.

198 Concerning minor cases, the police have the authority to caution suspected offenders, issue a fixed penalty notice, or refer them to the CPS. Regarding more grave circumstances, the police refer such offenders to the CPS to decide whether to prosecute. See Crown Prosecution Service, 'The Criminal Justice System' <www.cps.gov.uk/about-cps/criminal-justice-system> accessed 28 February 2022.

199 Whilst MASAK can provide information to LEAs spontaneously, it is authorised to provide information to the CE on request only.

200 It is necessary to note that the CPS personnel (i.e., public prosecutors in the UK) are not actively involved in criminal prosecutions as they primarily function as a decision mechanism concerning whether to prosecute or not. Additionally, the CPS has personnel embedded in the NECC (see Chapter 6).

The contribution of LEAs in Türkiye concerning tackling tax evasion originates predominantly from their intervention in smuggling crimes, including but not limited to fuel, alcohol, and tobacco smuggling.[201] In other words, their organisational structures do not comprise specialised units or tax experts entrusted primarily with undertaking tax inspections, albeit LEA personnel operating in KOM units, in particular, are trained in identifying tax offences. For example, the Directorate of Tax Inspection Board, in cooperation with TADOC and LEAs, provides LEA personnel with countering tax evasion courses.[202] As a result of LEA operations targeting tax evasion, they intervened in approximately 3,000 tax offences between 2016 and 2020, with the most substantial contribution in this end belonging to the GDS (see Table 8.4), whereby they secured the prosecution of roughly 5,000 tax offenders. Whilst the GDS made the most considerable proportion of these interventions, the GCG intervened in at least[203] 57 tax evasion incidents (34 in 2020[204] and 23 in 2021[205]) in the last two years, albeit data on the associated offenders detained/prosecuted are not available. Yet, similar to the VDK and GIB statistics, there is no information within the LEA statistics concerning whether these interventions have resulted in ML prosecutions.

Given that the only legal provision that sets forth an imprisonment sentence for tax offenders is Article 359 of TPL 1961, which determines the scope of tax evasion, examining judicial records and statistics reveals the effectiveness of judicial handling and incarceration rates of tax evaders. The relevant statistics indicate that 39,119 (38,234 in 2019) tax offences were filed at the criminal courts in 2020, and 8,045 (11,142 in 2019) offenders were sentenced to

201 EGM KOM Daire Başkanlığı, 'Kaçakçılık ve Organize Suçlarla Mücadele 2020 Raporu' (September 2021) 31–32 <www.egm.gov.tr/kurumlar/egm.gov.tr/IcSite/kom/YAYINLARIMIZ/TÜRKÇE/2020-RAPORU-TURKCE.pdf> accessed 7 February 2023; TC İçişleri Bakanlığı Jandarma Genel Komutanlığı (n 53) 21–23; Sahil Güvenlik Komutanlığı (n 91) 40; GMGM (n 189) 18–40.

202 Vergi Denetim Kurulu Başkanlığı (n 159) 100–1.

203 The relevant monthly statistics regarding 2021 do not contain data relating to June and September.

204 The GCG provides monthly statistics on the incidents they intervened in, including tax evasion. However, such statistics have been available since April 2019 (as of 7 February 2022), albeit 2019 data does not contain any information on tax offences. See TC İçişleri Bakanlığı Jandarma Genel Komutanlığı, '2019 Yılı Verileri' <www.jandarma.gov.tr/2019-yili-verileri> accessed 7 February 2023; TC İçişleri Bakanlığı Jandarma Genel Komutanlığı, '2020 Yılı Verileri' <www.jandarma.gov.tr/2020-yili-verileri> accessed 7 February 2022.

205 TC İçişleri Bakanlığı Jandarma Genel Komutanlığı, '2021 Yılı Verileri' <www.jandarma.gov.tr/2021-yili-verileri> accessed 7 February 2023.

Table 8.4 The number of tax evasion incidents and the associated suspects identified by the GDS KOM.[206]

2016		*2017*		*2018*		*2019*		*2020*		*Total*	
Incidents	Suspects	Incidents	Suspects	Incidents	Suspects	Incidents	Suspects	Incidents	Suspects	Incidents	Suspects
304	485	524	790	662	1,263	748	1,052	672	936	2,910	4,526

206 EGM KOM Daire Başkanlığı (n 201) 32.

an imprisonment term accordingly,[207] suggesting that approximately 20–25% of all tax cases result in the incarceration of tax offenders at criminal courts in Türkiye. Comparatively, 3,318 suspected tax evaders (i.e., natural persons) were prosecuted in the UK between 2017 and 2019 (i.e., 1,224 in 2017, 1,132 in 2018, and 962 in 2019), whereby 1,440 offenders were sentenced to a custodial sentence (692 of which suspended custodial sentences).[208] It is necessary to note that in terms of institutional (AML) amendments addressing the predicate crime of tax offences, Türkiye recently reinforced its judicial structure by introducing specialised criminal courts designated for hearing tax offences in November 2021.[209] Although the impact of this institutional amendment is yet to be seen, it indicates that Türkiye considers tax offences as a serious threat requiring targeted counter-measures. Additionally, it is worth emphasising here that these judicial statistics signify the differences in the two jurisdictions' priorities in approaching tax offenders. More specifically, the relevant data from the UK indicate that tax investigations led by the HMRC resulted only in 163 (691 in 2019–2020) prosecutions in 2020–2021, and the number of charging decisions (i.e., not only incarceration) made by the judicial authorities concerning tax fraud was only 304 (573 in 2019–2020) in the same period.[210] Early statistics denote similar prosecution/conviction rates: following three-digit prosecution figures in the first four years of the last decade (420 in 2010–2011, 525 in 2011–2012, 770 in 2012–2013, 915 in 2013–2014), HMRC referred 1,288 cases for prosecution to the CPS in 2015, whereby 32% of such cases (i.e., 412 suits) resulted in the custody of tax offenders,[211] suggesting the historical infrequency of tax cases before the prosecution

207 Ministry of Justice General Directorate of Judicial Record and Statistics, 'Judicial Statistics 2020' (September 2021) 99, 122 <https://adlisicil.adalet.gov.tr/Resimler/SayfaDokuman/16920211620l1adalet_ist-2020.pdf> accessed 1 February 2023; Ministry of Justice General Directorate of Judicial Record and Statistics, 'Judicial Statistics 2019' (August 2020) 99, 122 <https://adlisicil.adalet.gov.tr/Resimler/SayfaDokuman/1092020162733adalet_ist-2019.pdf> accessed 1 February 2023.

208 OECD, *Fighting Tax Crime – The Ten Global Principles: Country Chapters* (2nd edn, OECD Publishing 2021) 360 <www.oecd.org/tax/crime/fighting-tax-crime-the-ten-global-principles-second-edition-country-chapters.pdf?_ga=2.247447682.740417271.1644849908-1796273601.1644849908> accessed 1 February 2023.

209 Hakimler ve Savcılar Kurulu, 'Hakimler ve Savcılar Kurulu Birinci Dairesinin Kararı' (Decision No 1227 dated 25 November 2021) <www.hsk.gov.tr/Eklentiler/30112021092825112021-1227pdf.pdf> accessed 5 February 2023. It is necessary to note that these courts are not Tax Courts that handle civil tax disputes discussed in Chapter 5 previously.

210 HMRC, 'HM Revenue and Customs Annual Report and Accounts 2020 to 2021' (HC 696, November 2021) 53 <https://assets.publishing.service.gov.uk/government/uploads/system/uploads/attachment_data/file/1035550/HMRC_Annual_Report_and_Accounts_2020_to_2021__Print_.pdf> accessed 23 February 2022.

211 National Audit Office, 'Tackling Tax Fraud: How HMRC Responds to Tax Evasion, the Hidden Economy and Criminal Attacks' (HC 610, December 2015) 33–35 <www.nao.org.uk/wp-content/uploads/2015/12/Tackling-tax-fraud-how-HMRC-responds-to-tax-evasion-the-hidden-economy-and-criminal-attacks.pdf> accessed 23 February 2023.

authorities in the UK.[212] Although the relative increase secured in 2015 has been maintained by the HMRC, thereby yielding approximately 3,700 criminal convictions between 2016 and 2021,[213] these figures are still considerably lower than the conviction rates in Türkiye. This significant difference stems from the fact that the collection of revenue, rather than seeking criminal prosecution in the first place, has been a primary objective for the tax authorities in the UK (i.e., HMRC and its predecessor, the Inland Revenue).[214] Accordingly, among other reasons, considering the cost-effectiveness of applying to civil investigation procedures in settling tax liabilities,[215] HMRC reserves its criminal investigation powers only for pursuing a limited number of fraudulent tax practices and opts for the civil enforcement route for most cases.[216] The substantial disparity between prosecution/conviction figures regarding tax offenders between the two jurisdictions can also be attributable to the Contractual Disclosure Facility (CDF), a unique tax fraud investigation procedure utilised by the HMRC as determined under the Code of Practice 9 (COP9).[217] Similar to the DPAs (see Chapter 4), entering into a CDF contract and complying with its requirements (i.e., terminating deliberate conduct, disclosing the loss of tax caused, reimbursing the total loss) eliminates for offenders the risk of being criminally investigated by HMRC with a view to prosecution.[218] Whilst assessing which approach is more appropriate is beyond the scope of this book,[219] these statistics signify the effectiveness levels of the tax authorities in securing a successful judicial sentencing ***modus operandi*** for tax evaders in the two jurisdictions. However, given the higher imprisonment sentencing figures and the associated monetary penalties imposed (i.e., threefold of the tax loss caused, as touched upon previously) in Türkiye, it can be argued that Türkiye's legal regime addressing tax offenders seems to impose more severe sanctions to offenders (i.e., the loss of liberty) thus may act as a better deterrent. Yet, such statistics cannot be regarded as evidence of how competent

212 HMRC has always been criticised for securing low prosecution rates. See, for instance, Committee of Public Accounts, 'Tackling Tax Fraud' (Thirty-Fourth Report of Session 2015–16, HC 674, April 2016) <https://publications.parliament.uk/pa/cm201516/cmselect/cmpubacc/674/674.pdf> accessed 23 February 2023.

213 Simon York, 'HMRC's Response to the Rise of the Enabler' (*Tax Journal*, 26 March2021)<www.taxjournal.com/articles/-hmrc-s-response-to-the-rise-of-the-enabler-44236> accessed 23 February 2023.

214 For a more detailed discussion on the evolution of HMRC's enforcement approach to tax offenders, see Turksen and others (n 119) 96.

215 Peter Alldridge and Ann Mumford, 'Tax Evasion and the Proceeds of Crime Act 2002' (2005) 25(3) Legal Studies 353.

216 HMRC (n 188).

217 HMRC, 'Code of Practice 9' (June 2014) <https://assets.publishing.service.gov.uk/government/uploads/system/uploads/attachment_data/file/494808/COP9_06_14.pdf> accessed 23 February 2023.

218 ibid.

219 For a more comprehensive commentary on the appropriateness/ramifications of applying civil remedies to economic crime, including tax offences, see Mary Michelle Gallant, *Money Laundering and the Proceeds of Crime: Economic Crime and Civil Remedies* (Edward Elgar Publishing 2005).

authorities in the two jurisdictions perform regarding tackling the associated ML problem. Therefore, such an inquiry requires a closer examination of the annual reports published by MASAK and the UKFIU, thereby identifying the magnitude of tax-related STRs/SARs and the associated obliged entities that made such disclosures.

Obliged entities in Türkiye made a total of 237,531 STRs in 2020, 39.72% of which were within the scope of tax evasion.[220] Given that MASAK has direct access to databases held by tax authorities,[221] this relatively high proportion of STRs submitted within the scope of potential tax evasion provides MASAK with an opportunity to render such STRs more meaningful, thereby detecting associated ML practices. However, it is necessary to note that HMRC has personnel embedded in the UKFIU; and HMRC and the UKFIU recently formed a SARs Tax Evasion Group,[222] suggesting that the SAR database is fully exploitable in countering tax offences in the UK. That being the case where such STRs originate from (i.e., the quality of such disclosures) becomes more significant for Türkiye as each obliged entity does not have technical expertise in distinguishing between tax crimes and unethical but *still legal* tax noncompliance. The role tax examiners/auditors play as a part of their professions (i.e., checking the accuracy of taxpayers' books and records) renders their contribution to the STR/SAR submission practices more crucial in identifying tax crimes and the associated ML.[223] Nevertheless, whilst Turkish accountants and tax advisers did not submit a single STR, notaries and independent audit institutions submitted a total of seven STRs to MASAK in 2020,[224] suggesting that MASAK gets informed of suspicions regarding the phenomenon predominantly through other obliged entities, such as banks. Although the UKFIU does not keep statistics by predicate offence due to its all-crimes approach, the volume of SARs made alone by accountants and tax advisers (5,347) and independent legal professionals (3,006)[225] in the same period signifies that the relevant obliged entities in the UK are more sensitive to ML deriving from tax offences than those operating in Türkiye. Considering the functionality of enablers in perpetrating tax offences as recently well documented by the previously mentioned prominent scandals and research projects, such as PROTAX, it gives the impression that the current state of affairs relating to STR submission *modus operandi* in this context is unaccommodating in Türkiye. The

220 MASAK (n 4) 20–21. Please note that the percentage shows the distribution among selected STRs.
221 OECD (n 183) 72.
222 NCA (n 4) 12.
223 OECD, *Money Laundering and Terrorist Financing Awareness Handbook for Tax Examiners and Tax Auditors* (OECD Publishing 2019) 27 <www.oecd.org/tax/crime/money-laundering-and-terrorist-financing-awareness-handbook-for-tax-examiners-and-tax-auditors.pdf> accessed 1 February 2023.
224 MASAK (n 4) 20.
225 NCA (n 4) 9.

meagre STR submission practices of pertinent obliged entities (e.g., accountants) therein can be attributable to various reasons, such as tax amnesties,[226] as discussed in Chapter 7 in detail previously. However, within the scope of this chapter, it is necessary to underline the differences between legal provisions addressing professional enablers envisaged in Türkiye and the UK in this context. Furthermore, it is necessary to note also that this chapter does not devote any consideration to 'fiscal corruption' whereby public officials that operate within tax authorities or LEAs may be party to 'organised tax fraud' schemes as enablers of tax offences.[227]

OECD defines professional enablers of tax crimes, such as accountants, lawyers, and notaries, to name a few, widely as intermediaries with specific knowledge and expertise who provide fraudulent (non)taxpayers with sophisticated means of tax evasion/fraud.[228] However, similar to the heterogeneity in defining what constitutes ML or tax evasion/fraud (i.e., predicate crimes as a whole) across jurisdictions, including Türkiye and the UK, there is no uniformity regarding the legal definition of professional enablers, if any. For example, the (fiscal) legislation in Türkiye refers to the general provisions of TCC 2004 envisaged for jointly committed offences (i.e., *suça iştirak*)[229] in determining penalties for such enablers[230] as there is no specific definition or consideration for the involvement of those professionals as enablers/facilitators in tax crimes across *jus scriptum*. Accordingly, persons, amongst others, who (i) encourage (or reinforce the decision regarding) the commission of an offence; (ii) provide counsel as to how to commit a specific crime or supply the means used for its commission; and (iii) facilitate by assisting its execution are considered culpable as an *assistant* under TCC 2004.[231] In other words, although TPL 1961 stipulates a monetary penalty of tax loss caused for enablers of fraudulent tax arrangements,[232] Türkiye addresses them through general provisions applicable to all accomplices regardless of the type of the crime relating to determining entailing penalties. Therefore, in light of

226 Umut Turksen, Ismail U Misirlioglu and Osman Yukselturk, 'Anti-Money Laundering Law of Turkey and the EU: An Example of Convergence?' (2011) 14(3) Journal of Money Laundering Control 279; Turksen (n 120); Engin Erken, 'Institutional Corruption and Avoidance of Taxation – VIRTEU Roundtable' (*The Corporate Social Responsibility and Business Ethics Blog*, 26 March 2021) <https://corporatesocialresponsibilityblogcom.files.wordpress.com/2021/03/virteu-roundtable-session-4-institutional-corruption-1.pdf> accessed 21 February 2023.

227 Umut Turksen and others, *Tax Crimes and Enforcement in the European Union: Solutions for Law, Policy and Practice* (OUP 2023).

228 OECD, 'Ending the Shell Game: Cracking Down On the Professionals Who Enable Tax and White Collar Crimes' (2021) 10 <www.oecd.org/tax/crime/ending-the-shell-game-cracking-down-on-the-professionals-who-enable-tax-and-white-collar-crime.pdf> accessed 24 February 2023.

229 Law No 5237 (Turkish Criminal Code) 2004, arts 37–41.

230 Law No 213 (Tax Procedure Law) 1961, art 360.

231 Law No 5237 (Turkish Criminal Code) 2004, art 39(2).

232 Law No 213 (Tax Procedure Law) 1961, art 344(2).

relevant provisions of TPL 1961 (i.e., Article 360) and TCC 2004 (i.e., Article 39), in addition to the monetary penalty specified previously, the maximum imprisonment sentence term leviable on an enabler in Türkiye is 30 months, approximately one-third of the prison term envisaged in the UK.

Whilst Türkiye deals with enablers through *lex generalis*, the UK exploits a wide range of legal instruments (see, for instance, Schedule 38 of the Finance Act 2012 that stipulates provisions for dishonest conduct undertaken by 'tax agents'),[233] including common law,[234] in establishing the scope of enablers of tax crimes. The penal framework in the UK further addresses enablers of abusive tax practices (i.e., tax avoidance) that consist of persons who design, manage, market the arrangements or who are enabling participant(s) in the arrangements or financial enabler(s) concerning the arrangements.[235] Accordingly, a professional enabler in the UK (concerning income tax evasion, for instance) can face a maximum imprisonment sentence of seven years and/or an unlimited fine,[236] suggesting a more severe penal framework envisaged for enablers compared to Türkiye. It is worth underlining the differences in the severity of penalties in the two jurisdictions because an empirical study conducted on behalf of HMRC in the UK documented that imprisonment of individuals in the organisation complicit in the tax evasion is the most effective sanction perceived for enablers and facilitators of tax evasion.[237] That is not to say that it is a frequently utilised sanction mechanism in the UK[238] if any, but the presence of such penalties serves as a deterrent, at least theoretically. Therefore, introducing more severe thus deterrent sanctions for enablers of fraudulent tax practices under *lex specialis* (i.e., TPL 1961) in Türkiye would increase the contribution of pertinent obliged entities (e.g., accountants) to the national AML efforts (e.g., STR submission exercises) of the jurisdiction. It is also necessary to state that, as per the associated threat posed by professional enablers, the UK established the Enabler Practitioners Group (EPG), an Intelligence Sharing Expert Working Group (ISEWG), which became operational under the auspices of the NECC in 2019.[239] Similar to how JMLIT

233 Finance Act (FA) 2012, sch 38.

234 *Scott v Metropolitan Police Commissioner* [1975] AC 819.

235 Finance (No 2) Act 2017, sch 16(7).

236 Taxes Management Act (TMA) 1970, s 106A.

237 IFF Research, 'Enablers and Facilitators of Tax Evasion' (HMRC Research Report 600, June 2019) 65 <https://assets.publishing.service.gov.uk/government/uploads/system/uploads/attachment_data/file/938747/Research_report_600_Enablers_and_Facilitators_of_Tax_Evasion.pdf> accessed 27 February 2023.

238 For example, according to the IFF Report (see ibid), whilst imprisonment serves as the most deterrent sanction, most study participants also mentioned that they believe it is the least likely penalty to be imposed.

239 OPBAS, 'Anti-Money Laundering Supervision by the Legal and Accountancy Professional Body Supervisors: Progress and Themes from 2019' (March 2020) 19 <www.fca.org.uk/publication/opbas/supervisory-report-progress-themes-2019.pdf> accessed 25 February 2023.

serves, the EPG facilitates sharing of information between competent authorities relating to identifying cases involving professional enablers.[240] That is to say that the tax (enforcement) regime addressing professional enablers in the UK is tailored to unique threats posed by them accordingly, which renders it more effective than in Türkiye in detecting, punishing where appropriate, and deterring dishonest services for enabling tax crimes. For example, according to a Freedom of Information Act 2000 release communicated by the HMRC on 14 May 2021, HMRC declared that it was then investigating 153 suspected enablers of tax evasion, including but not limited to unregulated tax advisors,[241] whereby more than 60 were prosecuted since April 2017.[242] Concerning such tax advisors in Türkiye, although Türkiye has designated tax offences as predicate crimes since 1996, certified public accountants operating independently (i.e., without an employer) in Türkiye became obliged entities only in 2015[243] due to legal actions taken by TURMOB.[244] Given the role of TURMOB in setting professional standards for its members (i.e., accounting and auditing professionals), as discussed in Chapter 7 previously, this unenthusiastic approach they presented signifies the potential reasons for the inadequate STR submissions of such obliged entities. Therefore, it can be argued that there is considerable room for improving the AML ecosystem in Türkiye in terms of addressing the predicate crimes of tax offences.

Given the transnational and sophisticated nature of tax offences,[245] establishing a holistic approach to tackling tax crimes requires intrinsically ensuring that international cooperation mechanisms are available for national tax authorities (see Principle 9 of the TGPs).[246] As per this principle, in addition to the HMRC's global network of Fiscal Crime Liaison Officers (see Chapter 6), the UK further reinforced its capabilities in exchanging intelligence

240 ibid.

241 Michelle Sloane and Alice Kemp, 'HMRC Targets Enablers of Tax Evasion' (*RPC*, 27 October 2021) <www.rpc.co.uk/perspectives/tax-take/hmrc-targets-enablers-of-tax-evasion/> accessed 24 February 2023.

242 York (n 213).

243 See the Council of State decision dated 11 February 2015 (i.e., Danıştay İdari Dava Daireleri Genel Kurulu Kararı (Esas Sayısı: 2014/3871, Karar Sayısı: 2015/330).

244 It is necessary to state that although certified public accountants have been regarded as obliged entities since 2008 as per ROM 2008 (art 4(1)(t)), TURMOB filed a lawsuit in the Council of State for the annulment of the relevant provisions of ROM 2008 and the stay of execution, thereby rendering the process prolonged. For a more detailed discussion on the process relating to the designation of accounting and auditing professionals as obliged entities, see TURMOB, 'Serbest Muhasebeci Mali Müşavirlerin 5549 Sayılı Suç Gelirlerinin Aklanmasının Önlenmesi Hakkında Kanun Kapsamındaki Yükümlülükleri' (February 2017) 13–14 <www.turmob.org.tr/ekutuphane/detailPdf/11cf6ac2-7e4f-4f0d-a99d-b8e0660350aa/serbest-muhasebeci-mali-musavirlerin-5549-sayili-suc-gelirlerinin-aklanmasinin-onlenmesi-hakkinda-ka> 25 February 2023.

245 Friedrich Schneider, 'The Financial Flows of Transnational Crime and Tax Fraud in OECD Countries: What Do We (Not) Know?' (2013) 41(5) Public Finance Review 677.

246 OECD (n 129).

and expertise internationally by allying with tax enforcement bodies from Australia, Canada, the Netherlands, and the USA in 2018.[247] This alliance, namely the Joint Chiefs of Global Tax Enforcement (J5), has enabled its partners to proactively exchange more information than the previous decade combined since its inception.[248] It is worth noting that tackling ML deriving from tax evasion enabled by professionals constitutes one of the primary focus areas of the J5,[249] suggesting that the UK has extended its national efforts addressing professional enablers to the international tax enforcement sphere as well. HMRC contributes to the J5 predominantly through its Offshore, Corporate and Wealthy (OCW) Unit,[250] a component of the special task force created in response to the Panama Papers scandal in 2016.[251] The Panama Papers Taskforce has secured the investigation of at least 66 suspects relating to tax evasion, whereby HMRC has arrested at least four offenders accordingly.[252] From a more concentrated perspective, the OCW Unit of HMRC ensured a three times increase in prison sentences envisaged for convicted tax evaders in 2020–2021 (67 years) compared to the previous year (23 years),[253] signifying the effectiveness of its international cooperation mechanisms. On the other hand, although Türkiye has signed 95 bilateral treaties within the scope of taxation, these agreements primarily concern the principle of *ne bis in idem* and aim to prevent double taxation.[254] Remarkably, Türkiye has also signed 'exchange of information treaties on tax matters' with Jersey, Bermuda, Guernsey, the Isle of Man, and Gibraltar,[255] prominent tax havens[256] known

247 HMRC, 'Tax Chiefs Unite to Tackle International Tax Crime' (*Press Release*, 2 July 2018) <www.gov.uk/government/news/tax-chiefs-unite-to-tackle-international-tax-crime> accessed 25 February 2023.

248 IRS, 'Joint Chiefs of Global Tax Enforcement Successes' (June 2021) <www.irs.gov/pub/foia/ig/ci/j5-one-pager-07-14-2020.pdf> accessed 25 February 2023.

249 ibid.

250 Andrew Sackey, 'The J5: Tax Enforcement Without Borders' (*Tax Journal*, 20 January 2020) <www.taxjournal.com/articles/the-j5-tax-enforcement-without-borders> accessed 25 February 2023.

251 HM Treasury and others, 'UK Launches Cross-Government Taskforce on the "Panama Papers"' (*Press Release*, 10 April 2016) <www.gov.uk/government/news/uk-launches-cross-government-taskforce-on-the-panama-papers> accessed 31 May 2023.

252 Seely (n 124) 109.

253 Tax Journal, 'HMRC's OCW Unit Secures Increase in Prison Time for Evaders' (*Tax Journal*, 4 August 2021) <www.taxjournal.com/articles/hmrc-s-ocw-unit-secures-increase-in-prison-time-for-evaders> accessed 25 February 2023.

254 Gelir İdaresi Başkanlığı (n 173) 114. For a more detailed discussion on the principle of *ne bis in idem* and double taxation, see Peter J Wattel, 'Ne Bis in Idem and Tax Offences in EU Law and ECHR Law' in Bas van Bockel (ed), *Ne Bis in Idem in EU Law* (CUP 2016).

255 Gelir İdaresi Başkanlığı (n 173) 116.

256 Norman Mugarura, 'Tax Havens, Offshore Financial Centres and the Current Sanctions Regimes' (2017) 24(2) Journal of Financial Crime 200.

as tax evasion and ML centres in the world.[257] However, there are no data available as to whether Türkiye has benefited from the information-sharing partnerships established with such jurisdictions relating to, amongst others, identifying ML or underlying tax crimes, thereby securing convictions and confiscations. Whilst these initiatives can be considered Türkiye's efforts for ensuring an international cooperation mechanism as per the TGPs (Principle 9), Türkiye does not have any liaison officer abroad that would enhance its capabilities in addressing the border-free nature of tax offences. That is to say that undertaking more concrete steps (e.g., stationing liaison officers in key jurisdictions abroad) would help Türkiye create a more effective international network in this context, thereby tackling tax offences and the associated ML more effectively.

8.4 Conclusion

The scope of predicate crimes has gradually enlarged as per the emerging (financial) threats and the priority attached to those menaces globally. Jurisdictions have originally established their national AML structures concerning targeting drug-related offences, the first recognised predicate crime internationally. Despite more and more crimes (e.g., from tax evasion/fraud to terrorism and cybercrime) having been considered as predicate offences, states have endeavoured to tackle the plethora of predicate crimes by the identical AML compositions established to address ML deriving from the drug predicament at the outset. Given that the different nature of such offences with unique characteristics may prevent competent authorities from performing unvaryingly effectively, investigating the law in action in Türkiye and the UK relating to tackling the riskiest predicate crimes therein (i.e., drug trafficking and tax offences) provides insights into the effectiveness and appropriateness of AML frameworks in addressing dissimilar violations of the law.

Among other characteristics (e.g., demographics), the geographical position of Türkiye (i.e., transit and target country) and the UK (i.e., destination jurisdiction) render them more vulnerable to a high-level ML threat deriving from illicit drug trafficking as the two components of the Balkan Route and EU-neighbouring jurisdictions. Accordingly, Türkiye and the UK have placed several national strategy documents and action plans and introduced legal (e.g., increase in the penalties envisaged) and institutional responses (e.g., the creation of TADOC in Türkiye) addressing the root of the problem. From an AML perspective, as per the spirit of the National Strategy Document and Action Plan on Combatting Drugs 2018–2023, Türkiye has reinforced its institutional AML armada targeting illicit drug trafficking by creating, *inter alia*, the Bureau of Combatting Proceeds of Crime (GDS), the

257 Nicholas Shaxson, *Treasure Islands: Tax Havens – Tax Havens and the Men Who Stole the World* (Bodley Head 2011).

Counter Narcotics Training Academy, the Narcotics Crime Department and NARKOKIMs (CE), albeit failing to establish a separate unit within MASAK dedicated to the identification of the proceeds of drug trafficking. On par with these institutional amendments, Türkiye has increasingly identified more illicit drug trafficking and the associated ML incidents, suggesting the functionality of such AML modifications in addressing particular predicate crimes. Similarly, JITs established with domestic and international counterparts concerning illicit drug trafficking have ensured LEAs in Türkiye to secure the confiscation of a monetary amount that equals approximately the value of confiscation orders made in the UK concerning all crimes in recent years. That is to say that introducing AML amendments that have a direct and practical impact as to how the law operates in action can help jurisdictions curb underlying predicate crimes, thereby enhancing the overall AML effectiveness. Nevertheless, Türkiye would further benefit from adhering to its strategic plan of forming a dedicated unit under the auspices of MASAK and introducing far-reaching legal provisions (e.g., similar to the UK's notion of criminal lifestyle offences and the associated recovery powers) to be even more productive in this context. In other words, the current AML structure in Türkiye seems to be effective in addressing illicit drug trafficking (and similar *conventional* predicate crimes) and the associated ML predicament, albeit there is more opportunity to become even more efficacious in this context.

Unlike many other ML predicates, the technical expertise required for committing, identifying, and tackling tax offences renders these predicate crimes unique in many ways. That being the case, both perpetrating and countering criminal tax compliance necessitate the active involvement of expert individuals, such as enablers for the former and financial investigators for the latter, on most occasions, if not all. Accordingly, such attributes of tax crimes render it more crucial to establish an effective inter-agency cooperation and communication mechanism both domestically and internationally for countering these transnational offences. Equally important is the accountability of enablers. For any national legal regime to be effective in the fight against tax offences and the associated ML, legal provisions envisaged for enablers must be deterrent, adhered to, and implemented decisively. Whilst unique characteristics of a national AML structure embraced may be effective in detecting and countering ML deriving from certain predicate crimes, such as smuggling offences, it may show deficiencies in addressing others with more sophisticated elements. Although Türkiye and the UK designated tax offences as a predicate crime for ML in the 1990s, long before there was an international commitment to do so, their pertinent legal and institutional frameworks manifest significant differences regarding inter-agency cooperation and the handling of tax offenders and enablers. Whilst the fiscal regimes adopted in Türkiye and the UK, excluding the failure to prevent the facilitation of tax evasion as envisaged for corporations in the latter, stipulate similar provisions in establishing tax crimes, the penal framework in the UK provides for stiffer criminal sanctions both for tax offenders and enablers. Additionally, as per the associated skills required for countering tax crimes, whilst the UK has bestowed LEA powers and direct access ability to the FIU data on its tax enforcement authority, tackling tax offences and the associated ML in Türkiye necessitates an integrated operational approach created between MASAK, LEAs, tax authorities, and public prosecutors due to the relatively limited/restricted set of legal powers granted on each agency separately. Although Türkiye, considering the expertise requiring nature of the predicament, established specialised criminal tax courts and, notwithstanding its legal conventions, requires the *obiter dictum* of tax officials for opening a criminal case regarding tax evasion/fraud, these measures pertain to the judicial handling of such offenders. Therefore, such amendments and considerations have nothing to do with proactively tackling ML and its underlying tax offences, albeit may explain the increased sentencing figures and the related judicial efficiency. Such judicial outcomes also signify the differences in the two jurisdictions' priorities in approaching tax offenders, where the revenue collection has historically been the primary objective for the tax authorities in the UK. That is not to say that tax authorities in Türkiye do not seek to collect revenue in the first place, but the UK has introduced novel procedures (e.g., CDF) that replace criminal investigation conditionally. Nevertheless, considering the substantial difference in the imprisonment sentencing figures and the associated monetary penalties imposed in favour of Türkiye, Türkiye's legal regime addressing tax offenders can be considered as more deterrent, albeit the associated AML performance is not certain. Whilst introducing the General Directorate of Risk Analysis has enabled competent authorities in Türkiye to address the problem on an RBA, embedding VDK representatives in MASAK would eliminate the risk of potential disconnectedness in the information flow between agencies and help fully exploit the STR database. The UK's SARs Tax Evasion Group, which brings experts from HMRC and the UKFIU together, constitutes a remarkable good practice in this context.

This chapter has investigated and compared the AML structures adopted by Türkiye and the UK as to whether and how the unique characteristics of AML frameworks impact their effectiveness in addressing distinct predicate crimes differently. It has also dwelled on whether and how legal and institutional AML amendments introduced in these jurisdictions have affected the fight against ML predicates. Although well-developed information that establishes a direct link between predicate crimes and ML does not exist, available data from Türkiye indicate that institutional AML amendments have increased its AML effectiveness concerning drug-related offences in particular. However, as far as a tax evasion/fraud-related ML problem is concerned, the AML composition adopted in Türkiye seems to be far from achieving a similar effectiveness to its efficacy in countering illicit drug trafficking and the associated ML problem. This predicate crime-related difference is not evident concerning the UK's AML framework. It suggests, amongst others, that institutional choices in structuring AML compositions (e.g., the type of FIU adopted), the accessibility of STR/SAR databases, and the presence of permanent JITs are key determiners of the success in countering all predicate crimes regardless of their nature. The insufficient contribution of particular obliged entities (e.g., accountants and auditors), the discretion right in providing information granted to competent authorities with different legal powers and priorities, and the lack of national and international liaison networks (e.g., FCLO and J5) and working groups (e.g., EPG) constitute the principal reasons for the discrepancy observed in tackling predicate crime effectiveness in Türkiye. Therefore, in order to address all predicate crimes effectively, jurisdictions need to dwell on the unique nature of each underlying ML offence and act accordingly. Last but not least, both Türkiye and the UK would benefit from collecting/capturing relevant statistics and rendering them accessible, thereby enabling a more transparent/healthy crime/success evaluation.

Reference List

Alldridge P, 'Tax Avoidance, Tax Evasion, Money Laundering and the Problem of "Offshore"' in S Rose-Ackerman and P Lagunes (eds), *Greed, Corruption, and the Modern State* (Edward Elgar Publishing 2015)

——— and Mumford A, 'Tax Evasion and the Proceeds of Crime Act 2002' (2005) 25(3) Legal Studies 353

Basaranel BU and Turksen U, *Counter-Terrorist Financing Law and Policy: An Analysis of Turkey* (Routledge 2019)

Björnehed E, 'Narco-Terrorism: The Merger of the War on Drugs and the War on Terror' (2004) 6(3–4) Global Crime 305

Black DC, 'Review of Drugs: Summary (Accessible Version)' (Home Office Independent Report, February 2020) <www.gov.uk/government/publications/review-of-drugs-phase-one-report/review-of-drugs-summary> accessed 8 March 2023

Braithwaite V, *Taxing Democracy: Understanding Tax Avoidance and Evasion* (Routledge 2003)

Cilluffo F, 'The Threat Posed from the Convergence of Organized Crime, Drug Trafficking, and Terrorism' (Testimony of the Deputy Director of Global Organized Crime Program and the Director of Counterterrorism Task Force, Centre for Strategic and International Studies to the US House Committee on the Judiciary Subcommittee on Crime, 13 December 2000) <http://csis-website-prod.s3.amazonaws.com/s3fs-public/legacy_files/files/attachments/ts001213_cilluffo.pdf> accessed 18 January 2023

Clarke CP, 'Drugs and Thugs: Funding Terrorism Through Narcotics Trafficking' (2016) 9(3) Journal of Strategic Security 1

Committee of Public Accounts, 'Tackling Tax Fraud' (Thirty-Fourth Report of Session 2015–16, HC 674, April 2016) <https://publications.parliament.uk/pa/cm201516/cmselect/cmpubacc/674/674.pdf> accessed 23 February 2023

Crown Prosecution Service, 'The Criminal Justice System' <www.cps.gov.uk/about-cps/criminal-justice-system> accessed 28 February 2023

EGM, '07.02.2022 Tarihli Basın Açıklaması' (7 February 2022) <www.egm.gov.tr/07022022-tarihli-basin-aciklamasi> accessed 7 February 2022

EGM KOM Daire Başkanlığı, 'EMCDDA Türkiye Ulusal Raporu: Yeni Gelişmeler, Trendler, Seçilmiş Konular' (2013) <www.narkotik.pol.tr/kurumlar/narkotik.pol.tr/Arsiv/TUBIM/Documents/TURKIYE%20UYUSTURUCU%20RAPORU%202013.pdf> accessed 24 January 2023

——— 'EMCDDA Türkiye Ulusal Raporu: Yeni Gelişmeler, Trendler, Seçilmiş Konular' (2014) <www.narkotik.pol.tr/kurumlar/narkotik.pol.tr/Arsiv/TUBIM/Documents/TURKIYE%20UYUSTURUCU%20RAPORU%202014.pdf> accessed 24 January 2023

——— 'Kaçakçılık ve Organize Suçlarla Mücadele 2020 Raporu' (September2021)<www.egm.gov.tr/kurumlar/egm.gov.tr/IcSite/kom/YAYINLARIMIZ/ÜRKÇE/2020-RAPORU-TURKCE.pdf> accessed 7 February 2023

EGM Narkotik Suçlarla Mücadele Daire Başkanlığı, 'Narkotik Suçlarla Mücadele Eğitim Akademisi: Our Organization' <www.narkotik.pol.tr/nea/kurulusumuz> accessed 23 January 2023

——— 'Hakkımızda' <www.narkotik.pol.tr/narkotik-suclarla-mucadele-daire-baskanligi-hakkinda> accessed 17 February 2023

EMCDDA, 'European Drug Report 2021: Trends and Developments' (Publications Office of the European Union 2021) <www.emcdda.europa.eu/system/files/publications/13838/TDAT21001ENN.pdf> accessed 18 January 2023

——— 'EU Drug Market: Cocaine' (2022) <www.emcdda.europa.eu/publications/eu-drug-markets/cocaine_en> accessed 19 May 2023

——— 'EU Drug Market: Methamphetamine' (2022) <www.emcdda.europa.eu/publications/eu-drug-markets/methamphetamine_en> accessed 19 May 2023

——— 'Turkish National Focal Point' <www.emcdda.europa.eu/about/partners/reitox/turkey_en> accessed 17 February 2023

Erken E, 'Institutional Corruption and Avoidance of Taxation – VIRTEU Roundtable' (*The Corporate Social Responsibility and Business Ethics Blog*, 26 March 2021) <https://corporatesocialresponsibilityblogcom.files.wordpress.com/2021/03/virteu-roundtable-session-4-institutional-corruption-1.pdf> accessed 21 February 2023

Europol, 'European Union Serious and Organised Crime Threat Assessment (EU SOCTA 2021) – A Corrupting Influence: The Infiltration and Undermining of Europe's Economy and Society by Organised Crime' (2021) <www.europol.europa.eu/cms/sites/default/files/documents/socta2021_1.pdf> accessed 16 February 2023

FATF, 'Anti-Money Laundering and Counter-Terrorist Financing Measures – United Kingdom: Mutual Evaluation Report' (December 2018) <www.fatf-gafi.org/media/fatf/documents/reports/mer4/MER-United-Kingdom-2018.pdf> accessed 18 January 2023

——— 'Anti-Money Laundering and Counter-Terrorist Financing Measures – Turkey: Mutual Evaluation Report' (December 2019) <www.fatf-gafi.org/media/fatf/documents/reports/mer4/Mutual-Evaluation-Report-Turkey-2019.pdf> accessed 18 January 2023

——— 'International Standards on Combatting Money Laundering and the Financing of Terrorism & Proliferation: The FATF Recommendations' (Updated March 2022) <www.fatf-gafi.org/media/fatf/documents/recommendations/pdfs/FATF%20Recommendations%202012.pdf> accessed 26 June 2023

Fisher J and Clifford A, *The Criminal Finances Act 2017* (Informa Law 2018)

Fitzgibbon W and Hudson M, 'Five Years Later, Panama Papers Still Having a Big Impact ' (*ICIJ*, 3 April 2021) <www.icij.org/investigations/panama-papers/five-years-later-panama-papers-still-having-a-big-impact/> accessed 6 February 2023

Galizia MC and others, 'Explore the Documents: Luxembourg Leaks Database ' (*ICIJ*, 5 November 2014) <www.icij.org/investigations/luxembourg-leaks/explore-documents-luxembourg-leaks-database/> accessed 6 February 2023

Gallant MM, *Money Laundering and the Proceeds of Crime: Economic Crime and Civil Remedies* (Edward Elgar Publishing 2005)

Gelir İdaresi Başkanlığı, '2020 Faaliyet Raporu' (February 2021) <www.gib.gov.tr/sites/default/files/fileadmin/faaliyetraporlari/2020/2020_faaliyet_raporu.pdf> accessed 7 February 2023

GMGM, '2020 Faaliyet Raporu' (2021) <https://muhafaza.ticaret.gov.tr/data/5d31b1ee13b876092c062161/faaliyet%20raporu%202020.pdf> accessed 9 February 2023

——— 'Gümrük Muhafazadan Avrupa'da Ses Getiren Uluslararası Uyuşturucu Operasyonu' (7 February 2022) <https://muhafaza.ticaret.gov.tr/haberler/

kacakcilikla-mucadele/gumruk-muhafazadan-avrupada-ses-getiren-uluslararasi-uyusturucu-operasyonu> accessed 7 February 2023

Harrison K and Ryder N, 'The Avoidance and Evasion of Tax' in K Harrison and N Ryder (eds), *The Law Relating to Financial Crime in the United Kingdom* (2nd edn, Routledge 2016)

HJI Panayi C, *Advanced Issues in International and European Tax Law* (Hart Publishing 2015)

HMRC, 'Code of Practice 9' (June 2014) <https://assets.publishing.service.gov.uk/government/uploads/system/uploads/attachment_data/file/494808/COP9_06_14.pdf> accessed 23 February 2023

——— 'Tax Chiefs Unite to Tackle International Tax Crime' (*Press Release*, 2 July 2018) <www.gov.uk/government/news/tax-chiefs-unite-to-tackle-international-tax-crime> accessed 25 February 2023

——— 'Guidance: HMRC's Criminal Investigation Policy' (Updated 13 July 2021) <www.gov.uk/government/publications/criminal-investigation/hmrc-criminal-investigation-policy> accessed 12 February 2023

——— 'Guidance: HMRC's Criminal Investigation Powers and Safeguards' (Updated 13 July 2021) <www.gov.uk/government/publications/criminal-investigation/criminal-investigation> accessed 12 February 2023

——— 'Measuring Tax Gaps 2021 Edition – Tax Gap Estimates for 2019 to 2020' (September 2021) <www.gov.uk/government/statistics/measuring-tax-gaps/measuring-tax-gaps-2021-edition-tax-gap-estimates-for-2019-to-2020> accessed 1 February 2023

——— 'HM Revenue and Customs Annual Report and Accounts 2020 to 2021' (HC 696, November 2021) <https://assets.publishing.service.gov.uk/government/uploads/system/uploads/attachment_data/file/1035550/HMRC_Annual_Report_and_Accounts_2020_to_2021__Print_.pdf> accessed 23 February 2023

——— 'Counter Fraud in HMRC' <https://fraudinvestigationjobs.hmrc.gov.uk/criminal-justice-in-hmrc/overview/> accessed 12 February 2023

HM Treasury and HMRC, 'Tackling Tax Avoidance, Evasion, and Other Forms of Non-Compliance' (March 2019) <https://assets.publishing.service.gov.uk/government/uploads/system/uploads/attachment_data/file/785551/tackling_tax_avoidance_evasion_and_other_forms_of_non-compliance_web.pdf> accessed 2 February 2023

HM Treasury and Home Office, 'National Risk Assessment of Money Laundering and Terrorist Financing 2020' (December 2020) <https://assets.publishing.service.gov.uk/government/uploads/system/uploads/attachment_data/file/945411/NRA_2020_v1.2_FOR_PUBLICATION.pdf> accessed 26 June 2023

——— 'Economic Crime Plan, 2019 to 2022' (Policy Paper, updated 4 May 2021) <www.gov.uk/government/publications/economic-crime-plan-2019-to-2022/economic-crime-plan-2019-to-2022-accessible-version> accessed 9 February 2023

HM Treasury and others, 'UK Launches Cross-Government Taskforce on the "Panama Papers"' (*Press Release*, 10 April 2016) <www.gov.uk/government/news/uk-launches-cross-government-taskforce-on-the-panama-papers> accessed 31 May 2023

Home Office, 'Asset Recovery Statistical Bulletin: Financial Years Ending 2016 to 2021' (September 2021) <www.gov.uk/government/statistics/asset-recovery-statistical-bulletin-financial-years-ending-2016-to-2021/asset-recovery-statistical-bulletin-financial-years-ending-2016-to-2021> accessed 19 August 2023

——— and others, 'United Kingdom Drug Situation 2019: Focal Point Annual Report' (Updated 31 March 2021) <www.gov.uk/government/publications/united-kingdom-drug-situation-focal-point-annual-report/united-kingdom-drug-situation-focal-point-annual-report-2019> accessed 4 April 2023

ICIJ, 'Offshore Havens and Hidden Riches of World Leaders and Billionaires Exposed in Unprecedented Leak' (*ICIJ*, 3 October 2021) <www.icij.org/investigations/pandora-papers/global-investigation-tax-havens-offshore/> accessed 6 February 2023

IFF Research, 'Enablers and Facilitators of Tax Evasion' (HMRC Research Report 600, June 2019) <https://assets.publishing.service.gov.uk/government/uploads/system/uploads/attachment_data/file/938747/Research_report_600_Enablers_and_Facilitators_of_Tax_Evasion.pdf> accessed 27 February 2023

International Narcotics Control Board, 'Precursors and Chemicals Frequently Used in the Illicit Manufacture of Narcotic Drugs and Psychotropic Substances' (Report of the International Narcotics Control Board for 2020 on the Implementation of Article 12 of the United Nations Convention Against Illicit Traffic in Narcotic Drugs and Psychotropic Substances of 1988, January 2021) <www.incb.org/documents/PRECURSORS/TECHNICAL_REPORTS/2020/AR_with_Annexes/Precursors_with_annex_E_eBook_final_rev.pdf> accessed 28 January 2023

IRS, 'Joint Chiefs of Global Tax Enforcement Successes' (June 2021) <www.irs.gov/pub/foia/ig/ci/j5-one-pager-07-14-2020.pdf> accessed 25 February 2023

KOM Anti-Smuggling and Organized Crime Department, 'Turkish International Academy Against Drugs and Organized Crime Bulletin 2019–2020' (2020) <www.egm.gov.tr/kurumlar/egm.gov.tr/IcSite/tadoc/2019_20_BulletinENGLISH.pdf> accessed 17 February 2023

Lewis R, 'Drugs, War and Crime in the Post-Soviet Balkans' in V Ruggiero, N South and IR Taylor (eds), *The New European Criminology: Crime and Social Order in Europe* (Routledge 1998)

MASAK, 'Faaliyet Raporu 2020' (2021) <https://ms.hmb.gov.tr/uploads/sites/12/2021/09/Faaliyet-Raporu-2020.pdf> accessed 18 January 2023

McBain G, 'Modernising the Common Law Offence of Cheating the Public Revenue' (2015) 8(1) Journal of Politics and Law 40

Ministry of Justice General Directorate of Judicial Record and Statistics, 'Judicial Statistics 2019' (August 2020) <https://adlisicil.adalet.gov.tr/Resimler/SayfaDokuman/1092020162733adalet_ist-2019.pdf> accessed 1 February 2023

——— 'Judicial Statistics 2020' (September 2021) <https://adlisicil.adalet.gov.tr/Resimler/SayfaDokuman/1692021162011adalet_ist-2020.pdf> accessed 1 February 2023

Mugarura N, 'Tax Havens, Offshore Financial Centres and the Current Sanctions Regimes' (2017) 24(2) Journal of Financial Crime 200

National Audit Office, 'Tackling Tax Fraud: How HMRC Responds to Tax Evasion, the Hidden Economy and Criminal Attacks' (HC 610, December 2015) <www.nao.org.uk/wp-content/uploads/2015/12/Tackling-tax-fraud-how-HMRC-responds-to-tax-evasion-the-hidden-economy-and-criminal-attacks.pdf> accessed 23 February 2023

NCA, 'UK Financial Intelligence Unit Suspicious Activity Reports Annual Report 2020' (April 2020) <www.nationalcrimeagency.gov.uk/who-we-are/publications/480-sars-annual-report-2020/file> accessed 24 February 2023

——— 'NCA Secures First Serious Organised Crime Unexplained Wealth Order for Property Worth £10 Million' (*Press Release*, 25 March 2022) <www.nationalcrimeagency.gov.uk/news/nca-secures-first-serious-organised-crime-unexplained-wealth-order-for-property-worth-10-million> accessed 4 April 2023

OECD, 'Money Laundering Awareness Handbook for Tax Examiners and Tax Auditors' (2009) <www.oecd.org/ctp/crime/money-laundering-awareness-handbook-for-tax-examiners-and-tax-auditors.pdf> accessed 6 February 2023

——— 'Improving Co-operation Between Tax and Anti-Money Laundering Authorities: Access by Tax Administrations to Information Held by Financial Intelligence Units for Criminal and Civil Purposes' (September 2015) <www.oecd.org/ctp/crime/

report-improving-cooperation-between-tax-anti-money-laundering-authorities.pdf> accessed 12 February 2023

——— *Effective Inter-Agency Co-Operation in Fighting Tax Crimes and Other Financial Crimes* (3rd edn, OECD Publishing 2017) <www.oecd.org/tax/crime/effective-inter-agency-co-operation-in-fighting-tax-crimes-and-other-financial-crimes-third-edition.pdf> accessed 14 February 2023

——— *Money Laundering and Terrorist Financing Awareness Handbook for Tax Examiners and Tax Auditors* (OECD Publishing 2019) <www.oecd.org/tax/crime/money-laundering-and-terrorist-financing-awareness-handbook-for-tax-examiners-and-tax-auditors.pdf> accessed 1 February 2023

——— 'Tax Crime Investigation Maturity Model' (2020) <www.oecd.org/tax/crime/tax-crime-investigation-maturity-model.pdf> accessed 12 February 2023

——— 'Ending the Shell Game: Cracking Down On the Professionals Who Enable Tax and White Collar Crimes' (2021) <www.oecd.org/tax/crime/ending-the-shell-game-cracking-down-on-the-professionals-who-enable-tax-and-white-collar-crime.pdf> accessed 24 February 2023

——— *Fighting Tax Crime: The Ten Global Principles* (2nd edn, OECD Publishing 2021) <www.oecd-ilibrary.org/sites/006a6512-en/index.html?itemId=/content/publication/006a6512-en> accessed 14 February 2023

——— *Fighting Tax Crime – The Ten Global Principles: Country Chapters* (2nd edn, OECD Publishing 2021) <www.oecd.org/tax/crime/fighting-tax-crime-the-ten-global-principles-second-edition-country-chapters.pdf?_ga=2.247447682.740417271.1644849908-1796273601.1644849908> accessed 1 February 2023

——— 'List of OECD Member Countries – Ratification of the Convention on the OECD' <www.oecd.org/about/document/ratification-oecd-convention.htm> accessed 8 March 2022

——— 'Glossary of Tax Terms' <www.oecd.org/ctp/glossaryoftaxterms.htm#T> accessed 2 February 2023

Office for National Statistics, 'Crime in England and Wales: Appendix Tables – Table A4' (November 2021) <www.ons.gov.uk/file?uri=%2fpeoplepopulationandcommunity%2fcrimeandjustice%2fdatasets%2fcrimeinenglandandwalesappendixtables%2fyearendingjune2021/appendixtablejun21final.xlsx> accessed 24 January 2023

Omerod D, 'Cheating the Public Revenue' [1998] Criminal Law Review 627

OPBAS, 'Anti-Money Laundering Supervision by the Legal and Accountancy Professional Body Supervisors: Progress and Themes from 2019' (March 2020) <www.fca.org.uk/publication/opbas/supervisory-report-progress-themes-2019.pdf> accessed 25 February 2023

Raczkowski K and Mroz B, 'The Tax Gap in the Global Economy' (2018) 21(4) Journal of Money Laundering Control 567

Revenue Administration, <www.gib.gov.tr/en> accessed 7 February 2023

Robins P, 'Public Policy Making in Turkey: Faltering Attempts to Generate a National Drugs Policy' (2009) 37(2) Policy and Politics 289

Rossel L, Unger B and Ferwerda J, 'Shedding Light Inside the Black Box of Implementation: Tax Crimes as a Predicate Crime for Money Laundering' (2021) 16 Regulation & Governance <https://doi.org/10.1111/rego.12407> accessed 3 February 2023

Rossel L and others, 'The Implications of Making Tax Crimes a Predicate Crime for Money Laundering in the EU: Building a Legal Dataset of Tax Crimes and Money Laundering in the European Union' in B Unger, L Rossel and J Ferwerda (eds), *Combatting Fiscal Fraud and Empowering Regulators: Bringing Tax Money Back into the COFFERS* (OUP 2021)

Ryder N, *Financial Crimes in the 21st Century: Law and Policy* (Edward Elgar Publishing 2011)

Ryle G and others, 'About This Project: Swiss Leaks' (*ICIJ*, 8 February 2015) <www.icij.org/investigations/swiss-leaks/about-project-swiss-leaks/> accessed 6 February 2023

Sackey A, 'The J5: Tax Enforcement Without Borders' (*Tax Journal*, 20 January 2020) <www.taxjournal.com/articles/the-j5-tax-enforcement-without-borders> accessed 25 February 2023

Sahil Güvenlik Komutanlığı, '2020 Yılı İdare Faaliyet Raporu' (2021) <www.sg.gov.tr/kurumlar/sg.gov.tr/komutanlik/yayinlar/2020-Yili-Idare-Faaliyet-Raporu.pdf> accessed 20 January 2023

Schneider F, 'The Financial Flows of Transnational Crime and Tax Fraud in OECD Countries: What Do We (Not) Know?' (2013) 41(5) Public Finance Review 677

Seely A, 'Tax Avoidance and Tax Evasion' (UK Parliament Research Briefing Paper No 7948, November 2021) <https://researchbriefings.files.parliament.uk/documents/CBP-7948/CBP-7948.pdf> accessed 6 February 2023

Selby J, 'UK Is the Largest Consumer of Cocaine in Europe, National Crime Agency Says' *Inews* (16 May 2020) <https://inews.co.uk/news/uk-largest-consumer-cocaine-europe-national-crime-agency-428521> accessed 8 March 2023

Sentencing Council, 'Revenue Fraud' <www.sentencingcouncil.org.uk/offences/magistrates-court/item/revenue-fraud/> accessed 5 February 2023

——— 'Drug Offences' <www.sentencingcouncil.org.uk/outlines/drug-offences/> accessed 17 February 2023

Shalchi A, 'Unexplained Wealth Orders' (UK Parliament Research Briefing Paper No 9098, February 2022) <https://researchbriefings.files.parliament.uk/documents/CBP-9098/CBP-9098.pdf> accessed 4 April 2023

Shaxson N, *Treasure Islands: Tax Havens and the Men Who Stole the World* (Bodley Head 2011)

Sloane M and Kemp A, 'HMRC Targets Enablers of Tax Evasion' (*RPC*, 27 October 2021) <www.rpc.co.uk/perspectives/tax-take/hmrc-targets-enablers-of-tax-evasion/> accessed 24 February 2023

Tax Journal, 'HMRC's OCW Unit Secures Increase in Prison Time for Evaders' (*Tax Journal*, 4 August 2021) <www.taxjournal.com/articles/hmrc-s-ocw-unit-secures-increase-in-prison-time-for-evaders> accessed 25 February 2023

Tax Justice Network, 'The State of Tax Justice 2021' (November 2021) <https://taxjustice.net/wp-content/uploads/2021/11/State_of_Tax_Justice_Report_2021_ENGLISH.pdf> accessed 9 February 2023

TC Başbakanlık, 'Ulusal Uyuşturucu ile Mücadele Ulusal Strateji Belgesi ve Eylem Planı 2018–2023' (2018) <https://hsgm.saglik.gov.tr/depo/birimler/tutun-mucadele-bagimlilik-db/haberler/uyusturucu_eylem_plani/2018-2023_Uyusturucu_ile_Mucadele_Ulusal_Strateji_Belgesi_ve_Eylem_Plani.pdf> accessed 19 January 2023

TC Hazine ve Maliye Bakanlığı, '2020 Yılı Faaliyet Raporu' (February 2021) <https://ms.hmb.gov.tr/uploads/2021/03/2020-HMB-Idare-Faaliyet-Raporu.pdf> accessed 9 February 2023

——— 'Vergi Denetim Kurulu Başkanlığı' <www.hmb.gov.tr/vergi-denetim-kurulu-baskanligi> accessed 7 February 2023

——— 'TC Hazine ve Maliye Bakanlığı 2019–2023 Stratejik Planı' <https://ms.hmb.gov.tr/uploads/2020/03/2019-2023-Maliye-Bakanlığı-Stratejik-Planı_Basılacak-Versiyon.28.02.2020.pdf> accessed 9 February 2023

TC Hazine ve Maliye Bakanlığı GIB, 'Kayıt Dışı Ekonomiyle Mücadele Stratejisi Eylem Planı (2019–2021)' (2019) <www.gib.gov.tr/sites/default/files/fileadmin/user_upload/Kayit_Disi_Ekonomiyle_Mucadele_Stratejisi_Eylem_Plani_2019_2021.pdf> accessed 9 February 2023

TC İçişleri Bakanlığı, *Bağımlılık Yapıcı Maddeler ve Bağımlılıkla Mücadelede Ulusal Politika ve Strateji Belgesi 2006–2012* (TC İçişleri Bakanlığı 2006)

——— *Bağımlılık Yapıcı Maddeler ve Bağımlılıkla Mücadelede Ulusal Politika ve Strateji Belgesinin Uygulanması İçin Eylem Planı 2007–2009* (TC İçişleri Bakanlığı 2007)

——— 'Ulusal Uyuşturucu ile Mücadele Strateji Belgesi' (2015) <www.narkotik.pol.tr/kurumlar/narkotik.pol.tr/Arsiv/TUBIM/Documents/1-STRATEJİ%20BELGESİ_EYLEM%20PLANI_İL%20KURULLARI_2015_TR.pdf> accessed 19 January 2023

——— 'Türkiye Cumhuriyeti Uyuşturucu ile Mücadele Yüksek Kurulu Ulusal Uyuşturucu ile Mücadele Eylem Planı 2016–2018' <www.narkotik.pol.tr/kurumlar/narkotik.pol.tr/Arsiv/TUBIM/Documents/EYLEM%20PLANI_2016-2018_TR.pdf> accessed 19 January 2023

TC İçişleri Bakanlığı Jandarma Genel Komutanlığı, '2019 Yılı Verileri' <www.jandarma.gov.tr/2019-yili-verileri> accessed 7 February 2023

——— '2020 Yılı Faaliyet Raporu' (January 2021) <www.jandarma.gov.tr/kurumlar/jandarma.gov.tr/Duyurular/subat-2021/JANDARMA-GENEL-KOMUTANLIGI-2020-YILI-FAALIYET-RAPORU.pdf> accessed 9 February 2023

——— '2020 Yılı Verileri' <www.jandarma.gov.tr/2020-yili-verileri> accessed 7 February 2023

——— '2021 Yılı Verileri' <www.jandarma.gov.tr/2021-yili-verileri> accessed 7 February 2023

TC Ticaret Bakanlığı, '2018 Faaliyet Raporu' (2019) <https://muhafaza.ticaret.gov.tr/data/5d31b1ee13b876092c062161/2018%20FALİYET%20RAPORU.pdf> accessed 20 January 2023

Thomas JE, 'Narco-Terrorism: Could the Legislative and Prosecutorial Responses Threaten Our Civil Liberties?' (2009) 66(4) Washington and Lee Law Review 1881

TRTWorld, 'Turkey Carries Out Its Largest-Ever Narcotics Operation, Arrests Dozens' (*TRT World*, 30 June 2020) <www.trtworld.com/turkey/turkey-carries-out-its-largest-ever-narcotics-operation-arrests-dozens-37750> accessed 20 January 2023

Turkish National Police Counter Narcotics Department, '2015 Turkish National Drug Report' (2017) <www.narkotik.pol.tr/kurumlar/narkotik.pol.tr/Arsiv/TUBIM/Documents/2015%20TURKISH%20NATIONAL%20DRUG%20REPORT.pdf> accessed 24 January 2023

——— '2016 Turkish National Drug Report' (2017) <www.narkotik.pol.tr/kurumlar/narkotik.pol.tr/Arsiv/TUBIM/Documents/2016%20TURKISH%20NATIONAL%20DRUG%20REPORT.pdf> accessed 24 January 2023

——— '2017 Turkish National Drug Report' (2017) <www.narkotik.pol.tr/kurumlar/narkotik.pol.tr/Arsiv/TUBIM/Documents/2017%20TURKISH%20NATIONAL%20DRUG%20REPORT.pdf> accessed 24 January 2023

——— '2018 Turkish National Drug Report' (2018) <www.narkotik.pol.tr/kurumlar/narkotik.pol.tr/TUBİM/Ulusal%20Yayınlar/2018-Turkish-Drug-Report.pdf> accessed 24 January 2023

——— 'Turkish Drug Report 2019' (2019) <www.narkotik.pol.tr/kurumlar/narkotik.pol.tr/TUBİM/Ulusal%20Yayınlar/2019-TURKISH-DRUG-REPORT_30122019.pdf> accessed 24 January 2023

——— 'Turkish Drug Report: Trends and Developments' (2020) <www.narkotik.pol.tr/kurumlar/narkotik.pol.tr/TUBİM/Uluslar-Arasi-Yayinlar/2020uyusturucuraporuENG.pdf> accessed 24 January 2023

——— 'Turkish Drug Report: Trends and Developments' (2021) <www.narkotik.pol.tr/kurumlar/narkotik.pol.tr/TUBİM/2021-TURKISH-DRUG-REPORT.pdf> accessed 24 January 2023

Turksen U, 'Implications of Anti-Money Laundering Law for Accountancy in the European Union – A Comparative Study' in N Ryder, U Turksen and S Hassler (eds), *Fighting Financial Crime in the Global Economic Crisis* (1st edn, Routledge 2014)

——— *Countering Tax Crime in the European Union: Benchmarking the OECD's Ten Global Principles* (Hart Publishing 2021)

——— Misirlioglu IU and Yukselturk O, 'Anti-Money Laundering Law of Turkey and the EU: An Example of Convergence?' (2011) 14(3) Journal of Money Laundering Control 279

Turksen U and Abukari A, 'OECD's Global Principles and EU's Tax Crime Measures' (2021) 28(2) Journal of Financial Crime 406

Turksen U and others, 'Case Studies of Tax Crimes in the European Union' (787098 PROTAX EU H2020 Project D1.2, October 2018) <https://protaxwebtoolkit.eu/index.php/2021/04/23/case-studies-of-tax-crimes-in-the-eu/> accessed 12 February 2023

——— *Tax Crimes and Enforcement in the European Union: Solutions for Law, Policy and Practice* (OUP 2023)

TURMOB, 'Serbest Muhasebeci Mali Müşavirlerin 5549 Sayılı Suç Gelirlerinin Aklanmasının Önlenmesi Hakkında Kanun Kapsamındaki Yükümlülükleri' (February 2017) <www.turmob.org.tr/ekutuphane/detailPdf/11cf6ac2-7e4f-4f0d-a99d-b8e0660350aa/serbest-muhasebeci-mali-musavirlerin-5549-sayili-suc-gelirlerinin-aklanmasinin-onlenmesi-hakkinda-ka> 25 February 2023

UNODC, 'Drug Money: The Illicit Proceeds of Opiates Trafficked on the Balkan Route' (2015) <www.unodc.org/documents/rpanc/Publications/other_publications/Balkan_route_web.pdf> accessed 18 January 2023

——— 'Organized Crime' <www.unodc.org/unodc/en/organized-crime/intro.html> accessed 8 March 2023

——— *World Drug Report 2021 – Covid-19 and Drugs: Impact Outlook* (United Nations Publication, June 2021) <www.unodc.org/res/wdr2021/field/WDR21_Booklet_5.pdf> accessed 18 January 2023

——— *World Drug Report 2021 – Drug Market Trends: Cannabis Opioids* (United Nations Publication, June 2021) <www.unodc.org/res/wdr2021/field/WDR21_Booklet_3.pdf> accessed 18 January 2023

——— *World Drug Report 2021 – Drug Market Trends: Cocaine Amphetamine-Type Stimulants* (United Nations Publication, June 2021) <www.unodc.org/res/wdr2021/field/WDR21_Booklet_4.pdf> accessed 18 January 2023

——— *World Drug Report 2021 – Statistical Annex: Seizures of Illicit Drugs by Region and High-Ranking Countries* (United Nations Publication, June 2021) <https://dataunodc.un.org/data/drugs/Global%20Seizures> accessed 18 January 2023

van Duyne PC and Levi M, *Drugs and Money: Managing the Drug Trade and Crime Money in Europe* (Routledge 2005)

Vergi Denetim Kurulu Başkanlığı, 'Faaliyet Raporu 2018' (2019) <https://ms.hmb.gov.tr/uploads/2019/04/VDK-2018-Birim-Faaliyet-Raporu-1102019-002.pdf> accessed 7 February 2023

Wattel PJ, 'Ne Bis in Idem and Tax Offences in EU Law and ECHR Law' in B van Bockel (ed), *Ne Bis in Idem in EU Law* (CUP 2016)

Xe Currency Converter, 'Historical Rate Tables' <www.xe.com/currencytables/?from=TRY&date=2019-12-31#table-section> accessed 20 January 2023

——— <www.xe.com/currencyconverter/convert/?Amount=2000000&From=TRY&To=GBP> accessed 17 February 2023

——— <www.xe.com/currencyconverter/convert/?Amount=2000000000&From=TRY&To=GBP> accessed 20 January 2023

——— <www.xe.com/currencyconverter/convert/?Amount=66658208&From=TRY&To=GBP> accessed 7 February 2023

York S, 'HMRC's Response to the Rise of the Enabler' (*Tax Journal*, 26 March 2021) <www.taxjournal.com/articles/-hmrc-s-response-to-the-rise-of-the-enabler-44236> accessed 23 February 2023

Legal Instruments

International

UNGA A/RES/42/112 (7 December 1987)

United Nations Convention Against Illicit Traffic in Narcotic Drugs and Psychotropic Substances 1988

European Union

Directive (EU) 2015/849 of the European Parliament and of the Council of 20 May 2015 on the Prevention of the Use of the Financial System for the Purposes of Money Laundering or Terrorist Financing, Amending Regulation (EU) No 648/2012 of the European Parliament and of the Council, and Repealing Directive 2005/60/EC of the European Parliament and of the Council and Commission Directive 2006/70/EC (Text with EEA Relevance) [2015] OJ L 141/73

Türkiye

Constitution of the Republic of Türkiye 1982

Hakimler ve Savcılar Kurulu, 'Hakimler ve Savcılar Kurulu Birinci Dairesinin Kararı' (Decision No 1227 dated 25 November 2021) <www.hsk.gov.tr/Eklentiler/30112021092825112021-1227pdf.pdf> accessed 5 February 2023

Law No 213 (Tax Procedure Law) 1961

Law No 2313 on the Control of Narcotic Drugs 1933

Law No 3298 on the Narcotic Drugs 1986

Law No 4208 on the Prevention of Money Laundering 1996

Law No 5237 (Turkish Criminal Code) 2004

Official Gazette No 29174 dated 13 November 2014, 'Genelge 2014/19: Uyuşturucu ile Mücadele' <www.resmigazete.gov.tr/eskiler/2014/11/20141113-13.htm> accessed 19 January 2023

Official Gazette No 31103 dated 18 April 2020, 'Cumhurbaşkanlığı Kararnamesi (Kararname No 60)' <www.resmigazete.gov.tr/eskiler/2020/04/20200418-1.pdf> accessed 9 February 2023

Official Gazette No 31544 dated 17 July 2021, 'Genelge 2021/16: Türkiye'de Suç Gelirlerinin Aklanması ve Terörizmin Finansmanı ile Mücadele ve Müsadere Uygulamalarında Etkinliğin Arttırılması Strateji Belgesi (2021–2025)' <www.resmigazete.gov.tr/eskiler/2021/07/20210717-10.pdf> accessed 10 June 2023

Presidential Decree No 1 on the Organisation of the Presidency 2018

Presidential Decree No 4 2018

Regulation on Measures Regarding Prevention of Laundering the Proceeds of Crime and Financing of Terrorism (ROM) 2008

Tax Audit Board Regulation 2021

United Kingdom

Criminal Finances Act 2017

Criminal Justice Act 1988

Criminal Justice (International Co-operation) Act 1990

Customs and Excise Management Act 1979

Finance Act (FA) 2012

Finance Act (No 2) 2017

Investigatory Powers Act 2016
Misuse of Drugs Act 1971
Police and Criminal Evidence Act (PACE) 1984
Proceeds of Crime Act 2002
Serious Crime Act 2007
Taxes Management Act (TMA) 1970
Theft Act 1968
Value Added Tax Act (VATA) 1994

Cases (Türkiye)

Anayasa Mahkemesi, *Anayasa Mahkemesi Kararlar Dergisi* (Sayı: 49, 1. Cilt, Anayasa Mahkemesi Yayınları 2012) <https://anayasa.gov.tr/media/4890/kararlar_dergisi_49_1.pdf> accessed 21 February 2022
Danıştay İdari Dava Daireleri Genel Kurulu Kararı (Esas Sayısı: 2014/3871, Karar Sayısı: 2015/330, Karar Günü: 11.02.2015)

Cases (United Kingdom)

R v Hudson [1956] 2 QB 252
R v Less [1993] (unreported case)
R v Mavji [1987] 84 Cr App R 34
R v Mulligan [1990] BTC 135
Scott v Metropolitan Police Commissioner [1975] AC 819

9 Conclusion

9.1 Introduction

Among many security challenges, such as terrorism and organised crime, ML has been at the heart of the global policy agenda for decades.[1] Notably, the elevated levels of the international drug trade and associated concerns in the 1980s have motivated governments to address the phenomenon collaboratively and recognise illicit drug trafficking as a predicate crime for ML.[2] The UN-led global AML initiatives in the 1980s gave rise, amongst others, to the establishment of the FATF in 1989 and FATF Recommendations (i.e., 1990, 1996, 2003, and 2012), which have been used as a blueprint in orchestrating AML efforts globally by states since then. Whilst FATF Recommendations have widened the scope of predicate offences, many countries have endeavoured to tackle the plethora of predicate crimes with unique characteristics by the same AML compositions established to address ML deriving from the drug predicament at the outset. In other words, the effectiveness and efficiency of AML frameworks in tackling ever-growing distinctive criminal schemes depend intrinsically on the unique features of legal and institutional national AML structures designed originally for countering illicit drug trafficking, determining the overall AML capacity of a given jurisdiction concerning all predicate crimes.

Although extant literature has investigated the role of national AML structures in preventing ML offences,[3] surprisingly, their respective function in impeding predicate crimes (if any) is un(der)explored. Therefore, the main aim of this research has been to demonstrate whether and how differences between the legal and institutional AML structures may impact the effectiveness in

1 Frank Madsen, *Transnational Organized Crime* (1st edn, Routledge 2009).

2 William C Gilmore, *Dirty Money: The Evolution of International Measures to Counter Money Laundering and the Financing of Terrorism* (3rd edn, Council of Europe Publishing 2004).

3 Nicholas Ryder, *Money Laundering – An Endless Cycle? A Comparative Analysis of the Anti-Money Laundering Policies in the United States of America, the United Kingdom, Australia and Canada* (1st edn, Routledge 2012).

DOI: 10.4324/9781003466680-9

tackling and the prevalence of predicate crimes, thereby underlining the unique features of an optimum AML regime. Furthermore, given the scarcity of comparative studies devoted to the analysis of common law and civil law jurisdictions and the lack of studies comparing Türkiye and the UK in this context, a critical examination of the effectiveness of AML frameworks adopted by these jurisdictions in tackling predicate crimes is of critical importance. At this point, it is worth reiterating why this study has concentrated on Türkiye and the UK. Firstly, whilst Türkiye has always aspired to align its national AML composition with the requirements of international AML standards, there have been deficiencies as identified by the FATF.[4] Secondly, despite some challenges,[5] the UK is considered as one of the best jurisdictions in the AML domain, as documented, for instance, by the last MER of the UK conducted by the FATF,[6] constituting a sound point of reference for identifying more effective AML solutions for Türkiye. Finally, whilst there are salient differences between the two jurisdictions, Türkiye and the UK have repeatedly demonstrated similarities in approaching international matters as the two EU-neighbouring countries. In these circumstances, comparative examination of the national AML regimes of Türkiye and the UK in detail could help identify principal heterogeneities between the two jurisdictions and explain their corresponding impacts on the prevalence of divergent predicate crimes in these countries.

This book, as per its objectives, has aimed (i) to reveal the underlying reasons associated with the relevant AML legal frameworks accounting for the prevalence of different types of predicate crimes in Türkiye and the UK; (ii) to unveil the essential divergence points between the two institutional AML structures adopted by Türkiye and the UK and their impact on the prevalence of varying predicate crimes in these jurisdictions; and (iii) to shed light on the areas in need of reform, thereby enhancing the effectiveness in the fight against ML and its underlying predicate offences. Accordingly, this study has addressed three research questions investigating (i) whether the differences between the AML legal frameworks adopted by Türkiye and the UK impact the prevalence of predicate crimes (if so, how?); (ii) the unique characteristics of the two institutional AML structures that result in dissimilar predicate

4 See, for instance, FATF, 'Jurisdictions Under Increased Monitoring' (October 2021) <www.fatf-gafi.org/publications/high-risk-and-other-monitored-jurisdictions/documents/increased-monitoring-october-2021.html#turkey> accessed 24 May 2023.

5 Oliver Bullough, 'How Britain Can Help You Get Away with Stealing Millions: A Five-Step Guide' *The Guardian* (5 July 2019) <www.theguardian.com/world/2019/jul/05/how-britain-can-help-you-get-away-with-stealing-millions-a-five-step-guide> accessed 24 May 2022.

6 FATF, 'Anti-Money Laundering and Counter-Terrorist Financing Measures: United Kingdom – Mutual Evaluation Report' (December 2018) <www.fatf-gafi.org/media/fatf/documents/reports/mer4/MER-United-Kingdom-2018.pdf> accessed 18 January 2022.

crime prevalence; and (iii) the necessary steps to be taken to ensure the optimum AML composition, thereby reducing predicate crimes and increasing the recovery of criminal assets through a fit-for-purpose AML mechanism. Correspondingly, as a starting point, the study has first outlined the global AML regime, international AML actors, and their arguably limited roles in forming national AML structures. It has then examined the national AML legal frameworks established in Türkiye and the UK. Subsequently, the study has explored the institutional AML compositions adopted in these jurisdictions. In light of legal and institutional AML differences identified in the previous chapters and based on concrete empirical evidence from Türkiye and the UK (e.g., the number of STRs/SARs, prosecutions/convictions secured, and the asset recovery figures), it has thematically compared performance indicators of national AML authorities. After outlining the overall AML effectiveness of Türkiye and the UK associated with their structural AML differences, the study has concluded by investigating (the potential) impacts of discrepancies between the two AML regimes on predicate crimes, thereby underlining the areas in need of improvement.

In this framework, in what follows, the chapter first synthesises findings of this study, thereby answering the first two research questions. In doing so, it discusses both theoretical and practical implications for competent stakeholders. Last but not least, the study concludes by putting forward tentative solutions and policy recommendations for ensuring an optimum AML effectiveness regarding tackling all predicate offences regardless of their nature, be it conventional (e.g., smuggling offences) or with more sophisticated elements (e.g., tax crimes). By that means, it addresses the third research question inquiring into how to ensure an optimum and fit-for-purpose AML mechanism. The study also points out areas for further research that would enrich the literature in this context.

9.2 Synthesis of Findings

Understanding why the legal and institutional national AML structures diverge across jurisdictions, including Türkiye and the UK, requires, as a prerequisite, understanding the underlying reasons for such heterogeneities. There is no doubt that the unique characteristics of a nation-state impact its structural standpoint regarding any international matters, including its AML composition, but comprehending the roots of the AML differences beyond such factual features entails further investigation. Accordingly, given that jurisdictions that seek to maintain their integrity with the global financial ecosystem harmonise their AML regimes in tandem with the global AML ecosystem, the international and supranational (i.e., the EU) AML efforts and standards in this context have been discussed in Chapter 2. In doing so, the authorities of AML organisations at such levels, the nature of legal instruments they introduce (e.g., soft law), and their effects on the creation/forming of national AML structures have been examined.

Consistent with the literature (see, for instance, Turksen),[7] what emerges from the analysis conducted in this part of the study is that the harmonisation efforts of the global actors devoted to creating a more consistent AML regime across the world are far from generating a uniform AML legal and institutional framework. Furthermore, despite residing in a supranational regime, even the EU MS have failed to ensure consistency in this context, albeit following the same benchmarks under the EU AMLDs.[8] It is necessary to note that although Türkiye is not an EU MS and the UK has left the EU, EU AMLDs have been relevant to the scope of this study because Türkiye, as a prolonged candidate for EU membership, has always followed the provisions set forth by the EU AMLDs.[9] Similarly, as a former EU MS, the UK has formed its AML structure in accordance with the EU AMLDs until its recent departure from the Union. Whilst the unevenness of the global regulatory landscape accounts to some extent for the global AML diversity,[10] it has been demonstrated that the flexibility provided by FATF Recommendations (e.g., regarding the type of FIU to be adopted) results in diverse AML structures embraced by each jurisdiction. For example, concerning predicate crimes, whilst the FATF Recommendations provide a list for these designated categories of offences, the decision on the definitions of such criminal acts and the circumstances that render them *serious* have been handed over to governments.[11] Additionally, the FATF Recommendations allow jurisdictions to embrace either an all-crimes approach, a threshold approach, a list-based approach, or a combination of such procedures to predicate offences.[12] Similarly, at a regional level, EU AMLDs fail to provide interpretations for most of the predicate crimes; and the *directive* form of EU legal instruments in this context leaves it to the national

7 Umut Turksen, 'Implications of Anti-Money Laundering Law for Accountancy in the European Union – A Comparative Study' in Nicholas Ryder, Umut Turksen and Sabine Hassler (eds), *Fighting Financial Crime in the Global Economic Crisis* (1st edn, Routledge 2014). See also Emmanuel Ebikake, 'Money Laundering' (2016) 19(4) Journal of Money Laundering Control 346.

8 Melissa van den Broek, 'The EU's Preventive AML/CFT Policy: Asymmetrical Harmonisation' (2011) 14(2) Journal of Money Laundering Control 170.

9 See, for instance, Türkiye Büyük Millet Meclisi, 'Mali Suçları Araştırma Kurumunun Teşkilat ve Görevleri ile Suç Gelirlerinin Aklanmasının Önlenmesi Hakkında Kanun Tasarısı ve Avrupa Birliği Uyum ile Plan ve Bütçe' (Komisyon Raporları 1/1053, 2005) <www5.tbmm.gov.tr/sirasayi/donem22/yil01/ss1201m.htm> accessed 24 May 2022; Avrupa Birliği Bakanlığı, 'Fasıl 4: Sermayenin Serbest Dolaşımı' (October 2011) <www.ab.gov.tr/files/EMPB/sermayenin_serbest_dolasimi_sunumu__ekim_2011_pptx__otomatik_kaydedilme_.pdf> accessed 24 May 2022.

10 Norman Mugarura, *The Global Anti-Money Laundering Regulatory Landscape in Less Developed Countries* (Taylor & Francis Group 2012).

11 FATF, 'International Standards on Combatting Money Laundering and the Financing of Terrorism & Proliferation: The FATF Recommendations' (Updated March 2022) <www.fatf-gafi.org/media/fatf/documents/recommendations/pdfs/FATF%20Recommendations%202012.pdf> accessed 26 June 2023.

12 ibid. See Recommendation 3 and the interpretive note to Recommendation 3.

authorities to decide on such criteria.[13] Therefore, Chapter 2 has concluded that the freedom provided by international and supranational legal instruments causes diversified AML regimes and definitions of predicate offences adopted across jurisdictions, thereby undermining the global AML ecosystem relating, amongst others, to cross-border JITs[14] and forum shopping.[15]

After outlining the root causes of the structural AML differences observed across jurisdictions, Chapters 3 and 4 have examined whether and how such underlying reasons have generated different national AML legal frameworks as constructed by Türkiye and the UK, respectively. By doing so, this study has identified the potential impacts of such discrepancies on different predicate crimes in the two jurisdictions, as examined in Chapters 7 and 8 subsequently. This critical and novel analysis has revealed that although both administrations have followed the minimum global AML standards set out by the FATF and other pertinent international legal instruments (e.g., the relevant UN Conventions and EU AMLDs), their AML compositions present significant differences.

Firstly, whilst the Turkish regulatory AML composition consists of several dispersed legal instruments with slight variances across *jus scriptum*,[16] POCA 2002 in the UK serves as a comprehensive single legal instrument, thereby addressing the needs of all relevant stakeholders in the UK without any confusion. In addition to slight inconsistencies detected amongst the Turkish AML legal instruments, the analysis has also revealed ethereal nuances between particular legal provisions,[17] impeding the AML effectiveness of Türkiye. The trials that start within the ambit of ML but eventually result in verdicts relating to the incarceration of suspected money launderers for other crimes, such as robbery, indicate such hurdles in identifying and gathering the evidence necessary to ensure an effective ML prosecution in Türkiye.

13 Consolidated version of the Treaty on the Functioning of the European Union Part Six – Institutional and Financial Provisions Title I – Institutional Provisions Chapter 2 – Legal Acts of the Union, Adoption Procedures and Other Provisions Section 1 – The Legal Acts of the Union Article 288 (ex-Article 249 TEC) [2016] OJ C202/171.

14 Selina Keesoony, 'International Anti-Money Laundering Laws: The Problems with Enforcement' (2016) 19(2) Journal of Money Laundering Control 130.

15 Marco Arnone and Leonardo Borlini, 'International Anti-Money Laundering Programs: Empirical Assessment and Issues in Criminal Regulation' (2010) 13(3) Journal of Money Laundering Control 226.

16 See, for instance, Law No 5271 (CPC) 2004, art 128 and Law No 5549 2006, art 17. Whilst both provisions regulate the circumstances regarding obtaining a seizure decision, they set forth them differently: The former empowers only judges in this context, whereas the latter also authorises public prosecutors to order such verdicts.

17 See, for instance, Law No 5237 (TCC) 2004, arts 165 and 282(2). Although these articles address two different groups of offenders, their semantic distinction is ethereal, as they are almost a verbatim copy of each other. In other words, the wording of these provisions makes it an arduous task for competent authorities to distinguish between money launderers and other criminals, thereby upholding suitable sanctions against the perpetrators.

The second principal difference identified between the two AML legal frameworks relates to the criminal liability of legal entities where the Turkish legal regime, unlike the UK's legal composition, has not established such legal responsibility. Considering that the breaching of AML regulations only results in confiscation and security measures (e.g., the revocation of the operational permit) for legal entities in Türkiye, this relatively more lenient AML legal framework can attract legal entities whose agenda gestate ML activities. That being the case, the lack of criminal prosecution envisaged for legal entities consequently increases the prevalence of predicate crimes that are more likely committed by such entities, as evident in Türkiye relating to tax crimes committed by legal entities. Comparatively, similar to the liability of natural persons, the elements of *mens rea* and *actus reus* apply to companies (i.e., legal entities) in the UK.[18]

Last but not least, the examination of the two AML legal structures has identified the heterogeneities between the asset recovery powers determined by the national AML legal regimes adopted in Türkiye and the UK as one of the most crucial differences. It has been found that competent authorities in Türkiye encounter problems in the effective use of criminal confiscation, which is the only asset recovery means available therein, as evident in the scarce confiscation decisions given by the judiciary. This trend stems from the fact that whilst the use of asset recovery powers in Türkiye fundamentally requires *grounds for strong suspicion based on concrete evidence*, *reasonable grounds to suspect* that the crime has benefited the defendant is sufficient to trigger the relevant legal proceedings in the UK. This relatively undemanding proving onus, accompanied by incentive programmes, such as ARIS,[19] serves contestably as an inducing factor for competent authorities in the UK to pursue ML and its underlying predicates. Additionally, the precondition of conviction and the requirement for establishing a direct connection between the offence under consideration and the criminal proceedings to order confiscation and *in rem* characteristics of such verdicts account for the relatively limited Turkish AML effectiveness. Comparatively, along with UWOs and lifestyle provisions, the AML legal framework in the UK offers a myriad of asset recovery means that can be opted as per the circumstances depending on the evidence and offender, such as confiscation, taxation, and civil recovery by pulling the leverages accordingly. In other words, the analysis has revealed that the unique features of the AML legal regime in the UK, as reinforced,

18 For a more detailed discussion on the criminal liability established for legal entities in the UK, see Ali Shalchi, 'Corporate Criminal Liability in England and Wales' (UK Parliament Research Briefing Paper No 9027, February 2022) <https://researchbriefings.files.parliament.uk/documents/CBP-9027/CBP-9027.pdf> accessed 24 May 2023.

19 On the potential impacts of incentivisation of LEAs in this context, see Peter Sproat, 'The New Policing of Assets and the New Assets of Policing: A Tentative Financial Cost-Benefit Analysis of the UK's Anti-Money Laundering and Asset Recovery Regime' (2007) 10(3) Journal of Money Laundering Control 277.

amongst others, by DPAs, leave (almost) no room for offenders of financial crimes to benefit from such illegal profits. Therefore, from a criminological/crime deterrence viewpoint,[20] comparatively insufficient Turkish asset recovery capabilities encourage potential money launderers, such as legal entities, as they may perceive the confiscation threat as very low or absent, thereby contributing to the predicate crime prevalence.

From the perspective of predicate crimes, which has been one of the core foci of study, the difference in respective approaches to predicate offences is the most striking element between these jurisdictions. It is necessary to note that Türkiye and the UK homogenously recognise ML as a separate and independent crime from its predicates. Additionally, considering the transnational nature of these offences,[21] based on a similar locational approach, they do not make any distinctions between the crimes committed abroad or at home in criminalising ML. However, it has been deduced that Türkiye's threshold approach to predicate crimes intrinsically fails to encompass ML deriving from certain criminal conduct unless they do not entail a minimum imprisonment term, thereby qualifying as predicate offences. Comparatively, the UK's all-crimes strategy, at least in theory, can capture any ML activities regardless of the underlying crimes that have generated such illegal proceeds, constituting the crux of the heterogeneity between the two AML legal regimes in this context. Therefore, in light of these principal points of divergence mentioned earlier, Chapters 3 and 4 have concluded that the differences between the AML legal frameworks adopted by Türkiye and the UK do impact the prevalence of predicate crimes, answering the first research question of this study. Concerning the third research question, the analysis undertaken in these chapters has also deduced that the sole recovery means of confiscation and the legal thresholds/requirements envisaged for its implementation in Türkiye fail to effectively ensure depriving offenders of illicit proceeds obtained from predicate crimes. The findings emerging from the analysis undertaken in Chapters 7 and 8 corroborate this conclusion based on statistical evidence from Türkiye and the UK.

In order to address the second research question of this study, Chapters 5 and 6 have examined the unique characteristics of the two institutional AML structures that result in dissimilar predicate crime prevalence in Türkiye and the UK. In this regard, Chapters 5 and 6 have investigated the judicial structure (i.e., courts that have jurisdiction over ML and its underlying predicates), the legal sources (i.e., the law-making process), and the institutional frameworks relating to LEAs and FIUs in Türkiye and the UK, respectively. This analysis has revealed that similar to the heterogeneities observed in the two national AML legal frameworks, Türkiye and the UK have established their

20 Samuel Sittlington and Jackie Harvey, 'Prevention of Money Laundering and the Role of Asset Recovery' (2018) 70(4) Crime, Law, and Social Change 421.

21 Nikos Passas, *Transnational Financial Crime* (1st edn, Routledge 2013).

institutional AML structures with significant variances, albeit following the very same international and supranational AML legal instruments.

Concerning the judicial compositions of Türkiye and the UK, they do not comprise specific courts dealing only with ML or associated predicate crime cases.[22] The scrutiny of the two judicial structures in this context has revealed that the Criminal Courts of General Jurisdiction in Türkiye encounter problems in handling of ML/predicate crime cases promptly as they are overwhelmed with the excessive workload of criminal law hearings. Comparatively, Magistrates' Courts in the UK serve as a legal filter by handling most of the criminal cases, thereby allowing the Crown Court to devote more time and energy to dealing with ML and its underlying predicate crime trials. In other words, the judicial process in Türkiye is rather decelerated compared to the UK, where the completion period of a pertinent court case in the Crown Court takes approximately half of the time required in Türkiye. More importantly, the comparison of the judiciary in these jurisdictions has revealed that the most 'inexperienced' judge eligible for trying ML cases in the UK is (inherently) more experienced than their Turkish counterparts.[23] An additional significant difference identified in this context is that the AML regime in the UK ensures the training of *all* prosecutors in AML matters. Given the sophisticated nature of ML offences,[24] this part of the analysis has concluded that the characteristics of a judicial ecosystem (i.e., the experience and the expertise the judiciary might have) impact the prevalence of predicate crimes. That is to say, consistent with the relevant literature,[25] any failure in identifying such offences associated with problems in establishing a link between crimes under consideration and a probable ML connection result in inaccuracy in this context.

Regarding the legal sources and the law-making process in the two jurisdictions, the principal difference relates to the law systems (i.e., civil law and common law)[26] embraced in Türkiye and the UK. The analysis of this dichotomy has revealed that the binding nature of the legal precedent in the UK associated with being a common-law jurisdiction intrinsically renders court

22 Türkiye recently assigned certain Criminal Courts of General Jurisdiction as specialised money laundering courts on 24 June 2021. However, the impacts of this institutional amendment are yet to be seen. See Official Gazette No 31522 dated 25 June 2021, 'Hakimler ve Savcılar Kurulu Birinci Dairesinin Kararı – Karar No 485' <www.resmigazete.gov.tr/eskiler/2021/06/20210625-15.pdf> accessed 28 May 2023.

23 As discussed in Chapter 6 previously, the judiciary in the UK consists of legal practitioners, such as lawyers, with at least five to ten years of experience and additional practical knowledge. On the other hand, a recently graduated judge in Türkiye can hear ML/predicate crime cases.

24 Michael Levi, 'Money for Crime and Money from Crime: Financing Crime and Laundering Crime Proceeds' (2015) 21(2) European Journal on Criminal Policy and Research 275; Jeffrey Simser, 'Money Laundering: Emerging Threats and Trends' (2012) 16(1) Journal of Money Laundering Control 41.

25 Kenneth Murray, 'A Suitable Case for Treatment: Money Laundering and Knowledge' (2012) 15(2) Journal of Money Laundering Control 188.

26 Thomas Lundmark, *Charting the Divide Between Common and Civil Law* (OUP 2012).

decisions on legal proceedings, including ML and its underlying predicate crime cases, more homogenous across the jurisdiction. Additionally, whilst the monist characteristic of the legal system in Türkiye helps the jurisdiction keep pace with international AML reforms at least in theory, this study has identified that Türkiye has not always been prompt in ensuring its AML harmony with such global changes.[27] Concerning the legal instruments made by legislative bodies in Türkiye (i.e., GNAT) and the UK (i.e., the UK Parliament), the most striking divergence point of this legislative process is the public consultation process in the UK. The analysis herein has found that the UK government has repeatedly consulted the public (particularly the relevant stakeholders) relating to Draft AML Bills through White and Green Papers,[28] enabling the competent AML authorities and obliged entities to take an active role in the codification process. That being the case, this part of the analysis has concluded that AML legal instruments in the UK are more likely to be more effective and fit-for-purpose in the fight against the phenomenon as they consider recommendations made by AML stakeholders based on their operational AML experiences in practice.

As far as LEAs are concerned, the most salient difference between the two institutional AML frameworks is that whilst tackling ML and its underlying predicates is the responsibility of the conventional LEAs in Türkiye, this duty is incumbent on a broad range of agencies in the UK. Orchestrated by the NCA, each competent authority has crime-specific responsibilities and operational priorities congruent with and tailored to the highest risk predicate crimes identified in the NRA (e.g., fraud (SFO), tax offences (HMRC), cybercrime (the City of London Police)).[29] In addition to this copious institutional armada consisting of a myriad of organisations with specific expertise and legal powers that address particular aspects of the predicament, each conventional police force in the UK, including ROCUs, incorporates specialist economic crime teams. In other words, although Türkiye has established specific departments, namely KOMs, whose responsibilities *also include* tackling ML and its underlying predicates, in broader terms, it relinquishes the

27 As discussed in Chapter 3 previously, the development of the domestic AML framework of the country indicates that Türkiye's initial steps in this context (e.g., criminalising ML in 1996) were not undertaken promptly.

28 See, for instance, Home Office, 'Government Consultation: Changes to Bodies Granted Investigatory and Other Powers Under the Proceeds of Crime Act 2002' (January 2021) <https://assets.publishing.service.gov.uk/government/uploads/system/uploads/attachment_data/file/956309/AFI_Order_Consultation_V8.pdf> accessed 28 May 2023; Law Commission, 'Anti-Money Laundering: the SARS Regime Consultation Paper' (Consultation Paper No 236, 20 July 2018) <www.cicm.com/wp-content/uploads/2018/09/Anti-Money-Laundering-the-SARS-Regime-Consultation-paper.pdf> accessed 30 November 2023.

29 HM Treasury and Home Office, 'National Risk Assessment of Money Laundering and Terrorist Financing 2020' (December 2020) <https://assets.publishing.service.gov.uk/government/uploads/system/uploads/attachment_data/file/945411/NRA_2020_v1.2_FOR_PUBLICATION.pdf> accessed 26 June 2023.

fight against the phenomenon to its mainstream LEAs.[30] Consequently, the knowledge and expertise developed by LEA personnel in Türkiye may fail to reach sufficient levels required for countering each predicate crime and the associated ML effectively. Furthermore, the status of interagency cooperation networks both nationally and internationally created by the two jurisdictions constitutes another significant difference between the two institutional AML regimes. Whilst AML authorities in Türkiye cluster at the CBCFC meetings biannually,[31] amongst other platforms, the NECC[32] and the JFAC hosted by the NCA[33] ensure uninterrupted communication and cooperation between AML stakeholders in the UK by physically mustering their representatives under the same roof. Similarly, interinstitutional collaboration networks established with foreign counterparts[34] reinforce this interconnectedness globally. Comparatively, Türkiye neither has liaison officers abroad nor provides permanent multi-agency domestic working platforms regarding AML matters. Given the crucial role of developing proficiency and effective interagency cooperation in this context,[35] this part of the study has concluded that the institutional AML framework in the UK, at least in theory, furnishes more opportunities for developing more efficacious AML responses than in Türkiye.

Lastly, a comparison of FIUs in Türkiye and the UK has revealed additional noteworthy divergence points between the two institutional AML compositions. Whilst the administrative nature of the Turkish FIU renders MASAK

30 As discussed in Chapter 5 previously, LEAs in Türkiye do not uniformly comprise specialist economic crime teams. For a detailed discussion on how such specialist professionals (e.g., forensic accountants) assist LEAs in the UK, see Kenneth Murray, 'Dismantling Organised Crime Groups through Enforcement of the POCA Money Laundering Offences' (2010) 13(1) Journal of Money Laundering Control 7.

31 Presidential Decree No 1 on the Organisation of the Presidency 2018, art 232. It is worth reiterating here that the CBCFC does not incorporate any representatives of the GCG and the CGC, two critical LEAs of the jurisdiction (see Chapter 5).

32 As discussed in Chapter 6 previously, the NECC brings together all components of the fight against ML, including LEAs (e.g., NCA), justice agencies (e.g., CPS), government departments (e.g., Home Office), regulatory bodies (e.g., FCA), and the private sector. See NCA, 'National Economic Crime Centre' <www.nationalcrimeagency.gov.uk/what-we-do/national-economic-crime-centre> accessed 31 May 2023.

33 As discussed in Chapter 6 previously, initially launched in response to the Panama Papers leak, the JFAC brings together representatives of the NCA, HMRC, the FCA, and the SFO. See HM Treasury and others, 'UK Launches Cross-Government Taskforce on the "Panama Papers"' (*Press Release*, 10 April 2016) <www.gov.uk/government/news/uk-launches-cross-government-taskforce-on-the-panama-papers> accessed 31 May 2023.

34 As discussed in Chapter 6 previously, among other networks, the international network of liaison officers (NCA) enables uninterrupted communication and exchange of intelligence between the British AML organisational armada and their representatives, which operate abroad in higher-risk jurisdictions in this context. See NCA, 'International Network' <www.nationalcrimeagency.gov.uk/what-we-do/how-we-work/providing-specialist-capabilities-for-law-enforcement/international-network> accessed 31 May 2023.

35 Nikola Dujovski and Snezana Mojsoska, 'The Role of the Police in Anti-Money Laundering' (2019) 22(1) Journal of Money Laundering Control 145.

devoid of law enforcement and judicial powers, the law enforcement characteristic of the UKFIU enables it to utilise already existing LEA infrastructure (i.e., NCA) and legal powers available to LEAs. That being the case, unlike MASAK, the UKFIU can promptly access criminal intelligence databases held by LEAs and process/share SARs with other LEAs along with the relevant criminal intelligence. Whilst these abilities allow the UKFIU to generate prospective risk assessments relating to ML and its underlying predicates, the lack of such capabilities (i.e., the inability of simultaneous use of criminal intelligence) compels MASAK to exploit STRs in most cases retrospectively. Given the crucial role of predictive intelligence in countering the predicament,[36] MASAK intrinsically may fail to forecast potential ML threats based on criminal records and the relevant intelligence held by LEAs relating to (predicate) crimes. In other words, as Axelrod correctly opines, '[h]aving law enforcement examine financial institution data around known criminal enterprises could help financial institutions better pair suspicious activity with criminal activity, and thus provide better assistance to law enforcement'.[37] This relatively unconnected intelligence gathering/exploitation *modus operandi* adopted in Türkiye renders it crucial to establish an effective information flow between MASAK and the remaining national AML authorities of the jurisdiction. However, along with the centralised organisational structure of MASAK, the discretion right in providing information granted to competent authorities with different legal powers and priorities, which are organisationally dispersed throughout the jurisdiction, impede the sharing of relevant data and generating a prompt response addressing predicate crimes. The UKFIU, on the other hand, has established dedicated working groups addressing particular predicate crimes, such as the SARs Tax Evasion Group,[38] thereby reinforcing its interagency cooperation even further.

Another critical difference between the two FIUs is that whilst MASAK harnesses a monopolised supervisory responsibility, the UKFIU benefits from the contribution of other supervisory bodies, such as OPBAS. Among other reasons, this relatively meagre supervision mechanism results in the insufficient participation of particular obliged entities, such as legal professionals and the accountancy sector, in the national AML efforts in Türkiye, as confirmed by the research findings emerging from the analysis undertaken in Chapters 7 and 8. However, it is necessary to note that whilst MASAK is the core financial intelligence authority in Türkiye, the UKFIU shares its authority in gathering,

36 Richard John Lowe, 'Anti-Money Laundering – the Need for Intelligence' (2017) 24(3) Journal of Financial Crime 472.

37 Robert Michael Axelrod, 'Criminality and Suspicious Activity Reports' (2017) 24(3) Journal of Financial Crime 461, 469.

38 As discussed in Chapter 8 previously, the SARs Tax Evasion Group brings experts from HMRC and the UKFIU together. See NCA, 'UK Financial Intelligence Unit Suspicious Activity Reports Annual Report 2020' (April 2020) 12 <www.nationalcrimeagency.gov.uk/who-we-are/publications/480-sars-annual-report-2020/file> accessed 24 February 2023.

analysing, and disseminating such intelligence with several LEAs along with five thousand officers working in the NCA. Notwithstanding its higher workload, UKFIU has a smaller workforce than MASAK. These facts render its effectiveness questionable as the central AML unit and signify that the NCA may exploit the UKFIU by following its agency-specific priorities rather than the highest-risk predicate crime threats and the associated ML problem. For instance, the FATF's recent follow-up report on the UK MER published in May 2022 points out concerns about the operational independence of the UKFIU.[39] Last but not least, whilst the STR submission constitutes the only manifest contribution of the private sector in tackling the phenomenon in Türkiye, PPPs established in the UK, such as JMLIT, ensure the active involvement of the private sector in the AML efforts beyond the sole practice of SAR reporting. Therefore, in light of these cardinal institutional AML disparities between the two jurisdictions mentioned previously, Chapters 5 and 6 have concluded that such differences may contribute to the effectiveness in tackling and the prevalence of predicate crimes in Türkiye and the UK, answering the second research question. Concerning the third research question, the analysis undertaken in these chapters has also deduced that the lack of ***dedicated*** institutional asset recovery armada in Türkiye[40] contributes to the relative insufficiency of the jurisdiction regarding criminal asset recovery practices. The analysis undertaken in Chapters 7 and 8, as discussed subsequently, corroborates this conclusion based on concrete evidence from Türkiye and the UK.

Next, bearing in mind legal and institutional AML differences between the two jurisdictions mentioned previously, based on thematic comparisons, such as obliged entities and obligations, Chapter 7 explored the overall AML effectiveness of Türkiye and the UK. Whilst the core focus of research questions has been to identify the impacts of AML heterogeneities on the prevalence of predicate crimes, Chapter 7, from a broader AML perspective, has endeavoured to provide a solid basis for a predicate-crime-specific investigation. In other words, it has served as a strong foundation for the research interests.

A thematic comparison of obliged entities in Türkiye and the UK has revealed that whilst both jurisdictions require similar FIs and DNFBPs to comply with AML obligations, given the exclusion of particular sectors and the

39 FATF, 'Anti-Money Laundering and Counter-Terrorist Financing Measures – United Kingdom: Follow-Up Report and Technical Compliance Re-Rating' (May 2022) <www.fatf-gafi.org/media/fatf/documents/reports/fur/Follow-Up-Report-United-Kingdom-2022.pdf> accessed 12 June 2023.

40 Comparatively and as discussed in Chapter 6 previously, along with competent LEAs, the UK has established dedicated asset recovery units, such as Asset Confiscation Enforcement Teams, created in all ROCUs. See Home Office, 'Policy Paper: Asset Recovery Action Plan' (Updated 13 September 2019) <www.gov.uk/government/publications/asset-recovery-action-plan/asset-recovery-action-plan> accessed 8 June 2023.

recent inclusion of certain professions,[41] obliged entities in Türkiye are narrow in scope. This limited ambit of obliged entities in Türkiye offers offenders of predicate crimes exploitable gaps, thereby enabling them to launder the proceeds from their crimes. For example, given the astronomic increases in the rental accommodation prices in Türkiye,[42] where letting agents are excluded from the scope of obliged entities,[43] it would not be unreasonable to expect such criminals to abuse letting agencies as an intermediary for laundering their illicit gains. Therefore, it has been inferred that the extent of obliged entities in a given jurisdiction (i.e., including or excluding particular FIs and DNFBPs) is one of the determiners of the overall AML effectiveness therein.

In order to identify the divergence points between the two AML regimes regarding obligations stipulated for obliged entities, the implementation of KYC standards, record-keeping practices, and reporting *modus operandi* have been thematically compared. The juxtaposition of the application of CDD principles in Türkiye and the UK has revealed that the most striking difference between the two AML regimes relates to implementing these principles on an RBA. Whilst obliged entities in both jurisdictions abide by similar national provisions, the AML regime in the UK requires particular sectors, such as high-value dealers, to follow more rigid rules commensurate with the associated risks.[44] Similarly, in alignment with the RBA, unlike the AML ecosystem in Türkiye, the UK requires obliged entities to implement enhanced CDD measures regarding PEPs, albeit not immune from criticism regarding its implementation.[45] In other words, Türkiye has not been able to introduce an effective RBA in this context, preventing obliged entities from devoting AML efforts proportionate to the sectoral/circumstantial risks. Although posing some challenges,[46] considering the crucial role of implementing an RBA

41 As discussed in Chapter 7, letting agents, for instance, do not fall within the ambit of obliged entities in Türkiye. Similarly, lawyers have been subject to FATF Recommendations only since 31 December 2020. In relation to lawyers, see Official Gazette No 31351 dated 31 December 2020, 'Kitle İmha Silahlarının Yayılmasının Finansmanının Önlenmesine İlişkin Kanun' <www.resmigazete.gov.tr/eskiler/2020/12/20201231M5-19.htm> accessed 2 June 2023.

42 Neyran Elden, 'Satılık ve Kiralık Ev Fiyatları Neden Artıyor?' *BBC News* (30 April 2022) <www.bbc.com/turkce/haberler-turkiye-61285237> accessed 2 June 2023.

43 For a more detailed discussion on money laundering threats posed by the abuse of letting agents see Ilaria Zavoli and Colin King, 'New Development: Estate Agents' Perspectives of Anti-Money Laundering Compliance – Four Key Issues in the UK Property Market' (2020) 40(5) Public Money and Management 415.

44 For a more detailed discussion in this context (e.g., ML threats posed by high-value portable commodities), see Nicholas Gilmour, 'Blindingly Obvious and Frequently Exploitable' (2017) 20(2) Journal of Money Laundering Control 105.

45 Mario Menz, 'Show Me the Money: Managing Politically Exposed Persons (PEPs) Risk in UK Financial Services' (2021) 28(4) Journal of Financial Crime 968.

46 Norman Mugarura, 'Customer Due Diligence (CDD) Mandate and the Propensity of Its Application as a Global AML Paradigm' (2014) 17(1) Journal of Money Laundering Control 76.

in this context[47] and given the threats associated with PEPs,[48] it has been deduced that such anomalies impede the overall AML effectiveness of Türkiye.

In terms of differences in record-keeping practices undertaken by obliged entities in Türkiye and the UK, the comparison of the two methodologies has pointed out the extended retention period (i.e., eight years) and the more comprehensive documentation framework determined in Türkiye. This part of the analysis has concluded that whilst these relatively stiffer measures intrinsically increase the amount of information for competent authorities to investigate, contributing, in theory, to the AML effectiveness, they add an extra burden to obliged entities regarding compliance costs.[49]

As far as suspicious transaction/activity reporting procedures are concerned, the most significant heterogeneity between the AML regimes adopted in Türkiye and the UK has been identified as the time limit envisaged for fulfilling reporting obligations in these jurisdictions. Whilst obliged entities in Türkiye must file their suspicions with MASAK in *ten workdays* starting from the date suspicion occurred, FIs and DNFBPs in the UK must act *as soon as practicable* to inform the UKFIU of potential ML activities. Given the rapidity of ML offences,[50] what this dissimilarity implies is that Türkiye may fail to keep pace with the swift asset movements and financial transactions through a series of transactions between numerous accounts and jurisdictions where offenders add additional layers to hide the proceeds of their crimes. Stiffer sanctions envisaged for non-compliant obliged entities and the lower suspicion threshold set by the case law in the UK have also been identified as paramount differences between the two AML regimes. Against this background, the analysis has revealed that obliged entities in the UK submitted approximately 2.5 times higher number of SARs to the UKFIU in the last five years compared to STRs reported by FIs and DNFBPs in Türkiye in the same period. A closer examination of STRs/SARs made by particular sectors, such as banks and lawyers

47 Jos de Wit, 'A Risk-Based Approach to AML: A Controversy Between Financial Institutions and Regulators' (2007) 15(2) Journal of Financial Regulation and Compliance 156.

48 Mario Serio, 'Politically Exposed Persons' (2008) 11(3) Journal of Money Laundering Control 269; Kim-Kwang Raymond Choo, 'Politically Exposed Persons (PEPs): Risks and Mitigation' (2008) 11(4) Journal of Money Laundering Control 371; Kim-Kwang Raymond Choo, 'Challenges in Dealing with Politically Exposed Persons' (2010) 386 Trends and Issues in Crime and Criminal Justice 1; Joy Geary, 'PEPs – Let's Get Serious' (2010) 13(2) Journal of Money Laundering Control 103.

49 AML compliance requires a substantial budget. For instance, as estimated by LexisNexis® Risk Solutions, it costs £28.7bn for obliged entities in the UK annually (i.e., the figure shows 2020 expenditures). See Georgia Richardson, 'AML Compliance Costs Firms £28.7bn Annually – Which Is Half of Entire UK Defence Budget' *Harrington Starr* (August 2021) <www.harringtonstarr.com/blog/2021/08/aml-compliance-costs-firms-ps28-dot-7bn-annually-which-is-half-of-entire-uk-defence-budget?source=google.com> accessed 8 June 2023.

50 James Whisker and Mark Eshwar Lokanan, 'Anti-Money Laundering and Counter-Terrorist Financing Threats Posed by Mobile Money' (2019) 22(1) Journal of Money Laundering Control 158.

and accountants, in the two jurisdictions has found stark differences in the reporting figures of these FIs and DNFBPs regarding lawyers and accountants in particular. Given the scarcity of disclosures reported by legal professionals and the accountancy sector in Türkiye, it has been deduced that a plethora of factors, such as frequent tax amnesties, the fear of losing clients/losing the confidence of their clients (i.e., professional privilege issues),[51] the lack of trust and confidence in the STR *modus operandi*, the lack of knowledge/awareness concerning AML obligations, the lack of a dedicated AML supervisory body addressing these obliged entities, to name a few, result in such dearth of use of the STR mechanism. Therefore, given that ML investigations are triggered by STRs/SARs in most cases[52] and that the reporting regime constitutes the crux of AML efforts,[53] the current disclosure practices of obliged entities in Türkiye may overlook potential ML attempts. It can be argued that as offenders, including money launderers and those who commit predicate crimes, act rationally,[54] this *relatively* lower detection probability may attract them to carry out such unlawful conduct in jurisdictions that present AML deficiencies, including Türkiye. In other words, as Ferwerda aptly posits, ensuring a stricter AML policy, amongst others, by 'increasing the probability of being caught for money laundering and the predicate crime' can be functional in reducing crimes, including predicate offences.[55]

Concerning the quest that has inquired into the overall AML effectiveness of national AML authorities in Türkiye and the UK, the number of cases disseminated by FIUs to competent authorities for further investigation, the number of prosecutions/convictions secured, and the asset recovery figures in these jurisdictions have been compared. The analysis of the number of suspects reported by MASAK for prosecution has revealed a correlation between the personal count of the FIU and associated capacity as the reduction in the MASAK workforce significantly decreased the number of files opened for examination. Although such data are not available concerning the UKFIU, it has been found that MASAK has contributed to the prosecution and probably

51 Ping He, 'Lawyers, Notaries, Accountants and Money Laundering' (2006) 9(1) Journal of Money Laundering Control 62.

52 However, it is necessary to state that 'prosecution attitude, competence and resources' are additional determiners of initiating an ML investigation. See Michael Levi, Peter Reuter and Terence Halliday, 'Can the AML System Be Evaluated Without Better Data?' (2017) 69(2) Crime, Law, and Social Change 307, 320.

53 Gauri Sinha, 'To Suspect or Not to Suspect: Analysing the Pressure on Banks to Be "Policemen"' (2014) 15(1) Journal of Banking Regulation 75.

54 Nicholas Gilmour, 'Understanding the Practices Behind Money Laundering: A Rationale Choice Interpretation' (2016) 44(1) International Journal of Crime and Justice 1. Additionally, as it signifies rational choices made by this group of offenders, for a detailed discussion on how AML policies affect money launderers and their networks, see Peter Gerbrands and others, 'The Effect of Anti-Money Laundering Policies: An Empirical Network Analysis' (2022) 11(1) EPJ Data Science 1.

55 Joras Ferwerda, 'The Economics of Crime and Money Laundering: Does Anti-Money Laundering Policy Reduce Crime?' (2009) 5(2) Review of Law and Economics 903, 923.

to the conviction of more than 1,000 offenders in the last five years. As a point of comparison, FinCEN, the FIU of USA, secured similar judicial outcomes in three years.[56] However, it has been noted that both Türkiye and the UK AML regime either fail to collect conviction statistics in this context or to render them publicly available, diminishing the transparency and impeding an objective crime/success evaluation. Therefore, it has been concluded, in alignment with the literature,[57] that the personal capacity of an FIU and the lack/presence of feedback received from judicial authorities regarding the judicial outcomes of ML cases impact the overall AML effectiveness in a given jurisdiction.

The juxtaposition of ML cases and the judicial outcomes in Türkiye and the UK have revealed that whilst only 10% of ML cases result in a criminal sentence decision in Türkiye,[58] such verdicts constitute approximately 71% of ML trials in the UK. Similarly, it has been unveiled that whilst court decisions from the two jurisdictions present similar custody percentages, incarceration rates in the UK are significantly higher (i.e., four to 30 times) than the ratio of money launderers charged with imprisonment decisions in Türkiye. More importantly, due to hurdles in proving criminality associated with ML,[59] it has been found that approximately 4% of offenders have been incarcerated for other offences in Türkiye in the last five years, albeit their trials were within the ambit of ML. The analysis has highlighted the substantial commonalities between Articles 165 (i.e., purchasing or accepting property acquired through the commission of an offence) and 282(2) of TCC 2004 as the most critical issue for competent AML authorities in Türkiye that hamper their effective application of the appropriate legal procedures. In light of these divergence points between the two criminal justice systems, it has been deduced that although having some issues,[60] the accuracy of the detection and collection of

56 Internal Revenue Service: Criminal Investigation, 'Annual Report 2021' (2021) 48 <www.irs.gov/pub/irs-pdf/p3583.pdf> accessed 3 June 2023. It is necessary to note that several FIUs operating across the EU, such as Belgium, Chechia, and France, disseminated more than 2000 cases to competent authorities in a single year (i.e., 2019). See Corina-Narcisa (Bodescu) Cotoc and others, 'Efficiency of Money Laundering Countermeasures: Case Studies from European Union Member States' (2021) 9(6) Risks 120.

57 Jayesh D'Souza, 'Financial Intelligence Units: Monitoring Resource and Process Outcomes' in Jayesh D'Souza (ed), *Terrorist Financing, Money Laundering and Tax Evasion* (1st edn, CRC Press 2012). See also Shirin Sultana, 'Role of Financial Intelligence Unit (FIU) in Anti-Money Laundering Quest' (2020) 23(4) Journal of Money Laundering Control 931.

58 Sentence decisions comprise imprisonment, fine, suspended sentence, security measures, and other imprisonment sentence decisions. See Table 7.6 in Chapter 7.

59 These problems stem, amongst others, from the cryptic nature of particular provisions with close meanings (i.e., Law No 5237 (TCC) 2004, arts 165 and 282(2)). As discussed earlier, this almost indistinguishable wording of relevant articles undermines the accurate detection of crimes under consideration as it is not an easy task to identify criminal intent.

60 Kenneth Murray, 'In the Shadow of the Dark Twin: Proving Criminality in Money Laundering Cases' (2016) 19(4) Journal of Money Laundering Control 447. See also RE Bell, 'Proving the Criminal Origin of Property in Money-Laundering Prosecutions' (2000) 4(1) Journal of Money Laundering Control 4.

evidence required for ensuring an effective ML prosecution renders the UK more effective than Türkiye in this context.

Regarding the judicial handling of legal entities in Türkiye and the UK, this study has identified that despite the relatively lenient Turkish AML legal framework in this context, 15 legal entities were involved in ML prosecutions at the criminal courts between 2016 and 2020.[61] Comparatively, notwithstanding the criminal liability established for legal entities in the UK, there has not been a single legal entity prosecuted for ML under criminal law in the corresponding period therein.[62] However, it has been inferred that the availability of alternative legal powers in the UK, such as DPAs, may compensate for the scarcity of corporate criminal prosecutions.

The comparison of asset recovery figures obtained in Türkiye and the UK has indicated an enormous difference between the monetary value of assets recovered in the two jurisdictions. The analysis has underlined that only 0.5% of annual ML court verdicts have included confiscation decisions at the criminal courts in Türkiye since 2016, which led to a maximum recovery of approximately GBP 1.5m in 2017.[63] Comparatively, since 2016, the application of confiscation powers alone (i.e., excluding civil recovery, taxation, and similar legal tools) has consistently ensured the denial of at least approximately GBP 140m proceeds of crime to money launderers in the UK annually. In light of this immense disparity, it has been deduced that competent AML authorities in Türkiye encounter problems in the effective use of the *sole* asset recovery means of confiscation, *inter alia*, due to *in rem* characteristics of such verdicts. Accordingly, it has been concluded that the whole set of asset recovery tools and its frequent application as an integrated part of the sentencing *modus operandi* render the UK more effective than Türkiye in this context.

As far as sanctions levied on money launderers are concerned, it has been found that notwithstanding the relatively stiffer sanction mechanism envisaged

61 See Ministry of Justice General Directorate of Judicial Record and Statistics, 'Judicial Statistics 2016' (November 2017) 99 <https://adlisicil.adalet.gov.tr/Resimler/SayfaDokuman/2082019114041Adalet_ist_2016.pdf> accessed 28 October 2023; Ministry of Justice General Directorate of Judicial Record and Statistics, 'Judicial Statistics 2017' (August 2018) 97 <https://adlisicil.adalet.gov.tr/Resimler/SayfaDokuman/2082019114010Adalet_ist_2017.pdf> accessed 28 October 2023; Ministry of Justice General Directorate of Judicial Record and Statistics, 'Judicial Statistics 2018' (August 2019) 97 <https://adlisicil.adalet.gov.tr/Resimler/SayfaDokuman/1792019103654adalet_ist_2018.pdf> accessed 28 October 2023; Ministry of Justice General Directorate of Judicial Record and Statistics, 'Judicial Statistics 2020' (September 2021) 97 <https://adlisicil.adalet.gov.tr/Resimler/SayfaDokuman/1692021162011adalet_ist-2020.pdf> accessed 1 February 2023.

62 The first criminal prosecution (commenced by the FCA) against a company (i.e., National Westminster Bank Plc) was secured in 2021. See Chapter 6.

63 It is worth reiterating that there are not any publicly available and integrated data on ML cases and associated confiscation figures in Türkiye. As mentioned in Chapter 7, the relevant statistics were extracted from the FATF's Mutual Evaluation Report (MER) on Türkiye. Thus, such information is limited to three years, encompassing 2016 and 2018.

for money launderers in the UK, it has been more lenient than Türkiye concerning the prison sentences given by courts. It has been unveiled that the Turkish Criminal Justice System charges (i.e., 53 months on average) this group of offenders with approximately two times longer imprisonment terms than its British counterpart (i.e., around 28 months). In addition to these prolonged incarceration sentences, it has been identified that the judiciary in Türkiye applies (administrative and judicial) fines more frequently than in the UK, wherein an annual average amount has been less than GBP 500 consistently. Given the shorter confinement penalties and the modest fines levied on money launderers in the UK, it has been deduced that the law in action in Türkiye in this context (i.e., the sanctioning mechanism) is more deterrent than in the UK. However, Chapter 7 has concluded that divergence points between the scope of obliged entities, obligations, or in broader terms, the legal and institutional AML differences between the two jurisdictions render the UK more effective than Türkiye in the AML domain. The plethora of novel strategies constituting examples of best practices, such as the notion of Super SARs, the foundation of OPBAS, and the creation of PPPs (e.g., JMLIT) and asset recovery practices, including common databases in this context (e.g., JARD), in particular, lead us to such a conclusion.

Following the examination of how legal and institutional AML differences between the two jurisdictions impact the overall AML effectiveness of Türkiye and the UK, the study has investigated in Chapter 8 whether and how such variances in the law in the books generate diverse outcomes regarding the law in action concerning predicate crimes. Accordingly, it has focused on two of the most prevalent/highest risk predicate crimes for the two jurisdictions as case studies, namely illicit drug trafficking and tax offences. The underlying rationale for concentrating on these particular predicate offences has been manifold, including but not limited to their prevalence, unique characteristics (i.e., the dichotomy between conventional and white-collar crimes), the time difference between their recognition as predicate offences, and the geographical locations of Türkiye and the UK (e.g., the Balkan Route and EU neighbouring jurisdictions).

The investigation of the effectiveness of AML frameworks adopted in Türkiye and the UK in countering illicit drug trafficking has revealed that the differences between the two AML regimes do not seem to generate significant discrepancies in effectively tackling this particular predicate crime. Whilst the notion of criminal lifestyle[64] adopted in the UK theoretically renders the jurisdiction more effective than Türkiye regarding asset recovery practices, the investigation of statistical evidence from these jurisdictions has identified that this theoretical superiority of the UK AML regime is not evident regarding the law in operation. It has been found that recent AML amendments introduced

64 As discussed previously, illicit drug trafficking is considered one of the criminal lifestyle offences under the UK AML regime.

following the last pertinent national strategy document in Türkiye,[65] such as the establishment of the Bureau of Combatting Proceeds of Crime within the GDS Counter Narcotics Department, have been a gamechanger for the country. Whilst only 0.0005% of illicit drug trafficking cases had led to an ML investigation in Türkiye, recent AML amendments have ensured an effective enforcement ecosystem where LEAs have secured at least equal confiscation figures to those achieved in the UK in recent years.[66] In other words, regarding illicit drug trafficking, this study has concluded that recent AML amendments in Türkiye have been fit for their purpose, and modifications addressing deficiencies regarding how the law operates in action can be functional in controlling underlying predicate crimes.

However, the juxtaposition of the two AML regimes in tackling tax crimes has unveiled that the unique features of the AML frameworks embraced in Türkiye and the UK produce substantial AML differences. The most remarkable difference between the two AML legal compositions has been identified as the criminal offence of the failure to prevent the facilitation of tax evasion as envisaged for legal entities in the UK.[67] It has been concluded that the lack of criminal liability established for legal entities in Türkiye can encourage domestic corporations and magnetise international companies whose schedules gestate fraudulent tax practices and associated ML to engage in such unlawful conduct. Additionally, despite the threat posed by professional enablers, such as lawyers[68] and accountants,[69] the investigation of the differences between legal provisions addressing such obliged entities in the two jurisdictions has revealed that the Turkish *jus scriptum* does not devote a specific consideration to those professionals as enablers or facilitators. Along with other reasons, due to this lack of attentiveness, it has been found that whilst tax advisers and independent legal professionals seldomly submit STRs to MASAK (e.g., *only seven* in 2020), such experts file thousands of SARs with the UKFIU

65 As discussed in Chapter 8, Türkiye has been amending its AML structure to address illicit drug trafficking as per the National Strategy Document and Action Plan on Combatting Drugs 2018–2023.

66 See, for instance, Operation Swamp discussed in Chapter 8.

67 For a commentary on the potential benefits of establishing corporate criminal liability, see Liz Campbell, 'Corporate Liability and the Criminalisation of Failure' (2018) 12(2) Law and Financial Markets Review 57.

68 Michael Levi, Hans Nelen and Francien Lankhorst, 'Lawyers as Crime Facilitators in Europe: An Introduction and Overview' (2005) 42(2–3) Crime, Law, and Social Change 117; David J Middleton, 'Lawyers and Client Accounts: Sand Through a Colander' (2008) 11(1) Journal of Money Laundering Control 34; Michael Levi, 'Lawyers as Money Laundering Enablers? An Evolving and Contentious Relationship' (2022) 23(2) Global Crime 126.

69 A Mitchell, Prem Sikka and Hugh Willmott, 'Sweeping It Under the Carpet: The Role of Accountancy Firms in Money Laundering' (1998) 23(5) Accounting, Organizations and Society 589; Jeffrey Simser, 'Tax Evasion and Avoidance Typologies' (2008) 11(2) Journal of Money Laundering Control 123; Prem Sikka and Hugh Willmott, 'Regulating Money Laundering: A Case Study of the UK Experience' in Glenn Morgan and Lars Engwall (eds), *Regulation and Organizations* (1st edn, Routledge 1999).

(e.g., approximately 10,000 in 2020) annually. In other words, the analysis of the statistical evidence from the two jurisdictions in this context has identified such weaknesses in the AML regime in Türkiye concerning effectively tackling ML deriving from tax offences. In comparison, interagency working groups established as per the associated threats both nationally (e.g., the Enabler Practitioners Group and SARs Tax Evasion Group) and internationally (e.g., the HMRC's global network of Fiscal Crime Liaison Officers and the Joint Chiefs of Global Tax Enforcement), along with stiffer sanctions provided for tax offenders, including professional enablers, render the UK AML regime more tailored to unique ML risks than Türkiye.

As far as the two institutional AML structures are concerned, differences between legal powers harnessed by the tax enforcement authorities in Türkiye (i.e., VDK/GIB) and the UK (i.e., HMRC) constitute the most striking heterogeneity for the two jurisdictions in this context. It has been identified that whilst HMRC can address ML deriving from tax crimes for the most part singlehandedly, tackling the phenomenon in Türkiye entails multi-layered and integrated operational approaches established between MASAK, LEAs, and the tax authorities as directed by the public prosecutors. It has also been revealed that the relatively limited set of legal powers that tax inspectors/auditors possess in Türkiye is further aggravated by the restricted information flow (i.e., discretion rights) between the competent AML authorities therein. However, notwithstanding the relatively more autonomous tax enforcement mechanism adopted in the UK, the inquiry on the judicial handling process of tax evaders has pointed out the historical infrequency of tax cases before the prosecution authorities therein.[70] Whilst approximately 40,000 tax offenders are prosecuted with an incarceration rate of around 20–25% at the criminal courts in Türkiye annually, the UK tax enforcement regime only secures roughly 1,000 criminal prosecutions in a year. Türkiye has further reinforced its judicial practices by the recent introduction of specialised criminal courts designated for hearing tax offences in November 2021.[71] Nevertheless, it has been inferred that the availability of alternative legal tools in the UK, such as CDFs, may compensate for the infrequency of criminal prosecutions in this context as they have, along with criminal powers, enabled HMRC to recover more than GBP 1bn since 2016.[72] On the other hand, there is no available evidence of whether any tax offence prosecution has resulted in an ML

70 See also Samantha Bourton, 'A Critical and Comparative Analysis of the Prevention of Tax Evasion Through the Application of Law and Enforcement Policies in the United Kingdom and United States of America' (PhD thesis, University of the West of England 2021) <https://uwe-repository.worktribe.com/output/7316976> accessed 17 August 2023.

71 Additionally, it is worth reiterating here that given the complexity of tax offences and the technical expertise required for identifying such crimes, Türkiye, departing from its legal conventions, requires an *obiter dictum* of tax officials to initiate a criminal case (see Chapter 8).

72 HMRC, 'HMRC Fraud Squad Takes Back £1 Billion from Offenders' (*Press Release*, 30 December 2021) <www.gov.uk/government/news/hmrc-fraud-squad-takes-back-1-billion-from-offenders> accessed 6 June 2023.

investigation in Türkiye, thereby securing convictions/recovering illicit proceeds through confiscations. Although well-developed/integrated information that establishes a direct link between predicate crimes and ML exists neither in Türkiye nor in the UK, these research findings address the first two research questions. More specifically, unique characteristics of legal (i.e., question 1) and institutional (i.e., question 2) AML structures impact the prevalence of and the effectiveness in countering predicate crimes. The statistics from Türkiye indicate that whilst AML amendments have increased its AML effectiveness concerning drug-related offences, such modifications have been far from securing a similar efficacy in countering ML deriving from tax offences. It has been concluded that whilst unique characteristics of a national AML structure may be effective in countering ML deriving from particular predicate offences (i.e., *conventional* crimes), it may show deficiencies in tackling others with more sophisticated elements. This disparity in effectively tackling ML deriving from different predicate offences stems from the fact, as correctly observed by Soudijn, that '[c]ombating money laundering is sometimes a job for specialists . . . , but many forms . . . can easily be left to ordinary investigative officers without a background in finance'[73] or financial forensics. Given that the UK AML regime has not demonstrated such substantial discrepancies concerning distinct predicate crimes, it has been deduced that jurisdictions, including Türkiye, need to consider the unique features of *each* predicate crime in designing their national AML structures. If we regard a national AML framework as a spider's web and predicate crimes as different insects to be captured by such a web, the net needs to be, above all, strong and durable, which can be achieved by creating a thick-sown design. That is to say, regarding each competent AML authority as individual silks to be spun, national choices in structuring AML compositions, especially in the absence of sufficient dedicated/specialised LEAs, are of utmost importance in this context. In this regard, the type of FIU adopted, the accessibility of criminal and intelligence (e.g., STR/SAR) databases, and the presence of PPPs and (permanent) multiagency working groups/JITs are key determiners of the success in countering all predicate crimes regardless of their nature. The insufficient contribution of particular obliged entities, the discretion right in providing information granted to competent authorities with different legal powers and priorities, and the lack of national and international liaison networks/working groups constitute the principal reasons for the discrepancy observed in the effectiveness regarding tackling distinct predicate crimes in Türkiye. Last but not least, the higher evidentiary threshold and the unproductive asset recovery mechanism adopted by Türkiye impede the overall AML effectiveness of the jurisdiction regardless of predicate crimes committed.

73 Melvin RJ Soudijn, 'Rethinking Money Laundering and Drug Trafficking: Some Implications for Investigators, Policy Makers and Researchers' (2016) 19(3) Journal of Money Laundering Control 298, 307.

——— 'Judicial Statistics 2020' (September 2021) <https://adlisicil.adalet.gov.tr/Resimler/SayfaDokuman/1692021162011adalet_ist-2020.pdf> accessed 1 February 2023
Mitchell A, Sikka P and Willmott H, 'Sweeping It Under the Carpet: The Role of Accountancy Firms in Money Laundering' (1998) 23(5) Accounting, Organizations and Society 589
Mugarura N, 'The Global Anti-Money Laundering Court as A Judicial and Institutional Imperative' (2011) 14(1) Journal of Money Laundering Control 60
——— *The Global Anti-Money Laundering Regulatory Landscape in Less Developed Countries* (Taylor & Francis Group 2012)
——— 'Customer Due Diligence (CDD) Mandate and the Propensity of Its Application as a Global AML Paradigm' (2014) 17(1) Journal of Money Laundering Control 76
Murray K, 'Dismantling Organised Crime Groups through Enforcement of the POCA Money Laundering Offences' (2010) 13(1) Journal of Money Laundering Control 7
——— 'A Suitable Case for Treatment: Money Laundering and Knowledge' (2012) 15(2) Journal of Money Laundering Control 188
——— 'In the Shadow of the Dark Twin: Proving Criminality in Money Laundering Cases' (2016) 19(4) Journal of Money Laundering Control 447
NCA, 'UK Financial Intelligence Unit Suspicious Activity Reports Annual Report 2020' (April 2020) <www.nationalcrimeagency.gov.uk/who-we-are/publications/480-sars-annual-report-2020/file> accessed 24 February 2023
——— 'International Network' <www.nationalcrimeagency.gov.uk/what-we-do/how-we-work/providing-specialist-capabilities-for-law-enforcement/international-network> accessed 31 May 2023
——— 'National Economic Crime Centre' <www.nationalcrimeagency.gov.uk/what-we-do/national-economic-crime-centre> accessed 31 May 2023
Passas N, *Transnational Financial Crime* (1st edn, Routledge 2013)
Pieth M, 'The Prevention of Money Laundering: A Comparative Analysis' (1998) 6(2) European Journal of Crime, Criminal Law, and Criminal Justice 159
PROTAX <https://protax-project.eu> accessed 16 August 2023
Richardson G, 'AML Compliance Costs Firms £28.7bn Annually – Which Is Half of Entire UK Defence Budget' *Harrington Starr* (August 2021) <www.harringtonstarr.com/blog/2021/08/aml-compliance-costs-firms-ps28-dot-7bn-annually-which-is-half-of-entire-uk-defence-budget?source=google.com> accessed 8 June 2023
Ross S and Hannan M, 'Money Laundering Regulation and Risk-Based Decision Making' (2007) 10(1) Journal of Money Laundering Control 106
Ryder N, *Money Laundering – An Endless Cycle? A Comparative Analysis of the Anti-Money Laundering Policies in the United States of America, the United Kingdom, Australia and Canada* (1st edn, Routledge 2012)
Schneider J and Schneider P, 'The Anthropology of Crime and Criminalization' (2008) 37(1) Annual Review of Anthropology 351
Serio M, 'Politically Exposed Persons' (2008) 11(3) Journal of Money Laundering Control 269
Shalchi A, 'Corporate Criminal Liability in England and Wales' (UK Parliament Research Briefing Paper No 9027, February 2022) <https://researchbriefings.files.parliament.uk/documents/CBP-9027/CBP-9027.pdf> accessed 24 May 2023
Sikka P and Willmott H, 'Regulating Money Laundering: A Case Study of the UK Experience' in G Morgan and L Engwall (eds), *Regulation and Organizations* (1st edn, Routledge 1999)
Simser J, 'Tax Evasion and Avoidance Typologies' (2008) 11(2) Journal of Money Laundering Control 123

9.3 Suggestions for Policy Makers, Practitioners, and Future Research

The comparative analysis of the AML structures adopted in Türkiye and the UK has identified various legal and institutional AML differences between the two jurisdictions that impact the predicate crime prevalence and the effectiveness in tackling such diverse criminal conduct. It has underlined the potential weaknesses and strengths of each AML ecosystem where the primary focus has been on the AML regime in Türkiye (i.e., the UK AML regime has been regarded, in broader terms, as a point of reference). As the principal conclusion of this book, given that '*[c]eteris paribus*, tighter AML provisions lead to higher production and transaction costs of the predicate crime [and] . . . therefore influence the predicate offender',[74] Türkiye would benefit from reinforcing its AML composition.

In securing an optimum AML regime, jurisdictions, including Türkiye, must ensure that legal instruments are uncomplicated, fit for purpose, and in harmony with the international AML legal and enforcement ecosystem. Additionally, given the adaptability of money launderers and predicate offenders,[75] they must equip the national AML armada with a flexible legal arsenal comprising versatile legal tools capable of generating effective AML responses as per the circumstances. In other words, as Bell correctly posits, '[a]s crime evolves, investigative practice must also evolve'.[76] Admittedly, consulting with all AML stakeholders (e.g., the judiciary, LEAs, the FIU, and obliged entities) and benefiting from their real-life AML experiences in the codification process of AML legal instruments would increase the fitness of the AML regulation in this context. Concerning the overall AML legal framework in Türkiye, eliminating the dispersed nature of legal instruments addressing the phenomenon and the indistinguishable wording of pertinent provisions would be a fundamental step in this context. Similarly, introducing novel legal powers available for the judiciary and LEAs, such as UWOs and lifestyle provisions, would help lessen the proving onus in establishing criminal liability for money launderers, thereby increasing the asset recovery effectiveness of Türkiye. Remarkably, Türkiye recently introduced a national strategy paper on 17 July 2021 that aims to strengthen its efficacy in this context.[77] However, it has not helped dis-

74 Hans Geiger and Oliver Wuensch, 'The Fight Against Money Laundering: An Economic Analysis of Cost-Benefit Paradoxon' (2007) 10(1) Journal of Money Laundering Control 91, 94.

75 Brigitte Unger and Johan den Hertog, 'Water Always Finds Its Way: Identifying New Forms of Money Laundering' (2012) 57(3) Crime, Law and Social Change 287.

76 RE Bell, 'Discretion and Decision Making in Money Laundering Prosecutions' (2001) 5(1) Journal of Money Laundering Control 42, 49.

77 Official Gazette No 31544 dated 17 July 2021, 'Genelge 2021/16: Türkiye'de Suç Gelirlerinin Aklanması ve Terörizmin Finansmanı ile Mücadele ve Müsadere Uygulamalarında Etkinliğin Arttırılması Strateji Belgesi (2021–2025)' <www.resmigazete.gov.tr/eskiler/2021/07/20210717-10.pdf> accessed 10 June 2023.

suade the FATF from incorporating Türkiye into the list of jurisdictions under increased monitoring (due to the remaining deficiencies) in March 2022.[78] Therefore, accompanying this master plan with civil powers bestowed on competent AML authorities would enhance the flexibility of AML responses and secure an augmented redemption of illicit proceeds. Concerning the AML legal regime from a predicate crimes perspective, whilst Türkiye has enlarged its standpoint by departing from a list-based approach to a threshold strategy,[79] the study does not notice any impediment refraining Türkiye from adopting an all-crimes policy. As Cassella, concerning the global AML standpoint, aptly puts forward,[80] Türkiye would benefit from adopting an all-crimes approach to predicate crimes.

From an institutional AML perspective, the sophisticated nature of ML and its underlying predicates[81] renders it inevitable to create well-organised specialised AML units with expert personnel and intensified interagency communication/cooperation capabilities. In other words, '[c]ommunication among all parties is essential to making the [AML] system work'.[82] However, the study has identified that the discretion right in providing information granted to competent authorities with different legal powers/priorities and the lack of national/international liaison networks/(permanent) multiagency working platforms prevent Türkiye from ensuring such a strong communication network. More importantly, the study has revealed that such deficiencies constitute the principal reasons for the discrepancy observed in tackling distinct predicate crime effectiveness in Türkiye. Whilst this relatively weak interinstitutional connectedness may not adversely impact the effectiveness in tackling certain predicate crimes (e.g., *conventional* crimes), its weaknesses may be manifest in countering crimes with more sophisticated elements (e.g., tax crimes and cybercrime). Therefore, an optimum AML composition entails considering the unique characteristics of each predicate offence, introducing dedicated AML units, including a specialised asset recovery armada, with a proficient workforce, and ensuring uninterrupted interagency communication and collaboration practices.

Given the pivotal role of FIUs in AML, including asset recovery practices,[83] revising the administrative nature of MASAK, thereby rendering it an LEA or

78 FATF, 'Jurisdictions Under Increased Monitoring – March 2022' <www.fatf-gafi.org/publications/high-risk-and-other-monitored-jurisdictions/documents/increased-monitoring-march-2022.html#turkey> accessed 10 June 2022.

79 See Chapter 3.

80 Stefan D Cassella, 'Toward a New Model of Money Laundering: Is the "Placement, Layering, Integration" Model Obsolete?' (2018) 21(4) Journal of Money Laundering Control 494.

81 Michael Levi and Melvin Soudijn, 'Understanding the Laundering of Organized Crime Money' (2020) 49(1) Crime and Justice 579.

82 D'Souza (n 57) 153.

83 Egmont Group, 'Asset Recovery – The Role of FIUs' <https://egmontgroup.org/wp-content/uploads/2022/05/Sanitized-Asset-Recovery-Report-2.pdf> accessed 11 June 2023.

a hybrid type of FIU, would undoubtedly ensure an increased information flow between the AML authorities. Although converting the characteristics of MASAK may not be practicable in this context, Türkiye would benefit from adhering to its strategic plan of forming predicate-crime-specific dedicated units under the auspices of MASAK.[84] Similarly, creating affiliated branches to MASAK across the jurisdiction[85] would reinforce information-sharing practices among national competent AML authorities dispersed across the country. Therefore, an optimum AML mechanism necessitates improving the central/crucial role of any FIU, including MASAK.

Given the complexity of prosecuting ML offences,[86] the specialisation efforts also need to cover the judiciary/courts and prosecution authorities. Notably, Türkiye recently designated certain Criminal Courts of General Jurisdiction as specialised ML courts on 24 June 2021.[87] However, concerning the sentencing *modus operandi* of such courts, where a newly graduated judge can hear such cases singlehandedly, this is an early stage for evaluating whether such an amendment fits its purpose. This trend suggests that Türkiye considers ML cases less grave than some predicate crimes. Additionally, training in AML is crucial for prosecutors,[88] especially in jurisdictions where they direct LEA operations, as it is the case in Türkiye. Hence, an optimum AML composition requires the judiciary and prosecution authorities to harness the essential knowledge and expertise to tackle the predicament effectively. Last but not least, given the complexity of cross-border crimes and challenges in analysing the multitude of datasets revealed by the aforementioned scandals (e.g., Panama Papers, Paradise Papers) and research projects (e.g., PROTAX),[89] the capacity/tech tools to analyse large and complex sets of data involved in ML schemes (e.g., TRACE)[90] should be another component of an optimum AML structure.

Concerning obliged entities and their AML obligations, an optimum AML mechanism needs to be comprehensive enough to encompass each exploitable sector in this context (e.g., letting agencies in Türkiye) and to ensure obligations are adhered to and implemented effectively. Whilst the vague characteristics of the RBA (i.e., the conceptualism of risk) recommended by the FATF

84 TC Başbakanlık, 'Ulusal Uyuşturucu ile Mücadele Ulusal Strateji Belgesi ve Eylem Planı 2018–2023' (2018) <https://hsgm.saglik.gov.tr/depo/birimler/tutun-mucadele-bagimlilik-db/haberler/uyusturucu_eylem_plani/2018-2023_Uyusturucu_ile_Mucadele_Ulusal_Strateji_Belgesi_ve_Eylem_Plani.pdf> accessed 19 January 2023.

85 Presidential Decree No 1 on the Organisation of the Presidency 2018, art 231(6).

86 Norman Mugarura, 'The Global Anti-Money Laundering Court as a Judicial and Institutional Imperative' (2011) 14(1) Journal of Money Laundering Control 60.

87 See (n 22).

88 Bell (n 76).

89 PROTAX <https://protax-project.eu> accessed 16 August 2023.

90 TRACE <https://trace-illicit-money-flows.eu> accessed 16 August 2023

are not immune to criticism,[91] Türkiye must embrace and implement existing RBA principles effectively in the first place to reinforce its AML mechanism. Concerning CDD principles, whilst preventing financial exclusion,[92] Türkiye would benefit from reformulating such KYC standards with care, thereby adopting an effective RBA that (also) considers the unique threats posed by PEPs and particular sectors in this context. It should be borne in mind that for an effective implementation of RBA principles, competent AML authorities (e.g., FIUs) must provide obliged entities (i.e., the non-bank sector in particular) with sufficient data in this context.[93] As far as record-keeping practices are concerned, given that '*ceteris paribus*, [compliance costs] are likely to be higher, the more extensive the regulation',[94] aligning these requirements with the FATF Recommendations would eliminate the gratuitous burden of prolonged retention periods. In other words, given that '[t]he cost of AML implementation . . . dwarfs the quantity of crime proceeds recovered',[95] jurisdictions, including Türkiye, must refrain from imposing unwarranted obligations. With regards to the STR submission *modus operandi*, the current period of *ten workdays* benefits no one but potential offenders. Accordingly, given the swiftness of the ML process nowadays (e.g., technology-enhanced ML),[96] any national AML regime, including Türkiye, needs to create at least prompt countermeasures by devising a rapid warning system (i.e., STR/SAR) that triggers the whole AML mechanism. In alignment, in order for such a reporting regime to be meaningful and effective, jurisdictions must ensure that all obliged entities, including legal professionals, accountants, and auditors (i.e., professional enablers),[97] are actively involved in the reporting practices, thereby securing an optimum benefit in this context. Furthermore, as Pieth opines, 'the fight against money laundering entirely depends on the co-operation of the financial

91 Stuart Ross and Michelle Hannan, 'Money Laundering Regulation and Risk-Based Decision Making' (2007) 10(1) Journal of Money Laundering Control 106; Louis de Koker, 'Identifying and Managing Low Money Laundering Risk' (2009) 16(4) Journal of Financial Crime 334; Abdullahi Usman Bello and Jackie Harvey, 'From a Risk-Based to an Uncertainty-Based Approach to Anti-Money Laundering Compliance' (2017) 30(1) Security Journal 24.

92 Louis de Koker, 'Money Laundering Control and Suppression of Financing of Terrorism: Some Thoughts on the Impact of Customer Due Diligence Measures on Financial Exclusion' (2006) 13(1) Journal of Financial Crime 26.

93 Joy Geary, 'Light Is the Best Antidote' (2009) 12(3) Journal of Money Laundering Control 215.

94 Jackie Harvey, 'Compliance and Reporting Issues Arising for Financial Institutions from Money Laundering Regulations: A Preliminary Cost Benefit Study' (2004) 7(4) Journal of Money Laundering Control 333, 335.

95 Michael Levi, 'Evaluating the Control of Money Laundering and Its Underlying Offences: The Search for Meaningful Data' (2020) 15 Asian Journal of Criminology 301–2.

96 Nicholas Gilmour, 'Illustrating the Incentivised Steps Criminals Take to Launder Cash While Avoiding Government Anti-Money Laundering Measures' (2020) 23(2) Journal of Money Laundering Control 515.

97 Katie Benson, 'Money Laundering, Anti-Money Laundering and the Legal Profession' in Colin King, Clive Walker and Jimmy Gurulé (eds), *The Palgrave Handbook of Criminal and Terrorism Financing Law* (Springer 2018).

sector with law enforcement'.[98] Thus, creating an optimum AML regime entails ensuring the active involvement of the private sector in the fight against the phenomenon, which could be achieved by creating PPPs (e.g., JMLIT), thereby increasing their contribution beyond the sole practice of STR/SAR submission. It could also be achieved by revising the monopolised supervisory responsibility of MASAK and by creating sector-specific supervision bodies or designating already existing organisations (e.g., TÜRMOB for the accountancy sector and the Union of Turkish Bar Associations for the legal services sector) with supervisory AML responsibilities. OPBAS in the UK constitutes a remarkable example in this context. Whilst these tentative recommendations address the third research question inquiring into the essential characteristics of an optimum AML composition, there remain areas that need to be investigated even further.

This study has only concentrated on the legal and institutional AML structures of two jurisdictions which present significant differences. Future researchers may want to compare AML frameworks adopted by a comprehensive set of administrations or AML compositions with similar characteristics in more and/or other jurisdictions. Such studies would help confirm or increase the validity of the research findings of this study. Additionally, this study has focused only on two predicate offences as case studies. Accordingly, examining the impacts of AML structures on broader types of predicate crimes (i.e., at least two conventional, such as illicit arms trafficking and smuggling offences in general, and two more complex crimes, such as tax crimes and online fraud/cybercrime) would similarly help reinforce the justifiability of the research findings. Due to the hurdles brought along by the pandemic, it was not possible to conduct face to face interviews with key stakeholders in Türkiye or in the UK. Therefore, future studies may want to adopt a more comprehensive research design that includes, for instance, interviews with AML stakeholders in public and private sectors. Furthermore, given the role of anthropological,[99] social,[100] and cultural factors[101] in tackling any criminal scheme, including ML and its underlying predicates, future scholars may want to investigate the function of such notions in addressing the predicament. Last but not least, given the recent significant AML developments in Türkiye, such as the designation of certain courts as specialised ML courts, future researchers, who are interested in the AML effectiveness of Türkiye, may want to examine the impacts of such evolutions.

98 Mark Pieth, 'The Prevention of Money Laundering: A Comparative Analysis' (1998) 6(2) European Journal of Crime, Criminal Law, and Criminal Justice 159.

99 Jane Schneider and Peter Schneider, 'The Anthropology of Crime and Criminalization' (2008) 37(1) Annual Review of Anthropology 351.

100 Sally Cameron and Edward Newman, *Trafficking in Humans Social, Cultural and Political Dimensions* (United Nations UP 2008).

101 Otto Klineberg, 'Culture and Delinquency: An Overview' in TCN Gibbens, Robert H Ahrenfeldt and World Federation for Mental Health (eds), *Cultural Factors in Delinquency* (Routledge 2001).

Reference List

Arnone M and Borlini L, 'International Anti-Money Laundering Programs: Empirical Assessment and Issues in Criminal Regulation' (2010) 13(3) Journal of Money Laundering Control 226

Avrupa Birliği Bakanlığı, 'Fasıl 4: Sermayenin Serbest Dolaşımı' (October 2011) <www.ab.gov.tr/files/EMPB/sermayenin_serbest_dolasimi_sunumu__ekim_2011_pptx__otomatik_kaydedilme_.pdf> accessed 24 May 2023

Axelrod RM, 'Criminality and Suspicious Activity Reports' (2017) 24(3) Journal of Financial Crime 461

Bell RE, 'Proving the Criminal Origin of Property in Money-Laundering Prosecutions' (2000) 4(1) Journal of Money Laundering Control 4

——— 'Discretion and Decision Making in Money Laundering Prosecutions' (2001) 5(1) Journal of Money Laundering Control 42

Bello AU and Harvey J, 'From a Risk-Based to an Uncertainty-Based Approach to Anti-Money Laundering Compliance' (2017) 30(1) Security Journal 24

Benson K, 'Money Laundering, Anti-Money Laundering and the Legal Profession' in C King, C Walker and J Gurulé (eds), *The Palgrave Handbook of Criminal and Terrorism Financing Law* (Springer 2018)

Bourton S, 'A Critical and Comparative Analysis of the Prevention of Tax Evasion Through the Application of Law and Enforcement Policies in the United Kingdom and United States of America' (PhD thesis, University of the West of England 2021) <https://uwe-repository.worktribe.com/output/7316976> accessed 17 August 2023

Bullough O, 'How Britain Can Help You Get Away with Stealing Millions: A Five-Step Guide' *The Guardian* (5 July 2019) <www.theguardian.com/world/2019/jul/05/how-britain-can-help-you-get-away-with-stealing-millions-a-five-step-guide> accessed 24 May 2023

Cameron S and Newman E, *Trafficking in Humans Social, Cultural and Political Dimensions* (United Nations UP 2008)

Campbell L, 'Corporate Liability and the Criminalisation of Failure' (2018) 12(2) Law and Financial Markets Review 57

Cassella SD, 'Toward a New Model of Money Laundering: Is the "Placement, Layering, Integration" Model Obsolete?' (2018) 21(4) Journal of Money Laundering Control 494

Choo KKR, 'Politically Exposed Persons (PEPs): Risks and Mitigation' (2008) 11(4) Journal of Money Laundering Control 371

——— 'Challenges in Dealing with Politically Exposed Persons' (2010) 386 Trends and Issues in Crime and Criminal Justice 1

Cotoc CN and others, 'Efficiency of Money Laundering Countermeasures: Case Studies from European Union Member States' (2021) 9(6) Risks 120

de Koker L, 'Money Laundering Control and Suppression of Financing of Terrorism: Some Thoughts on the Impact of Customer Due Diligence Measures on Financial Exclusion' (2006) 13(1) Journal of Financial Crime 26

——— 'Identifying and Managing Low Money Laundering Risk' (2009) 16(4) Journal of Financial Crime 334

de Wit J, 'A Risk-Based Approach to AML: A Controversy Between Financial Institutions and Regulators' (2007) 15(2) Journal of Financial Regulation and Compliance 156

D'Souza J, 'Financial Intelligence Units: Monitoring Resource and Process Outcomes' in J D'Souza (ed), *Terrorist Financing, Money Laundering and Tax Evasion* (1st edn, CRC Press 2012)

Dujovski N and Mojsoska S, 'The Role of the Police in Anti-Money Laundering' (2019) 22(1) Journal of Money Laundering Control 145

Ebikake E, 'Money Laundering' (2016) 19(4) Journal of Money Laundering Control 346

Egmont Group, 'Asset Recovery – The Role of FIUs' <https://egmontgroup.org/wp-content/uploads/2022/05/Sanitized-Asset-Recovery-Report-2.pdf> accessed 11 June 2023

Elden N, 'Satılık ve Kiralık Ev Fiyatları Neden Artıyor?' *BBC News* (30 April 2022) <www.bbc.com/turkce/haberler-turkiye-61285237> accessed 2 June 2023

FATF, 'Anti-Money Laundering and Counter-Terrorist Financing Measures – United Kingdom: Mutual Evaluation Report' (December 2018) <www.fatf-gafi.org/media/fatf/documents/reports/mer4/MER-United-Kingdom-2018.pdf> accessed 18 January 2023

——— 'Jurisdictions Under Increased Monitoring' (October 2021) <www.fatf-gafi.org/publications/high-risk-and-other-monitored-jurisdictions/documents/increased-monitoring-october-2021.html#turkey> accessed 24 May 2023

——— 'International Standards on Combatting Money Laundering and the Financing of Terrorism & Proliferation: The FATF Recommendations' (Updated March 2022) <www.fatf-gafi.org/media/fatf/documents/recommendations/pdfs/FATF%20Recommendations%202012.pdf> accessed 26 June 2023

——— 'Anti-Money Laundering and Counter-Terrorist Financing Measures – United Kingdom: Follow-Up Report and Technical Compliance Re-Rating' (May 2022) <www.fatf-gafi.org/media/fatf/documents/reports/fur/Follow-Up-Report-United-Kingdom-2022.pdf> accessed 12 June 2023

——— 'Jurisdictions Under Increased Monitoring – March 2022' <www.fatf-gafi.org/publications/high-risk-and-other-monitored-jurisdictions/documents/increased-monitoring-march-2022.html#turkey> accessed 10 June 2023

Ferwerda J, 'The Economics of Crime and Money Laundering: Does Anti-Money Laundering Policy Reduce Crime?' (2009) 5(2) Review of Law and Economics 903

Geary J, 'Light Is the Best Antidote' (2009) 12(3) Journal of Money Laundering Control 215

——— 'PEPs – Let's Get Serious' (2010) 13(2) Journal of Money Laundering Control 103

Geiger H and Wuensch O, 'The Fight against Money Laundering: An Economic Analysis of Cost-Benefit Paradoxon' (2007) 10(1) Journal of Money Laundering Control 91

Gerbrands P and others, 'The Effect of Anti-Money Laundering Policies: An Empirical Network Analysis' (2022) 11(1) EPJ Data Science 1

Gilmore WC, *Dirty Money: The Evolution of International Measures to Counter Money Laundering and the Financing of Terrorism* (3rd edn, Council of Europe Publishing 2004)

Gilmour N, 'Understanding the Practices Behind Money Laundering: A Rationale Choice Interpretation' (2016) 44(1) International Journal of Crime and Justice 1

——— 'Blindingly Obvious and Frequently Exploitable' (2017) 20(2) Journal of Money Laundering Control 105

——— 'Illustrating the Incentivised Steps Criminals Take to Launder Cash While Avoiding Government Anti-Money Laundering Measures' (2020) 23(2) Journal of Money Laundering Control 515

Harvey J, 'Compliance and Reporting Issues Arising for Financial Institutions from Money Laundering Regulations: A Preliminary Cost Benefit Study' (2004) 7(4) Journal of Money Laundering Control 333

He P, 'Lawyers, Notaries, Accountants and Money Laundering' (2006) 9(1) Journal of Money Laundering Control 62

HMRC, 'HMRC Fraud Squad Takes Back £1 Billion from Offenders' (*Press Release*, 30 December 2021) <www.gov.uk/government/news/hmrc-fraud-squad-takes-back-1-billion-from-offenders> accessed 6 June 2023

HM Treasury and Home Office, 'National Risk Assessment of Money Laundering and Terrorist Financing 2020' (December 2020) <https://assets.publishing.service.gov.uk/government/uploads/system/uploads/attachment_data/file/945411/NRA_2020_v1.2_FOR_PUBLICATION.pdf> accessed 26 June 2023

HM Treasury and others, 'UK Launches Cross-Government Taskforce on the "Panama Papers"' (*Press Release*, 10 April 2016) <www.gov.uk/government/news/uk-launches-cross-government-taskforce-on-the-panama-papers> accessed 31 May 2023

Home Office, 'Policy Paper: Asset Recovery Action Plan' (Updated 13 September2019)<www.gov.uk/government/publications/asset-recovery-action-plan/asset-recovery-action-plan> accessed 8 June 2023

——— 'Government Consultation: Changes to Bodies Granted Investigatory and Other Powers Under the Proceeds of Crime Act 2002' (January 2021) <https://assets.publishing.service.gov.uk/government/uploads/system/uploads/attachment_data/file/956309/AFI_Order_Consultation_V8.pdf> accessed 28 May 2023

Internal Revenue Service: Criminal Investigation, 'Annual Report 2021' (2021) <www.irs.gov/pub/irs-pdf/p3583.pdf> accessed 3 June 2023

Keesoony S, 'International Anti-Money Laundering Laws: The Problems with Enforcement' (2016) 19(2) Journal of Money Laundering Control 130

Klineberg O, 'Culture and Delinquency: An Overview' in TCN Gibbens, RH Ahrenfeldt and World Federation for Mental Health (eds), *Cultural Factors in Delinquency* (Routledge 2001)

Law Commission, 'Anti-Money Laundering: The SARS Regime Consultation Paper' (Consultation Paper No 236, 20 July 2018) <www.cicm.com/wp-content/uploads/2018/09/Anti-Money-Laundering-the-SARS-Regime-Consultation-paper.pdf> accessed 30 November 2023

Levi M, 'Money for Crime and Money from Crime: Financing Crime and Laundering Crime Proceeds' (2015) 21(2) European Journal on Criminal Policy and Research 275

——— 'Evaluating the Control of Money Laundering and Its Underlying Offences: The Search for Meaningful Data' (2020) 15 Asian Journal of Criminology 301

——— 'Lawyers as Money Laundering Enablers? An Evolving and Contentious Relationship' (2022) 23(2) Global Crime 126

——— Nelen H and Lankhorst F, 'Lawyers as Crime Facilitators in Europe: An Introduction and Overview' (2005) 42(2–3) Crime, Law, and Social Change 117

Levi M, Reuter P and Halliday T, 'Can the AML System Be Evaluated without Better Data?' (2017) 69(2) Crime, Law, and Social Change 307

Levi M and Soudijn M, 'Understanding the Laundering of Organized Crime Money' (2020) 49(1) Crime and Justice 579

Lowe RJ, 'Anti-Money Laundering – the Need for Intelligence' (2017) 24(3) Journal of Financial Crime 472

Lundmark T, *Charting the Divide Between Common and Civil Law* (OUP 2012)

Madsen F, *Transnational Organized Crime* (1st edn, Routledge 2009)

Menz M, 'Show Me the Money: Managing Politically Exposed Persons (PEPs) Risk in UK Financial Services' (2021) 28(4) Journal of Financial Crime 968

Middleton DJ, 'Lawyers and Client Accounts: Sand through A Colander' (2008) 11(1) Journal of Money Laundering Control 34

Ministry of Justice General Directorate of Judicial Record and Statistics, 'Judicial Statistics 2016' (November 2017) <https://adlisicil.adalet.gov.tr/Resimler/SayfaDokuman/2082019114041Adalet_ist_2016.pdf> accessed 28 October 2023

——— 'Judicial Statistics 2017' (August 2018) <https://adlisicil.adalet.gov.tr/Resimler/SayfaDokuman/2082019114010Adalet_ist_2017.pdf> accessed 28 October 2023

——— 'Judicial Statistics 2018' (August 2019) <https://adlisicil.adalet.gov.tr/Resimler/SayfaDokuman/1792019103654adalet_ist_2018.pdf> accessed 28 October 2023

——— 'Money Laundering: Emerging Threats and Trends' (2012) 16(1) Journal of Money Laundering Control 41

Sinha G, 'To Suspect or Not to Suspect: Analysing the Pressure on Banks to Be "Policemen"' (2014) 15(1) Journal of Banking Regulation 75

Sittlington S and Harvey J, 'Prevention of Money Laundering and the Role of Asset Recovery' (2018) 70(4) Crime, Law, and Social Change 421

Soudijn MRJ, 'Rethinking Money Laundering and Drug Trafficking: Some Implications for Investigators, Policy Makers and Researchers' (2016) 19(3) Journal of Money Laundering Control 298

Sproat P, 'The New Policing of Assets and the New Assets of Policing: A Tentative Financial Cost-Benefit Analysis of the UK's Anti-Money Laundering and Asset Recovery Regime' (2007) 10(3) Journal of Money Laundering Control 277

Sultana S, 'Role of Financial Intelligence Unit (FIU) in Anti-Money Laundering Quest' (2020) 23(4) Journal of Money Laundering Control 931

TC Başbakanlık, 'Ulusal Uyuşturucu ile Mücadele Ulusal Strateji Belgesi ve Eylem Planı 2018–2023' (2018) <https://hsgm.saglik.gov.tr/depo/birimler/tutun-mucadele-bagimlilik-db/haberler/uyusturucu_eylem_plani/2018-2023_Uyusturucu_ile_Mucadele_Ulusal_Strateji_Belgesi_ve_Eylem_Plani.pdf> accessed 19 January 2023

TRACE <https://trace-illicit-money-flows.eu> accessed 16 August 2023

Türkiye Büyük Millet Meclisi, 'Mali Suçları Araştırma Kurumunun Teşkilat ve Görevleri ile Suç Gelirlerinin Aklanmasının Önlenmesi Hakkında Kanun Tasarısı ve Avrupa Birliği Uyum ile Plan ve Bütçe' (Komisyon Raporları 1/1053, 2005) <www5.tbmm.gov.tr/sirasayi/donem22/yil01/ss1201m.htm> accessed 24 May 2023

Turksen U, 'Implications of Anti-Money Laundering Law for Accountancy in the European Union – A Comparative Study' in N Ryder, U Turksen and S Hassler (eds), *Fighting Financial Crime in the Global Economic Crisis* (1st edn, Routledge 2014)

Unger B and Hertog J, 'Water Always Finds Its Way: Identifying New Forms of Money Laundering' (2012) 57(3) Crime, Law and Social Change 287

van den Broek M, 'The EU's Preventive AML/CFT Policy: Asymmetrical Harmonisation' (2011) 14(2) Journal of Money Laundering Control 170

Whisker J and Lokanan ME, 'Anti-Money Laundering and Counter-Terrorist Financing Threats Posed by Mobile Money' (2019) 22(1) Journal of Money Laundering Control 158

Zavoli I and King C, 'New Development: Estate Agents' Perspectives of Anti-Money Laundering Compliance – Four Key Issues in the UK Property Market' (2020) 40(5) Public Money and Management 415

Legal Instruments

European Union

Consolidated Version of the Treaty on the Functioning of the European Union Part Six – Institutional and Financial Provisions Title I – Institutional Provisions Chapter 2 – Legal Acts of the Union, Adoption Procedures And Other Provisions Section 1 – The Legal Acts of the Union Article 288 (ex-Article 249 TEC) [2016] OJ C202/171

Türkiye

Law No 5237 (Turkish Criminal Code) 2004
Law No 5271 (Criminal Procedure Code) 2004
Presidential Decree No 1 on the Organisation of the Presidency 2018
Official Gazette No 31351 dated 31 December 2020, 'Kitle İmha Silahlarının Yayılmasının Finansmanının Önlenmesine İlişkin Kanun' <www.resmigazete.gov.tr/eskiler/2020/12/20201231M5-19.htm> accessed 2 June 2023
Official Gazette No 31522 dated 25 June 2021, 'Hakimler ve Savcılar Kurulu Birinci Dairesinin Kararı – Karar No 485' <www.resmigazete.gov.tr/eskiler/2021/06/20210625-15.pdf> accessed 28 May 2023
Official Gazette No 31544 dated 17 July 2021, 'Genelge 2021/16: Türkiye'de Suç Gelirlerinin Aklanması ve Terörizmin Finansmanı ile Mücadele ve Müsadere Uygulamalarında Etkinliğin Arttırılması Strateji Belgesi (2021–2025)' <www.resmigazete.gov.tr/eskiler/2021/07/20210717-10.pdf> accessed 10 June 2023

Index

Note: Page numbers in **bold** indicate a table on the corresponding page.

FSC
www.fsc.org
MIX
Papier | Fördert
gute Waldnutzung
FSC® C083411

Kolibri 360 GmbH
Ferdinand-Jühlke-Straße 7
99095 Erfurt, Deutschland
produktsicherheit@kolibri360.de